Human Resource Management

Human Resource Management

Sixth Edition

George T. Milkovich
John W. Boudreau

both of Cornell University
with the assistance of Carolyn Milkovich

IRWIN

Homewood, IL 60430
Boston, MA 02116

Cover and interior marble photographs: © M. Angelo/Westlight
The previous edition of this book was published under the title of *Personnel/Human Resource Management: A Diagnostic Approach.*

© RICHARD D. IRWIN, INC., 1974, 1978, 1982, 1985, 1988, and 1991

Sponsoring editor: Karen Johnson
Developmental editor: Kama Brockmann
Project editor: Ethel Shiell
Production manager: Irene H. Sotiroff
Designer: Maureen McCutcheon
Artist: Progressive Typographers, Inc.
Compositor: Weimer Typesetting Co., Inc.
Typeface: 10/12 Times Roman
Printer: R. R. Donnelley & Sons Company

Library of Congress Cataloging-in-Publicaton Data

Milkovich, George T.
   Human resource management / George T. Milkovich, John W. Boudreau.
  —6th ed.
     p.   cm.
   Rev. ed. of: Personnel/human resource management. 5th ed. 1988.
   Includes bibliographical references and index.
   ISBN 0-256-08153-0
   1. Personnel management. I. Boudreau, John W. II. Milkovich,
George T. Personnel/human resource management. III. Title.
HF5549.M4736 1991
658.3—dc20   90–44216

PREFACE

Managers are rethinking how they manage employees. They have discovered that their own success, as well as the success of their organizations, depends on their decisions about employees. We wrote this book based on that basic premise—*decisions about managing human resources make a difference*. The decisions you will make as a manager will affect the types of employees who work for you, their performance and satisfaction, their sense of fair treatment and, ultimately, the efficiency and effectiveness of the entire organization.

Managers' decisions about human resources do not occur in a vacuum. Managers face constant economic pressures to improve productivity, boost the quality of products and services, and control labor costs. In addition to economic pressures, there are social pressures stemming from growing employee diversity, shifting expectations, and expanding government regulations. Shifts in technology and globalization of production, marketing, and finance also influence managers' decisions about employees.

Faced with these pressures, managers are urged to take actions. Advice is plentiful, and solutions appear simple. These superficial solutions suggest that flatter and trimmer organization designs with fewer layers are in, anything that hints of hierarchy is out. Pay linked to performance is in, any concern for fair treatment and equity is out. Managers acting as team leaders who foster trust among employees are in, autocratic managerial styles are out. Multiskilled, flexible employees are desired, specialists are not. Adversarial relations with unions that balance power between employees and employers are to be replaced with cooperation, teamwork, and the search for mutuality of interest.

It all sounds simple enough, on what is this advice based, and does it pay off? Or are we like birds on a fence—when one flies, we all fly. Are we simply replacing one set of managerial myths with other, more contemporary myths? Were past managers misguided when they specified hiring and pay procedures that are now conventional? Or were these conventional approaches the thoughtful responses to pressures and objectives faced at the time? Procedures in one set of circumstances may be inappropriate in another; however, advocating wholesale change runs the risk of simply replacing current approaches with trendier ones.

Employees, the human resources, are vital to any organization's success. It follows that they should be managed with at least the same care and logic as financial, capital and material resources. Yet, all too often, managing human resources is regarded as the "soft" function, the one that has little effect on either the organization's ability to serve its customers and clients or its profitability. This is unfortunate, because the potential returns from making effective decisions about employees can match and often surpass those from decisions on other resources.

ABOUT THIS BOOK

The design of this book is largely based on four basic phases of the diagnostic model of human resources management. As the model in Chapter 1 illustrates, these phases include: (1) assessing the conditions, both external and internal to the organization, that face managers of human resources; (2) planning and setting human resources objectives for the organization that are based on these conditions; (3) choosing the appropriate human resources actions that will achieve these desired objectives; and (4) evaluating the results. The major sections in the book examine these phases and discuss the major human resource issues involved.

The heart of the book examines how to make effective decisions about human resources. It achieves this by analyzing the prevailing pressures and human resource issues facing managers; discussing the concepts, theories, and research related to these issues; and describing the actions taken by leading organizations to achieve their objectives. Examples of the issues covered include: the effects of demographic shifts and work force diversity (Chapter 2); international developments, such as Europe 1992 (integrated throughout the book—see Chapter 17 as an example); quality teams and new approaches to employee relations (Chapter 15); recent Supreme Court decisions and equal opportunity (Chapter 6); pay incentives and health care costs (Chapters 13 and 14); college student recruiting (Chapter 7); work force reductions and layoffs (Chapter 9); managing careers (Chapter 10); establishing the link between business strategies and human resource decisions (Chapter 5); and more.

Our objective is to help you prepare to make effective decisions about human resources. To achieve this objective, this book undertakes three basic tasks.

The first is to examine the current theory and research related to human resource management. We draw upon theory and research from organization behavior, psychology, economics, sociology, and the law. This discussion is supported by extensive up-to-date references, which offer the opportunity to dig into topics beyond what is provided in the text discussion.

The next task is to examine the rapidly changing state of practices among employers. Here we draw upon practices actually used by a wide variety of employers; examples from public and private, large and small, as well as domestic and international firms, are included. Those practices illustrate new developments, as well as established approaches, to human resource management.

Finally, this book offers an opportunity for you to develop your own decision-making skills of exercises based on actual events. One option is "Your Turn," included in each chapter. "Your Turn" presents a short real-life human resource problem. You make your decision and compare it to the actions actually taken by managers in the real organization.

Next, three computer applications with software specifically designed for this text are included. These applications focus on human resource decision making, not data entry, and are based on our work with leading employers.

A series of integrated cases (nine of them) set within one firm are another option. It gives you the opportunity to dig into situations and work through more involved projects. In addition, there are other cases, role-playing exercises, and discussion topics.

Our intention is to offer you a menu of exercises from which to choose. Completing these exercises will help you better understand the concepts and issues discussed in the book and help as you develop skills readily transferable to future jobs.

George T. Milkovich
John W. Boudreau

ACKNOWLEDGMENTS

We relied on the contributions of many people in the preparation of this book. We owe a special debt to our students who continue to challenge and motivate us.

We appreciate the contributions of the many managers who shared their ideas and practices with us. While we can't here recognize all of them, a few who went beyond the call include:

Stewart M. Aronowitz, M.D.	*IBM Corporation*
Robert Berg	*Colgate-Palmolive*
John Boroski	*Eastman Kodak Company*
John Bronson	*PepsiCo*
Walton E. Burdick	*IBM Corporation*
James Curnow	*3M*
William Colucci	*IBM Corporation*
Larry Doyle	*Union Carbide*
Derek Harvey	*Mobil Oil Company*
Layton King, Jr.	*Mobil Oil Company*
William Maltarich	*TRW Corporation*
Rooney Mereness	*NCR Corporation*
Ray Olsen	*TRW*
Larry Phillips	*General Electric*
Walt Read	*IBM Corporation*
Lew Sears	*TRW Corporation*
William Stopper	*IBM Corporation*
Jay Stright	*Chevron Corporation*
Christopher Wheeler	*3M*
R. Alicia Whitaker	*Colgate-Palmolive*

Several academic colleagues were also very helpful in the preparation of this edition.

Reviewers of previous editions:

Marick Masters	*U. of Pittsburgh*
Richard Lutz	*U. of Akron*
Anne S. Tsui	*U. of Cal.–Irvine*
Mark Singer	*James Madison University*
Steve Motowidlo	*U. of Florida–Gainesville*
James Rush	*University of Western Ontario*
Gerald Ferris	*Texas A&M University*

Tom Bergmann	*U. of Wisconsin–Eau Claire*
Judy Olian	*U. of Maryland–College Park*
Francis Gallagher	*Bloomsburg State College*
Alan Cabelley	*Portland State University*
Linda Krefting	*Texas Tech University*
Joanne Loomba	*California State U.–Hayward*
R. Kelley	*Governors State University*
James Bitter	*U. of Northern Colorado*
Solomon Montoya	*St. John's U., NY*
Sara Rynes	*University of Iowa*

Reviewers of current edition:

Moshe Banai	*Baruch College*
Richard Leake	*Luther College*
Deborah Cain Good	*University of Pittsburgh*
Daniel J. Koys	*DePaul University*
Joseph F. Salamone	*State University of New York–Buffalo*

The comments of the following were especially appreciated:

Robert Risley	*Cornell University*

We want to give a special acknowledgment to Joe Salamone of SUNY Buffalo, who offered significant commentary and provided many of the cases and "Your Turn exercises." We also wish to thank Megan Boudreau for her assistance.

G.T.M
J.W.B

CONTENTS

CHAPTER 1
The Diagnostic Approach   1

Why Human Resources Are Important   2
  Valuing Human Resources   3
The HR Professional   4
Multiple Stakeholders in HR Decisions   5
HR Issues Vary   6
  Decisions Vary over Time   6
  Decisions Vary across Organizations   6
  Decisions Vary across Countries   7
A Diagnostic Approach to Human Resource Management   8
  An HR Example   10
  A Proactive Perspective   10
  Combining the Approach with Theoretical and Technical Knowledge   11
Assess Conditions   11
  External Conditions   11
  Organization Conditions   12
  Employee Characteristics   13
Set HR Objectives   13
  Efficiency   13
  Equity   14
  Integrating Efficiency and Equity through Planning   14
HRM Activities   15
  Staffing   15
  Development   15
  Compensation   15
  Employee/Union Relations   15

Evaluating Results   16

Summary   16

Discussion and Review Questions   17

Appendix: Specialization in HRM   17

Notes and References   18

PART ONE
ASSESS CONDITIONS   20

CHAPTER 2
External Conditions   23

Assessing External Pressures   25

Environmental Scanning   25
   Monitoring the Environment   26
   Screening Information   26
   Researching Issues   26
   Develop Plans   27

Social/Demographic Changes   28
   Population, Labor Force, and Participation Rates   29

A Changing Population: Aging   30

A Changing Population: Immigration   33

The Feminization of the Labor Force   33

HR Effects of Social/Demographic Changes   34

Quality of the Labor Force   35

Economic Conditions   35
   Labor Market Conditions   35
   Product/Service Market Conditions   37

Inflationary Pressures   38

The Globalization of Markets   38
   Europe 1992   38
   International Management   39
   Foreign Product Market Competition   39

Technological Changes   41

Government Influences: Laws, Regulations, and Policies   43

Unions   46

Differential Impact and Responses to Uncertainties 46

Shaping the External Environment 47

Summary 47

Discussion and Review Questions 48

Your Turn: Managing Diversity 48

Notes and References 49

CHAPTER 3

Organization Conditions   52

Organization-Level Factors 54

Financial Conditions 54

Strategy 55

  HR Issues and Business Strategy 56

  Strategic Human Resource Management (HRM) 57

Technology 60

Culture/Philosophy 61

  Culture and Strategy 61

Management Style 62

The State of Research 65

The Nature of Work 65

Work-Level Factors 66

  Content 66

  Qualifications 66

  Rewards and Returns 66

Job Analysis 67

  Assessing Job Content 68

  Conventional Job Analysis 70

  Quantitative Job Analysis 73

  Job Descriptions 74

  Is Job Analysis Useful? 75

Job Design 76

  Scientific Management 76

  Human Relations 77

  Job Characteristics 78

  Sociotechnical Perspective 79

  Work Teams 79

Summary 80

Discussion and Review Questions   81

Your Turn: Restructuring Blues   82

Appendix: Procedures Job Analysis   82

Notes and References   86

CHAPTER 4
Employee Conditions   89

Assessing Employee Characteristics   90

Assessing Performance   91

  Why Assess Performance?   92

  What Performance to Assess?   94

  How to Measure Performance?   96

  Who Should Assess Performance?   104

  When to Assess Performance?   107

  How to Communicate Performance Assessment?   107

  Evaluating Performance Assessment and Resolving Disputes   108

  The Role of the Human Resource Function in Performance
  Assessment   111

Assessing Absenteeism   111

Assessing Separations and Turnover   113

Assessing Employee Attitudes/Opinions   113

Assessing Employee Demographic Characteristics   115

Summary   115

Discussion and Review Questions   115

Your Turn: Appraising "Quality" Performance at Ford Motor
Company   116

Notes and References   117

PART TWO
PLANNING AND SETTING OBJECTIVES   124

CHAPTER 5
Planning, Objectives, and Evaluation   127

Planning, Setting Objectives, and Evaluating Results   129

  Planning Is Diagnostic Decision Making   130

The Relationship between Objectives and Evaluation
Standards 132
    What Makes a Good Objective/Standard? 133
    Why Perform Human Resource Planning? 134

How Human Resource Planning Fits the Broader Planning
Process 135
    The External Level 136
    The Organizational Level 136
    Human Resource Department/Function Level 138
    Human Resource Quantity and Deployment 140
    Specific Human Resource Management Activities 140

Planning the Human Resource Department and Function 141

Auditing Human Resource Activities 141
    Human Resource Budgets 142
    Activity, Cost, or Headcount Ratios 142
    Human Resource Accounting 142
    Return on Investment in Human Resources 143
    Client Opinions/Perceptions 143

Employment Planning: The Quality and Deployment of Human
Resources 145
    Demand Analysis: "Where Do We Want to Be?" 145
    Internal Supply Analysis: "Where Are We Now, Where Will We
Be?" 149
    External Supply Analysis: "Who Is Joining the Organization, Who Will
Be Joining?" 153
    Reconciling Supply and Demand: Setting Objectives and Choosing
Activities 153

Planning Specific Human Resource Activities 155
    The Human Resource "Investment": Quantity, Quality, and Cost 155

Summary 157

Discussion and Review Questions 158

Your Turn: Planning for the Oil Industry Engineer Shortage 158

Appendix: Human Resource Information Systems 159

Notes and References 170

CHAPTER 6
Equal Employment Opportunity   173

The Need for Equal Employment Opportunity (EEO) 175
    Occupational Attainment 176
    Earnings Gap 176

The Equal Pay Act   180
   Definition of Equal   180
   Factors Defining Equal Work   181
Title VII of the Civil Rights Act of 1964   181
   Defining Discrimination   181
   Exceptions to Title VII   184
Executive Order 11246   186
Age Discrimination in Employment Act   187
Vocational Rehabilitation Act and Americans with Disabilities Act   188
Sexual Harassment   188
Evaluating EEO Performance   189
   Work Force Analysis   190
   Availability Analysis   191
   Establish Goals   195
   Programming to Achieve Goals   196
Settling Disputes   197
   EEOC   197
   Office of Federal Contract Compliance   198
   Internal Resolution   198
EEO in the 1990s   200
   Reverse Discrimination   200
   Proving Disparate Impact   201
   The Civil Rights Act of 1990   201
Summary   202
Discussion and Review Questions   202
Your Turn: Diane Joyce   203
Notes and References   204

PART THREE
EXTERNAL STAFFING   208

CHAPTER 7
External Recruiting   215

Recruiting: The Beginning of the Staffing Process   217
The Applicant's Job-Search Process   218
   Choosing an Occupation   219

Seeking Information about Jobs/Organizations   219
Choosing a Job/Organization   221

Choosing Required Applicant Qualifications   222
Tapping the Older Work Force   222
Creating Opportunities for the Disabled   223
Removing Housing and Transportation Barriers   223
Tapping Applicants with Minimum English Literacy Requirements   223

Choosing Recruitment Sources and Communication Channels   224
Walk-ins   224
Employee Referrals   224
College Recruiting   226
Other Educational Institutions   228
Employment Agencies and Professional Societies   228
Advertising   229
Temporary Employees   231
Immigrants   232

Choosing Inducements   233

Choosing the Message: Realism versus Flypaper   233

Choosing and Preparing Recruiters   235

International Perspectives on Recruiting   237

Evaluating Recruitment   238
Efficiency   238
Equity   239
Actual Recruiting Evaluation Practices   240

Summary   241

Discussion and Review Questions   241

Your Turn: Happy Meal Recruitment Advertising   243

Appendix: A Diagnostic Approach to Your Own Job Search   243

Notes and References   252

CHAPTER 8
External Employee Selection   258

External Employee Selection   260
Setting Objectives for External Selection Activities   260
Validity: How Well Does Information Predict the Future?   262
Choosing Selection Techniques   265
Application Forms and Résumés   268

Reference and Background Checks   269
Life-History Information   270
Interviews   274
Ability Tests   284
Job Knowledge Tests, Work Samples, and Job Tryouts   287
Physical/Physiological Requirements   288
Personality, Honesty, and Graphology Tests   291
Constructing the External Selection Process   293
Single-Job Selection versus Classification   293
Gathering and Scoring Predictor Information   294
Combining Multiple Selection Procedures   294
Validating the Selection Process to Determine What Works   296
Criterion-Related Validation Approaches   297
Content-Based Validation   301
Extent of Test Validation   301
Government Regulation of Validation   302
International Perspectives on External Selection   302
Evaluating External Selection Activities   303
Efficiency   303
Equity   307
Summary   308
Discussion and Review Questions   308
Your Turn: Drug Testing at IBM   309
Notes and References   310

CHAPTER 9
Employee Separations, Work Force Reduction, and Retention   318

Employee Separations, Work Force Reduction, and Retention   320
A Diagnostic Approach to Work Force Reduction and
Retention   320
Efficiency   320
Equity   321
The Role of Employee Separations in the Staffing Process   322
Separations Initiated by Employees versus Employers   323
Measuring the Separation Rate   323
The Concept of Validity in Separations/Retentions   324
Managing Resignations   327
Quits   327
Retirements   331

Managing Employee Dismissals   334

   Discharges   334

   Layoffs   338

International Perspectives on Employee Separations, Work Force
Reduction, and Retention   343

Evaluating Employee Separations, Work Force Reduction, and
Retention   344

   Efficiency   345

   Equity   346

Summary   346

Discussion and Review Questions   347

Your Turn: Employment Security at Digital Equipment
Corporation   348

Notes and References   349

PART IV
EMPLOYEE DEVELOPMENT   356

CHAPTER 10
Internal Staffing and Career Development   361

Internal Staffing and Careers   363

   Setting Objectives for Internal Staffing and Careers   365

Role of Internal Employee Movement in the Staffing Process   366

   Internal Staffing Effects in Source and Destination Jobs   369

Career Management and Career Planning   371

Career Planning: Employees Finding and Pursuing Their
Goals   373

   Career Orientation   373

   Career Stages   374

   Implications for Career Development   376

Recruitment in Career Management   376

   Job Posting   377

   Skills Inventories   377

   Replacement and Succession Planning   378

   Nomination by the Employees' Superiors and Mentors   382

   Nomination by the Employees Themselves   382

Selection in Career Management 383

Past Performance, Experience, and Seniority 383

Selection Procedures Used for Internal Staffing 386

Assessment Centers 386

Separation/Retention in Career Management 387

Plateaued Careers 388

Dual-Ladder Career Progressions 389

Is the "Mommy Track" an Opportunity or a Betrayal for Women Managers? 391

Chief Executive Officer (CEO) Succession 391

International Perspectives on Internal Staffing and Careers 393

Japanese Management Career Paths 393

International Management Assignments 394

Evaluating Internal Staffing and Careers 394

Efficiency 394

Equity 395

Summary 396

Discussion and Review Questions 396

Your Turn: Breaking the Glass Ceiling at Corning Glass Works 397

Notes and References 398

CHAPTER 11
Training, Orientation, and Development 404

Training and the Employee Development Process 405

A Diagnostic Approach to Training 408

Assessing Training Needs 409

Organization Analysis 409

Job, Task, and Knowledge-Skill-Ability Analysis 410

Person Analysis 410

Comparison and Use of Needs Assessment Methods 411

Identifying Training Objectives 411

Selection and Design of Training Programs 412

Establishing Supportive Conditions for Learning 413

Choosing the Content of Training 417

Choosing Training Delivery Methods 421

International Perspectives on Training, Orientation, and Development   427

Evaluating Training Outcomes   428

  Evaluation Criteria   428

  Efficiency: Costs   429

  Efficiency: Benefits   432

  Break-Even Analysis   433

  Equity   436

Summary   437

Discussion and Review Questions   438

Your Turn: Basic Skills Training at Swift Textiles   439

Notes and References   439

PART V
HUMAN RESOURCE ACTIVITIES: COMPENSATION   444

CHAPTER 12
External and Internal Comparisons   451

Multiple Perspectives   452

Forms of Pay   453

Compensation Legislation   453

  Wage Controls and Guidelines   454

  Wage and Hour Regulations   454

  Prevailing Wage Laws   455

Setting Compensation Objectives   456

  A Pay Model   456

  Compensation Objectives   456

Basic Policy Decisions   457

  Balancing Policy Decisions   459

Translating Policy into Practice   460

External Competitiveness   460

  Pay Level Effects   460

  Market Surveys   461

Internal Consistency   463

  Pay Structure Effects   464

  Levels and Size of Pay Differences   465

Criteria for Pay Structures   466
   Structures Built on Employee Attributes   468
   Job-Based Structures   470

Job Evaluation Decisions   471
   Purpose   471
   Who to Involve?   471
   Methods   472
   Results of Job Evaluation   476

Summary   479

Discussion and Review Questions   479

Your Turn: Evaluating Jobs   480

Appendix: A Skill-Based Job Evaluation Plan for Manufacturing
Jobs   486

Notes and References   491

CHAPTER 13
Paying Individual Employees   494

Employee Contributions   495

Recognizing Employee Differences with Pay   496

Individual Pay Techniques   496
   Flat Rates   496
   Pay Ranges   497
   Pay Increase Guidelines   499
   Merit Awards   500
   Lump-Sum Payments   501

Incentives   501
   Individual Incentives   501
   Group Incentives   503
   Gainsharing   504
   Profit Sharing   507

Evaluating the Results of Pay for Performance Systems   507
   Efficiency: Pay for Performance   508
   Equity: Pay Satisfaction   511

Pay Administration   512
   Cost Controls   512
   Communication and Appeals   513

Participation   514
Special Groups   514

Executive Pay   515
Compensation Decisions   515
The Critics   517

International Differentials   519

Comparable Worth   519
Earnings Gap   519
A Definition   520
Critics, Politics, and Costs   521

Summary   522

Discussion and Review Questions   523

Your Turn: Executive Pay at Disney   524

Appendix/AFSCME: Pay Equity Study   524

Notes and References   526

CHAPTER 14
Benefits   529

The Growth of Benefits   531
Unions   531

Setting Benefit Objectives and Strategies   532
Integrate with Human Resource Objectives   533
Entitlements versus Contributions   533
A Benefits Gap   534

Benefit Decisions   535

Competitiveness   535
Cost Comparisons   535
Actuarial Valuation   536

Compliance   537
Civil Rights Laws   539
Fiduciary Responsibility   540
Mandated Benefits   542

Coverage   543
Employer-Purchased Insurance   544
Paid Time Away from Work   545
Employee Services   546
Retirement Income   546

Communication   548

Choice   548

How Flexi Benefits Work   549

Advantages   549

Flexible Benefits as a Cost Reduction Strategy   551

Evaluating the Results of Benefit Decisions   551

Effects on Costs   552

Effects on Employee Behavior   554

Effects on Equity   555

Summary   555

Discussion and Review Questions   556

Your Turn: National Health Insurance   556

Notes and References   557

PART VI

HUMAN RESOURCE ACTIVITIES: EMPLOYEE/LABOR
RELATIONS   562

CHAPTER 15
Employee Relations   567

Set Employee Relations Objectives and Strategies   569

Communication   570

Protection   571

Safety and Health Hazards   572

Co-Worker Relations   574

Employee Assistance   578

Approaches to Employee Assistance   579

Family/Job Conflict   580

Stress   586

Cooperation   586

Conflict and Discipline   591

Disciplinary Process   591

Conflict Resolution   593

Evaluating Results   595

Efficiency   595

Equity   596

Summary   597

Discussion and Review Questions   598

Your Turn: Tradition or Team Approaches   599

Notes and References   599

CHAPTER 16

Collective Bargaining   603

The Legal Framework for Collective Bargaining   605

The Organizing Campaign   608

   Authorization Cards   608

   Hearings   609

   Holding the Election   609

   Success of Campaign Tactics   610

Negotiating a Contract   612

   Preparation   612

   Negotiation Issues   613

   Refusal to Bargain   616

   Bargaining Structures   617

   Formalizing the Contract   618

Impasses in Collective Bargaining   618

   Conciliation and Mediation   618

   Strikes and Lockouts   619

   Who Strikes—And Why?   621

Contract Administration   622

   Steps in the Grievance Process   623

   Arbitration   623

Summary   625

Discussion and Review Questions   626

Your Turn: Arbitrating a Grievance   626

Notes and References   627

CHAPTER 17

Labor Relations Objectives and Evaluation   630

Labor Relations Objectives   632

   Union Suppression   632

   Maintain a Union-Free Status   634

   Collaboration   635

Why Employees Join Unions 637
  Why People Don't Join Unions 637
  Union Jobs 638

The Union Organization 638
  The Local Union 639
  Union Leaders 639

Union Strategies 640
  Involvement in Employer's Strategic Decisions 641
  Cooperative Programs 642
  Alternative Forms of Representation 643

Public Sector Unions 644

Labor Relations in Other Countries 645

Interaction of Business, Labor, and Government 645

Evaluating the Effects of Labor Relations Activities 648
  Efficiency: Union Impact on Wages 648
  Efficiency: Union Impact on Productivity 651
  Equity: Union Impact on Employees' Voice 652

Summary 652

Discussion and Review Questions 653

Your Turn: Play or Pay 654

Notes and References 654

CASES   658

Human Resource Management at Ithaca's Own 660
  Starting Salary: Introduction to the PC 660
  Background Description of Ithaca's Own 664
  Strategies and Staff 668
  Setting Objectives 670
  Employment Planning 671
  Choosing Colleges for Recruiting: Using the PC 673
  Developing New Managers 680
  Merit Pay Decisions: Using the PC 681
  Compression and External Experienced Hiring 686
  The Jack Freelance Affair 686

Stand-Alone Cases 693
  Strategic Human Resource Planning 693

Job Analysis   695

Ralph's Genuine French Cuisine   696

Gigantic Aircraft Company   698

Training Cost/Benefit Analysis at Massive Manufacturing Corporation   699

State Government   703

Lori Petersen   705

Collective Bargaining   706

Contract Costing   708

Name Index   711

Subject Index   725

The Diagnostic Approach

Why Human Resources Are Important
Valuing Human Resources

The HR Professional

Multiple Stakeholders in HR Decisions

HR Issues Vary
Decisions Vary over Time
Decisions Vary across Organizations
Decisions Vary across Countries

A Diagnostic Approach to HRM
An HR Example
A Proactive Perspective
*Combining the Approach with Theoretical
and Technical Knowledge*

Assess Conditions
External Conditions
Organizational Conditions
Employee Characteristics

Set HR Objectives
Efficiency
Equity

HRM Activities

Evaluating Results

Appendix: Specialization in HRM

As you read the daily newspaper, or watch a newscast, you are already confronting issues in human resource management (HRM). Drug abuse, public education, the trade deficit—all are issues that impinge on organizations. Can human resource managers ensure a drug-free (or smoke-free) workplace while protecting individual employee rights? Will the HR manager be able to hire enough qualified employees in the future? What will foreign imports do to product markets? Conditions in the product market affect both an employer's need for workers and its ability to pay meaningful wages.

Even the sports pages deal with HR issues. Professional athletes negotiate contracts with their teams. Will raising a key player's pay cause dissension among teammates? HR decisions are among the most difficult that managers must make. The political, cultural, and economic forces in society are interwoven in them.

WHY HUMAN RESOURCES ARE IMPORTANT

Although plant, equipment, and financial assets are also resources required by organizations, employees—the human resources—are particularly important. Human resources provide the creative spark in any organization. People design and produce the goods and services, control quality, market the products, allocate financial resources, and set overall strategies and objectives for the organization. Without effective people it is simply impossible for an organization to achieve its objectives. The HR manager's job is to influence this relationship between an organization and its employees.

Human resource management is a series of decisions about the employment relationship that influence the effectiveness of employees and organizations.

Today's employees have different expectations about the work they are willing to perform.[1] Some employees want to be involved in managing their jobs, and they wish to share in the financial gains achieved by the organization. Others have so few marketable skills that employers must redesign jobs and offer extensive training before they can be hired. Demographics of the population and labor force are also changing.[2] Women's increased participation in the work force, dual-career families, single-parent families, and influx of immigrants and undocumented workers, and the aging of the labor force are all examples of demographic changes. During the years 1985 to 2000, 62 percent of the new entrants to the workplace will be female, 30 percent will be black or Hispanic, and only 15 percent of the new entrants will be American-born white males. These changes make managing HR more complex. Employees are not interchangeable economic units that can be plugged into narrowly defined jobs. Yet they are absolutely essential for every organization's success.

Valuing Human Resources

Human resources can also be expensive. For some organizations, such as General Foods Corporation and Texaco, wages, benefits, training, and the like can range from 20 to 30 percent of total operating expenses. But for others, such as H&R Block, Inc., and Citicorp, labor expenses can be over 50 percent of operating expenses. In most organizations, that percentage is growing.

Most important decisions are made by examining costs and benefits. But generally accepted decision-making methods are seldom applied to making HR decisions.[3] Human resources are often only treated as an expense. The benefits or payoffs tend to be discounted. This has had an important impact on HR management.

Information on costs and benefits can make a decision process more systematic, more rational, and hopefully, more effective. Thus, when the college board of regents considers adding a dormitory, the regents want to see projected enrollment figures and cash flow statements to determine if the new building is within the college's resources.

When it comes to making decisions about investments in personnel, however, a quite different process has evolved. Because data on the *payoffs* of HR programs are not usually available, the HR manager is at a disadvantage. Only the expenses are clear.

If HR managers do not try to show the probable future returns on the investment for retraining workers, for example, available funds may be spent on equipment maintenance at the expense of human maintenance. If managers simply sold off materials inventory, this would improve short-run profits, but accountants would notice and everyone would know that the organization's operating position had not improved. But throwing away investments in human resources by laying off employees or letting them work in jobs that don't use all their capabilities leads to no short-run penalty, since these investments don't appear on the balance sheet. In fact, laying off employees will improve a balance sheet, since it will cut expenses. The potential negative effects of layoffs on revenues—new products not developed, new marketing strategies not devised—are overlooked. This may explain why so many HR decisions are made incorrectly.

An example will illustrate the point. Consider a training program taken by 100 engineers. If each engineer stays with the organization for seven years, this training program will affect 700 person-years of productivity. If the training produces an average of $1,000 worth of improved engineering productivity per person in each year, this single program is worth $700,000 to the organization. Imagine the impact of ongoing HR programs affecting thousands of person-years of productivity. Clearly, the impact of HR decisions rivals the impact of decisions in finance, plant and equipment, inventories, and marketing.

THE HR PROFESSIONAL

Managing human resources is a central concern of every single manager in every single organization. For example, the manager of a plant that manufactures personal computers needs to coordinate electronic components (the raw materials), production designs, and financial budgets. This coordination depends on effective human resource management. Even though HR professionals may be on the staff to offer advice and expertise, other managers, such as the designer, the purchaser, and the financial officer, actually manage human resources.

However, other managers may have different orientations or even different objectives. For example, a production manager may wish to minimize costs by paying only the minimum wage necessary to attract sufficient workers to do the job at minimum levels of competence. On paper, the plan may look good. But over time, resentful workers may take out their frustrations on product quality and equipment; inferior goods or services may drive away formerly loyal customers. Profits may plummet, but by then the shortsighted manager has moved to a new location. In contrast, human resource managers ought to recommend decisions that recognize both the payoffs and the costs of those decisions. Ideally, the human resource professionals and other managers complement each other, rather than compete.

HR professionals combine many skills. They must understand the business of the organization, possess expertise in the technical and theoretical aspects of HRM, and work productively with employees at all levels of the organization. These skills combine in a number of different roles.

Business Partner

The foremost objective for the HR manager is to link HR programs with an organization's business directions, to ensure that all HR programs are consistent with the organization's needs.[4] For example, if a company is trying to reduce its number of employees, it would be inconsistent to base managers' pay on the number of people they supervise. Programs must also be internally consistent. Rates of pay, for example, affect firms' ability to hire and retain employees. They also affect employees' willingness to take on the training and extra responsibilities involved in a promotion, or to vote to certify a union for collective bargaining. No single program stands on its own. It is up to the HR manager to consider these interrelationships and to manage programs to achieve overall organization objectives. This aspect of HRM is becoming increasingly important as global competition is boosting the cost of inefficient activities. To fulfill this role, HR managers must fully understand an organization's business and its finances.

Communicator

Keeping on top of currents outside the organization is a major HR responsibility. But being informed is not sufficient. Grasping the HR implications of trends and educating top management and employees about these implications are also required. The HR professional must also communicate the organization's position to those outside the organization.

Similarly, HR managers must be in touch with the work force, to tell top management what employees are thinking or feeling and to be a credible source of information for employees on what the organization is experiencing. So the HR professional must facilitate communication among levels of employees within the organization and between the organization and the rest of society.[5]

Advocate

A good HR manager tries to ensure that all employees are treated fairly.[6] Decisions about who to hire, promote, and train, about how much to pay, and about how to assist dissatisfied employees must be made with the objective of fairness in mind. A sense of inequity among employees affects their work attitudes and behaviors. Absenteeism, low motivation, lack of concern for the quality of products or services, withholding suggestions for improvements, lack of commitment, and even sabotage may result. These attitudes and behaviors affect costs, productivity, profits, and, hence, the market value of the firm's stock. So the HR professional works toward the organization's success by being a business partner, communicator, and advocate. The appendix to this chapter contains additional information on becoming an HR professional.

MULTIPLE STAKEHOLDERS IN HR DECISIONS

Employees and managers are not the only ones who have a stake, or an interest, in HR decisions. All of us as consumers are affected. In the 1960s, many new car buyers refused to accept cars assembled on a Monday. Monday cars were reputed to be plagued by defects that resulted from high absenteeism or inattention from employees who spent the weekend trying to rid themselves of the frustrations of the assembly line. People who can't get telephones connected during a strike by the Communications Workers of America are acutely aware of how HR decisions affect consumers.

Others also have a stake in the quality of HR decisions. Stockholders, regulatory agencies, and unions may all hold the HR function accountable for achieving objectives that they consider important.[7] For example, stockholders expect personnel decisions to increase the value of the firm and enhance their investment. They may support a decision to lay off workers as a way to reduce labor costs. But regulatory agencies and unions may feel that layoffs should be permitted only as a last resort, because the disruption to individuals, families, and communities is so great. These stakeholders expect personnel decisions to be consistent with broad social objectives.

So we all have a stake in HR decisions, whether we are consumers, stockholders, members of society, employees, or managers. And we all have unique expectations of the HR manager.

HR ISSUES VARY

The importance of HR management ebbs and flows in response to pressures faced by the organization.[8] Prior to 1900, first-line supervisors handled personnel problems. But this system permitted abuses. For example, supervisors could vary the pay rates and job assignments among favored workers. Some supervisors even demanded a kickback from new employees in exchange for being hired. As these abuses and the costs associated with them became intolerable, separate personnel departments were created to help regulate HR decisions. Labor legislation in the late 1930s and the World War II labor shortages created a new demand for better management. Equal employment legislation required new personnel specialists in the 1960s and 1970s who possessed the analytical skills to assure compliance with government regulations. In the 1980s and 1990s, HR management continues to gain in importance. This time, many organizations are finding that HR management can help them manage changes with a diversified work force in a global economy.

Decisions Vary over Time

Today, HR professionals deal with a variety of issues. They recruit new employees, formulate guidelines for selecting them, and design training, pay, communication, and retirement programs. Specific issues vary with the needs of the organization, and will vary over time. Exhibit 1.1 captures the change in emphasis in HR functions over time. Compensation remains an important responsibility, but HR strategic planning—fitting HR programs to the business needs of the organization—is now the most important issue. While the same issue will continue to be important, no doubt the ordering will continue to change, as organization and employee needs change.

Decisions Vary across Organizations

Patterns of HR decisions also vary among companies, and sometimes even among units within a company. For example, TRW is organized into three main sectors, each with its own human resource staff. Each sector makes HR deci-

EXHIBIT 1.1   How Has the Emphasis Shifted?*

	1980	1985	1990
1.	Compensation	Compensation	Planning
2.	Staffing	Planning	Compensation
3.	Labor Relations	Staffing	Benefits
4.	Employee Relations	Management Development	Work Force Management Diversity Education and Training Motivation
5.	EEO	Benefits	Management Development
6.	Benefits	Employee Relations	Staffing
7.	Management Development	Work Force Management	Employee Relations
8.	Planning	Communications	EEO
9.	Training	Labor Relations	Labor Relations

* Rankings taken from a variety of consultant surveys.

sions that suit its needs. So the TRW Oilwell Cable Division in Lawrence, Kansas, implemented a knowledge-based pay system, which is a nontraditional approach to compensation. The TRW Motor Division in nearby Manhattan, Kansas, considered knowledge-based pay, but it decided that a pay-for-performance system better suited its needs. HR decisions varied across organization units, as each unit sought to increase its effectiveness.

Decision Vary across Countries

Exhibit 1.2 shows the results of a survey of 450 companies in 11 countries. The relative importance of HR functions varies by country. While management and executive development was listed as one of the top three functions in all the countries, only one country (Germany) listed employee development as a top priority. Recruiting and employment (staffing) and compensation are numbers 2 and 3 overall in this survey.

An underlying premise in this book is that all these variations—over time and across organizations—make a difference. While HR administrators are just as likely as others to play "follow the leader" in adopting currently popular programs, most HR decisions are made after considering organization and employee needs. What determines these variations? What difference do these variations make? These are the major issues for students of HRM. They are repeated throughout this book. Our diagnostic model provides a framework for addressing them.

EXHIBIT 1.2   Three Functions Most Frequently Rated as a Top Priority by Country

HR Function	Europe				North America		Asia/ Pacific		Latin America		
	FR	GER	ITA	UK	CAN	US	AUS	JPN	ARG	BRZ	MEX
Work force planning	X		X					X			
Labor cost management											
Work force productivity				X			X				
Compensation			X		X	X			X	X*	X
Flexible benefits											
Participative management					X*					X	
Mgmt./exec. development	X	X	X	X	X	X	X	X	X	X	X
Succession planning							X			X*	
Retirement strategies											
Work/family programs											
Recruiting/employment	X	X		X		X		X	X		X*
Employee relations					X*						X*
Performance appraisal											
Employee communications											
Corporate citizenship											
Employee development		X									
Equal opportunity											
Health											

* Indicates tied vote for third place.

A DIAGNOSTIC APPROACH TO HUMAN RESOURCE MANAGEMENT

Exhibit 1.3 illustrates the diagnostic approach used in this book. The model includes four phases: (1) assess human resource conditions, (2) set objectives based on the assessment, (3) choose a course of action from alternatives generated to achieve the objectives, and (4) evaluate the results. Evaluating the results provides feedback on the success of the actions. HR actions lead to new HR conditions. Actions can be continued or revised, depending on these new conditions.

This diagnostic approach applies to any number of situations. For instance, think of a particularly effective physician you may have visited. The general objective is to maintain or improve your health. The physician examines your medical history, interviews you regarding your symptoms, or conducts laboratory tests. This assessment phase results in more specific health objectives, which probably differ in their importance or priority. The physician next con-

EXHIBIT 1.3   The Diagnostic Model

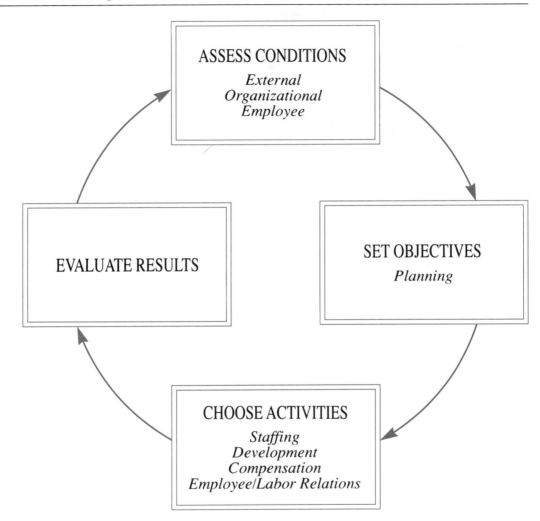

siders alternative treatments. A treatment is chosen, based on the various health objectives, the knowledge of the physician, and your own preferences.

If the treatment fails to yield the desired results, the physician reassesses and considers a new or revised treatment. This process of assessing the situation, setting objectives, choosing among alternatives, and evaluating results continues throughout your relationship with the physician. Sometimes, a crisis (e.g., stop the bleeding) forces the physician to weigh alternatives and make choices rapidly, based on limited information. At other times, the objectives may be broader and less immediate (e.g., lose 15 pounds). Then alternatives are considered with more deliberation.

An HR Example

Apply the same diagnostic approach to an HR problem. Say that a manufacturing unit experiences a drop in productivity. The manager of the unit will gather and analyze information on possible equipment malfunctions, raw material quality, and production histories to better identify the nature of the problem and to suggest possible causes. Perhaps the problem lies with the employees (e.g., frequent absences or omitting certain tasks). If this is the case, then the problem becomes a human resource management issue because it stems from the relationship with employees. Possible remedies include training employees to better perform the job, linking the job behaviors to pay, hiring new employees who are better qualified, or redesigning the jobs to better fit employee behaviors. Based on the available information, the priorities of different objectives, and any evidence regarding the effectiveness of different alternatives, the manager could choose one or more options to correct the situation. After the options are implemented, their effects become additional information. If the first program doesn't solve the problem, the manager can try something else. To choose the best option, the manager weighs relative costs, feasibility, and chances of success. While a complex cost/benefit analysis of each option is possible, the choice is frequently based on the manager's experience and knowledge of HR management. But because human behavior is so variable, what works one time may not work in slightly different circumstances. That is why the process is not complete until the results are evaluated. Evaluation tells the manager if a program is successful. It also may provide information on additional problems.

A Proactive Perspective

In addition to simply reacting to a problem after it occurs, managers must also anticipate and prevent issues from arising. They must be proactive. This is becoming an increasingly important part of a manager's job. Suppose a business machine manufacturer concludes that declining sales of electric typewriters will result in the need for fewer engineers. The plant's human resource manager could freeze hiring and let naturally occurring turnover solve the engineer surplus.

But change is seldom that simple. If electric typewriter sales are declining, top management may decide to enter the electronic typewriter and word processor business. This strategic market decision has a cascading effect on human resource decisions. Current engineers may not possess the skills to design these new products. These engineers can be retrained, encouraged to take early retirement, or offered help in seeking other employment. At the same time, new engineers with different skills will be hired. This is not a hypothetical example. It is a description of Smith-Corona's HR actions in the 1980s. When a business strategy shifts, HR actions must change, too.

Combining the Approach with Theoretical and Technical Knowledge

We have described the diagnostic approach for considering information on which HR decisions will be based. Much of the rest of the book will discuss the theoretical and technical knowledge necessary to make those decisions.

The organization of this book parallels the diagnostic approach. Part One describes external, organizational, and employee conditions relevant to human resource decisions. Part Two describes the planning process in which objectives are specified and the ways to evaluate the results of HR actions are considered. The book then goes into detail about the human resource activities, including staffing, development, compensation and employee/union relations. Keep the diagnostic model in mind as you progress through the book. It provides a framework for combining the decision-making process with the technical and theoretical knowledge that makes up human resource management.

ASSESS CONDITIONS

Conditions of particular interest to HR management fall into three broad categories: external conditions, organization conditions, and employee characteristics.

External Conditions

Conditions outside the organization influence and restrict what actions an organization can take.

Economic

Organization decisions to hire additional people, to lay off current employees, or to grant a cost-of-living wage increase are all influenced by economic conditions. Economic conditions also influence employees. For example, high unemployment rates make many employees reluctant to quit their present jobs, because they are afraid they won't find another one. This reduces turnover. Or workers squeezed by inflation may ask for extra hours of work to fatten paychecks.

International

In recent years, economic markets have become global to an unprecedented extent. Few of us realize how tightly interwoven our economies have become. Pick up any product and trace its history, its manufacture, or its raw materials. Chances are good there is a foreign connection. Is the company that produced it foreign-owned? Does it have divisions that operate in foreign countries? Is the product also exported? (This textbook is exported to several countries, which by now you might think is a pretty good idea.) If no other foreign connection exists, there is always money. Every single business in every single country is affected by currency fluctuations. Obviously, companies that operate in many countries will pay closer attention to international conditions than will Ralph's Pretty Good Grocery in Lake Wobegon, Minnesota. But even Ralph's customers probably listened to the grain market reports before they drove into town, and the grain market plays a central role in international trade.

Government Regulations
Laws reflect a society's response to social, political, or economic problems. A growing share of business decisions—one estimate is as many as half—are shaped by federal, state, and local regulations. Equal employment opportunity legislation and employment-at-will decisions are especially significant examples. These laws require examination of every single personnel policy and program to ensure compliance. As more companies operate in many different countries, simultaneously complying with regulations of many countries poses an additional challenge.

Unions
In many cases, unions have forced employers to adopt sound human resource programs. However, the presence of a union reduces employers' flexibility in designing human resource programs. Therefore, many organizations wish to maintain or achieve a union-free status. How organizations respond to unions (if they are unionized) or the threat of unionization becomes an extremely important factor in HR decisions.

Organization Conditions

Several factors make up the nature of the organization: its strategies and objectives, financial situation, technology, and culture are examples.

Strategy refers to the fundamental direction of the organization. Strategies guide the deployment of all resources, including human resources. Let us use PepsiCo to illustrate organization strategy and the diagnostic model. Until the early 1980s PepsiCo, the overall corporation, was organized into several business units: Pizza Hut, Frito Lay, Taco Bell, and Pepsi-Cola. The actual soft drink was manufactured by local independently owned bottlers throughout the United States and the world. The Pepsi-Cola unit of PepsiCo focused on marketing the soft drink. Recently, PepsiCo began to acquire these independent bottlers, thereby transforming the Pepsi-Cola unit into a manufacturing as well as a marketing organization.

This vertical integration reflects a fundamental change in business strategy. Organization resources—financial, capital, and human—will need to be deployed in a manner consistent with this new direction. Managers in the Pepsi-Cola business, for example, now face decisions about running bottling plants, including negotiating with unions, hiring and supervising production workers, and learning how to design and manage employee production teams. None of these issues were faced when the unit's business focused on marketing. They are the result of the change in the business strategy of the organization.

To a great extent, the technology used in an organization determines the nature of the jobs. Obviously, the work at Iowa Beef Processors differs from the work at the New York Metropolitan Museum of Art. Each organization requires human resources, but the differences in the work require different human resource management systems. The jobs to be performed influence the skill and training required, the compensation offered, the job design, and other human resource activities.

Employee Characteristics

Information about employees is critical for setting objectives and shaping human resource decisions. Each employee has unique experiences, skills, abilities, needs, and motivations. Individual differences relevant to human resource management include possession of highly sought skills, career preferences, and performance. Information can be obtained on each individual and on the entire work force. Relevant work force data include attitudes, experience, wages, and performance levels.

So the diagnostic approach assesses employee characteristics as well as organization and external conditions. Management analyzes information in these categories to set objectives for human resource management.

SET HR OBJECTIVES

Knowing where we are is the first step. Knowing where we want to be is the second. Discrepancies between the desired conditions and actual or likely future conditions are the source of objectives. Objectives stimulate decisions on which actions to take to reduce the discrepancies. An organization can have many objectives. Two general categories of objectives are efficiency and equity.

Efficiency

Every organization operates by combining resources in a way that produces marketable products or services. If we think of the resources (raw materials, data, technology, and human resources) as inputs and the products/services that result as outputs, then efficiency refers to the comparison between inputs and outputs. Efficient organizations maximize outputs while minimizing inputs. HR decisions affect an organization's efficiency by employing the work force in the most efficient manner.

Measures of human resource efficiency may focus on the organization (market share, return on investment, or quality of public service), or on employees (job performance, pay rates, absenteeism, accident costs, or quit rates).

Equity

Equity is the perceived fairness of both the *procedures* used to make human resource decisions and the *decisions*. Many stakeholders are interested in the rules and procedures used to decide pay increases, hiring, layoffs or promotions, as well as the effects of those decisions. Employees, managers, government regulatory agencies, and society judge the equity of employment decisions.

Measures of equity are less well developed than efficiency measures. Like efficiency, equity may be assessed from the perspective of the organization or the employee. Equity at the organization level may be indicated by the percentage of employees who are members of minority groups and how that compares to the percentages of minority group members in the labor market, and whether the public views the organization as a good place to work or a good community citizen. At the employee level, equity is usually assessed through attitude surveys or by rates of employee grievances.

Integrating Efficiency and Equity through Planning

Efficiency and equity are interrelated. For example, many organizations believe that an equity policy of no layoffs enables them to operate more efficiently. They reason that if employees do not fear losing their jobs, they will be more willing to accept retraining or relocation or to offer productivity improvement suggestions. On the other hand, efficiency and equity are not always maximized by the same decisions. For example, layoffs designed to retain younger employees who possess more up-to-date skills may seem unfair to senior employees who feel that their loyalty to the organization should be worth greater consideration. Although all management functions face questions of efficiency and equity, some of the most vivid, important, and exciting issues fall squarely within HR management.

Balancing equity and efficiency is a constant challenge. Planning is required to meet this challenge. Planning focuses on how an organization should move from its current human resource conditions to its desired human resource conditions—how to achieve its objectives of efficiency and equity. Planning links the human resource objectives with the organization's overall objectives. It also integrates all HR decisions into an overall HR strategy.

So, establishing HR objectives and planning to achieve them is the second phase of the diagnostic model. Objectives become the goals for HRM activities, the third phase of the model.

HRM ACTIVITIES

HRM activities are the programs designed in response to HR objectives and managed to achieve those objectives. We have identified four broad categories of activities.

Staffing

Staffing determines the composition of an organization's human resources. How many people should we employ? What skills, abilities, and experiences should they possess? When and how should people be transferred, recruited, or laid off? How do we select the correct individuals in each case? These are all staffing issues.

Development

Employee development and training activities are among the most common and costly HR activities. These activities teach new skills, refine existing skills, and affect employees attitudes. For example, newly hired employees typically undergo an orientation session soon after joining the organization. Orientation involves some training in job skills, but it also makes new employees feel part of the group. Development activities are a powerful means to enhance the efficiency and equity of the organization, especially when they are integrated with other HR activities.

Compensation

Exhibit 1.1 shows that many HR managers believe that compensation is their most important HR activity. Positioning the organization's pay relative to its competitors' pay, ensuring equitable pay differences among employees, and deciding whether pay increases should be based on individual, team, or organization performance measures are all compensation issues.

Employee/Union Relations

Employee relations activities promote harmonious relationships among managers and employees. The relationship with unions, including collective bargaining and contract administration, is the most visible aspect of employee relations. For some managers, employee relations means reducing hostilities, or at least reducing dissatisfaction to a tolerable murmur. Others aim higher: they seek to design and manage HR activities to ensure fair and equitable treatment of all employees. Employment security provisions, grievance procedures, and provisions for child care and drug counseling may all be part of employee relations activities.

These, then, are the four major human resource activities listed in the diagnostic approach: staffing, development, compensation, and employee/union relations. How these activities are designed and managed depends on the previous two phases of the model: the human resource conditions the organization faces, and the objectives it has established. Decisions on these activities make up the organization's human resource strategy. Results of these activities are evaluated as part of the process of monitoring conditions.

EVALUATING RESULTS

Evaluation determines the effects of human resource activities. Did its activities help the organization achieve its human resource objectives? For example, efficiency might be evaluated by comparing the labor costs after a staffing or training program to the labor costs before the program. Or they may compare performance and absenteeism before and after a new pay system. Equity may be evaluated by comparing the number of minorities and females hired as a result of a more aggressive recruiting approach to affirmative action objectives.

HR activities change the organization's environment and lead to new conditions. This leads us back to the first phase of the diagnostic model: assess and evaluate conditions. The components of the diagnostic model are thus interrelated, and their influence can be multi-dimensional.

The model will provide the framework for the rest of the book. In the next chapter, we will look in greater detail at the external conditions that affect HRM.

SUMMARY

Human resource management is a fascinating and important subject. The fascination lies in the fact that it involves people and decisions involving people at work. It is important because human resources *are* the organization. People make the decisions, set the objectives, and design, assemble, and sell the products.

The basic premise underlying this book is that decisions about how people are managed make a difference. Making decisions about human resources involves both process and content. The process refers to how decisions get made and includes assessing human resource conditions, setting objectives, choosing and applying programs, and reviewing the results obtained.

The diagnostic model offers a framework combining theoretical and technical knowledge with the diagnostic approach. In our model, external and also within organization conditions, as well as employees, affect human resource decisions and their effectiveness in achieving objectives. Objectives include organizational efficiency and equity. These objectives are standards for evaluating the results of decisions.

We should emphasize that the diagnostic model in Exhibit 1.3 is not static. Changing conditions dictate ongoing assessment and flexible decision making. Nor do the relationships always proceed in one direction. Human resource activities can affect external conditions (such as changing the labor market by attracting more candidates), and organization conditions (such as identifying strategic directions best suited to the skills and motivations of employees), as well as employees. Managing such a dynamic process is what makes HRM so important and challenging.

DISCUSSION AND REVIEW QUESTIONS

1. What are some HRM issues that have been in the news in the past two months?
2. How has the role of the HR manager changed over time?
3. Discuss the interests of various groups inside and outside the organization in HRM. In what circumstances might these interests conflict? Whose interests should prevail?
4. Describe the *process* of HRM described in this chapter.
5. Tell what is meant by a "proactive" approach and give some examples.
6. What particular problems does cost/benefit analysis present for HRM?
7. How would you evaluate HR decisions?
8. When might efficiency and equity conflict?
9. Describe the interaction of operating and HR managers in making decisions.
10. Why is managing human resources so complex?

APPENDIX
Specialization in HRM

The human resource function has been moving toward greater education and professionalism. College training includes such courses as personnel management, human resource planning, equal employment opportunity, compensation administration, training, recruiting, staffing, labor law, and collective bargaining. Those who wish to become more specialized may join an association like the Society for Human Resource Management (SHRM), attend meetings, read professional journals listed in the notes and references in this book, or seek accreditation.

The Society for Human Resource Management has set up an accreditation institute to offer executives the opportunity to be accredited as specialists (in functional areas, such as employment, placement and planning, or training and development) or as generalists (multiple specialties). This institute is a nonprofit organization formed for the purpose of accrediting human resource professionals.

Accreditation is based on mastery of a body of knowledge, as demonstrated by passing a comprehensive written examination and on varying amounts of full-time

---

EXHIBIT 1.4   Specialties of the Personnel Administration and Industrial Relations Field as Defined by the Society for Human Resource Management

---

1. **Staffing:** Screening, interviewing, recruitment, testing, personnel records, job analysis, job description, staffing tables, promotion, transfer, job enlargement, and the like.

2. **Personnel Maintenance:** Counseling, personnel appraisal inventories, turnover, health services and accident prevention, employee benefits and services, and so on.

3. **Labor Relations:** Group relationships with organized or unorganized employees; negotiations, contract administration, grievances, arbitration, third-party involvement, mutual aid pacts, and so forth.

4. **Training/Development:** Job training, supervisor training, manager and executive development, pre-employment and special-purpose training, retraining, and so on.

5. **Compensation:** Wage and salary surveys, incentive pay plans, profit sharing, stock ownership, financial and nonfinancial rewards, job enrichment, wage and salary controls, etcetera.

6. **Employment Communications:** House organ, employee handbook, rumor control, listening, attitude, morale and expectations surveys, feedback analysis, and so on.

7. **Organization:** Structural design, planning and evaluation, innovation, utilization of formal and informal approaches to reducing conflict, overcoming resistance to organizational change, and the like.

8. **Administrator:** Explanation and interpretation of options—authoritative, consultative, participative, self-management styles, assistance in change, and so forth.

9. **Personnel Policy and Planning:** Defining organizational goals, policy guidelines and strategies; identifying, translating, and complying with public HR policy; forecasting HR needs, selecting optional courses, etcetera.

10. **Review, Audit, Research:** Program reporting recording; evaluation of policies and programs; theory testing, innovation, experimentation, cost/benefit studies, and so on.

---

professional experience in the field, as practitioners, consultants, educators, or researchers. Individuals must currently be serving in the role appropriate to the type of accreditation they seek. Accreditation can be changed or upgraded as roles change and experience accumulates. A generalist must pass examination on five areas in order to demonstrate broad knowledge, whereas the specialist is expected to possess greater in-depth knowledge. Information and application materials are obtained from the Society for Human Resource Management, 606 North Washington Street, Alexandria, Virginia 22314. Exhibit 1.4 lists areas of specialization in HR management.

NOTES AND REFERENCES

1. Robert Leverinig, *A Great Place to Work* (New York: Random House, 1988);   Daniel W. Kendall, "Rights across the Waters," *Personnel Administrator,* March 1988, pp. 58–61;   James Fraze and Martha I. Finney, "Employee Rights between Our Shores," *Personnel Administrator,* March 1988, pp. 50–54, 79.

2. Sheila B. Kamerman and Alfred J. Kahn, *The Responsive Workplace: Employees and a Changing Labor Force* (New York: Columbia University Press, 1987).

3. John W. Boudreau, "Utility Analysis," in *Human Resource Management: Evolving Roles and Responsibilities,* ed. Lee Dyer and Gerald W. Holder (Washington, D.C.: Bureau of National Affairs, 1988), pp. 1.125–1.186.

4. Lee Dyer and Gerald W. Holder, "A Strategic Perspective of Human Resource Management," in *Human Resource Management: Evolving Roles and Responsibilities,* ed. Dyer and Holder (Washington, D.C.: Bureau of National Affairs, 1988), pp. 1.1–1.46. David Ulrich and Arthur Yeung, "A Shared Mindset," *Personnel Administrator*, March 1989, pp. 38–45.

5. Alan Farnham, "The Trust Gap," *Fortune,* December 4, 1989, pp. 56–75.

6. Patricia H. Werhane, *Persons, Rights and Corporations* (Englewood Cliffs, N.J.: Prentice-Hall, 1985).

7. George Lodge and Richard Walton, "The American Corporation and Its New Relationships," *California Management Review*, Spring 1989, pp. 9–24.

8. James N. Baron, Frank R. Dobbin, and P. Devereaux Jennings, "War and Peace: The Evolution of Modern Personnel Administration in U.S. Industry," *American Journal of Sociology*, September 1986, pp. 350–83.

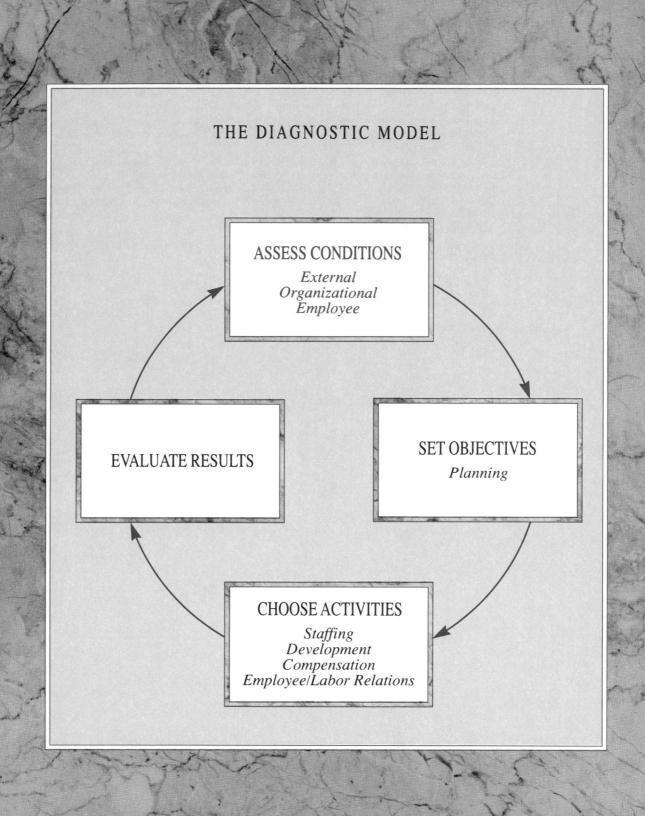

THE DIAGNOSTIC MODEL

ASSESS CONDITIONS

External
Organizational
Employee

SET OBJECTIVES

Planning

EVALUATE RESULTS

CHOOSE ACTIVITIES

Staffing
Development
Compensation
Employee/Labor Relations

PART ONE

ASSESS CONDITIONS

Part One analyzes the relevant factors that influence human resource management (HRM). The diagnostic model on the previous page groups these factors into three categories: external, organization, and employee conditions. This grouping provides a framework for Part One.

Chapter Two covers external conditions: social/demographic, economic, international, and technological conditions, and their implications for HRM. Government influence through law, regulation, and policy is covered throughout the book. However, its general influence is touched on here.

Chapter Three moves from the external to the internal. Organization conditions are assessed, as well as how to link organization objectives with HR activities. Chapter Three also discusses the nature of work in the organization—how tasks, behaviors, responsibilities and outcomes are assigned to different jobs, and how jobs relate to each other.

Assess Conditions Concluded

Chapter Four moves to the level of the individual employee. Assessing performance is crucial to the success of the organization, and it is an activity in which HR managers are heavily involved. Other work outcomes, such as absenteeism and turnover, are also discussed, as is assessing employee attitudes, since attitudes are believed to affect performance.

CHAPTER
TWO

External Conditions

Assessing External Pressures

Environmental Scanning
Monitoring the Environment
Screening Information
Researching Issues
Develop Plans

Social/Demographic Changes
Population, Labor Force, Participation Rates
A Changing Population: Aging
A Changing Population: Immigration
The Feminization of the Labor Force
HR Effects of Social/Demographic Changes
Quality of the Labor Force

Economic Conditions
Labor Market Conditions
Product/Service Market Conditions

Inflationary Pressures

The Globalization of Markets
Europe 1992
International Management
Foreign Product Market Competition

Technological Changes

Government Influences: Laws, Regulations, Policies

Unions

Differential Impact and Responses to
Uncertainties

Shaping the External Environment

Your Turn: Managing Diversity

◆

McCullagh Coffee is a 120-years-old importer, roaster, and distributor of premium-grade, high-quality and specialty products. The company produces its own blends of regular and decaffeinated coffees to customer specifications and sells them to colleges, hospitals, nursing homes, and restaurants throughout western New York, eastern Pennsylvania, and northeastern Ohio. McCullagh is a small business; it employs only 50–60 people. But with a 1988 acquisition of its major competitor, McCullagh is now the major independent coffee roasting firm in the region, and its CEO, Warren Emblidge, has turned his attention to future growth possibilities.

After an assessment of the potential market in Syracuse and Albany, New York, Pittsburgh, and Cleveland, he has concluded that major expansion south, east, and west is not feasible because of entrenched competition already in those markets. Emblidge is therefore focusing his expansion plans north, in Canada. The U.S.-Canadian Free Trade Agreement reached in 1989 is supposed to remove all trade barriers between the United States and Canada within 10 years. Toronto's growing metropolitan area at the western end of Lake Ontario has created a 4.5 to 5 million person marketplace as compared to the 1.5 million marketplace of western New York. Emblidge's assessment is that the market in Canada is overpriced and underserviced. Therefore, he believes there is a real opportunity for major expansion. However, there are some major business and HR issues which need to be resolved before undertaking the expansion.

In spite of its small size, McCullagh faces many of the same issues faced by Boeing, Hewlett-Packard, or Allied-Signal. What type of personnel should be employed? Should they be Canadian or U.S. citizens, or both? What skills will be needed? How are these people to be located? Who will make the major decisions on which products should be sold, and where those products should be purchased (in the United States or in Canada)? How will those U.S. employees who have been with McCullagh for 20 years feel as a result of the Canadian effort? Are special efforts needed to retain their loyalty? Should they be transferred to Canada? Or should they be encouraged to retire? How will Canadian employees feel about working for a foreign-owned company? What will be required to fit the company into the Canadian culture and comply with Canadian laws?

EXHIBIT 2.1 Techniques to Diagnose External Conditions for Key Human Resource Programs

Device	→	External Conditions Analyzed	→	Human Resource Programs
Environmental scanning		Social/demographic changes Economic conditions International competition Technological change Governmental regulations Unions		Human resource planning
Salary surveys		Wages and benefits paid by competitors in labor and product markets		Compensation and benefits
Availability analysis		Availability of potential employees with required skills and experience Availability of women and minorities with required skills and experience		Recruiting Employment planning Affirmative action planning Selection
Labor settlement surveys		Recent contract settlement provisions among relevant unions and employers		Labor relations

ASSESSING EXTERNAL PRESSURES

Just as McCullagh Coffee is forced to come up with new HR approaches to deal with external conditions (changing legislation, new product market), part of the job of today's HR managers is to be aware of trends in the external environment, to identify those of particular relevance to their organization, and to design possible responses to these pressures. But how does a manager identify or anticipate significant external change? Exhibit 2.1 lists some techniques. As you can see, three of them are designed for specific HR activities. Availability analysis provides labor market information for staffing and recruiting. Labor settlement surveys identify patterns of agreements negotiated by various unions and employers. Salary surveys tell how much competing employers are paying. One procedure, environmental scanning, is flexible enough to assess a wide range of trends relevant to HRM.[1]

ENVIRONMENTAL SCANNING

Environmental scanning systematically surveys, identifies, and interprets relevant events and conditions. Its purpose is to answer the question, "What's coming and what will it mean to us?"

Scanning for general business purposes is reasonably well developed, but HRM applications are less common. The process is shown in Exhibit 2.2.

EXHIBIT 2.2 The Scanning Process

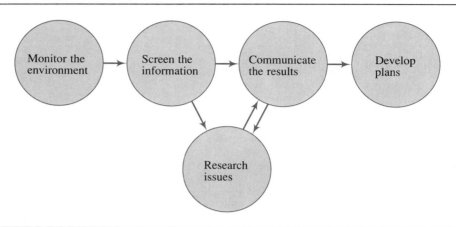

Source: G. Milkovich, L. Dyer, T. Mahoney, "HRM Planning," in *Human Resources Management in the 1980s,* ed. Stephen J. Carroll and Randall S. Schuler (Washington, D.C.: Bureau of National Affairs, 1983), pp. 2–18. Copyright ©1983 by The Bureau of National Affairs, Inc. Reprinted by permission.

Monitoring the Environment

Issues can be monitored through newspapers, specialized newsletters, journals, and the like. For example, 100 life insurance managers read publications in four general areas (economic and business conditions, governmental/political trends, social developments, and technological and scientific trends) for the Trend Analysis Program (TAP) of the American Council of Life Insurance.[2] The readers identify and abstract relevant articles, then forward them with comments to a screening committee.

Screening Information

Monitoring turns up more information than can be used. Further, the information comes in bits and pieces, whereas managers need the pieces assembled into patterns or changes in patterns. Screening separates the wheat from the chaff and organizes the information around issues. A second committee then prepares trend reports to be sent to member companies.

Researching Issues

Inside a company, information will be further screened and then integrated into business plans as McCullagh did with its information on potential new markets. Not all trends will be important to all companies. Of those trends that are important, further research may be required to develop HRM implications in light of a particular organization's business and HR plans. For example, proposed changes in immigration policy may be of great interest to Sunkist, which employs migrant labor, but less so for Weyerhaeuser, which does not. Sunkist would monitor and research this topic, and probably share its views by lobbying relevant government officials. Weyerhaeuser would pay greater attention to proposed changes in the Occupational Safety and Health Administration regulations, since Weyerhaeuser employs loggers, a notoriously dangerous occupation. Both companies monitor government regulations, but in different areas.

Exhibit 2.3 provides a framework for research on external trends. It recommends defining trends, projecting them into the future, and predicting the consequences for a particular organization. But as my mother always says, "It is difficult to predict, especially the future." One way to deal with uncertainties of projections is to include multiple viewpoints—involve people from different organization functions (HR, finance, production) in the process.[3]

Many companies prioritize external issues according to their impact on the organization. Honeywell uses a matrix, shown in Exhibit 2.4, that includes likelihood of an event actually occurring, the magnitude of impact, and time frame, to establish priorities. Thus, an event with large impact but low likelihood (e.g., being bought out by another company) can be planned for and, perhaps, a contingency plan developed.

Develop Plans

The purpose of all this research and analysis is to improve managers' decisions. So, the result must be transmitted to them on a timely basis and in an understandable and usable form. Written reports, abstracts, or seminars are typically used to spell out the HR implications of a trend for a specific firm.

Exhibit 2.5 shows how PepsiCo considers external information in formulating its HR plans. PepsiCo has calculated its staffing needs through the year 2000. These figures are derived from PepsiCo's business plans for its three main business lines: beverages (Pepsi-Cola), snacks (Frito-Lay), and restaurants (Pizza Hut). To obtain its growth targets, PepsiCo plans to expand employment in its restaurant business from 158,000 in 1990 to 308,000 in 2000, and to maintain present employment levels in its beverages (23,000) and snacks (27,000). Additionally, annual turnover rates—replacing employees who leave—are 15 percent in beverages and snacks and 150 percent in restaurants. Projecting these turnover rates and combining them with growth rates means that PepsiCo needs to hire almost 3.7 million people in the 1990s if it is to achieve its business plan.

But at the same time that PepsiCo's business plan requires a 72 percent increase in its work force, its research on external trends reveals that the U.S. labor force will grow by only 13 percent. Therefore, PepsiCo must attract more than its share of new employees. And that's what PepsiCo's HR people are working on. They are considering ways to open up new sources of employees.

EXHIBIT 2.3   A Framework for Research on External Issues

Data Analysis

---

1. Define Trends
   + Data inspection
   + Statistical analysis
   + Graphic presentation
2. Project the Future
   + Data extrapolation
   + Limiting factors
   + Best-case/Worst-case
3. Predict Consequences
   + Key organizational concerns
   + Gross impact analysis

4. Prioritize Implications
   + Likelihood of occurrence
   + Magnitude of impact
5. Identify Issues
   + Input from decision makers
   + Cite examples
   + Pose as questions
6. Rank Issues
7. Document/Disseminate Finds

Source: Adapted from Lorenz P. Schrenk, "Environmental Scanning," in *Human Resource Management: Evolving Roles and Responsibilities,* ASPA–BNA Series, vol. 1, ed. Lee Dyer (Washington, D.C.: Bureau of National Affairs, 1988), pp. 1.88–1.124.

Day care, part-time jobs, training programs, and other HR programs may make PepsiCo an attractive employer for people who otherwise would not have considered it.

So, at PepsiCo as well as other organizations, environmental scanning identifies, monitors, researches, and communicates external trends that affect the organization. HR managers draw out the HR implications of trends, integrate them into the organization's business plans, and plan HR actions based on this information.

Although environmental scanning can track trends across the entire external environment, those trends of widest interest for HRM include social/demographic changes, economic pressures, international competition, technological change, and governmental regulations.

SOCIAL/DEMOGRAPHIC CHANGES

Demographic changes affect the labor force, which affect an organization's supply of labor, and hence its HR decisions. Exhibit 2.6 summarizes some of the demographic predictions for the United States in the decade ahead.[4] These include continued population growth and aging, with above-average growth rates among black, Hispanic, and Asian populations. The labor force participation rates for women and minorities will continue to rise, so these groups, along with immigrants, will account for 82 percent of the increase in the labor force between 1985 and 2000.

EXHIBIT 2.4   Issue Prioritization Matrix

Probability	Impact: High	Impact: Medium	Impact: Low	Time Frame
High				
Medium				Immediate
Low		C		
High				
Medium		C		Immediate
Low	C			
High		C		
Medium	C			Long range
Low	C			

C = Consider contingency plan.

Source: Lorenz Schrenk, "Environmental Scanning," in *Human Resource Management: Evolving Roles and Responsibilities* ASPA–BNA Series, vol. 1, ed. Lee Dyer (Washington, D.C.: Bureau of National Affairs, 1988), pp. 1.88–1.124.

Population, Labor Force, and Participation Rates

People who are either working, looking for work, or in the armed services make up the *labor force*. Labor force is a subset of an area or country's *population*. In addition to the population/labor force distinction, a third statistic has already been mentioned: labor force participation rates. The *labor force participation rate* is the percent of those eligible to work (over 15 years of age and not in a prison, hospital, or other institution), who are working, looking for work, or in the armed services—that is, actually in the labor force.

EXHIBIT 2.5   Analyzing Demographic Trends at PepsiCo, 1990–2000

Estimates of PepsiCo New Hires

	Beverage	Snack	Restaurant	Total
1989 estimate headcount	23,000	27,000	158,000	208,000
1990–2000 new hires	34,500	40,500	3,595,000	3,670,000
2000 estimate headcount	23,000	27,000	308,000	358,000
Net increase	0	0	150,000	150,000

Issues

✦ Will work force availability stunt our growth? (Our work force must grow 71% while U.S. work force grows 13%.)

✦ Where will our 3,670,000 new hires come from?

✦ How do we ensure our share of the 15 million new workers?

✦ How do we help our franchisees get their share?

Distinguishing among these three statistics is important for employment planning. For example, while the population of the United States is projected to increase annually by a rate of 0.7 percent a year until 2000, the labor force will increase by 1.2 percent a year.[5] So the labor force is expanding faster as a percent than the population, though not in absolute numbers. The reason for this discrepancy is that a greater percent of the population is working—the participation rate has increased. Let us look at some of the demographic predictions to understand what this will mean for HRM.

A CHANGING POPULATION: AGING

Owing to past fluctuations in the birthrate, there are many more people in some age categories than others. Exhibit 2.7 projects U.S. population/age distributions into the year 2030. Low birthrates in the 1960s and 1970s have combined with medical improvements to produce a substantially older population in the 21st century. Medical advances have meant that people 65 and over increased by almost 80 percent between 1960 and 1987, and those 85 and over grew even faster—over 200 percent. The 85+ group is growing at a rate faster than any other age category.[6]

However, few people over 65 are still in the labor force. In fact, the average retirement age has been steadily dropping. This trend toward earlier retirement is fueled in part by better pension plans and additional financial inducements offered by downsizing employers. So the labor force is not aging as rapidly as the population.

EXHIBIT 2.6   Growing Roles in the Labor Force, 1985–2000

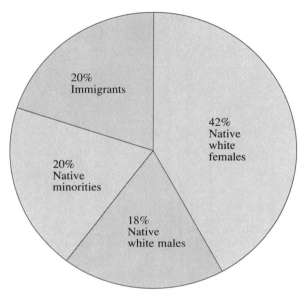

20% Immigrants

42% Native white females

20% Native minorities

18% Native white males

. . . And Their Causes

✦ Continual population growth.

✦ Steady aging of the population.

✦ Rising participation of minorities and women in the population.

✦ Increase in immigrants, particularly Asians and Hispanics.

Source for data: Hudson Institute estimates, based on BLS and census data.

In addition to people living longer, they are having fewer children. Between 1960 and 1990, the absolute number of Americans under age 15 declined by 9 million. The shortage of young people means that labor force expansion will be slower than it has been in the past. Fast-food chains, retailers, and hotels are already becoming hard-pressed to fill entry-level (typically low-paying) jobs that require little experience. Higher wages, improved benefits, and better training and career opportunities are some HR strategies to cope with the shortage. Other employers are looking to new technologies to improve productivity. Still others are turning to retirees as a source of well-trained, experienced employees. IBM and Combustion Engineering have established a "job bank" to create flexible relationships with older, experienced workers who no longer wish to work full time but don't want to stop working. Almost half the men 65 and over, and more than half the women in that age group, favor part-time employment after they retire.

EXHIBIT 2.7   Age Distribution of the U.S. Population: 1987, 2000, 2010, and 2030

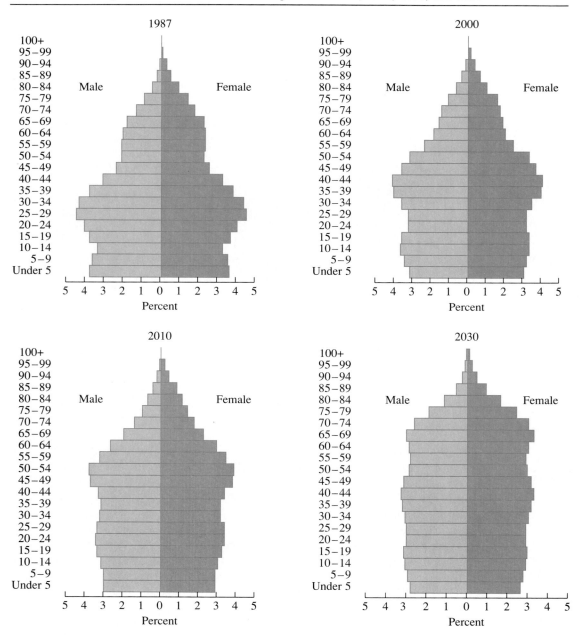

Source: Bureau of the Census, *Current Population Reports Projections of the Population of the United States, by Age, Sex, and Race: 1988 to 2080,* by Gregory Spencer.

A CHANGING POPULATION: IMMIGRATION

In the 1980s, immigration became as important as birthrates in shaping the look of the U.S. population: it now represents a major factor in the labor supply. Rates of immigration in the 1980s were higher than at any time since 1925. About half a million people arrive legally each year and perhaps another 1.5 million illegally.[7] Future immigration trends are difficult to predict, because the U.S. immigration policy is typically set in response to national and international political pressure. Economic implications of rulings that change the size and composition of the flow of immigrants are seldom researched.[8] Rather, decisions are made on humanitarian and political grounds. Shortages in certain occupations, particularly teachers and nurses, have led to intense recruitment campaigns. New York City, for example, recruits public school teachers in Spain. The city pays relocation costs in exchange for a two-year commitment to teach in the New York City public schools. These bilingual teachers are considered an asset in a city where 30 percent of the residents are foreign-born.

Most of today's immigrants are from very different cultures—predominantly Mexican, and Latin American. Cultural misunderstandings among employees and with customers inevitably increase as interactions occur among people who do not understand or value other people's ways of doing things. Managing diversity is becoming increasingly important in all organizations.

The United States and Canada are already the most diverse countries in the world. The challenge is to turn this diversity into an asset. A vice president for Procter & Gamble says, "The first companies that achieve a true multicultural environment will have a competitive edge. Diversity provides a much richer environment, a variety of viewpoints, greater productivity."[9] Creativity and innovation can result from combining different perspectives. But diversity also requires greater sensitivity from managers. Managers may overprotect some employees or, alternatively, judge them more harshly. They may make assumptions based on stereotypes or be unable to openly communicate and share information with people whose styles are different from their own. Differences need to be recognized and appreciated through training programs and by holding managers accountable for behaviors.

THE FEMINIZATION OF THE LABOR FORCE

The most significant long-term demographic change in the past 50 years is the dramatic increase in women's participation in the labor force. In 1949, 26 percent of married women between the ages of 25 and 44 held jobs. By 1981, the rate was 63 percent and, by 1989, it was 67 percent. Few predicted the magnitude or persistence of this change, or the changes in HR practice that would be required.[10] Hiring procedures, even hiring sources, pay practices, training programs—all needed reexamination to determine if they were unfair or had a negative impact on opportunities for women.[11]

The labor force participation rate for women continues to go up, although the rate of increase has slowed. As Exhibit 2.6 shows, women will enjoy the largest share of labor force growth through 2000. Women's participation rates are becoming more like men's for all age groups.

HR EFFECTS OF SOCIAL/DEMOGRAPHIC CHANGES

While discussion of changes may (or may not) be interesting, the real question is, What difference will it make for HRM?

An older work force will be more experienced but also more expensive, since wages are highly correlated with age.[12] Pensions and health insurance, heavily financed by employers, will also become more expensive.

For example, men aged 50 to 64 submit an average of $1,897 a year in medical expense claims that are reimbursed by their employers' health insurance plans. This is more than triple the claim rate of men aged 20 to 35. Women 50 to 64 submit $1,867 a year, 51 percent more than their younger counterparts.

The implications of an aging work force go beyond costs: an aging work force requires additional training to prevent obsolescence, phased retirements, and job redesign to accommodate changing physical needs and simultaneously capitalize on workers' experiences. (As textbook authors age, many argue—perhaps wistfully—that the experience and productivity of older employees, including authors, more than offset these adjustments.)

The increased role of women in the labor force is affecting every human resource decision.[13] It has increased interest in equal opportunity, pay discrimination, day-care benefits, and flexible work schedules. Today, over 65 percent of U.S. families have two or more wage earners. When there are employed spouses, disruption to a second career may make employees less flexible in accepting job assignments that require relocation. Two-career families may want to work fewer hours or have flexible schedules that accommodate family demands.[14] Many readers of this book can expect to face these issues as employees.

Combining the increased labor force participation rate of women and minorities with the flood of immigrants will produce a labor force that is increasingly diverse in gender, race, and culture. Sensitivity and respect for this diversity will be required.[15] All groups must feel they are viewed as equals by their employers: equal opportunities for promotions, pay increases, and equal opportunities to influence HR actions.

Women, minorities, and immigrants have traditionally suffered labor market problems, including discrimination. The demographic trends may provide a unique opportunity to narrow income gaps among ethnic groups and distribute women and minorities among a wider range of jobs than in the past. HR managers will be uniquely positioned to act on this opportunity.

QUALITY OF THE LABOR FORCE

In addition to greater cultural diversity, the U.S. population is diverging educationally. While Americans of both sexes and all ages enjoy high levels of educational attainment, the U.S. Department of Education reports that 17 million to 21 million adults cannot read well enough to cope with everyday life. While many of these are recent immigrants unable to understand or speak English, illiteracy is a problem even among high school graduates. For example, Blue Cross of Massachusetts discovered that 50 percent of its clerical workers tested for promotion read below a 12th grade level. Twenty-two percent of employees at a General Motors Corporation division asked for training in understanding simple words, signs, and labels; 31 percent needed help understanding basic written directions, charts, and instructions. Thus, more and more training programs inside organizations are forced to cover basic reading, math, and computer literacy.[16]

Many employers are trying to change this situation by getting directly involved in public schools.[17] One group is trying to develop a standardized test for high school graduates to measure basic skills. At present, all students who enter the labor force right after high school receive on average the same pay and get the same jobs regardless of high school performance.[18] Employers say that, if they can document students' reading and quantitative skills, they can pay differential wages based on those skills. Being paid for skills could provide a financial incentive for students to take their high school performance more seriously. Linking high school performance to pay can ensure a better work force, and also improve public education.

ECONOMIC CONDITIONS

Social and demographic changes affect an organization's supply of labor. Other labor market conditions also affect organizations.

Labor Market Conditions

Exchanges between employers and potential employees occur in the labor market. Information is exchanged about opportunities, skills, and requirements. When parties reach an agreement acceptable to all participants, a formal or implied contract is executed, and employees are hired for various jobs at various rates of pay.[19]

While an employer must be aware of conditions in the labor market, it is impossible to know about every single exchange. Instead, we use the concept of relevant labor market. Three factors usually define the relevant labor market:

Occupation (qualifications and skills required).
Geography (distances employees are willing to relocate or commute).
Competing employers with similar products and services.

EXHIBIT 2.8 Relevant Labor Markets, by Geographic and Employee Groups

	Employee Groups/Occupations					
Geographic Scope	**Production**	**Office and Clerical**	**Technicians**	**Scientists and Engineers**	**Managerial Professional**	**Executive**
Local: within relatively small areas, such as cities or MSAs (Metropolitan Statistical areas; e.g., Dallas metropolitan area)	Most likely	Most likely	Most likely	—	—	—
Regional: within a particular area of the state or county or several states (e.g., Greater Boston area)	Only if in short supply or critical	Only if in short supply or critical	Most likely	Likely	Likely	—
National: across the country	—	—	—	Most likely	Most likely	Most likely
International: across several countries	—	—	—	Only for critical skills or those in very short supply	Only for critical skills or those in very short supply	Likely

Source: George T. Milkovich and Jerry Newman, *Compensation*, 3rd ed. (Homewood, Ill.: Richard D. Irwin, 1990).

Occupations Skills and qualifications regulate mobility among occupations. Licensing and certification requirements, as well as training and education, set limits on who is in a labor market for a specific occupation. Accountants, for example, cannot legally do the work of barbers. However, accountants do not share this protection. With the exception of certified public accountants, anyone, including barbers, can legally do the work of accountants.

Geography Qualifications interact with geography to further narrow the relevant labor markets (see Exhibit 2.8). Degreed professionals (accountants, engineers, physicians) are recruited nationally and internationally; technicians, craft workers, and operatives are recruited regionally; and office workers locally. As the importance and complexity of job qualifications increase, the geographic scope increases.

Competing Employers The exchanges of greatest interest to a particular employer involve nearby employers of people with similar qualifications. Salary surveys (see Exhibit 2.1) would include these exchanges.

However, the geographic scope is not fixed. It changes in response to workers' willingness to relocate or to commute certain distances. This propensity to move may in turn be affected by personal and economic circumstances, as well as job conditions. Additionally, the geographic limits may not be the same for all in a broad skill group. Some firms, such as insurance and utilities, recruit MBAs regionally, others, such as consulting and research-and-development-intensive firms, recruit internationally.

Although labor market conditions do affect human resource decisions, the exact nature of their effect cannot be specified without further information on the organization, its employees, its strategies, and its objectives.

Product/Service Market Conditions

Labor market conditions put a floor on wages: an employer must pay wages sufficient to attract employees. Product market conditions put a ceiling on wages by limiting an employer's ability to pay. An employer must over time generate enough revenues to cover expenses, including pay and other human resource programs.[20] Thus, an employer's ability to hire, train, and promote employees is constrained by its ability to compete in its product market. Demand for a firm's products also affects staffing decisions. This is true for nonprofit, for-profit, and government organizations. Increased college enrollments (demand for services) eventually affect the number of professors and teaching assistants employed. Consequently, managers use product demand and productivity data to decide how many employees possessing which skills are needed.

INFLATIONARY PRESSURES

Inflation is the rate of change in prices we pay for goods and services. Its most direct effect on HR decisions is on cost-of-living adjustments (COLAs) to wages and pension plans.

Although inflation was reasonably low for most of the 1980s, its effects are cumulative. So, if you made $30,000 in 1985, you would need to make $36,000 in 1990 just to keep up with the cumulative effect of inflation during that time. Inflation also influences HR in less obvious ways. For example, a study by Exxon reports that relocating a transferred employee costs the company almost $75,000 in mortgage assistance, "bridge" loans, new home, and moving costs.

THE GLOBALIZATION OF MARKETS

International competition in domestic and foreign markets may be the key external condition affecting HRM in the 1990s.[21] At the end of World War II, America was the premier mass market for the world's goods and services. Relative to the rest of the world, its large population possessed sufficient skills to command high disposable incomes. The American product market was eight time larger than the next largest market. While the United States and Canada remain each other's largest trading partner, the unification of Europe into a common market (European Economic Community), scheduled to occur in 1992, has the potential to produce a market of 320 million people with incomes approximately equal to those of the 250 million Americans.[22]

Europe 1992

The purpose of the European common market is to create "an area without internal frontiers in which the free movement of goods, persons, services, and capital is insured."[23] Some companies see the single market as an opportunity to reduce costs through lower distribution expenses, but others express concern that new products and markets will undermine existing businesses. For example, West German workers, who are heavily unionized, enjoy some of the world's highest wages and shortest working hours.[24] But German employers and employees are already feeling pressure due to anticipated changes. Employers are pressing to continue operations on weekends. Currently, most unions do not allow weekend work. So, when one West German printer receives a rush order late in the week, he ships it to a French partner to meet a Monday delivery deadline back in Germany. Already, Volkswagen has increased its investments in its Spanish facility and has announced plans to boost production there.

The common market's Charter of Fundamental Social Rights calls for "information, consultation, and participation for workers" when an organization makes a substantial change—restructures, merges, introduces major technological change, or goes bankrupt.[25] The document also stresses the importance of collective bargaining, and it leaves open the possibility of Europeanwide agreements.

International Management

The unification of the European Economic Community raises the possibility for emergence of truly international managers.[26] At present, most companies staff top positions in their overseas operations largely with nationals from the parent country, rather than the host country or a third company (i.e., U.S. companies use American executives in Spain, rather than Spanish, French, or Japanese employees). Inside U.S. companies there is debate over the effect of overseas job assignments on a manager's career. In some companies, overseas experience enhances the likelihood of promotion into senior management positions. But in others, an overseas position takes a manager out of the mainstream of company decisions. Worse, there may be no procedures in place when managers return from overseas assignments to capitalize on their experience and knowledge gained.

Internationalization brings us back to the issue of valuing diversity. For example, Exhibit 2.9 lists some of the problems that may result from cultural differences between the United States and Japan. The most dangerous stumbling blocks involve information exchange. Americans are used to thrashing out issues, sometimes through heated exchange, in formal meetings. Japanese work out disagreements in private. Information is exchanged and consensus built in casual discussions that occur over lunch or after work. These are the kinds of differences that must be recognized for an international organization to effectively manage its employees. So, globalization presents a host of HR challenges to ensure that employees and employers are able to capitalize on new opportunities.

Foreign Product Market Competition

U.S. companies are not the only ones seeking overseas markets. Pacific Rim countries, particularly South Korea, Taiwan, Singapore, and Malaysia, combine lower wages with the latest technologies to become prime competitors. However, as the industrialization process continues in these countries, wage rates tend to rise. Exhibit 2.10 shows the considerable variation in average wage rates among countries. As you can see, Japan, which is heavily industrialized, no longer has the wage advantage it enjoyed up through the 1980s. While Singapore, Korea, and Taiwan still pay extremely low rates relative to the United States, Canada, Germany, and Japan, wage rates there are rising faster than in those countries with older industrial bases. However, caution is required in interpreting international wage comparisons, since government-provided benefits (e.g., health care in Canada and large layoff awards in West Germany) are not

---

EXHIBIT 2.9   An Example of Cultural Differences in International Organizations

---

United States	Japan
Personal priorities	
Family might come ahead of work.	Company loyalty is top priority.
Personal relations	
Emphasis on individuality and independence.	Group membership is paramount.
Communication style	
Explicitness is necessary.	Vagueness, ambiguity are essential.
Work relations	
Emphasis on talent, experience, and aggressiveness.	Getting along and versatility are essential.
Job promotion	
Based on merit, skill, and tenacity.	Based on seniority, skill, and deference.
Decision making	
Process is swift and from the top down.	Process is slow and built on bottom-to-top consensus.
Confrontations	
Showdowns are considered inevitable.	Conflict must be avoided at all costs.
Time orientation	
Based on bottom line financially.	Past, present, and future considered.

Source: Adapted from Deborah Okuma Associates, a placement company in Millbrae, Calif.

included, nor are changes due to monetary fluctuations.[27] Nevertheless, the exhibit shows that the wage advantage of foreign competitors is narrowing.

Employer forays into international markets can range from exporting one piece of equipment to participating in joint ventures to becoming a worldwide household name.[28] For example, the Holland Hitch Company of Holland, Michigan, not a household name, already earns 60 percent of its revenues by selling tractor trailer coupling devices to Renault and Daimler-Benz. At the other extreme, European users of Digital Equipment Corporation's computer software can check their spelling in a number of different languages before they go home to heat up their Weight-Watcher dinners and drink Diet Cokes.

Whatever the extent, globalization brings up a host of new HR issues. Moving U.S. employees raises questions of housing, schools, health facilities, and a pay arrangement that may seek to maintain the employee and family at approximately the same living standard as in the United States, although many companies are moving away from this "parity" approach. At the minimum, human resources at facilities in other countries must be managed in a style consistent with the cultural, social, and legal conditions of the countries in which they are

EXHIBIT 2.10   Hourly Compensation Costs in U.S. Dollars for Production Workers in Manufacturing

Country	1975		1980		1983		1985		1987		1988	
	Cost	%	Cost	%	Cost	%	Cost	%	Cost	%	Cost	%
U.S.	$6.36	100%	$9.84	100%	$12.10	100%	$12.96	100%	$13.46	100%	$13.90	100%
Canada	$5.79	91	$8.37	85	$10.85	90	$10.81	83	$11.97	89	$13.58	98
Germany	$6.35	100	$12.33	125	$10.23	85	$9.56	74	$16.87	125	$18.07	130
U.K.	$3.32	52	$7.43	76	$6.39	53	$6.19	48	$8.97	67	$10.56	76
Japan	$3.05	48	$5.61	57	$6.13	51	$6.47	50	$11.14	83	$13.14	95
Singapore	$0.84	13	$1.49	15	$2.21	18	$2.47	19	$2.31	17	$2.67	19
Korea	$0.35	6	$1.02	10	$1.23	10	$1.36	10	$1.79	13	$2.46	18
Taiwan	$0.39	6	$0.98	10	$1.27	10	$1.46	11	$2.19	16	$2.71	19
Brazil	$0.86	14	$1.39	14	$1.26	10	$1.22	9	$1.49	11	—	—
Mexico	$2.00	31	$2.96	30	$1.85	15	$2.09	16	$1.57	12	—	—

Source: *International Comparisons of Hourly Compensation Costs for Production Workers in Manufacturing*, U.S. Department of Labor, Bureau of Labor Statistics, August 1990.

located.[29] Exhibit 2.11 presents a "snapshot" of the labor force in a number of different countries. As you can see, literacy rates vary from 50 percent (Guatemala) to 100 percent (Luxembourg). Unionization rates range from 5 percent (Indonesia) to 90 percent (Virgin Islands); and English is the most common business language. HR managers need to monitor Europeanwide and even worldwide social, legal, and economic trends.

TECHNOLOGICAL CHANGES

Technological change alters jobs, creates new skills, makes occupations obsolete, and revises what employees need to learn and be trained to do. At the macro level, technological change occurs constantly, although its rate may fluctuate. For example, at the beginning of this century, farm workers were the most numerous occupation in the United States. By 1910, the Industrial Revolution gave manual workers preeminence. By the 1990s, blue-collar work gave way to a service and information economy requiring professional, managerial, and technical workers. These groups are projected to have the most rapid expansion among occupational groups up to the mid-90s.[30] Exhibits 2.12 and 2.13 lists occupations expected to grow rapidly in the 1990s, as well as those expected to decline.

While technological change in the overall economy is continuous, it can be a sudden jolt that causes extreme disruption for an organization and its employees. Managing this change can be difficult.[31] Studies show that change is better

EXHIBIT 2.11   International Economic Comparisons

	Population	Gross National Product	Percent of Unemployment	Business Language	Literacy Rate	Percent of Organized Labor
Pacific Rim						
Japan	123.2MM	2,805.5B	2.8%	English	99%	29%
South Korea	45.0MM	154.6B	3	English	92	10
Taiwan	19.8MM	95.8B	2.5	English	94	18
Hong Kong	5.6MM	45.7B	2.8	English	88	15
China	1.1 billion	269.4B	N/A	Mandarin	70	65
Thailand	55MM	51.1B	8	English	89	N/A
Vietnam	66.7MM	2.2B	N/A	French, English	94	N/A
Malaysia	16.9MM	34.1B	N/A	English	80	10
Singapore	2.7MM	23.8B	6	Chinese, Malay, English	87	17
Indonesia	187.7MM	63.4B	N/A	Bahasa, Indonesia	72	5
Philippines	61.9MM	32.6B	N/A	Philipino, English	88	N/A
Australia	16.5MM	196.8B	7.8	English	99	62
Europe—EC92						
Great Britain	56.8MM	670.0B	8.7	English	99	37
Netherlands	14.7MM	213.0B	10	English	99	29
Denmark	5.1MM	101.0B	6.5	English	99	65
Ireland	3.5MM	29.0B	17.6	English	99	36
West Germany	60.1MM	1,118.0B	6.4	English	99	34
Belgium	9.9MM	139.0B	10.8	English	98	70
France	55.0MM	880.0B	10.4	English	99	20
Luxembourg	0.4MM	6.0B	2.5	English	100	N/A
Portugal	10.2MM	37.0B	5.9	English	83	55
Spain	38.7MM	289.0B	19.8	English	97	25
Italy	57.3MM	758.0B	12.4	English	93	40
Greece	10.0MM	47.0B	8	English	95	20
Carribean/Central						
Guatemala	8.8MM	9.2B	50	English, Spanish	50	8
Honduras	5.0MM	2.6B	12	English, Spanish	56	40
Belizz	171,000	193MM	14	English, Spanish	93	15
Bahamas	242,000	2.1B	30	English	95	25
El Salvador	5.4MM	4.36B	45	English, Spanish	65	15
Jamaica	2.5MM	2.4B	22	English	74	24
Costa Rica	2.9MM	4.2B	65	English, Spanish	93	15
Haiti	6.3MM	2.1B	<50	English, French	99	N/A
Dominican Republic	7.2MM	5.6B	N/A	English, Spanish	74	15
Puerto Rico	3.4MM	14.8B	21	English, Spanish	89	N/A
St. Vincent & Grenadines	107,000	95MM	35	English	82	10
Grenada	84,000	129MM	20	English	85	20
Guyano	765,000	519MM	30	English	85	34
Montserrat	12,000	37.1MM	7	English	77	30
Virgin Islands	112,000	1.0B	3.5	English	90	90

EXHIBIT 2.11 *(concluded)*

	Population	Gross National Product	Percent of Unemployment	Business Language	Literacy Rate	Percent of Organized Labor
Antigoa & Barbuda	71,000	173MM	20	English	90	N/A
St. Christopher & Nevis	37,000	70MM	N/A	English	80	30
Domenica	98,000	91MM	20	English	80	25
St. Lucia	136,500	158MM	30	English	78	20
Barbados	256,700	1.2B	N/A	English	99	32
Trinidad/Tobago	1.3MM	5.0B	17	English	98	24
Mexico	83.6MM	127.2MM	18	English, Spanish	82	35

N/A means not available; MM means millions; B means billion.
HRPlanning Newsletters 4 and 5, vol. II, issue 2, February 1990.

accepted and more successful if affected employees help determine when, how, and where the changes are to be made.

Sometimes new technologies require new job designs. For example, work teams whose members share responsibility for tasks may be more appropriate than individual workers with separate responsibilities.[32]

At the other extreme, some technologies isolate workers.[33] Computer networks permit people's living rooms to be their work sites. While decentralization carried to this extreme may fit the needs of many employees, it also decreases interaction with colleagues and may diminish commitment to the organization. So, at the minimum, technological change creates uncertainty. It may also create the need for new ways to manage employees.

GOVERNMENT INFLUENCES: LAWS, REGULATIONS, AND POLICIES

Governments are major players in the management of human resources. Their laws and regulations have a direct effect. Examples are readily apparent: the Fair Labor Standards Act specifies a minimum wage for the nation, although individual states may set higher standards. The Wagner Act establishes the National Labor Relations Board to oversee collective bargaining. The Civil Rights Act establishes the Equal Employment Opportunity Commission to deal with allegations of discrimination.

Assessing trends in government is not a simple task. Federal, state, and local jurisdictions are all involved and often move in somewhat different directions. The current status of comparable worth is a case in point. Proposed legislation generally requires that jobs within an organization that are in some sense *comparable* should be paid the same, whether or not their job content is equal.[34] The issue most frequently arises in comparing clerical and blue-collar jobs.

EXHIBIT 2.12   Fastest-Growing Jobs in the 1990s

Help Wanted

Most of the fastest growing jobs of the 1990s will be in medical support fields, such as therapists, technicians, and aides.

FASTEST GROWING

(Employed labor force aged 16 and older, ranked by percent change; numbers in thousands; 1988–2000)	Number of Workers		Percent Change 1988–2000
	2000	1968	
Paralegals	145	83	75.3%
Medical assistants	253	149	70.0
Home health aides	397	236	67.9
Radiologic technologists and technicians	218	132	66.0
Data processing equipment repairers	115	71	61.2
Medical records technicians	75	47	59.9
Medical secretaries	327	207	58.0
Physical therapists	107	68	57.0
Surgical technologists	55	35	56.4
Operations research analysts	85	55	55.4
Securities and financial services sales workers	309	200	54.8
Travel agents	219	142	54.1
Computer systems analysts	617	403	53.3
Physical and corrective therapy assistants	60	39	52.5
Social welfare service aides	138	91	51.5

BIGGEST GAINERS

The jobs gaining the most workers in the future will require specialized skills, although not necessarily advanced education.

(Employed labor force aged 16 and older, ranked by change in number of workers; numbers in thousands; 1988–2000)	Number of Workers		Change in Number 1988–2000
	2000	1988	
Salespersons, retail	4,564	3,834	730
Registered nurses	2,190	1,577	613
Janitors and cleaners, including maids	3,450	2,895	556
Waiters and waitresses	2,337	1,786	551
General managers and top executives	3,509	3,030	479
General office clerks	2,974	2,519	455
Secretaries, except legal and medical	3,288	2,903	385
Nursing aides, orderlies, and attendants	1,562	1,184	378
Truck drivers, light and heavy	2,768	2,399	369
Receptionists and information clerks	1,164	833	331
Cashiers	2,614	2,310	304
Guards	1,050	795	256
Computer programmers	769	519	250
Food counter, fountain and related	1,866	1,626	240
Food preparation workers	1,260	1,027	234

Source: Bureau of Labor Statistics, 1989.

EXHIBIT 2.13   Fastest Declining Occupations in the 1990s, 1986–2000

	Employment (000s)		
Occupation	1986	Projected, 2000	Percent Decline in Employment
Electrical and electronic assemblers	249	116	−53.7%
Electronic semiconductor processors	29	14	−51.1
Railroad conductors and yardmasters	29	17	−40.9
Railroad brake, signal, and switch operators	42	25	−39.9
Gas and petroleum plant and system occupations .	31	20	−34.3
Industrial truck and tractor operators	425	283	−33.6
Shoe sewing machine operators and tenders	27	18	−32.1
Station installers and repairers, telephone	58	40	−31.8
Chemical equipment controllers, operators and tenders	73	52	−29.7
Chemical plant and system operators	33	23	−29.6
Stenographers	178	128	−28.2
Farmers	1,182	850	−28.1
Statistical clerks	71	52	−26.4
Textile draw-out and winding machine operators and tenders	219	164	−25.2
Central office and PBX installers and repairers . . .	74	57	−23.1
Farm workers	940	750	−20.3
Coil winders, tapers and finishers	34	28	−18.5
Central office operators	42	34	−17.9
Directory assistance operators	32	27	−17.7
Compositors, typesetters, and arrangers, precision	30	25	−17.1

Source: George Silvestri and John Luka-Siewiez, "A Look at Occupational Employment Trends to the Year 2000," *Monthly Labor Review,* September 1987, p. 61.

While some states have passed and others are considering legislation, others have rejected the notion, and the federal government seems to be avoiding it.[35] In Canada, the provinces have passed wide-ranging laws that regulate both public and private sector employees regarding comparable worth.[36]

Since employers who operate internationally are required to be in compliance with the laws of the nations in which they operate, these laws will have far-reaching HR implications. For example, if General Motors can operationalize a comparable worth pay plan that complies with the law in Windsor, Ontario, why can't it do the same thing across the river in Detroit, Michigan?

While some employment legislation limits actions of employees, most of it restrains employers and specifies financial liability for failure to comply.[37] Moreover, record-keeping and reporting requirements can be expensive. For these reasons, most employers lobby against legislative initiatives or, at the minimum, try to shape them. An example of this shaping is the use of skill, effort, responsibility, and working conditions to define equal work in the 1967 Equal Pay Act. Employers informed Congress that these factors were already commonly used to evaluate jobs.

Employers also influence interpretation of legislation by defending their practices in the courts. Because this is a costly procedure, it is not one that many employers voluntarily seek.

Because government has such a pervasive effect on HRM, specific laws will be discussed throughout the book.

UNIONS

The presence of a union means many HR decisions must be negotiated with a third party. But unions have an effect beyond those employers whose workers are unionized. Many organizations make decisions as part of a strategy to remain nonunionized. Thus, they may match pay rates earned by union members, or they may locate facilities in geographic areas where unions' power is historically weak. It is no accident that the majority of foreign car makers who opened plants in the United States did so in rural areas or near small towns in the Midwest.

DIFFERENTIAL IMPACT AND RESPONSES TO UNCERTAINTIES

We have already mentioned the difficulties of predicting external pressures for an entire society, much less the impact on a specific organization. It is one thing to understand that the labor force in the entire United States is, on average, growing older or becoming more diverse or more susceptible to global competition. But the key question for human resource managers is what difference that trend will make to their particular organization. For example, in comparison to Toyota and Honda, the aging work force employed at Ford and General Motors not only is expensive but also limits promotion opportunities for younger employees. So Ford and General Motors may offer enhanced retirement programs to increase turnover among the older employees. In contrast, a rapid-growth organization, such as PepsiCo, may hire those newly retired workers to obtain reliable employees. So, repercussions of trends vary among organizations.

As a result of the variability and uncertainty facing firms, some HR managers feel it is sufficient simply to realize that the environment is changing and will continue to change.[38] Rather than designing elaborate procedures to forecast specific changes, they urge creation of a flexible work force and an adaptable organization structure that will permit the organization and employees to adapt when necessary to whatever significant environmental changes occur.

Thus, there are three possible ways HR managers can approach external uncertainties. One is to try to reduce uncertainty by implementing scanning, forecasting, and planning mechanisms. Another is to establish HR policies that create a flexible work force and an organization structure that can adapt when necessary to whatever happens. The third approach is to help shape external conditions.

SHAPING THE EXTERNAL ENVIRONMENT

In addition to external pressures shaping HR decisions, the diagnostic model shows that HR decisions also can shape the external environment. Lobbying the regulatory process is the obvious example. Other examples include working closely with technical schools and universities to affect the education and training of future employees and customers, and to improve literacy and math skills. Major grants of computer hardware and software to engineering and business schools are another example. Even corporate support of community cultural and charitable organizations is an initiative to shape the organization's human resource environment, because the attractiveness of a community affects the ease of recruiting.

So, external conditions set the stage for the management of human resources. They influence the decisions that organizations make; the decisions, in turn, influence these conditions. But not all conditions affect all organizations the same. Thus, organization responses vary. So, while we can say that external factors affect HRM, and that these factors vary over time, consequences of these variations and the specifics of their impact on HR activities are not well studied or understood.

SUMMARY

External conditions set the stage for management of human resources. They influence the decisions organizations make; the decisions, in turn, influence these conditions. So, assessing external conditions is a crucial element in the diagnostic model.

Although the nature of the external conditions can be discussed in general terms, it is sometimes difficult to discuss specifics. This is so for several reasons.

First, the external conditions are interrelated, and constantly changing. For example, we have classified relevant conditions as social/demographic, economic, international, technological, and governmental in our diagnostic model. Yet, demographic changes not only affect organizations, they also affect government, the economy, and all of society. So, as one factor changes, the others inevitably change, too.

Second, organizations differ, and they are constantly changing, too. So, the same external condition may have very different implications among organizations.

External pressures may be viewed as an opportunity to improve human resource effectiveness. Some managers use periods of recession to restructure their organizations and remove poor performers. Other organizations look to the human resource managers to buffer the organization from external pressures. Thus, the role of human resource managers with respect to external pressures also seems to vary across organizations.

While today's managers are increasingly sensitive to the influence of external factors on their organizations' human resource management, they may not be clear about how to come to grips with the factors that they recognize as being important. A helpful start is the concept of the environmental scanning system—a systematic procedure for searching the external environment for developments that are likely to become significant.

The diagnostic model identifies organization conditions as being additional determinant of HR activities. We shall discuss how organization conditions affect HR in the next chapter.

DISCUSSION AND REVIEW QUESTIONS

1. Why is it important for HR managers to keep track of external forces?
2. What are the possible disadvantages or problems with keeping track of external pressures?
3. There is some controversy over whether immigration is good or bad for the economy. What do you think, and why?
4. What difference do changes in labor force participation rates make?
5. Think back to when you were in high school. What kind of business interventions would you have welcomed? What objectives would you set for such interventions?
6. What is the difference between labor market and product market? What impact does each have on HRM?
7. What kind of skills do you think an international manager should possess?
8. Technological advances can make jobs safer and more interesting, but they can also make them more routine. Is technology good or bad for society?
9. How does inflation affect organizations?
10. In what ways would HRM be different if the labor force was shrinking, instead of expanding?

YOUR TURN
MANAGING DIVERSITY

Xerox, Procter & Gamble, Hughes Aircraft, Apple, Weyerhaeuser, the U.S. Food and Drug Administration, and other large organizations have already started to plan for and respond to the labor force of the next century. Projections of increased minority and growing female involvement have prompted organizations to recognize the impact these changes will likely have on operations.

Xerox is striving to become more sensitive to work-group communications involving minorities by using seminars, video tape, and role playing training; Procter & Gamble is stressing and exploiting the existence of cultural diversity in its labor force; Hughes Aircraft has been using consultants to assist with minority integration; Apple emphasizes recognition of and adjustment to employee differences rather than worker conformity; the FDA and Weyerhaeuser believe their success depends on reducing the internal prejudice and racism that hinders full utilization of their human resources.

In each of the above examples the initiative focuses on recognition and integration of the sociocultural differences of employees. Rather than wait and hastily react to external changes, some organizations have begun to actively explore and implement policy revisions to adjust to their changing labor force.

Assume you are a corporate director of HR for a specific company in your area. Describe your organization. What impact do you feel the labor force changes will have on your operations? What influence will sociocultural differences have on your human resource strategy? Why, how, and when would you address these differences among employees?

This case prepared by Joseph Salamone, SUNY Buffalo.

NOTES AND REFERENCES

1. Lorenz P. Schrenk, "Environmental Scanning," in *Human Resource Management: Evolving Roles and Responsibilities,* ASPA–BNA Series, vol. 1, ed. Lee Dyer (Washington, D.C.: Bureau of National Affairs, 1988), pp. 1.88–1.124.

2. George Milkovich, Lee Dyer, and Thomas Mahoney, "HR Planning," chap. 2 in *Human Resources Management in the 1980s,* ed. S. J. Carroll and R. S. Schuler (Washington, D.C.: Bureau of National Affairs, 1983), pp. 2-1, 2-28.

3. Schrenk, "Environmental Scanning."

4. "Outlook 2000," series of five articles printed in *Monthly Labor Review,* November 1989, pp. 3–74.

5. Ibid.

6. Ibid.

7. Ibid.

8. Vernon M. Briggs, Jr., *Immigration Policy and the American Labor Force* (Baltimore, Md.: Johns Hopkins University Press, 1984); Vernon M. Briggs, Jr., "The Growth and Composition of the U.S. Labor Force," *Science,* October 9, 1987, pp. 176–80; Julian L. Simon, *The Economic Consequences of Immigration* (New York: Basil Blackwell, 1990).

9. Gretchen Haight, "Managing Diversity," *Across the Board,* March 1990, pp. 22–29.

10. Helen Remick, ed., *Comparable Worth and Wage Discrimination* (Philadelphia: Temple University Press, 1984).

11. Victor R. Fuchs, *Women's Quest for Economic Equality* (Cambridge, Mass.: Harvard University Press, 1988).

12. Benson Rosen and Thomas H. Jerdee, *Older Employees: New Roles for Valued Resources* (Homewood, Ill.: Dow Jones-Irwin, 1985).

13. Fuchs, *Women's Quest for Economic Equality*.

14. Sheila B. Kamerman and Alfred J. Kahn, *The Responsive Workplace: Employers and a Changing Labor Force* (New York: Columbia University Press, 1987).

15. "Valuing Workforce Diversity," *Personnel*, June 1988; pp. 52–60.

16. Pat Choate and J. K. Linger, *The High-Flex Society* (New York: Alfred A. Knopf, 1986).

17. Nancy J. Perry, "How to Help America's Schools," *Fortune*, December 4, 1989, pp. 137–42.

18. John Bishop, "Why High School Students Learn So Little and What Can Be Done about It," Ithaca, New York, Cornell University Center for Advanced Human Resource Studies, Working Paper No. 88–01.

19. For a more extended discussion of labor markets, see Arne L. Kalleberg and Aage B. Sorensen, "The Sociology of Labor Markets," *Annual Review of Sociology*, 1979, pp. 351–79; Ronald G. Ehrenberg and Robert S. Smith, *Modern Labor Economics* (Glenview, Il.: Scott, Foresman, 1982), or Robert J. Flanagan, Robert S. Smith, and Ronald G. Ehrenberg, *Labor Economics and Labor Relations* (Glenview, Ill.: Scott, Foresman, 1984).

20. John Boudreau, "Utility Analysis," in Dyer, *Human Resource Management*, pp. 1.125–1.186.

21. Oded Shenkar and Yoram Zeira, "Human Resources Management in International Joint Ventures: Directions for Research," *Academy of Management Review* 12, no. 3 (1987), pp. 546–57.

22. John Young, "Responding to the New Reality of Global Competition," in *Competing Through Productivity and Quality*, ed. Y. K. Shetty and Vernon M. Buehler (Cambridge, Mass.: Productivity Press, 1988), pp. 79–93.

23. *Industrial Relations Europe*, a monthly newsletter, has covered the debate on the social charter for the Common Market.

24. "Reshaping Europe: 1992 and Beyond," *Business Week*, December 12, 1988, pp. 48–53; "Is the German Featherbed on Its Way Out?" *Business Week*, March 13, 1989, p. 62.

25. *Industrial Relations Europe*, March 1990, pp. 25–35.

26. Kenneth R. Sheets, "The 21st Century Executive," *U.S. News and World Report*, March 7, 1988, pp. 48–59; John F. Magee, "1992: Moves Americans Must Make," *Harvard Business Review*, May–June 1989, pp. 78–84.

27. Michael L. Dertouzos, Richard K. Lester, and Robert M. Solow, *Made in America* (Cambridge, Mass.: MIT Press, 1989).

28. "Reshaping Europe"; Preston Townley, "Global Business in the Next Decade," *Across the Board*, January–February 1990, pp. 13–19.

29. Peter J. Dowling, "International HRM," in *Human Resource Management: Evolving Roles and Responsibilities*, ASPA–BNA Series, vol. 1, ed. Lee Dyer (Washington, D.C.: Bureau of National Affairs, 1988), pp. 1.228–1.257.

30. Samuel M. Ehrenhalt, "Work Force Shifts in 80s," *New York Times*, August 15, 1986, p. 26.

31. Raymond E. Miles, "Adapting to Technology and Competition," *California Management Review*, Winter 1989, pp. 9–28.

32. Edgar H. Schein, "Corporate Teams and Totems," *Across the Board*, May 1989, pp. 12–17.

33. Guillermo J. Grenier, *Inhuman Relations* (Philadelphia: Temple University Press, 1988).

34. Donald J. Treiman and Heidi I. Hartmann, *Women, Work, and Wages* (Washington, D.C.: National Academy Press, 1981).

35. The National Committee on Pay Equity, Washington, D.C., publishes a member newsletter that reports activity at the national and state level.

36. "Pay Equity: The New Ontario Legislation," speech delivered by Edward T. McDermott to Canadian Bar Association, February 5, 1987.

37. Ursula Fairbairn and Michelle Mitchell, "The External Environments of Human Resources" (Armonk, N.J.: IBM Corporation, 1988).

38. Alan D. Meyer, "Adapting to Environmental Jolts," *Administrative Science Quarterly* 27 (December 1982), pp. 515–37.

CHAPTER THREE

Organization Conditions

Organizational-Level Factors

Financial Conditions

Strategy
HR Issues and Business Strategy
Strategic Human Resource Management

Technology

Culture/Philosophy

Management Style

The State of Research

The Nature of Work

Work-Level Factors

Job Analysis
Conventional Job Analysis
Quantitative Job Analysis
Job Descriptions

Job Design
Scientific Management
Human Relations
Job Characteristics
Sociotechnical Perspective
Work Teams

Your Turn: Restructuring Blues

Appendix: Job Analysis Procedures

I put on my hard hat, change into my safety shoes, put on my safety glasses, go to the bonderizer. They rake the metal, they wash it, they dip it in a paint solution, and we take it off. My arms get tired about the first half hour. After that, they don't get tired any more until maybe the last half hour at the end of the day.

Interview with steelworker, *Working,* by Studs Terkel[1]

Everything that happens in the market I see instantaneously. I have a machine in front of me that records and memorizes every transaction that takes place in the entire day. I watch 18 million, 20 million shares pass the tape. I look at every symbol, every transaction. I would go out of my mind, but my eye has been conditioned to screen maybe 200 stocks and ignore the others. I pick up with my eyes Goodrich, but I don't see ITT. There are over 3,200 symbols. I drop the other 3,000. Otherwise I'd go mad. I really put in an enormously exhausting day.

Interview with stockbroker, *Working,* by Studs Terkel[2]

Two people describe very different jobs in very different organizations. Most people spend a significant part of their adult lives inside work organizations, where they do an endless variety of tasks. For example, TRW, Inc., manufactures products ranging from electronic guidance systems for NASA to auto brakes for General Motors. The firm's Financial Services sector gathers credit data on consumers and markets it to retailers. To compete effectively in such diverse markets, TRW's three sectors—Electronics, Automotive, and Financial Services—are subdivided into divisions and plants located throughout the United States and the world. The external pressures and organization conditions in the three sectors differ. So do many of their human resource activities. For example, the Electronics sector needs electrical engineers and computer specialists. These skills are currently in very high demand, and salaries are escalating. Thus, Electronics is operating under highly competitive labor market conditions. At the same time, the Automotive sector has experienced less dependable markets and stiff foreign competition. Layoffs, retrenchment, changes in work rules, plant relocation and modernization, and controlled wage increases (even wage concessions) have been typical personnel activities in the Automotive business. Financial Services requires computer, financial, and marketing specialists. Since it is a new venture for TRW, its HRM decisions are tailored to its unique conditions.

Even though the work and HR activities across sectors vary, a number of tasks are similar across all three sectors. All three sectors need secretaries, accountants, managers, and financial analysts.

Furthermore, there are some similarities in their HR activities. All three sectors provide pension and health care insurance to employees, and all three sectors transfer people among them. So, at the same time that the sectors face different external pressures, they are bound together in a single organization. Policies set for the total corporation are binding on all sectors.

This chapter looks at organization conditions and work inside the organization. Both the organization and the nature of the work need to be considered when making HR decisions. We will begin this chapter with a discussion of organization factors. Later on, we will move to the work level.

ORGANIZATION-LEVEL FACTORS

A few years back, a book was published listing the 100 best organizations to work for.[3] The book did not categorize organizations by their size, what industry they were in, what organization design they followed, or how their financials looked. All of these organizational characteristics are important, and they deserve study. But the 100 best organizations to work for were chosen on the basis of their HR programs: opportunity for advancement (i.e., staffing and development), pay (i.e., compensation and benefits), challenging assignments (i.e., work design and career development), and how the corporation treated its employees (employee relations).

Researchers have compiled a lengthy list of organizational characteristics related to HR decisions. These include size, industry, geographic location, and even the importance of research and development in the firm's business strategy. For example, petroleum and drug firms like Mobil and Merck pay higher wages than do manufacturing or consumer product organizations.[4] Organizations that spend more than 5 percent of their revenues on research and development pay bigger bonuses and pay them to a larger percentage of their employees compared to other firms.[5] So, a number of organizational characteristics are related to HRM. A discussion of all of them is beyond the scope of this book. Instead, we are going to focus on five factors shown in Exhibit 3.1. These are:

Financial conditions
Business strategy
Technology
Culture/Philosophy
Management style

These factors were chosen because they exert a strong influence on the nature of work in organizations and on HRM.

FINANCIAL CONDITIONS

If an organization does not make enough money over time, it cannot pay employees, fund training or retraining programs, or provide laid-off employees assistance in finding new jobs.

EXHIBIT 3.1   Assessing Organization Conditions

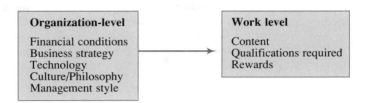

In most organizations, HR decisions, particularly those involving how many people to employ, how much to pay them, and whether to retrain them, account for a large share of expenses. Many organizations are taking steps to tie these decisions more closely to the organization's financial conditions.[6]

There are a number of different ways to do this. Union contracts, for example, frequently include specific details on what job search assistance and retraining are to be provided and what benefits are to be paid to laid-off workers.[7] They may even specify under what financial conditions layoffs are permitted. Legal settlements of allegations of discrimination often require specific HR activities.[8] Profit sharing plans allow pay to rise and fall with the firm's financial condition.

So, HRM decisions must be made with their affordability in mind.

STRATEGY

An organization's strategy focuses on such questions as *Which businesses should we compete in?* and *How should we compete?* Strategy sets long-term directions. It integrates decisions and directs them toward specific goals.

Corporate-Level Strategy

Strategic questions occur at various levels in the organization. The most fundamental question is at the corporate level: *What business(es) should we be in?* During the 1970s, the answer for many organizations was "diversify." Steel companies bought oil companies and hotels, and oil companies bought department stores, office equipment manufacturers, and movie studios. While the financial logic was to acquire product lines whose product cycles complemented each other, many organizations did not have the expertise to run their new businesses. So, the 1980s and early 1990s saw a new wave of realignments, as organizations reduced product diversity to focus on basic products and markets.[9]

Unit-Level Strategy

Unit-level decisions focus on parts of the organization, often called *profit centers, lines of business,* or *business units*. TRW's three sectors are examples. Strategic decisions at this level focus on deciding *how to compete in their specific markets*.

Functional-Level Strategy

Functional decisions involve particular components of the organization, such as marketing, finance, and, of course, human resource management. At this level, managers formulate a strategy that will *help their function contribute to the achievement of corporate and unit objectives*. So, for example, the appropriate inventory valuation and other accounting conventions are determined by corporate and unit needs. For HRM, a strategic approach translates into three tasks:[10]

1. Assure that HR issues are considered in formulating business strategies ("In what businesses should we compete?").
2. Establish HR goals and plans—an HR strategy—to support the business strategy ("How will HR decisions help us compete?").
3. Work with managers to ensure implementation of the HR plan ("How to translate policies into day-to-day actions").

HR Issues and Business Strategy

Strategic decisions involve choices, and these choices shape human resource decisions. USX's choices to reposition itself in specialty steels and to acquire Marathon Oil involved major redeployment of human resources. The effects were dramatic: 150 steel plants were closed; 100,000 employees were laid off or retired; remaining employees were forced to compete with new products in new markets.

Just as the business strategy shapes human resource decisions, so, too, do human resource decisions affect strategic choices. Perhaps the most clear-cut examples are the selection of chief executives and top managers. Since these people are so involved in formulating strategies, changes in their ranks can have significant effects.

The purchase of Eastern Airlines by Frank Lorenzo provides a vivid example of this interaction between HR decisions and business strategy. Lorenzo's strategy at Continental, an airline he had previously acquired, was to take the airline into bankruptcy to break union contracts, then restructure as a smaller, more profitable airline that paid lower wages. Afraid that they would become victims of this same business strategy, Eastern Airlines mechanics, pilots, and flight attendants teamed up to try to rebuff Lorenzo's efforts to acquire Eastern.[11] Human resource decisions beyond the selection of the executives can also affect business strategies.[12] Some argue that the terms General Motors negotiated with its union, UAW, have seriously limited its ability to make work rule changes necessary to compete. And Exxon dropped its office products business when it became clear that its chemical engineers weren't able to compete with other organizations in that rapidly changing product market.

Strategic Human Resource Management (HRM)

The premise behind strategic HRM is that HR decisions that "fit" the organization conditions will positively affect performance, as shown in Exhibit 3.2. Human resource strategy's purpose is to help guide managers' personnel decisions and thereby affect the success of the organization.

A number of typologies have been proposed to relate HR decisions to a specific strategy. Miles and Snow began with business strategies.[13] They classified organizations as:

Defenders: organizations operating in a few stable product markets.

Prospectors: organizations that continually search for new product and market opportunities and regularly take risks.

Analyzers: organizations that operate in many product markets, some relatively stable, others changing.

They then proposed HR activities that would complement each of these business strategies (see Exhibit 3.3). For example, the product market stability enjoyed by Defenders allows them the time to do formal and extensive planning, and to develop people internally to meet anticipated staffing needs. In contrast, Prospectors must be more adaptable, and so are more likely to recruit people with the skills they need from outside the organization. The uncertainties that Prospectors face make formal HR planning less useful. Rather, it is sufficient to have people who are flexible enough to respond to challenges as they arise.

Dyer and Holder identify three major HR strategies, which they refer to as *Inducement, Investment,* and *Involvement.*[14]

Inducement

Inducers compete in the product market on the basis of price or quality. They are characterized by a centralized organization structure and slow technological change. Reliability and dependability are the most valued employee characteristics, and jobs are narrowly defined and tightly controlled. Consistent, solid performance on specified tasks is valued in employees, not necessarily innovation, new ideas, or competence beyond that required for the present job.

To get this performance, Inducers rely on pay. Incentive plans, gainsharing, performance bonuses, and other approaches base pay on performance. Because of these multiple plans, pay is not necessarily low, even though labor costs are closely managed. The strong emphasis on labor costs also means that staffing tends to be lean. Lincoln Electric and UPS are cited as successful Inducers. These are the same companies that Miles and Snow labeled as Defenders.

Investment

Investors believe that product differentiation or unique features will allow wide profit margins. But this reliance on uniqueness increases their susceptibility to market changes and other external pressures. To buffer themselves, Investors

EXHIBIT 3.2 The Payoff of Strategic Human Resource Management

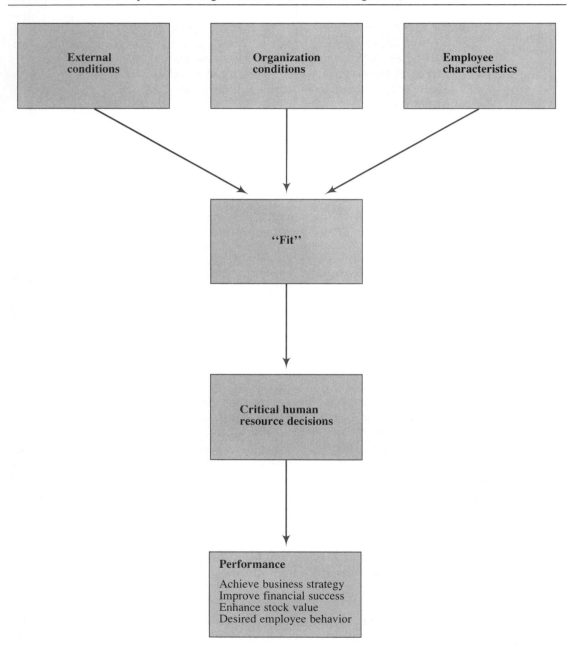

EXHIBIT 3.3   Organization Conditions and Human Resource Management Activities

	Type A (Defender)	Type B (Prospector)	Type C (Analyzer)
Organizational Characteristics			
Typical company	Lincoln Electric	Hewlett-Packard	Texas Instruments
Product-market strategy	Limited, stable product line; predictable markets	Broad, changing product line; changing markets	Stable and changing product line; predictable and changing markets
Research and development	Limited mostly to product improvement	Extensive; emphasis on "first-to-market"	Focused; emphasis on "second-to-market"
Production	High volume/low cost; emphasis on efficiency and process engineering	Customized; prototypical emphasis on effectiveness and product design	High volume/low cost; emphasis on process engineering
Marketing	Limited mostly to sales	Focused heavily on market research	Extensive marketing campaigns
Human Resource Management Activities			
Basic role	Maintenance	Entrepreneurial	Coordination
Human resource planning	Formal; extensive	Informal; limited	Formal; extensive
Recruitment, selection, and placement	Make	Buy	Make and buy
Training and development	Skill building	Skill identification and application	Skill-building and application
Compensation	Internal pay relationships; internal equity	External pay relationships; external competitiveness	Internal consistency and external competitiveness, a blend
Performance appraisal	Process-oriented; focus on training needs; individual/group performance	Results-oriented; focus on staffing needs, division/corporate performance	Mostly process-oriented; training and staffing needs, individual/group/division performance

tend to overstaff, which provides flexibility—but at a price. Their technologies tend to be so complex and changing that highly trained, innovative employees are required.

Training, development, and employee relations (e.g., communications and due process procedures) are important HR programs for Investors, and supervisors play a key role in carrying out these programs. Supervisors are given the training and resources to be highly supportive and effective deliverers of the organization's message of respect and equitable treatment for employees. Labor relations is almost a nonissue, because Investors are rarely unionized. IBM is the classic Investor.

Involvement

Involvers push decisions down to the lowest possible work level. Involvers assume that employees feel committed to decisions they help make, and that initiative, creativity, and flexibility flow from the commitment. Motorola and Colgate-Palmolive use this strategy.

The crucial HR focus in an Involvement strategy is job design. Self-managed work teams are common, with the supervisor assisting the team by providing information and resources. Training emphasizes communications, problem solving, and group dynamics. Pay and employee relations receive less attention; the rewards from involvement theoretically minimize the need for such programs.

There are a number of other approaches to categorizing HR strategies. They share the common objective of trying to relate or fit HR decisions to organization characteristics. The key premise underlying all this discussion of strategy is that HR decisions that fit the organization (and external conditions) are likely to be more effective.

TECHNOLOGY

Technology can be defined as the processes and techniques used to generate goods and services. Many of the dirty, dangerous, and boring aspects of work can be eliminated through applications of new technology. Computer-assisted design eliminates tedious drafting; scanners eliminate key punching routine information; robots lessen risk of exposure to dangers in the laboratory or the factory. But many employees view new technologies as a threat to their job security. Employee participation in decisions that affect how work is structured can help allay these fears and provide greater flexibility in adapting to continuing changes.[15]

While popular mythology of the 1980s depicted an aging steelworker being trained to program the robot that replaced him, most changes are far less drastic. New technologies have provided ways for small, start-up firms to compete against bigger, slow-moving rivals, thus fueling job creation. But on average, most new jobs created by technological change do require more skill than today's jobs. A serious challenge for organizations will be helping to ease the strain of change for older workers. Such older workers, many with employed spouses and family and financial obligations, are frequently less able to move about the country in search of new opportunities than younger workers.

There is some evidence that the economy is entering a new phase in technological change. Orders for new robots are declining, and orders for new mainframe computers are at their lowest levels since 1979. The emphasis may have switched to structuring organizations and designing jobs around new technical capacities to better integrate employees and technological processes.[16] We shall return to this point in the job design discussion later in this chapter.

CULTURE/PHILOSOPHY

Volumes have been written about the importance of corporate culture and philosophy in achieving employee and organization effectiveness. Still, debate continues on such fundamental issues as exactly what corporate culture really is, how it changes, and whether that change emanates from the top or bottom of an organization. To some, the culture of an organization is the bedrock that gives it identity and stability, and it is reflected in day-to-day practices. To others, culture is a force that drives an organization to its goals. As those goals change, so does the culture.

Culture and Strategy

The notion of culture has been used in a number of separate ways.[17]

1. *Culture as a social control system.* Shared expectations shape individual behavior. If we want to be accepted, we try to live according to these expectations. For example, in Japan, employees rarely take their full number of vacation days. Employees who return from vacation are made to feel that other employees have had to do their work in their absence. Thus, there is social pressure to forgo vacations. The expectations of co-workers come to control behavior.

2. *Culture as normative order.* In this interpretation, the norms regarding what is and is not appropriate do not focus on social acceptance. Rather, they exist around a corporatewide sense of "how things are done."[18] For example, Johnson & Johnson requires all its managers and supervisors to receive training on understanding the needs of their changing work force. Supervisors who understand Johnson & Johnson's commitment to working families will be flexible in dealing with family-related employee problems.

3. *Culture in promoting strategy.* In this interpretation, the norms of the organization help execute the business strategy. For example, if an organization's business strategy is to compete on innovation, rather than price, which norms actively promote the generation of new ideas and help implement new approaches? And which norms will hinder this strategy? A strategy requires an appropriate culture if it is to be successfully implemented. For example, the culture that made an electronics firm successful in the design and manufacture of satellites and other sophisticated equipment ultimately sabotaged its efforts to design a word processor. The firm's engineers had a strong ethic of "getting it right" and would not release the machine until they were satisfied. The window of opportunity for entry into the market passed, leaving the firm with a

$40 million write-off of their investment. So as firms grow and strategies change, the culture needs to reflect the new direction.

Exhibit 3.4 reflects the culture at Morse Automotive. Note it addresses financial conditions (quality workmanship at a competitive price), strategy (taking initiative), technology (innovation), and culture (working together). Its HR programs are designed to be consistent with and supportive of this philosophy.

MANAGEMENT STYLE

An organization's culture is translated into practice largely as a result of actions taken by managers, as Exhibit 3.5 shows. By their words and actions, managers call attention to what is important. Thus, the quality and style of managerial leadership is crucial in shaping perceptions that will support cultural values and, hence, the organization's strategy.

Considerable effort was once spent trying to identify what personality characteristics determined a successful leader. Such information would be helpful in selecting supervisors.[19] One group classified leaders by their decision-making style:

Authoritarian: the leader makes decisions alone and tells subordinates what they are to do.

Democratic: the leader actively involves subordinates in the decision-making process, sharing problems, soliciting input, and sharing authority.

Laissez-faire: the leader avoids making decisions whenever possible and leaves it up to subordinates to make individual decisions with little guidance either from the leader or from the rest of the group.

Research on the effectiveness of alternative leadership styles produced some interesting results. For example, individuals under democratic leadership were more satisfied, had higher morale, were more creative, and had better relationships with their superiors. However, the quantity of output produced by workers was highest under the authoritarian leadership style, slightly lower under democratic leadership, and lowest under laissez-faire leadership.

Authoritarian managers have seen their power erode, because HRM has taken over many of the decisions that were formerly made unilaterally by supervisors. For example, American Steel and Wire had over 100,000 pay classifications prior to 1900. Only supervisors knew how many people were employed in a department and what they were paid. This gave supervisors tremendous power to vary work assignments and pay rates.[20] Inevitably, that power over employees was abused. Consequently, HR systems and legislation have to a large extent usurped this power to reward and punish to ensure fair treatment of all employees. Today's managers must lead by persuasion, integrity, and their own performance.

Most researchers now agree that no single leadership style is universally associated with effectiveness. Rather, a *contingency approach* is advocated (i.e.,

EXHIBIT 3.4   Values of Morse Automotive, Ithaca Plant

Providing Quality Workmanship at a Competitive Price.   Our real success is in our customers' success; our reputation is based on it; our future relies on it. To our customers, the Morse name means quality workmanship at a competitive price, and our responsibility is to keep it that way. Our customers' cost competitiveness is dependent on our cost effectiveness, as well as that of our suppliers. Therefore, we must seek out every opportunity to reduce our costs and give our customers the edge they require in the worldwide automotive market.

Taking Initiative.   Each employee has the obligation to take initiative, whether it be by learning to do something new or contributing an idea during a problem-solving session. Taking initiative reflects our basic drive to act on our instincts, satisfy our thirst for information and to have a hand in making a difference. Taking initiative means going beyond the expected in search of the ideal, and that's what Morse Automotive is all about.

A Continuing Tradition of Innovation.   Our greatest tradition is innovation. We have come this far by combining the preservation of established systems with the introduction of fresh ideas, realizing that therein lies the heart of progress. We must support and encourage creativity in each other, knowing that from innovative thinking comes the concepts that will help us anticipate, respond to, and bring about change. In an ever-changing world, innovation is a fundamental building block in our leadership in the automotive industry.

Working Together.   Teamwork is the foundation upon which our success is built. Each of us offers effort, skill, and perspective; our special contribution is in blending these together as a means of achieving shared goals. Our commitment to doing individual jobs well must be matched if not exceeded by our dedication to seeking each other's input, keeping each other informed, and appreciating each other's viewpoints. Working together in this way enables us as a team to accomplish what no one could do alone.

Finding the Right People for the Right Job.   We are firmly committed to selecting and employing the most qualified person for every available position, without regard to sex, color, creed, age, or national origin. This commitment is enhanced and supported by a selection process that involves peers in interviewing and evaluating prospective employees. In this way, we strive to hire those best equipped both personally and professionally to do the job at hand.

Belonging to the Global Community.   At Morse Automotive, we accept seriously and with pride our obligation to conduct ourselves responsibly, ethically, and legally, in accordance with the highest standards of business practice throughout the world.

Epilogue.   These values are our standards, the benchmarks by which we will measure our achievements. They define our purpose and our principles, our mission and our meaning. Each day we have the opportunity to make something happen, to urge ourselves forward. Our purpose, our mission, is to seize the opportunity, to achieve our present goals and pursue the bright promise of our future. There is no doubt that we have the talents and abilities to do so. With these values to guide us, let us at Morse now make a commitment to do so, together.

EXHIBIT 3.5   The Process of Managing a Culture

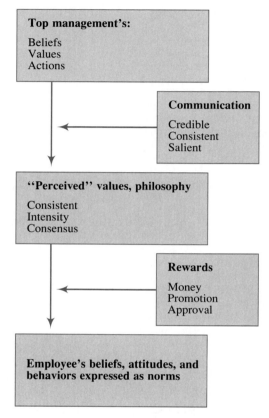

Source: Charles O'Reilly, "Corporations, Culture, and Commitment: Motivation and Social Control in Organizations," *California Management Review,* Summer 1989, pp. 9–25. Copyright © 1989 by The Regents of the University of California. Reprinted for the *California Management Review.* By permission of The Regents.

effective leadership depends on the circumstances). As Likert wrote 30 years ago:

> [Management] is . . . always a relative process. To be effective and to communicate as intended, a leader must always adapt his behavior to take into account the expectation, values, and interpersonal skills of those with whom he is interacting. . . . There can be no specific rules of supervision which will work well in all situations. Broad principles can be applied in the process of supervision and furnish valuable guides to behavior. These principles, however, must be applied in a manner that takes fully into account the characteristics of the specific situation and of the people involved.[21]

THE STATE OF RESEARCH

This completes our discussion of organization conditions that need to be considered when making HR decisions. Please recall that this list is not exhaustive. Other factors may be important. We've tried to analyze how the more important ones relate to managing HR.

Before turning to work-level factors, let us briefly consider the state of research on organization factors. This requires a note of caution. Research about which specific human resource strategy or which leadership style fits the various external and organization conditions is not well developed. Research suggests that differences in organizations are related to different HR strategies. We can even describe which HRM activities seem to fit with different organization conditions. But that is all we can do—describe the HR strategies that different organizations have adopted. Studies of the payoffs of various human resource strategies under different external and organization conditions have yet to be conducted.

THE NATURE OF WORK

Obviously, work and the way it is organized is critical in HRM. The skills and experience required to perform a job influence the kind of education and training people seek.[22] To a large extent, the job influences the pay that employees receive and, thus, their economic well-being. Many people find status and personal fulfillment at work. And the way we organize work into jobs affects the organization's ability to serve its customers.

An organization's basic decisions about technology, goods, or services and about business strategy delineate the nature of work in that particular plant. Allegheny Ludlum, for example, sells specialty steel that it produces from raw steel made from iron ore. Allegheny has many options. It can buy partially finished steel and finish it to customers' specifications, or it can buy iron ore to smelt in its own furnace. Many factors go into Allegheny's decision on which strategy to pursue, but whatever decision it makes determines the nature of the work done at Allegheny. All organizations face similar issues. The strategies and objectives chosen by managers affect the work to be performed and how that work is organized into jobs.

Look at Exhibit 3.1 again. The work done influences the organization's financial condition. A business strategy implies certain tasks of varying importance. Technology affects the nature of the tasks. And culture and management styles may influence how people feel about their jobs. To a large extent, organization conditions determine the nature of work.

The next section of this chapter will take a closer look at the elements of work: content, qualifications, and rewards. We will discuss how these elements can be measured (job analysis) and arranged (job design).

WORK-LEVEL FACTORS

We started this chapter with a steelworker and stockbroker describing their work. They commented on the tasks they perform, the abilities that are required, and the rewards (or lack of them) for doing the work. These are the same three types of information that human resource managers typically use to assess work.

◆

The nature of work includes:

1. The content—tasks, behaviors, duties, relationships, responsibilities.
2. The qualifications required to perform it—skills, abilities, experience.
3. Returns and rewards for performing it—pay, promotions, and intrinsic satisfaction.

Content

Work content can focus on specific *tasks*—their purpose and what they accomplish, or on *behaviors* (e.g., advising, negotiating, writing, lifting, assembling).

Qualifications

Qualifications describe the skills, abilities, and knowledge required to satisfactorily perform work. Data about these qualifications are necessary to recruit, select, pay, and train employees. It would be impossible to match individuals with work without details on the precise qualifications required for different jobs.

Rewards and Returns

The rewards and returns from work may be *extrinsic* or *intrinsic*. Extrinsic rewards are relatively concrete: pay, benefits, promotions, praise, pleasant working conditions, and so on. Intrinsic rewards are less observable and, to some extent, are less controllable by others. Examples include feelings of accomplishment, freedom, or autonomy.

However, because people do not always agree on what is intrinsically and extrinsically rewarding, people with differing educations, backgrounds, or aspirations may see the content, qualifications, and rewards of work differently. This variety is what makes HRM so dynamic.

Job content, qualifications, and rewards are usually used to assess work. These data, in turn, are used in two procedures: job design and job analysis.

EXHIBIT 3.6   Job Analysis Terminology

Task	Smallest unit of analysis, a specific statement of what a person does; for example, operates an Apple II terminal, answers the telephone.
Position	Next level of analysis, *a group of tasks* performed by *one* person; for example, all tasks done by a computer operator or secretary.
Job	Many positions, all with the same basic tasks and with several people performing them.
Occupation	Grouping of jobs with broadly similar content; for example, managerial, technical, crafts.
Job descriptions	Systematic summary of the information collected in the job analysis.
Job specifications	The minimum skills, knowledge, and abilities required to perform the job.

Source: E. J. McCormick, "Job and Task Analysis," in *Handbook of Industrial and Organizational Psychology,* ed. M. D. Dunnette, © 1976, John Wiley & Sons, Inc. Reprinted by permission.

Job design assigns job content and responsibilities to members of the organization. Job analysis collects information about jobs and the relationships among jobs so human resource decisions can be made in a systematic way.

JOB ANALYSIS

◆

Job analysis is a systematic process of collecting data and making judgments about the nature of a specific job.

Exhibit 3.6 summarizes some job analysis terminology. Job analysis usually collects information about specific tasks. A group of tasks performed by one person makes up a position. Identical positions make a job, and broadly similar jobs combine into an occupation.

Job analysis provides information for many HR activities. Exhibit 3.7 lists some of the uses and the data needed for each purpose. For example, training requires information on qualifications and job content so programs can be tailored to the actual qualifications required to perform the jobs. Hiring and promotion standards can be based on this same information. Job analysis information allows interviewers to assess the match between job candidates and the job, and it can help candidates decide if they are really interested in a job vacancy.

Job analysis is often the first step in deciding what to pay people. In performance evaluation, both employees and supervisors look to the required behaviors and results expected in a job. Job analysis also helps document the

EXHIBIT 3.7   Uses of Job Analysis Information

Function	Job Analysis		
	Information		Result
Job design	Tasks, qualifications, rewards, expected results	→	Organization structure
Recruitment and selection	Required qualifications	→	Selection and promotion standards
Training and development	Tasks, behaviors	→	Training programs
Performance appraisal	Behavior standards or expected results	→	Performance appraisal criteria
Compensation	Tasks, abilities, behaviors	→	Similarities and differences in the work; job descriptions

work-relatedness of HR decisions, which is important to ensure nondiscrimination. So, we will be referring to job analysis throughout the text.

But a proper job analysis can be time consuming and expensive.[23] Consequently, it is important that the reasons for conducting job analysis be well thought out and properly understood before beginning the process.

Assessing Job Content

There are three basic categories of job information collected for analysis: task data, behavioral data, and abilities data. Job analysis methodologies vary on which they emphasize.

Task Data

Task data are subparts of a job, with emphasis on the purpose of each task. An excerpt from a job analysis questionnaire that collects task data is shown in Exhibit 3.8. While the aspect of work being assessed in this exhibit is "communication," the questionnaire describes the elemental units of communication (e.g., "read technical publications" and "consult with coworkers"). The objective of the task (e.g., "read technical publications to keep current on industry" and "consult with co-workers to exchange ideas and techniques") is also emphasized. Task data reveal the actual work performed and why it is performed. This excerpt, from Control Data Corporation's Position Description Questionnaire, also measures time spent doing a task. Other possible measures are degree of importance of the task and prior experience required.

EXHIBIT 3.8 Job Analysis Questionnaire Using Task Data (excerpt)

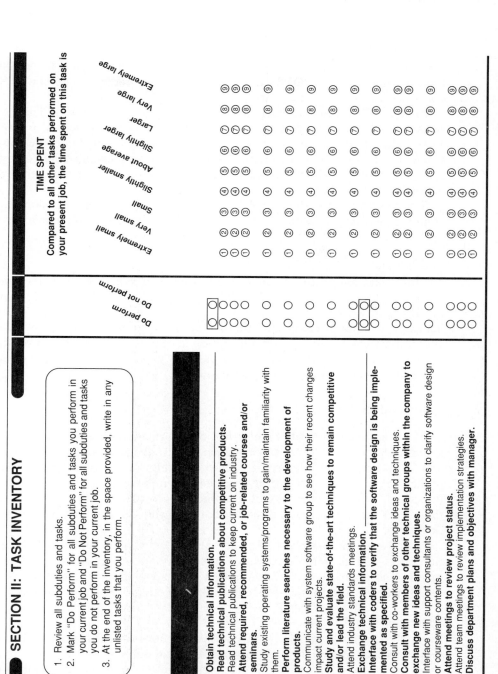

SECTION II: TASK INVENTORY

1. Review all subduties and tasks.
2. Mark "Do Perform" for all subduties and tasks you perform in your current job and "Do Not Perform" for all subduties and tasks you do not perform in your current job.
3. At the end of the inventory, in the space provided, write in any unlisted tasks that you perform.

TIME SPENT
Compared to all other tasks performed on your present job, the time spent on this task is

Scale (left to right): Extremely small (1), Very small (2), Small (3), Slightly smaller (4), About average (5), Slightly larger (6), Larger (7), Very large (8), Extremely large (9)

Do perform / Do not perform

Obtain technical information.
421. **Read technical publications about competitive products.**
422. Read technical publications to keep current on industry.
423. **Attend required, recommended, or job-related courses and/or seminars.**
424. Study existing operating systems/programs to gain/maintain familiarity with them.
425. **Perform literature searches necessary to the development of products.**
426. Communicate with system software group to see how their recent changes impact current projects.
427. **Study and evaluate state-of-the-art techniques to remain competitive and/or lead the field.**
428. Attend industry standards meetings.
Exchange technical information.
429. **Interface with coders to verify that the software design is being implemented as specified.**
430. Consult with co-workers to exchange ideas and techniques.
431. **Consult with members of other technical groups within the company to exchange new ideas and techniques.**
432. Interface with support consultants or organizations to clarify software design or courseware contents.
433. **Attend meetings to review project status.**
434. Attend team meetings to review implementation strategies.
435. **Discuss department plans and objectives with manager.**

Behavioral Data

Behavioral data use verbs describing the behaviors that occur on the job. Exhibit 3.9 shows such behavioral observations. This time, "communications" is described as advising, negotiating, persuading, and so on.

Exhibit 3.9 is from the Position Analysis Questionnaire (PAQ). The PAQ describes similarities and differences among jobs, using seven factors: Information Input, Mental Processes, Work Output, Relationships with Other Persons, Job Context, Other Job Characteristics, and General Dimensions. The communications behavior in Exhibit 3.9 is part of the "Relationships with Other Persons" factor.[24]

Some users caution that the PAQ has a high reading comprehension level and complex instructions, which make it difficult for employees to complete without assistance.

Abilities Data

Abilities data assess the underlying knowledge or skill a worker must possess for satisfactory job performance. Abilities may be (1) psychomotor, (2) physical, or (3) cognitive. Exhibit 3.10 shows a scale used by AT&T to assess "Comprehension." Comprehension and another factor, Expression (not shown), correspond most closely to the communication aspect of work examined on the two previous exhibits. Notice that this assessment can be done with or without reference to specific tasks or behaviors in a job.

Conventional Job Analysis

The conventional method of collecting job information involves an analyst using a questionnaire to interview job holders and supervisors. The questionnaires and interviews are structured to achieve a uniform response format. The approach requires considerable involvement of employees and supervisors, which increases their understanding of the process, provides an opportunity to clarify their work expectations, and increases the likelihood that they will accept the results.

Usually, an analyst translates the data collected to a summary job description sheet. Often, both employees and supervisors are given an opportunity to modify and approve the job description. The appendix at the end of this chapter provides a step-by-step procedure for collecting data and a questionnaire.

Functional Job Analysis

Probably the most detailed conventional procedure is functional job analysis (FJA). While commonly used by public-sector employers, few private-sector employers have adopted it. It is a refinement of Department of Labor job analysis methodology developed in the 1930s.[25]

FJA describes jobs by the complexity of their relationships to *data, people,* and *things*. For example, the simplest relationship to people requires taking in-

---

EXHIBIT 3.9   Job Analysis Questionnaire Using Behavioral Data (excerpt)

Section 4 Relationships with Other Persons.

This section deals with different aspects of interaction between people involved in various kinds of work.

> *Code Importance to This Job (1)*
> N   Does not apply
> 1   Very minor
> 2   Low
> 3   Average
> 4   High
> 5   Extreme

4.1 Communications
Rate the following in terms of how *important* the activity is to the completion of the job. Some jobs may involve several or all of the items in this section.

4.1.1 Oral (communicating by speaking)
99 ____ Advising (dealing with individuals in order to counsel and/or guide them with regard to problems that may be resolved by legal, financial, scientific, technical, clinical, spiritual, and/or other professional principles).

100 ____ Negotiating (dealing with others in order to reach an agreement or solution; for example, labor bargaining, diplomatic relations, etc.).

101 ____ Persuading (dealing with others in order to influence them toward some action or point of view; for example, selling, political campaigning, etc.).

102 ____ Instructing (the teaching of knowledge or skills, in either an informal or a formal manner, to others; for example, a public school teacher, a machinist teaching an apprentice, etc.).

103 ____ Interviewing (conducting interviews directed toward some specific objective; for example, interviewing job applicants, census taking, etc.).

104 ____ Routine information exchange: job related (the giving and/or receiving of *job related* information of a routine nature; for example, ticket agent, taxicab dispatcher, receptionist, etc.).

105 ____ Nonroutine information exchange (the giving and/or receiving of *job-related* information of a nonroutine or unusual nature; for example, professional committee meetings, engineers discussing new product design, etc.).

106 ____ Public speaking (making speeches or formal presentations before relatively large audiences; for example, political addresses, radio/TV broadcasting, delivering a sermon, etc.).

4.1.2 Written (communicating by written/printed material)
107 ____ Writing (for example, writing or dictating letters, reports, etc., writing copy for ads, writing newspaper articles, etc., do *not* include transcribing activities described in item 4.3, but only activities in which the incumbent creates the written material).

4.1.3 Other Communications
108 ____ Signaling (communicating by some type of signal; for example, hand signals, semaphore, whistles, horns, bells, lights, etc.).

109 ____ Code communications (telegraph, cryptography, etc.).

Source: PAQ Services, Inc., Logan, Utah. Copyright © 1969 by Purdue Research Foundation, West Lafayette, Indiana 47906.

EXHIBIT 3.10   Job Analysis Questionnaire Using Ability Data (excerpt)

Written Comprehension
This is the ability to understand written sentences and paragraphs.

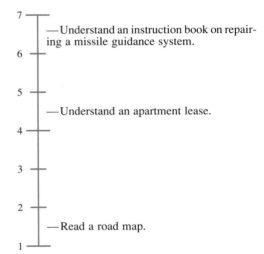

Requires understanding complex or detailed information *in writing*, containing unusual words and phrases and involving fine distinctions in meaning among words.

7 — Understand an instruction book on repairing a missile guidance system.

6

5 — Understand an apartment lease.

4

3

Requires understanding short, simple *written* information containing common words and phrases.

2

— Read a road map.

1

Oral Comprehension
This is the ability to understand spoken English words and sentences.

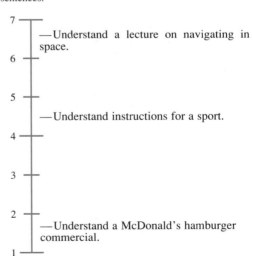

Requires understanding complex or detailed information, *presented orally*, containing unusual words and phrases and involving fine distinctions in meaning among words.

7 — Understand a lecture on navigating in space.

6

5 — Understand instructions for a sport.

4

3

Requires understanding short, simple, *spoken* information containing common words and phrases.

2 — Understand a McDonald's hamburger commercial.

1

Source: AT&T.

EXHIBIT 3.11   Job Description for a Personnel Manager

166.117-018 Manager, Personnel (professional and kindred)

Plans and carries out policies relating to all phases of personnel activity. Recruits, interviews, and selects employees to fill vacant positions. Plans and conducts new employee orientation to foster positive attitude toward company goals. Keeps record of insurance coverage, pension plan, and personnel transactions, such as hires, promotions, transfers, and terminations. Investigates accidents and prepares reports for insurance carrier. Conducts wage survey within labor market to determine competitive wage rate. Prepares budget of personnel operations. Meets with shop stewards and supervisors to resolve grievances. Writes separation notices for employees separating with cause and conducts exit interviews to determine reasons behind separations. Prepares reports and recommends procedures to reduce absenteeism and turnover. Contracts with outside suppliers to provide employee services, such as canteen, transportation, or relocation service. May keep records of hired employee characteristics for governmental reporting purposes. May negotiate collective bargaining agreement with *business representative labor union* (professional and kindred).

Source: U.S. Department of Labor, *Dictionary of Occupational Titles,* 4th ed. (Washington, D.C.: U.S. Government Printing Office, 1977).

---

structions or serving. The most complex is mentoring, defined as serving as a role model or counselor.[26] Exhibit 3.11 is a job description written from information developed with conventional job analysis.[27]

Conventional methods place considerable reliance upon analysts' abilities to understand the work performed and to translate it into a job description. One writer describes the process: "We all know the classic procedures. One [worker] watched and noted the actions of another . . . at work on [the] job. The actions of both are biased, and the resulting information varied with the wind, especially the political wind.[28]

New techniques to quantify and computerize job data have been developed.[29] Such developments minimize errors in data collection and, insofar as possible, increase the chances that jobs are analyzed on work-related factors. Reducing subjectivity in job analysis is the primary goal of quantitative job analysis.[30] Additionally, a computerized job analysis may relieve the drudgery of collecting and translating job data.

Quantitative Job Analysis

Inventories are the core of quantitative job analysis. An inventory is essentially a structured questionnaire in which the task and behavior attributes relevant for the group of jobs to be analyzed are listed. Exhibit 3.8 and 3.9 are taken from quantitative job analysis inventories.

A major limitation of all quantitative analysis is cost. Nevertheless, the quality of job analysis has been improved with the development of quantitative ap-

---

EXHIBIT 3.12   Partial Description of Job of Nurse, Cleveland Lutheran Hospital, 1887

In addition to caring for your 50 patients each nurse will follow these regulations:

1. Daily sweep and mop the floors of your ward, dust the patient's furniture and window sills.
2. Maintain an even temperature in your ward by bringing in a scuttle of coal for the day's business.
3. Light is important to observe the patient's condition. Therefore, each day, fill kerosene lamps, clean chimneys, and trim wicks. Wash the windows once a week.
4. The nurse's notes are important in aiding the physician's work. Make your pens carefully, you may whittle nibs to your individual taste.
5. Each nurse on day duty will report every day at 7 A.M. and leave at 8 P.M. except on the Sabbath on which day you will be off from 12:00 noon to 2:00 P.M.
6. Graduate nurses in good standing with the director of nurses will be given an evening off each week for courting purposes, or two evenings a week if you go regularly to church.
7. Each nurse should lay aside from each pay day a goodly sum of her earnings for her benefits during her declining years, so that she will not become a burden. For example, if you earn $30 a month you should set aside $15.
8. Any nurse who smokes, uses liquor in any form, gets her hair done at a beauty shop, or frequents dance halls will give the director good reason to suspect her worth, intentions, and integrity.
9. The nurse who performs her labors and serves her patients and doctors faithfully and without fault for a period of five years will be given an increase by the hospital administration of five cents a day, provided there are no hospital debts that are outstanding.

---

proaches, and a number of factors are operating to increase their use. First, as more employers use them, the technology will become better understood and simpler to apply. Second, information about the nature of work and the requirements to perform it is the basic foundation for all HR decisions. The next chapter will discuss in more detail the assessment of employee requirements. Moreover, as we shall see in Chapter Six, challenges from employees, courts, and EEO agencies to verify the work-relatedness of decisions require job analysis.[31]

Job Descriptions

Because job analysis serves as the starting point for so many other HR activities, the data collected must be in a form that is usable to other people than the analyst. That form is the job description. Typical job descriptions contain three sections that identify, define, and describe the job.

1. *Identification.*   This section may contain the job title, number of incumbents, where it is located (department, work site) and job number, if any is

used. Its purpose is to clearly identify the job and to distinguish it from those with similar job titles or duties. The date of the analysis is also important. The job description in Exhibit 3.12 should indicate why.

2. *Definition.* This summary section reflects the purpose of the job: why the job exists, and how it fits in with other jobs and with the organization and its overall objectives. What constitutes satisfactory performance of this job may also be included. It ought to provide an accurate "word picture" of the job. The word picture of the nurse position in Exhibit 3.12, making the 5 cents per day raise contingent on a debt-free employer, reflects a century of change.

For managerial jobs, statistics on the size of the budget under the control of this job, the number (and job titles) of people supervised, and reporting relationships with other managers at both higher and lower organization levels are frequently included in the job definition, too. Financial and organizational data help locate a job in the organization's hierarchy.

3. *Description.* This section is an elaboration of items in the definition, or summary section. It indicates the major duties of this job, the specific work performed, how closely supervised it is, and what controls limit the actions of the jobholder. In addition to describing the tasks performed, the training and experience required to perform them may also be included here, or in a separate section called Job Specifications.

Is Job Analysis Useful?

The usefulness of job analysis information can be judged by a number of different standards.[32]

Reliability Reliability is a measure of the *consistency* of the results obtained, either from two different analysts of the same job, or from one analyst looking at a single job on two different occasions.

Validity Validity is a measure of the *accuracy* of the results obtained. It is quite possible for two analysts to agree completely and for both to be wrong as a result of incomplete information, biased interpretation, and the like. There is almost no way of showing statistically the extent to which a job analysis result is accurate or valid, particularly as one moves to more complex jobs. The most common method of ensuring accuracy is to collect data from multiple job holders or supervisors, or both. Requiring job holders and supervisors to "sign off" on results may help ensure their validity.

Purpose of the analysis If there is a need for uniform job data at many locations, does the method provide it? Can the method provide documentable evidence of the work-relatedness of the pay structure? Does it adequately assess the subtle differences among jobs unique to our organization? Are both the typist and the vice president of marketing convinced that it fairly describes their jobs? These challenges to job analysis provide criteria to judge a method's usefulness. However, some analysts get so taken with their statistics and computers that they ignore the role that human judgment continues to play in job analysis. As Dunnette et al. state:

> I wish to emphasize the central role played in all these procedures by human judgment. I know of no methodology, statistical technique, or objective measurement that can negate the importance of, nor supplement, rational judgment as an important element in the process of deriving behavior and task information about jobs and of using that information to develop or justify human resources programs.[33]

Quantitative and more systematic approaches to job analysis do not remove the judgment; they only permit us to become more systematic in the way we make it.

So, job analysis provides the foundation for many HR decisions. We shall discuss job design—arranging the organization's tasks into jobs—in this chapter. In the next chapter we shall discuss how organizations assess employee characteristics by comparing employee behavior to the requirements of the jobs.

JOB DESIGN

◆

Job design integrates work content, qualifications, and rewards for each job in a way that meets the needs of employees and the organization.

Job design is often the key to whether a job alienates or energizes the jobholder. How much freedom of action or authority do jobholders enjoy? Do they feel committed to the products they make or the services they render? Is there anything about the job that hinders employee productivity? These issues can all be influenced by job design.[34] Exhibit 3.13 outlines advantages and disadvantages of the major job design approaches.

Scientific Management

Frederick W. Taylor was one of the first to specify systematic principles for the most efficient arrangement of work. His writings on scientific management have been the basis for many jobs and organizations since 1911.[35]

Taylor studied the technical aspects of the production process at the Midvale Iron Company in Pennsylvania. He also studied individual employees and the groups they form. Based on the systematic organization of this information, he calculated standards and specific methods for jobs.

EXHIBIT 3.13   Job Design Philosophies/Approaches

	Techniques	Advantages	Disadvantages
Scientific Management Philosophy	Work simplification	Creates jobs that are safe, simple, reliable. Minimizes the mental demands on employees.	Boring, demeaning.
	Job enlargement	Can reduce waiting time between tasks, enhance organization flexibility, reduce support staff needs.	May lose the advantages of work simplification without offsetting the disadvantages.
Human Relations Philosophy	Work groups	Recognizes importance of social needs of employees.	Gives little technical guidance.
Job Characteristics Approach	Job enrichment	Creates jobs that "engage" the employee, boost motivation, satisfaction, production.	Costly. Accident/error potential increases. May require additional employees. Control still rests with managers.
Sociotechnical Approach	Teams	Gives employees a great deal of control over jobs. Most successful in new plants, where it's compatible with the technology.	Requires compatible organization design, careful structuring of teams. Relationships among teams must be managed. Some work may still be boring. A lot of time devoted to nonproduction issues.

His approach was to reduce each job to its simplest tasks (job simplification) that were to be performed under close supervision. The assembly line epitomizes scientific management and its emphasis on efficient production.

But while Taylor's scientific management principles were an early systematic effort at job design, many managers distorted the principles. They focused on the close supervision and set standards that contained little flexibility. Rigidly enforced standards with little regard for employees' physical needs and safety, much less their psychological needs, led to boredom, dissatisfaction, alienation, and frustration.

Human Relations

The human relations movement was in large part a reaction against the dehumanizing aspects of scientific management carried to an extreme. Rather than emphasizing the production needs of the organization, the human relations movement looked at jobs from the perspective of the individual worker. The movement grew out of studies done in the 1920s, now referred to as the *Hawthorne studies*. The original goal of the studies at Western Electric Company's Hawthorne plant was to test how variations in working conditions affected productivity. The striking conclusions were that variations in the work environment (lighting, ventilation, temperature) were less important than the social interaction among co-workers.[36]

The researchers discovered that workers spontaneously organized the work environment, established standards, and enforced sanctions among themselves. Economic incentives, which scientific management viewed as the key motivator, were less important than employees' social needs, which were met by other employees in informal work groups. Both scientific management and human relations philosophies addressed the issue of efficiency, but the human relations movement advocated job design as a way to direct work groups toward the goals of the organization. Supportive work groups and nonauthoritarian supervisors were seen as keys to increasing worker motivation and, thus, productivity.

Quality circles and other worker participation programs may be viewed as recent applications of human relations ideas. However, about 75 percent of the participative programs begun in the late 1970s and early 1980s had been dropped by the 1990s.[37] The reasons for dropping programs vary. Sometimes expectations were unrealistically high. Other times, there was insufficient support for the programs at higher levels in the organization. Some critics charge that participatory systems only *look* like they transfer responsibility from managers to employees, but in actuality they fragment the work force to decrease the likelihood of unions forming.[38]

Job Characteristics

Scientific management focused on the job; the human relations movement focused on employees. The job characteristics model focuses on the psychological interaction between the employee and the job.[39] It advocates job enrichment: giving employees more responsibility, autonomy, and control in their jobs. The model identifies five job characteristics that can potentially motivate workers:

1. *Skill variety.* The degree to which the job requires a variety of different activities in carrying out the work and uses a number of an individual's skills and talents.

2. *Task identity.* The degree to which the job requires completion of a "whole" and identifiable piece of work—that is, doing a job from the beginning to end with a visible outcome.

3. *Task significance.* The degree to which the job has a substantial impact on the lives or work of other people.

4. *Autonomy.*   The degree to which the job provides substantial freedom, independence, and discretion to the individual in scheduling the work and in determining the procedures to be used in carrying it out.

5. *Feedback.*   The degree to which carrying out the work activities required by the job results in the individual's obtaining direct and clear information about the effectiveness of his or her performance.

The first three job characteristics influence whether an individual feels the work is important. Autonomy influences whether an individual feels personally responsible for good or poor performance. And feedback provides the individual with knowledge of the results of the work. The assumption is that proper arrangement of these characteristics can ensure job designs that are intrinsically rewarding. While the model has spawned a great deal of academic research, it is difficult for managers to apply, because it relies on psychological states that may or may not exist in individuals.[40]

Sociotechnical Perspective

Other job designers have tried to combine the philosophies of scientific management and human relations and avoid the pitfalls of identifying what each individual finds to be motivating. They take a sociotechnical approach, which recognizes the importance of the workplace sociology, as well as the productivity gains of optimum technological arrangements. The sociotechnical approach assumes that the two subsystems are related to one another, serve as constraints on one another, and must be effectively fit to one another to achieve optimal functioning.[41] The work team is an application of this approach.

Work Teams

A work team is a set of two or more people who are interdependent with one another for the accomplishment of a purpose and who communicate and interact with one another on a more or less continuous basis. In many cases (but not always) they work closely together physically. The team assumes responsibility for deciding how it will accomplish its primary task.

Members of a work team may not have a "job" in the traditional sense. Rather, they learn multiple skills and rotate through different tasks. The team has the authority to arrange tasks and assign roles among themselves in any way they choose. They are charged with responsibility for an end product, and they are free, within technological and budgetary restrictions, to manage this responsibility as they see fit. Thus, the team manager's responsibility is not to design jobs that will be intrinsically motivating. The manager, instead, seeks to form work teams whose members possess the qualifications to accomplish the tasks, are compatible, and whose objectives will correspond to those of the organization.

Properly structured work teams take advantage of new technologies. For example, Corning makes ceramic components for automotive catalytic converters in both Blacksburg, Virginia, and Erwin, New York. The Blacksburg plant, which had been closed in 1984, reopened in 1988 with a new technology that permits small production runs and can switch relatively easily from one component model to another. Employees in teams rotate among the tasks required by each production run. There are only two job classifications: operations associate and maintenance engineer. In contrast, the Erwin plant, which uses an older technology to produce a similar product, has 49 job classifications. The flexibility of the Blacksburg plant has allowed Corning to capture new business that the firm would previously have conceded to competitors.[42]

At Jamestown, New York, the Cummins Engine Company uses self-managed work teams to manufacture and test diesel engines. Here, too, the plant was purposely designed to allow for work teams that would have greater responsibility and authority than traditional manufacturing facilities allowed.[43] The original expectation was that as teams "matured," they would exercise ever-greater autonomy. But that has not been the case. While employees can be given great latitude, strong leadership and direction from team leaders is still required after 10 years of team experience. Additionally, teams have typically looked to leaders to enforce discipline and to handle performance difficulties.[44] While work teams are currently very popular, they are not appropriate for all organizations nor all employees.

So, we have seen that organizations come in different sizes and shapes, and each organization has its own flavor. That flavor is the result of many factors, a few of which we discussed in this chapter. Work, too, comes in many flavors. The variety in work gives every organization a great deal of latitude in how to structure and organize work. This variety in work both reflects and contributes to the nature of the organization, an important factor in the diagnostic model.

SUMMARY

Organizations adopt different approaches to human resources: Some promote from within, while others hire experienced people; some seek cooperative relations with unions, while others aggressively avoid them. Some offer employment security and retraining, others do not; and some base pay on group performance and profit sharing, while others use individual performance schemes. These differences are not simply the result of varying external conditions. Even though pressures in the external environment affect human resource decisions, organization factors also play a significant role. To better understand differences in human resource decisions, we need to assess differences in organizations, as well as external conditions.

With a diagnostic approach, managers assess the conditions of the organization before they make human resource decisions. We analyzed four important conditions in this chapter: financial, strategic, technological, cultural, and managerial style.

Strategies are integrated patterns of decisions made about employees. Strategic human resource management links external pressures discussed in the previous chapter with the conditions faced within the organization.

Continuing our examination of organization factors that influence human resource management, we concentrated on assessing the nature of work and how this work affects employees as well as organizations. The *content* (duties, tasks, behaviors, functions, responsibilities), the *qualifications* required to perform it (skills, abilities, experience), and *returns and rewards* for performing it (pay, promotions, challenging work) constitute the nature of work.

Job analysis assesses the content of jobs. Its results provide input for a variety of human resource activities, including job design. Although job analysis is a basic assessment process, not all organizations do it. Job analysis can be tedious, time consuming, and expensive. Recent advances in computerizing the process may eliminate some of these drawbacks, but not all of them. Computerization raises the possibility of collecting a great deal of job information for a variety of purposes. Unfortunately, the amount of data may outrun its usefulness. Informed human judgment can never be omitted from the work assessment process.

Job design is concerned with alternative arrangements of the content, qualifications, and rewards. Currently, work teams using a sociotechnical model is a popular approach; however, any job design approach is limited by the technology of the workplace.

The basic premise of this chapter is that the nature of work plays a critical role in the management of human resources. Job analysis and job design are important tools in the process of matching the nature of the individual with the nature of the work. This matching process helps achieve employee and organizational objectives.

DISCUSSION AND REVIEW QUESTIONS

1. Give some examples of how financial conditions affect HRM, and how HRM can affect financial conditions.
2. How are HR strategy and business strategy linked?
3. Discuss what is meant by "fit" in the strategic perspective. How might a researcher measure the fit to determine if, in fact, a strategic perspective makes any difference?
4. How does the HR strategies of Inducers, Investors, and Involvers differ?
5. What are some key HR issues at each strategic level?
6. How can an organization try to ensure that the social influences in work groups are directed toward positive organization objectives?
7. Contrast the perspectives of scientific management and human relations.
8. Give some concrete examples of the kind of job information necessary for the paying of people. Do the same for a training program.

9. What is the critical advantage of quantitative job analysis? Why is this important?
10. Describe the interaction among external pressures, organization-level factors, and work-level factors.

YOUR TURN
RESTRUCTURING BLUES

In 1986, in response to collapsing oil prices, Exxon Corporation eliminated some operations, peeled away layers of management, and talked many people into leaving the company. For those retained, employee workloads increased, jobs were enlarged, promotion opportunities dried up, work group size shrunk, supervision became aggressive, and certain operations were understaffed. One employee viewed the changes as "economic blackmail, a lack of care and equity." As a result of the restructuring, Exxon's operating costs decreased, earnings and stock prices began recovering, and annual revenue approached $96 billion. The restructuring and downsizing appeared successful.

In 1989, articles praising Exxon's recovery ceased to appear. Instead, Exxon made the news because of the Valdez oil spill, the Bayway Refinery pipeline break, the Baton Rouge refinery explosions, its New Jersey oil spill indictment, and its Baytown, Texas refinery fires. Observers of Exxon's situation place great emphasis on the "human error" associated with each of the disasters. It seems the restructuring has increased more than just Exxon's revenue.

What role can HR play in designing and implementing business strategy? Prepare a presentation of the potentially positive and negative results of reducing layers of management and downsizing. How would Exxon's restructuring change the activities of its human resources department?

Case prepared by Joseph Salamone, SUNY Buffalo.

APPENDIX
Job Analysis Procedures

OVERVIEW

A combination of on-site observations, interviews, and preinterview preparation and study is used to develop the necessary job information. An illustrative schedule of on-site job study activities is shown in Exhibit 3A.1.

The schedule is intended to illustrate one way of sequencing the interviews and job visits. The schedule may be modified to accommodate the complexity of the job being studied, the job analyst's familiarity with the job, and unforeseen operating exigencies.

EXHIBIT 3A.1 General Procedures

Step		Things to Remember or Do
1. Develop preliminary job information	*a.*	Review existing documents in order to develop an initial "big picture" familiarity with the job: its main mission, its major duties or functions, work flow patterns.
	b.	Prepare a preliminary list of duties that will serve as a framework for conducting the interviews.
	c.	Make a note of major items that are unclear, or ambiguous, or that need to be clarified during the data-gathering process.
2. Conduct interviews	*a.*	It is recommended that the first interview be conducted with someone who can provide an overview of the job and how the major duties fit together—a supervisor or experienced employee.
	b.	The interviewees are considered subject matter experts by virtue of the fact that they perform the job (in the case of job incumbents) or are responsible for getting the job done (in the case of first-level supervisors).
	c.	The job incumbent to be interviewed should represent the *typical* employee who is knowledgeable about the job (*not* the trainee who is just learning the ropes *nor* the outstanding member of the work unit).
	d.	Whenever feasible, the interviewees should be selected with a view towards obtaining an appropriate race/sex mix.
3. Consolidate job information	*a.*	The consolidation phase of the job study involves piecing together into one coherent and comprehensive job description the data obtained from several sources: supervisor, jobholders, on-site tours, and written materials about the job.
	b.	A subject matter expert should be accessible as a resource person to the job analyst during the consolidation phase.
	c.	Check your initial preliminary list of duties and questions—all must be answered or confirmed.
4. Verify job description	*a.*	The verification phase involves bringing all the interviewees together for the purpose of determining if the consolidated job description is accurate and complete.
	b.	The verification process is conducted in a group setting. Typed or legibly written copies of the job description (narrative description of the work setting *and* list of task statements) are distributed to the first-level supervisor and the job incumbent interviewees.
	c.	Line by line, the job analyst goes through the entire job description and makes notes of any omissions, ambiguities, or needed clarifications.

DATA SOURCES

Sources of information for developing the job description include:

- ✦ Existing documents, such as job briefs, previously developed task lists, and training manuals.
- ✦ On-site observations of work operations.
- ✦ Interviews with first-level supervisors and job incumbents.

Job Analysis Report

Date __2-23-90__

Job Analyst __C. Davis__

1. Job Title __Executive Secretary__
2. Department __General Headquarters__
3. No. incumbents __2__   Interviewed __2__

4. Relation to other jobs:
   Promotion: From __Secretary-D__   To __Executive Secretary__
   Transfer: From __Administrative Assistant__   To __Executive Secretary__
   Supervision received __From President and/or Chairman of the Board.__
   __Works under minimal supervision.__
   Supervision given __Regularly to other clerical personnel.__

5. Summary of Job:

   Personal Secretary to President and/or Chairman of the Board. Exercises discretion in handling confidential and specialized information, screening telephone calls and letters, arranging meetings,
   and handling inquiries during superior's absence. Performs variety
   of secretarial and clerical duties including filing, routing mail,
   as well as answering telephone and written inquiries.

6. Equipment used: Typewriter, word processor, and telephone.

Working conditions:
   Hazards (list): N/A
   Work space and quarters: Office enviroment
   Noise exposure: None
   Lighting: Good
   Temperature: Regulated office environment
   Miscellaneous: —

Job training:
   A. Required experience: (include other jobs)
      Four years of secretarial-stenographic experience or the
      equivalent.
   B. Outside educational courses:

		Time in semester/quarters
Vocational courses:	Typing, stenography	2 semesters
High school courses:	Graduate	6-8 semesters
College courses:		None
Continuing education required:		None

   C. In-house training courses:

	Time in months
Courses: Basic and Advanced Word Processing	1/2 month

Task Statement Worksheet

Task Statement: Opens and organizes mail addressed to superior.

1. Equipment used —
2. Knowledge required Must be well versed on superior's responsibilities, how superior's job fits into overall organization.
3. Skills required —
4. Abilities required Discretion. Organization skills.
5. Time spent and frequency of task performance (hourly, daily, monthly)
   Time varies by assignment. Weekly frequency.
6. Level of difficulty/consequence of error
   Relatively difficult, little effect of error.

Task Statement: Establishes, maintains, and revises files.

1. Equipment used Typewriter, word processor.
2. Knowledge required
   Understanding of organization and responsibilities of superior.
3. Skills required Typing and word processing, filing.
4. Abilities required Ability to organize and categorize information.
5. Time spent and frequency of task performance (hourly, daily, monthly)
   One hour spent daily.
6. Level of difficulty/consequence of error Relatively easy, but moderate to serious consequences if information mishandled.

NOTES AND REFERENCES

1. Studs Terkel, *Working* (New York: Random House, 1974).
2. Ibid.
3. Robert Levering, *One Hundred Best Companies to Work for* (New York: Random House, 1984).
4. Erica Groshen, "Why Do Wages Vary among Employers?" *Economic Review,* quarter 1, 1988, pp. 19–38.
5. George Milkovich, Barry Gerhart, and John Hannon, "Use of Incentive Pay in R&D Firms," Ithaca, N.Y.; Center for Advanced Study of Human Resource Management, Cornell University, Working Paper, January 1990.
6. Jerry Newman, "Selecting Incentive Plans to Complement Organization Strategy," in *Current Trends in Compensation Research and Practice,* ed. L. Gomez-Mejia and D. Balkin (Englewood Cliffs, N.J.: Prentice Hall, 1987), pp. 14–24.
7. John Dunlop, "Have the 1980s Changed U.S. Industrial Relations?" *Monthly Labor Review,* May 1988, pp. 29–34.
8. "EEOC and General Motors Sign," *Fair Employment Practices Manual* (Washington, D.C.: Bureau of National Affairs, November 3, 1983), pp. 3–4.
9. Thomas J. Peters and Robert H. Waterman, Jr., *In Search of Excellence* (New York: Harper & Row, 1983).
10. Lee Dyer and Gerald Holder, "A Strategic Perspective of Human Resource Management," in *Human Resource Management: Evolving Roles and Responsibilities,* ed. Lee Dyer and Gerald Holder (Washington, D.C.: Bureau of National Affairs, 1988), pp. 1.125–1.186.
11. George Lodge and Richard Walton, "The American Corporation and Its New Relationships," *California Management Review,* Spring 1989, pp. 9–24. Although the unions were unable to stop Lorenzo from acquiring Eastern, they have taken him to court to reverse his efforts to move assets from unionized to nonunionized sectors.
12. Cynthia A. Lengnick-Hall and Mark L. Lengnick-Hall, "Strategic Human Resource Management: A Review of the Literature and a Proposed Typology," *Academy of Management Review* 13, 3, 1988, pp. 454–70.
13. R. E. Miles and C. C. Snow, *Organizational Strategy, Structure, and Processes* (New York: McGraw-Hill, 1978); C. C. Snow and R. E. Miles, "Organizational Strategy, Design, and Human Resource Management" (paper presented at National Academy of Management meetings, Dallas, 1983).
14. Dyer and Holder, "Strategic Perspective."
15. Howard Schwartz and Stanley M. Davis, "Matching Corporate Culture and Business Strategy," *Organizational Dynamics,* Summer 1981, pp. 36–48; Gloria deBejar and George Milkovich, "Human Resource Strategy at the Business Level" (paper presented at National Academy of Management Meetings, Chicago, August 1986); C. W. Hofer and D. Schendel, *Strategy Formulation: Analytical Concepts* (St. Paul, Minn.: West Publishing, 1978).
16. Roy B. Helfgott, *Computerized Manufacturing and Human Resources* (Lexington, Mass.: Lexington Books, 1988).
17. Charles O'Reilly, "Corporations, Culture, and Commitment: Motivation and Social Control in Organizations," *California Management Review,* Summer 1989, pp. 9–25.
18. Daniel J. Koys, "Human Resource Management and a Culture of Respect," *Employee Responsibilities and Rights Journal* 1, no. 1 (1988), pp. 57–68.
19. Fred E. Fiedler and Joseph Garcia, *New Approaches to Effective Leadership: Cognitive Resources and Organization Performance* (New York: John Wiley & Sons, 1987).

20. Sanford M. Jacoby, "Development of Internal Labor Markets," in *Internal Labor Markets,* ed. P. Osterman (Cambridge, Mass.: MIT Press, 1984), pp. 23–70.

21. R. Likert, *New Patterns of Management* (New York: McGraw-Hill, 1961), p. 95. For a sampling of current theory and research on leadership, see: John P. Kotter, *The Leadership Factor* (New York: Free Press, 1988; James Krantz, "The Managerial Couple: Superior-Subordinate Relationships as a Unit of Analysis," *Human Resource Management,* Summer 1989, pp. 161–75; Noel Tichy and Mary Anne Devanna, *The Transformational Leader* (New York: John Wiley & Sons, 1986); Andrew Crouch and Philip Yetton, "Manager-Subordinate Dyads: Relationships among Task and Social Contact, Manager Friendliness and Subordinate Performance in Management Groups," *Organizational Behavior and Human Decision Processes* 41 (1988), pp. 65–28; Belle Rose Ragins, "Power and Gender Congruency Effect in Evaluations of Male and Female Managers," *Journal of Management* 15, no. 1 (1989), pp. 65–76; Dean Tjosvold, "Interdependence and Power between Managers and Employees: A Study of the Leader Relationship," *Journal of Management* 15, no. 1 (1989), pp. 49–62; Warren Bennis, *Why Leaders Can't Lead* (San Francisco: Jossey-Bass, 1989); Bernard M. Bass, *Leadership and Performance beyond Expectations* (New York: Free Press, 1985); Harold W. Berkman and Linda L. Neider, *The Human Relations of Organizations* (Boston: Kent, 1987); Lawrence H. Peters, Darrell D. Hartke, and John T. Pohlmann, "Fiedler's Contingency Theory of Leadership: An Application of the Meta-Analysis Procedures of Schmidt and Hunter," *Psychology Bulletin* 97 (1985), pp. 274–85.

22. R. P. Rumelt, *Strategy, Structure, and Economic Performance* (Boston: Harvard Business School, 1974); and M. Leontiades, *Strategies for Diversification and Change* (Boston: Little, Brown, 1980).

23. R. C. Mecham, E. J. McCormick, and P. R. Jeanneret, *Technical Manual for the Position Analysis Questionnaire (PAQ) System* (Logan, Utah: PAQ Services, 1977; E. T. Cornelius III, T. J. Carron, and M. M. Collins, "Job Analysis Models and Job Classification," *Personnel Psychology* 32 (1979), pp. 693–708; also see R. W. Lissitz, J. L. Mendoza, C. J. Huberty, and V. H. Markos, "Some Ideas on a Methodology for Determining Job Similarities/Differences," *Personnel Psychology* 32 (1979), pp. 517–28; and JoAnn Lee and Jorge L. Mendoza, "A Comparison of Techniques Which Test for Job Difference," *Personnel Psychology* 34 (1981), pp. 731–48.

24. E. A. Fleishman, *Structure and Measurement of Physical Fitness* (Englewood Cliffs, N.J.: Prentice-Hall, 1964); E. A. Fleishman, "Toward a Taxonomy of Human Performance," *American Psychologist* 30 (1975), pp. 1017–32; E. A. Fleishman, "Evaluating Physical Abilities Required by Jobs," *The Personnel Administrator* 24 (1979), pp. 82–92.

25. U.S. Department of Labor, Manpower Administration, *Handbook for Analyzing Jobs* (Washington, D.C.: Government Printing Office, 1972); S. A. Fine and W. W. Wiley, *An Introduction to Fundamental Job Analysis,* monograph no. 4 (Kalamazoo, Mich.: W. E. Upjohn Institute for Employment Research, 1971).

26. Fine and Wiley, *Job Analysis.*

27. Ernest J. McCormick, "Job Information: Its Development and Applications," in *Handbook of Personnel and Industrial Relations,* ed. D. Yoder and H. G. Heneman, Jr. (Washington, D.C.: Bureau of National Affairs, 1979).

28. E. M. Ramras, "Discussion," *Proceedings of Division of Military Psychology Symposium: Collecting, Analyzing, and Reporting Information Describing Jobs and Occupations,* 77th Annual Convention of the American Psychological Association, Lackland Air Force Base, Texas, September 1969, pp. 75–76.

29. Luis R. Gomez-Mejia, Ronald C. Page, and Walter W. Tornow, "A Comparison of the Practical Utility of Traditional, Statistical, and Hybrid Job Evaluation Approaches,"

Academy of Management Journal 25, no. 4 (1982), pp. 790–809; Edward L. Levine, Francis Sistrunk, Kathryn J. McNutt, and Sidney Gael, "Exemplary Job Analysis Systems in Selected Organizations: A Description of Process and Outcomes," *Journal of Business and Psychology,* Fall 1988, pp. 3–21.

30. Paul Sparks, "Job Analysis," in *Personnel Management,* ed. K. Rowland and G. Ferris (Boston: Allyn & Bacon, 1982).

31. *Pay Equity Implementation* (Toronto, Ontario: The Pay Equity Commission, 1989).

32. Ronald A. Ash and Edward L. Levine, "A Framework for Evaluating Job Analysis Methods," *Personnel* 57, no. 6 (November–December 1980), pp. 53–59; E. L. Levine, R. A. Ash, H. Hall, and F. Sistrunk, "Evaluation of Job Analysis Methods by Experienced Job Analysts," *Academy of Management Journal,* no. 2 (1983), pp. 339–48.

33. M. D. Dunnette, L. M. Hough, and R. L. Rosse, "Task and Job Taxonomies as a Basis for Identifying Labor Supply Sources and Evaluating Employment Qualifications," in *Affirmative Action Planning,* ed. George T. Milkovich and Lee Dyer (New York: Human Resource Planning Society, 1979), pp. 37–51.

34. Robert Levering, *A Great Place to Work* (New York: Random House, 1988); Michael A. Campion, "How Do You Design a Job?" *Personnel Journal,* January 1989, pp. 43–46; John W. Kendrick, *Improving Company Productivity* (Baltimore: Johns Hopkins University Press, 1984).

35. Frederick W. Taylor, "On the Art of Cutting Metals," *Transactions of the American Society of Mechanical Engineers* 28 (1907); F. W. Taylor, *Principles of Scientific Management* (New York: Harper & Row, 1911); Edwin A. Locke, "The Ideas of Frederick W. Taylor: An Evaluation," *Academy of Management Review* 7, no. 1 (1982), pp. 14–25.

36. E. Mayo, *The Human Problems of an Industrial Civilization* (New York: Macmillan, 1933).

37. Levering, *Great Place to Work.*

38. Guillermo J. Grenier, *Inhuman Relations: Quality Circles and Anti-Unionism in American Industry* (Philadelphia: Temple University Press, 1988).

39. J. R. Hackman and G. R. Oldham, *Work Redesign* (Reading, Mass.: Addison Wesley, 1979).

40. K. Roberts and W. Glick, "The Job Characteristics Approach to Task Design: A Critical Review," *Journal of Applied Psychology* 66 (1981), pp. 193–217; Yitzhak Fried and Gerald Ferris, "The Validity of the Job Characteristics Model: A Review and Meta-Analysis," *Personnel Psychology,* Summer 1987, pp. 287–322; Michael A. Campion and Paul W. Thayer, "Development and Field Evaluation of an Interdisciplinary Measure of Job Design," *Journal of Applied Psychology* 70 (1985), pp. 29–43.

41. Edgar H. Schein, "Corporate Teams and Totems," *Across the Board,* May 1989, pp. 12–17; Victor H. Vroom and Arthur G. Jago, *The New Leadership: Managing Participation in Organizations* (Englewood Cliffs, N.J.: Prentice-Hall, 1988).

42. John Holusha, "Beating Japan at Its Own Game," *New York Times,* F–1, F–8.

43. Robert H. Guest, "Team Management under Stress," *Across the Board,* May 1989, pp. 30–35; Paul Chance, "Redefining the Supervisor's Role," *Across the Board,* May 1989, pp. 36–37; Paul Chance, "Great Experiments in Team Chemistry," *Across the Board,* May 1989, pp. 18–25.

44. Elliot Jaques, "In Praise of Hierarchies," *Harvard Business Review,* January–February 1990.

CHAPTER FOUR

Employee Conditions

Assessing Employee Characteristics

Assessing Performance
Why Assess Performance?
What Performance to Assess?
How to Measure Performance?
Who Should Assess Performance?
When to Assess Performance?
*How to Communicate Performance
Assessment?*
*Evaluating Performance Assessment and
Resolving Disputes*
*The Role of the Human Resource Function in
Performance Assessment*

Assessing Absenteeism

Assessing Separations and Turnover

Assessing Employee Attitudes/Opinions

Assessing Employee Demographic
Characteristics

Summary

Your Turn: Appraising "Quality"
Performance at Ford Motor Company

Imagine that your human resource management class is a job, and the students are employees. Also, your college can record whatever information it wishes about the class's employees (you and your fellow students). The information will be used to make decisions, such as who gets into or advances in the class, allocating rewards among students, changing the class design, and assessing whether the class is achieving its objectives for its employees, its organization, and its environment. Finally, imagine that you have been hired (at an astronomical fee) as a consultant to recommend what information to collect about employees.

Would you recommend assessing the "performance" of the students? Should performance be measured by comparing students to each other, by comparing their behaviors to specified standards, or by comparing their ultimate achievements to goals? What should be measured—effort, behaviors, knowledge, leadership, dependability, or something else? Who should assess performance—each individual student, the instructor, the entire class, an outside expert, or some combination? Is it enough to perform well while at work (in class), or would you recommend tracking each student's attendance as well? What about their out-of-class habits? What's the best way to inform students of their performance?

Should you suggest tracking the attitudes and opinions of the students regarding their work and their organization? Such opinions could be important in identifying opportunities for improvement. Moreover, student attitudes may be clues to future performance problems in the making. How would you decide what factors to include in the attitude/opinion measurement system? Would you use surveys, interviews, or some other approach? How would you ensure honesty?

Would you track any personal characteristics about the students? A huge number of such characteristics could be measured, including height, weight, eye color, hair color, sex, age, and race. Would it be appropriate to design a personnel management class differently if the students are older, have previous work experience, and support families than if the students are under 20 years old, have little previous work experience, and are single?

ASSESSING EMPLOYEE CHARACTERISTICS

HR managers use information about their employees just as they use information about external and organizational conditions—to make better decisions. As you saw in the example, it's hardly obvious exactly what employee characteristics to track or how to measure them. Unlike other resources, such as raw materials or financial instruments, you can't just order employees with a particular desired set of characteristics. People are bundles of characteristics that affect the success of HR decisions. Sometimes, to get the characteristics it needs, the organization must also accommodate other characteristics. For example, parents of school-age children have proven to be reliable and diligent workers in many retail and fast-food operations. Organizations can accommodate these workers' needs with flexible work hours and training for managers to help them understand parents' special needs and circumstances.

Employee characteristics are important, because they affect employees' *ability* to carry out job requirements, as well as employees' *motivation* to exert effort toward job requirements. Perhaps the most obvious employee characteristic that must be measured is employee performance—the degree to which employees accomplish work requirements. Performance measurement is an important HR activity. Informal and formal performance measurement occupies a great deal of time for HR professionals and the managers they support. This chapter will describe performance measurement in detail, because performance information is fundamental to every HR activity discussed in later chapters.

However, employee performance reflects mainly *efficiency* objectives. Most organizations are also concerned with employee perceptions of *equity,* and employee attitudes and opinions about their work. Moreover, if organizations tracked only employee performance, it would be difficult to determine how to improve that performance. Performance measures alone cannot reveal whether low performance is due to poor attendance, to low motivation, to performance barriers related to handicap or physical strength, or to a lack of skills and abilities. In addition to measuring performance, HR managers must help the organization identify and measure other employee characteristics that support decisions about HR activities.

There is an infinite variety of physical, mental and emotional employee characteristics, so it would be impossible to list and discuss them all in one chapter (or even in one book!). Later chapters, focusing on specific HR activities, will expand the description of the employee characteristics that are most relevant to those activities. Ability measures will be discussed in the chapters on recruiting and hiring employees. Motivation will be discussed in the chapters on pay. This chapter will describe employee characteristics that are assessed because of their relevance to many HR decisions: employee performance, employee absenteeism, employee separations and turnover, employee attitudes/opinions, and employee demographic characteristics.

ASSESSING PERFORMANCE

Performance assessment, or *performance appraisal,* is the process that measures employee performance. *Employee performance* is the degree to which employees accomplish work requirements.

EXHIBIT 4.1   Six Key Questions in Performance Assessment

Why assess performance?
What performance to assess?
How to assess performance?
Who should assess performance?
When to assess performance?
How to communicate performance assessments?

Virtually all organizations assess employee performance. Designing and implementing performance assessment systems requires answering six key questions, as shown in Exhibit 4.1.

Why Assess Performance?

At first, it may seem obvious that an organization needs to measure employee performance, but some have suggested that performance assessment systems do little good and some harm. Managers in one study perceived no consequences nor any practical value in conducting formal performance appraisals.[1] Many Japanese factories follow the urgings of W. Edward Deming to cease all individual performance assessments and to evaluate unit or plant level performance, instead, focusing on assisting those who are out of line with the system. Also, performance assessment involves costs: costs to develop the system, to have managers and employees carry it out, and to process the results. A 1978 study estimated the four-year cost of developing and implementing a performance assessment system at over $300,000. That's nearly $500,000 at today's prices. Performance assessment should not be undertaken lightly.

On the other hand, differences in individual performance can make a huge difference to the organization. The U.S. army recently estimated that it takes only 9 tanks commanded by superior tank commanders to accomplish the same task as 17 tanks commanded by average tank commanders.[2] When human error caused the Exxon tanker *Valdez* to run aground, causing the largest oil spill in Alaska, the difference between good and poor tanker commander performance became all too apparent. So, as Exhibit 4.2 shows, most organizations have many uses for performance appraisal systems, primarily in determining wage and salary adjustments, making promotion decisions, and communicating between supervisors and subordinates.

Exhibit 4.3 summarizes the two general purposes of performance appraisal—providing feedback/counseling and allocating rewards/opportunities. The arrows in the exhibit signify potential conflicts in performance assessment that arise because it serves such different purposes.[3] Within-organization conflict exists because, to satisfy the organization's goals related to allocating rewards and

EXHIBIT 4.2   Uses of Performance Appraisal Information Ranked in Order of Importance

Most Important: Improving work performance.
Administering pay based on merit.
Advising employees of work expectations.
Making promotion decisions.
Counseling employees.
Motivating employees.
Assessing employee potential.
Identifying training needs.
Better working relations between managers and employees.
Helping employees set career goals.
Assigning work more efficiently.
Making transfer decisions.
Making layoff or termination decisions.
Assisting in long-range planning.
Least Important: Evaluating hiring procedures.

Source: Robert D. Bretz, Jr., and George T. Milkovich, "Performance Appraisal in Large Organizations: Practice and Research Implications," Working Paper no. 89-17, Center for Advanced Human Resource Studies, Ithaca, New York, 1989.

EXHIBIT 4.3   Potential Conflicts Caused by the Two Purposes of Performance Assessment

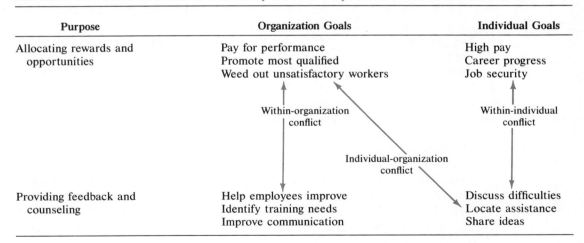

Purpose	Organization Goals	Individual Goals
Allocating rewards and opportunities	Pay for performance Promote most qualified Weed out unsatisfactory workers	High pay Career progress Job security
Providing feedback and counseling	Help employees improve Identify training needs Improve communication	Discuss difficulties Locate assistance Share ideas

Within-organization conflict

Within-individual conflict

Individual-organization conflict

opportunities, performance assessments must compare individuals to each other, consider job specifications, and focus on objective observable outcomes achieved in the past. But, to satisfy the organization's goals related to providing feedback and counseling, performance assessments must focus on each individual independently, must consider such job requirements as skills and abilities

---

EXHIBIT 4.4   Types of Performance Criteria and Examples

Skills/Abilities/Needs/Traits	Behaviors	Results
Job knowledge	Perform tasks	Sales
Strength	Obey instructions	Production levels
Eye-hand coordination	Report problems	Production quality
Licenses	Maintain equipment	Wastage/scrap
Business knowledge	Maintain records	Accidents
Desire to achieve	Follow rules	Equipment repairs
Social needs	Attend regularly	Customers served
Dependability	Submit suggestions	Customer satisfaction
Loyalty	Smoking abstinence	
Honesty	Drug abstinence	
Creativity		
Leadership		

---

that are often not easily observed, and must focus on improving the individual's potential for the future.

Within-individual conflict exists because, to satisfy the individual's goals of obtaining high rewards and opportunities, individuals want to be favorably evaluated, and they may want to present their performance in the best possible light by denying problems and inflating accomplishments. But, to satisfy employee goals related to feedback/counseling, they must receive accurate and helpful guidance, which requires that they honestly share difficulties and ideas for improvement.

Finally, individual-organizational conflict exists between the individual's goals of obtaining rewards and opportunities and both types of organizational goals. The organization's goals require complete and accurate information about both job behaviors and ways to help individuals improve, but providing such information may not maximize the individual's rewards and recognition. The conflict is especially sharp for poor performers, which may explain why poor performance ratings are rare and difficult.

Despite these conflicts, most organizations assess performance, and attempt to achieve both purposes to some degree. HR managers play an important role in designing the assessment systems and interpreting their results, and work closely with line managers who actually carry out the performance assessments. The next step is deciding what to measure.

What Performance to Assess?

Exhibit 4.4 suggests the wide range of criteria that might be measured when assessing performance. Skills, abilities, needs, and traits are individual characteristics that interact with the nature of the work and the organization to produce behaviors, which, in turn, affect results. Performance assessments can contain any combination of these criteria, and often contain several different criteria. A Bureau of National Affairs study found that the following criteria were used for white-collar workers: 93 percent of firms used quality of work; 90 percent used quantity of work; 87 percent used initiative; 87 percent used cooperation; 86 percent used dependability; 85 percent used job knowledge; 79 percent used attendance; and 67 percent used need for supervision.[4] Organizations monitor smoking, drug use, telephone conversations, and even excess wiggling among computer operators.[5] Employee theft is usually monitored as part of employee performance, especially because theft costs U.S. employers between $15 and $25 billion per year.[6] Managers should choose what to assess by considering the purposes of performance assessment, as discussed above, and the organization and work, as discussed in Chapter Three. The overriding consideration should be the ability of the performance information to support decisions by managers, employees, and the organization.

Criteria Reflect Organizational Conditions

Chapter Three showed the challenges and opportunities for HR management created by organization conditions. At PepsiCo, they want managers who "act like owners, run lean, and get big results." CEO Wayne Calloway says, "We take eagles and teach them to fly in formation," and the corporate culture puts a premium on honesty and openness among managers. The performance assessment process for managers includes an annual performance review between a superior and each of his or her subordinate managers, focusing on "what the manager actually did this year to make a big difference in the business, not whether he's a nice guy or wears the right color socks. Did he make his sales target? Did he develop a successful new taco chip or soda commercial?" Notice the emphasis on outcomes, rather than only behaviors. PepsiCo combines these outcome-oriented appraisals with a feedback program in which the bosses get evaluated by their subordinates in confidential reports.[7]

Criteria Reflect the Job

Job analysis (see Chapter Three) guides the choice of performance criteria, by specifying the tasks, objectives, and skill requirements for the job, as well as how it relates to other jobs in the organization. Simply listing these factors is not enough, however. The feasibility of measuring each criterion must be assessed.[8] Such traits as dependability, honesty, and loyalty may make fine criteria for evaluating Boy Scouts and may be quite desirable in employees, but it's difficult to measure them reliably.[9] Different jobs also afford different opportunities to achieve performance. Factors outside the individual's control, such as supervision, leadership, group processes, and resources/constraints, should be considered in choosing criteria.

EXHIBIT 4.5   Approaches to Performance Assessment and Examples

Comparison to Agreed Objectives	Comparison to Job Standards	Comparison between Individuals
Management by objectives (MBO)	Physical observation Checklists Rating scales Critical incidents Behaviorally anchored rating scale (BARS) Essays/diaries	Ranking Forced distribution

Criteria Reflect Employee Characteristics

Even in the same job, individuals perform differently under different conditions. One study found very little relationship between individuals' maximum performance (when they knew they were being evaluated and were encouraged to perform at their best) and their typical performance as supermarket cashiers. On the same job, some individuals were good at maximum performance but poor at typical performance, and vice versa.[10]

We have seen that an important purpose of performance assessment is communication between the appraiser and the person being appraised. Counseling and developing employees may require measuring employee characteristics, such as skills, performance patterns across different tasks, or other factors that could provide clues to help employees improve. Measuring only the results of an employee's work may give insufficient information. Employees with special requirements, such as single parents, might be served by tracking whether their performance is affected by their use of assistance opportunities, such as company-provided day care.

How to Measure Performance?

Once the organization has chosen performance criteria, it must decide how to observe and record the criteria. With so many possible performance criteria, it's not surprising to find a wide variety of performance assessment techniques. Exhibit 4.5 describes approaches to measuring performance in terms of comparisons—comparison to agreed objectives, comparisons to job standards, and comparisons between individuals—and lists some of the more well-known and widely used measurement techniques for each approach.

Like performance criteria, different performance measurement approaches are often combined, and techniques differ, depending on the type of organization, work, and employee involved. Exhibit 4.6 shows how assessment techniques differ across jobs.

EXHIBIT 4.6 Usage of Performance Assessment Techniques across Different Types of Jobs

	Nonexempt			Exempt			
	Production (119)	Office Clerical (232)	Professional Technical (222)	Professional Technical (225)	Supervisors (first-level) (238)	Middle Management (228)	Top Management (167)
Methods used in performance evaluation process for each employee group							
◆ Rating scale	67%	67%	65%	55%	56%	50%	46%
◆ Essay	48	53	55	60	59	63	61
◆ Checklist	40	34	35	28	28	25	21
◆ Critical incident	18	18	19	19	19	18	19
◆ Management by objectives (MBO)	11	22	24	44	44	49	56
◆ Ranking	10	7	9	8	7	8	7
◆ Other	3	3	3	4	3	4	4

Source: The Bureau of National Affairs, Inc., "Performance Appraisal Practices," *Personnel Policies Forum, Survey no. 135* (1983), p. 6.

EXHIBIT 4.7   Management by Objectives (MBO) Performance Report for Salespeople

Objectives Set	Period Objective	Accomplish-ments	Variance
1. Number of sales calls.	100	104	104%
2. Number of new customers contacted.	20	18	90
3. Number of wholesalers stocking new product 117.	30	30	100
4. Sales of product 12.	10,000	9,750	97.5
5. Sales of product 17.	17,000	18,700	110
6. Customer complaints/service calls.	35	11	30
7. Number of sales correspondence courses successfully completed.	4	2	50
8. Number of sales reports in home office within one day of end of month.	12	10	80

Comparison to Agreed Objectives

Management by objectives (MBO) involves the employee and his or her superior jointly setting objectives in advance for the employee to try to achieve during a specified period. The technique encourages, or even requires, them to phrase these objectives primarily in terms of measurable, observable outcomes or results. The evaluation consists of a joint review of the degree to which objectives are achieved. Exhibit 4.7 shows typical MBO objectives that might be developed for a salesperson, and a hypothetical summary of their achievement. A vital part of MBO is goal setting, and research consistently suggests that goal setting is effective in increasing productivity, especially when goals are specific, challenging, and accepted. However, MBO also involves ongoing monitoring, planning, and rewards. MBO research typically shows positive effects, but they are weaker and less frequent than experimental studies focusing only on goal setting.[11] Also, if not closely monitored, MBO techniques can eventually produce performance standards that alter fundamental job requirements, producing performance assessments that no longer reflect the organization's purpose.[12]

Comparison to Job Standards

To ensure that performance consistently reflects established job requirements, some performance assessment methods compare employee behaviors, traits and other characteristics to objective standards describing job performance.

Physical observation   Though relatively rare, direct physical observation of results, employee behaviors, physical conditions, or habits has generated a great deal of controversy. Polygraph (lie detector) tests were severely restricted in

EXHIBIT 4.8   Checklist Using Job Behaviors

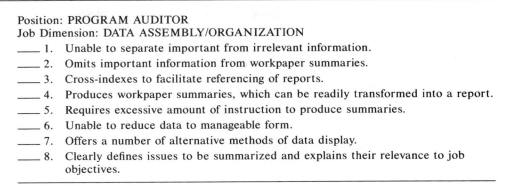

Position: PROGRAM AUDITOR
Job Dimension: DATA ASSEMBLY/ORGANIZATION

_____ 1.   Unable to separate important from irrelevant information.

_____ 2.   Omits important information from workpaper summaries.

_____ 3.   Cross-indexes to facilitate referencing of reports.

_____ 4.   Produces workpaper summaries, which can be readily transformed into a report.

_____ 5.   Requires excessive amount of instruction to produce summaries.

_____ 6.   Unable to reduce data to manageable form.

_____ 7.   Offers a number of alternative methods of data display.

_____ 8.   Clearly defines issues to be summarized and explains their relevance to job objectives.

Source: Stephen J. Carroll and Craig E. Schneier, *Performance Appraisal and Review Systems* (Glenview, Ill.: Scott, Foresman 1982). Copyright © 1982 by Scott, Foresman and Company. Reprinted by permission.

1988 by the Employee Polygraph Protection Act (EPPA).[13] Still, a *Business Week* magazine article asks, "Is your boss spying on you?" describing techniques that included hidden cameras, recording computer keystrokes, using special chairs to detect wiggling ("wigglers aren't working"), and electronic recording of truck driving speed, oil pressure, engine RPMs, and idling time.[14] The Office of Technology Assessment estimated that between 6 and 7 million office employees are monitored by computers for performance assessment.[15] A 1986 Executive Order (EO 12564) subjects more than 1 million U.S. government employees to random testing for illegal drug use, though courts tend to allow such testing only where it affects safety or national security.[16] In the private sector, Southern Pacific Transportation Company credits pre-employment and post-accident drug tests with reducing injuries by 60 percent in 1984.[17] The legality and value of such practices will undoubtedly continue to be debated.[18] Some research suggests that negative effects of electronic monitoring can be reduced through careful feedback and attention to equity in the use of the information.[19]

Checklists   Checklists present the evaluator with a set of behaviors, adjectives, or descriptive statements. If the rater believes the statement describes the person being evaluated, she or he checks the item; if not, she or he leaves it blank. Each statement is given a score reflecting its importance and its positive or negative impact on job performance. The performance rating is the sum of the weights for the items checked. Exhibit 4.8 shows a checklist based on work behaviors, in which the performance score is the number of positive items checked.

EXHIBIT 4.9 Typical Graphic Rating Scale

Name _____ Dept. _____ Date _____

	Outstanding	Good	Satisfactory	Fair	Unsatisfactory
Quality of work Thoroughness (neatness and accuracy of work) Comments:	☐	☐	☐	☐	☐
Knowledge of job Clear understanding of the facts or factors pertinent to the job Comments:	☐	☐	☐	☐	☐
Personal qualities Personality, appearance, sociability, leadership, integrity Comments:	☐	☐	☐	☐	☐
Cooperation Ability and willingness to work with associates, supervisors, and subordinates toward common goals Comments:	☐	☐	☐	☐	☐
Dependability Conscientious, thorough, accurate, reliable with respect to attendance, lunch periods, reliefs, etc. Comments:	☐	☐	☐	☐	☐
Initiative Earnestness in seeking increased responsibilities. Self-starting, unafraid to proceed alone? Comments:	☐	☐	☐	☐	☐

Rating scales One of the oldest and most widely used assessment techniques is the rating scale, sometimes called a *graphic rating scale* when it appears as a graph or line or series of boxes along which performance levels are marked. Exhibit 4.9 shows an example of a graphic rating scale that covers several of the criteria discussed above. The evaluator marks the box best describing the evaluated person's level of each criterion. If desired, each level could be assigned a number, perhaps ranging from Outstanding = 5 to Unsatisfactory = 1, and each criterion could be assigned a weight according to its importance, and every person's evaluation could be expressed as the sum of the importance

EXHIBIT 4.10   Behaviorally Anchored Rating Scale (BARS) for a Residence Hall Advisor

Performance Dimension

Concern for individual dorm residents: attempts to get to know individual dorm residents and responds to their individual needs with genuine interest. This resident adviser could be expected to:

Rating Scale

Good (1)	(2)	(3)	(4)	(5) Poor
Recognize when a floor member appears depressed and ask if person has problem he or she wants to discuss.	Offer floor members tips on how to study for a course he or she has already taken.	See person and recognize him/her as a floor member and say "hi."	Be friendly with a floor member; get into discussion on problems, but fail to follow up on the problem later on with student.	Criticize a floor member for not being able to solve his or her own problems.

weights times the level of each criterion achieved. *Summated scales* can be constructed using more sophisticated statistical methods for assigning values to such items.[20] *Mixed standard scales* include not only the criteria but several statements describing each criterion, which the evaluator may choose to describe performance, such as (1) "This person is a real self-starter and always takes the initiative," (2) "Although this person generally shows initiative, an occasional prod from the superior is required to get the work done," and (3) "This person has a tendency to sit around and wait for directions."

Critical incidents   *Critical incidents* are statements describing very effective and very ineffective behaviors that are critical to each performance dimension.[21] Critical incidents can be used as part of a number of different performance assessment techniques.

Behaviorally anchored rating scales (BARS)   This approach starts with a rating scale like those described earlier, but it uses critical incidents to provide examples or "anchors" for different points on the rating scale.[22] These anchors make the rating scale more job-specific and, hopefully, less subjective and less error-prone. Exhibit 4.10 shows a BARS that might be applied to a residence hall advisor. The steps in developing a BARS are:

1. Supervisors identify "performance dimensions," or categories of activities that make up the job.
2. Supervisors write a set of critical incidents for each job dimension.

3. An independent group of supervisors sorts the incidents into dimensions and rates each incident along a favorable/unfavorable performance scale.

4. Incidents that were consistently placed in each dimension are kept, and scales are constructed for each dimension, anchored with incidents showing good and bad performance.

Researchers have developed variations on BARS, including behavioral observation scales (BOS), which assess the frequency of behavior, and behavior discrimination scales (BDS), which compare the actual frequency of behavior to the opportunity to exhibit the behavior, and the expected frequency of the behavior.[23] Although variations can offer some advantages, no evidence has established the general superiority of BARS or its variations over more easily developed appraisal techniques.[24]

Essays/diaries   Performance can be assessed by having evaluators write an essay describing the strong and weak aspects of the employee's behavior over a time period. The essay can be completely open-ended, but usually follows guidelines specifying the topics and purpose of the essay. Essays can be constructed from diaries of observed critical incidents kept by the evaluator during the performance assessment period. Essays can also be used in conjunction with rating scales or BARS to provide documentation and elaborate on the ratings.

Comparison between Individuals

Some personnel decisions, such as pay increases, giving an award to the top performer, and choosing who gets promoted, involve allocating a fixed set of opportunities among employees. Such decisions require comparing individuals to each other. These comparisons are frequently based on only a general judgment, but they can also be based on more detailed information by using any of the techniques discussed earlier. Several methods for making the comparisons have been used.

Ranking   Ordering performers from highest to lowest is simple, fast, easy to understand, and inexpensive. With large numbers of employees, ranking can become complex. Alternation ranking and paired comparisons can simplify the process. With *alternation ranking,* you first determine who is the highest performer, then who is the lowest performer, then who is the second highest, the second lowest, and so on. *Paired-comparison* ranking involves comparing each possible pair of employees and deciding which of the pair is the best performer. The one with the most best-of-the-pair choices is ranked highest, and so on.

Forced distribution   This technique is similar to grading on a curve. A fixed distribution of ratings is required, such as 10 percent unsatisfactory, 20 percent needs improvement, 40 percent satisfactory, 20 percent good, and 10 percent outstanding. The evaluator must give this distribution of ratings. Forced distributions can alleviate problems, such as inflated ratings, or the tendency to rate everyone near the middle of the scale. However, it assumes that performance levels follow the distribution. This may not be true for outstanding groups of employees or for very small groups of employees and may produce frustration among both the raters and those they rate.

Drawbacks of comparisons between individuals Simple rankings are seldom appropriate for performance assessment.[25] Rankings are often based on crudely defined criteria (or no defined criteria) and can become very subjective and difficult to explain and justify in work-related terms. These simple, easy, and inexpensive techniques may create problems that are very costly to solve. American Cyanamid Company discovered that its 10-category forced distribution appraisal system seemed arbitrary and caused great frustration among its research scientists. Managers felt obligated to dwell on trivial shortcomings to justify putting the required number of employees in the *needs improvement* category. After implementing a new appraisal system with only three categories (*superior, quality,* and *needs improvement*), mutually agreed specific objectives, and employee involvement in the process, both the scientists and their managers expressed increased satisfaction.[26]

Tailor Appraisal Methods to the Situation

Choosing appraisal techniques depends on the nature of the appraisal situation. Exhibit 4.11 illustrates how the nature of the work, employee characteristics, and organizational characteristics can be used to guide such choices. Generally, the more routine task, the lower the employee desire for independence, and the more stable the environment, the more appropriate are techniques based on comparisons to job standards and specific behaviors, such as rating scales. At moderate levels of routinization, desire for independence, or environmental stability, it becomes more appropriate to focus on achieving objectives (perhaps using MBO), because employees desire independence and they may have to change behaviors in response to changing conditions. At extremely high levels of desired independence, on very nonroutine work, and in volatile environments, one is forced to make very unstructured comparisons, perhaps using diaries or essays.[27] These relationships are similar to those faced by an instructor when deciding how to test learning in a class. Very objective material might be tested with multiple-choice questions or mathematical problems. Moderately objective material, where answers could be expressed in many ways, might be tested by using short-answer questions. General material involving ethics, values, and opinions are best tested by using essays or papers that give the student the maximum flexibility and that impose little structure.

EXHIBIT 4.11   How Characteristics of the Work, the Employees, and the Environment Affect
Performance Assessment Techniques

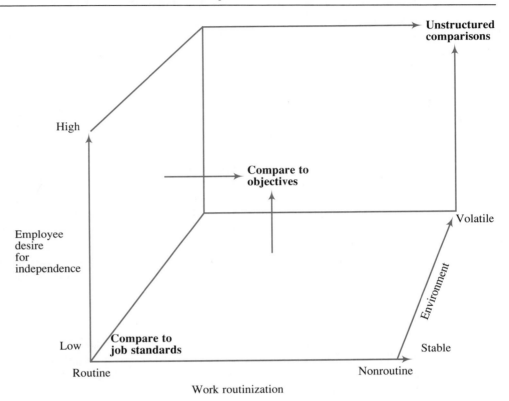

Who Should Assess Performance?

Choosing the right persons to assess performance is at least as important as choosing the right performance criteria and assessment techniques. Exhibit 4.12 illustrates the variety of appraiser choices, including self-appraisal, which has shown mixed results. Many appraisal systems use several appraisers, but the vast majority rely primarily on the supervisor or a higher-level manager, or both.[28] Evidence is mixed regarding which approach works best in which situation.[29] The best appraisers will have three characteristics: opportunity to observe performance; ability to translate observations into useful assessments; and motivation to provide useful performance assessments.

Opportunity to Observe Performance
If the immediate supervisor works closely with the subordinates, he or she will have ample opportunity to observe their behaviors. However, others may have

EXHIBIT 4.12   Alternative Performance Assessors

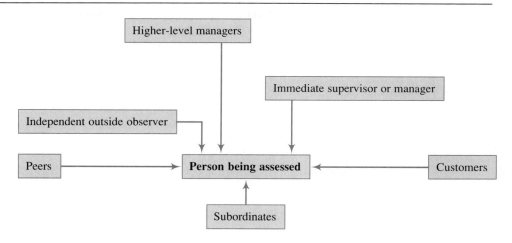

more opportunity to observe other aspects of performance. In China, employment is guaranteed, so the Xian Department Store needed an alternative to dismissal as a way to motivate poor-performing clerks. They initiated a public award for the "40 Worst Employees," and they found shoppers eager to report instances of clerks throwing merchandise, being rude, and leaving their posts.[30] Some employers increasingly feel that every employee should be evaluated by a "customer" or a "client," whether it is an actual buyer, another employee who depends on that employee's performance, or a manager. Student evaluations of instructors are a kind of customer-focused evaluation. Subordinates and peers can often provide more accurate information than managers, because they see more of the person's behaviors.[31]

Ability to Translate Observations into Useful Assessments

Observing performance is only useful if the observer can recall, organize, and report those observations as useful performance assessments. The goals of performance appraisal shown in Exhibit 4.3 can only be reached if assessors understand them and endeavor to gather and report the information in a useful way. A great deal of research by psychologists has focused on the factors affecting appraisal abilities, including mental or "cognitive" processes (such as memory), prior expectations, and prior knowledge.[32] Other factors that can affect appraisals include the appraisal purpose and the age, sex, race, and attractiveness of appraisers or those appraised.[33] One innovation to improve performance appraisal uses personal computers, programmed with "expert systems" that guide the appraiser through a series of questions that expert appraisers have found to be useful. A program called *Performance Mentor* guides the appraiser and then offers advice on how to handle the performance discussion with the employee, depending on the employee, the appraiser and the situation.[34] Appraiser training, discussed below, can also affect some aspects of appraisal ability, but it is difficult to provide such training to some appraisers (such as customers).

Motivation to Provide Useful Performance Assessments

Appraisers are more likely to be motivated to provide useful performance assessments when they see a clear link between the quality of those assessments and outcomes that are important to them.[35] Motivation can be enhanced by linking appraiser rewards to the quality of their assessments, increasing appraisers' trust in the process, requiring appraisers to justify appraisals, and training appraisers to handle undesirable reactions to negative appraisals. As logical as these tactics may sound, it is uncommon for organizations to evaluate appraisers on the quality of their appraisals.[36] Moreover, while these tactics are appropriate for supervisors, it may be difficult to apply them when using other appraisers, such as peers, subordinates, or customers.

Errors in Performance Assessment

Because performance assessment is often subjective, there has been a good deal of research on errors and biases. Extreme errors and biases can reduce the value of performance assessments by affecting personnel decisions. Any measurement system strives for *reliability*—consistency, as well as *validity*—an ability to reflect what it's supposed to measure. Errors can detract from reliability and validity. The most frequently studied measurement errors are: halo, leniency, severity, and central tendency.[37] Halo error involves incorrectly giving similar ratings on different performance criteria based on an overall impression, such as rating a person high on job knowledge just because they have good social skills. Halo can tend to inflate or deflate ratings, depending on the direction of the overall impression. Leniency error involves giving overly favorable ratings to an entire group; severity error is the opposite. Central tendency error involves incorrectly giving ratings near the middle of the scale to the entire group, such as when an instructor gives grades ranging only between $B-$ and $B+$, even though there were large differences in student performance. Research suggests that biases reflecting race and gender are reduced when appraisals are based on specific task performance, though age, attractiveness, and similarity to the person being appraised do affect ratings.[38] Yet, for all the attention to rating errors, there is little convincing evidence that they actually affect rating accuracy.[39]

Training and Rewarding Performance Appraisers

Most of the largest U.S. firms train their performance appraisers, emphasizing how to communicate appraisal results, how to use the forms, how to set performance standards, how to recognize good performance, and how to avoid making rating errors. A much smaller proportion of the firms (22 percent) reported they track appraisal quality or reward good appraisers.[40] Research has shown that training can reduce errors, but it may also reduce accuracy.[41] Some have suggested that training should emphasize observation and decision-making skills, rather than error reduction.[42] Given the important role that the person being appraised plays in the proper interpretation and use of the appraisal, it is surprising that there appears to be very little training for employees in this area.

When to Assess Performance?

Most organizations conduct formal performance appraisals once a year on employees, often on each employee's hiring anniversary date.[43] Though this provides administrative efficiency, more frequent appraisals occurring at the end of important projects or tasks would probably improve accuracy by reducing possible memory lapses. Diary-keeping can also help here. Aside from increasing the appraiser's accuracy and memory, however, providing performance feedback closer to the performance event is likely to increase employee awareness and motivation. Most students, for example, prefer feedback on their progress throughout a class, rather than receiving their grade based on one final examination or paper at the end.

How to Communicate Performance Assessment?

In quantum physics, the way scientists observe the effects of laser light on ions affects how the ions behave—a watched pot may never boil.[44] People, too, react differently, depending on how their behavior is measured. So, deciding what, how, who, and when to measure performance is only part of the picture. How the information is communicated is just as important.[45] Even positive feedback given in the wrong way can provoke hostile reactions from employees. Imagine how you would feel if your professor said, "Well, you *finally* got a decent grade on a test." Research evidence suggests that specific feedback based on specific performance goals can improve performance.[46] It also shows that subordinates perceive the appraisal more favorably and are motivated to improve when they feel they have participated in the process, when the feedback is positive, and when the source of the appraisal is viewed as expert, reliable, and attractive.[47] Exhibit 4.13 shows how communication enters into each phase of performance evaluation at Bank of America.

Even when an organization provides opportunities to communicate performance appraisal, managers may be reluctant to use them. This is especially likely when the performance appraisal is negative. However, failure to communicate performance results undermines many of the goals of the process, so HR managers must strive to ensure that communication is encouraged and rewarded.

EXHIBIT 4.13   Performance Communication at Bank of America

Step One: Performance Planning

Your manager should work with you to develop your performance plan based on the goals of your unit. He or she should sit down with you to discuss it and answer any questions you may have. The objectives should be: *Traceable,* related to the unit's goals; *Results-Oriented,* focusing on outcomes, not just activities; *Specific* about the required results; *Measurable,* providing you with a way of quantifying and monitoring the quality or quantity of your performance; *Time Bound,* including target dates by which you are to achieve the planned results. The discussion should also summarize your ongoing activities, as well as any *developmental activities* you should undertake to improve your current skills.

Step Two: Coaching

Your manager should observe and talk with you about your performance using *informal coaching,* which involves ongoing observation, feedback, and informing you of changes in the job. *Formal coaching* is when your manager holds periodic sessions with you, preferably once each quarter, to assess your performance compared to your plan, give positive feedback on your performance that meets or exceeds your objectives, develop ideas about how your performance can be maintained or improved, and revise your performance plan if necessary. During coaching *you* should listen carefully to your manager's assessment, discuss your own view of your progress if it differs from your manager's, and discuss and clarify any misunderstandings.

Step Three: Evaluation

You will be formally evaluated once a year, either on January 1 or on your anniversary date. During your performance evaluation, your manager should rate the results of your performance, document the evaluation on the Performance Planning, Coaching, and Evaluation (PPC&E) form, and review and summarize the results with you. The discussion should cover Objectives, Ongoing Responsibilities, Developmental Accomplishments, and Unplanned Activities. You and your manager should discuss your strengths and suggested improvements. You should sign and date the form, writing your comments in the space provided on the back of the form. If you disagree with your evaluation, you may contact Personnel Relations.

Unsatisfactory job performance is performance that is rated "Met Some Not All" (MSNA) or "Did Not Meet" (DNM). If your rating is MSNA, your manager should set a period for you to improve your performance to a "Met" level. If your rating is DNM, your manager should put you on an appropriate measured assignment. If you do not improve to "Met" within the period or by the end of the assignment, you will be terminated or demoted/reassigned.

Source: Copyright © February 1987 Bank of America NT&SA, San Francisco, California. Produced by Management Development #3636, EXEC–1170.

Evaluating Performance Assessment and Resolving Disputes

Like all HR activities, performance assessment should be evaluated for its contribution to organizational goals. Among the largest U.S. organizations, the most important goals for performance assessment were: (1) that the system be accepted by those being rated; (2) that employees have a sense of being treated

EXHIBIT 4.14 Evaluations of Performance Assessment Techniques

Technique	Providing Feedback and Counseling	Allocating Rewards and Opportunities	Minimizing Costs	Avoiding Rating Errors
Management by objectives (MBO)	*Excellent:* Specific problems, deficiencies, and plans are identified.	*Poor:* Nonstandard objectives across employees and units makes comparisons difficult.	*Poor:* Expensive to develop. Time consuming to use.	*Good:* Tied to observations, reflects job content, low errors.
Checklist	*Average:* General problems identified, but little specific guidance for improvement.	*Good–Average:* Comparative scores available, and dimensions can be weighted.	*Average:* Expensive development, but inexpensive to use.	*Good:* Techniques available to increase job-relatedness and reduce errors.
Graphic rating scale	*Average:* Identifies problem areas, and some information on behaviors/ outcomes needing improvement.	*Average:* Comparative scores available but not easily documented and defended.	*Good:* Inexpensive to develop and use.	*Average:* Substantial opportunity for errors, though they can be linked to specific dimensions.
Behaviorally anchored rating scales (BARS)	*Good:* Identifies specific behaviors leading to problems.	*Good:* Scores available, documented, and behavior-based.	*Average:* Expensive development, but inexpensive to use.	*Good:* Based on job behaviors, can reduce errors.
Essay	*Unknown:* Depends on essay topics chosen by evaluators.	*Poor:* No overall score available, not comparable across employees.	*Average:* Inexpensive development, but expensive to use.	*Unknown:* Good observation can reduce errors, but lack of structure poses a danger.
Comparing individuals (ranking, forced distribution)	*Poor:* Based on general factors, with few specifics.	*Poor–Average:* Overall score available, but difficult to defend.	*Good:* Inexpensive to develop and to use.	*Average:* Usually consistent, but subject to halo error and artificiality.

fairly; (3) that employees believe the results are fair; (4) that useful feedback be given in the appraisal interview; and (5) that it be a useful tool for managing performance and productivity.[48] Appraisal errors were not frequently mentioned concerns. Exhibit 4.14 compares selected assessment techniques on several evaluation criteria.

The Bottom-line Value of Performance Assessment

Research suggests that the difference in performance between average and superior performers is very likely to be more than 40 percent of average salary, and it may be much more.[49] One study estimated that introducing performance feedback for 500 managers could produce a $5.3 million return in each subsequent year.[50] If you've ever worked in a fast-food store, you know how easy it is for mistakes to waste food and time. A study of college-age counter workers in a Florida frozen yogurt shop found that objective performance appraisal and feedback (putting a scale on the counter to weigh the yogurt servings) could double yearly profits through reduced waste.[51] Imagine the potential value of effective performance appraisal on jobs where employees handle materials even more valuable than frozen yogurt!

Dispute Resolution

Performance appraisal systems usually include a method for resolving disputes when employees disagree with the assessment.[52] Sixty-four percent of the largest U.S. firms recently reported having at least informal systems, while an additional 25 percent reported having a formal dispute-resolution process. Only 10 percent reported having no appeals process at all.[53] A useful dispute resolution process will provide ample opportunities for all parties to express their views, will involve parties with many different views (such as employees, managers, and unions), and will clearly stipulate the duties and possible outcomes of each stage of the process.

Legal Considerations, EEO, and Performance Assessment

When John Chamberlain, a 23-year employee and manager of manufacturing engineering at Bissell, Inc., was denied a wage increase due to performance problems, his superior failed to inform him that he was in danger of termination. When he was subsequently fired for poor performance and attitude (which had been discussed with him in his appraisal interview), he successfully sued Bissell, Inc., for over $61,000.[54] EEO legislation frequently treats performance assessments as tests, upon which future promotion decisions are based. Because such tests are legally required to avoid discrimination against protected groups, they should be carefully designed and administered. A review of court cases suggests the following practical guidelines:[55]

1. Base performance appraisal on job analysis.
2. Provide performance raters with written standards of job performance based on job analysis.
3. Train raters to use the rating instrument properly.
4. Provide a formal appeal mechanism and review of ratings by upper-level personnel.
5. Document evaluations and instances of poor performance.

6. Provide performance counseling and guidance to assist poor performers to improve.

The Role of the Human Resource Function in Performance Assessment

The performance appraisal process involves managers, employees, and sometimes customers. HR professionals usually play a key role by: auditing the completed appraisal forms, measuring appraiser's behavior, consulting in developing appraisal forms and procedures, providing appraiser training, administering the appeals process, and evaluating results. Policy decisions about performance appraisal are usually made at the top level of the organization, through a collaboration between line managers and HR professionals. However, a sizable number of organizations design specific appraisal programs for each business unit.[56] In either case, HR professionals are likely to be actively involved in both the design and implementation of such systems. This role offers opportunities to add value and contribute to organizational goals.

ASSESSING ABSENTEEISM

Performance assessment usually reflects not only employee behaviors and outcomes when they are at work but also how reliably and often they come to work. Even the best employees become less valuable if they miss work frequently.

---◆---

Absenteeism is the frequency, or duration, or both, of work time lost when employees do not come to work. *Attendance*, the opposite of absenteeism, is how often an employee is available for work.

Absenteeism is often subject to discipline and dismissal, because it is such an observable and obviously detrimental behavior. The formula for absence used by the Bureau of National Affairs (BNA) is:

$$\frac{\text{Worker days lost through job absence during the month}}{\text{Average number of employees} \times \text{Number of work days in month}}$$

This formula reflects both the number of absent employees and the duration of their absence. BNA does not include absences for jury duty, scheduled disciplinary time off, long-term disabilities (after the first four days), or excused absences scheduled in advance.[57] However, to support their particular decisions, organizations may choose to measure absenteeism differently. Some organizations might include any missed work days, in an effort to capture the cost of

---

EXHIBIT 4.15   A Diagnostic Model of Employee Attendance

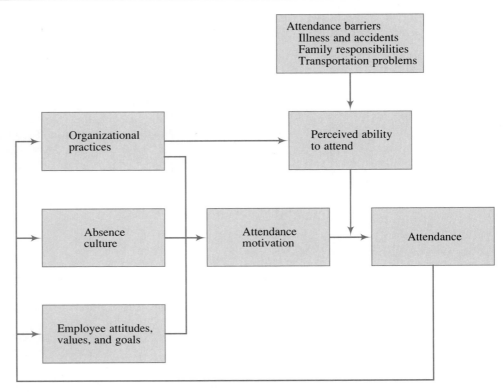

Source: Susan R. Rhodes and Richard M. Steers, *Managing Employee Absenteeism* (Reading, Mass.: Addison-Wesley, 1990), p. 57. © 1990 by Addison-Wesley Publishing Co. Reprinted by permission.

absence. Others might include only absence under the employees control, in an effort to capture intentionally poor attendance.[58] The BNA reports quarterly absence statistics, which show higher rates in larger and nonprofit organizations.[59]

Psychologists have long studied the causes and consequences of absence. Absence is affected by both the employee's ability and motivation to attend, and by both on-the-job and off-the-job factors.[60] Exhibit 4.15 shows a diagnostic model of employee attendance. Attendance is affected by the employee's perceived ability to attend, which can be reduced by attendance barriers, such as illness and accidents, family responsibilities, and transportation problems. Attendance is also affected by the employee's attendance motivation, which is affected by organizational practices, such as attendance penalties or rewards; the absence culture, which reflects whether absence is considered acceptable or unacceptable; and employee attitudes, values, and goals, such as how satisfied or committed the employee is to the organization. One research review suggests that absence frequency and duration are related to work satisfaction, though the relationship is not extremely strong. The greater the proportion of females, the stronger the relationship between absence and satisfaction.[61] This points out the importance of having information on many employee characteristics to effectively manage HR outcomes.

Absence-control programs must address the broad causes of absenteeism. Organizations can discipline absent employees, verify medical excuses, better communicate rules regarding excusable absences, and reward good attendance records. Dealing with other absence causes, such as family responsibilities, is much more difficult. Nonetheless, effectively managing employee attendance can be valuable. The costs of employee absenteeism for 800 insurance employees paid an average of $9.21 per hour was estimated to be $876,859, or $1,096 per employee.[62]

ASSESSING SEPARATIONS AND TURNOVER

Organizations assess how many of their employees are leaving, whether such departures are initiated by the organization or the individual, and how long employees stay in the organization. When employees separate, new employees must be hired and trained, so assessing and predicting separations is essential to planning future hiring strategies, as discussed in Chapter Five. The costs of separations include not only the costs of selecting and hiring replacements but also the lost productivity if a position remains vacant, the extra burden on employees who must fill in, and the extra supervisory activity devoted to managing the separation and replacement process. Not surprisingly, many organizations consider separations a problem to be reduced. However, such an approach is shortsighted and can lead to incorrect decisions. This is such an important issue that Chapter Eight will show how to measure, manage, and evaluate employee separations. One factor that consistently relates to employee separations is their attitude about their work.

ASSESSING EMPLOYEE ATTITUDES/OPINIONS

Organizations have long assessed their employees' attitudes and opinions about work. In an early 17th century study in Modena, Italy, Ramazzini noted looks of dismay on the faces of men cleaning out the city cesspool, interviewed the workers, and wrote a report about their sentiments (or should we say "scent"-iments).[63] Today, many large organizations conduct periodic attitude and opinion surveys, some even put such surveys on personal computers. Equifax, Inc., asks employees what they would do if they were president.[64] Such assessments usually focus on three related concepts: satisfaction, commitment, and opinions.

◆

Job satisfaction is a pleasurable or positive emotional reaction to a person's job experiences.[65] *Organizational commitment* is a strong belief in the organization's goals and values, a willingness to exert considerable effort on behalf of the organization, and a strong desire to remain a member of the organization.[66] *Employee opinions* are personal evaluations of specific organizational characteristics, such as policies, procedures, and relationships.

Organizations assess employee attitudes and opinions, because they place a strong philosophical and ethical value on maintaining an attractive and equitable workplace, or because they believe that attitudes and opinions are related to other behaviors, such as performance, absenteeism, separations, and willingness to accept changes.[67] An appealing notion is that employee satisfaction and performance are related, and that making employees more satisfied will enhance their productivity. In fact, after thousands of studies, there is little support for this general notion.[68] Research suggests that satisfaction relates to citizenship-type behaviors, such as cooperation, helping co-workers, attendance, separation, and complying with rules; but that satisfaction associates less with production-related behaviors and outcomes.[69]

Most theories suggest that satisfaction depends on the match between the individual's needs and the returns provided by the organization and the job, with more important needs affecting satisfaction more strongly. Commitment is affected by the match between the individuals values and beliefs and the organization and job environment, as well as the availability of alternative opportunities. Thus, organizations can affect satisfaction and commitment by influencing organizational, job, and employee characteristics.[70] There may be limits to the organization's ability to affect employee attitudes. Recent research on twins who grew up apart suggest that up to 30 percent of job satisfaction differences may be explained by inherited genetic factors.[71] Nonetheless, employee attitudes remain an important and highly visible employee characteristic. HR professionals are often called upon to assist managers in managing attitudes effectively.

Organizations contemplating attitude/opinion surveys should carefully consider their potential costs and benefits. Assessing employee attitudes can be useful; for example, Motorola learned its workers craved recognition, and Ashland Oil learned employees find the grapevine the best source of information. But, employees will likely expect to be informed of the results of their surveys and expect that the organization will do something about any problems that are identified. As Corning believes, they can become "big traps if used to provide all the answers."[72]

ASSESSING EMPLOYEE DEMOGRAPHIC CHARACTERISTICS

Chapter Two described changes in the demographic characteristics of the external labor market that affect HR management decisions. Organizations also routinely assess the demographic characteristics of their own employees. One reason is that the U.S. government requires its contractors to demonstrate equitable representation, employment opportunities, and pay for employees, based on protected characteristics, such as race, gender, age, and handicap. Even without these requirements, managing an increasingly diverse work force requires keeping a close watch on internal demographic trends. As the work force ages, and it includes more females, single parents, and cultural differences, old policies geared toward white males become less effective, and managing "diversity" requires awareness of changes.[73]

SUMMARY

Performance, attendance, retention, attitudes, and demographics. There's certainly no shortage of employee characteristics that organizations can assess, and it's often up to the HR manager to provide the logic and guidance that shapes what and how they are measured. The recurring themes in this chapter are that managers should consider how this information can support and shape important decisions, and that the process of gathering and communicating this information may be even more important than the information itself. When you combine the characteristics in this chapter with the external and organizational characteristics discussed in Chapters Two and Three, the dangers of information overload are clear. Managers must have a framework for choosing and using this information. The next part—Planning and Objectives—will show how the diagnostic model provides such a framework. But first, try your hand at solving a real performance appraisal problem in the next section.

DISCUSSION AND REVIEW QUESTIONS

1. What are some goals of performance assessment? What decisions can performance assessment affect within an organization?

2. What are the positive and negative aspects of performance appraisal from the organization's point of view as well as the employee's? When does performance appraisal put the organization's goals at odds with the employee's? What can be done to reduce this conflict?

3. How could different jobs require different assessment criteria? How could the use of different criteria in performance assessment alter decisions about pay, promotion, and hiring procedures? What problems could be caused by using different criteria on different jobs?

4. What purpose could be served by tracking such employee characteristics as gender, age, marital and parental status, as well as health habits?

5. Discuss the differences between MBO, checklist, and graphic rating scales as techniques of performance appraisal. Would they be equally useful in assessing different jobs, positions, or levels within the same organization? Why or why not?

6. What types of measurement error can affect performance assessments? How can errors be minimized? What factors should be considered before spending resources to alleviate rating errors?

7. Imagine that your instructor chooses to assess your personnel management class's performance at midterm. List the criteria you would use. Would you try to maximize your classmates' development with accurate feedback, allocate grades equitably, or both? What techniques would you adopt to accomplish your goals? How would you evaluate your system to see if it was successful?

8. Summarize reasons why absenteeism can be costly to an organization. Using the absenteeism model in Exhibit 4.15, briefly summarize what might cause members of your study group to be absent more frequently from your scheduled meetings. What would you do about it, and how does this fit with the chapter's discussion of absenteeism?

9. If employees are doing their jobs, why would an organization want to measure their attitudes/opinions? How can such information affect decisions that really have an impact on the organization? Considering the uses and effects of attitude/opinion surveys, what are the advantages and disadvantages of the common practice of measuring student opinions about a class at the end of the class?

10. Discuss how knowing employee demographics might affect decisions about HR. How could such decisions affect the larger organization's success?

YOUR TURN
APPRAISING "QUALITY" PERFORMANCE AT FORD MOTOR COMPANY

"Quality is Job 1," the familiar slogan of Ford Motor Company, goes beyond the typical focus on instituting employee involvement teams, reducing manufacturing defects, analyzing production processes with statistical process control, and ensuring high-quality materials from suppliers. As early as 1985, William Scherkenbach, Ford's executive in charge of implementing quality companywide, recognized the critical importance of the performance appraisal system in any quality enhancement effort.

Mr. Scherkenbach states that "in my opinion, the performance appraisal system is the biggest inhibitor to continuing improvement in any organization."[74] There are at least five major reasons why:

1. *It destroys teamwork,* because each business function and each individual employee is evaluated on meeting performance goals that focus on their particular area. For example, manufacturing employees get rewarded for reducing product failures, which may take more time. But, buyers get rewarded for negotiating many contracts, which is harder if the time costs of production go up.

2. *It fosters mediocrity,* because appraisals focus on setting and meeting objectives. The person being appraised has an incentive to try to set the objective as low

as reasonably possible so they can be sure to meet it. Employees will implement their ideas for improvement only slowly so they can use them to meet objectives over several years, rather than exceed the first objective and risk not meeting later objectives.

3. *It increases the variability of people's performance,* because most appraisal systems have too many performance categories, and appraisers are forced to make impossibly fine distinctions, such as "outstanding," "superior," "above average," "below average," "needs improvement," and "poor." Forced distribution systems also require placing a certain proportion of employees in every category, which may force appraisers to make finer distinctions than necessary. These unrealistically fine distinctions cause employees to constantly try to change their behavior to get into the next-highest category, even if their current performance is generally quite satisfactory. The system becomes chaotic because a large proportion of employees are changing behaviors that really don't need changing at all.

4. *It confounds the contribution of people with the contribution of other resources,* because performance standards, such as sales, productivity, scrap levels, and so on, depend on both the employee's behaviors and other factors, such as material quality, equipment reliability, and advertising. Employees may get credit for good performance that they did not cause, and they may get blamed for poor performance caused by other factors.

5. *It focuses on the short-term,* because performance goals often reflect an arbitrarily limited period, and the behaviors that can improve performance in the short run, such as using low-quality but inexpensive materials, can often damage long-run quality.

Imagine that you are an HR professional working for Ford Motor Company and given the assignment to respond to Mr. Scherkenbach's comments and recommend areas for improving the performance appraisal system. The following questions may be helpful as a guide to your thinking.

1. What goals should be emphasized in the appraisal system? Which of Mr. Scherkenbach's five problems are caused by the conflict between appraisal goals?

2. What are the most important performance criteria in an environment emphasizing "quality improvement"? What would be the best measures of these criteria?

3. How could the appraisal rating scale be improved to alleviate existing problems?

4. Who should be involved in observing and communicating appraisal results?

5. What changes in other HR activities may be required to make your new appraisal system work?

Your instructor has additional information about Ford's performance appraisal system and about some of the improvements that Ford is attempting to make.

NOTES AND REFERENCES

1. N. K. Napier and Gary P. Latham, "Outcome Expectancies of People Who Conduct Performance Appraisals," *Personnel Psychology* 39 (1986), pp. 827–37.
2. N. Kent Eaton, Hilda Wing, and K. J. Mitchell, "Alternate Methods of Estimating the Dollar Value of Performance," *Personnel Psychology* 38 (1985), pp. 27–40.

3. Allan M. Mohrman, Jr., Susan M. Resnick-West, and Edward E. Lawler III, *Designing Performance Appraisal Systems* (San Francisco: Jossey-Bass, 1989), chap. 1.

4. Bureau of National Affairs, "Performance Appraisal Programs," *Personnel Policies Forum,* Survey no. 135, February 1983.

5. Jeffrey Rothfeder, Michele Galen, and Lisa Driscoll, "Is Your Boss Spying on You?" *Business Week,* January 15, 1990, pp. 74–75.

6. Ira Michael Shepard and Robert Duston, *Thieves at Work* (Washington, D.C.: Bureau of National Affairs, 1988).

7. Brian Dumaine, "Those Highflying PepsiCo Managers," *Fortune,* April 10, 1989, pp. 78–84.

8. E. T. Cornelius, M. D. Hakel, and P. R. Sackett, "A Methodological Approach to Job Classification for Performance Appraisal Purposes," *Personnel Psychology* 32 (1979), pp. 283–97.

9. H. John Bernardin and Richard W. Beatty, "Performance Appraisal: Assessing Human Behavior at Work" (Boston: Kent Publishing, 1984), p. 65.

10. Paul R. Sackett, Sheldon Zedeck, and Larry Fogli, "Relations between Measures of Typical and Maximum Job Performance," *Journal of Applied Psychology* 78, no. 3 (1988), pp. 482–486.

11. John P. Campbell, Richard J. Campbell & Associates, "Productivity in Organizations" (San Francisco: Jossey-Bass, 1988); L. Cummings Lawrence, *Improving Human Resource Effectiveness* (Berea, Ohio: ASPA Foundation, 1982); Richard A. Guzzo, R. D. Jette, and R. A. Katzell, "The Effects of Psychologically Based Intervention Programs on Worker Productivity: A Meta-Analysis," *Personnel Psychology* 38 (1985), pp. 275–91; R. E. Kopelman, *Managing Productivity in Organizations* (New York: McGraw-Hill, 1986); Gary P. Latham and T. W. Lee, "Goal Setting" in *Generalizing from Laboratory to Field Settings,* ed. Edward A. Locke (Lexington, Mass.: Lexington Books, 1986); M. E. Tubbs, "Goal Setting: A Meta-Analysis Examination of the Empirical Evidence," *Journal of Applied Psychology* 71 (1986), pp. 474–83.

12. Jeffrey S. Kane and Kimberly A. Freeman, "MBO and Performance Appraisal: A Mixture That's Not a Solution, Part 1," *Personnel* 63, no. 12 (December 1986), pp. 26–36; Jeffrey S. Kane and Kimberly A. Freeman, "MBO and Performance Appraisal: A Mixture That's Not a Solution, Part 2," *Personnel* 64, no. 2 (February 1987), pp. 26–32.

13. "Ban on Lie Detector Tests to Go into Effect December 27," *Daily Labor Report,* no. 246, December 22, 1988 (Washington, D.C.: Bureau of National Affairs); James G. Frierson, "Labor Relations: New Polygraph Test Limits," *Personnel Journal,* December 1988, pp. 40–45; David E. Nagle, "The Polygraph Shield," *Personnel Administrator,* February 1989, pp. 34–39.

14. Rothfeder, Galen, and Driscoll, "Is Your Boss Spying on You?"

15. U.S. Congress, Office of Technology Assessment, *The Electronic Supervisor: New Technology, New Tensions* (Washington, D.C.: U.S. Government Printing Office, September 1987), p. 28.

16. For example, see "Court Denies Federal Union Challenges to Validity of Random Testing Order," *BNA Labor Relations Week* 4, no. 2 (1989) (Washington, D.C.: Bureau of National Affairs).

17. Andrew Kupfer, "Is Drug Testing Good or Bad?" *Fortune,* December 19, 1988, pp. 133–40.

18. Peter A. Susser, "Electronic Monitoring in the Private Sector: How Closely Should Employers Supervise Their Workers?" *Employee Relations Law Journal* 13 (Spring 1988), pp. 575–98.

19. John Chalykoff and Thomas A. Kochan, "Computer-Aided Monitoring: Its Influence on Employee Job Satisfaction and Turnover," *Personnel Psychology* 42 (1989), pp. 807–34.

20. Bernardin and Beatty, "Performance Appraisal," pp. 68–71.

21. Patricia Smith, "Behaviors, Results, and Organizational Effectiveness," in *Handbook of Industrial and Organizational Psychology,* ed. M. Dunnette (Chicago: Rand McNally, 1976).

22. George Rosinger, Louis B. Myers, Girard W. Levy, Michael Loar, Susan Morhman, and John R. Stock, "Development of a Behaviorally Based Performance Appraisal System," *Personnel Psychology,* Spring 1982, pp. 75–88; Richard W. Beatty, Craig Schneier, and James Beatty, "An Empirical Investigation of Perceptions of Ratee Behavior Frequency and Ratee Behavior Change Using Behavioral Expectation Studies (BES)," *Personnel Psychology* 30 (1977), pp. 647–58; K. R. Murphy, C. Martin, and M. Garcia, "Do Behavioral Observation Scales Measure Observation?" *Journal of Applied Psychology* 67 (1982), pp. 652–67; J. S. Kane and H. J. Bernardin, "Behavioral Observational Scales and the Evaluation of Performance Appraisal Effectiveness," *Journal of Applied Psychology* 35 (1982), pp. 635–41.

23. Jeffrey Kane, "Performance Distribution Assessment: A New Breed of Appraisal Methodology," in Bernardin and Beatty, *Performance Appraisal*; H. J. Bernardin, "Behavioral Expectation Scales versus Summated Scales: A Fairer Comparison," *Journal of Applied Psychology* 62 (1977), pp. 422–27; H. J. Bernardin and J. S. Kane, "A Second Look at Behavioral Observation Scales," *Personnel Psychology* 33 (1980), pp. 809–14; G. P. Latham, C. H. Fay, and L. M. Saari, "The Development of Behavioral Observation Scales for Appraising the Performance of Foremen," *Personnel Psychology* 32 (1979), pp. 299–311; G. P. Latham, C. Fay, and L. M. Saari, "BOS, BES, and Baloney: Raising Kane with Bernardin," *Personnel Psychology,* Winter 1980, pp. 815–22.

24. P. O. Kingstrom and A. R. Bass, "A Critical Analysis of Studies Comparing Behaviorally Anchored Rating Scales (BARS) and Other Rating Formats," *Personnel Psychology* 34 (1981), pp. 263–89; H. J. Bernardin and P. C. Smith, "A Clarification of Some Issues Regarding the Development and Use of Behaviorally Anchored Rating Scales," *Journal of Applied Psychology* 66 (1981), pp. 458–63; Thomas A. DeCotiis, "An Analysis of the External Validity and Applied Relevance of Three Rating Formats," *Organizational Behavior and Human Performance* 19 (1977), pp. 247–66; Kevin R. Murphy and Joseph I. Constans, "Behavioral Anchors as a Source of Bias in Rating," *Journal of Applied Psychology* 73, no. 4 (1988), pp. 573–77.

25. "Performance Appraisal Pitfalls," in *Fair Employment Practices: Summary of Latest Developments,* October 20, 1983 (Washington, D.C.: Bureau of National Affairs).

26. Saul W. Gellerman and William G. Hodgson, "Cyanamid's New Take on Performance Appraisal," *Harvard Business Review,* May–June 1988, pp. 36–41.

27. Allan M. Mohrman, Jr., Susan M. Resnick-West, and Edward E. Lawler III, *Designing Performance Appraisal Systems*.

28. Bretz and Milkovich, "Performance Appraisal in Large Organizations," Working Paper no. 89-17.

29. J. L. Farh, J. D. Werbel, and Arthur G. Bedeian, "An Empirical Investigation of Self-Appraisal-Based Performance Evaluation," *Personnel Psychology* 41 (1988), pp. 141–56; Michael M. Harris and J. Schaubroeck, "A Meta-Analysis of Self-Supervisor, Self-Peer, and Peer-Supervisor Ratings," *Personnel Psychology* 41 (1988), pp. 43–62; R. J. Vance, R. C. MacCallum, M. D. Coovert, and J. W. Hedge, "Construct Validity of Multiple Job Performance Measures Using Confirmatory Factor Analysis," *Journal of Applied Psychology* 73, no. 1 (1988), pp. 74–80.

30. Adi Ignatius, "Now, If Ms. Wong Insults a Customer, She Gets an Award," *The Wall Street Journal,* January 24, 1989, p. A1.

31. Mohrman et al., *Designing Performance Appraisal Systems,* chap. 4; G. M. McEvoy and P. F. Buller, "User Reactions to a Peer Appraisal System in an Industrial Setting," paper presented at the annual meeting of the Academy of Management, New Orleans, August 1987; H. John Bernardin and Richard W. Beatty, "Can Subordinate Appraisals Enhance Managerial Productivity?," *Sloan Management Review* 28, no. 4 (1987), pp. 63–73.

32. Angelo S. DeNisi and K. J. Williams, "Cognitive Approaches to Performance Appraisal," in *Research in Personnel and Human Resources Management* 6, eds. Kendrith M. Rowland and Gerald R. Ferris (Greenwich, Conn.: JAI Press, 1988), pp. 109–55.

33. See Bretz and Milkovich's "Performance Appraisal Research and Practice" for a recent review.

34. Peter H. Lewis, "I'm Sorry; My Machine Doesn't Like Your Work" *New York Times,* February 4, 1990, p. 27.

35. Bernardin and Beatty, "Performance Appraisal," pp. 267–68.

36. Bretz and Milkovich, "Performance Appraisal Research and Practice," p. 26.

37. W. H. Cooper, "Ubiquitous Halo," *Psychological Bulletin* 90 (1981), pp. 218–44; Charles L. Hulin, "Some Reflections on General Performance Dimensions and Halo Rating Error," *Journal of Applied Psychology* 67, no. 2 (1982), pp. 165–70; Bernardin and Beatty, "Performance Appraisal," 1983.

38. Bretz and Milkovich, "Performance Appraisal Research and Practice," pp. 10–11.

39. Kevin R. Murphy and William K. Balzer, "Rater Errors and Rating Accuracy," *Journal of Applied Psychology* 74, no. 4 (1989), pp. 619–24.

40. Bretz and Milkovich, "Performance Appraisal Research and Practice," p. 26.

41. D. E. Smith, "Training Programs for Performance Appraisal: A Review," *Academy of Management Review* 11, no. 1 (1986), pp. 22–40.

42. J. W. Hedge and Michael J. Kavanagh, "Improving the Accuracy of Performance Evaluations: Comparison of Three Methods of Performance Appraiser Training," *Journal of Applied Psychology* 73 (1988), pp. 68–73.

43. Bretz and Milkovich, "Performance Appraisal Research and Practice," p. 27.

44. Robert Pool, "Quantum Pot Watching," *Science* 246, November 17, 1989, p. 888.

45. John F. Kikoaki and Joseph A. Litterer, "Effective Communication in the Performance Appraisal Interview," *Public Personnel Management,* Spring 1983, pp. 33–42; Douglas Cederblom, "The Performance Appraisal Interview"; R. J. Burke and D. S. Wilcox, "Characteristics of Effective Employee Performance Reviews and Development Interviews," *Personnel Psychology* 22 (1980), pp. 291–305.

46. Anthony J. Mento, Robert P. Steele, and Ronald J. Karren, "A Meta-Analysis of Goal Setting and Feedback," *Organizational Behavior and Human Decision Processes* 39 (1987), pp. 52–83.

47. MaryBeth DeGregorio and Cynthia D. Fisher, "Providing Performance Feedback: Reactions to Alternate Methods," *Journal of Management* 14, no. 4 (1988), pp. 605–16; Donald B. Fedor, Robert W. Eder, and M. Ronald Buckley, "The Contributory Effects of Supervisor Intentions on Subordinate Feedback Responses," *Organizational Behavior and Human Decision Processes* 44 (1989), pp. 396–414.

48. Bretz and Milkovich, "Performance Appraisal Research and Practice," p. 29.

49. John W. Boudreau, "Utility Analysis for Human Resource Management Decisions," Working Paper no. 88–21, Center for Advanced Human Resource Studies, Cornell Uni-

versity, 1988. Forthcoming in Marvin D. Dunnette, *Handbook of Industrial-Organizational Psychology* (2nd ed.).

50. Frank J. Landy, James L. Farr, and Rick R. Jacobs, "Utility Concepts in Performance Measurement," *Organizational Behavior and Human Performance* 30 (1982), pp. 15–40.

51. Beth C. Florin-Thuma and John W. Boudreau, "Performance Feedback Utility Effects on Managerial Decision Processes," *Personnel Psychology,* 1988.

52. Jerry Greenberg, "Using Explanations to Manage Impressions of Performance Appraisal Fairness," in Jerry Greenberg and R. Bies (chairs), "Communicating Fairness in Organizations," symposium presented at the annual meeting of the Academy of Management, Anaheim, Calif., August 1988; Jerry Greenberg, "Determinants of Perceived Fairness of Performance Evaluations," *Journal of Applied Psychology* 71 (1986), pp. 340–42.

53. Bretz and Milkovich, "Performance Appraisal Research and Practice," p. 28.

54. David C. Martin, "Performance Appraisal 2: Improving the Rater's Effectiveness," *Personnel,* August 1986, pp. 28–33.

55. Gerald V. Barrett and Mary C. Kernan, "Performance Appraisal and Terminations: A Review of Court Decisions since Brito v. Zia, with Implications for Personnel Practices," *Personnel Psychology* 40 (1987), pp. 489–503; see also, Hubert S. Field and William H. Holley, "The Relationship of Performance Appraisal Cases," *Academy of Management Journal* 25, no. 2 (1982), pp. 392–406.

56. Bretz and Milkovich, "Performance Appraisal Research and Practice," p. 25.

57. Bureau of National Affairs, "Quarterly Report on the Employment Outlook, Job Absence, and Turnover" (Washington, D.C.: Bureau of National Affairs, 1986).

58. Susan R. Rhodes and Richard M. Steers, *Managing Employee Absenteeism* (Reading, Mass.: Addison-Wesley, 1990).

59. Ibid.

60. See Richard M. Steers and Susan R. Rhodes, "Major Influences on Employee Attendance: A Process Model," *Journal of Applied Psychology* 63, no. 4 (1978), pp. 390–96.

61. Rick D. Hackett, "Work Attitudes and Employee Absenteeism: A Synthesis of the Literature," *Journal of Occupational Psychology* 62 (1989), pp. 235–48.

62. Susan R. Rhodes and Richard M. Steers, "Managing Employee Absenteeism."

63. Walter Keichel III, "How Important is Morale, Really?" *Fortune,* February 13, 1989, pp. 121–22.

64. "Labor Letter," *The Wall Street Journal,* September 19, 1989, p. A1.

65. Edwin A. Locke, "The Nature and Causes of Job Satisfaction," in *Handbook of Industrial and Organizational Psychology,* ed. Marvin D. Dunnette (Chicago: Rand McNally, 1976).

66. Richard Mowday, Lyman Porter, and Richard Steers, *Organizational Linkages: The Psychology of Commitment, Absenteeism and Turnover* (New York: Academic Press, 1982).

67. Sanford M. Jacoby, "Employee Attitude Surveys in Historical Perspective," *Industrial Relations* 27, no. 1 (Winter 1988), pp. 74–93.

68. M. T. Iaffaldano and Paul M. Muchinsky, "Job Satisfaction and Job Performance: A Meta-Analysis" *Psychological Bulletin* 97 (1985), pp. 251–73; M. M. Petty, G. W. McGee, and J. W. Cavender, "A Meta-Analysis of the Relationships between Job Satisfaction and Individual Performance," *Academy of Management Review* 9 (1984), pp. 712–21.

69. Dennis W. Organ, "A Restatement of the Satisfaction-Performance Hypothesis," *Journal of Management* 14, no. 4 (1988), pp. 547–57.

70. Edwin A. Locke, "The Nature and Causes of Job Satisfaction"; Mowday, Porter, and Steers, "Organizational Linkages"; Charles Glisson and Mark Durick, "Predictors of Job Satisfaction and Organizational Commitment in Human Service Organizations," *Administrative Quarterly* 33 (1988), pp. 61–81.

71. Richard D. Arvey, Thomas J. Bouchard, Jr., Nancy L. Segal, and Lauren M. Abraham, "Job Satisfaction: Environmental and Genetic Components," *Journal of Applied Psychology* no. 2 (April 1989), pp. 187–92.

72. "Labor Letter," *The Wall Street Journal*.

73. Jolie Solomon, "Firms Address Workers' Cultural Variety," *The Wall Street Journal,* February 10, 1989, p. B1; Charlene Marmer Soloman, "The Corporate Response to Work Force Diversity," *Personnel Journal,* August 1989, pp. 43–53; Susan Butruille, Eleanor Haller, Lynn Lannon, and Joan Sourenian, "Four by Four: Women in the Workplace," *Training and Development Journal,* November 1989, pp. 21–30; Amanda Bennett, "The Baby Busters: New Generation Asks More Than Its Elders of the Corporate World," *The Wall Street Journal,* October 26, 1988, p. A1; Jolie Soloman, "Firms Grapple with Language Barriers," *The Wall Street Journal,* November 7, 1989, p. B1.

74. William W. Scherkenbach, "Performance Appraisal and Quality: Ford's New Philosophy," *Quality Progress,* April 1985, pp. 40–46.

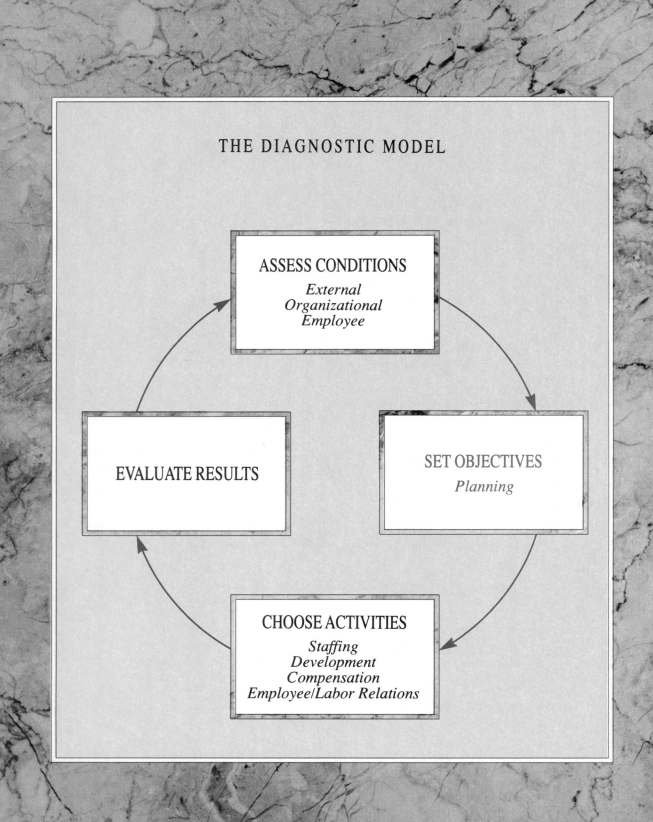

THE DIAGNOSTIC MODEL

ASSESS CONDITIONS
External
Organizational
Employee

SET OBJECTIVES
Planning

EVALUATE RESULTS

CHOOSE ACTIVITIES
Staffing
Development
Compensation
Employee/Labor Relations

PART TWO

PLANNING AND SETTING OBJECTIVES

Throughout this book, we discuss the need to set objectives for HR activities and weigh the results of those activities against the objectives. Indeed, the process of gathering data to set objectives and then evaluating progress against the objectives is the heart of the diagnostic approach. The exhibit shows how the process of setting objectives begins with the assessments of external, organizational, and employee conditions (Part One). In Part Two, we discuss how those assessments are translated into objectives to guide the choices among HR activities.

Chapter Five describes planning, setting objectives, and evaluating results. It shows how information is used to formulate plans, which produce standards for evaluating HR decisions. It also shows that HR planning is part of a broader planning and evaluation process that constantly occurs within the organization. The planning principles discussed

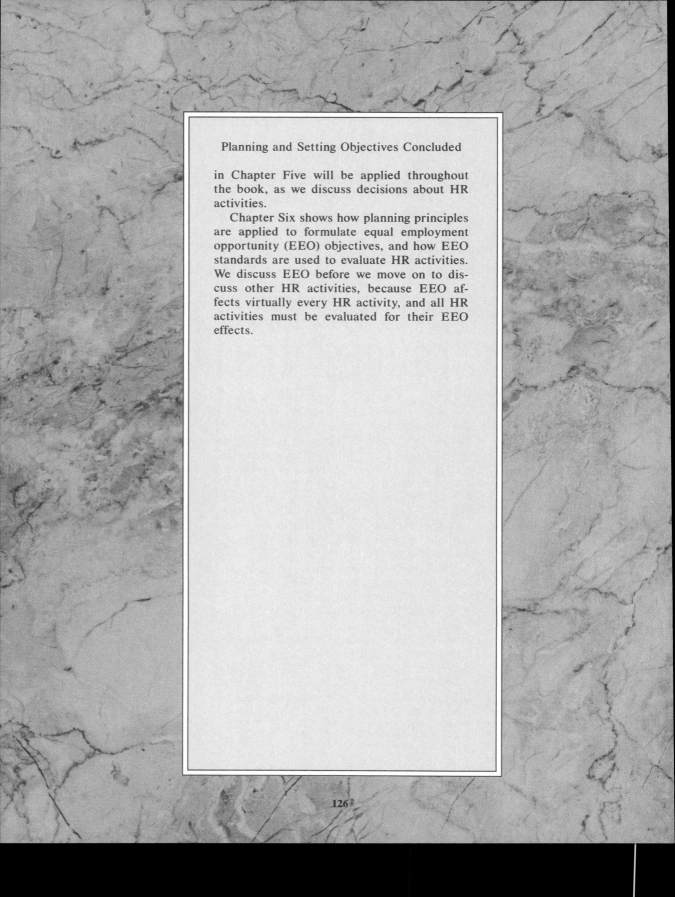

Planning and Setting Objectives Concluded

in Chapter Five will be applied throughout the book, as we discuss decisions about HR activities.

Chapter Six shows how planning principles are applied to formulate equal employment opportunity (EEO) objectives, and how EEO standards are used to evaluate HR activities. We discuss EEO before we move on to discuss other HR activities, because EEO affects virtually every HR activity, and all HR activities must be evaluated for their EEO effects.

Planning, Objectives, and Evaluation

Planning, Setting Objectives, and
Evaluating Results
Planning Is Diagnostic Decision Making
*The Relationship between Objectives and
Evaluation Standards*
What Makes a Good Objective/Standard?
Why Perform Human Resource Planning?

HR Planning In the Broader Planning Process
The External Level
The Organization Level
Human Resource Department/Function Level
Human Resource Quantity and Deployment
Specific HRM Activities

Planning the HR Department and Function
Auditing Human Resource Activities
Human Resource Budgets
Activity, Cost, or Headcount Ratios
Human Resource Accounting
Return on Investment in Human Resources
Client Opinions/Perceptions

Employment Planning: The Quantity and
Deployment of Human Resources

Planning Specific Human Resource Activities

Your Turn: Planning for the Oil Industry
Engineer Shortage

In the late 1970s and early 1980s, major U.S. oil companies vividly encountered the importance of human resources. They had weathered the storm of the OPEC oil embargoes, the prospects of a more robust U.S. and world economies were raising oil prices, and most oil companies had plans for major new exploration and production (E&P) activities, such as opening new oil fields in Abu Dhabi and expanding transportation capacity. Meticulous attention was paid to such things as geological forecasts, projected price levels, and transportation but not to HR supply and demand patterns. The petroleum and chemical industry is not very labor intensive, and these companies had always managed to adequately staff past operations.

Soon their Middle East divisions began requesting the drilling engineers necessary to staff their expanded operations. Even a large drilling operation requires only a handful of these people, so Middle East divisions typically request six or nine drilling engineers from the U.S. E&P divisions. Top management didn't place great importance on assuring a supply of this resource. To their surprise, the U.S. divisions often responded, "We can't spare them." Could it really be possible that oil property investments by some of the world's financially strongest, most technologically intensive and largest organizations (Exxon employs 104,000 people worldwide) could be affected by an internal request for six or nine people? Yet, if staff was unavailable, multi-million-dollar business decisions would have to be changed: perhaps the companies would develop the fields with local engineers, perhaps they would just buy financial rights in fields operated by others, perhaps they would just offer technical assistance.

Top management put this question to their HR planners, who made it their top priority. First, they established the goal—to adequately staff Middle East operations with six to nine drilling engineers.

Second, they compared current conditions to the goal—most companies only had 30 or so drilling engineers in their entire organization, so this represented a gap of 33 to 67 percent. Work permits in the Middle East require five years' experience, so new engineers could not be used. Engineers with high-school-age children had seldom taken foreign assignments, so that eliminated those over 45. Yet, the age distribution of existing engineers was bimodel—lots of engineers under 30 and lots of them over 50. Finally, more drilling engineers than ever were leaving, because the high demand for their skills in the labor market was driving up salaries. Comparing the goal to the current work force, there was a serious gap between demand in the Middle East and supply in the United States. The planners considered the longer-run gap: oil demand was expected to rise into the 1990s. By then, the present over-45 engineers would be retired and the present under-30 engineers would be in their 40s.

Third, the planners considered options that might close these gaps. How about recruiting experienced engineers? This would require drastically raising drilling engineer pay levels, which would be costly and might foster feelings of inequity among other engineers. Moreover, in three months everyone else would have raised pay as well, so you'd just have higher pay and no competitive advantage. How about adding career and other incentives? This would be costly, and it would change career progressions. How about training? Drilling engineers need very special skills, which are learned through experience, so very few could be created this way.

Closing the long-run gap required creating a group of young engineers before the mid-1980s. How about recruiting from colleges? Enrollments in drilling engineer programs had dropped during the oil industry slowdown in the 50s and 60s. In the entire United States, only 100 such engineers graduated per year. You just couldn't expect to hire more than 10 or 12.

PLANNING, SETTING OBJECTIVES, AND EVALUATING RESULTS

What would you have done as one of these HR planners? Is there other information about external, organizational, or employee conditions you would gather? Are there other options you would have considered? Could these options be combined in some integrated way that creates an effect greater than any one option alone? How would you measure your success—filling the jobs, keeping costs under control, avoiding employee inequity, enhancing company profits?

Part of the HR manager's job is to anticipate and plan for exactly such contingencies, to choose the most relevant information on which to base forecasts, and to establish objectives and evaluate results. After reading Chapter Two, Three, and Four, you're probably thinking that there must be thousands of pieces of information that might be used to assess conditions, and you're right. Most large organizations' computerized information systems have thousands of data elements on thousands of current and former employees, covering years of employment history. How do you identify the important information and analyze it in a way that supports key decisions, and lets you evaluate how you did? HR planning is the process that does this. HR planning, like other HR activities, occurs informally and formally at all levels of the organization, virtually all the time.

Human resource planning is gathering and using information to support decisions about investing resources in HR activities.

EXHIBIT 5.1   The Planning Process at the Heart of the Diagnostic Approach

---

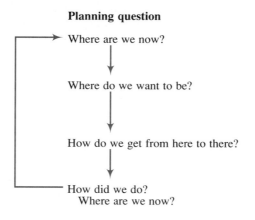

Planning question	**Diagnostic approach**
Where are we now?	*Assessing* external and organizational conditions, and employee characteristics.
Where do we want to be?	*Set human resource objectives,* based on efficiency and equity, according to dimensions that matter to the key stakeholders.
How do we get from here to there?	*Choose human resource activities,* and expend resources necessary.
How did we do? Where are we now?	*Evaluate results,* by assessing new conditions according to the objectives, and start the process again.

You might think that computerized information systems and technology automatically choose and analyze such information, so it's not necessary for HR managers to do it, but that's not true. One of the most pressing problems in large organizations is that only a handful of their top HR planners are able to think creatively about the information and to use it to support practical HR decisions.[1] The appendix following this chapter describes how computerized HR information systems are designed and used. Such systems actually enhance the importance of HR planning because, without skilled planners who know how to use them, information systems can produce information overload.

Planning Is Diagnostic Decision Making

Decisions are choices based on information. Every decision involves expending resources and is usually directed to achieve some goal. You make decisions every day, such as deciding whether to come to class or not. Your decision to attend class means that you will spend your time and energy in class, and you will give up whatever else you might have done instead. Your decision is probably directed toward some goal, such as listening to a fascinating lecture, learning intriguing facts about HR management, or perhaps getting to meet a visiting corporate executive who will later be recruiting on campus. Finally, your decision is based on information, such as the quality of past lectures, the material assigned for that day, or the rumor that the recruiter said she or he is especially interested in people with military experience, which you have.

HR planning supports decisions about how to allocate the organization's resources to manage its employees and to produce outcomes that are valuable. The planning process can be represented by four questions, as shown in Exhibit 5.1. The planning process fits closely with the diagnostic process. Indeed, the planning process is the heart of the diagnostic model.

Where are we now?   Chapter Two, Three, and Four have shown you the vast array of external, organizational, and individual factors that could be used to measure the current status of HR management. The planning process takes that information and uses it to set goals and to make choices.

Where do we want to be?   Deciding where we want to be is the first step in identifying the desired conditions. Then we identify gaps between where we are now and where we want to be. The gaps that are large and important enough to remedy become our objectives. One of the most important parts of objective-setting is deciding what conditions you're really trying to change, and what changes to use as measures of success. For example, would you call attending class a success if you just see the corporate recruiter? If you also talk to him or her? If she or he takes your résumé? Or, must you get invited to interview with him or her?

How do we get from here to there?   We choose to expend resources on HR activities aimed at meeting the objectives. The chapters in the rest of the book will provide you with detailed descriptions of the various activities that can be mixed and matched to reach a wide variety of objectives. This chapter will show how planning provides the framework for choosing and integrating them.

How did we do?   After we've spent our resources and implemented our chosen activities, we can ask whether we have met the objective. The standards that we use to determine success usually reflect the standards that we used to set the objectives. As we compare our achievements with our objectives, we're back to assessing conditions, and we make more plans based on the new gap between where we are and where we want to be.

---◆---

Human resource decisions are choices about how to expend resources on HR activities aimed at meeting objectives. Decisions require: (1) *objectives,* which establish the gaps to be reduced; (2) *alternatives,* which are the available choices, each requiring resources and producing an anticipated set of outcomes; (3) *attributes,* which are the characteristics of the alternatives that relate to the objectives and are compared in choosing among alternatives; and (4) *evaluation standards,* which are the outcomes measured to assess success and should reflect the original objectives.

EXHIBIT 5.2   How Objectives and Evaluation Standards Are Determined

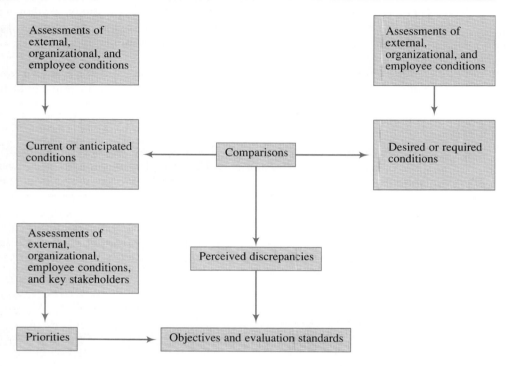

A *human resource plan* specifies the alternatives selected through HR decisions, and the attributes of the standards that will be used to evaluate them.

The Relationship between Objectives and Evaluation Standards

Exhibit 5.2 describes how objectives and evaluation standards are established. It may seem unusual to discuss objectives and evaluation standards together. Shouldn't we discuss objectives now, before we discuss the HR activities, and then discuss evaluation at the end of the book? Even experienced HR managers often proceed this way, establishing such broad objectives as quality, profitability, safety, and legal compliance during the "planning process" and then evaluating their strategies on different criteria, such as costs, employee reactions, management opinions, and activity summaries. It's not that these latter objectives are inappropriate, but they may or may not reflect the broader objectives. It's possible to stay within a budget, have employees say they like your activities, and carry out all of the activities you said you would and still fail to enhance product quality, safety, and legal compliance. Thus, separating objectives from evaluation standards carries real risks. Therefore, we will treat objectives and evaluation standards as going hand in hand. The same criteria and gaps that define objectives should be suitable criteria for evaluation. Throughout this chapter we will refer to both the objectives and the evaluation standards simply as *standards*.

The top half of Exhibit 5.2 shows that setting standards begins with assessments of conditions as described in earlier chapters. This information is used to make comparisons between the current conditions and the desired or required future conditions. The oil companies, for example, compared the number and quality of available petroleum engineers to what they desired to pursue overseas operations. These comparisons will identify discrepancies or gaps between current and desired or required conditions. The bottom of Exhibit 5.2 shows, however, that HR managers cannot and should not try to correct every discrepancy they identify. Available resources are seldom sufficient to attempt to achieve perfection. Also, some of the discrepancies will be so small that reducing them would not be worth the effort.

Priorities must be established. These priorities should reflect how seriously the discrepancies may affect organizational goals, so they, too, are based on assessments of conditions. In addition, priorities must reflect the beliefs and values of "key stakeholders." These stakeholders also define the attributes along which alternatives should be judged when choices are made to reduce the gaps.

◆

Stakeholders are the groups and individuals who establish organizational goals. External stakeholders are not organizational members, and they include customers, communities, regulators, unions and investors. Internal stakeholders are organizational members, and they include employees, as well as HR and non-HR managers.

In the oil company example at the beginning of this chapter, the original financial analysis anticipated only small labor shortages (only six to nine people out of thousands), and they were not given high priority. Only when a key stakeholder—top management—realized the strategic importance of the gap did it become a vital objective. HR planners measured the gap, forecasted its effects, and helped key stakeholders understand the importance of investing resources to address it.

What Makes a Good Objective/Standard?

Information is an investment, just like any other resource, and the value of gathering information on a particular objective/standard is related to its usefulness. Some standards are established because an outside force requires them—

inspection reports are required by government agencies, financial statements are required by the Security and Exchange Commission. Organizations gather information on these standards because, without it, they can't continue to operate. On the other hand, many standards are established because someone inside the organization wants that information. Surprisingly, activity to gather information supporting these standards is often wasted, because no one really knows what to do with it.

The value of information supporting standards is a function of two factors:

1. How many decisions will be corrected by having information on the objective/standard?
2. How much value will each corrected decision produce?

Some standards create value by correcting only a few decisions, which have very important consequences. For example, standards showing how executives are paid may only cause changes in the executive pay system once every several years. However, every change can have multimillion-dollar consequences because the quality and performance of top executives affects fundamental business decisions. Some standards create value by correcting many decisions, each with modest value. For example, standards reflecting individual employee medical claims may detect thousands of mistakes that might have caused overpayments. Though each overpayment avoided may only save less than $1,000, correcting thousands of such incorrect decisions can save on organization millions of dollars.

The final factor affecting the value of an objective/standard is the cost of gathering and using the information it requires, including processing, analysis time, communication, and other factors. Even an objective/standard with high value may not be worth having if the costs of tracking it are prohibitive. For example, tracking the precise genetic susceptibility to skin rashes of every applicant for a chemical production job might be useful in screening out applicants who will file more injury claims. However, the dollar cost and privacy violations of individual genetic screening probably vastly outweigh the likely benefits of such avoided claims.

Notice the importance of decisions in determining information value. If an objective/standard doesn't correct a decision, it doesn't have value. Even potentially useful standards can have little value if no one knows how to use them to make better decisions. A good objective/standard is measurable, timely, accurate, and clearly related to the decision-making process. It is also measured at a level of precision that is high enough to support decisions, but it is not so high that it's cost exceeds its value.

Why Perform Human Resource Planning?

Planning is a time-consuming and expensive process, and it seldom produces perfectly accurate predictions or perfectly correct choices. So, why would any organization invest in HR planning activities? Planning provides links between actions and consequences. Without planning, we have no way of knowing what assessments are useful, whether we're moving in the right direction, which of our actions are achieving the greatest results, and how to integrate the different activities so that they complement one another. Without planning, HR management can become just a collection of activities, each one independent of the others and focusing on its own goals: staffing activities might focus only on filling vacancies quickly, compensation activities might focus only on making sure payroll costs are as low as possible, training activities might focus on delivering standard activities at low cost. When HR management is just a collection of activities, long-run and integrated standards are seldom established, and results of decisions are seldom compared to the standards that motivated them.

The diagnostic approach reveals that HR management is not simply a set of activities but an integrated strategy to manage human resources in concert with other resources to achieve efficiency and equity. Activities must be directed toward standards and be systematically evaluated on whether they achieve them. They must also be integrated, for combinations of activities often can accomplish more than the sum of the individual activities. In the oil company example at the beginning of this chapter, planning showed that the real objective was not simply filling drilling engineer vacancies nor simply controlling compensation costs. Rather, it was to achieve a stable and qualified engineering work force, sufficient for present and future business needs, at a reasonable cost. With this in mind, an *increase* in compensation might actually have been the best strategy, because it would attract better and more qualified employees, and higher compensation costs will be offset by higher productivity and lower staffing and training costs.

Not only does HR planning link and integrate choices about *human resource* activities, it also links the HR choices to the broader strategic choices of the *organization*. In a very real sense, internal and external stakeholders judge HR management by its standards. Ideally, stakeholders should be involved in shaping the standards. If HR managers focus on costs, the function will be judged as a cost center. If HR managers focus on carrying out activities as planned, it will be judged as a group of activities. If HR managers link their decisions to organizational goals, it will be judged as an integral contributor to the organization.

HOW HUMAN RESOURCE PLANNING FITS THE BROADER PLANNING PROCESS

HR decisions must fit within the broader organization planning framework. HR plans provide a link between broad organizational plans and specific HR activity choices. Exhibit 5.3 shows five levels of analysis at which HR planning can take place. Each level of analysis suggests different standards for HR planning. These different standards are reflected in different types of planning activities. And each level of analysis emphasizes different types of decisions. From the top to the bottom of Exhibit 5.3, the level of analysis becomes more specific to HR activities. Still, planning for specific human resource activities, shown at the bottom of Exhibit 5.3, should draw on and support more broadly focused planning at the external and organization level, in the top of the exhibit.

The External Level

The top of Exhibit 5.3 shows standards derived from external conditions. Because these are external standards, they are determined by stakeholders outside the organization, such as governments, unions, communities and customers, suppliers, and investors. Information to set such standards is gathered through external scanning, as discussed in Chapter Two. Specific standards that might be established here include:

- Achieve an increase in our stock price of 3 percent above the industry average in 18 months.
- Upgrade the rating on our corporate bonds from AA to AAA in six months.
- Achieve a satisfactory compliance rating by the Occupational Safety Commission in all production units by the end of the year.
- Avoid a strike during the next upcoming labor contract negotiations.
- Be a finalist in this year's "Good Community Citizen" ratings by the local news media.
- Reduce customer complaints by 30 percent before the end of the fiscal year.

Notice how each of these standards ultimately requires that an external stakeholder judge whether it is met.

HR decisions certainly affect external standards—but to different degrees. HR activities directly affect safety, equal employment opportunity, and community relations. On the other hand, it's seldom appropriate to give HR management decisions full credit or blame for changes in stock prices or debt ratings, though evidence suggests that financial markets do react to them.[2]

The Organization Level

The second level of standard focuses on decisions about the organization. The *organization* usually refers to the entire firm; but in very large or decentralized organizations, it might refer to subunits, such as divisions, regions, profit centers, branches, or agencies. The key stakeholders setting organization-level standards are the top managers responsible for directing and achieving organizational goals. Chapter Three described organizational characteristics and how they are assessed. The process of identifying organization-level standards and decisions to reach them is called *business planning*. Organization-level standards might include:

EXHIBIT 5.3   How Human Resource Planning Fits into the Broader Planning Process

Level of Analysis	Standards	Type of Planning Activities	Typical Decisions
Environment (Chapter Two)	Financial (stock price, debt rating) Government (agency ratings) Unions (strikes, organizing, grievances) Community (attitudes, opinions)	External scanning	
Organization (Chapter Three)	Hierarchy structure Norms/culture Profit Market share Quality of product	Business planning	What business should we be in? What market, process, technology, and organization design does this imply?
Human resource department/function	Budget Activities Client opinions	HR strategic planning	How does HR management contribute to the business? How much resources should we use? What broad directions should we emphasize?
Human resource quantity/deployment	Quantity of employees Assignment to jobs Labor cost levels	Employment planning	What is future HR demand and supply? What gaps should we try to reconcile?
Specific human resource management activities	Quantity of affected employees Activity costs Activity results Payoff/utility	HR action plans	What specific activities should we implement? How extensive should each activity be?

+ Achieve an organizational hierarchy and structure congruent with our product/market strategy, within three years.
+ Get all employees to understand and accept the organization's norms and corporate culture by the end of the year.
+ Achieve a 15 percent increase in organizational profit levels within 18 months.

♦ Introduce five new products before the end of the year.

♦ Achieve a 10 percent increase in our share of the market for our products/ services within six months.

♦ Implement team-based robotic production processes before the end of this year.

Notice how these standards can be assessed by stakeholders within the organization and do not require a direct assessment by external stakeholders. Yet, these standards focus on organization or unitwide outcomes.

The last column of Exhibit 5.3 shows example decisions that are made as part of organizational strategic planning, but can HR decisions affect organization-level standards? Decisions about job design and career management directly affect the organization's hierarchy and structure. Communication activities affect employee understanding and the acceptance of norms and cultural values, especially in such companies as IBM, where this is considered a primary task for all managers. The effects of HR decisions on market share, profits, product quality, production processes, and customer satisfaction may be less obvious, but they are no less real, as the oil company example at the beginning of this chapter showed.

One prevailing organization-level objective, especially among U.S. corporations, is *quality*. In 1987, the U.S. Congress established the Malcolm Baldrige National Quality Award to recognize and publicize successful quality achievements. Exhibit 5.4 contains the qualifying criteria for the award, which was won in 1988 by Motorola, Inc., Globe Metallurgical, Inc., and Westinghouse Electric Corporation's Commercial Nuclear Fuel Division, and, in 1989, by Milliken & Company and Xerox's Business Products and Systems. Notice how prominently "human resource utilization" appears in the criteria, and consider the influence of HR management decisions on all of the criteria. Which HR decisions do HR managers think affect organization-level standards most? When 440 HR executives were asked which of their activities did the most to increase their organization's "competitive advantage," they named: (1) protecting the company against lawsuits for discrimination and wrongful discharge, (2) building employee team orientation, and (3) designing performance appraisal systems to achieve business goals.[3]

Human Resource Department/Function Level

Planning at the external and organization levels produces standards and decisions reflecting broad success and survival. While HR management decisions can and should reflect standards at this level, such standards may not reveal whether success was achieved because of, or in spite of, a well-managed HR department/function. Therefore, HR planners typically establish standards for how the department/function itself is managed, whether the level and mix of resources correspond to plans, and whether key stakeholders within the orga-

---

EXHIBIT 5.4   An Organization-Level Goal, The Malcolm Baldrige National Quality Award

---

**Qualifying Criteria for
the Malcolm Baldrige National Quality Award**

Only companies incorporated and located in the United States are eligible. Qualifying companies may be privately or publicly owned. Up to two awards may be given in each of three categories: large manufacturing companies or subsidiaries, large service companies, and smaller companies engaged either in manufacturing or services.

Criteria are rigorous, with an emphasis on systems for quality improvement not just quality achievements. Examiners will consider the following seven categories:

- *Leadership*—The senior management's success in creating and sustaining a quality culture.
- *Information and analysis*—The effectiveness of the company's collection and analysis of information for quality improvement and planning.
- *Planning*—The effectiveness of integration of quality requirements into the company's business plans.
- *HR utilization*—The success of the company's efforts to utilize the full potential of the work force for quality.
- *Quality assurance results*—The company's results in quality achievement and quality improvement, demonstrated through quantitative measures.
- *Customer satisfaction*—The effectiveness of the company's systems to determine customer requirements and demonstrated success in meeting them. Finalists are subject to an on-site visit by examiners to verify their quality activities.

The National Institute of Standards and Technology is responsible for developing and administering the awards.

Source: M. Katherine Glover, "Malcolm Baldrige National Quality Award," *Business America,* November 20, 1989, pp. 2–3.

nization generally hold the department/function in high regard. This level of planning is called *human resource strategic planning,* and it establishes the broad standards within which specific HR decisions are made. Standards at this level of analysis might include:

- Allocate funds so we achieve no more than a 1 percent deviation from planned budgets at the end of the fiscal year.
- Conduct five new literacy training programs in the next eight months.
- Implement a recruiting program targeted to older workers within three months.
- Achieve a 90 percent approval rating in the annual survey of managers and employees who use HR management services.

Notice how each of these standards focuses on the mix of HR activities chosen and their combined effects, rather than on broad organizational or external outcomes.

Exhibit 5.3 shows typical decisions made at this level of planning. HR strategic planning translates the organizational strategic plan into specific choices about the general emphasis and direction of the HR function. HR strategic planning standards are certainly useful, but not complete. Standards at the organization level and even the HR function level can be affected by many factors besides HR decisions, including finances, technology, marketing, and raw materials. Also, budgets, activities, and stakeholder opinions may not reveal specific ways to improve HR management quality.

Human Resource Quantity and Deployment

To further isolate the effects of HR decisions, planners typically consider the size of the work force and how it is deployed across different organizational jobs. This is called *employment planning*. Typical standards in employment planning might include:

+ Reduce the size of our work force by 5 percent within six months.
+ Reduce employees in headquarters staff jobs by 5,000 and redeploy at least 4,000 of them into sales/marketing jobs within two years.
+ Maintain this year's labor costs at their current level, despite inflation in overall price levels.

Notice how these standards focus on whether the number, costs, and qualities of employees match needs, rather than focusing on the ultimate effects of matching those needs or on the mix of programs used. Exhibit 5.3 shows that employment planning decisions focus on identifying discrepancies between the future demand and supply of employees, and then making choices to reconcile the two.

Specific Human Resource Management Activities

Perhaps the most obvious way to plan and assess HR decisions is to ask, "Are our activities being carried out and producing the immediate results we want?" *Human resource action plans* consider the likely effects of specific HR activities. Typical standards at this level of analysis might include:

+ Extend long-term medical benefits to all employees identified as at risk for long-term disabilities, before July 30.
+ Implement the new merit pay plan recognizing high performance, without increasing the compensation budget by more than $100,000, before the end of the year.
+ Have every participant in literacy training pass a minimum reading competency test by the end of the year.
+ Demonstrate that the benefits exceed the costs of the new team-building and worker-involvement seminar series, by more than 120 percent.

Notice how these standards isolate specific HR activities, the resources they use, or the immediate outcomes they achieve.

Exhibit 5.3 shows that typical decisions in HR action planning include whether to implement particular activities and how extensive each activity should be. Action plans translate the work force size and deployment standards of employment planning into specific activities. Action plan standards often reflect many of the individual characteristics discussed in Chapter Four. HR action planning can provide very specific guidance for continuing, expanding, or eliminating activities. However, it must also reflect broader standards. For example, training 200 production workers in hydraulics may satisfy an action plan, but it provides little value if the demand for hydraulic skills is falling.

PLANNING THE HUMAN RESOURCE DEPARTMENT AND FUNCTION

Human resource strategic planning focuses on making sure the broad directions of the HR department and function are consistent with the organization's direction and objectives. This requires that the mix of HR activities and resources correspond to the structure, norms, culture, market, and production goals of the organization. For example, labor-intensive organizations forecasting labor shortages, such as Hilton and Marriott, want a mix of HR activities that emphasizes aggressive external staffing and employee retention. Firms with surpluses of labor, such as manufacturing organizations, want a mix of HR activities that emphasize the providing of equitable opportunities for employees to leave the organization and the retention of the most valued employees. Organizations with strong cultural norms, such as IBM, desire HR activities that communicate and reward values, including respect for the individual and customer service. There are several ways to assess whether the HR function is establishing the appropriate role and mix of activities, and whether the function itself is adding value.

Auditing Human Resource Activities

HR audits, like financial or tax audits, examine whether HR policies and practices are in place and being followed.[4] Audits might track whether performance appraisals are completed on all employees by the required date, whether exit interviews with departing employees are conducted, whether insurance enrollments are properly processed when employees join, and whether planning involves the appropriate individuals. Virtually any activity or procedure can be audited, by measuring whether it occurs as planned, is carried out according to procedures, and involves the recommended individuals. One study gathered data from archives, such as separation percentages, payroll complaints per employee, and compensation increases, to determine how they related to organizational performance, executive and employee satisfaction, and personnel budget allocation per employee.[5] Audit information can help establish goals based on following practices and procedures more closely, and it can help identify how those who manage personnel spend their time. However, audits don't necessarily tell whether the practices are appropriate, nor whether they relate to accomplishing organizational objectives. For example, if procedures call for conducting exit interviews with every separating employee, an audit can show whether the exit interviews are indeed carried out. But, do the interviews help reduce or change the separation pattern to be more favorable? An audit is necessary to this analysis, but it doesn't tell the whole story.

Human Resource Budgets

Budgets reflect dollar amounts spent on different HR activities. While it might seem obvious that organizations track their expenditures for HR activities, many organizations track only activities that eventually show up on the financial income statement or balance sheet, such as pay and benefits. More complete budgets can reveal where resources are really spent in managing HR. An organization may believe that it emphasizes training but finds that it spends only 5 percent of it's budget on training activities, and that it spends $500 per employee on training compared to others in its industry who spend $2,000. Such information may cause it to reevaluate the true nature of its activities and try to bring them more in line with its stated goals.

Activity, Cost, or Headcount Ratios

A method of combining the audit and budgeting approaches is to construct ratios comparing activities, costs, and headcount levels. Typical ratios include the number of total employees to HR staff employees, training costs per trainee, staffing costs per new hire, merit pay per person, days to fill job vacancies, and the like.[6] There is an infinite variety of ratios that could be constructed and combined using standards at all organizational levels. Just imagine the number of ratios that might be constructed using the standards shown in Exhibit 5.3. Many organizations compute such ratios and subscribe to surveys through consulting firms or professional societies to compare their ratios to others. Like audits, however, such ratios do not tell the whole story. For example, if an organization's ratio of HR staff to employees is higher than the industry average, that could indicate excessive HR staff levels, but it could also mean that the organization has found unique ways to make that extra staff produce valuable contributions.

Human Resource Accounting

Some accountants have long recognized that HR activities generally appear on financial statements simply as costs of doing business, or unspecified "overhead" expenses that are arbitrarily allocated to business units. HR accounting

(HRA) can trace its roots to the 1970s, when accountants began to explore the possibility of estimating the "asset value" of people, according to how much it costs to obtain their services, or by projecting the dollar value of their expected economic activity in the organization.[7] While this idea is intriguing, because it would value human resources similarly to financial and capital resources, it has not been widely applied and can be very complex to implement. This is not to say that HR activities do not directly affect the organization's financial performance, but that tracing these effects often requires working from the activity to the financial outcome, rather than measuring the financial outcome directly. Nonetheless, work on HRA has clarified the structure for measuring the costs of acquiring, training, and separating employees, as will be discussed in later chapters.

Return on Investment in Human Resources

Just as HR accountants recognize that it would be useful to measure the investment in human resources, some have suggested that the results of HR decisions be expressed as "return on investment."[8] Typical return-on-investment measures might include:

+ Sales revenue divided by total employees.
+ Sales revenue divided by total employee-related costs.
+ Pretax earnings divided by total personnel expenses.
+ After-tax earnings divided by total personnel expenses.
+ Total asset value divided by the number of employees.
+ Total yearly profit divided by the investment in employees.

Exhibit 5.5 shows the concept of "value-added," which is the difference between the total sales revenue generated by an organization or unit, minus the cost of the raw materials and purchased services it consumes to produce that sales revenue. Value-added is used to pay for costs of maintaining and acquiring capital, such as buildings, plants, and machinery. It is also used to pay for employee costs, and the remaining amount becomes pretax earnings. Value-added can also be used in return on investment ratios, such as value-added per employee or value-added per employee cost.

Client Opinions/Perceptions

Cliff Ehrlich, senior vice president of human resources for the Mariott Corporation, bases decisions on "what's fair" to employees, and he actively markets the value of HR to employees.[9] He is very concerned that employees have high opinions of the HR function and uses their opinions in his planning. Employees are only one of many groups of stakeholders whose opinions might make useful standards for HR planning. Other key stakeholders include the top personnel executives, line managers of business operations, production managers, and ex-

EXHIBIT 5.5   The Relationship between Employee Costs and Value-Added

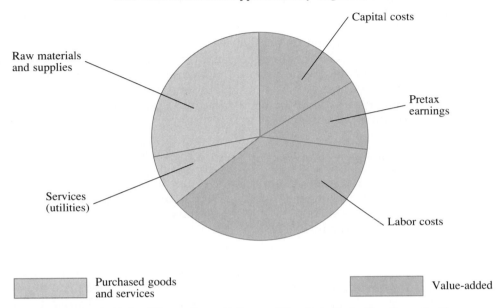

How Sales Revenue Is Apportioned by Organizations

Source: Henry L. Dahl, Jr., "Human Resource Cost and Benefit Analysis: New Power for Human Resource Approaches," *Human Resource Planning* 11, no. 2 (1988), p. 75.

ternal groups, such as unions and governments. The premise of the reputational approach is that these client perceptions determine the effectiveness of the HR department and its decisions.[10] Research has sought constituent opinions on:

+ Responsiveness (quick answers to questions, cooperation, objectivity, and neutrality).
+ Proactivity and innovativeness (creative policies, evaluations against goals, support for line management).
+ Overall effectiveness.

Reputational evaluations can be useful in identifying sources of dissatisfaction, and they explicitly recognize the fact that standards must reflect the values of the key stakeholders in the HR function.

Audits, budgets, cost/headcount ratios, HR accounting, return on investment, and client opinions all can be useful, if they correct decisions that have important consequences. Used alone, however, they provide little guidance without a broader framework based on using information to support decisions. If cost ratios go up, or are higher than competitors, what action should be taken? Is it always bad to have high or rising HR staff-to-employee ratios? What if the higher-than-average ratios produce much more valuable outcomes? Do the clients really understand what's good for the organization? Such questions require that HR planners look not only at whether the function is well managed and well regarded but at specific outcomes of HR decisions. One such outcome is the quantity and deployment of Human Resources within the firm, discussed next.

EMPLOYMENT PLANNING: THE QUANTITY AND DEPLOYMENT OF HUMAN RESOURCES

Employment planning aims to get the right numbers and types of employees doing the right work at the right time. Exhibit 5.6 shows the employment planning process. Employment planning involves three basic phases: (1) analyzing HR demand, (2) analyzing HR supply, and (3) reconciling important discrepancies between demand and supply by maintaining or changing HR activities. Notice how this process parallels the general planning process described in Exhibit 5.1. *Demand analysis* asks "Where do we want to be?" *Supply analysis* asks "Where are we now?" and "Where will we be?" by considering both the *internal supply* (current employees), and the *external supply* (employees who join the organization from outside). The sum of internal and external supply is then compared with the projected demand. Gaps are identified, and the process shown in Exhibit 5.2 is applied to them—priorities are established, and the most important gaps become HR standards. In employment planning, the standards reflect the quantity and deployment of employees. Finally, the standards are *reconciled* by choosing HR activities to address the gaps, and the process starts again.

Demand Analysis: "Where Do We Want to Be?"

Demand analysis describes how many employees are needed in each job in the organization and what each employee needs to do in that job. It may also include what characteristics each employee should have to do the job and what labor costs are allocated to induce and support that employee's efforts. HR demand is derived from the organization's business plan (organizational strategic planning) and the HR strategic plan, as shown in Exhibit 5.3.

Actual demand forecasts don't try to predict future needs down to every single employee. They summarize these factors for key groups of employees, and they focus on the most critical individual characteristics and costs. In the oil company example at the beginning of the chapter, business plans dictated continuing levels of U.S. exploration and production, with expanded Middle East oil field development. This translated into U.S. division *demands* to maintain their existing 30 to 50 drilling engineers, and Middle East division *demands* for

EXHIBIT 5.6   Employment Planning Process: Three Phases

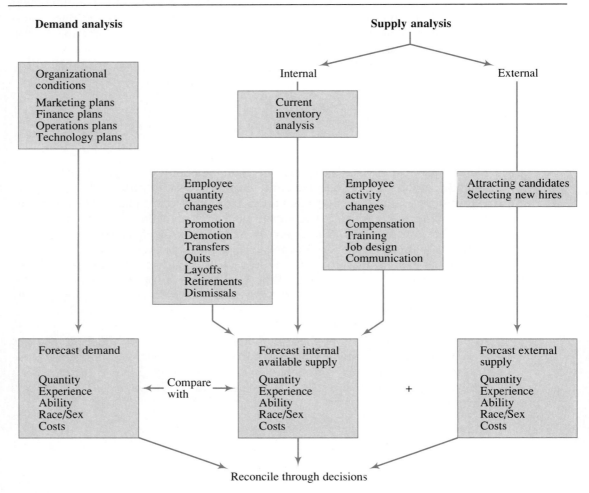

six to nine new drilling engineers. Willingness to relocate and whether employees had high-school-age children emerged as critical individual characteristics. Where did these numbers come from? They were derived from the link between business activity and HR requirements supporting that activity.

Linking Business Plans to Human Resource Requirements

Increased hiring by the rapidly expanding hotel industry and the frequent layoffs and "restructuring" by the auto industry are vivid examples of the relationship between planned business activity and HR requirements. If business

---

EXHIBIT 5.7   The Link between Business Activity and Human Resource Demand

---

General Formula

| **Business activity** | **= Quantity of human resources** $\times$ **Productivity per employee** |

General Examples

Sales revenues	= Number of salespeople	$\times$ Sales dollars per salesperson
Production levels	= Number of production hours worked	$\times$ Output per production hour
Operating costs	= Number of employees	$\times$ Labor cost per employee

Oil Company Example

New oil fields under production	= Number of engineers +	$\times$ Engineer productivity
	Number of operators +	$\times$ Operator productivity
	Number of managers +	$\times$ Manager productivity
	Number of others	$\times$ Other productivity

---

expands, then the performance capability of human resources must increase to support it, and vice versa. But, specifically, how does business translate activity levels into specific numbers and types of employees?

The general logic is described in Exhibit 5.7. The level of business activity that can be supported is the product of the quantity of employees and the amount of time they work, times the average business activity per person or work time. The general examples show several of the many ways that business activity, quantities of employees, and business activity per employee can be defined. Examples of measurements of activity levels per employee or work time are:

+ The 3M Company uses gross sales revenues.[11]
+ State Farm Insurance companies use insurance policies in force.[12]
+ Upjohn Company uses return on investment, and still other firms use estimated production volumes or value-added (the difference between the cost of raw materials and the price of the final product).[13]

Business activity can also be defined as costs, in which case the goal is usually to achieve a reduced level of activity. A layoff, or "downsizing," is often motivated by a business goal to cut labor costs to boost efficiency.[14]

The bottom of Exhibit 5.7 shows how oil company HR planners might have linked the business plan to open new oil fields to the quantity and deployment of human resources across several different skill categories. This "skill mix"

EXHIBIT 5.8   How Business Activity Goals Can Lead to Different Combinations of Human Resource Demand Levels

---

Business activity = Quantity of employees × Productivity per employee
or work time   or work time

Business Strategy	Human Resource Demand	HRM Example
Large increase in activity	Increase employee activity faster than increases in employee quantity.	Increase sales or production per employee or per hour, and add employees or person-hours.
Moderate increase in activity	Increase employee activity while holding employee quantity stable.	Increase sales or production per person or per hour but make no net additions to staff, replace only those who leave.
Moderate increase in activity	Hold employee activity stable while increasing employee quantity.	Maintain existing employee production or sales levels but add staff in the same proportion to the increase in business activity.
Large decrease in activity	Decrease employee activity while decreasing employee quantity.	Reduce the amount of scheduled overtime and do not replace employees who choose to leave.
Moderate decrease in activity followed by an increase in activity	Decrease employee activity while maintaining employee quantity, then increase employee activity.	Reduce overtime and encourage employees to take vacation time in the short run, but replace those who leave. When activity rises, add overtime and reduce vacations.

---

issue is central to HR planning, and it is approached in different ways. Some firms estimate needs for critical-skill employees first, and then they estimate the needed quantity of support staff (accountants, HR professionals, secretaries) as a function of the quantity of critical-skill employees required.[15] For example, where engineering skills are critical, such as Hewlett-Packard Company or Rockwell International, planners might use a ratio of two secretaries, one-half an accountant, and one HR professional for every 10 engineers.

Because the level of business activity is a function of the product of the quantity of human resources and the business activity per person or work time, HR demand forecasts must account for both the quantity and productivity. A given business activity level can be reached by changing the number of people, the time worked, or the cost or productivity per person. Exhibit 5.8 shows how several different combinations of quantity and productivity levels could support different levels of business activity. Notice, in the bottom example, that the organization must not only consider the short run, but must look ahead. With highly skilled or experienced employees, it may not be prudent to reduce staff sizes in response to a short run downturn only to find that the staff must be rehired again when demand picks up.

Demand analysis produces the desired amount of people (or time) and their deployment to different jobs to support business activities. The next step is to determine the existing quantity, productivity, and deployment of the current and projected work force.

Internal Supply Analysis: "Where Are We Now, Where Will We Be?"

Supply analysis focuses both internally and externally to the organization. As shown in Exhibit 5.6, internal analysis begins by asking "Where are we now?" and examining the *current internal inventory* of employees. Then, it asks "Where will we be" by *forecasting internal supply,* assuming current activities are continued. This forecast accounts for movement inside the organization (promotion/demotions/transfers) and out of the organization (quits, layoffs, retirements, dismissals). The result is a summary of the current and projected work force, which can reflect size, experience, ability, race/sex, costs or other characteristics of interest.[16]

In principle, internal supply analysis is very simple. Just determine how many people you have in each job now. Then, for each job, estimate how many will stay where they are, how many will move to other jobs, and how many will leave their job and the organization. Add up all of these movements and departures, and you get a projection of how many people you will have in each job after all the movements are finished. The reality, however, is more complex. Will you keep the same array of jobs as you have now, or will you remove some, combine some to create new jobs, or add new jobs? Will you assume that movements between jobs and out of jobs will occur in the same pattern as before? Will you assume that every employee who moves to a new job is just as productive as the person who was there before? While answers to such questions are often a matter of judgment, several forecasting techniques are used to make internal supply analysis more systematic and grounded in experience.

Skill Inventories

A skill inventory is a list of employees, showing characteristics that relate to their ability to perform different jobs.[17] These characteristics might include training classes attended, previous experience, licenses obtained, tests passed, supervisory judgments of ability, and even strength or endurance. A skill inventory can help planners estimate the likelihood that a given employee will move to a new job, based on his or her qualifications for that job.

EXHIBIT 5.9 Transition Probability Matrix for Projecting Internal Labor Supply*

Job States†		Destination States Time Period 2										Exit	Total
		A	B	C	D	E	F	G	H	I	J		
Source States Time Period 1	A	1.00										—	1.00
	B	.15	.80									.05	1.00
	C		.16	.76	.04		◀ Organizational career I					.04	1.00
	D		.01	.23	.73							.03	1.00
	E					.85	.05					.10	1.00
	F					.25	.65	.05				.05	1.00
	G		Organizational career II ▶				.40	.50	.03			.07	1.00
	H						.02	.15	.75			.08	1.00
	I								.20	.50		.30	1.00
	J					Organizational career III ▶				.50		.50	1.00

* Cell entries are proportions.
† A to J job states are different jobs arranged hierarchically.

Replacement Charts

While skill inventories list skills for individuals, replacement charts list the individuals who could move into key jobs in the organization. They list the employees who could be promoted or transferred into the job, as well as the employees' current jobs, their level of readiness, their skill/abilities, and their willingness to move into the new job. Replacement charts help planners forecast movement between jobs by identifying the most likely and willing candidates.

Transitional Matrices

Rather than looking at particular individuals or jobs, transitional matrix analysis examines the overall pattern of movement into jobs, between jobs, and out of the organization.[18] These patterns are then applied to the current inventory of employees, to determine where they will be if they follow the past movement pattern.

Exhibit 5.9 shows the three elements of a transitional probability matrix:

1. *"State" definitions:*   States are the divisions the planner uses to segment

the organization for analysis. States may be jobs, salary grades, performance levels, or other characteristics to be analyzed. In Exhibit 5.9, the letters A to J represent jobs, with A at the top of the organization and J at the bottom. Jobs A, B, C, and D might be a sales career path, such as assistant product sales manager (job D), product sales manager (job C), assistant regional marketing manager (job B), and regional marketing manager (job A). Jobs E through I might be a manufacturing career path, such as process operator (job I), process foreman (job H), production supervisor (job G), assistant plant manager (job F), and plant manager (job E). Job J might be a position outside the other career paths, such as truck driver. The right-hand column labeled *Exit* represents the state of having left the organization.

2. *Time interval:* Movement occurs over time, so the matrix must specify a time period for analysis. The rows of the matrix (Time Period 1) describe the states at the beginning of the analysis, which may represent some past period, the current period, or even a projected future period. The columns of the matrix (Time Period 2) describe the states at the end of the analyzed time period. The time period of analysis may be a day, month, year, business cycle, or whatever time period the planner feels is most relevant to the supply forecast.

3. *Cell entries:* Each cell of the matrix is an intersection of a row and column—a job at Time Period 1 with a job at Time Period 2. Into these cells are entered the proportion of employees who were in the Source State (row) at Time Period 1, and in the Destination State (column) at Time Period 2. For example, Cell AA has an entry of 1.00, meaning that 100 percent of the employees in job A at Time Period 1 were still in job A at Time Period 2. Cell BA has an entry of .15, meaning that 15 percent of the employees in job B at Time Period 1 had moved up to job A at Time Period 2. The cells along the diagonal (AA, BB, CC, and so on) represent the probability of remaining in the same job over the time period of analysis. Each probability is computed by counting the number of employees who moved from the Row state to the Column state, and dividing that number by the original number of employees in the Row state at the beginning of the analysis. Cell entries can reflect actual past movements, or they can be hypothetical what-if possibilities that we wish to achieve in the future.

What can the transitional probability matrix tell us?   First, it can identify career patterns. Movement from job D to C to B to A is a career path, because there is movement among these jobs, but no movement between these jobs and others. Another career pattern has job E as the top job and job I as its entry-level job. State J, on the other hand, isn't involved in between-job movement. Fifty percent of those in state J at the beginning of the analysis are still there at the end, while the other 50 percent leave the organization.

Second, transitional matrices can identify the effects of separations across the organization. The numbers in the Exit column represent the separation rate for each of the states. States I and J have particularly high separation rates. State A has a zero separation rate, in the time period used in this analysis. At first this may seem like good news, but remember that state A is the top job in the ABCD career pattern. A lack of separations from state A may be a bottleneck preventing employees from advancing.

How can the transitional matrix forecast the future internal supply?   Simulating the future tells what the employer can expect if people continue to move through and out of the organization according to the same patterns as before. A simulation starts with the actual or assumed number of employees in each state at the beginning of the analysis (Time Period 1). Then, the beginning number in each Source State is multiplied by each probability across the row, to give the movement from that Source to each Destination, including Exit. Finally, the forecasted number of employees staying or moving into each state is the sum down the column, including the diagonal. The total movement out of each state is the sum across the row, excluding the diagonal. For example, suppose the starting number of employees was 100 in job A, 200 in B, 300 in C, and 400 in D. What is the projected number of employees staying or moving into job B at the end of the time period? The number of employees staying in job B is 160 (200 times .80). The number moving from A to B is 0, from C to B is 48 (300 times .16), and from D to B is 4 (400 times .01). Adding these numbers give the predicted number of people staying or moving into job B— 212. We project 30 employees moving from B to A (200 times .15) and 10 employees leaving the organization from job B (200 times .05), for a total of 40. The net projected number of employees in state B at the end of the analysis is 212 minus 40, or 172.

Transitional matrices can also be used to do multiperiod analysis, by simply substituting the ending numbers of employees from the Time Period 2 as the new beginning numbers, and redoing the analysis described above. For example, the projected number of Exits among the 172 employees in state B during Time Period 3 is 8.6 (172 times .05). Though these calculations are somewhat lengthy, today's personal computers can easily accomplish them.[19]

Many organizations routinely use transitional matrices, including AT&T, Merck, and Weyerhaeuser.[20] As you've probably guessed, the actual numbers and assumptions that go into such matrices are seldom extremely precise. Such projections certainly do not forecast the future perfectly, but this is not their main purpose. Their greatest value is in providing an organized framework for describing the movement process within the organization so that different possible future outcomes can be quickly and systematically explored. They assist in affirmative action planning, where the states are defined to emphasize legally protected groups, such as sex, race, age, and handicap.[21] Affirmative action planning will be discussed in Chapter Six.

With projected internal supplies established, the planner is part way to identifying the gaps between demand forecasts and projected supply. Now, the effects of hiring employees from outside the organization must be factored in.

External Supply Analysis: "Who Is Joining the Organization, Who Will Be Joining?"

External supply is created by the organization's activities that attract and select job candidates. Chapters Seven and Eight will discuss this process in detail. External supply analysis is similar to internal supply analysis, because it forecasts the quantity, productivity, and deployment of human resources. Unlike internal supply analysis, however, external supply analysis focuses on the supply of employees projected to join the organization from *outside,* assuming that current activities to attract and select employees are continued.[22] Past hiring patterns will suggest how many employees will be entering the organization in different jobs. These entering individuals can be analyzed according to their quantity, experience, abilities, race/sex, and labor costs. External scanning, discussed in Chapter Two, can provide useful information for forecasting the likely availability of different types of employees at different future time periods. Oil company planners used external scanning to determine the numbers of graduates of university drilling engineer programs, who might be attracted and hired under current policies. External supply analysis can focus on "states" similar to those used in transition matrix analysis. Just as with internal supply analysis, the numbers are seldom perfectly accurate. Like the transitional matrix, external supply forecasting does not produce perfect predictions. It's value lies in providing an organized framework for considering where employees are obtained and where they enter the organization.

As Exhibit 5.6 shows, the total projected supply is the sum of the supply expected from internal sources and external sources. Demand analysis has now answered the question "Where do we want to be?" Supply analysis has answered the question "Where are we now, and where will we be?" It's now possible to identify the gaps, establish standards, and consider how to achieve them.

Reconciling Supply and Demand: Setting Objectives and Choosing Activities

Comparing demand and supply can produce three outcomes: (1) demand and supply will closely match, (2) demand will exceed supply indicating possible shortages, or (3) supply will exceed demand indicating possible surpluses. These comparisons reflect not only the quantities of employees, but their experience, abilities, race/sex, cost levels, and, perhaps, other factors. So, the projected quantity of demand and supply may match, but the skill levels, race/sex composition, or labor costs may not. So, gaps and objectives may reflect several different standards, as indicated in Exhibit 5.3.

Gaps will also emerge at different levels, with some parts of the organization in good balance while others are out of balance. Also, not every gap will justify action. The stakeholders must be consulted, priorities set, and standards established that reflect the most critical gaps.

Choosing Activities to Address Shortages

When the projected demand exceeds supply, an obvious solution is to hire more employees. This might involve recruiting at new sources, more aggressively pursuing job candidates, lowering entrance requirements, and expanding the use of temporary or older workers. Chapters Seven and Eight will discuss these options in detail. Organizations are often reluctant to add new jobs, unless it's absolutely necessary. For example, before Upjohn Corporation's managers can add new employees, they must answer the following questions:

1. What purposes does the new job serve?
2. Which alternatives were considered to accomplish the same purposes?
3. If the job is filled, what are the projected five-year costs?
4. What impact will this job have on sales, earnings, improved HR utilization.[23]

As Exhibit 5.8 shows, a second way to deal with a shortage is to expand the level of productivity per employee or time worked. Training, job design, compensation, benefits, and employee relations are often used to expand employees' ability or motivation. Subsequent chapters will discuss these activities in detail.

Choosing Activities when Forecasts Indicate a Surplus

A surplus exists when the organization's supply of human resources exceeds its demands. Surpluses entail some of the most difficult planning choices, because employees are seldom responsible for the surplus, yet they may bear the brunt of its effects. Reducing overtime or work hours, encouraging early retirement, reducing hiring so attrition diminishes the work force, and relying on less-expensive temporary employees may be considered. As a last resort, organizations may consider layoffs. Subsequent chapters will describe each of these options in detail.

Using Surpluses to Address Shortages

Organizations could conduct employment planning on a unit-by-unit or job-by-job basis to produce an estimate of shortages/surpluses for each unit or job. But, a comprehensive plan that considers the entire organization can use surpluses in one area to offset shortages in other areas. For example, IBM faced a surplus of managerial and production staff in the mid 1980s and a shortage of programmers and salespeople. Rather than treat them separately, IBM trained and transferred employees from managerial and production jobs into programming and sales jobs.

Employment planning can identify the shortages or surpluses and even give clues to what activities should be used to address them. Ultimately, however, decisions must be made about what resources to spend on what specific activities. So, planners usually include standards geared to specific HR activities in their analysis.

PLANNING SPECIFIC HUMAN RESOURCE ACTIVITIES

Human resource action planning involves deciding what specific activities will be used to achieve standards. Such activities include staffing, training, compensation, and benefit activities. The subsequent chapters in this book will discuss each activity of HR management and how to evaluate the effectiveness of each activity. However, it's important to understand how such activity-specific planning fits into the broader framework. Activity-specific planning asks, "What did this particular activity actually do?" Evaluation standards can come from many levels of analysis. Activities might be evaluated for their effects on sales or profit, achieving safety levels, ensuring the appropriate quantity/deployment of employees, or by their effects on employee characteristics, such as skills, abilities, attitudes, performance, and absenteeism.

The Human Resource "Investment": Quantity, Quality, and Cost

Evaluating the efficiency of HR management activities is similar to evaluating investments in new production facilities, marketing campaigns, or financial instruments. HR investments consume inputs, such as time, money, and materials, and employee involvement. They use these inputs to create experiences for employees or to change the nature of their relationship with the organization. Compensation activities use money and management time to change the relationship between employee behaviors and their pay. Training activities use money, trainer time, and training materials to create experiences that alter trainees' skill, ability, or motivation. Staffing activities use money, tests, and managers as interviewers to improve the quality of those who are allowed to join the organization.

Exhibit 5.10 draws the analogy between evaluating an investment and evaluating HR activities. The key variables are: (1) the quantity of employees and work time affected by the activity, (2) the quality enhancement produced by the activity, and (3) the activity's costs. The bottom of Exhibit 5.10 summarizes the results of a hypothetical activity to train 1,000 salespeople and give them an extra 10 percent sales bonus for four years.

Quantity

For HR activities, the quantity of productive effort affected by an activity is not just the number of employees who go through the activity but also how long the activity affects their performance. In the example of Exhibit 5.10, we assume that the 1,000 salespeople are trained at the same time, but that the effects of the training last four years. Therefore, the true quantity of productive

---

EXHIBIT 5.10   Human Resource Activities as Investments

Formula for Calculating the Value Created by an Investment

Value	= [Quantity	× Quality]	− Costs
Profit	= Number of units produced	× Price per unit sold	− Materials + Capital + Labor

Formula for Calculating the Value Created by Human Resource Activities

Value	= [Quantity	× Quality]	− Costs
Utility	= Number of employees and time periods affected	× Increased dollar value per employee and time period	− Time Money Materials Managers' involvement

Numerical Example of Applying the Cost/Benefit Formula

Value	= [Quantity	× Quality]	− Costs
	1,000 Salespeople for 4 years	× $1,000 Additional sales per person-year	− 10% Sales bonus + $200 Training cost + $400,000 Administration
Utility	= [4,000	× $1,000]	− $400,000 + $200,000 + $400,000
$3,000,000 =		$4,000,000	− $1,000,000

---

activity affected is 4,000 person-years. When HR activities last a long time, their effects are often much more substantial than many realize. The common practice of computing costs per trainee or reporting the number of employees going through training ignores these long-run effects.

Quality
The quality created by HR activities can be measured in many ways, as discussed in Chapter Three. In Exhibit 5.10 we focus on the additional sales generated by each trained employee who receives the bonus. Based on previous experience with activities like this one, management forecasts, or scientific studies, planners might estimate that each salesperson will average $1,000 in additional sales per year in response to the training and bonus. Another way to measure activity effects is to examine the dollar value of preventing unwanted employee activities such as smoking, absenteeism, theft, or separations. This approach is called *behavioral costing*.[24]

Information about quality increases might come from past productivity or sales records, management opinions, process engineering studies, or industry reports. This information often is not perfectly precise and can be difficult to obtain. However, the value of this analysis is not in precisely forecasting actual dollar values but in presenting HR activities as investments, rather than simply costs or activities.

Cost

The costs of HR activities are the resources necessary to carry out the activity. In Exhibit 5.10, these costs include the costs of training (assumed to be $200 per person), the costs of the extra bonus (10 percent of the total additional sales), and the costs of administering and managing the training and bonus activity (assumed to be $400,000 over the four-year period).

Utility Analysis

The total "utility," or usefulness, of the activity is calculated by multiplying the quantity by the quality, and then subtracting total costs. As Exhibit 5.10 shows, this hypothetical training and compensation activity produces $4 million in additional sales over the four-year period, at a cost of $1 million in costs, for a $3 million total utility value. This is a 300 percent return on the $1 million investment.

While this analysis is simplified, these concepts have been applied to HR activities in virtually every functional area. Generally, the reported returns from HR activities range from slightly to extremely positive. Utility analysis can be applied to individual activities or combinations of HR activities.[25] Later chapters will contain applications of utility analysis to training, staffing and performance management.

SUMMARY

The diagnostic model says that HR management involves using information from assessments of conditions to set objectives and evaluation standards, and to use the standards to make decisions about investing resources in HR activities. HR planning is at the heart of the diagnostic process, because planning gathers and uses the information to make decisions. We have seen that standards and planning activities can focus on many different levels of analysis, and that each level of analysis contributes to improved decision making—and must support the others.

While planning, objective setting, and evaluation seem essential to effective HR management, evaluation often is not very systematic or extensive. Reasons may include: (1) fear that evaluation results will reveal problems, (2) unclear purposes of evaluation, (3) difficulty and costs of measurement, (4) lack of agreement on the level of analysis, and (5) lack of a framework for understanding evaluation.[26] These reasons argue for more careful attention and more specific goals for planning and evaluation. The diagnostic model shows that planning and evaluation activities are investments, with specific features that create value. Understanding the investment value of planning is the key to making it relevant and important to organizational goals.

This chapter, and Chapter Two, Three, and Four have discussed many different specific measures that can be used to support HR planning. Many of these reflect efficiency (such as profits, productivity levels, costs, performance ratings, and sales). Many others reflect equity (such as legal compliance, community relations, organizational culture, and employee attitudes). Subsequent chapters will show how standards can be used to assess effectiveness in each HR area. In a very real sense, HR management is judged according to the standards it sets.

DISCUSSION AND REVIEW QUESTIONS

1. Discuss why the four questions that represent the planning process provide a never-ending series of activities.
2. What four things do HR decisions require? How do they correspond to the four planning process questions?
3. What factors determine the value of an objective/standard? Should every objective/standard be used? Why or why not?
4. Why would an organization spend the time and money to use HR planning?
5. Is it fair to judge an HR activity by the organizations' standards?
6. If information gathered can't be used to predict with total accuracy, is it valuable to the organization to use it at all? Why or why not?
7. Which constituency should be used to determine an objective/standard of success? Would different constituencies in the organization have the same opinion about the value of an activity? Give examples.
8. Discuss the use of skill inventories, succession charts, and transitional matrices in forecasting an organization's internal supply of employees.
9. Is it fair to expect an HR planner to address both efficiency and equity when developing an HR activity? What conflicts could arise?
10. Describe how utility analysis can be used to forecast the value of HR activities before they are chosen. How accurate does the forecast have to be to affect a decision?

YOUR TURN
PLANNING FOR THE OIL INDUSTRY ENGINEER SHORTAGE

In case you're wondering whether the oil industry HR planners came up with a strategy for addressing their drilling engineer shortage, they did. Try your hand at HR planning by rereading the opening situation described at the beginning of the chapter and formulating an approach for identifying the gaps, the possible HR activity choices, and the standards for evaluating success. The following questions may guide you:

1. What are the nature of the gaps between desired and anticipated conditions? Are the gaps different in the short versus the long run? Do they mainly reflect headcount gaps, or are there gaps in other employee characteristics as well?

2. Even though you haven't read about the particular HR activities covered in later chapters, what are your general ideas on how to reduce the gaps you identified in question 1? What are the likely synergies you could attain by combining HR activities in different areas (such as tailoring a training activity to the compensation strategy)?

3. How would you measure your success? Who are the key stakeholders to be considered as you evaluate your performance? How will you combine short-run and long-run standards? Do your standards link back to the gaps you identified in question 1?

Your instructor has additional information about what the oil company planners did.

APPENDIX
Human Resource Information Systems

The diagnostic process in the accompanying exhibit shows that human resource management (HRM) uses information to assess conditions, identify objectives, make choices among activities, and evaluate outcomes. Just as doctors have developed technological tools to make their diagnoses, human resource managers have also progressed toward more sophisticated systems for gathering, using, and presenting information about human resources. Not surprisingly, human resource managers have yet to develop systems as sophisticated as CAT scanners, magnetic resonance imagers, or computerized "expert systems" that mimic the diagnostic logic of experts. The majority of human resource managers use information technology that is more similar to the accounting and billing software that you might find when you pay your doctor's bill.

Nonetheless, human resource managers, universities, and consulting firms are all developing knowledge and experience to produce new tools for the human resource manager every day. These tools now virtually always rely on some form of computer—ranging from a simple personal computer (PC) on a manager's desktop to a worldwide information network, with PCs connected via satellite or cable to many large mainframe computers 24 hours a day. The number and variety of different information tools is so large that it would be impractical to list them or even attempt to describe the different "computer applications" that exist. Leading professional journals, such as *Personnel Journal, Personnel,* and *Personnel Administrator,* all have regular reviews of the latest software and run a yearly "Buyers' Guide" for human resource managers.

This appendix will highlight the major components of a human resource information system (HRIS), including systems that are computerized and those that are not.

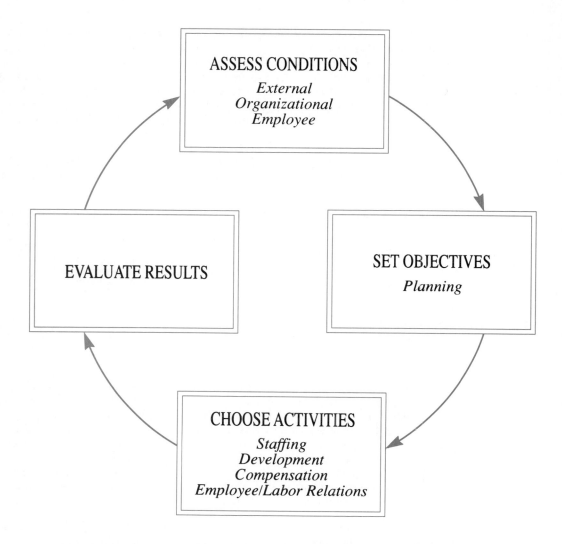

These basic principles will provide you with a foundation to understand and explore how computerized and noncomputerized information can assist the human resource professional to achieve HR objectives. The computer software and cases that are included with this book allow you to experience first-hand how a PC can be used to support real HR decisions.

---◆---

A human resource information system (HRIS) is a systematic procedure for collecting, storing, maintaining, retrieving, and validating data needed by an organization about its human resources, personnel activities, and organization unit characteristics.[27]

An HRIS need not be complex or even computerized. The HRIS can be as informal as the payroll records and time cards of a small boutique or restaurant, or they can be as extensive and formal as the computerized HR data banks of major manufacturers, banks, and governments. HRISs can support planning, with information for labor supply and demand forecasts; staffing, with information on equal employment, separations, and applicant qualifications; and development, with information on training program costs and trainee work performance. HRISs can also support compensation, with information on pay increases, salary forecasts, and pay budgets; and labor/employee relations, with information on contract negotiations and employee assistance needs. In every case, their purpose is to provide information that is either required by HR stakeholders or supports HR decisions.

THE PURPOSES OF HUMAN RESOURCE INFORMATION

Chapter Five discussed the value of information in supporting and setting standards. Some information is gathered to satisfy an external stakeholder's requirement. Examples of this information include EEO forms describing minority and female representation, pay and benefit information related to unemployment compensation, wages and hours, or pension regulation. Other information is gathered because it is required to fulfill the employment relationship. Examples of this kind of information include payroll and employee benefit information needed to issue employee paychecks. Most information systems begin with this required information, and many of the computerized enhancements to information systems are designed to produce this information faster or at a lower cost. The benefits of the information are obvious—the organization would not be allowed to continue in business if it didn't use the information to produce the required reports or payments. So, attention focuses on lowering the costs of the information.

In contrast, a large amount of information gathered by organizations is not required. Presumably, it is gathered because someone in the organization looks at it, uses it, and makes better decisions because it is available. Chapter Five showed that the value of such information is a function of two factors:

1. How many decisions will be corrected by having the information?
2. How much value will each corrected decision produce?

The value of information must then be weighed against the cost of the information to determine whether the information represents a good investment.

An HRIS is also an investment. There is an infinite variety of information that could be gathered and tracked about employees, so it is necessary for human resource managers to carefully consider the likely value of the information they include in the HRIS. The question of whether to computerize an HRIS is often presented in terms of how much cost will be saved by reduced mailing, printing, and administration. These savings are compared to the investment necessary to acquire and use the computer system. In addition to considering how information can save costs, a manager should also look at the value side of the equation. A computer system may enhance value by making it easier to get and use information. It can also reduce information value by intimidating information users or by requiring so much expertise that it is impractical to use. So, understanding how HRISs contribute to HR management is just an extension of understanding what makes information valuable.

BASIC COMPONENTS OF AN HRIS

It is convenient to consider these three major functional components in any HRIS:[28]

Input Function

The input function provides the entry of personnel information into the HRIS. This includes the procedures required to collect the data, such as who collects data, when, and how data is processed. In the past, data entry was often a laborious process requiring clerical staff to sit at a machine like a typewriter that punched patterns of holes in cards. Only one line of 80 columns could be included on each card. More recently, electronic linkages between computers allowed data entry to proceed by typing in the information at a computer terminal and then electronically sending it to the computer. Today, scanning technology exists that allows computers to scan and store the actual image of the original document, including signatures and handwritten notes. Some scanners are like copy machines, but, instead of making a paper copy, they can "read" typed documents and feed the information directly to a computer just as if it had been typed in by a person.[29] Telephone companies, such as NYNEX, use touch-tone systems through which employees or managers can input information by following directions and touching the keys on their telephones.

Data Maintenance Function

After the data have been entered into the information system, the data maintenance function updates and adds the new data to the data base. Noncomputerized systems may do this by hand, filing paper documents in the appropriate places and making the appropriate entries in the files. Computerized systems can accomplish this function accurately and rapidly, often making the new data available only seconds after it has been input.

Output Function

The most visible function of an HRIS is the output generated. To generate valuable output for computer users, the HRIS must process that output, make the necessary calculations, and then format the presentation in a way that the user can understand. Noncomputerized systems may do this by manually compiling statistics and typing reports. Highly computerized systems may do this by using sophisticated programs to do thousands of calculations in minutes, produce color graphics, and simultaneously direct the results via cable and satellite to the PCs on the desks of executives worldwide.

You have probably used computers that allow you to make choices by touching a screen, perhaps to find the location of a product in a store, or to find information about attractions in a certain city. This same technology now allows HR managers to

---

EXHIBIT 5A.1   Levels of User Activity and HRIS Functions

User Activity Continuum

Inactive ← ——————————————————————————————→ *Active*

EDP	MIS	DSS
Data and files storage	Information retrieval	Interactive for user
Transaction processing	Analyzing data	"What-if" analyses
Summary reports transactions	Inquiry and report generation	Generation of decision alternatives

---

Note: EDP—electronic data processing; MIS—management information system; DSS—decision support system.

Adapted from Michael J. Kavanagh, Hal G. Gueutal, and Scott I. Tannenbaum, *Human Resource Information Systems: Development and Application* (Boston, Mass.: Kent, 1990).

---

touch their screens to call up information about their operation. This information is usually about financial or market outcomes, but in leading companies it also includes information about the status and plans for human resources. A touch-screen is obviously much more pleasant and interesting than waiting several weeks for a typed paper report. However, no matter how compelling the technology, the information presented is still the heart of a system's value. Beautiful output that is incorrect or of the wrong type only makes it more likely that more people will rely on the information and make mistakes. Therefore, considering the user is critical to a successful HRIS.

TAILORING THE HRIS TO THE USER

The user of an HRIS in the past was typically a technically trained systems analyst whose tasks were to generate paychecks, government reports, and financial summaries with precise specifications at specific times during the year. In many of today's organizations, employees, line managers, and a variety of human resource and other staff use the information in the HRIS directly through their PCs, telephones, or in written form. This trend is likely to continue, with users demanding a more active role in the input, maintenance, and output functions of the HRIS.

Exhibit 5A.1 shows three types of user activity that can be supported by an HRIS. The activity level ranges from relatively passive or "inactive" on the left, to highly involved or "active" on the right. In the relatively inactive electronic data processing (EDP) relationship, the user simply provides input to standard transactions and receives standardized periodic reports. In the moderately active management information system (MIS) relationship, the user can conduct some analyses, usually by requesting experts to do special computer runs that inquire and report particular information. In the highly active decision support system (DSS) relationship, the computerized information system interacts with the user, providing immediate answers to "what-if" questions and generating possible decision alternatives. While any of

---

EXHIBIT 5A.2   The HRIS Design Process at TRW

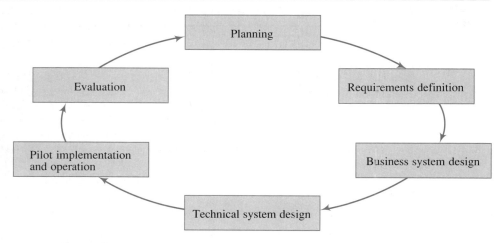

Source: TRW Task Force Report on employee information system, 1983.

these systems is appropriate, depending on the needs of the user, the trend is clearly toward a more active relationship made possible by advances in computer technology and cost reductions.

HRIS DESIGN PROCESS

No best approach to the design process has emerged. Exhibit 5A.2 shows the process used by TRW, Inc., to design its fairly common system. The first and most important step involves specifying the system requirements. These specifications are the heart of the system and include such decisions as the type of data to collect, the amount of data to collect, how to collect it, and when to collect it.[30]

The next step in TRW's design process is the business system design. It involves answering questions about who will use the system, how will they access it, how will it be updated, and so on. Technical design includes software system development and programming. Then the system is tested at certain locations and evaluated. Once in operation, the system is evaluated, improvements are planned, and the process begins again.

THREE PATTERNS OF HRIS DESIGN

Many attempts to develop an HRIS start and stop at trying to determine the data requirements. Typically, a newly hired personnel specialist's first assignment is to visit all possible users and find out their data needs. An enormous wish list can result, containing so many items that the project is crushed by its own weight. Exhibit

5A.3 lists typical data elements for an HRIS in alphabetical order. Clearly, the principles of information value should be used to guide the choice of information to be included in an HRIS. The design of the HRIS must also account for organizational and user characteristics.

A recent study conducted extensive interviews with the executives in charge of HRIS at Aetna, ALCOA, Armstrong World, AT&T, Becton-Dickinson, Chevron, Data General, Digital Equipment Corporation, Mobil Oil Corporation, and NCR. The results showed that eight dimensions were important to the value added by HRIS, and that three patterns of HRIS development could be identified across the organizations.[31] The results are summarized in Exhibit 5A.4. The four "System Development Dimensions" reflect attributes of the HRIS itself, including:

1. How much data is included.
2. How widely available is the data.
3. How much decision support is provided.
4. The degree of integration among the different data base components.

The four "Organization Development Dimensions" reflect:

1. How closely the HR function coordinates with the organization's information systems (IS) experts who design its other computer-based systems.
2. How much effort is devoted to managing HR users' expectations for the system.
3. How much effort is devoted to enhancing HR users' knowledge of the system's capabilities.
4. How closely the system designers try to link the technology used in the HRIS with the technology used in other parts of the organization.

All organizations found that there was a threshold of automation required just to survive. They had all computerized their payroll functions, for example, or had found external organizations who handled this task. Beyond this threshold, the study found three profiles. Though no organization followed one pattern exclusively, three distinct patterns did emerge, as shown in the columns of Exhibit 5A.4.

Profile One (Traditional, Central Mainframe) describes organizations that started computerizing their HRIS early, when large and centralized mainframes were the state of the art. The organizations centralized their HR decisions, so the highest value-added for computers was in processing large amounts of data for a relatively few high-level executives or in efficiently accomplishing corporate administrative tasks affecting large numbers of employees (such as payroll). Thus, the systems contain comprehensive data, are available to both HR and non-HR users at corporate offices, focus on administrative decisions, and are integrated at a mainframe computer (this is a very large computer requiring a maintenance staff and climate control). There are strong links to the organization's IS group and strong links to the organization's existing technology base. Because corporate managers preapproved the computer system, the effort devoted to managing user expectations is not high, and any training tends to focus on how to use a specific application.

Profile Two (PC-Based, Distributed) describes very different organizations, where the key HR decisions are made at each individual unit (such as a division or even a

---

EXHIBIT 5A.3   Typical Data Elements in a Human Resource Information System

---

Address (work)	Garnishments	Salary change type
Address (home)	Grievance (type)	Salary
Birthdate	Grievance (outcome)	Salary range
Birthplace	Grievance (filing date)	Schools attended
Child support deductions	Handicap status	Service date
Citizenship	Health plan coverage	Service branch
Claim pending (description)	Health plan (no. dependents)	Service discharge type
Claim pending (outcome)	Injury date	Service ending rank
Claim pending (court)	Injury type	Service discharge date
Claim pending (date)	Job location	Sex
Date on current job	Job preference	Sick leave used
Department	Job position number	Sick leave available
Dependent (sex)	Job title	Skill function (type)
Dependent (number of)	Job location	Skill subfunction (type)
Dependent (relationship)	Leave of absence start date	Skill (number of years)
Dependent (birthdate)	Leave of absence end date	Skill (proficiency level)
Dependent (name)	Leave of absence type	Skill (date last used)
Discipline (appeal date)	Life insurance coverage	Skill (location)
Discipline (type of charge)	Marital status	Skill (supervisory)
Discipline (appeal outcome)	Marriage date	Social Security number
Discipline (date of charge)	Medical exam (date)	Spouse's employment
Discipline (outcome)	Medical exam (restrictions)	Spouse's date of death
Discipline (hearing date)	Medical exam (blood type)	Spouse's name
Division	Medical exam (outcome)	Spouse's birthdate
Driver's license (number)	Miscellaneous deductions	Spouse's sex
Driver's license (state)	Name	Spouse's Social Security
Driver's license (exp. date)	Organizational property	number
Education in progress (date)	Pay status	Start date
Education in progress (type)	Pension plan membership	Stock plan membership
Educational degree (date)	Performance rating	Supervisor's name
Educational degree (type)	Performance increase ($)	Supervisor's work address
Educational minor (minor)	Performance increase (%)	Supervisor's work phone
Educational level attained	Phone number (work)	Supervisor's title
Educational field (major)	Phone number (home)	Termination date
EEO–1 code	Prior service (term. date)	Termination reason
Emergency contact (phone)	Prior service (hire date)	Training schools attended
Emergency contact (name)	Prior service (term. reason)	Training schools (date)
Emergency contact (relation)	Professional license (type)	Training schools (field)
Emergency contact (address)	Professional license (date)	Training schools completed
Employee weight	Race	Transfer date
Employee number	Rehire code	Transfer reason
Employee code	Religious preference	Union code
Employee status	Salary points	Union deductions
Employee height	Salary compa ratio	United Way deductions
Employee date of death	Salary (previous)	Vacation leave available
Federal job code	Salary change date	Vacation leave used
Full-time/part-time code	Salary change reason	Veteran status

Reprinted by permission of the publisher from "A Matter of Privacy: Managing Personnel Data in Company Computers," Donald Harris, *Personnel*, February 1987, p. 37. © 1987 American Management Associations, New York. All rights reserved.

EXHIBIT 5A.4   Three Profiles of HRIS Development

	Profile One: Traditional, Central Mainframe	Profile Two: PC-Based, Distributed	Profile Three: Central Mainframe, End User Development Focus
System Development Dimensions			
1. Database(s) coverage	Comprehensive	Application specific	Comprehensive with local additions
2. Availability	Extensive, HR and non-HR users	Application specific, most HR business units	Extensive for HR users
3. Decision support	Focus on simpler, administrative decisions	Support range of HR decisions from simple to complex	Focus on simpler administrative decisions
4. Integration	Full	Stand alone	Relational
Organization Development Dimensions			
5. HR–IS bridges	HR manages HRIS, but IS influence high	HR controls HRIS	HR control HRIS, HR staff in units given HRIS duties
6. HR expectations	Low investments	High, informal investments	Very high, formal investments
7. HR knowledge	HR training specific to applications	HR training specific to applications; investment to bring in new skills	Across-the-board training, mostly required
8. HR–Org. technology links	Formal links, high investments in internal development	Informal links, moderate investments in vendors and internal development	Formal links, high investments in vendors

Source: Renae Broderick and John W. Boudreau, *Human Resource Automation for Competitive Advantage: Case Studies of Ten Leaders* (Ithaca, N.Y.: Center for Advanced Human Resource Studies, Working Paper no. 90-04, 1990).

plant), so the value of computerization is in being flexible enough to develop applications that units find valuable, even if they are not applicable to every other unit in the organization—or even if top management does not use them. The key is to provide very fast and customized support for specific unit-level needs. Therefore, organizations following this profile will construct many separate data bases, each one designed to support a particular application. Availability of systems is also application-specific, depending on which unit can use the application. The applications may simply process administrative information, but they can also be quite sophisticated in their ability to support decisions, depending on what the individual unit needs and is willing to pay for. These applications also stand alone and are not tied together in any centralized way. Organizationally, the HRIS staff controls and directs system de-

---

EXHIBIT 5A.5   Ten Most Common Mistakes in Developing a Computer-Based HRIS

---

1. Being all things to all people, all at once.
2. No personnel expertise on the project team.
3. Separate systems for each personnel activity.
4. Too much complexity.
5. Insufficient operating management support.
6. No participation in design.
7. Technical marvels, but not "user-oriented."
8. Loose design project control.
9. Promising savings that don't occur.
10. Building, when you can buy.

Source: A. J. Walker, "The 10 Most Common Mistakes in Developing Computer-Based Personnel Systems," *Personnel Administrator,* July 1980, pp. 39–42.

velopment, with only informal links to the organization's centralized IS technology. Profile Two organizations spend more resources managing the users' expectations and "selling" the value of the applications, and they also invest more in training than Profile One organizations.

Profile Three (Central Mainframe, End User Development Focus) is the most recent of the three profiles to emerge. This profile faces both a strong centralized HR executive group, as well as strong decentralized unit-level HR organizations. All of these HR users are well aware of computer technology and want support for both centralized administration (like Profile One) as well as unit-level customization (like Profile Two). Therefore, the data base has a comprehensive "core," with the ability to allow local units to add their own customized data. It is available to all HR users, but currently focuses on administrative decisions, because it is a new system. The different unit-level data bases are so "related" to the central data base that all the information is available to all users, even though different pieces of information may come from different unit data bases. Organizationally, there is very strong direction from HR executives, with the HRIS assignments becoming part of the standard career path for HR professionals. To be successful, Profile Three HRIS organizations must get support from all stakeholders, because they are trying to satisfy both corporate and unit-level managers. Therefore, they make high investments in enhancing the users' expectations of the system and in training them to use it. They also rely on the expertise of the organization's information systems experts. Profile Three HRIS organizations would not have been possible 10 years ago due to the limitations of computers. However, with technology advances, even Profile One and Profile Two organizations see themselves evolving toward the characteristics of Profile Three.

COMMON MISTAKES

Exhibit 5A.5 lists the 10 most common mistakes in installing computer-based HRISs, according to one leading consultant who installed them for over 15 years. Many of these mistakes parallel the dimensions listed in Exhibit 5A.4, and they reflect the general information value principles discussed earlier. It is important that HRISs provide value to users. This means knowing what computerized information users need to make better decisions, but it may also mean helping users see how they can use computers more effectively. Having top management support, requiring user participation in design, and making sure the system has the right amount of complexity and user orientation are all valuable ways to achieve this. As Exhibit 5A.4 shows, it is also important not to try to be all things to all people immediately. Even in Profile Three, the most successful organizations focused on achieving initial successes with applications that clearly solved important administrative issues and reduced costs.

THE ROLE OF PERSONAL COMPUTERS IN THE HRIS

PCs have definitely arrived in HR management. Hundreds of software programs exist to help HR managers be more effective and more are on the way. As PC technology becomes cheaper and more powerful, the number of feasible applications increases. Many organizations or units with less than 10,000 employees can store their entire HR data base on a PC. When PCs are combined with traditional mainframe computers, the power to use the advantages of both presents revolutionary possibilities. PCs are very good at graphic presentation of information, interactive data analysis, and providing a high degree of individual control of the analysis. Mainframe computers are good at storing, retrieving, and calculating large amounts of information, which tends to be very time consuming on a PC.

By including PCs in the HRIS design, organizations can provide a much more user-friendly environment. They can use technology such as touch-screens, voice-activated responses, telephone or cable connections between locations, scanning technology, and sophisticated graphics that make relationships clearer. Many experts forecast that the PC will become a central tool for all HR professionals in the future.[32] Leading universities have already incorporated PC training into their curriculum for future HR professionals.[33] The computer cases and software that are included with this book can give you hands-on experience with PCs and their role in personnel management.

THE ISSUE OF SECURITY AND PRIVACY

While the benefits of ready access to computerized HR information are often quite compelling, the advance of this technology creates new obligations and responsibilities for the HR professional. Much of the data stored on computerized systems is confidential and private and should be accessible only to approved individuals under controlled conditions. Controlling access is easier when the data reside on a mainframe system that requires having special programming skills to access. Easier data access means that even a novice computer user may be able to get information and combine it in ways no one anticipated. For example, information on marital status, medical claim history, and age might be used to identify potential AIDS victims. Because HR professionals increasingly lead the development of HRISs, they will undoubtedly be expected to shoulder the responsibility for achieving equity objectives by ensuring the privacy of individual information, and access to that information only by those with a legitimate need to know.[34]

NOTES AND REFERENCES

1. Renae L. Broderick and John W. Boudreau, "Making HR Automation Work: The Experience of 10 Industry Leaders," Working Paper no. 90-04, Center for Advanced Human Resource Studies, Cornell University, Ithaca, New York, 1990.

2. John M. Abowd, George T. Milkovich, and John M. Hannon, "Effects of Human Resource Management Decisions on Shareholder Value," Center for Advanced Human Resource Studies, Working Paper no. 89-20, 1989.

3. "Around the World of Work," *Work in America* 14, no. 10 (October 1989), p. 5.

4. G. E. Biles, "Auditing HRM Practices," *Personnel Administrator,* December 1986, pp. 89–93; G. E. Biles and Randall S. Schuler, *Audit Handbook of Human Resource Management Practices* (Alexandria, Va.: American Society for Personnel Administration); Walter R. Mahler, "Auditing PAIR," in *ASPA Handbook of Personnel and Industrial Relations,* ed. D. Yoder and H. Heneman, Jr. (Washington, D.C.: Bureau of National Affairs, 1979), pp. 2–103; Geneva Seybold, *Personnel Audits and Reports to Top Management,* Studies in Personnel Policy 191 (New York: The Conference Board, 1964).

5. Luis R. Gomez-Mejia, "Dimensions and Correlates of the Personnel Audit as an Organizational Assessment Tool," *Personnel Psychology* 38 (1985), pp. 293–308.

6. Jac Fitz-Enz, *How to Measure Human Resources Management* (New York: McGraw-Hill, 1980).

7. E. Flamholtz, "Replacement Cost as a Surrogate Measure of Human Resource Value: A Field Study" (AIS Working Paper no. 74–1, July 1973, mimeographed); E. Flamholtz, "Human Resource Accounting: Measuring Positional Replacement Costs," *Human Resource Management,* Spring 1972, pp. 8–16; Eric G. Flamholtz, *Human Resource Accounting,* 2nd ed. (San Francisco: Jossey-Bass, 1985); R. Likert, *The Human Organization: Its Management and Value* (New York: McGraw-Hill, 1967); R. Likert and D. G. Bowers, "Organizational Theory and Human Resource Accounting," *American Psychologist,* September 1969, pp. 585–92; James A. Craft, "Resource Accounting and Manpower Management: A Review and Assessment of Current Applicability," *Journal of Economics and Business* 1 (1980), pp. 42–50.

8. Henry L. Dahl, Jr., "Human Resource Cost and Benefit Analysis: New Power for Human Resource Approaches," *Human Resource Planning* 11, no. 2 (1988), pp. 69–76.

9. Martha Finney, "Profiles in Success: Fair Game," *Personnel Administrator,* February 1989, pp. 44–48.

10. Anne S. Tsui, "Defining the Activities and Effectiveness of the Human Resource Department: A Multiple Constituency Approach," *Human Resource Management* 26, no. 1 (Spring 1987), pp. 35–69; Terry Connelly, E. J. Conlon, and S. J. Deutsch, "A Multiple Constituency Approach of Organizational Effectiveness," *Academy of Management Review* 5, no. 2 (1980), pp. 211–18; Michael Keeley, "Impartiality and Participant-Interest Theories of Organizational Effectiveness," *Administration Science Quarterly* 29, no. 1 (1984), pp. 1–26; Michael Hitt, R. D. Ireland, B. W. Keats, and A. Vianna, "Measuring Subunit Effectiveness," *Decision Sciences,* January 1983, pp. 87–102; Michael Keeley, "A Social Justice Approach to Evaluation," *Administrative Science Quarterly,* June 1978, pp. 272–92; Anne S. Tsui, "A Tri-partite Approach to Research on Personnel Department Effectiveness," *Industrial Relations,* Spring 1984, pp. 188–97.

11. Burton, "Manpower Planning."

12. See Milkovich and Mahoney, "HRP and PAIR Policy."

13. Henry Dahl and K. S. Morgan, *Return on Investment in Human Resources* (Kalamazoo, Mich.: Upjohn Company report, 1982).

14. Marilyn Chase, "Ashton-Tate Is Cutting Its Work Force 15 Percent to 20 Percent, Predicting Wider Losses," *The Wall Street Journal,* August 16, 1989, p. B4; Vindu P. Goel, "Campbell Soup Plans to Cut 2,800 Jobs in Restructuring to Boost Efficiency," *The Wall Street Journal,* August 25, 1989, p. A3; G. Pascal Zachary and Richard B. Schmitt, "PC Price Battles Are Taking Toll on Businessland," *The Wall Street Journal,* January 11, 1990, p. B1.

15. Vetter, *Manpower Planning;* W. Rudelius, "Lagged Manpower Relationships in Development Projects," *IEEE Transactions on Engineering Management,* December 1976, pp. 188–95.

16. L. Dyer, "Human Resource Planning," in *Personnel Management,* ed. K. Rowland and G. Ferris (Boston: Allyn & Bacon, 1982), pp. 52–77; D. M. Atwater, E. S. Bres III, R. J. Niehaus, and J. A. Sheridan, "An Application of Integrated Human Resources Planning Supply-Demand Model," *Human Resource Planning* 5, no. 1 (1982), pp. 1–15; B. W. Holz and J. M. Wroth, "Improving Strengths Forecasts: Support for Army Manpower Management," *Interfaces* 10, no. 6 (1980), pp. 37–52; and J. R. Hinrichs and R. F. Morrison, "Human Resource Planning in Support of Research and Development," *Human Resource Planning* 3, no. 4 (1980), pp. 201–10.

17. R. G. Murdick and F. Schuster, "Computerized Information Support for the Human Resource Function," *Human Resource Planning* 6, no. 1 (1983), pp. 25–35.

18. Several references exist on this subject: the advanced reader is directed to R. C. Grinold and K. T. Marshall, *Manpower Planning Models* (New York: Elsevier North-Holland Publishing, 1977); D. J. Bartholomew, *Stochastic Models for Social Processes,* 2nd ed. (New York: John Wiley & Sons, 1973); and Harrison White, *Chains of Opportunity: System Models of Mobility in Organizations* (Cambridge, Mass.: Harvard University Press, 1970). Students new to this topic are directed to Thomas A. Mahoney, George T. Milkovich, and Nan Weiner, "A Stock and Flow Model for Improved Human Resources Measurement," *Personnel,* May–June 1977, pp. 57–66; and Victor H. Vroom and K. R. MacCrimmon, "Towards a Stochastic Model of Management Careers," *Administrative Science Quarterly,* June 1968, pp. 26–46; K. M. Rowland and M. G. Sovereign, "Markov-Chain Analysis of Internal Manpower Supply." *Industrial Relations* 9, no. 1 (1969), pp. 88–89; T. Mahoney and G. Milkovich, "Markov Chains and Manpower Forecasts," Office of Naval Research Technical Report NR 151–323–7002, 1970; and D. J. Bartholomew and A. R. Smith, eds., *Manpower and Management Science* (London: English University Press, 1970).

19. John W. Boudreau and George T. Milkovich, "User's Corner: Employment Planning Using the PC" *Computers in HR Management* 1, no. 5 (May 1990); John W. Boudreau and George T. Milkovich, *Personal Computer (PC) Exercises for Personnel/Human Resource Management* (Homewood, Ill.: Richard D. Irwin, 1988), chap. 4.

20. Several examples of application have been reported in the literature. See notes and references 18.

21. Niehaus, "Computer-Assisted Manpower Planning"; Mahoney and Milkovich, "Markov Chains and Manpower Forecasts"; Jackson F. Gillespie, Wayne E. Leininger, and Harvey Kahalas, "A Human Resource Planning and Valuation Model," *Academy of Management Journal,* December 1976, pp. 650–56; E. S. Bres III, R. J. Niehaus, A. P. Schinnar, and P. Steinbuch, "Efficiency Evaluation of EEO Program Management," *Human Resource Planning* 6, no. 4 (1983), pp. 223–47; F. Krzystofiak, "Estimating EEO Liability," *Decision Sciences* 2, no. 3 (1982), pp. 10–17; J. Ledvinka and R. L. LaForge, "A Staffing Model of Affirmative Action Planning," *Human Resource*

Planning, 1978, pp. 135–50; and G. Milkovich and F. Krzystofiak, "Simulation and Affirmative Action Planning," *Human Resource Planning* 2, no. 1 (1979), pp. 71–80.

22. Dyer, "Human Resource Planning."

23. Henry Dahl and K. S. Morgan, *Return on Investment in Human Resources* (Kalamazoo, Mich.: Upjohn Company report, 1982).

24. Wayne F. Cascio, *Costing Human Resources,* 2nd ed. (Boston: Kent, 1987).

25. John W. Boudreau, "Utility Analysis," chap. 1.4, in Lee D. Dyer, ed., *Human Resource Management Evolving Roles & Responsibilities* (Washington, D.C.: Bureau of National Affairs, 1988).

26. Anne S. Tsui and Luis R. Gomez-Mejia, "Evaluating Human Resource Effectiveness," chap. 1.5, in Lee D. Dyer, ed., *Human Resource Management Evolving Roles and Responsibilities* (Washington, D.C.: Bureau of National Affairs, 1988).

27. This definition is adapted from A. J. Walker, *HRIS Development* (New York: Van Nostrand Reinhold, 1982).

28. Sidney H. Simon, "The HRIS: What Capabilities Must It Have?" *Personnel,* September–October 1983, pp. 36–49.

29. Phillip Robinson, "TruScan and OnmiPage Offer Page-Recognition Capabilities for the Mac or AT," *BYTE,* May 1989, pp. 203–08.

30. Walker, *HRIS Development*; also see Lyman Seamans, Jr., "Establishing the Human Resource System Data Base," *Personnel Administrator,* November 1977, pp. 44–49; V. Ceriello, "A Guide for Building a Human Resource Data System," *Personnel Journal,* September 1978, pp. 496–503; Mary Jo Lavin, "HRDIS: A Computerized Human Resource Development Information System," *Human Resource Planning,* 14, no. 1 (1981), pp. 25–35; William B. Miller, "Building an Effective Information Systems Function," *MIS Quarterly,* June 1980, pp. 21–30.

31. Renae Broderick and John W. Boudreau, *Human Resource Automation for Competitive Advantage: Case Studies of Ten Leaders* (Ithaca, N.Y.: Center for Advanced Human Resource Studies, Working Paper no. 90-04, 1990).

32. For an excellent discussion of the future of PCs in HR management, see the special issue of *HR/PC,* "How Will PC Technology Affect Human Resources in the 1990's?", vol. 4.6, July 1–August 15, 1989.

33. John W. Boudreau, *Building a PC-Based Human Resource Management Curriculum at the School of Industrial and Labor Relations,* presented at the national meeting of the Industrial Relations Research Association, Atlanta, Ga., December 1989.

34. Donald Harris, "A Matter of Privacy: Managing Personal Data in Company Computers," *Personnel,* February 1987, pp. 34–43.

CHAPTER
SIX

Equal Employment Opportunity

The Need for Equal Employment
Opportunity (EEO)
Occupational Attainment
Earnings Gap

The Equal Pay Act
Definition of Equal
Factors Defining Equal Work

Title VII of the Civil Rights Act

Executive Order 11246

Age Discrimination in Employment Act

Vocational Rehabilitation Act and Americans
with Disabilities Act

Sexual Harassment

Evaluating EEO Performance
Work Force Analysis
Availability Analysis
Establish Goals
Programming to Achieve Goals

Settling Disputes

EEO in the 1990s
Reverse Discrimination
Proving Disparate Impact
The Civil Rights Act of 1990

Your Turn: Diane Joyce

After Diane Joyce had spent four years on the road crew for the Santa Clara (California) Transportation Agency, a notice for dispatcher was posted. Both Joyce and Paul Johnson applied at once.

There were two checkpoints to cross to get the job. The first was a 15-minute quiz on job duties. Applicants with the seven highest scores went on to an interview. Because the grades of the top seven candidates are generally so close, it is county hiring policy to consider all top seven equally qualified.

Next, three male road superintendents interviewed each of the seven candidates. They ranked Johnson first, Joyce third. Joyce had had previous run-ins with two of them. In court, one of them would later say he considered Joyce a "rebel-rousing, skirt-wearing person" and "not a lady."[1]

When rumors began circulating that Johnson had the job, Joyce called the affirmative action office. Her complaint reached James Graebner, the newly appointed director of the Santa Clara Transportation Agency. "What it boiled down to," says Graebner, "is we clearly needed to make some progress." He overruled the director of roads operations and gave the job to Joyce. She got the job as part of an affirmative action plan to achieve a work force that reflected the race and gender composition of the county's work force. Despite having a plan in place for years, the county had made little progress. The county had failed to hire women in virtually all of the higher-paying traditionally male jobs: mechanics, equipment operators, carpenters. On the other hand, women filled 90 percent of the clerical and secretarial slots, the lowest-paid positions.

When Joyce got the job, Johnson sued the county for reverse discrimination. The Justice Department sided with Johnson, alleging that hiring preferences could be used only by employers who admitted past discrimination. The county was not legally required to have an affirmative action plan, nor did it ever acknowledge any past discrimination. To give preference to people who were not personally victims of discrimination violated Title VII of the Civil Rights Act, according to Johnson and the Justice Department.

But the Supreme Court rejected this view. Title VII does outlaw discrimination on the basis of sex or race. But giving preference to women and minorities to integrate previously segregated job categories is legel.

In light of the fact that none of the county's 238 skilled jobs were held by women, the county's action was justified and did not constitute reverse discrimination.

Legal rights of various employees can conflict, and many of these conflicts involve EEO. For instance, Memphis's contract with its fire-fighters' union specified promotions and layoffs based on seniority. In a court-ordered consent decree, the city also agreed to an affirmative action plan for minority employees. When budgetary problems forced layoffs, however, the affirmative action decree and the union contract were in conflict. A district court ordered the city to keep less senior minorities on the staff, so whites with greater seniority were laid off. This action was consistent with the affirmative action decree but not with the union contract. The Supreme Court ruled that, in this case, the seniority system could *not* be ignored.[2] Unless minorities could prove they had been actual victims of discrimination, seniority rights prevailed over affirmative action in layoffs.

These cases reflect how complex managing equal employment opportunity (EEO) and affirmative action (AA) is today. They are part of a stream of cases beginning in the 1960s, in which the courts and the country explored how equal opportunity and affirmative action should be implemented. As we saw in the previous chapter, planning is an important part of the human resource management process (HRM). Planning for EEO is an important activity in all organizations, because EEO influences every HR activity. Every HR activity must be evaluated for its EEO implications.

THE NEED FOR EQUAL EMPLOYMENT OPPORTUNITY (EEO)

The Civil Rights Act of 1964 became law almost three decades ago. In the 1960s, most employers and unions ignored EEO legislation. No one was quite sure how it would be enforced or how it would affect personnel practices.[3] Equal employment opportunity seemed to direct managers to prepare minorities and women to take advantage of job opportunities and to remove the informal barriers which prevented them from doing so. This approach focused on good faith efforts.

The 1970s saw the emphasis shift to affirmative action policies requiring a proactive approach: seeking out minorities and women to actively and affirmatively share job opportunities. Agencies argued that affirmative efforts were necessary to overcome past discrimination.

Affirmative action is the activities employers use to ensure that current decisions and practices enhance the employment, upgrading, and retention of minorities and women. Such actions go beyond refraining from practices that discriminate. They include positive steps to seek out, encourage, and prepare minorities and women to take advantage of job opportunities.

By the late 70s, most employers and unions were sensitive to their roles in achieving equal employment opportunity. The change in employers' and unions' approaches to EEO was due to many factors. Employers recognized that huge supplies of skilled, talented people had been systematically excluded from employment opportunities. These underutilized people represented wasted human resources. There was also a growing awareness of how costly discriminatory practices could be—not only in back-pay awards, but also in the loss of government contracts and poor public relations.[4] Nothing rivets corporate attention like a multimillion dollar lawsuit!

The 80s brought an increasing awareness of conflicting claims between those seeking jobs and promotions and those with seniority-based claims. Court orders prescribing promotions and entrance to training programs for minorities frequently conflicted with seniority-based systems.[5] Reductions in work force in reverse order of hire, which favored seniority, were likely to result in layoffs of recently hired minorities, thus negating the effects of affirmative action plans. In the 90s, new legislation has been passed directing employers to take greater steps to assist those with disabilities to become fully employed. So, as a society, our sense of what is equal treatment and who is entitled to it continues to expand. There is not always agreement on whose claims take precedence, particularly in the workplace.[6]

Although EEO and affirmative action are accepted and progress has been made, signs of inequality persist, particularly in occupational attainment and earnings.

Occupational Attainment

The distribution of ethnic and gender groups among occupations remains uneven, with women concentrated in clerical jobs and blacks and Hispanics in semiskilled and unskilled occupations.[7] Exhibit 6.1 shows the uneven occupational attainment. In 1989, 28 percent of working women worked in clerical (administrative support) occupations, and over half of all blacks and Hispanics were in semiskilled and unskilled occupations. Compare these data to the distribution of all employees—fewer than one fifth in clerical and one third in semiskilled and unskilled occupations. However, there has been a marked change in some occupations. For example, in 1970, 30 percent of insurance adjusters were women, compared to 60 percent in 1980. Exhibit 6.2 shows some of the change in occupational attainment for women over a 10-year period.

Earnings Gap

Not only are the races and sexes unevenly distributed among occupations but there is also a gap in their earnings.[8] The median weekly earnings of women working full time in 1989 is approximately 70 percent of men's.[9] This gap exists for black and Hispanic men and women, too. Even in traditionally female occupations, such as clerical, men's earnings have been consistently higher than women's. Among blacks, the earnings gap between women and men is narrowing. In 1955, black women earned about 55 percent of what black men made, while in 1980 they earned 74 percent as much as black males. Despite this gain, black women remain at the bottom of the earnings scale. Even though black men have made progress in narrowing the gap between their earnings and those

EXHIBIT 6.1 Employment Distribution of Gender and Racial Groups among Jobs

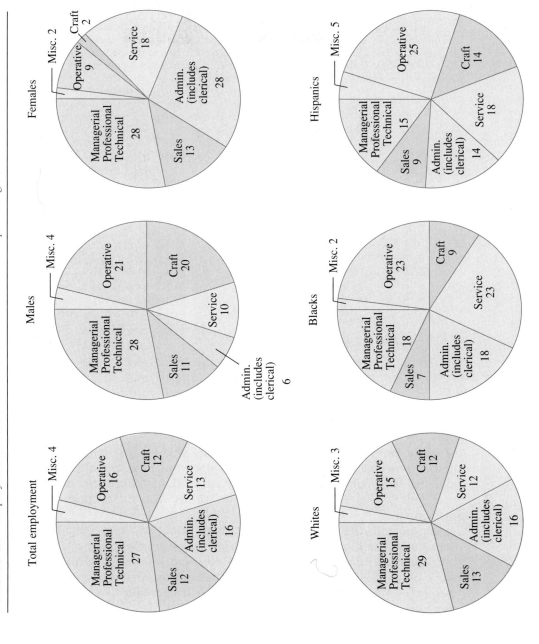

Total employment

Managerial Professional Technical 27
Sales 12
Admin. (includes clerical) 16
Service 13
Craft 12
Operative 16
Misc. 4

Males

Managerial Professional Technical 28
Sales 11
Admin. (includes clerical)
Service 10
Craft 20
Operative 21
Misc. 4

Females

Managerial Professional Technical 28
Sales 13
Admin. (includes clerical) 28
Service 18
Craft 2
Operative 9
Misc. 2

Whites

Managerial Professional Technical 29
Sales 13
Admin. (includes clerical) 16
Service 12
Craft 12
Operative 15
Misc. 3

Blacks

Managerial Professional Technical 18
Sales 7
Admin. (includes clerical) 18
Service 23
Craft 9
Operative 23
Misc. 2

Hispanics

Managerial Professional Technical 15
Sales 9
Admin. (includes clerical) 14
Service 18
Craft 14
Operative 25
Misc. 5

6

EXHIBIT 6.2   A Pink-Collar Ghetto?

This chart shows the percentage of women in some traditionally male-dominated occupations. The jobs are ones in which the number of women employees increased dramatically between 1970 and 1980. A male occupation is defined as one with less than 40 percent females in 1970. A disproportionate increase is 9.2 percent, or twice women's increased representation in the labor force as a whole.

	1970	1980	Change in %
Wholesale and retail trade buyers, except farm products	27.8%	44.5%	16.7%
Operations and systems researchers and analysis	11.1	27.7	16.6
Public relations specialists	26.6	48.8	22.2
Advertising and related sales occupations	20.5	41.6	21.1
News vendors	17.1	33.3	16.2
Computer operators	33.9	59.1	25.2
Dispatchers	14.6	31.5	16.9
Production coordinators	20.2	44.4	24.2
Expediters	35.4	54.1	18.7
Insurance adjusters, examiners, and investigators	29.6	60.2	30.6
Bartenders	21.2	44.3	23.1
Bakers	25.4	40.7	15.3
Typesetters and compositors	16.8	55.7	38.9
Bus drivers	28.3	45.8	17.5

---

of white males, the percent of black males who are participating in the labor market has declined substantially. This drop has occurred at all age and educational levels. In fact, a 1989 report states that, "Since the early 1970s, the economic status of blacks relative to whites has, on average, stagnated or deteriorated."[10]

We cannot attribute the fact that there is not an equal distribution among occupations and wages solely to discriminatory personnel practices. Other factors, such as educational attainment, personal interests and preferences, and work patterns, also play a role. Nevertheless, the existence of differences creates pressures in society for change. One instrument for this change is to ensure that personnel decisions do not discriminate.

On the face of it, equal employment opportunity and discrimination seem so simple and intuitive that their definitions would be obvious to all. Yet considering the enormous volume of regulatory paperwork and the continuing litiga-

EXHIBIT 6.3 Employment Discrimination Legislation

Law	Prohibits	Covers
Equal Pay Act of 1963	Sex differences in pay for substantially equal work.	Private employers (state and local governments uncertain).
Title VII of the 1964 Civil Rights Act	Discrimination or segregation based on race, color, religion, sex, or national origin.	Private employers with 15 or more employees; federal, state, and local governments; unions and apprenticeship committees; employment agencies.
Executive Orders 11246 and 11375 (1965)	Discrimination based on race, color, religion, sex, or national origin (affirmative action required).	Federal contractors and subcontractors.
Executive Order 11478 (1969)	Discrimination based on race, color, religion, sex, national origin, political affiliation, marital status, or physical handicap.	Federal government.
Age Discrimination in Employment Act of 1967	Discrimination against employees age 40 and over.	Private employers with 20 or more employees, unions with 25 or more members, employment agencies, apprenticeship and training programs (state and local governments uncertain).
Rehabilitation Act of 1973; Executive Order No. 11914 (1974)	Discrimination based on physical or mental handicap (affirmative action required).	Federal contractors, federal government.
Vietnam-era Veterans Readjustment Act of 1974	Discrimination against disabled veterans and Vietnam-era veterans (affirmative action required).	Federal contractors, federal government.
Americans with Disabilities Act of 1990	Discrimination against disabled persons qualified to perform the essential elements of a job.	Takes effect in 1992 for employers with 25 or more employees. In 1994, covers employers with 15 or more employees.
State laws	Similar to Title VII.	Vary by state; passed in about 85 percent of states.

tion, these concepts are anything but simple in the real world. In fact, the Civil Rights Act provided no definition for discrimination, leaving the task to courts and regulatory agencies.

Exhibit 6.3 gives a brief description of some of the U.S. laws and executive orders that prohibit discrimination. Groups protected by EEO legislation include women, blacks, Hispanics, American Indians, Pacific Islanders, people age 40 and over, the handicapped, and veterans. Understanding these laws is a necessary part of managing human resources.

THE EQUAL PAY ACT

Passed after nearly two years of congressional debate, the Equal Pay Act (EPA) forbids wage discrimination:

> between employees on the basis of sex when employees perform equal work on jobs in the same establishment requiring equal skill, effort, and responsibility and performed under similar working conditions. . . . Pay differences between equal jobs can be justified when that differential is based on (1) a seniority system; (2) a merit system; (3) a system measuring earnings by quality or quantity of production; or (4) any factor other than sex.

Thus, the EPA embodies for women the "equal work" definition of pay discrimination. Pay discrimination against minorities is covered under Title VII. In fact, both women and minorities can bring suit over pay discrimination under Title VII. Equal work is defined by *four factors:* (1) equal skill, (2) equal effort, (3) equal responsibility, and (4) equal working conditions. However, the EPA permits pay differences between men and women engaged in equal work if there are also differences (1) in seniority, (2) in quality of performance, (3) in quality or quantity of production, or (4) some factor other than sex.

Although the definition of equal work contained in the Equal Pay Act and the exceptions are relatively specific, numerous cases have required the courts to interpret the law. Some important issues raised include:

+ How equal is equal?
+ What is meant by equal skill, effort, responsibility, and working conditions?

Definition of Equal

Schultz v. *Wheaton Glass Company* provided some guidelines to define equal work in 1970.[11] Wheaton Glass Company maintained male and female job classifications for selector packers in its production department. The female job class carried a pay rate 10 percent below that of the male job class. The company claimed that the male job class included additional tasks that justified the pay differential, such as shoveling broken glass, opening warehouse doors, and doing heavy lifting. The plaintiff claimed that the extra tasks were infrequently performed, and not all men did them. Did the additional tasks performed by some members of one job class render the jobs unequal? The court decided not, and ruled that the equal work standard required only that jobs be *substantially* equal, not identical. The extra duties performed by some of the men did not justify paying all of the men 10 percent more than the women. The concept "equal pay for substantially equal work" has been recognized in cases following *Schultz* v. *Wheaton Glass Company*.

Factors Defining Equal Work

The Department of Labor provides these definitions of the four factors that define equal work.

Skill—Experience, training, education, and ability as measured by the performance requirements of a particular job.

Effort—(Mental or physical) the amount or degree of effort, not type of effort, actually expended in the performance of a job.

Responsibility—The degree of accountability required in the performance of a job.

Working conditions—The physical surroundings and hazards of a job, including dimensions such as inside versus outside work, heat, cold, poor ventilation.

The courts have consistently held that overall time, effort, or skill required must be substantially greater in one of the jobs to support any claim of unequal work, and that all of the higher-paid workers must actually perform the additional tasks to justify any pay differential. Hence, any system of valuing jobs must specify these distinctions. We return to the discussion of pay discrimination and the idea of equal pay for jobs of "comparable" value (as contrasted with *substantially similar*) in the chapters about compensation.

TITLE VII OF THE CIVIL RIGHTS ACT OF 1964

Title VII prohibits discrimination on the basis of sex, race, color, religion, or national origin in any employment condition, including hiring, firing, promotion, transfer, compensation, and admission to training programs.[12] Title VII was amended in 1972 and 1978. The 1972 amendments strengthened enforcement and expanded coverage to include employees of government and educational institutions, as well as private employers of more than 15 persons. The pregnancy amendment of 1978 made it illegal to discriminate because of pregnancy, childbirth, or related conditions.[13]

Defining Discrimination

Since 1964 the courts have ruled that several different behaviors by employers and unions are unlawful under Title VII. These fall into two basic behaviors: disparate treatment and disparate impact. Exhibit 6.4 contrasts the two behaviors.[14]

Disparate Treatment

Personnel practices that treat protected group members less favorably than others constitute disparate treatment. A practice is unlawful if it applies different or unequal standards to different employees; for example, rejecting female but not male job applicants who have school-age children.

EXHIBIT 6.4   Discriminatory Behavior

Disparate Treatment	Disparate Impact
Different standards for different individuals or groups.	Same standards have differing consequences.
Impact on individual claimants, not classwide.	Impact is classwide on all similarly situated employees.
Intent to discriminate may be inferred.	Discriminatory intent need not be present.
Group statistics not useful.	General statistical impact of specific practice may show discrimination.
Individual actions scrutinized.	Business practices, not individual actions, examined.

However, simply prohibiting disparate treatment does not ensure that the results for all groups will be equal. Even though many common job requirements are applied to all groups equally, they may have adverse impact on certain groups. For example, some blacks may be less able to meet educational requirements for employment—even if those requirements have no relationship to the job in question. Permitting such requirements to exist threatened to leave blacks and other minorities in the same disadvantaged status that prevailed prior to Title VII. Thus, courts and government agencies adopted a more stringent definition of discrimination—disparate impact.

Disparate Impact

Personnel practices that have a differential *effect* on certain groups are illegal, unless the differences can be justified as necessary to the safe and efficient operation of the business, or are work-related. The major case which established this interpretation of Title VII is *Griggs* v. *Duke Power Company*. In this case, the court struck down employment tests and educational requirements that screened out a greater proportion of blacks than whites. The requirements in question were that applicants be high school graduates and score above a certain level on a general intelligence test. The requirements were imposed "on the Company's judgment that they generally would improve the overall quality of the work force." But the court concluded that:

> The evidence shows that employees who have not completed high school or taken the tests have continued to perform satisfactorily and make progress in departments for which the high school and test criteria are now used. The promotion record of present employees who would not be able to meet the new criteria thus suggests the possibility that the requirements may not be needed. . . .
>
> Good intent or absence of discriminatory intent does not redeem employment procedures or testing mechanisms that operate as "built-in headwinds" for minority groups and are unrelated to measuring job capacity.[15]

The standards were certainly applied equally: both white and blacks had to pass them. The practices were prohibited, because (1) they had the consequence of excluding blacks in greater number than whites and (2) they were not related to the jobs in question.

The unequal impact definition is important to managers, because many traditional personnel practices have a built-in unequal impact. Examples are numerous: the minimum height and weight requirements of many police departments tended to screen out women, Orientals, and Hispanics disproportionately. Such requirements have been struck down by the courts. The same is true of automatically rejecting job applicants with arrest records or even criminal records.

The unequal impact definition differs from the unequal treatment definition. Under unequal or disparate impact, whether or not the employer intended to discriminate is irrelevant. A personnel practice can *seem* neutral; but if the results of it are unequal, as shown through statistical analysis, the employer must demonstrate that there is a legitimate business reason for the decision.

The courts have also ruled that every single step of the hiring/promotion process must be job-related if the process has disparate impact. In *Connecticut v. Teal,* the employer had used a multi-stage promotion process.[16] Applicants provisionally promoted to supervisory positions had to pass written tests and receive satisfactory performance ratings and supervisor recommendations to receive permanent promotion to the positions. Failure to pass the test precluded an applicant from further consideration, no matter how outstanding the work record may have been. When blacks failed the test in greater proportions than whites, the employer applied an affirmative action program so the net outcome of the promotion process was more favorable to blacks than to whites. But the Court said this bottom-line result did not protect the employer from charges of discrimination at an earlier stage of the process.

Even if the final outcome of the promotion process was equal for all protected groups, if one stage of the process has disparate impact, that stage must be shown to be job-related.

In 1989, the courts refined the procedures on using statistical comparisons to show disparate impact. The case involved the Wards Cove Packing Company, an Alaskan cannery.[17] Jobs at the cannery are of two general types: unskilled jobs on the cannery line, filled predominantly by nonwhites, and noncannery jobs, mostly classified as skilled positions, and filled predominantly with white workers. The nonwhite cannery workers pointed out the statistical discrepancy between the racial composition of the cannery line workers and the noncannery line workers, and charged that the employer's hiring and employment practices led to this racial stratification. The company responded that its practices were racially neutral, and that the reason for the stratification was because cannery-line jobs were filled under a hiring agreement with a predominantly nonwhite union. Therefore, a valid business reason existed.

The Supreme Court held that merely demonstrating a statistical disparity between the two groups of workers did not constitute proof of disparate impact, for two reasons. First, because the cannery and noncannery jobs differ, it makes no sense to assume that the racial composition of the group of people interested in one group of job would be the same as people interested in the other group of jobs. (Dissenters pointed out that since all the jobs were seasonal and in a remote area of Alaska, it made less sense to assume that the two groups of people available would be as racially segregated as the Wards Cove work force.) Second, identifying several *likely* causes of the racial stratification is insufficient. Plaintiffs had charged that the lack of minorities in the skilled jobs was the result of cronyism, nepotism, and a failure to promote from within. Instead, the Court held that plaintiffs must specify which employment practice had the adverse impact and "link causally" that practice with the resulting racial imbalance. In response to this ruling, legislators have introduced the Civil Rights Act of 1990, which is discussed in detail at the end of this chapter.

Exceptions to Title VII

Several specific exceptions to the definitions of discrimination have emerged from the courts' interpretations of Title VII. Among these are work-related requirements, bona fide occupational qualifications, seniority systems, and preferential quota systems.

Job-Related

Even if an employment practice has disparate impact on the groups covered by Title VII, an employer can successfully defend its use by showing that it is job-related. It may sound easy for a company to show that its practices are job-related—if they were not, why would the company continue to use them? In fact, employers have had a difficult time defending their practices in court. Courts have held employers to a very demanding standard of job-relatedness. For example, the U.S. Supreme Court has said that employers wishing to defend tests that have unequal impact must follow the *Uniform Guidelines on Employee Selection,* issued by the Equal Employment Opportunity Commission.[18] The guidelines require the employer to undertake extensive, expensive research.

Nevertheless, if an employment practice serves a legitimate need, and if there is no alternative that has less of an adverse impact, it may be worthwhile for the organization to try to defend that practice. While the Wards Cove case may appear to ease the standard that employers must meet, it is still not yet clear what the courts will consider legitimate.

Bona fide occupational qualifications (BFOQ)

In circumstances where race, religion, gender, color, or national origin is "reasonably necessary to the normal operations of the particular business or enterprise," such factors may be used in employment decisions. In the late 1960s and early 70s, state laws protected women from certain occupations considered in earlier periods to be too dangerous, too dirty, or inconvenient. But the courts (*Rosenfeld* v. *Southern Pacific*) decided these "protective laws" were in conflict with Title VII and thus null and void.[19] Some employers also thought that BFOQ exceptions precluded hiring men for jobs that women supposedly performed better. The most celebrated example of this reasoning was the *Diaz* v. *Pan American Airways* decision, in which the court ruled that an airline could not limit its employment of flight attendants to women.[20] At the time, the idea of a male flight attendant was unheard of but the court ruled against the airline.

A current application of BFOQ is being reviewed by the Supreme Court. At Johnson Controls, women who are capable of bearing children are not permitted to use chemicals that have been linked to birth defects. These chemicals have no known harmful effects on adults. Critics of the policy say it bars women from higher-paying jobs and is another example of protective legislation that does economic harm to women. Johnson Controls alleges that no safer technology exists.

BFOQ is still recognized in cases of age discrimination, especially where public safety is involved. For example, it is legal to set an upper age limit for admission to police, fire-fighting, and bus driver training programs. But gender, race, or religion as a BFOQ is not very common.

Seniority System Exception

To be considered bona fide, a seniority system must have a nondiscriminatory purpose behind its creation. So long as a seniority system was not conceived out of an intent to discriminate, it is not unlawful under Title VII, even though it may result in restrictions of employment opportunities. As we saw in the Memphis fire-fighter's case, sometimes a seniority system can have unequal impact. If blacks were not hired into an employer's work force until recently, a seniority system that bases promotions on seniority would have an unequal impact on black promotions, and one that bases layoffs on a "last hired, first fired" rule would adversely affect black employment when the work force is reduced.[21]

But the Supreme Court ruled that an employer may not be ordered to ignore a seniority system when making layoffs, even if the effect will be to reduce the number of women or minorities hired under a court-mandated affirmative action plan.[22]

Preferential-Quota System Exception

Preferential treatment systems set aside a portion of opportunities for groups who have been discriminated against. The objective is to overcome the long history of discrimination that has relegated certain groups to a lower-economic status. The systems do so by instituting employment preferences for members of such groups. For example, a specific share (say, 20 percent) of openings in a training program may be set aside for minorities or women.

Quota systems are a source of controversy. However, the U.S. Supreme Court has consistently ruled that employers can voluntarily give *temporary* preference to qualified members of underrepresented protected groups. In the first such case, *Weber* v. *Kaiser Aluminum and Chemicals,* an employer and union had collectively bargained access to an in-plant training program that was required to attain higher-paying jobs. Separate lists of black and white workers eligible to receive the training were maintained. Fifty percent of the openings in the training program were reserved for blacks. The result was that qualified blacks experienced shorter waits for training than qualified whites. The court ruled such a plan was legal, noting that

> the plan does not unnecessarily trammel the interests of the white employees. The plan does not require the discharge of white workers and their replacement with new black hires. . . . Nor does the plan create an absolute bar to the advancement of white employees; half of those trained in the program will be white. Moreover, the plan is a temporary measure; it is not intended to maintain racial balance, but simply to eliminate a manifest racial imbalance. Preferential selection of craft trainees at the plant will end as soon as the percentage of black skilled craft workers in the plant approximates the percentage of blacks in the local labor force.[23]

Additional cases since *Weber,* including the *Johnson* case discussed in the beginning of this chapter, have upheld affirmative action plans, providing they are "narrowly tailored" to correct serious imbalances among race and sex groups in a comparison to their availability.

The importance of being "narrowly tailored" cannot be overemphasized. In 1989, the Supreme Court struck down a Richmond, Virginia, program that set aside 30 percent of public construction funds for minority business enterprises, on the grounds that the city had not laid the proper groundwork for such a rigid approach.[24] The city had not identified or documented any discrimination suffered by particular groups; therefore, their program could not have been designed to remedy any specific discrimination. Before using rigid numerical goals, an employer must show that other, more race-neutral remedies would not be sufficient to correct the effects of past discrimination.

Thus, Title VII permits unequal impact of personnel decisions if the practice is legitimately job-related or is defensible as a bona fide occupational qualification, as the result of a seniority system, or as a preferential quota system designed to overcome past discrimination.

EXECUTIVE ORDER 11246

Executive Order 11246 requires that all firms with government contracts of $100,000 or more and 100 or more employees must agree not to discriminate and to take affirmative action to ensure equal opportunity in employment. While Executive Order 11246 was the original source of the concept of affirmative action, many employers voluntarily act affirmatively to rectify the effects of past practices, or to anticipate and avoid future problems. We shall discuss specific affirmative action plans later in this chapter.

AGE DISCRIMINATION IN EMPLOYMENT ACT

Organization downsizing resulting in layoffs and the early retirement of older workers has increased interest in age discrimination. In recent years, age discrimination complaints have grown at a faster rate than any other discrimination issue. Congress enacted the Age Discrimination in Employment Act (ADEA) in 1967 to protect persons between the ages of 40 and 70 against arbitrary discrimination in employment practices. A subsequent amendment which took effect in 1987 removed the upper age boundary. ADEA's prohibitions are similar to those of Title VII. Its purpose is to promote employment of older persons on their ability, rather than age; to prohibit arbitrary age discrimination in employment; to help employers and workers find ways of meeting problems arising from the impact of age on employment. The law forbids:

◆ Mandatory retirement based on age (with the exception of fire fighters, police officers, and tenured professors).

◆ Limiting or classifying employees in any way that would adversely affect their status because of age.

◆ Reducing any employee's wage rate to comply with the act.

◆ Discriminating in compensation or terms of employment because of age.

Public safety employees (police and fire fighters) are exempt from the law until 1994. The exemption provides time to study whether tests can be developed to adequately evaluate job-related mental or physical fitness. If such tests are feasible, then these measures would be used in lieu of age to evaluate individual qualifications to continue work.

Practices which would otherwise be prohibited are permissible if (1) age is a bona fide occupational qualification, (2) the differentiation is on reasonable other factors than age, (3) the employer is observing a bona fide seniority or benefit plan, (4) the employer is disciplining or discharging an employee for just cause, or (5) the employee is a top executive or policymaker.

Employers face a particularly complex set of issues in attempting to diagnose age discrimination. For example, when promotion rates of older and younger workers are compared, older workers tend to have lower rates. This may be due to differences in job opportunities available—older, more senior workers tend to be in higher-level positions where fewer promotion possibilities exist. Or, older workers may have reached a job level that matches their competence. Or, there may, indeed, be age discrimination.

ADEA is discussed again in the chapter on benefits, because it has implications for early retirement and pension plans.

VOCATIONAL REHABILITATION ACT AND AMERICANS WITH DISABILITIES ACT

The Rehabilitation Act of 1973 prohibits discrimination on the basis of physical or mental disability. Employers with federal contracts of over $2,500 are required to take affirmative action for the employment and promotion of qualified handicapped individuals. The Americans with Disabilities Act (1990) extends these prohibitions to all employers with 25 or more employees, effective in 1992. In 1994, the law becomes effective for all employers with 15 or more employees.

In many ways, these laws are similar to Title VII—but there are significant differences. One major difference is that affirmative action plans for the disabled, unlike those for women and minority groups, need not set specific numerical hiring goals based on population figures. A second important difference is that, although neither plan requires the hiring of unqualified workers, employers must take steps to reasonably accommodate workers with disabilities so they can hold jobs they otherwise could not perform. Reasonable accommodation may include redesigning jobs, constructing ramps, installing phones with special adaptations, installing elevators to all floors, and examining training and promotion opportunities for jobs from which the disabled may have been excluded but for which they are qualified. Because the Americans with Disabilities Act is so new, a lot of uncertainty exists over its enforcement. The law states that disabled people must be considered for employment if they can perform the essential elements of a job, but it is not yet clear who will decide what is and is not an essential element in a job and what degree of accommodation is required.

The appropriate treatment of employees with acquired immunodeficiency syndrome (AIDS) is another contemporary issue. Experts advise employers to treat AIDS as an employee disability and to avoid discriminating against employees who have the disease. Other protective measures include training supervisors about the company's position on the issue, reviewing related policies on personal leave, disability plans, and health insurance for consistency with the policy on AIDS and reviewing safety procedures in such settings as hospital laboratories where a risk of exposure may exist. Chapter Fifteen, Employee Relations, contains further discussion of this sensitive topic.

SEXUAL HARASSMENT

Government agencies issue a variety of guidelines intended to interpret the equal employment opportunity law and executive orders. These guidelines are frequently the subject of considerable interest and controversy, because they are the rules used to implement the law's intent. One example of federal guidelines deals with sexual harassment as a violation of Title VII of the Civil Rights

Act. These guidelines hold that the employer is responsible for the actions of its employees.

According to the guidelines, sexual harassment can take many forms, which involve verbal or nonverbal behavior that is subtle and therefore difficult to recognize. While no conscious intent to harass may be involved, behavior acceptable in a social setting may be inappropriate in the workplace. Under these guidelines, an employer is liable for the sexual harassment acts of its supervisors and agents "regardless of whether the specific acts complained of were authorized or even forbidden by the employer and regardless of whether the employer knew or should have known of their occurrence."[25] However, an employer can reduce liability by having a well-defined and publicized policy forbidding harassment and by following up immediately on complaints.

Two categories of sexual harassment claims exist: *quid pro quo harassment,* where an employee is forced to choose between giving in to a superior's sexual demands or forfeiting an economic benefit (pay increase, promotion, continued employment), and *hostile environment,* where sexual conduct unreasonably interferes with an individual's performance or creates an intimidating, hostile, or offensive working environment.

Saying that an employee suffered no economic loss, or that an employer was unaware of the harassment, is no defense against charges of hostile environment. If the conduct is unwelcome, and occurs with sufficient frequency to create an abusive work environment (i.e., is not an isolated incident) then the employer is responsible for changing the environment by warning, reprimanding, and even firing the harasser.

A nonprofit organization that helps women obtain and keep jobs in the coal mining industry offers the advice in Exhibit 6.5 to those who feel they are victims of harassment. Harassment is discussed again in Chapter 15.

EVALUATING EEO PERFORMANCE

Every major human resource activity (staffing, compensation, training, labor relations) needs to be evaluted for its EEO implications. Here, however, we discuss how to evaluate only the overall employment patterns of an organization. We examine the EEO implications for specific human resource activities in the appropriate chapters.

EEO analysis has four steps:

1. *Analyze the work force* to determine representation (percentage) of minorities and women in each job group in the organization.
2. *Analyze availability* in the relevant labor force to determine the proportion of minorities and women qualified and interested in the job opportunities.
3. *Establish EEO goals* by comparing the present work force to availability. Goals are the percentages of job opportunities to be shared with women

---

EXHIBIT 6.5

If You Are Being Harassed . . .

1. DON'T QUIT YOUR JOB. It won't solve anything, and you'll be out of a paycheck. Quitting may also work against you if you file an EEOC complaint, for the company will be under no pressure to negotiate. If the harassment intensifies because of your complaint, that only strengthens your case.

2. ACT QUICKLY. The best defense to harassment is a strong offense. Confront the harasser. Tell him his behavior is offensive to you, and ask him to stop.

3. GET SUPPORT FROM YOUR CO-WORKERS. Make sure the men and women who work with you are aware of the situation and your efforts to remedy it. Many men find sexual harassment as offensive as women.

4. RIDICULE THE HARASSER. Public exposure of sexual harassment can be the most effective way of stopping it. You may ask the harasser, "Does it make you feel like a big man to pick on a woman?" Or, "Do you speak to your wife like that? Maybe I'll have to call her and ask."

5. USE YOUR UNION GRIEVANCE PROCEDURE. Union women have more protection than their nonunion sisters, under an antidiscrimination clause that is part of most contracts. Contact your union representative immediately and consider filing a grievance.

6. NOTIFY THE COMPANY, whether your harasser is a supervisor or a co-worker. If you don't, your employer can claim ignorance and deny responsibility for the behavior. Put it in writing, and keep a copy!

7. KEEP A DIARY. Indicate dates, times, names of witnesses. Write exact quotes, if possible. The more evidence, the better.

8. FIND OTHER VICTIMS If you can build evidence that the harasser has abused other women, or that harassment has been condoned by management, your case will be strengthened.

Source: Marat Moore and Connie White, *Sexual Harassment in the Mines* (Oak Ridge, Tenn.: Coal Employment Project, no date).

and minorities to increase their representation in jobs in which they are underrepresented, where their percentage in a job is less than their percentage in the relevant availability.

4. *Prepare EEO programs* specifying how the EEO goals are to be achieved and a proposed timetable for achievement.

Work Force Analysis

The EEO work force analysis is relatively straightforward and objective. It simply involves determining representation rates, the proportions of employees in each job group of each gender who are members of various racial groups. Work force analysis may also focus on how employees flow into and through the organization by calculating hiring and promotion rates, the percentage of each protected group hired or promoted into specific job groups. Exhibit 6.6 shows part of legally required EEO form used as part of this analysis.

If certain employee groups are scarce in a group of jobs, such as in the Santa Clara Transportation Agency's laborers, drivers, and dispatchers, or in the Ward Cove noncannery line employees, what does this tell us? How great is the extent of any underrepresentation? What should the gender and race composition have been? The answer is found in availability analysis.

Availability Analysis

Availability analysis determines the proportions of employees in the relevant labor force who are members of various protected groups and who are *qualified* and *interested* in specific job opportunities.[26] Availability is the standard against which actual representation, hiring, and promotion rates are compared for evidence of discrimination. The availability of specific skills in each race and gender category is presumed to reflect approximately what the race and gender composition of the employer's work force would be were it not for discrimination.

In the Wards Cove case mentioned previously, plaintiffs used the racial composition of the cannery workers as the standard for determining what the racial composition of the noncannery workers should be. But the Supreme Court found that this comparison did not constitute proof of disparate impact. The cannery work force did not represent the pool of qualified applicants or the qualified population in the external work force—the relevant labor market—for noncannery jobs.

Determining availability involves considerable judgment. Hence, the results are open to controversy. Data provided by the Bureau of the Census are often too broad and, typically, only serve as a starting point. Further refinements may be based on geographical factors (commuting patterns), information on enrollments in local trade schools or other training institutions, or any other factors that appear to affect the supply of labor. Availabilities are merely estimates.

Measuring Availability

Exhibit 6.7 gives some alternative measures of availability and the assumptions that underlie each measure. Let us use the job of arc welding at the Boeing plant in Seattle, Washington, as an example. Not everyone in the entire U.S. population, the first category in the exhibit, is qualified to be an arc welder in the aircraft industry, nor is the entire civilian labor force, the second category. So we narrow the relevant availability to those qualified. But all those qualified may not be available or interested—some may already be employed, others may live too far away and not wish to relocate. The next step may be to narrow availability to applicants, and consider the percentage of minorities and women

EXHIBIT 6.6 Part of an EEO Form

Section D- EMPLOYMENT DATA

Employment at this establishment—Report all permanent, temporary, or part-time employees including apprentices and on-the-job trainees unless specifically excluded as set forth in the instructions. Enter the appropriate figures on all lines and in all columns. Blank spaces will be considered as zeros.

JOB CATEGORIES	OVERALL TOTAL (SUM OF COL. B THRU K) A	MALE					FEMALE				
		WHITE NOT OF HISPANIC ORIGIN B	BLACK NOT OF HISPANIC ORIGIN C	HISPANIC D	ASIAN OR PACIFIC ISLANDER E	AMERICAN INDIAN OR ALASKAN NATIVE F	WHITE NOT OF HISPANIC ORIGIN G	BLACK NOT OF HISPANIC ORIGIN H	HISPANIC I	ASIAN OR PACIFIC ISLANDER J	AMERICAN INDIAN OR ALASKAN NATIVE K
Officials and Managers	700	572	10	1	3		105	7		2	
Professionals	261	198	6	2	1		51	2		1	
Technicians	71	40		1			30				
Sales Workers	40	35	3				2				
Office and Clerical	544	30	1				502	10		1	
Craft Workers (Skilled)	5	5									
Operatives (Semi-Skilled)	4	3					1				
Laborers (Unskilled)	2						2				
Service Workers	19	9	2				8				
TOTAL	1646	892	22	4	4		701	19		4	
Total employment reported in previous EEO-1 report	1696	904	31	4	3		732	16		5	1

(The trainees below should also be included in the figure for the appropriate occupational categories above)

| Formal On-the-job trainees | White collar | 27 | 17 | 3 | | | | 7 | | | | |
| | Production | | | | | | | | | | | |

1. NOTE: On consolidated report, skip questions 2-5 and Section E.
2. How was information as to race or ethnic group in Section D obtained?
   1 ☐ Visual Survey   3 ☐ Other-Specify . . . .
   . . . .
   2 ☒ Employment Record
3. Dates of payroll period used- 2/28/90

4. Pay period of last report submitted for this establishment
   _____2/28/89_____
5. Does this establishment employ apprentices?
   This year? 1 ☐ Yes   2 ☒ No
   Last year? 1 ☐ Yes   2 ☒ No

who actually apply for jobs as arc welders. Each time we move to a narrower category in the exhibit, the numbers become more specific. But how much narrowing of the definition of availabilities is reasonable? For example, do we assume that only those who actually apply for the welder's job and can demonstrate that they can weld should be included in an availability estimate? In doing so, we have limited our estimate to welders actively seeking employment, which may not reflect the actual subpopulation of minority and women welders. Some people may not be aware of the job opportunity, or may be discouraged from applying due to past discrimination. Additionally, we have ignored those who are interested in becoming welders and who could gain the

EXHIBIT 6.7   Assumptions Characterizing Alternative Availability Estimates

Alternative Labor Pools	Assumptions		
	Available	**Interested**	**Qualified**
Population	All persons are equally available for employment.	Job interests are equally distributed across population.	All persons possess requisite job skills.
Civilian labor force	Both employed and unemployed are available; excludes institutional inmates, retirees, housewives, young children, and those in the armed services.	Persons not working or not looking for work are not interested; interests are equally distributed across those in the civilian labor force.	All persons in the civilian labor force possess requisite job skills.
Qualified labor force	Both employed and unemployed are available.	All persons employed or looking for employment are equally interested.	Persons employed or looking for employ-ment in the occupa-tional categories which correspond to employer's job group possess necessary skills.
Applicants	Those who apply are available for employment.	Only those who apply are interested, and interests are equally distributed.	All applicants possess the necessary skills.
Qualified applicants	Those who apply are available for employment.	Only those who apply for employment are interested, and interests are equally distributed.	Only applicants possessing the necessary skills are qualified.

Source: Patricia Snider, "External Data for Affirmative Action Planning," *Human Resources Planning* 2, no. 1 (1979), p. 8.

necessary skill within a reasonable time period. This group is called *quali-fiable,* and estimating their numbers and whether to include them is an addi-tional complication. Clearly, there is no best approach to estimating availabilities. All availability statistics have limitations. Recognizing the limita-tions allows an employer to make a best estimate that is useful and workable.

Exhibit 6.8 models the process for disaggregating (separating) the population in order to calculate availability. The model shows how people in the labor re-serve (neither employed or looking for work) may sometimes be considered

EXHIBIT 6.8 Availability in the External Labor Market

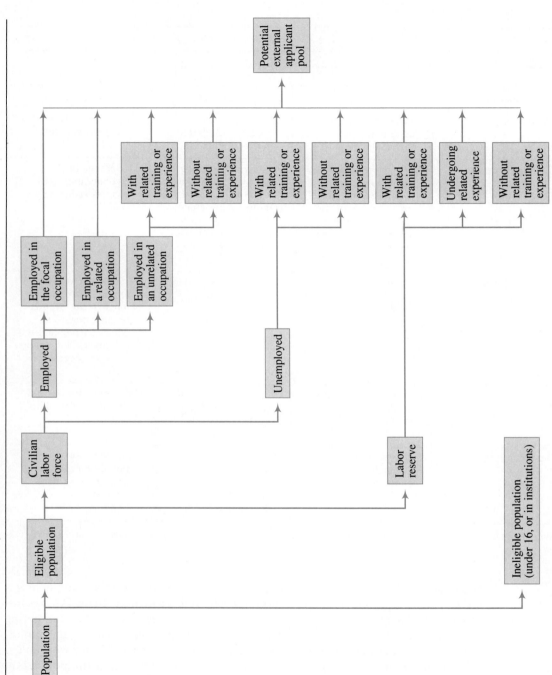

Source: Adapted from F. Krzystofiak and J. Newman, "Evaluating Employment Outcomes: Availability Models and Measures," *Industrial Relations*, Fall 1982, pp. 277–92.

part of the pool of potenital employees. People who are already employed in related occupations probably constitute the largest segment of the availability pool.

Establish Goals

Comparing the representation, hiring, and/or promotion rates of minorities and women in each job to their relevant availability may produce three outcomes:

1. *Underutilization*—the representation, hiring, and/or promotion rate is below the relevant availability.
2. *Parity*—the representation, hiring, and/or promotion rate is approximately equal to the relevant availability.
3. *Overutilization*—the representation, hiring, and/or promotion rate is above the relevant availability.

Based on this outcome, the employer may establish hiring or promotion goals for future HR activity. Underutilization is usually regarded as the most serious outcome, but overutilization can signal possible reverse discrimination against whites or males.

For parity, how equal is approximately equal? How much must the representation, hiring, or promotion rate fall below availability to indicate a problem? There is no simple answer. Courts and regulatory agencies have adopted several tests, including: (1) whether the difference in rates is statistically significant (not due to chance) and (2) whether the representation, hiring, or promotion rate is less than four fifths of the availability.

The Four-Fifths Rule

As an example of the four-fifths, or 80 percent, rule, assume that 40 qualified females and 40 qualified males apply for 12 carpenter positions. If gender is not a factor in the employment decisions, probability would suggest that half of the employees hired will be female. This is based on the fact that half of the applicants for the positions are female. Actually, only five females are hired, resulting in a selection rate of five out of 40, or 12.5 percent. Consequently, seven out of 40 males were hired, resulting in a selection rate of 17.5 percent.

Applying the 80 percent rule, the adverse impact calculation would be:

$$\frac{0.125 \text{ Selection rate for females}}{0.175 \text{ Selection rate for males}} = 71.4\%$$

Thus, this selection procedure appears to have adverse impact against females, in that the selection rate for females in less than 80 percent of the selection rate for males.

Programming to Achieve Goals

Human resource managers must diagnose the causes of underrepresentation (lower percentages) of women and minorities in the company's work force. In this way they will know what practices must be changed in order to increase representation of women and minorities. For example, the underrepresentation may be attributed to a host of factors, including the employer's reputation or a location that is considered unsafe. Once potential causes are diagnosed, then programs may be designed to increase the representation. Perhaps flexible work schedules, day-care programs, or escorted transportation home are options. Without knowing the cause, however, managers may attempt to increase the representation by lowering the hiring requirements or granting transfers to members of protected groups while refusing to grant them to other employees. This would not only increase the risk of reverse discrimination charges, it may also contribute to morale problems and foster resentment in the company.

At AT&T, research to redesign the outside-craft jobs so women could perform them more readily was conducted as part of affirmative action efforts. This research found problems with an extension ladder that was hard for women to handle and with a safety harness used by workers in climbing telephone poles. Also, a particularly grueling training program was redesigned by spreading out the hard physical labor over a longer time—to the benefit of men as well as women.

EEO programs can entail a substantial change in the way a company manages its personnel program. Still, the barriers to full employment for women and minorities can be deeply ingrained in the organization's practices, and it may take a substantial expenditure of both time and money to identify and eliminate them.

Most affirmative action plans involve the use of goals and timetables. For example, the San Francisco Fire Department recently agreed to a plan that sets a long-term goal of 40 percent minorities and 10 percent women in the department, and goals of 55 percent minority hiring through 1994. In other words, of every 100 vacancies, 55 are expected to go to minorities until the 40 percent goal is reached. So San Francisco is going to have to go out of its way to attract and help qualify minority applicants. The department also agreed to prepare a new, unbiased examination for hiring and promotion. Other possible actions that employers can take to achieve EEO goals are discussed in later chapters.

Many companies help ensure that EEO goals are met by making them a basis for evaluating managers' performance. For example, all IBM managers are given goals for each job category in their IBM facility. These goals are based on availability and utilization information determined from published data and internal personnel records. Where underutilization is a problem, managers are asked to set goals and timetables to eliminate the underutilization. Progress toward these goals is monitored quarterly.

SETTLING DISPUTES

The courts are not the only interpreters of EEO laws; several governmental agencies also interpret and enforce the laws. Regulatory agencies are an important factor in the organization's external environment. Compliance agents often make site visits and require explanations of firms' EEO performance.

EEOC

The lead agency in most EEO matters is the Equal Employment Opportunity Commission (EEOC). The EEOC has several responsibilities. It interprets the law through guidelines that have the effect of law. Guidelines dealing with sexual harassment as a violation of Title VII are an example. EEOC also processes discrimination charges and files lawsuits in federal court on behalf of alleged victims of discrimination. Enforcement of the Age Discrimination Act, Equal Pay Act, and Title VII of the Civil Rights Act all fall within EEOC jurisdiction.

EEOC's Major Activities

EEOC's major activity is the processing of charges made by those who believe they are victims of discrimination. EEOC interviews each complainant to determine whether the complaint falls within the coverage of legislation. If it does, then the charge is turned over to the state or local fair employment practice agency. If there is no agency with adequate powers in the state, EEOC investigates by interviewing the parties concerned with the alleged discrimination and collecting facts that might have a bearing on the charge. Ordinarily, those investigators are the first EEOC personnel with whom the employer comes into contact.

Conciliation

If there appears to be some truth to the accusations against the employer, EEOC attempts to bring about an out-of-court agreement between the employer and the charging party. This process is called *conciliation*. If the employer and EEOC accept the settlement, then the matter ends. But if conciliation efforts fail, the complainant or EEOC, or both, may file in federal district court.

The EEOC itself cannot order a remedy or impose a settlement. It can only negotiate settlements with employers, or, failing that, turn to the courts.

EEO-1 Reports

All employers subject to Title VII with 100 or more employees must submit to EEOC a form (EEO-1), such as the one shown in Exhibit 6.7. This form reports employment by sex and race for each of several broad job classifications. Multiple-establishment enterprises must file a report for each establishment of 50 or more employers. These data indicate, at least initially, whether an employer is complying with Title VII.

Office of Federal Contract Compliance (OFCCP)

The Office of Federal Contract Compliance is that part of the Department of Labor which administers affirmative action plans required under Executive Order 11246. OFCCP issues its own guidelines and goals for compliance. Its regulations stress that goals are "not rigid quotas which the contractor must achieve regardless of employment circumstance," but rather are "targets to be affirmately pursued." Like EEOC, OFCCP appears to be moving away from reliance on rigid quotas and statistics, and is encouraging innovation and flexibility in hiring and training programs.[27]

Internal Resolution

Whether required by a union contract or not, most employers agree that some sort of internal grievance process is desirable for all personnel issues, but especially for EEO issues.[28] Supervisors who have open communication with their workers may avoid or satisfy many complaints, grievances, and even lawsuits.

Employers

Three elements are necessary to successfully deal with EEO disputes: The first is a published policy advising employees how to bring a complaint within the organization. Such a policy should also include the company's stance on sexual harassment and equal opportunity. The system must be flexible enough that, in cases of sexual harassment, the offender, who may be the immediate supervisor, is not the organization's representative with whom the victim must file the complaint.

Second, every complaint lodged should be thoroughly investigated. Investigators may be the human resource staff, other employees, or neutral parties.

Third, employees must be kept informed on the investigation's progress. If an investigation is inconclusive, accusing employees should be informed and advised of their alternatives or opportunities to present further evidence. If cause is found for the complaint, then disciplinary action applied in other offenses should be required.

But if internal resolution does not work, what are the options? A discrimination suit can be resolved by coming to an agreement with the person involved, or going through a formal trial. If the EEOC is involved, management's options are reduced. EEOC may try to negotiate an agreement both before and after a suit is filed, or it may seek court orders requiring specific actions. Court remedies typically include back pay awards, changes in hiring/promotion or other job practices, and attorney's fees and legal costs.

Supervisors

The supervisor may play the most important role in an organization's EEO program. The supervisor translates much policy into action, and the supervisor's actions often determine whether employees believe they are being treated fairly.

When EEO goals require changes in procedures, problems may arise in getting supervisors to buy into the need for these changes. Occupational role stereotyping, societal racism and sexism, and sexual harassment have sometimes made it difficult for organizations to implement affirmative action programs.[29] Supervisors and co-workers may be unable to objectively appraise the work performance of employees from differing backgrounds or accept their occupational competence. If this is the case, the organization must communicate to the supervisor why changes are necessary and how they can benefit the organization. Most managers pay attention to the criteria on which their own job performance ratings are based. Therefore, a good way to get managers to help implement EEO policy is to review their performance on the basis of their unit's EEO behavior.

Unions

Executive Order 11246 also requires that unions lend a hand in employers' affirmative action efforts. A nondiscrimination clause is included in virtually all collective bargaining agreements. Affirmative action efforts are often constrained, however, by the seniority provisions found in many contracts. One alternative is *inverse seniority* where, in a layoff situation, the most senior person is allowed to elect a temporary layoff with substantial compensation and the right to return to work at some future time. This alternative to the "last hired, first fired" allows the employer to temporarily reduce the work force and still retain the minorities and women who may have lower seniority. However, the inducement to get senior employee's cooperation may be very costly, and is not a long-term solution. Clearly, a combined effort is required by both employers and unions to attain affirmative action goals.

Union's attitudes and responses to equal employment vary as much as employers' attitudes and actions.[30] Construction unions have contributed to the shortage of women in that industry, by their control over hiring. Unlawful racial practices by some unions in the 1930s and 1940s, including segregating members by race and racial discrimination in collective bargaining activities, may have contributed to subsequent erosion of union membership.

At the other extreme, unions in industries with a large percent of women members, especially those in the public sector, have been on the forefront of women's issues. Many unions have championed equal opportunity and the comparable worth concept discussed in later chapters.

Employees

Discrimination and harassment are against the law. But is the law the best way to deal with the problem? Litigation costs money, and can take years. Many women and minorities have found that unions offer a faster, easier route to complaint resolution than the courts. Union support on a complaint may help decrease the imbalance in power between an aggrieved employee and employer. Additionally, the Supreme Court has upheld an employee's right to still file a complaint if the result of the grievance procedure is unsatisfactory.

EEO IN THE 1990s

We pointed out earlier in this chapter that, in spite of a quarter of a century of experience with EEO issues, questions remain. Two issues that have received recent public attention include reverse discrimination and proving disparate impact.

Reverse Discrimination

In its efforts to undo effects of any past discrimination, how does an organization ensure that it does not discriminate against employees who are not members of protected groups? Several court cases have dealt with this issue. Most of them concern pay adjustments for women. The courts have ruled that a one-time adjustment to overcome past discrimination is not a permanent change in the compensation system and, therefore, need not be applied to men.[31] But a permanent change not tailored to correct past discrimination must be applied equally to all employees in the system, regardless of gender.[32]

Reverse discrimination is also an issue in affirmative action. A 1989 Supreme Court decision has raised concern among civil rights activists that lawsuits claiming reverse discrimination will be able to prevent companies from carrying out affirmative action.[33] The case, *Martin* v. *Wilks,* grew out of an earlier lawsuit alleging that the city of Birmingham, Alabama, had discriminated against blacks in hiring and promoting fire fighters. City officials settled the case by signing a consent decree, in which they agreed to an affirmative action plan that included hiring and promotion goals for blacks. A group of white fire fighters then filed a separate lawsuit alleging that, as a result of this settlement, they were being denied promotions in favor of less-qualified blacks solely on the basis of race. The Supreme Court ruled that the consent decree that settled the original lawsuit was not binding on persons who had not been parties to the proceedings in which it was negotiated. Since the white fire fighters had not been parties to the consent decree, they were free to challenge it.

Many employers feel that this ruling will increase the difficulty of settling discrimination lawsuits. For most employers, one of the main incentives to settle is to avoid further legal action. But if, by settling with one group of plaintiffs, an employer opens the door to lawsuits from other groups in the workforce, much of the incentive to settle is lost. To identify every person whose interests could be affected and make them all parties to the settlement appears prohibitively costly and time consuming—if not impossible.

This decision returns the issue of affirmative action to the legislators. Civil rights activists are trying to mount a campaign for remedial legislation. In the meantime, employers must focus on structuring settlements that will withstand challenge from employee groups. Such settlements require that:

✦ An imbalance in a traditionally segregated job category must be documented.

✦ Preferences for protected group members must be narrowly tailored to eliminate the imbalance without trammeling on the rights of nonprotected employees.

✦ Race or gender can be only one factor, but not the sole determinant, of hiring and promotion decisions.

✦ Preferences must be eliminated, once balance is achieved.

Proving Disparate Impact

Prior to 1989, procedures had been fairly well established for proving discrimination on the basis of disparate impact. A statistical showing of disparate impact of a neutral policy was considered sufficient to force the employer to prove that its challenged employment practices were a "business necessity" essential to effective job performance. Plaintiffs then could try to rebut efforts to prove business necessity by showing that other available employment practices could have met the employer's needs without similar discriminatory consequences.

But the 1989 *Wards Cove* case muddled this interpretation. The Supreme Court made it clear that the burden of proof at all times remains with the plaintiffs.[34] Additionally, the plaintiffs must indicate which specific practice caused the disparate impact, and why that practice lacks a business justification. It doesn't matter if other practices would have served the same purpose without the discriminatory consequences. A practice need not be "essential" or "indispensable" to be legal, merely "legitimate."

The Civil Rights Act of 1990

Legislation has already been introduced to reestablish standards in use before the *Wards Cove* case.[35] The Civil Rights Act of 1990 (1) returns to the employer the responsibility for persuading the courts that a practice is a "business necessity" that is "essential to effective job performance" rather than merely "legitimate" and (2) removes the requirement that plaintiffs must specify which practice results in the disparate impact. Supporters of the legislation observe that the employers have the best access to the information that went into the HR decisions; therefore, they ought to shoulder the more stringent burden of proof in lawsuits. The bill also permits employees to sue for punitive damages. Critics say this reduces the incentive to fashion out-of-court settlements that include remedial programs that benefit all employees.

SUMMARY

Equal employment opportunity affects all human resource decisions. In one sense, EEO legislation and regulations simply require employers to adopt sound human resource practices. The treatment employees receive must be based on work and business factors, rather than on race or sex. This not only makes good business sense but also ensures compliance with the law.

Dispute continues over whether we as a nation have made any progress at eliminating employment discrimination. Although differences in occupational attainment and earnings among protected groups remain, some studies suggest progress has been made. Yet unexplained differences remain, and some of this is the result of discriminatory practices in the workplace.

There are no magical cures for these problems, but one proposition that does seem to go a long way is *involvement*. Too often, EEO is treated as the exclusive province of the personnel department. If this can be changed by involving operating managers in planning and goal setting, attainment of EEO objectives should increase.

To make EEO programs work, top management must not only communicate its desires but also build EEO effectiveness into the reward system for managers. The goal is to make the EEO program ethical, workable, and in full compliance with the law.

General Electric Company requires its managers to report their progress in achieving EEO goals. Their degree of goal achievement in EEO affects their compensation, as does their progress in cost control. This system has helped General Electric meet its EEO goals. This kind of communication and control system is more likely to achieve courtproof EEO systems than memos or other such means.

In sum, top managers must get involved in EEO programs to make sure that the enterprise is, in fact, an equal employment opportunity employer and that the EEO–AA program meets the letter as well as the spirit of the law.

DISCUSSION AND REVIEW QUESTIONS

1. What does *availability* mean? Why is it so important in EEO analysis to define relevant availability?
2. Compare and contrast equality of opportunity and equality of results. What application does this have for HRM?
3. How would you recognize discriminatory employment behavior? What are the two basic definitions?

4. How are EEO disputes settled?

5. What is the legal status of seniority systems?

6. How does affirmative action planning relate to HR planning?

7. Compare reverse discrimination and affirmative action.

8. What is the role of the supervisor in EEO?

9. Are affirmative action programs socially desirable? Why or why not? Who might they help? Who might they hurt?

10. What should employees who feel discriminated against do?

YOUR TURN:
DIANE JOYCE

On March 25, 1987, the U.S. Supreme Court decided, six to three, that Diane Joyce could indeed have her job—seven years after she got it. When she was promoted to the post in 1980, Joyce became the first woman in Santa Clara County's work force to fill one of the Transportation Agency's 238 skilled crafts jobs.

When word came of the Supreme Court's decision, a crowd of supporters swarmed around Diane Joyce, pumping her hand. "A big win for us," one women's group leader declared. Of course, the "us"—the Washington professional women, the lawyers, politicians, and journalists—were not going back to the transportation yard.

The day after the Court ruled, Diane Joyce was in the dispatch office when a bouquet of two dozen carnations arrived from one of the supporters. Joyce arranged the flowers in a plastic bleach bottle—the closest object she had to a vase. A day later, the carnations had vanished. "I drop-kicked them across the yard," a roads foreman told her. Joyce found the flowers in a garbage bin, dug them out, and put them back in the bottle.

"I know someone who would break your arm or leg for a price," was how a Santa Clara County female maintenance worker was greeted on her first day of work. Another woman was purposely taught the wrong, and dangerous, way to use brakes on county trucks. Still another was ordered by her supervisor to clean a transit bus—only to find that the men had left her a gift: feces smeared on the seats.

In all the oratory on the Supreme Court steps, political leaders overlooked something fundamental: a woman's place in the blue-collar work world has barely changed. While about 49 percent of the professional work force is now female, only 8.6 percent of precision, production, crafts, and repairs jobs are held by women. While middle-class women have made dramatic inroads into management—a 77 percent increase from 1975—working-class women represent only 3 percent of mechanics, 1.5 percent of construction workers.

It is not true, as some would assert, that there are so few women in skilled crafts and trades because women don't want these jobs. Union leaders report that many women apply for craft apprenticeships, but contractors won't hire them.

Women who do break into blue-collar work must face, as Diane Joyce did and does, ostracism, hazing, harassment, threats, physical abuse.

"The mainstream feminist movement," says Mary Ellen Boyd, executive director of Non-Traditional Employment for Women, a national advocacy group, "continues to focus on the concerns of its original proponents, mostly white, middle-class women." The "concerns" of blue-collar women like Diane Joyce have less to do with the old anthems of personal fulfillment or self-discovery, and more to do with making it to the end of the month. "I needed the money, pure and simple," Diane Joyce says. "I'm not the pioneer people have made me out to be."

Questions

You are the HR director for Santa Clara County.

1. How do EEO laws affect your decisions and options?
2. How do the laws affect your employees Diane Joyce and Paul Johnson?
3. How would you deal with the tension among county employees?

Source: Text excerpted from Susan Faludi, "Diane Joyce," *MS.*, January 1988, pp. 62–65, 90–92.

NOTES AND REFERENCES

1. *Johnson* v. *Transportation Agency, Santa Clara County, California,* No. 85–1129 (March 25, 1987).
2. *Firefighters Local 1784* v. *Stotts,* 104 Sup. Ct. 2576 (1984).
3. Uncertainty accompanied passage of the original EEO legislation, too. See, for example, George T. Milkovich, "The Emerging Debate" in *Comparable Worth: Issues and Alternatives,* ed. E. R. Livernash (Washington, D.C.: Equal Employment Advisory Council, 1978).
4. *Promoting Minorities and Women: A Practical Guide to Affirmative Action for the 1990s.* BNA Special Report. Washington, D.C.: Bureau of National Affairs, 1989.
5. Conflict between seniority and EEO was an issue in *Teamsters* v. *United States,* 431 U.S. 324 (1977); and *Boston Fire Fighters Union, Local 718* v. *Boston Chapter, NAACP,* No. 82–185 (May 16, 1983); *Williams* v. *City of New Orleans,* 18 FEP Cases 345 (E. D. La. 1976).
6. David L. Kirp, Mark G. Yudof, and Marlene Strong Franks, *Gender Justice* (Chicago: University of Chicago Press, 1986); *Women in the American Economy,* Current Population Reports Special Series P-23, No. 146 (Washington, D.C.: Superintendent of Documents, U.S. Goverment Printing Office, 1987).
7. F. D. Blau and M. A. Ferber, "Occupations and Earnings of Women Workers," in *Working Women,* ed. K. S. Koziara, M. H. Moskow, and L. D. Tanner (Washington, D.C.: Bureau of National Affairs, 1987).
8. H. Remick, ed., *Comparable Worth and Wage Discrimination* (Philadelphia: Temple University Press, 1984); D. J. Treiman and H. I. Hartmann, ed., *Women, Work, and Wages* (Washington, D.C.: National Academy of Science, 1984).
9. Council of Economic Advisers, 1989 *Annual Report* (Washington, D.C.: U.S. Government Printing Office, 1989).
10. R. B. Freeman, "Have Black Labor Market Gains Post-1964 Been Permanent or Transitory?" (Working Paper 751, National Bureau of Economic Research, 1981); Thomas

Sowell, *Markets and Minorities* (New York: Basic Books, 1981); James P. Smith and Finis R. Welch, *Closing the Gap: Forty Years of Economic Progress for Blacks* (Santa Monica, Calif.: The Rand Corporation, 1986); G. D. Jaynes and R. M. Williams, Jr., eds. *Blacks and American Society* (Washington, D.C.: National Academy Press, 1989).

11. *Schultz* v. *Wheaton Glass Co.,* 421 F.2d 259, 3rd Cir. (1970).

12. Ruth G. Shaeffer, *Nondiscrimination in Employment—And Beyond,* Report No. 782 (New York: The Conference Board, 1980).

13. *General Electric Co.* v. *Gilbert,* 429 U.S. 125 (1977). But see *Cleveland Board of Education* v. *Lafleur,* 414 U.S. 632, 5 FEP 1253 (1974); and *Holthaus* v. *Compton & Sons, Inc.,* 514 F.2d 651, 10 FEP 601 8th Circuit (1975); also see Ruth Shaeffer, *Nondiscrimination and Beyond.*

14. The Spring 1990 issue of *ILR Report* is devoted exclusively to the 1989 Supreme Court rulings on discrimination and disparate impact.

15. *Griggs* v. *Duke Power Co.,* 401 U.S. 424 (1971).

16. *Connecticut* v. *Teal,* 112 S.Ct. 2525, U.S. Sup. Ct. 29 EPD, 32, 870 (1982).

17. *Wards Cove Packing Co.* v. *Atonio* 109 S.Ct. 2115 (1989).

18. *Uniform Guidelines on Employee Selection Procedures,* 29 Code of Federal Regulations, Part 1607; *Federal Register* 43, no. 166 (1978), pp. 38295–309.

19. *Rosenfeld* v. *Southern Pacific Company,* 9th Cir. 444 F.2d 1219 (1971).

20. *Diaz* v. *Pan American World Airways, Inc.,* 5th Cir. 422 F.2d 385 (1971).

21. Marcia Graham, "Seniority Systems and Title VII: Reanalysis and Redirection," *Employee Relations Law Journal* 9, pp. 81–102; Michael E. Gordon and William A. Johnson, "Seniority: A Review of Its Legal and Scientific Standing," *Personnel Psychology* 35, no. 2 (1982), pp. 255–80.

22. *Firefighters Local 1784* v. *Stotts,* 104 U.S. 2576 (1984).

23. *Weber* v. *Kaiser Aluminum and Chemical Corp.,* 415 F. Sup. 761, 12 CCH *Employment Practices Decisions* 91 11,115, S.D. La. (1976).

24. *City of Richmond* v. *J.A. Croson Co.,* 109 S.Ct. 706 (1989).

25. *Meritor Savings Bank* v. *Vinson,* Sup. Ct. 40 FEP Cases 1826 (1986).

26. *Equal Employment Advisory Council Perspectives on Availability* (Washington, D.C.: 1978); Pat Snider, "External Data for Affirmative Action Planning," in *Affirmative Action Planning,* ed. George Milkovich and Lee Dyer (New York: Human Resources Planning Society, 1979); *Fair Employment Practices,* OFCCP Rules Revision, no. 467 (Washington: Bureau of National Affairs, 1983).

27. Joseph N. Cooper, "New Directions within OFCCP," *Labor Law Journal,* January 1986, pp. 3–5.

28. David Ewing, *Justice on the Job* (Boston: Harvard Business School Press, 1989).

29. Marvin D. Dunnette and Stephan J. Motowidlo, "Estimating Benefits and Costs of Antisexist Training Programs in Organizations," *Woman in the Work Force,* ed. H. John Bernardin (New York: Praeger Publishers, 1982), chap. 7.

30. Herbert Hill, "The AFL and the Black Worker: Twenty-Five Years after the Merger," *The Journal of Intergroup Relations,* Spring 1982, pp. 5–79; Richard Freeman and Jonathan Leonard, *Union Maids: Unions and the Female Workforce* (Cambridge, Mass.: National Bureau of Economic Research, 1985); *Ourself: Women and Unions* (Washington, D.C.: Food and Beverage and Trades Department, AFL-CIO, 1981); American Federation of State, County and Municipal Employers, *You've Come a Long Way—Maybe* (Washington, D.C.: AFL-CIO, 1984); Lisa Portman, Joy

Ann Grune, and Eve Johnson, "The Role of Labor," in *Comparable Worth and Wage Discrimination,* ed. H. Remick (Philadelphia: Temple University Press, 1984).

31. *Ende* v. *Board of Regents of Northern Illinois University,* 37 FEP Cases 575 (7th Cir. 1985).

32. *Board of Regents of University of Nebraska* v. *Dawes,* 522 F.2d 380, II FEP Case 283 (8th Cir. 1976).

33. *Martin* v. *Wilks,* 109 S.Ct. 2180 (1989).

34. Robert E. Williams, "The Supreme Court's 1989 Employment Decisions—Civil Rights and Illusions of Armageddon," *ILR Report,* June 1990.

35. Howard M. Metzenbaum and Albert F. Cacozza, Jr., "The Fair Employment Reinstatement Act—Restoring the Balance," *ILR Report,* June 1990.

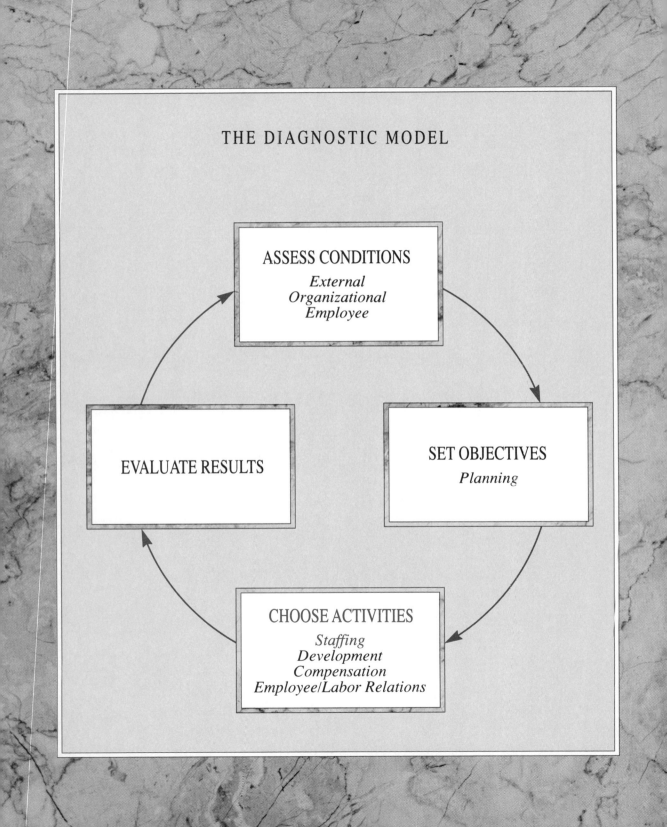

PART
THREE

EXTERNAL STAFFING

Employees are constantly joining, moving within, and leaving organizations. Managing this employee movement is one of the most important and influential human resource management (HRM) activities. The best-designed organization in terms of jobs, structure, and reward systems cannot function unless the right numbers and types of employees join, get assigned to the right positions, and remain with the organization.

Staffing is the process of moving employees into, through, and out of the organization, to produce the desired quantity and types of employee assignments.

External staffing focuses on moving employees into the organization from outside, and on the pattern of employee separations from the organization.

Internal staffing focuses on moving employees between positions within the organization.

The internal staffing process is discussed in Part Four, on Employee Development, because it is closely linked to training and developing employee skills and abilities. In Part Three, we focus on the external staffing process of attracting, choosing, and retaining employees.

A DIAGNOSTIC APPROACH TO EXTERNAL STAFFING

The exhibit shows how external staffing fits the diagnostic approach. External staffing brings human resource management into direct contact with external labor and product markets and matches the organization's requirements to them. Thus, its success is keenly affected by effective diagnosis, assessing conditions, and objectives/standards that reflect both efficiency and equity.

External Conditions

Labor markets The number of science and engineering baccalaureates are expected to fall increasingly short of the demand for these skills throughout the 1990s and into the next century. Labor shortages have forced hospitals to cut services and to send patients to other hospitals. The American Hotel and Motel Association suggests that travel and tourism is predicted to be the country's number one employer by the year 2000, requiring "more than three quarters of a million new work-ers every year," according to its president. Already, businesses that traditionally relied on younger workers are facing shortages, and the pool of younger workers will fall by almost two million, or 8 percent, between 1990 and the year 2000. The U.S. work force is growing more slowly, and becoming more "diverse," with increasing percentages of nonwhites, immigrants, and women.

These labor market trends mean that external staffing will often be very different in the 1990s than before. Traditional recruitment methods, such as advertisements and employee recommendations, which worked well with an abundant supply of white males, are less effective in the new labor market. Attracting sufficient applicants receives much greater emphasis relative to choosing among applicants. When labor is short, the emphasis shifts to attracting sufficient employees and, perhaps, using training to create the necessary skills. Regarding employee separations and retention, downturns in the demand for a company's products can motivate early retirement incentives or even layoffs to reduce the work force. Dissatisfied employees are less likely to voluntarily leave when unemployment is high than when it is low.

Governments and society Legislation and litigation affect the external staffing process more every year. Equal employment opportunity legislation and related court cases (see Chapter Six) allow government agencies to review recruitment, selection, and retention practices for adverse effects on protected minority and other groups. The pool of candidates attracted by recruiting activities often is used to define the availability of minorities and females in the organization's labor market. Because as these groups comprise a greater proportion of the work force, organizations will be expected to attract, hire, and retain more of them. The devices used to select candidates also come under government scrutiny, to ensure that they are job-related or do not reject a disproportionate number of minority or female candidates. Failure to consider these requirements can be costly. Burlington Northern, Inc., agreed to a $40 million settlement, primarily due to its inability to demonstrate that its selection programs were job-related. The increasing frequency of organizational downsizing has prompted legislators to call for expanding the role of the Equal Employment Opportunity Commission in monitoring discharge and layoff procedures for adverse effects on protected groups.

Non-EEO legislation also affects external staffing activities. Polygraph (lie detector) tests were severely restricted in 1988 by the Employee Polygraph Protection Act. Protection for "whistleblowers," who report organizational wrongdoing, and for veterans' rights, drug abuse, polygraph tests, and plant closings are just a few of the controversial issues that Congress dealt with in recent legislation. Increasingly, courts and state legislatures also have had profound effects on legal requirements for external staffing. Many state courts have awarded damages to fired employees who claimed that statements made during selection interviews or in employee handbooks guaranteed them employment, pension, or severance benefits.

Unions Whether unionized or not, organizations must consider the effects of organized labor on staffing activities. National union lobbying is influential in shaping such legislation as early warnings of factory closings, bans and limits on drug and lie detector tests, and changes in minimum wage legislation. More directly, unions still comprise the main applicant pool for some crafts, and labor agreements stipulate specific procedures and rules about the timing and order of employee layoffs and dismissals.

Organizational and Work Conditions

As Chapter Five showed, the organization's financial and market position directly affects external staffing activities, by determining the types and quantities of employee needed. Areas of growing demand will require activities be focused on extensive hiring and retention, while areas of slowing demand may focus on very selective hiring (or none at all) and encourage early retirement. Yet, simple supply and demand doesn't fully explain organizational effects. Organizational reputation can help with recruiting as Merck & Company discovered that being named *Fortune* magazine's most admired company drew in "over 100,000 applications for jobs from New Jersey alone." Dominant management coalitions or even customers may shape external staffing policies. A study of hospitals found that, when the revenues came mainly from private insurance carriers, administrators with accounting backgrounds were selected more often; but, when private donations provided most of the revenue, administrators were selected for their business and professional contacts. Organization values will also influence external staffing policies, as IBM's values of "respect for the individual" lead to corporate policies that motivate its managers to avoid layoffs as a way to reduce the work force. Often, those within the organization consciously or unconsciously choose applicants similar to themselves.

The nature of the work directly affects external staffing activities by establishing the qualifications needed for performance. It also determines whether applicants will generally find the job and the general employment relationship attractive or unattractive, which determines how easily job candidates can be found. Finally, if the work is unpleasant or difficult, employees may be more apt to leave when another opportunity comes along.

Employee Characteristics

Applicant characteristics, such as skills, experience, and abilities, are the signals organizations use to decide who should get an employment offer. Employee characteristics, such as job performance, attitudes, absenteeism, separations, and race/gender, are often measured to determine the success of external staffing. Employee demographic characteristics can also determine external staffing needs. As those born during the baby boom age, current workers will retire and vacancies may emerge even with little increase in business activity. On the other hand, the immediate future will see many workers entering their most productive years (between 30 and 50), so it may be possible to support business activity with fewer workers. Finally, employee

attitudes/opinions affect external staffing decisions, as when the perceived fairness of a layoff or plant closing leads to extensive retraining or outplacement assistance.

Evaluating External Staffing Results

The most obvious objective/standard for external staffing is whether the organization can obtain and retain employees. However, filling vacancies is not enough, because the quality of the work force will also determine productivity and efficiency. External staffing activities are costly and time consuming, and they should be evaluated for their return on investment, just as other organization activities. Increasingly, evaluations are focusing beyond the staffing process to determine the effects of external staffing on profits, market share, and sales. External staffing decisions often have multimillion-dollar effects, because they affect the pay, benefits, and performance of employees who may spend decades as organizational members. Perhaps the most intriguing issue is how to *combine* external staffing activities to achieve objectives. In tight labor markets, for example, it may often be more effective to focus not only on filling vacancies but on ensuring that the right employees remain with the organization so the organizations don't have to fill vacancies as often. Spending too much on recruiting may actually be counterproductive without corresponding attention to employee retention.

Equal employment opportunity is typically the most important equity objective/standard for external staffing. Ensuring that employment candidates and employees are treated without bias toward race/

gender, handicap, age, and other protected characteristics is a key goal of external staffing activities. External staffing is an important factor in avoiding adverse impact (see Chapter Six), and the relative numbers of employees in protected groups is closely monitored when making decisions about how and where to select new employees, as well as how and where to reduce the work force. However, external staffing activities reflect equity considerations in other ways. For example, some organizations work hard to maintain employee job security. This is certainly driven by the belief that such efforts contribute to efficiency, but it is also often driven by a fundamental organization value—respect for the individual.

Part Three describes the external staffing process, with three chapters. Chapter Seven describes external recruiting—the activity that attracts the pool of employment candidates. Chapter Eight describes external selection—the activity that chooses which of the candidates will receive employment offers. Chapter Nine describes retention—the activity that determines who will stay and who will leave the organization.

CHAPTER SEVEN

External Recruiting

Recruiting Begins the Staffing Process

The Applicant's Job-Search Process
Choosing an Occupation
Seeking Information about Jobs/Organizations
Choosing a Job/Organization

Choosing Required Applicant Qualifications
The Older Work Force
Opportunities for the Disabled
Housing and Transportation Barriers
Applicants with Minimum English Literacy

Choosing Recruitment Sources and
Communication Channels
Walk-ins
Employee Referrals
College Recruiting
Other Educational Institutions
Employment Agencies and Professional Societies
Advertising
Temporary Employees
Immigrants

Choosing Inducements

The Message: Realism versus Flypaper

Choosing and Preparing Recruiters

International Perspectives on Recruiting

Evaluating Recruitment
Efficiency and Equity
Actual Recruiting Evaluation Practices

Appendix: Your Own Job Search

Your Turn: Happy Meal Recruitment Ads

———————◆———————

A new Pizza Hut restaurant is due to open in Paramus, New Jersey, but it can't because there aren't enough workers in the area, despite jobs promising as much as $7 an hour, more than twice the federal minimum wage. The problem is that Paramus is a wealthy suburb of New York City, and the Pizza Hut manager estimates that "most of the kids around here make more than that in allowance."[1]

Simpson Construction Company in Rochester, Vermont, used to add people to keep up with increased building construction orders. The company must now use expensive prefabricated wall panels purchased from Alabama because, as the president states, "We can't build them ourselves, because we can't get the people."

Harmonium Moving & Storage of Boston charged its customers $76 an hour in 1989, up from $42 in 1987, to recover the increased recruiting and compensation costs necessary to attract sufficient workers. "We've priced ourselves out of many markets," says the president of Harmonium.[2]

The vice president of Automatic Laundry Service of Newton, Massachusetts, needed a new field-service worker to repair the equipment his company sells and leases. He placed a help-wanted ad that offered a starting wage of up to $9 an hour, profit sharing, a pension plan, and full medical benefits. Three weeks later, only five people had applied. One had a severe drinking problem, three could not speak or read English, and the last one wanted $12 an hour. Three months later, the job remained unfilled.[3]

The National Science Foundation predicts that the number of science and engineering baccalaureates in 1996 will fall short of the demand by 45,000 and, by 2010, the shortfall will be 700,000. The American Hospital Association says that labor shortages have forced one fourth of hospitals to cut services and 13 percent to send patients to other hospitals.[4]

What would you do to combat these problems? Greater use of traditional methods, such as advertisements, employment agencies, and employee recommendations, often won't be sufficient. Some firms are busing employees from the inner city to jobs in the suburbs.[5] Some firms will change job qualifications to make more people eligible—Days Inns recently began hiring the homeless and older workers in Atlanta.[6] Would you simply raise pay? That can be expensive, and, if matched by other companies, it may provide only a short-run advantage. Would you give applicants a real taste of the job, including the bad parts, or would you try to hide the bad parts in hopes of getting people to take the job?

RECRUITING: THE BEGINNING OF THE STAFFING PROCESS

These problems show how important it has become to attract a qualified and motivated pool of individuals from which to select employees. The issue often isn't whom to choose but how to get enough people to apply for job vacancies, and the problem will probably worsen before it gets better. One fourth or more of all 707 organizations responding to a survey by the American Society for Personnel Administration about labor shortages said they were having "great" or "very great" difficulty in finding all kinds of employees except for executives/managers and sales people.[7] We shall discuss how recruitment activities must consider not only the quality of applicants but also ensure that a sufficient quantity of applicants is attracted.[8]

◆

Recruiting is the process of identifying and attracting a pool of candidates, from which some will later be selected to receive employment offers.

Exhibit 7.1 shows the role of recruiting in the external staffing process. Notice how the staffing process sequentially filters individuals through a series of hurdles. As the examples at the beginning of the chapter showed, even the most accurate and effective selection and retention activities will be of little use unless the recruitment process generates a sufficiently large pool of qualified applicants to select from and to replace those who leave. Not only does recruitment affect employee qualifications, it is also a key to effective equal employment opportunity. If sufficient minorities and females don't apply for jobs, there's no way to hire enough of them to meet affirmative action goals. The U.S. work force is growing more slowly and becoming more "diverse," with increasing percentages of nonwhites, immigrants, and women.[9]

Recruitment is not just important to the organization, however. It's a two-way communication process. Applicants desire accurate information about what it would be like to work in the organization. Organizations desire accurate information about what kind of employee the applicant would make if he or she were hired. Both candidates for employment and the organization send signals about the employment relationship. Applicants want to send signals that suggest they are attractive candidates and should receive job offers, and applicants try to get the organization to give them information to determine if they want to join. The organization wants to send signals that suggests it is a good place to work, and it wants to get signals from applicants that will give a true picture of their potential value as employees.

So, understanding the recruitment process is also important when you become a job candidate. Knowing how the search process works, and how you can influence it, are important tools no matter what kind of career you pursue. The end of the chapter contains an appendix to help you begin thinking about

---

EXHIBIT 7.1   The Staffing Process as a Series of Filters

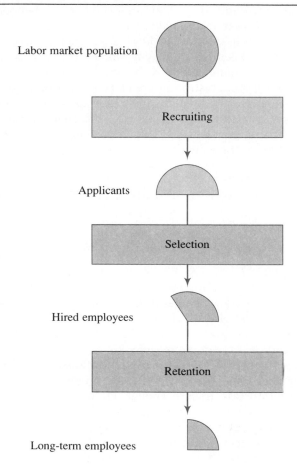

Labor market population

Recruiting

Applicants

Selection

Hired employees

Retention

Long-term employees

your own job search. Next, however, we discuss the applicant search process, to show its implications for how organizations conduct recruiting activities.

THE APPLICANT'S JOB-SEARCH PROCESS

Though organizations generally recruit applicants for particular jobs, choosing a job in a particular organization is actually the second step in most applicant's job-search process. A person must first make an occupational choice, which defines the general types of jobs he or she will pursue, such as engineering, business, music, photography, and so forth. Then, the person chooses an organization that offers a job in that occupation.

Choosing an Occupation

Occupational choice is influenced by individual as well as environmental characteristics. Psychologists have argued that people try to choose jobs that are congruent with their self-concept, classifying jobs and people as artistic, investigative, conventional, realistic, social, or enterprising.[10] Sociologists emphasize how the family, educational system, peer group, and guidance agencies might influence and constrain occupational choice. However, occupational choice is also influenced by the realities of labor markets and by the individual's capabilities and resources. Economists describe occupational choice in terms of how people seek to maximize their future income flow and to minimize the time and effort it takes to obtain it. There is no simple formula to predict occupational choice, but it usually occurs early in an individual's life, about the time they take their first job.

Organizations have only limited influence on most factors affecting occupational choice, but they can influence some factors directly. Many organizations encourage their employees to actively work with elementary and secondary schools and to foster students' interest and ability in math and science. Dow Chemical awarded scholarships and summer job guarantees to four students at Chicago's High School for Agricultural Sciences. Forecasting a need for 7,000 more mechanics by 1995, Toyota gives tools, cars, trucks, and scholarships to 55 U.S. vocational schools and colleges. Hewlett-Packard and Lockheed Missile & Space Company work with the Sequoia Union High School District to start vocational programs in computers and electronics for students at high risk for dropping out of school.[11]

The *Strong Vocational Interest Blank* and the *Kuder Occupational Interest Survey* are questionnaires that measure a person's interests and values, and that determine their similarity to different groups of people in different kinds of occupations.[12] The idea is that people tend to enter and stay in an occupation that fits their interests and values. Many college and professional placement services administer these questionnaires to help job seekers find the group that is similar to them, and to help them locate an appropriate occupation. Your own placement service may offer this service.

Occupational choice narrows the field of job choices. The next step is choosing what job/organization to join.

Seeking Information about Jobs/Organizations

Before a person can choose a job/occupation, she or he must gather information to determine what employment opportunities exist. The method and extent of this activity seem to vary according to individual and situational factors. A review of 22 studies on information gathering by job seekers found that much job information is acquired on an informal basis. Friends and relatives are the most frequent source, with direct application (walk-ins) a close second.[13] Methods vary by occupation, with managerial and clerical job seekers more likely to use a private employment service than are blue-collar job seekers.[14] It appears that persons in less financially secure situations search more. Unemployed persons with nonwage income or who are receiving unemployment benefits spend fewer hours per week looking for jobs.[15] Among applicants for life insurance agent jobs, female and nonwhite applicants tended to use "formal" information sources, such as employment agencies, newspaper ads, and school placement offices, while white males relied on "informal" sources, such as referrals by employees and acquaintances.[16] One study of students found that some emphasized the attractiveness of the job when choosing companies to interview with, while others emphasized the probability of receiving an offer.[17]

In terms of the outcomes of job-search activity, it appears that those who search longer or more intensively are more satisfied with their jobs and obtain higher salary increases.[18] One study found that male users of public employment services remained unemployed longer than those using other search methods. Those who got help from friends and relatives got jobs more quickly but took a lower wage than they were earning previously.[19]

One recent study of undergraduate business students measured both job-search behavior and outcomes. Job-search behavior was described by its focus, intentions to be systematic, environmental exploration, and confidence that the search would lead to good placement outcomes. The study also asked students how many interviews they had on campus, how many interviews they had on company sites, the number of job offers they received, their job satisfaction, and how much stress they encountered in the search process. The study found that students who performed better in school expressed more certainty in their search activity, females were more certain and reported more focused search, and type A behavior tendencies associated with more focused search and greater intentions to search systematically. Yet, more focused and systematic search did not relate to job-search outcomes. School performance, environmental exploration, and certainty related positively to the number of interviews on campus. Students with greater type A tendencies went on more company-site interviews, and the number of site interviews was strongly related to the number of job offers received. Those who got more job offers were more satisfied on their jobs. High levels of environmental exploration were associated with greater job satisfaction and less search stress.[20]

Computers may make it easier to gather and consider large amounts of information about jobs. Programs now exist that can provide both career counseling and organize the more clerical aspects of sending and tracking résumés and letters.[21] Once an applicant has gathered the information, it must be evaluated to make a choice.

Choosing a Job/Organization

A *compensatory,* or economically "rational," approach to job choice involves gathering complete information on every job offered and then comparing every offer to all other offers on all of the important criteria, and finally, choosing the one with maximum overall value. Offers low on some criteria could compensate by being very high on others. But people are seldom this systematic or rational, so the *bounded rationality* approach describes the search process as limited by the mental capacity of the searcher. According to bounded rationality, people can rarely keep track of all possible comparisons between all important factors on all jobs, so they resort to simplifying strategies, such as eliminating all offers that are below some standard on a couple of important factors (location, salary), and then choosing among the remaining offers using a more complete comparison process.[22] Economists use the term *reservation wage* to describe the minimum level of pay required to make a job offer acceptable.[23] Bounded rationality is a *noncompensatory* approach, because job offers that fail to meet the initial minimum standard are eliminated and cannot compensate by being especially good on other factors.

What strategy do you think will describe your own job search? Students' approaches to job search have been classified as (1) *maximizers,* who took as many interviews as possible, get as many job offers as possible, and then rationally chose the best one based on self-specified criteria; (2) *satisfiers,* who took the first offer they got, believing that one company was about the same as any other; and (3) *validators,* who gathered offers until they got an acceptable one and then got one more, just to see if their favorite was good, before taking the favorite offer.[24]

One increasingly important issue in applicant job searches is the *dual-career* issue. With more women entering the work force, married job seekers often require a job for both spouses. Organizations may attempt to provide both spouses with a job in their organization or to provide assistance in locating a job elsewhere for the applicant's spouse. The dual-career factor is likely to become increasingly important in applicant job-search decisions.

Clearly, there is no single model of job-search behavior, nor do we know what kind of search works best under different circumstances. Also, most research on job search and choice has been done with graduating college students, who often have the opportunity to gather several offers before making a choice. In many other situations, such as with unemployed individuals, or those who are changing jobs, there may be pressure to take the first good offer before it expires.

For organizations, understanding the applicant-search process can provide guidance in designing recruitment activities. For example, an organization that can pay high starting salaries but in a less desirable location might require a very quick response to its job offer. Requiring a quick decision will reduce the chance of applicants finding better offers. It may also cause the applicant to use a noncompensatory search process that accepts the minimally desirable location and emphasizes the high salary offer.

Designing a complete recruitment strategy, however, requires considering more than just the timing of the job offer. It involves choosing applicant qualifications, communication channels/sources, inducements, messages, and recruiters. These choices interact with each other (e.g., very stringent qualifications are also frequently combined with attractive inducements) to create the recruiting strategy.

CHOOSING REQUIRED APPLICANT QUALIFICATIONS

Before recruiting can begin, the organization must decide on the nature of the employment vacancy and on the qualifications required to fill it. Employment planning (see Chapter Five) helps to identify the number and types of jobs that will be needed. Job analysis (see Chapter Four) helps to identify the needed job behaviors and the employee characteristics required to carry them out.

As Exhibit 7.1 showed, recruiting acts as the first filter in determining who joins the organization. We have seen that recruiting activities can affect the applicant's search process and, thereby, determine who applies for jobs. Recruiting also filters applicants directly by choosing required applicant qualifications. An organization might try for the cream of the crop by setting stringent qualifications and spending lots of time and money looking for the best candidate. Or, because of a very tight labor market or the desire to reduce recruiting costs, the organization might consider lower-quality candidates, creating a larger applicant pool. Research has found that increasing qualifications reduces the number of applicants but often increases their quality.[25]

An essential choice in recruiting is the level and type of qualifications that will be required before applicants are given further consideration. *Screening* is the process of rejecting clearly unqualified candidates at the recruitment stage, and it is actually the first step in the selection process, discussed in Chapter Eight. Screening devices, such as drug tests, honesty tests, and licensing requirements, will be discussed there, along with other traditional methods of selection, such as interviews. However, organizations are increasingly exploring ways to attract job candidates from nontraditional sources by tapping groups whose qualifications are often overlooked. These include applicants who are older, disabled, remotely located, or minimally English-literate.

Tapping the Older Work Force

As Chapter Two showed, the number of people over 50 years old will increase dramatically, and health and longevity mean that many of these people will be willing and able to work long after they have retired or left their previous organization.[26] Maximum age requirements for jobs are illegal under the Age Discrimination in Employment Act (ADEA), but past attention has focused mostly on how older employees were dismissed or retired.[27] Long-held biases about the availability and ability of older workers often prevent organizations from tapping a valuable applicant source.[28] Yet, such efforts as McDonald's "Mc-Masters," Kelly Girls' "Encore," and Kentucky Fried Chicken's "the Colonel's Tradition" generate significant increases in qualified applicants by recognizing the special requirements and contributions of older workers.[29]

Creating Opportunities for the Disabled

Technological advances and increasingly sophisticated medical treatments are opening opportunities for mentally and physically disabled persons at a rapid pace. The Job Accommodation Network is a national information network and consulting service of the President's Committee on Employment of People with Disabilities that provides a toll-free number advising employers on how to accommodate employees and applicants. A variety of workplace modifications can be used to reduce barriers due to disabilities and, thus, enable the organization to loosen applicant qualification requirements that might have excluded disabled individuals.[30] Holiday Inns, Wyse Technology, Equifax, Inc., Dominoes Pizza, and Weyerhaeuser Company are among the companies profiting from such strategies.[31]

Removing Housing and Transportation Barriers

Should the ability to find transportation to work be a minimum qualification for employment? Many organizations have found that relaxing this requirement by providing transportation, relocating jobs, or other accommodations can increase the available applicant pool. Days Inns recruits homeless workers in Atlanta, housing four of the nine workers in a motel within walking distance of their work.[32] Providing transportation is another option being used more frequently, especially in suburbs of large cities.[33]

Tapping Applicants with Minimum English Literacy Requirements

Should the ability to speak and write English be a minimum qualification for applicants? Some employers have found that this requirement increasingly means severe shortages of qualified applicants. In 1987, 57,000 applicants took the New York Telephone Company's entry-level exam, a simple test measuring basic skills in math, reading, and reasoning—and 54,900 flunked. In Washington, D.C., about 90 percent of young people who apply for jobs with the Chesapeake and Potomac Telephone Company fail its entry-level employment test, set at about the 9th- or 10th-grade reading level.[34] Chapter Eleven, Training, will discuss organizational efforts to implement literacy training to reduce the need for all applicants to have such skills before being hired. Barden, a Connecticut ball-bearing maker, responded to a demand for 125 new workers in a single year by initiating a buddy system and special courses in English to enable the firm to tap applicants representing a "veritable United Nations from such diverse countries as Cambodia, Laos, Colombia, Brazil, the Dominican Republic, Guatemala, Chile, Lebanon, Pakistan, Thailand, and Yemen" who had good educations in their home countries but lacked sufficient English to look up operating procedures in manuals.[35]

CHOOSING RECRUITMENT SOURCES AND COMMUNICATION CHANNELS

Whatever the qualifications, applicants must know that employment opportunities exist. Choosing the types of applicants to inform of vacancies and the communication channels to use determines who will learn about available employment opportunities. Recruiting channels/sources should produce a sufficient number of high-quality applicants at a reasonable cost. They are also often chosen based on company tradition or past practice. Exhibit 7.2 shows the percentage of organizations that use different recruitment sources for jobs including professional/technical jobs (such as scientists, computer programmers, or lawyers), and manager/supervisor jobs. The results come from a survey of 245 organizations by the Bureau of National Affairs. "Promotion from within" is used by virtually everyone, and will be discussed in Chapter Ten, on Internal Staffing. The next sections discuss the most prevalent and well known of the other external recruitment sources.

Walk-ins

Walk-ins are simply people who come to an organization seeking employment, often responding to help-wanted notices posted in the work site. This is a very inexpensive source of recruits, especially for jobs filled primarily through the local labor market. As Exhibit 7.2 shows, it is used very frequently, but less often for professional/technical, sales, and managerial/supervisor positions. It is likely to yield the most applicants when local unemployment is high, though their quality may be mixed. An *open house* can increase walk-in applicants by inviting members of the community, college students, or others to visit the organization's site and learn about its products and technology.

Employee Referrals

Did you ever recommend one of your friends as a job candidate to your boss? If so, you provided an employee referral. As Exhibit 7.2 shows, this is a very frequently used recruitment method, even for professional/technical jobs. It is particularly likely to be used for new and unfamiliar positions, which are frequently harder to fill.[36] Evidence suggests that applicants from employee referrals are less likely to leave the organization in the first year, though not in companies with low morale or substandard working conditions.[37] Perhaps the

EXHIBIT 7.2 Recruiting Sources Used by Employers

	Percent of Companies					
	Any Job Category*	Office/ Clerical	Production/ Service	Professional/ Technical	Commissioned Sales	Managers/ Supervisors
(Number of companies)	(245)	(245)	(221)	(237)	(96)	(243)
Internal sources						
Promotion from within	99%	94%	86%	89%	75%	95%
Employee referrals	91	87	83	78	76	64
Walk-in applicants	91	86	87	64	52	46
Advertising						
Newspapers	97	84	77	94	84	85
Journals/magazines	64	6	7	54	33	50
Direct mail	17	4	3	16	6	8
Radio/television	9	3	6	3	3	2
Outside referral sources						
Colleges/universities	86	24	15	81	38	45
Technical/vocational institutes	78	48	51	47	5	8
High schools/trade schools	68	60	54	16	5	2
Professional societies	55	4	1	51	19	37
Community agencies	39	33	32	20	16	9
Unions	10	1	11	1	—	1
Employment services						
State employment service	73	66	68	38	30	23
Private employment agencies	72	28	11	58	44	60
Search firms	67	1	†	36	26	63
U.S. Employment Service	22	19	20	11	7	7
Employee leasing firms	20	16	10	6	2	†
Computerized resume service	4	†	—	4	—	2
Video interviewing service	2	†	†	1	—	1
Special events						
Career conferences/job fairs	53	20	17	44	19	19
Open house	22	10	8	17	8	7
Other	9	5	5	7	6	7

Note: Percentages for each job category are based on the number of organizations that provided data for that category, as shown by the numbers in parentheses.

* Percentages in this column show the proportion of all responding organizations that use a recruiting source for any one of the job categories.

† Less than 0.5 percent.

Source: Reprinted with permission from *Recruiting and Selection Procedures,* Personnel Policies Forum Survey no. 146, p. 7 (May 1988). Copyright, 1988 by the Bureau of National Affairs, Inc.

"referrer" prescreens the new employee to be sure the referrer doesn't get associated with a failure, or perhaps the referrer tells the job applicant what to expect from the job, or maybe the referrer exerts pressure on the referred person to do well and not make the referrer look bad. However, referrals are influenced by personal characteristics, such as age, gender, and race, which may eventually contribute to difficulties in meeting EEO goals if nonwhite applicants and females are not referred for jobs held predominantly by white males.[38]

Organizational incentives can often increase the quantity and quality of employee referrals. When employees or retirees refer someone who gets hired, the "Referralot" program at Lockheed Missiles and Space Company gives them a cash award, a promotional gift, and an eligibility in a quarterly drawing where four winners receive two $1,000 savings bonds.[39] At Merck, the most admired company for its ability to build talent, its chairman Roy Vagelos acts as his own chief talent scout, and he often greets his managers with "Who have you recruited lately?" The vice president for clinical research boasts that he recently enticed Merck's new head of infectious diseases away from Yale Medical School.[40]

College Recruiting

The appendix to this chapter describes how you can use the college placement process to get a job. There are also self-help books, and college placement offices frequently provide assistance. Here, we discuss college recruitment from the employer's perspective.

As Exhibit 7.2 shows, colleges represent an important source of new talent. College recruiting also represents a large investment. One 1986 study estimated that an average employer spent $329,925 in one year to recruit 161 college graduates and devoted 16 percent of the personnel function budget and 17 percent of personnel head count to college recruiting activities.[41] Though this may seem expensive, organizations often believe that their presence on college campuses maintains an image with future customers. Also, by regularly visiting campuses even when there are few vacancies, organizations maintain the contacts they need to obtain applicants when their needs rise.

Designing a college recruiting program involves choosing schools and attracting applicants for campus interviews.

Choosing Schools

Schools are chosen based on the organization's resources and the type of position. Some organizations limit recruiting costs by visiting only local schools, while larger organizations recruit nationally. Professional/technical positions are frequently recruited from colleges, as Exhibit 7.2 shows, and are often the targets of intensive competition at specialized and prestigious schools. A survey of firms among the Fortune 1000 found that each organization recruited at an average of 47 campuses per year, with the most important factors in choosing schools being (1) reputation in critical skill areas, (2) general school reputation, (3) performance of previous hired from the school, (4) location, and (5) reputation of faculty in critical skill areas.[42]

The most prestigious schools are not always the most desirable, however. PepsiCo is renowned for the quality of its management talent that emphasizes understanding the business. Rather than recruit "hotshots" from Harvard or Stanford, PepsiCo "shops around at second-tier business schools for people willing to get their hands dirty." One recently-hired MBA from the University of Virginia toils as an assistant manager in a Pizza Hut restaurant in Washington, D.C., but can expect to move up in a year or two to regional manager, with 40 or so restaurants under him.[43]

Attracting Applicants

Simply choosing appropriate schools is not enough. Organizations must find ways to become known to students and to inform them about their company's opportunities. Many organizations, such as IBM, designate a small number of universities as "key" schools and assign high-level executives a responsibility for maintaining a liaison with the school. This executive is expected to get to know the faculty and placement officers and to help them understand the kind of positions and student qualifications that best fit her or his company. You may encounter one or several human resource executives as guest speakers in your personnel management class. In addition to giving executives the opportunity to interact with students, this is an excellent way to make students aware of employment opportunities in human resource management and other areas. It's also an excellent opportunity for you to express your interest in a possible future employer.

Organizations can also make donations of equipment, money, or sponsor scholarships. IBM has sponsored development of 10 personal computer human resource learning laboratories at major industrial relations centers across the United States.[44]

Job fairs are employer-sponsored gatherings where students can come to speak with representatives from one or several organizations about career opportunities. *Cooperative education (co-op) or internship programs* hire college students in the summer, to give the students a taste of corporate life and to give the company a chance to evaluate the student's potential. Travelers' Corporation, Cigna Corporation, Champion International Corporation, American Brands, and PepsiCo all have active internship programs, often placing special focus on minorities in technical specialties. At PepsiCo, 60 percent of the interns return after graduation, and top candidates get scholarships.[45] The recruiting process can include not only new graduates but also alumni. Stanford University advertises "ProNet," a database of career profiles of alumni, which costs $3,500 per year for 20 requests but is free to alumni.[46]

Other Educational Institutions

George Bush, during his 1988 campaign, stated, "You don't have to go to college to be a success." Organizations frequently use high schools, trade schools, and technical/vocational schools, as Exhibit 7.2 shows, though less frequently for professional/technical or manager/supervisor jobs. The dearth of young workers expected in the 1990s, combined with growing labor demands in such jobs as salesclerks, waiter/waitresses, nurses aides, technicians, and cashiers, means that employers will come to depend even more on workers without college degrees. Xerox CEO David Kearns has spoken and written extensively about the need to reform U.S. high schools.[47] A growing number of experts argues that one of the best ways to encourage higher academic standards in high school is for employers to scrutinize high school academic records more thoroughly, so there is a real incentive to do well for high school students who do not continue on to college.[48] Some have heralded vocational schools as a source of hope for filling technical job vacancies in the future.[49]

Employment Agencies and Professional Societies

State employment services, private employment agencies, search firms, professional societies, community agencies, and the U.S. Employment Service (USES) provide employee referrals, usually for a fee. As shown in Exhibit 7.2, state and private agencies are used much more frequently than the USES or community agencies.

Public Employment Agencies

The U.S. Employment Service operates over 2,400 employment agencies in the United States, with operating funds from the federal government. One survey found that smaller firms used USES more often than larger ones.[50] It has typically been used mainly to place clerical, unskilled laborers, production workers, and technicians. The USES has instituted more standardized testing and placement systems, which have recently been the subject of some controversy over the proper way to report test scores and avoid adverse impact against minorities.[51] This will be discussed in Chapter Eight.

Private Employment Agencies

These agencies usually specialize in one or more specific skills, ranging from secretaries to accountants to executives. Agencies maintain an inventory of applicants and are often able to fill jobs more quickly than the organization could through its own efforts. Agencies can also provide value by prescreening candidates, saving the time and money of considering unqualified applicants. High-level executive "headhunters" are constantly contacting employed executives to determine their interest in moving to new positions. One fourth of one survey's respondents used executive search firms for higher-salary managerial positions and used private agencies for entry-level and lower-salary positions.[52] A hiring organization usually pays a fee of about 30 percent of the first year's salary for candidates from search firms, with smaller fees to other agencies.

Professional Associations

The American Medical Association, American Dental Association, American Management Association, Society for Women Engineers, American Psychological Association, Society for Human Resource Management, and Academy of Management are professional societies. Their main purpose is to provide a forum through which members of their professions can share ideas, make acquaintances, and improve their professional skills. Most of them also maintain placement services, through which organizations can advertise position openings or attend professional meetings to meet with applicants. Many professors in universities are recruited this way. Your professor may be able to describe how this process worked when she or he was hired.

Advertising

Newspaper ads are one of the most frequently used communication methods for all sorts of jobs. Exhibit 7.2 shows that advertisements are also placed in trade journals or magazines, radio/television, and even mailed directly to people who seem to fit the profile of a likely applicant. Advertisements are seen not only by those seeking employment but by prospective future applicants, customers, and the community. Thus, their message must be carefully chosen and project an image of fairness. Exhibit 7.3 shows a flyer used by Pizza Hut to encourage its customers to find employees for it. The AMA survey found that larger firms used national advertising and spent more on advertising in every category than small firms. Though newspaper ads are almost unanimously used, studies have found this source to more frequently produce low-performing employees with high levels of separations.[53]

Advertisements can be targeted by borrowing techniques from marketing. NEC Information Systems (NECIS) in New England used focus groups (panels of marketing and technical applicants) to tell NECIS what they looked for in a company and in an employment advertisement. NECIS even used a "tachiscope evaluation" that exposed people to a slide of different recruitment ads at speeds of 1/125th, 1/30th, 1/8th and 1 second to see how easily it was to identify the company's name in the advertisement.[54] A recent innovation is computerized talent lists, such as Bank Executives Network, but organizations still do not use computerized résumés or video interviewing very much, as Exhibit 7.2 shows.[55]

Would you ever think to look for a job by reading the bathroom walls? At Chicago's Merchandise Mart, "managers live in dread of the day a prized female staffer announces, 'I'm just going to run to the ladies' room for a minute,'" because she may never return. The 26 women's restrooms at the mart

EXHIBIT 7.3   Recruitment Advertising to Customers at Pizza Hut

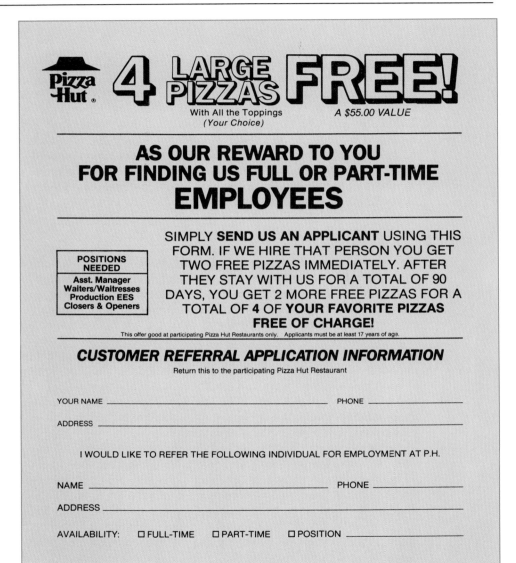

are lined with job notices placed by the home-furnishing and floor-covering wholesalers in the building. One administrative supervisor notes that it's a great prescreening tool, "because everyone using the washrooms has a knowledge of how Mart companies operate."[56]

Temporary Employees

An alternative to recruiting permanent workers is to fill short-term changes in employee needs with temporary employees, also called *contingent employees* or *nonpermanent employees*. Seasonal fluctuations, uncertainty about the future business climate, and unusually high vacations or illnesses often motivate companies to consider temporary employees. The recent growth in service industries, coupled with constant pressure to cut costs and remain flexible, have made temporary employees a virtually permanent fixture for most organizations. Temporary employee options include:

1. *Internal temporary pool,* where persons are on call as needed. The pool is managed internally by the company, and it may consist of former employees or external hires, or both.
2. *Temporary agency hires,* where persons are hired through a temporary service firm and are employees of that agency, not of the firm that contracts for them.
3. *Independent contractors,* who are self-employed workers hired for a finite time, such as free-lance writers or professors acting as consultants.
4. *Short-term hires,* where persons are hired only for a specific time period (such as a busy season) or for a specific project.

Although still less than 5 percent of total wage and salary employment, the use of temporary employees is growing. Between 1980 and 1988, the number of temporary workers employed in the United States each day rose from 416,100 to 1,042,000. Temporary help agency revenues rose from $4 billion in 1980 to $12 billion in 1988.[57] Roughly 35 percent of firms in manufacturing and services use internal temporary pools, over 80 percent use temporary agency hires, and about 60 percent use independent contractors.[58] Exhibit 7.4 shows how the use of temporary employees varies with different occupations.

Gone are the days when temporary workers were used only for secretarial work or Christmas retailing. Temporary help services now provide physicians, pharmacists, accountants, lawyers, and technical personnel.[59] The U.S. government has revised its hiring policies to encourage greater use of temporary employees.[60] Small firms are even hiring chief executives on short-term contracts to get through financial crises or to fill in for managers who suddenly die or become ill and leave no successors.[61] Talent Tree in Houston fill requests for Santas, Smurfs, and Abraham Lincolns.[62]

However, temporary employees are no "free lunch," and they can add to training and hiring costs. They often require creative efforts to adequately motivate them, and it may be more difficult to obtain high-quality work.[63]

Employee leasing involves a longer-term arrangement, whereby an employer dismisses its existing employees, who are then hired by a leasing company and leased back to the original employer. The leasing company takes full responsibility for the employees, including payroll, benefits, taxes, and government-required paperwork, and charges the leaser a fee covering these costs and

---

EXHIBIT 7.4 Use of Temporary Employees by Occupational Category

---

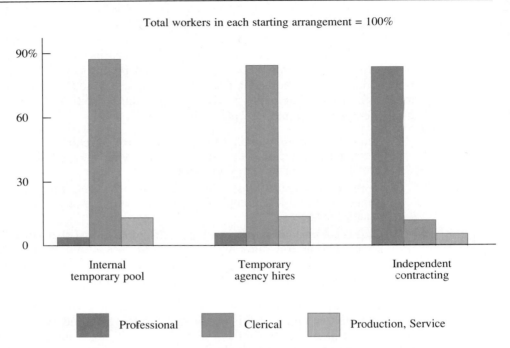

Total workers in each starting arrangement = 100%

Source: Reprinted with permission from Kathleen Cristensen, *Flexible Staffing and Scheduling in U.S. Corporations* (New York: The Conference Board, 1989), p. 8.

administration. Employee leasing increased after passage of the Tax Equity and Fiscal Responsibility Act (TEFRA) in 1982, as a way to establish a "safe harbor" for companies to pay lucrative pension plans to top executives but avoid the requirement of extending those benefits to their employees. Employers may also reap cost reductions, and employees may receive better benefits from the leasing firm than they would from their original company.[64]

Immigrants

Chapter Two noted the increasing proportion of immigrants in the work force. Recruiting this group often involves special efforts, such as advertising in foreign-language newspapers, busing from particular areas of communities, and using community agencies. The Immigration Reform and Control Act of 1986 reflects the increasing concern about the use of illegal aliens and prohibits employers from knowingly hiring, recruiting, or referring for work those aliens who have entered the country illegally or whose immigrant status does not permit their employment. Exhibit 7.5 summarizes the main points of this act. For organizations that recruit immigrants, the stakes are high. Piedmont Quilting, a South Carolina textile firm, was fined $580,000 for employing 85 illegal aliens, including minors, and for paperwork violations involving 400 other employees. Eleven company officers and supervisors were indicted in more than 100 counts, involving up to $5 million in fines and up to 653 years in jail for each if convicted.[65] Some in Congress are now arguing that such serious consequences may lead to discrimination against Hispanics and other minorities as employers refuse to hire anyone who might later turn out to be an illegal immigrant.

CHOOSING INDUCEMENTS

The main inducements for employment applicants involve the rewards, position requirements, and working conditions they will encounter if they join. Chapter Three discussed how jobs are analyzed and designed and how working conditions differ. Compensation and benefits are also powerful inducements, as will be discussed in later chapters.[66] Opportunities for career advancement, skill training, or scholarships are also frequently motivating factors and will be discussed in the chapters on employee development and training.

Certain inducements, however, are focused specifically on the recruiting process. Oil companies may provide loans to top candidates that can be forgiven if they stay more than three years with the company. Service industries, such as ski resorts, hotels, and fast-food restaurants, often offer free or reduced-cost services to new hires and employees. Signing bonuses, long used by sports teams, are also becoming more common among technical/professional and managerial occupations. One study asked 5,000 young men to estimate the probability that they would sign up for the armed services under present inducement levels versus an additional $2,000, $5,000, or $8,000 sign-on bonus. Those responding they would "probably" or "definitely" join were correspondingly 1.1 percent higher, 9.7 percent higher, and 18.3 percent higher.[67] Inducements must be chosen carefully to avoid feelings of inequity among current employees.

Another reason for choosing inducements carefully is that they can serve as signals regarding organization and job characteristics. One study of 30 undergraduate students found that those seeing hypothetical job descriptions with higher pay levels also believed the jobs would be more desirable in challenge, working conditions, skill requirements, and effort required.[68]

CHOOSING THE MESSAGE: REALISM VERSUS FLYPAPER

Would you rather an organization try to recruit you using a "flypaper" approach, which tells you only the most attractive dimension of the organization, or would you prefer a more "realistic" treatment, which includes both the po-

---

EXHIBIT 7.5 Synopsis of the Immigration Reform and Control Act of 1986

Purpose:

To curtail the flood of immigration by undocumented aliens into the United States by making the hiring of such aliens illegal for U.S. employers.

Employment eligibility verification requirements:

The law prohibits employers from knowingly hiring, recruiting, or referring for work aliens who are not authorized to work in the United States. The employer must ask for and examine evidence of prospective employees' identities and employment eligibility indicated by the following documents:

1. A United States passport.
2. A certificate of United States citizenship.
3. A certificate of naturalization.
4. An unexpired foreign passport, if the passport has an appropriate unexpired endorsement of the Attorney General authorizing the individual's employment in the United States.
5. A resident alien card or other alien registration card that contains a photograph or other personal identifying information and that is evidence of authorization for employment in the United States.

If none of the above are available, then the employer must ask for two documents, providing separate evidence of employment eligibility and identity.

Penalties for violations:

1. $250 to $2,000 for a first offense, for each alien involved.
2. $2,000 to $5,000 for a second offense, for each alien.
3. $3,000 to $10,000 for third offense, for each alien.
4. Criminal penalties of up to six months' imprisonment and/or a $3,000 fine for pattern or practice violations.
5. Civil fines of $100 to $1,000 for recordkeeping violations.

Sources: Reproduced with permission from HUMAN RESOURCES MANAGEMENT—IDEAS AND TRENDS IN PERSONNEL Issue No. 130, pages 177–78 (November 14, 1986), published and copyrighted by Commerce Clearing House, Inc., 4025 W. Peterson Avenue, Chicago, IL 60646, The Bureau of National Affairs, Inc., *Immigration Reform: A Practical Guide* (Washington, D.C.: Bureau of National Affairs, 1987).

---

itive and negative aspects? Would the organization be more successful by attracting lots of applicants with positive messages? or by having applicants obtain a more realistic idea so, if they join, they already know what to expect? This is by far the most frequently studied question in recruitment.[69]

The *realistic job preview (RJP)* is an approach that attempts to give recruits an accurate picture of the job and the organization, including negative aspects. RJPs can be delivered through recruiters, booklets, films, or any other communication means. A film for potential operators at Southern Bell made it clear that the work was closely supervised, repetitive, and sometimes required dealing with rude or unpleasant customers.

RJP's may work because (1) applicants with more accurate information "self-select" out of the running for a job if it doesn't suit them, (2) those who take the job have realistic expectations and aren't disappointed, (3) the information helps new employees cope with anticipated work problems, or (4) applicants find honest employers to be more credible and attractive.[70]

Key elements of an RJP include:[71]

1. *Accuracy* of the information is the most common aspect of RJPs and the most frequently studied, though there is little research to indicate whether recipients of RJPs find them accurate.

2. *Specificity* reflects how much the given information focuses on a particular job and on particular job characteristics. Many published RJPs focus on general organizational factors, such as overtime or vacation policies, and provide little information about the day-to-day job environment.

3. *Breadth* refers to the number of job and organizational factors that are covered in an RJP. Most published RJPs appear to focus on only a limited set of factors, omitting things like supervision, promotion opportunities, or department politics.

4. *Credibility* refers to the degree to which applicants believe the RJP information. Psychologists designing RJPs usually assume credibility, though it has seldom actually been measured.

5. *Importance* refers to whether the RJP contains information reflecting factors that applicants want to know about, and that they would not already know through other means. Most published RJPs appear to reflect only generally known job aspects, such as that bank tellers frequently work on their feet. They often do not cover hard-to-get information, such as relations with supervisors, co-workers, and work groups.

RJPs seem to increase employee satisfaction and reduce employee turnover (Chapter Nine will discuss the link between satisfaction and turnover). Exhibit 7.6 gives recommendation in five areas for improving RJP effectiveness. Your professor was probably recruited with an RJP. Most universities bring professor candidates to the school to participate in a series of meetings with deans, directors and potential colleagues.

CHOOSING AND PREPARING RECRUITERS

Virtually every recruitment process includes a meeting with one or more organization members who act as recruiters. This group virtually always includes a representative from the human resource management department, and it may include supervisors, co-workers, and even subordinates as well. Because so much about the organization and the job cannot be known in advance, applicants appear to use aspects of recruiters as signals about job attributes they cannot observe firsthand, and about the likelihood of receiving an offer.

Studies suggest that recruiters perceived as personable and informative seem to signal desirable job characteristics and work/company environments. Recruiters perceived as competent and informative were associated with higher

---

EXHIBIT 7.6   How to Improve Realistic Job Previews' Effectiveness

---

Content
Information should be as accurate, specific, broad, credible and important as possible.

Sources of information
Multiple sources should be used, including job incumbents, the immediate supervisor, the job description, employee manuals, personnel department representatives, and exit interviews with former employees.

Communication
Encourage two-way conversations with job incumbents that are "off the record." Use multiple methods, such as detailed job descriptions, tours of the work site, films portraying difficult job situations, and hands-on work simulations.

Target jobs
Don't restrict RJPs to lower-level jobs. Consider using them for professional/technical and managerial jobs, especially in the wake of restructuring or mergers.

Timing
If the RJP is inexpensive, give it to all applicants to maximize their chance to self-select out of jobs that don't fit them. If the RJP is expensive, prescreen applicants first and give the RJP only to clearly qualified candidates.

Source: James A. Breaugh and Robert S. Billings, "The Realistic Job Preview: Five Key Elements and Their Importance for Research and Practice," *Journal of Business and Psychology* 2, no. 4 (Summer 1988), pp. 291–305.

applicant regard for the company, while aggressive recruiters negatively affected applicants' perceived job attractiveness. When applicants perceived recruiters as more personable, they reported a higher expectancy of receiving a job offer and a higher intention to accept a job.[72] Several studies suggest that recruiters reveal far less about the job and organization than applicants would like to know, and this lack of informativeness has been linked to unfavorable applicant perceptions of their interview performance, lower intentions to accept job offers, and lower willingness to place follow-up phone calls after interviews.[73]

The ideal recruiter will be able and willing to accurately represent the organization in a way that kindles applicants' enthusiasm. Yet, research shows that recruiters frequently project poor personalities and inadequate preparation in campus interviews.[74] Even more disturbing are racial or sexist remarks. The University of Chicago Law School recently suspended the noted Chicago law firm of Baker & McKenzie after a black law school recruit was asked how she would react to being called a "nigger" or "black bitch" by adversaries or colleagues.[75] The U.S. Office of Personnel Management (OPM) has found that even the people who initially take applications or greet applicants are important. When one applicant filled out an application at the Labor Department and asked when she might hear whether she got a job, she was told "possibly never." When she asked a Labor Department employee how he got his job, she was told, "I'm lucky, my mother works downstairs." At the Department of Health and Human Services, applicants couldn't get in without a pass.[76]

With such high stakes, how do organizations determine who recruits? A survey of college recruiting managers favored such criteria as strong interpersonal skills, enthusiasm for the company, knowledge of the company and jobs, and credibility with students and co-workers. Formal credentials, such as recruiter training or seniority, were rated as considerably less important. Moreover, recruiter success was seldom systematically tracked or rewarded.[77] Yet, a few companies choose and train recruiters systematically. At Eastman Kodak Company, recruiters must be nominated by their managers and attend a training conference. Participants stage 20-minute mock interviews, which are videotaped and reviewed.[78]

INTERNATIONAL PERSPECTIVES ON RECRUITING

One of the most interesting and topical contrasts between recruiting in the United States and other countries is the emphasis placed on noncollege education institutions and student performance. In Japan, for example, high schools compete for student entrants, just as U.S. colleges do. The high schools recommend graduates to businesses with which they have cultivated relationships, basing their recommendations on extensive testing that taps not only grades but other indicators of skills and abilities. Businesses usually see only as many applicants as they have openings, and they usually hire all of them. The main screening occurs as high schools with the best business ties select the most talented students, and then as high schools match students with companies.[79]

Roughly 70 percent of West German high school students study a vocation. Grade school students are placed either into *Gymnasium* for college prep through grade 13, *Realschule* that readies tenth-grade students for apprenticeships or technical training, and *Hauptschule,* a lower-level school that prepares students for apprenticeships that begin after ninth or tenth grade. In West Germany, about 500,000 companies every year provide on-the-job training for 1.8 million teenage apprentices, comprising 6 percent of the work force, at a cost of roughly $10 billion. U.S. apprentices make up a mere 0.3 percent of the workers. One superintendent of vocational education observed, "We are committed to training people for college. They are committed to training people for work."[80]

Like their U.S. counterparts, Japanese and some European countries are facing labor shortages. In Japan, this has prompted some organizations to violate the "gentleman's agreement" not to start contacting students until August 20th every year. Japanese young people "don't want to do things that soil their hands," says a Labor Ministry official, which is leading construction companies to employ illegal immigrants.[81] Another result of the Japanese labor shortage is a change in the traditional two-track system that reserved managerial jobs for men and lower-level jobs for "office ladies."[82] One survey suggests that in Melbourne, Australia, organizations make much less use of employee referrals and walk-ins and share the U.S. tendency to use advertisements heavily.[83]

Evidence suggests that temporary agencies and employee leasing are increasingly used in Western Europe, with very different regulatory environments. At one extreme, Greece, Italy, and Spain forbid the operation of temporary work agencies and temporary work contracts altogether (though they exist illegally). Most other countries, such as Belgium, Denmark, France, West Germany, Ireland, Luxembourg, the Netherlands, and the United Kingdom require registration of temporary agencies. Portugal has no effective regulation of any kind.[84]

EVALUATING RECRUITMENT

Do recruiting decisions really make any difference? What organizational goals can they affect? How do organizations measure recruiting effectiveness? The evidence suggests that recruitment is both a costly and potentially valuable activity, but that it is not evaluated very carefully.

Efficiency

Costs

Exhibit 7.7 shows recruiting costs in 1986 dollars for three representative jobs. Recruiting costs vary greatly, according to the level of the job and the intensiveness of the recruiting activity. Costs also differ, depending on the number and type of recruiting sources used. Travel and relocation costs can be reduced by focusing on sources closer to the work site. Search firm fees can be reduced through careful shopping. *Personnel Journal* publishes a "Buyer's Guide" to recruiting organizations and products that can assist managers in identifying ways to lower costs or increase effectiveness.[85]

Productivity

Earlier, we discussed the evidence suggesting that employee referrals seem to generate employees who stay longer with the organization and sometimes perform better. Recent evidence suggests that this may be partly because such referrals tend to tap employees who are older and have more previous experience. It also suggests that referrals from other employees generate more productive employees, but that applicants generated through employment services, newspaper ads, walk-ins, and friends/relatives of employees are not significantly more productive.[86] RJPs can reduce employee separations, as we have seen. Other aspects of the recruiting process have received much less attention, so we know little about their productivity effects. Still, computer simulation has suggested that, when recruitment and selection are integrated, large dollar-valued outcomes are possible.[87] Employers are often less than optimistic about prospects of adequately filling positions. One survey found that only a third of

EXHIBIT 7.7   Recruiting Costs by Category for Three Job Groups

| | Job Titles (yearly salary) | | |
Cost category	General Manager ($80,000)	Purchasing Director ($50,000)	Computer Programmer ($28,000)
Employment agency fee	$16,000	$ 8,000	$4,550
Search firm fee	21,200	12,150	6,650
Referral awards	1,250	200	450
Advertising:			
Local	1,600	900	800
Regional	1,750	1,350	950
National	1,950	1,950	1,550
Trade	1,600	700	1,000
Travel/lodging:			
Candidate	2,450	1,150	650
Recruiter	1,300	400	400
Recruiter salary (per hire)	532	321	235
Relocation	23,200	7,000	8,900

Adapted by permission of the publisher from *Hiring Costs and Strategies*, an AMA Report, p. 13, ©1986 American Management Associations, New York. All rights reserved.

firms believed there was a 90 percent chance or better of adequately filling a position with the first selection, half rated their chances as better than 75 percent, and one 10th rated their chances as less than 75 percent. They were even less optimistic for high-level positions, despite spending more money on these positions.[88]

Equity

Perhaps the most obvious effect of recruitment is on generating a sufficient number of minority and female job candidates so that external selection activities can meet affirmative action and EEO goals. Recruitment success is frequently evaluated by the ease or difficulty of filling vacancies with qualified minorities and females. Government agencies recommend aggressive recruitment as a key method for achieving affirmative action goals.[89] If recruiting activities don't generate enough of these applicants, there is little chance that subsequent selection and career activities will succeed.

Recruitment decisions also affect employee, applicant, and community perceptions of the organization. Advertisements for Dow Chemical Corporation typically depict a new employee describing the company's work on treating ill-

---

EXHIBIT 7.8   Possible Measures to Evaluate Recruiting Activities

---

Attracting

Number of applicants.

Cost per applicant.

Time required to locate applicants.

$$\frac{\text{Qualified applicants}}{\text{Total applicants}}$$

$$\frac{\text{Minority and female applicants}}{\text{Total applicants}}$$

Offers and Hires

$$\frac{\text{Offers extended}}{\text{Visits accepted}}$$

$$\frac{\text{Offers extended}}{\text{Qualified applicants}}$$

$$\frac{\text{Offers accepted}}{\text{Offers extended}}$$

Costs per hire.

Time lapsed per hire.

Same ratios for minorities and females.

Screening

Total visits offered.

$$\frac{\text{Visits offered}}{\text{Applicants}}$$

$$\frac{\text{Qualified minorities and females}}{\text{Qualified applicants}}$$

$$\frac{\text{Visits offered to minorities and females}}{\text{Visits offered}}$$

Results

Performance rating of hires.

Tenure of hires.

Costs per level of performance.

Absenteeism per hire.

---

nesses or feeding populations, thereby creating a positive organizational image, as well as attracting recruits. RJPs can adjust applicant expectations, creating an image of openness and fairness, even among applicants who choose not to take job offers.

Actual Recruiting Evaluation Practices

Though studies are limited, they suggest that organizations do not carefully evaluate recruiting activities against objectives/standards. Although surveyed Fortune 1000 companies consistently indicated that such objective factors as costs, applicant quality, new-hire performance, and retention rates are important in evaluating recruiting strategies, less than 30 percent of responding companies actually recorded retention rates, recruiting costs by source, applicant qualifications by source, or performance differences across recruiters and sources. Filling job vacancies and following proper procedures dominate the evaluation information actually collected.[90]

Exhibit 7.8 describes several of the many measures that might be used to evaluate recruiting activities. They reflect the processes of attracting, making offers, initial screening, as well as the results. They reflect both efficiency and equity dimensions. It seems likely that, if organizations made efforts to collect such information, they might uncover relationships between important outcomes and the recruiting choices described here. Then, changes in recruiting strategies could be better planned and implemented.

Experience How Personal Computers Can Support Recruitment Planning and Evaluation

Personal computers are increasingly becoming the tool of choice for managing information about recruiting activities and their results. This book comes with a disk containing a software exercise that allows you to use any IBM-compatible personal computer to plan and evaluate college recruiting at a hypothetical company called *Ithaca's Own*. The case, "Recruitment Planning at Ithaca's Own" at the end of the book, explains how to use the software, and provides you with questions to guide your thinking.

SUMMARY

External recruiting attracts a pool of applicants from which some are chosen for employment offers. We have seen that this relatively simple-sounding activity requires a keen awareness of external and internal organizational conditions, such as increasing labor shortages and rapidly changing position requirements. Also, recruitment is a two-way process, with recruitment messages serving not only as signals to the organization regarding applicant quality but as signals to applicants, government agencies, and communities about the organization's image and philosophy. We have described the decisions involved in recruitment: (1) choosing required applicant qualifications, (2) choosing recruitment sources and communication channels, (3) choosing inducements, (4) choosing the message, and (5) choosing and preparing recruiters. While each was treated separately, they must blend to form an integrated strategy. Choices in one area imply opportunities and constraints in others.

Attracting a large and appropriately qualified applicant pool establishes the foundation for external staffing. The next step is to choose the applicants who should receive employment offers, which is the topic of Chapter Eight, External Selection.

DISCUSSION AND REVIEW QUESTIONS

1. How can recruiting help meet such organizational goals as EEO compliance and increasing productivity? Can it be used to reduce the number of employees? Explain.

2. What do job applicants expect from organizations recruiting them? Does this conflict with the organizations needs during the process?

3. Explain how understanding the various approaches to an applicant's job search could allow an organization to develop a more effective recruiting process.

EXHIBIT 7.9   Recruitment Advertising for Fast-Food Workers (actual advertisement included in McDonald's Happy Meals for Children, September 1988)

Dear Mom:

It's that time of year again. The kids have gone back to school and Christmas is just around the corner.

We at McDonald's would like to help you earn that extra spending money that would come in handy this season.

The nice thing about a job at McDonald's is that we need you when you want to work. If your kids are home, you can be also.

Our hours are flexible and can be changed with a short notice. Uniforms and meals are also provided.

Please stop in.

4. Discuss how setting applicant qualifications can be used to increase or decrease an applicant pool. As the traditional labor force shrinks, how can recruiters increase their effectiveness in finding workers?

5. Different external recruitment sources are more appropriate for different jobs. How does an organization choose which sources to use? Explain.

6. What sort of criteria helps an organization decide which schools to target while recruiting? How are these decisions likely to change as the traditional labor force shrinks?

7. What messages do recruiting inducements send to applicants? Can they be used to achieve organizational goals, such as EEO compliance and reducing turnover?

8. Compare the "realistic" and "flypaper" approaches to recruiting. Discuss the RJP and its effects.

9. Is the recruiter an important part of the process? What sorts of things can an individual recruiter affect?

10. Discuss the value of and criteria for evaluating recruitment.

◆

YOUR TURN
HAPPY MEAL RECRUITMENT ADVERTISING

Exhibit 7.9 contains an actual recruitment advertisement included in McDonald's Happy Meals for children in September 1988. Read the advertisement and consider how it might be used as part of a complete recruiting strategy. Imagine that you work at some other competing fast-food restaurant, and your manager has asked you if your organization should initiate a similar program. Your instructor has additional information about this case. The following questions can guide you:

1. What applicant-search process is McDonald's trying to appeal to? Does it involve both occupation and organizational choice? Why did McDonald's place the ad in Happy Meals in September?
2. What kinds of applicant qualifications and characteristics are likely to be generated by this kind of communication?
3. What changes in the working arrangements might need to be made if large numbers of applicants responding to this ad are hired?
4. What inducements are highlighted by the advertisement?
5. Does the advertisement adopt a "flypaper" or a "realistic" approach? What are the likely consequences of this?
6. What kinds of recruiters are respondents to this ad likely to encounter? Will this require any special selection or training for recruiters?
7. What are the likely effects of tapping this applicant pool on both efficiency and equity?

APPENDIX
A Diagnostic Approach to Your Own Job Search

The recruiting process takes on special significance as you prepare to find a job. This section uses the diagnostic approach to describe the steps in recruiting from a college student's perspective. Keep in mind, however, that most colleges have placement experts who can provide additional specialized information concerning their particular placement process.

DECIDING ON AN OCCUPATION/VOCATION

Chances are that you've already given some thought to the general kind of occupation you'd like to enter. You may have already chosen a major area of study that will lead to jobs in a specific occupation, such as chemical engineering, computer programming, marketing, or human resource management. Even within these broad occupational categories, however, there are many types of occupations offering very

EXHIBIT 7.10   Stages in the Job-Search Strategy

Assess Conditions	Prepare Your Case	Present Your Case	Consider Offers
You	Résumé	Interviews	Reply
Opportunities	Cover letter		
Environment	Job sources	Site visits	Accept/reject

different rewards and demands. A talk with a career counsellor or taking a career interest inventory may help you specify more precisely what it is you want out of your occupation. The beginning of Chapter Ten gives an example of a career interest inventory. A widely used book that provides a good starting point is *What Color Is Your Parachute,* by Richard Bolles. We'll assume that you've narrowed down your occupational choice, and now we discuss in detail the recruiting process for choosing a job and organization.

Exhibit 7.10 lists the four major steps in job search.

ASSESSING CONDITIONS

The first step is to carefully consider the conditions affecting your job search. These three major areas are yourself, the available jobs, and the external environment.

Assessing Yourself

The job you get must fit you. So, the first step is to carefully consider what you need and desire from your work. For most students, the job categories they consider are largely determined by their college training. But even within fairly specialized categories, such as personnel management, there is a wide variety of job types. A good match depends on how well you know what you want. Consider the following questions:

1. How hard do I like to work?
2. Do I like to be my own boss, or would I rather work for someone else?
3. Do I like to work alone, with a few others, or with large groups?
4. Do I like to work at an even pace or in bursts of energy?
5. Does location matter? Do I want to work near home? In warmer climates? In ski country? Am I willing to be mobile?
6. How much money do I want? Am I willing to work for less money but in a more interesting job?
7. Do I like to work in one place or many; indoors or outdoors?
8. How much variety do I want in work?

It is also important to consider what you want from an employer. The following questions illustrate issues to ponder:

1. Do I have a size preference?
2. Do I have a sector preference (private, not for profit, public sector)?
3. What kinds of industries interest me? (This is usually based on interests in company products or services.)
4. Have I checked to make sure that the sector or product or service has a good future and will lead to growth in opportunity?

Finally, it is important to carefully consider your own employment preparation. What do you have to offer an employer? For which jobs are your particular credentials suited? Specific areas of consideration parallel the parts of a résumé, so this process will help you prepare a résumé. At this stage it is also important to identify the job opportunities for which you are qualified.

Assess Job Opportunities

To assess the numbers and types of jobs available to you, you should use as many sources of jobs and job information as you can. The right sources for you are those best tailored to your particular job desires. Some of the sources you should consider include:

Newspapers and professional publications Read the media ads for the type of job you want, and read the professional publications and newspapers in the area you have selected. *The Wall Street Journal* and the *New York Times* are examples of where to look. Respond to ads that sound interesting.

College placement offices These offices have some job information, and they are the place where recruiters offer job interviews. Get to know the placement office people. Sign up for all interviews that sound interesting that you can work into your schedule.

Professional associations Many professional associations provide job placement services. Get your name in the placement application file. Job ads appear in their publications, too.

Private employment agencies and executive search firms Another source of jobs is the private employment agency. Generally, you should visit them and bring a résumé. They charge a fee, often payable by the employer, but sometimes payable by you. The fee can be as much as 15 percent of the first year's salary. Executive search firms tend to recruit middle managers and up (salaries in the $50,000 range).

Some firms also offer résumé preparation, testing services, and career counseling. They often charge up to $1,500, whether you get a job or not. Though this fee is usually paid by employers, ask about any costs that you must bear.

Personal Contacts   One of the best sources of jobs is to contact people working for the organization or who have worked there in the past. Develop your contacts from as many sources as you can: parents, relatives, friends, fraternity brothers, or sorority sisters. Some experts estimate that 80 percent of jobs are never advertised. Contacts get these jobs. You might consider conducting an "exploration interview" with someone who holds or previously held a job similar to one you are considering. Alumni from your school are often quite willing to participate in such interviews. Exhibit 7.11 lists several questions appropriate for such an interview.

Direct mail   It is useless to mail unsolicited résumés to personnel offices without a personal approach. One way that sometimes works is to write a personalized letter to the personnel manager of the organization explaining why you are applying to them. Find out the manager's name. Specify your preferences and advantages in the letter and tell the manager you will call in 10 days to two weeks for a job interview. Sitting back and waiting for an organization to come to you is not fruitful.

Assess Environmental Conditions

As discussed in Chapter Two, factors in the environment affect your job-seeking behavior. If jobs are scarce, you have to start looking earlier and look harder. You may need to compromise your expectations.

PREPARE YOUR CASE

With your job preferences established, and a firm grasp on the available job opportunities and what they offer, you are ready to begin preparing your case for employment.

Preparing a Résumé

A résumé is the first, and sometimes the only, glimpse a prospective employer has of a job applicant. It should present a professional, organized, competent image. Thus, it should be uncluttered, balanced, grammatical, accurate, and readable. Exhibit 7.12 contains a sample résumé for a human resource management student. Most résumés include the following information:[91]

1. Identification—name, address, and phone number.
2. Career or job objective.
3. Educational background (including directly related coursework).
4. Work experience (related to the job).
5. Activities or community involvement.
6. Interests and/or hobbies (where relevant to the job).
7. Published papers or articles.
8. A statement indicating references.

EXHIBIT 7.11   Questions for a Job Exploration Interview

Personal background
  1. When you were in college, what did you think your career was going to be? What was your undergraduate major field of study? What was your graduate field of study?

Preparation
  1. Which credentials, educational degrees, or licenses are required for entry into this kind of work?
  2. What kinds of prior experience are absolutely essential?
  3. How did *you* prepare yourself for this work?

Present job
  1. Describe what you do during a typical workweek.
  2. Which skills or talents are most essential for effectiveness in this job?
  3. What are the toughest problems with which you must deal?
  4. What do you find most rewarding about the work itself, apart from external motivators, such as salary, fringe benefits, or travel?

Prior experience
  1. Which of your past work experiences affect what you do now?
  2. Have any of your job changes been for reasons of lifestyle?

Career future
  1. If things develop as you'd like, what sort of ideal career do you see for yourself?
  2. If the work you do was suddenly eliminated, which different kinds of work could you do?
  3. How rapidly is your present career field growing? How would you describe or estimate future prospects?

Lifestyle
  1. What obligations does your work place on you, outside the regular workweek? Do you enjoy these obligations?
  2. How much flexibility do you have in dress, work hours, vacation schedules, and place of residence?

Advice
  1. How well is my background suited to this job?
  2. What additional educational preparation do you feel would be best?
  3. Which kinds of experiences, paid employment or other, would you recommend?
  4. If you were a college graduate and had it to do over again, what would you do differently?

Hiring criteria
  1. If you were hiring someone to work with you today, which factors would be most important in your hiring decision and why?

Adapted from *Student Job Search* (Ithaca, N.Y.: Cornell University of Career Services, NYSSILR, 1987).

EXHIBIT 7.12   Sample Résumé for a Human Resource Management Student

PROFESSIONAL OBJECTIVES:	A position in human resource management utilizing my education, training, and experience while gaining exposure to a wide range of personnel functions with particular emphasis on employee relations.
PERSONAL QUALIFICATIONS:	Excellent organizational skills, well-developed leadership abilities. Strong academic and practical background. Proven interpersonal skills with groups and individuals.
EDUCATION:	**Cornell University**, Ithaca, New York New York State School of Industrial and Labor Relations Bachelor of Science Degree, June 1, 1988 **Bucknell University**, Lewisburg, Pennsylvania School of Arts and Sciences, September 1984–May 1985

COURSE CONCENTRATIONS:

Organizational behavior and development	Compensation administration
Labor history, law, management, and economics	Employee staffing and supervision Human resource economics
Psychology	Statistics
	Collective bargaining

EMPLOYMENT EXPERIENCE:	**Resident Adviser** (August 1987–June 1988) Department of Residence Life, Cornell University Responsible for directly assisting 90 college freshmen adjust to university life by coordinating educational and social programming and providing personal and academic counseling. **Labor Relations Intern** (May 1987–August 1987) Central New York Bottle Company, a Division of Philip Morris, Inc., Auburn, New York. Administered corporate quality awareness program including a 30-day participation booster campaign, researched and compiled three-year analysis of grievances, worked with employee involvement implementation, grievance resolutions, workers' compensation, disability claims, and nonexempt attendance program maintenance. **Research Intern** (January 1987) Buffalo-Erie County Labor Management Council, Suite 407, Convention Tower, Buffalo, New York. Developed and administered several research techniques and compiled the information into a case study of labor/management participation in an abrasives company. **Marketing/Public Relations Supervisor** (May 1986–August 1986) Darien Lake Amusement Park, Corfu, New York. Composed and supervised the administration of consumer surveys. **Proposals Intern** (January 1985) GTE Sylvania, Mountain View, California. Organized and revamped the entire proposals department filing system. **Restaurant Supervisor** (Summer 1982–1985) Service Systems/Darien Lake, Corfu, New York. Sole supervisor of the largest fast-food stand in an amusement park.
ACTIVITIES:	Resident adviser Cornell dining employee Secretary–Treasurer, college student government American Society of Personnel Administrators N.Y.S. School of Industrial and Labor Relations Ambassador Volunteer at area nursing home; Traveling, skiing, socializing
REFERENCES:	Available on request

Source: *Student Job Search* (Ithaca, N.Y.: Cornell University, Office of Career Services, NYSSILR, 1986).

Preparing a Cover Letter

When you send your résumé to employers, include a cover letter. Your objective is to write a cover letter that will make the employer want to learn more from your résumé and, perhaps, through a subsequent job interview. Keep the following guidelines in mind:

1. Each letter should be a typed original, not a photocopy.
2. Grammar, spelling, and style should be perfect. Have someone else (preferably someone skilled in editing) proof it for you.
3. Send the letter to a *person,* not an office. If you know someone in the company, send it to them. If not, call and get the name of an executive in the area in which you want to work.
4. If someone encouraged you to apply, ask their permission to use their name in the letter.
5. Keep the letter simple. Express interest in the position. Briefly summarize your credentials, and request an interview.

Exhibit 7.13 contains a sample cover letter for a student in human resource management.

Interview Preparation

Initial employment interviews are usually a half hour long, so it is very important that you be well prepared to present your case. Several steps will help you prepare:[92]

1. *Research the employer.* This means more than reading the promotional brochure. You can check through the *New York Times Index* or recent issues of such business publications as *The Wall Street Journal* or *Business Week* for developments related to the area in which you want to work. Placement offices often collect annual reports and employment manuals for companies who recruit on campus regularly.
2. *Know your résumé and anticipate questions.* Have a friend or instructor read your résumé and identify obvious questions. Be prepared to emphasize your strengths and to discuss areas of weakness in a way that best represents your qualifications.
3. *Have questions in mind for the interviewer,* such as: "Please describe the job duties." "Why is the position open?" "Where does it fit in the organization's hierarchy?" "What have been the best results produced by others in this job?" "What do you like most about your job and this company?"
4. *Dress neatly* in clothes similar to those expected on the job.

PRESENT YOUR CASE

The moment of truth arrives. You are about to enter the office and begin the interview. If you have prepared carefully, you will be ready to get the most out of the interview and provide the interviewer with information that best represents your qualifications.

EXHIBIT 7.13   Example Cover Letter

725 State Street
Ithaca, NY 14850
February 8, 1988

Mr. Samuel Staples
Personnel Manager, Federal Mogul Corporation
198 Hollywood Blvd.
Los Angeles, CA 95678

Dear Mr. Staples:

I am currently a senior in the School of Industrial and Labor Relations at Cornell University and am seeking employment in the field of human resources. The Office of Career Services has informed me that your organization will be recruiting at our school this semester. I would very much like to meet with you to discuss employment opportunities at Federal Mogul. Because of the limited interviews and bidding system that further restricts the possibility of being successful in obtaining an interview, I would appreciate being included on your invitation list.

My main interest in human resources is in the areas of training and organizational development. These areas will provide me the opportunity to make a contribution in the development of an organization's human resources at both the individual and the unit levels, which I feel greatly influences operations. I plan to begin my career as a generalist or in the area of compensation to establish a solid grounding in the organization in which I am employed. Either position will provide an overall picture of an organization's human resource function as it relates to other operating functions. After reviewing the available information on the position at Federal Mogul, I believe it would provide this opportunity.

Additionally, my experience, as can be seen by my résumé, is very compatible with much of the industry in which your organization operates. Although limited, my knowledge of your firm will allow me to become a contributing member more rapidly. This knowledge has been acquired through several temporary part-time positions with Federal Mogul.

Once again, I am very interested in the opportunities at Federal Mogul. Thank you very much for your consideration. I look forward to hearing from you.

Cordially,

Source: *Student Job Search* (Ithaca, N.Y.: Cornell University, Office of Career Services, NYSSILR, 1987).

Interview

Though no two interviews are the same, campus interviews typically follow this sequence:

1. *Introduction,* initiated by the interviewer, involves personal introductions, some small talk to set the applicant at ease, and perhaps a plan for the interview.
2. *Interrogation,* also initiated by the interviewer, involves questions designed to probe the candidate's strengths and weaknesses and assess problem-solving abilities.
3. *Selling,* initiated by the applicant, provides a chance to describe qualifications in more detail, ask questions about the job and company, and demonstrate interest and knowledge about the company.
4. *Conclusion,* initiated by the recruiter, involves a description of the decision-making process, dates by which the candidate can expect to hear from the company (usually two to four weeks), and the end of the interview.

Interview Follow-Up

Be sure to keep a record of your contacts. Immediately after leaving the interview make the following notations:

◆ The name of the interviewer.
◆ The type of opportunity for which you were considered.
◆ Location of work.
◆ Your reaction and possible interest.
◆ *Your next action.*

Answers to Invitations for Visits

If you receive an invitation for a plant visit, acknowledge it in one of three ways:

1. Accept and set the date when you will be there.
2. Indicate your desire to accept at a later date if you need more time to consider.
3. Decline for whatever honest reason you have.

Follow-Up to Site Visit

If you make a site visit, as soon as you return send a letter of thanks to the individual who issued the invitation, as well as to any others you believe should receive a special note of appreciation.

CONSIDERING OFFERS

With hard work and luck, your efforts will pay off with one or several employment offers. Though you may think this is the end of the process, it still requires careful handling.

Replying to an Offer

Offers of employment may be made verbally, by telegram, or by letter, the last two being the most usual means.

Again, there are innumerable ways of handling an offer. Most companies do not expect an immediate acceptance or rejection, but they do expect an acknowledgment. *Therefore, be sure to reply within three days* after receiving the offer, thanking them and stating a time when you will send definite word, provided they have not already specified a deadline date. If they have, send a letter of acknowledgment and indicate your final answer will be forthcoming by the specific date.

Delaying a Final Answer

The occasion might arise when you need an extension of time. If so, send another letter and state quite frankly your reasons and request their indulgence. Remember always to keep in mind the employer's position as well as your own.

Accepting an Offer

It is probably unnecessary to go into detail on how to accept an offer beyond the fact that an enthusiastic note of appreciation should be sent, together with an indication of when you will report for work. This latter point, of course, is developed by mutual agreement.

Rejecting an Offer

Letters of rejection should be sent just as soon as you realize you are definitely not interested in accepting. It is not necessary to state your exact reasons for turning down an offer, or to say where you expect to go, but it is courteous to express your sincere thanks for having been favorably considered. It is helpful for the organization to know what your true feelings are regarding them, such as preference for a different location, another product, or different initial training.

NOTES AND REFERENCES

1. Jeffrey A. Tannenbaum, "Firms Try Busing to Ease Labor Shortage," *The Wall Street Journal,* December 30, 1988, p. B2.
2. Udayan Gupta and Jeffrey A. Tannenbaum, "Labor Shortages Force Changes at Small Firms," *The Wall Street Journal,* May 22, 1989, p. B1.

3. "All Hands on Deck!" *Time,* July 18, 1988, pp. 42–43.

4. Lynne F. McGee, "Innovative Labor Shortage Solutions," *Personnel Administrator,* December 1989, pp. 56–60.

5. Jeffrey A. Tannenbaum, "Firms Try Busing."

6. "Motel Franchiser Hires Homeless, Older Workers to Stem Labor Shortage," *BNA's Employee Relations Weekly,* May 15, 1989, pp. 637–38.

7. "Staffing Woes," *Human Resource Management News,* March 4, 1989, p. 2.

8. Sara L. Rynes and Alison E. Barber, "Applicant Attraction Strategies: An Organizational Perspective," *Academy of Management Review* 15, no. 2 (1990), pp. 286–310.

9. Amanda Bennett, "As Pool of Skilled Help Tightens, Firms Move to Broaden Their Role," *The Wall Street Journal,* May 8, 1989, p. B1; Linda Fernandez, ed., *Now Hiring: An Employer's Guide to Recruiting in a Tight Labor Market* (Washington, D.C.: Bureau of National Affairs, 1989).

10. J. L. Holland, *The Psychology of Vocational Choice* (New York: Blaisdell, 1966); D. Brown, "The Status of Holland's Theory of Vocational Choice," *Career Development Quarterly* 36, no. 1 (1988), pp. 13–23; J. Holland, "Current Theory of Holland's Theory of Careers: Another Perspective," *Career Development Quarterly* 36, no. 1 (1988), pp. 24–30.

11. Nancy J. Perry, "The New, Improved Vocational School," *Fortune,* June 19, 1989, pp. 127–38.

12. J. C. Hanson and D. P. Campbell, *Manual for the SVIB-SCII* (Stanford, Calif.: Stanford University Press, 1985); D. G. Zytowski, *Kuder Occupational Interest Survey for DD Manual Supplement* (Chicago: Science Research Associates, 1986).

13. D. W. Stevens, "A Reexamination of What Is Known about Job-Seeking Behavior in the United States," Paper presented to the Conference on Labor Market Intermediaries, sponsored by the National Commission for Manpower Policy, November 16–17, 1977.

14. C. Rosenfeld, "Job-Seeking Methods Used by American Workers," *Monthly Labor Review,* August 1975, pp. 39–42.

15. L. D. Dyer, "Job Search Success of Middle-Aged Managers and Engineers," *Industrial and Labor Relations Review,* January 1973, pp. 969–79; J. Barron and D. W. Gilley, "The Effect of Unemployment Insurance on the Search Process," *Industrial and Labor Relations Review,* March 1979, pp. 363–66; Martin Feldstein, "The Economics of the New Unemployment," *Public Interest,* Fall 1973, pp. 3–42; Ronald G. Ehrenberg and Ronald L. Oaxaca, "Unemployment Insurance, Duration of Unemployment and Subsequent Wage Gain," *American Economic Review,* December 1976, pp. 754–66; Finis Welch, "What Have We Learned from Empirical Studies of Unemployment Insurance," *Industrial and Labor Relations Review,* July 1977, pp. 451–61.

16. Jean Powell Kirnan, John A. Farley, and Kurt F. Geisinger, "The Relationship between Recruiting Source, Applicant Quality, and Hire Performance: An Analysis by Sex, Ethnicity, and Age," *Personnel Psychology* 42 (1989), pp. 293–308.

17. Sara L. Rynes and John Lawler, "A Policy-Capturing Investigation of the Role of Expectancies in Decisions to Pursue Job Alternatives," *Journal of Applied Psychology* 68, no. 4 (1983), pp. 620–31.

18. Thomas Gutteridge and Joseph Ullman, "On the Return to Job Search," in *Proceedings of Academy of Management,* Boston, August 1973, pp. 366–72; and J. C. Ullman and T. G. Gutteridge, "The Job Search," *Journal of College Placement* 33, no. 2 (1973), pp. 67–72, "The Higher the Pay the Longer the Job Hunt," *The Wall Street Journal,* December 15, 1989, p. B1.

19. *Empirical Analysis of the Search Behavior of Low-Income Workers* (Menlo Park, Calif.: Stanford Research Institute, 1975); G. L. Reid, "Job Search and the Effectiveness of Job-Finding Methods, *Industrial and Labor Relations Review,* June 1972, pp. 479–95.

20. Brian D. Steffy, Karyll N. Shaw, and Ann Wiggins Noe, "Antecedents and Consequences of Job Search Behaviors," *Journal of Vocational Behavior* 35 (1989), pp. 254–69.

21. Diane Cole, "Letting Computers Lend a High-Tech Helping Hand," *New York Times,* October 30, 1988, p. F15.

22. J. W. Payne, "Task Complexity and Contingent Processing in Decision Making: An Information Search and Protocol Analysis," *Organizational Behavior and Human Performance* 16 (1976), pp. 366–87.

23. Ronald G. Ehrenberg and Robert S. Smith, *Modern Labor Economics,* 3rd ed. (Glenview, Ill.: Scott, Foresman, 1988).

24. William Glueck, "Decision Making: Organization Choice," *Personnel Psychology,* Spring 1974, pp. 66–93; "How Recruiters Influence Job Choices on Campus," *Personnel,* March–April 1971, pp. 46–52.

25. L. V. Gerstner, "College Recruiting: Why the Good Ones Get Away," *Management Review* 55 (1966), pp. 4–12; F. T. Malm, "Hiring Procedures and Selection Standards in the San Francisco Bay Area," *Industrial and Labor Relations Review* 8 (1955), pp. 231–52; Judy D. Olian and Sara L. Rynes, "Organizational Staffing: Integrating Practice with Strategy," *Industrial Relations* 23 (1984), pp. 170–83; W. F. Gerson, "The Effects of a Demanding Application Process on the Applicant Pool for Teaching Positions," Ph.D. dissertation, University of Pennsylvania, 1975, *Dissertation Abstracts International* 36, 7773A; N. A. Mason and J. A. Belt, "Effectiveness of Specificity in Recruitment Advertising," presented at 45th annual meeting of the Academy of Management, San Diego, August 1985.

26. Michael E. Borus, Herbert S. Parnes, Steven H. Sandell, and Bert Seidman, eds., *The Older Worker* (Madison, Wis.: Industrial Relations Research Association, 1988).

27. Stephen S. Rappaport, *Age Discrimination* (Washington, D.C.: Bureau of National Affairs, 1989).

28. Jeanette N. Cleveland, Ronald M. Festa, and Linda Montgomery, "Applicant Pool Composition and Job Perception: Impact on Decisions Regarding an Older Applicant," *Journal of Vocational Behavior* 32 (1988), pp. 112–25; Dane E. Herz and Philip L. Rones, "Institutional Barriers to Employment of Older Workers," *Monthly Labor Review,* April 1989, pp. 14–21.

29. Linda Fernandez, "Now Hiring," p. 118.

30. Kevin R. Hopkins, Clint Bolick, and Susan L. Nestleroth, *Opportunity 2000: Creative Affirmative Action Strategies for a Changing Workforce* (Washington, D.C.: Employment and Standards Division of the U.S. Department of Labor).

31. "Hiring the Handicapped Gets New Emphasis in Bid to Staff Hard-to-Fill Jobs," *The Wall Street Journal,* October 3, 1989, p. A1.

32. "Motel Franchiser Hires Homeless, Older Workers to Stem Labor Shortage," *BNA's Employee Relations Weekly* 7 (May 15, 1989), pp. 637–38.

33. Jeffrey A. Tannenbaum, "Firms Try Busing to Ease Labor Shortage," *The Wall Street Journal,* December 30, 1988, p. B2.

34. David Whitman, Joseph P. Shapiro, Ronald A. Taylor, Amy Saltzman, and Bruce B. Auster, "The Forgotten Half," *U.S. News and World Report,* June 26, 1989, pp. 45–53; "National Alliance of Business Chief Sees Business Problems in Growing Shortage of Qualified Workers," *BNA's Labor Relations Week* 4, no. 2 (January 1990).

35. "Language Course Taps New Bank of Work Skills," *Human Resource Management News,* December 30, 1989, p. 2.

36. American Management Association, *Hiring Costs and Strategies: The AMA Report* (New York: American Management Association, 1986).

37. J. C. Ullman, "Employee Referrals: Prime Tool for Recruiting Workers," *Personnel* 43, no. 1 (1966), pp. 30–35; D. P. Schwab, "Recruiting and Organizational Participation," in *Personnel Management,* ed. K. Rowland and G. Ferris (Boston: Allyn & Bacon, 1982); P. J. Decker and E. T. Cornelius, "A Note on Recruiting Sources and Job Survival Rates," *Journal of Applied Psychology* 64, no. 3 (1979), pp. 463–64; M. J. Gannon, "Source of Referral and Employee Turnover," *Journal of Applied Psychology* 55, no. 1 (1971), pp. 226–28; R. E. Hill, "New Look at Employee Referrals as a Recruitment Channel," *Personnel Journal* 49, no. 1 (1970), pp. 144–48; D. F. Caldwell and W. A. Spivey, "The Relationship between Recruiting Source and Employee Success: An Analysis by Race," *Personnel Psychology* 36 (1983), pp. 67–72.

38. Harry J. Holzer, "Hiring Procedures in the Firm: Their Economic Determinants and Outcomes," in Morris M. Kleiner, Richard N. Block, Myron Roomkin, and Sidney W. Salsburg, eds., *Human Resources and the Performance of the Firm* (Madison, Wis.: Industrial Relations Research Association, 1987).

39. "Referral Payoff," *Human Resource Management News,* March 4, 1989, p. 2.

40. Faye Rice, "Leaders of the Most Admired," *Fortune,* January 29, 1990, p. 40.

41. Sara L. Rynes and John W. Boudreau, "College Recruiting in Large Organizations: Practice, Evaluation, and Research Implications," *Personnel Psychology* 39 (1986), pp. 729–57.

42. Rynes and Boudreau, "College Recruiting in Large Organizations."

43. Brian Dumaine, "Those Highflying PepsiCo Managers," *Fortune,* April 10, 1989.

44. John W. Boudreau, "Building a PC-Based Human Resource Management Curriculum at the School of Industrial and Labor Relations, Cornell University," presented at the National Industrial Relations Research Association Meeting, December 1989, Working Paper no. 90-03, Center for Advanced Human Resource Studies, Cornell University.

45. "Internship Programs Still Thrive," *The Wall Street Journal,* May 9, 1989, p. A1.

46. Anne R. Field, "Hunting Heads the High-Tech Way," *Business Week,* August 17, 1987.

47. David Whitman, Joseph P. Shapiro, Ronald A. Taylor, Amy A. Saltzman, and Bruce B. Auster, "The Forgotten Half," *U.S. News & World Report,* June 26, 1989, pp. 45–53.

48. John Bishop, "Productivity Consequences of What Is Learned in High School," *Journal of Curriculum Studies,* 1990, forthcoming.

49. Nancy J. Perry, "The New, Improved Vocational School."

50. American Management Association, "Hiring Costs and Strategies."

51. John A. Hartigan and Alexandra K. Wigdor, eds., *Fairness in Employment Testing* (Washington, D.C.: National Academy Press, 1989).

52. American Management Association, "Hiring Costs and Strategies."

53. James A. Breaugh, "Relationships between Recruiting Sources and Employee Performance, Absenteeism, and Work Attitudes," *Academy of Management Journal* 24 (1981), pp. 142–47; James A. Breaugh and R. B. Mann, "Recruiting Source Effects: A Test of Two Alternative Explanations," *Journal of Occupational Psychology* 57 (1984), pp. 261–67; Martin J. Gannon, "Sources of Referral and Employee Turnover," *Journal of Applied Psychology* 55 (1971), pp. 226–28; P. J. Decker and Edwin T. Cornelius III, "A Note on Recruiting Sources and Job Survival Rates," *Journal of Applied Psychology* 64 (1979), pp. 463–64; Donald P. Schwab, "Recruiting and Orga-

nizational Participation," in *Personnel Management,* ed. K. M. Rowland and G. Ferris (Boston: Allyn & Bacon, 1982).

54. Albert H. McCarthy, "Research Provides Advertising Focus," *Personnel Journal,* August 1989, pp. 82–87.

55. "Recruiting Data Bases May Be an Innovation Still Waiting for Its Day," *The Wall Street Journal,* December 5, 1989, p. A1.

56. Tony Lee, "Notice: All Employees Must Wash Hands before Applying for a Job," *The Wall Street Journal,* June 2, 1989, p. B1.

57. Richard Jaccoma, "Temporary Relief," *Human Resource Executive,* September 1989, pp. 25–29.

58. Kathleen Christensen, *Flexible Staffing and Scheduling in U.S. Corporations* (New York: The Conference Board, 1989);   Bureau of National Affairs. *The Changing Workplace: New Directions in Staffing and Scheduling* (Washington, D.C.: Bureau of National Affairs, Inc., 1986).

59. Richard Jaccoma, "Temporary Relief," Morton E. Grossman, "Temporary Services: A Permanent Way of Life," *Personnel Journal,* January 1989, pp. 38–40;   "Use of Temporary Employees Is Widespread among Respondents," *Resource,* October–December 1988;   David Kirkpatrick, "Smart New Ways to Use Temps," *Fortune,* February 15, 1988, pp. 110–16.

60. Michael J. McCarthy, "Temp-Services Industry Stands to Gain under New Federal Hiring Proposal," *The Wall Street Journal,* October 21, 1988, p. B2.

61. Selwyn Feinstein, "More Small Firms Get Help from Rent-a-Boss Services," *The Wall Street Journal,* January 25, 1989, p. B1.

62. Richard Jaccoma, "Temporary Relief."

63. Richard S. Belous, *The Contingent Economy* (Washington, D.C.: National Planning Association, 1989);   "Managers Predict More Benefits for Temporary Workers in 1990s," *BNA Labor Relations Week* 4, no. 2 (January 10, 1990).

64. George Munchus III, "Employee Leasing: Benefits and Threats," *Personnel,* July 1988, pp. 59–61;   Suzanne Woolley, "Give Your Employees a Break—by Leasing Them," *Business Week,* August 14, 1989, p. 135.

65. "INS Proposes Record Fine over Illegal Hiring at Textile Firm," *Daily Labor Report,* December 14, 1989, p. 1.

66. Sara L. Rynes, "Compensation Strategy in Recruiting," *Topics in Total Compensation* 1, no. 1 (1987).

67. David B. Balkin and S. Groenman, "The Effect of Incentive Compensation on Recruitment: The Case of the Military," *Personnel Administrator,* January 1985, pp. 29–34.

68. Alison Barber, "Pay as a Signal in Organizational Recruiting," presented at the National Meeting of the Academy of Management, Washington, D.C., August 1989.

69. S. L. Premack and John P. Wanous, "A Meta-Analysis of Realistic Job Preview Experiments," *Journal of Applied Psychology* 70 (1985), pp. 716–19.

70. Ibid.

71. James A. Breaugh and Robert S. Billings, "The Realistic Job Preview: Five Key Elements and Their Importance for Research and Practice," *Journal of Business and Psychology* 2, no. 4 (Summer 1988), pp. 291–305.

72. Michael M. Harris and Laurence S. Fink, "A Field Study of Applicant Reactions to Employment Opportunities: Does the Recruiter Make a Difference?" *Personnel Psychology* 40, no. 4 (1987), pp. 765–83;   Sara L. Rynes and H. E. Miller, "Recruiter and Job Influences on Candidates for Employment" *Journal of Applied Psychology* 68

(1983), pp. 147–54;   Schmitt, Neil, and Coyle, "Applicant Decisions in the Employment Interview," *Journal of Applied Psychology,* 61 (1976), pp. 184–92.

73. C. W. Downs, "Perceptions of the Selection Interview"; P. Herriott and C. Rothwell, "Organizational Choice and Decision Theory: Effects of Employers' Literature and Seleciton Interview," *Journal of Occupational Psychology* 54 (1981), pp. 17–31; M. Susan Taylor and Janet A. Sniezek, "The College Recruitment Interview: Topical Content and Applicant Reactions," *Journal of Occupational Psychology* 57 (1984), pp. 157–68;   Rynes and Miller, "Recruiter and Job Influences on Candidates for Employment";   Schmitt and Coyle, "Applicant Decisions in the Employment Interview."

74. C. W. Downs, "Perceptions of the Selection Interview," *Personnel Administration,* May–June 1969, pp. 8–23;   R. L. Hilgert and L. S. Eason, "How Students Weigh Recruiters," *Journal of College Placement* 28 (1968), pp. 99–102.

75. Clare Ansberry and Alecia Swasy, "Minority Job Applicants Say Slurs often Surface," *The Wall Street Journal,* February 10, 1989, p. B1.

76. Judith Havemann, "It's Getting Harder and Harder to Find Good Help These Days," *Washington Post National Weekly Edition,* June 24–30 1989, p. 34.

77. Rynes and Boudreau, "College Recruiting in Large Organizations."

78. Ansberry and Swasy, "Minority Job Applicants Say Slurs often Surface."

79. James E. Rosenbaum and Takehiko Kariya, "Market and Institutional Mechanisms for the High School to Work Transition in the U.S. and Japan," presented at the annual meeting of the American Sociological Association, Chicago, August 1987.

80. Nancy J. Perry, "The New, Improved Vocational School."

81. Massayoshi Kanabayashi, "Some Japanese Industries Face Prospect of Labor Shortage Amid Boom Times," *The Wall Street Journal,* August 1, 1989, p. A7.

82. Sally Solo, "Japan Discovers Woman Power," *Fortune,* June 19, 1989, pp. 153–58.

83. Margaret J. Nowak, "Information Theory and Employer Recruitment Practices," *Journal of Industrial Relations* 30, no. 2 (June 1988), pp. 277–93.

84. "Survey of Temporary Work Contracts," *European Industrial Relations Review,* March 1989, pp. 11–16.

85. "Recruitment Buyer's Guide," *Personnel Journal,* August 1989, pp. 95–137.

86. Harry J. Holzer, "Hiring Procedures in the Firm: Their Economic Determinants and Outcomes," chap. 7 in M. M. Kleiner, R. N. Block, M. Roomkin, and S. W. Salsburg, eds., *Human Resources and the Performance of the Firm* (Madison, Wis.: Industrial Relations Research Association, 1987).

87. John W. Boudreau, "Utility Analysis," chap. 14 in Lee D. Dyer, ed., *Human Resource Management Evolving Roles and Responsibilities* (Washington, D.C.: Bureau of National Affairs, 1988).

88. American Management Association, "Hiring Costs and Strategies."

89. James Ledvinka and Vida Scarpello, *Federal Regulation of Personnel and Human Resource Management,* 2nd ed. (Boston: Kent Publishing, 1990).

90. Sara L. Rynes and John W. Boudreau, "College Recruiting in Large Organizations."

91. NYSSILR, Office of Career Services, *Student Job Search* (Ithaca, N.Y.: Cornell University, 1987).

92. Ibid.

CHAPTER EIGHT

External Employee Selection

External Employee Selection
External Selection Objectives
Validity: Does Information Predict the Future?

Choosing Selection Techniques
Application Forms and Résumés
Reference and Background Checks
Life-History Information
Interviews
Ability Tests
Job Knowledge Tests, Work Samples, Job Tryouts
Physical/Physiological Requirements
Personality, Honesty, and Graphology Tests

Constructing the External Selection Process
Single-Job Selection versus Classification
Gathering and Scoring Predictor Information
Combining Multiple Selection Procedures

Validating Selection to Discover What Works
Criterion-Related Validation Approaches
Content-Based Validation
Extent of Test Validation
Government Regulation of Validation

International Perspectives on Selection

Evaluating External Selection Activities
Efficiency
Equity
Your Turn: Drug Testing at IBM

How would you pick a residence hall advisor? Your recruiting process has attracted an apparently bright and qualified group of candidates, but you've only got a few vacancies to fill. Some person or group must decide which candidates will receive employment offers.

You would probably start by examining the residence hall advisor's job itself to identify the important behaviors/outcomes, and the skills, abilities, and traits that seem necessary to carry out those behaviors and produce the outcomes. What criteria are you aiming to affect through selection? Is it enough that the person stay on the job for the whole year? Should you try to select those who will get high performance ratings from the residence hall administrator? Should you select based on their ability to understand student concerns and counsel students or on their ability to enforce rules and mediate conflicts? When you think about it, the job of residence hall advisor is pretty complex.

Once you've decided for what you're selecting, you must decide what selection techniques and information you will gather and use. The goal here is to find things you can measure before applicants are hired, that will predict their behaviors and achievements after they are hired. Would you consider previous job experiences? Would you call on references and, if you did, would you only call on the references listed by the applicant? Might a test of general mental abilities or specific job knowledge be appropriate? How about a personality test—do some personality "types" make better residence hall advisors than others? Should you screen out applicants who fail a drug or honesty test? Should you impose a gender requirement—male advisors in all-male residence halls and female advisors in all-female halls? If you do, the government requires you to demonstrate a clear performance-based reason for this preference.

Would you interview the job candidates? Who would conduct the interview—the advisor's boss, student residents, past residence advisors? Virtually every organization interviews applicants, most job candidates expect it, and most interviewers think they are good judges of people. Yet, unless an interview is constructed and carried out in a very structured way, interviewers may not do very well at selecting good performers.

What information would you use to tell what selection techniques are likely to work? Would you be satisfied if you found that your techniques were used by other universities with good results, or would you want to test the techniques on your particular group of candidates?

If you include several of the techniques described above, you'll be constructing a pretty involved and expensive selection process. Is it really worth all that time and effort just to find better residence hall advisors? Remember, the money you spend on selection could be used to improve residence hall security, install personal computers in student rooms, or (perhaps most important) improve the quality of the food/beverage vending machines in the student lounge.

On the other hand, selection mistakes may be very costly in terms of theft, student unrest, rule violations, and security problems. How would you assess the value of your proposed selection strategy?

EXTERNAL EMPLOYEE SELECTION

After external recruiting has produced an applicant pool, there are usually more applicants than job openings. A decision must be made to offer employment to some subset of the applicants, while rejecting or postponing an offer to others. Exhibit 8.1 shows that the selection process acts as the hurdle or filter in determining whether applicants actually become employees.

External selection gathers and uses information about externally recruited applicants to choose which of them will receive employment offers. It is often preceded by *screening,* which identifies obviously unqualified applicants before gathering additional selection information.

This chapter focuses on external selection, which is the process of choosing among applicants to join the organization. Chapter Ten, on internal staffing and careers, will show how a similar process occurs when candidates are considered for employment opportunities that involve moving between jobs within the organization. Many of the techniques and concepts that apply to external selection also apply to internal selection.

Human resource management (HRM) professionals play key roles in the external selection process. They are often called upon to recommend and design specific selection techniques and the processes that use them. They are also usually involved in conducting and interpreting the results of selection activities and ensuring that the activities meet legal and other requirements.

Setting Objectives for External Selection Activities

Efficiency

External selection activities determine who joins the organization. These new hires often will spend decades with the organization, and they will become the resource the organization depends on for performance, flexibility in changing times, innovation, and candidates for further job assignments throughout their careers. It's no exaggeration to say that the decision to hire each employee will

EXHIBIT 8.1   The Staffing Process as a Series of Filters

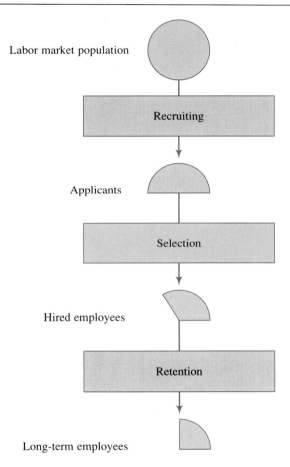

Labor market population

Recruiting

Applicants

Selection

Hired employees

Retention

Long-term employees

cost the organization thousands of dollars in pay, benefits, and other support costs. Selection activities can cost millions of dollars when applied to large numbers of employees.[1] However, because those employees affect organizational outcomes for many years, the one-time effort to select carefully can produce extraordinary returns on the investment.[2]

Equity

External selection activities are one of the most visible and important signals about the organization's commitment to fairness and legal compliance. Selection activities are often the first contact that applicants have with the organization, and they use the activities as signals about other organizational attributes.[3] EEO laws and court cases frequently focus on external selection

---

EXHIBIT 8.2   Selection as a Two-Way Signalling Process

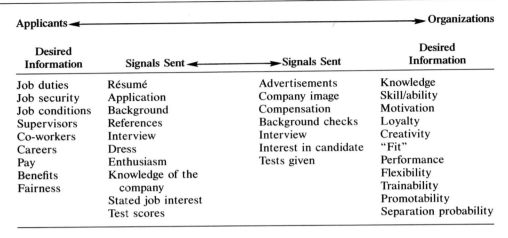

Applicants ◄————————————————————————————————————► Organizations			
Desired Information	**Signals Sent** ◄————►	**Signals Sent**	**Desired Information**
Job duties	Résumé	Advertisements	Knowledge
Job security	Application	Company image	Skill/ability
Job conditions	Background	Compensation	Motivation
Supervisors	References	Background checks	Loyalty
Co-workers	Interview	Interview	Creativity
Careers	Dress	Interest in candidate	"Fit"
Pay	Enthusiasm	Tests given	Performance
Benefits	Knowledge of the		Flexibility
Fairness	company		Trainability
	Stated job interest		Promotability
	Test scores		Separation probability

activities and are an important consideration in choosing and using external selection techniques. As Chapter Six described, when an organization's selection processes reject too many members of protected groups, courts or government agencies may require that the fairness and necessity of those selection procedures be carefully assessed, often with expensive and time-consuming data collection efforts. In fact, many organizations choose their external selection procedures based primarily on a desire to avoid those procedures that might reject protected groups, rather than to select the best applicants from among the pool.

As the example at the beginning of this chapter illustrated, designing an external selection strategy involves making the following choices: (1) what selection criteria and evidence to use in judging and assessing selection information about applicants, (2) which specific information-gathering techniques to use, (3) how the information will be used within the selection process, and (4) how to measure the results of selection.

VALIDITY: HOW WELL DOES INFORMATION PREDICT THE FUTURE?

External selection decisions are predictions. Based on applicant characteristics that can be observed before hiring, organizations try to predict how applicants will behave or perform if they are hired. The only way to really know for sure which applicants are the best would be to hire everyone who applies, let everyone perform on the job, and then keep only enough of the best employees to fill the organization's needs. Unfortunately, this approach is seldom practical, due to high costs, limited equipment availability, risks of damage or accidents, and applicants' reluctance to give up other opportunities during the probationary period. Even if it was feasible, it still would require making predictions about important outcomes, such as performance in higher-level positions or the likelihood of staying with the organization.

So, organizations must choose among applicants based on less-direct indicators of their future behaviors. Exhibit 8.2 depicts selection as a two-way signaling process, with the organization observing signals from applicants, such as their performance in interviews, their test scores, and their knowledge of the company. These signals are interpreted for their relationship to the desired information, such as applicants' knowledge, skill/ability, motivation, and other factors shown on the right-hand side of Exhibit 8.2. The signals are called the *predictors,* and the desired information elements are called the *criteria.* Evidence regarding how well predictors actually work is call *validity information.* Exhibit 8.2 also shows that the selection process acts as a signal to job applicants as well. Applicants will interpret what they encounter in the selection process as they form impressions about what it would be like to work in the organization.

Validity is the degree to which predictions from selection information are supported by evidence. *Validation* is the process of gathering information about predictor validity. *Reliability* is the accuracy and consistency with which a measure reflects an individual's characteristics. High reliability in both predictors and criteria is necessary, but it is not sufficient to achieve high validity.

Validation identifies the accuracy of selection predictions, allowing organizations to choose predictors that can improve the accuracy of the organization's selection decisions and the quality of those selected. Validation is also important from a legal perspective. As Chapter Six described, when predictors seem to exclude members of legally protected groups, EEO laws and courts will consider evidence that the predictors are related to job performance and, thus, necessary to the business. Validity information can provide evidence that selection processes are job-related.

Validity Coefficient

Exhibit 8.3 contains three graphs, called *scatterplots,* each one plotting the relationship between predictor scores on a selection technique (the horizontal axis) and criterion scores on a job behavior (the vertical axis). Every dot represents one person's score on the predictor and criterion. The ellipses represent the general pattern of dots for a sample of individuals. Figure 1, at the top, shows low validity, because any particular predictor score is associated with a wide range of possible criterion scores. Figure 2, in the middle, shows moderate

EXHIBIT 8.3 Scatterplots and Validity Coefficients for Different Predictor-Criterion Relationships

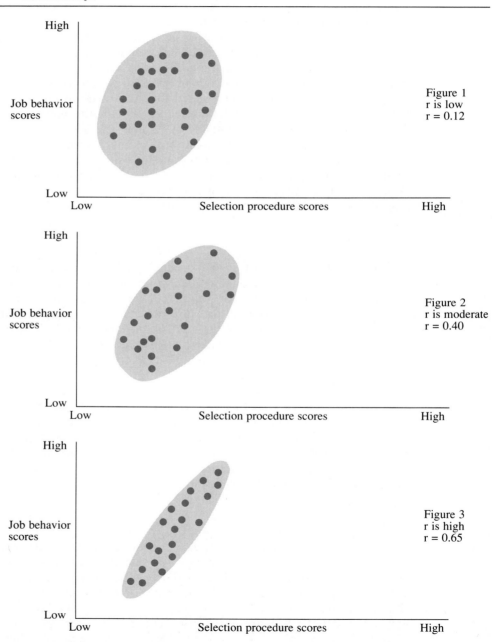

validity, because each predictor score associates with a narrower range of criterion scores. Figure 3, at the bottom, shows the highest level of validity, because the dots fall nearly on a straight line, with each predictor score associated with only a very narrow range of possible criterion scores.

The information in a scatterplot can be summarized by a single number called a *correlation coefficient*. In validation it is called a *validity coefficient*. It is represented by the symbol r, and the values for r can range from -1.0 (indicating that scores fall perfectly on a line sloping downward from left to right), to 0.0 (indicating that scores fall in a circle or have no linear relationship), to 1.0 (indicating that scores fall perfectly on a line sloping upward from left to right). In Exhibit 8.3, notice how the r values of 0.12 in Figure 1, 0.40 in Figure 2, and 0.65 in Figure 3 reflect this pattern.

A validity coefficient can be calculated for any set of paired scores, and it reflects the degree of relationship in that *particular* sample of scores. An important question is whether you would see a similar relationship in future samples of applicants. Statistical tests can determine if the relationship in one particular set of scores is strong enough to conclude that it is very unlikely to see it simply by chance if there was no real relationship. When the probability of an observed relationship being due to chance is very small, such as 1 out of 20, we say the validity coefficient is *statistically significant*. A statistically significant validity coefficient suggests you would see the relationship in similar situations with other applicant groups.

Later discussions will report validity coefficients for different selection procedures, and you may wonder how high a validity coefficient must be for the selection procedure to be "good." Unfortunately, there is no general rule, because the value of selection depends on the situation. Even selection procedures with low validity coefficients may be useful if applied to large numbers of selection decisions for very important jobs. We will discuss how validity affects selection value at the end of this chapter.

Now that you understand the general nature of selection validity, we will describe the procedures that organizations use to gather information about applicants. Later, we will describe how organizations can actually determine the validity of these procedures.

CHOOSING SELECTION TECHNIQUES

There is probably an infinite variety of ways to measure applicant information, and new ways are being developed every day. Computerized testing and genetic screening were virtually unheard of several years ago but now are used by many organizations, as we shall see. Still, traditional information-gathering techniques, such as the application form and the interview, enjoy the widest use.

Exhibit 8.4 presents a summary of the techniques we will discuss, as well as their validity, cost, legality, and popularity. Subsequent sections will show from

---

EXHIBIT 8.4   Characteristics of Different External Selection Techniques

Method	Validity	Cost	Legality	Popularity
Application forms and résumés	Less than 0.20 for academic achievement and experience ratings. Weighted application blanks reported as high as 0.56.	Low information acquisition cost, but higher if WAB is developed. Processing costs are moderate.	Defensible when job-related, but use of legally risky questions is common and may cause adverse impact.	Pervasive use in an unstructured way. About 11% of organizations use WABs.
Reference and background checks	In the range of 0.25.	Moderate, primarily costs of employee time or private investigators.	Risk of adverse impact can be reduced by avoiding risky questions, using release forms, and structuring to link to jobs.	Pervasive use of phone and mail checking. Less than 20% use outside investigators.
Life-history information	Biographical inventories and accomplishment records yield validity in the 0.30s or higher. Training and experience ratings show validity less than 0.20.	Moderate to high. Simple training and experience ratings involve employee time, while developing BIBs or accomplishment records can cost thousand of dollars.	General education or experience requirements can cause adverse impact, but clear links to job-related behaviors and structure can improve legality.	Very common to verify educational background. More structured and directive methods are rarely used.
Interview	Unstructured interviews can produce validity as high as the 0.30s, with structured interview validity in the 0.60s or higher.	Relatively high. Interviewer time and travel can easily amount to thousands of dollars per candidate. Developing structured interviews involves added development and processing costs.	Subjectivity is not automatically a problem unless it produces adverse impact. Structuring and interviewer training can reduce adverse impact likelihood.	Pervasive, but only about 35% of companies use structured interviews.

---

where the information in Exhibit 8.4 came. Clearly, selection technique popularity is not a simple matter of choosing the most valid or least-cost method. Many expensive techniques with modest validity are among the most popular, and vice versa. A better understanding of the techniques can help explain why.

EXHIBIT 8.4   *(concluded)*

Method	Validity	Cost	Legality	Popularity
Ability tests	Generally greater than 0.40, and can range as high as 0.80.	Relatively inexpensive to administer, costing less than $100 per person. Additional modest costs involved in processing and interpreting scores. Developing a new test can cost over $100,000.	Risk of adverse impact against low-scoring minorities, but validation evidence can be used as an effective defense.	Used by about 30% of organizations, with the greatest use for office/clerical positions.
Job knowledge tests, work samples, and job tryouts	Validities in the 0.40s are common.	Varies widely. Standard job-knowledge tests have costs equivalent to ability tests. However, developing work samples can cost thousands of dollars, and probationary periods involve costs of paid wages and additional supervision.	Relatively little risk of adverse impact for work samples, but higher risk for job-knowledge tests.	Skill tests or work samples used by over 60% of organizations, with 31% using job knowledge tests.
Physical and physiological requirements	Stringently developed ability tests have shown validities in the 0.50s. Validity for most physiological tests is low or evidence sketchy.	Varies widely. Medical examinations and lab work can cost about $1,000 per employee. Drug testing and AIDS screening can cost between $500 and $1,500 per test.	Very high risk of adverse impact against females and some minority groups. Physiological testing also risks litigation over invasion of privacy.	Medical examinations and drug tests are given by about half of all organizations. Less than 10% currently use other physiological tests.
Personality, honesty, and graphology tests	Very low validities reported in virtually all studies, though evidence is flawed in many cases.	Relatively inexpensive, as standard tests and scoring systems are available from consulting and testing firms. Costs per applicant probably less than $500.	Risks of adverse impact against religious groups. Risks based on invasion of privacy. Difficult to demonstrate relationships to job behaviors.	About 17% of organizations use personality tests, mostly for salespeople. Less than 10% use other types of tests.

Application Forms and Résumés

The first piece of information provided by most job candidates is a written sum-mary of their personal characteristics. For blue-collar, clerical, and non-managerial jobs, this information is typically gathered through an application form. Managers and professionals usually provide this information in the form of a résumé and cover letter, though an application form is typically part of the process for these people as well.

Application Forms

If you have applied for employment in any large organization, you were proba-bly asked to fill out some kind of application form. Application forms serve as a record of the employment application and as a way to keep track of the char-acteristics of applicants as future employment openings occur. In addition, ap-plication forms usually pose a series of questions that can be used to judge suitability for employment. Application forms virtually always request appli-cants' name, address, telephone, Social Security number, and citizenship or employment eligibility. They usually request information on the type of work desired and the preferences about scheduling (part-time, full-time, evenings, and so on). Application forms may request the names of references and prior work history.

Extensive application forms may also include questions about age, race, physical characteristics, religion, gender, marital and family status, physical health, military service, arrest/conviction records, education, credit rating, medical conditions, and estimated job skills/abilities. Though Title VII of the Civil Rights Act does not specifically prohibit particular types of questions, asking applicants questions that might be used to reject protected groups, such as gender, marital status, and religion, is risky. If a disproportionate number of protected-group members are rejected, the organization may be required to prove that such information is job-related and was not used to reject protected-group members. Many organizations simply refrain from asking such questions.

Application forms may contain a clause requiring the applicant to undergo further testing—also releasing former employers, credit sources, and references from legal liability for the information they furnish—accepting a probationary period, agreeing that the employment relationship may be terminated at any time, and stating that information provided on the form is accurate and truth-ful. Applicant signatures are obtained as evidence of understanding and agree-ment with these stipulations.[4]

An important factor in the usefulness and legal safety of application form information is the way it is used. Checklists can be constructed to ensure that relevant information is considered, depending on the type of employment being considered for the applicant. A very elaborate form of application blank scoring is the *weighed application blank* (WAB), that scores the responses to each ques-tion, multiplies each score by a weight reflecting that question's importance in predicting performance on the job being considered, and then adds up the weighed scores to produce a total score for each applicant.[5] About 11 percent of firms responding to a recent study indicated that they used weighted application blanks.[6]

Résumés

If you plan to pursue a managerial or professional job with an organization, you will undoubtedly need to prepare a résumé listing your qualifications and a cover letter. The appendix to Chapter Seven provides guidelines on preparing and using these tools to make your case to a prospective employer. From the organization's perspective, a cover letter and résumé can be used similarly to an application form. Selectors scan these documents for useful selection information. Checklists and weighting schemes can also be used to add structure and consistency to the résumé-scanning process.

Validity

Simple ratings of academic achievement or experience do not strongly relate to job performance, with validities below 0.20.[7] However, weighting has demonstrated an ability to improve predictive power, especially for such criteria as turnover.[8]

Legality

Considering the dangers that application form information may show different patterns for different legally protected groups, as discussed in Chapter Six, questions about such things as arrest records, credit ratings, race, age, and marital status are risky. Applicants may later claim that, by gathering such information, the organization consciously or unconsciously excluded one or more protected groups. One review of application forms in 151 Fortune 500 firms suggested widespread use of such risky questions.[9] Such allegations might force an employer to defend the collection and the use of this information.

Therefore, employers deciding what information to request on application forms should consider: (1) possible adverse impact, (2) information value in identifying qualified applicants, (3) possible conflict with court decisions or EEOC guidelines, (4) possible invasion of privacy, and (5) availability of evidence that the information relates to job performance.

Reference and Background Checks

Most organizations verify information on application forms and résumés, and they gather additional information from references supplied by the applicant or other sources, such as credit bureaus, previous employers, and educators. A survey of personnel executives in 245 U.S. organizations shows that virtually all organizations check the date of most recent job, the reason for leaving the most recent job, as well as information about jobs prior to the most recent, the salary and position in the most recent job, and the legal eligibility for employment (required by the U.S. Immigration Reform and Control Act of 1986). Other frequently checked information included: professional references, current supervisor's evaluation, educational background, personal references, medical history, and driving record. Most organizations conduct reference checks by mail or by phone, and some organizations use private investigators.[10] Such inquiries need not be limited to only the references recommended by the individual on their résumé or application blank.

Organizations also report finding it increasingly difficult to obtain information beyond basic employment facts. Employers fear slander suits, like the September 1989 case that produced a $25 million punitive damage award to Clifford Zalay from his former employer, John Hancock.[11] Members of the National Association of Corporate and Professional Recruiters reported that 81 percent of companies make reference checks before offering a job, but 41 percent of companies have written policies against giving out anything other than confirmation of employment. The rule often seems to be, "Even if you have something nice to say, don't say anything at all."[12] One way to encourage greater candor from references is to have applicants release references from liability or waive their right to see reference information. Exhibit 8.5 shows an example of a confidential reference request used by a large northeastern retail firm.

Validity
References recommended by applicants frequently give uniformly positive responses, which make it impossible to distinguish among the candidates. However, over many studies, reference checks have shown moderate validity in the vicinity of 0.25.[13] If references are willing, another way to increase the consistency and comparability of information is to ask references to rate candidates on scales reflecting such behaviors as attendance, punctuality, accepting authority, and safety.[14]

Legality
Like application blanks, reference and background checks can reduce legal vulnerability by demonstrating clear links to job-related factors and by avoiding risky questions. Having applicants sign release forms can minimize the risk of suits over invasion of privacy and slander.

Life-History Information

Did you ever build a model airplane that flew? This question turned out to be a very good predictor of pilot trainee performance.[15] It's an example of one kind of life-history information that goes beyond the information typically contained in application forms, résumés, or background checks but that still focus on aspects of the candidates' previous experience, including previous education, experiences, and accomplishments.

EXHIBIT 8.5   Confidential Reference Request Used by a Large Northeastern Retail Firm

CONFIDENTIAL REFERENCE REQUEST

TO BE COMPLETED BY APPLICANT	
NAME PRINT:	IF NAME DIFFERENT WHILE IN JOB/SCHOOL INDICATE
SOCIAL SECURITY NUMBER	I HAVE APPLIED FOR A POSITION AS:

I HAVE MADE APPLICATION FOR EMPLOYMENT AT _____ , I REQUEST AND AUTHORIZE YOU TO RELEASE ALL INFORMATION REQUESTED BELOW CONCERNING MY EMPLOYMENT RECORD, REASON FOR LEAVING YOUR EMPLOY, OR MY EDUCATION. I HEREBY RELEASE_____, MY PERSONAL REFERENCES, MY FORMER EMPLOYERS AND SCHOOLS, AND ALL INDIVIDUALS CONNECTED THEREWITH, FROM ALL LIABILITY FOR ANY DAMAGE WHATSOEVER FOR FURNISHING THIS INFORMATION.

SIGNATURE _____ DATE _____

SCHOOL REFERENCE:

DATES ATTENDED   FROM: TO: GRADUATED? ☐ Yes ☐ No   DEGREE AWARDED

EMPLOYMENT REFERENCE:

POSITION HELD   DEPARTMENT

IMMEDIATE SUPERVISOR'S NAME   EMPLOYMENT DATES: FROM   TO

REASON FOR LEAVING ☐ DISCHARGED ☐ RESIGNED ☐ LAID OFF   IF DISCHARGED EXPLAIN:

FORMER EMPLOYER OR SCHOOL—Please complete the following.   Thank You.

IS THE ABOVE INFORMATION CORRECT?
☐ YES ☐ NO   If not, give correct information: _____

PLEASE CHECK	EXCEL.	GOOD	FAIR	POOR	COMMENTS:
ATTITUDE					
QUALITY OF WORK					
COOPERATION					
ATTENDANCE					

WOULD YOU RECCOMMEND FOR EMPLOYMENT?   ☐ YES ☐ NO

EMPLOYER ONLY: LAST RATE OF PAY   WOULD YOU REHIRE? ☐ YES ☐ NO

ADDITIONAL COMMENTS: _____

SIGNATURE OF EMPLOYER OR SCHOOL REPRESENTATIVE   TITLE

Source: Bureau of National Affairs, *Recruiting and Selection Procedures,* PPF Survey no. 146, May 1988, p. 63. Reprinted by permission.

Education

Employers frequently examine the length and type of formal education reported by a job applicant, and they sometimes check with educators for background information. U.S. organizations emphasize college education and go to great lengths to develop relationships with university programs in such areas as engineering and management. In contrast, Japanese organizations emphasize long-term relationships with high schools, which compete for students and rigorously prepare them for recommendation to the businesses that have relationships with the high school.[16] As Chapter Seven noted, however, many of the applicants for future jobs in the United States will be those without college educations, trained primarily in high schools and vocational schools.[17]

Several researchers, reports, and government officials, including the Secretary of Labor, have emphasized the importance of properly assessing and rewarding noncollege training and experience. Hundreds of American companies are supporting efforts to develop standardized tests that could be used to assess basic skills and academic achievement.[18] The National Alliance of Business is working with the Educational Testing Service to create an "employee credentialing" system that would automatically track the experiences and education of noncollege-bound people (such as on-the-job learning, vocational training, and so forth) so employers could easily consider the full detail of their high school and subsequent performance, rather than simply checking to see if they have a high school diploma.[19] If businesses selected and rewarded high school students based on their performance in school, it could create a very strong incentive for better student and school performance.[20]

Biographical Information Blanks (BIBs)

Biographical information blanks ask applicants questions about their backgrounds, life experiences, attitudes, and interests. Typical questions might include: "How many hours per week did you work on an outside job while you were in college?" "How carefully do you account for and budget the money you spend?" "When in high school, how high were the standards you set for yourself?" These questions, for example, were related to supervisory performance in one study.[21]

Training, Experience, and Accomplishments

While an application blank or résumé can list the titles of classes taken, participation in activities or clubs, and awards/honors, it is often difficult to relate these to particular job requirements. If a person says he or she worked as a "fast-food manager," does that mean the person mainly made hamburgers or that he or she supervised a group of 10 food preparers and servers? *Training and experience (T&E) forms* and *accomplishment records* relate experiences directly to particular job or organizational requirements.

Training and experience forms provide a list of important tasks, generated through job analysis. Exhibit 8.6 shows a hypothetical T&E form that might be

---

EXHIBIT 8.6 Training and Experience Evaluation Form for the Job of Personnel Research Analyst

---

> *Directions:* Listed below are some important job tasks performed by a Personnel Research Analyst. Read each of the tasks. If you have had experience or training in performing a task, check the box marked "Yes." If you have not, then check the box marked "No." For the task(s) marked "Yes," please describe your experience and training. All of your responses are subject to review and verification.

Have you had
experience or training
with this task?

Task

Yes   No

☐   ☐

1. Computed and monitored applicant flow statistics for nonexempt job applicants using computerized statistical packages (for example, SPSS, SAS).

Experience

Employer: _____ Title: _____
Dates of employment: From ___ To ___
Describe your experience with this task: _____
_____
_____

Training

Formal coursework and location: _____
_____

Training programs attended and location: _____
_____

On-the-job training: _____
_____

☐   ☐

2. Designed and conducted test validation studies for entry-level jobs.

•   •
•   •
•   •

☐   ☐

3. Supervised research assistants in collecting data for human resource studies.

•   •
•   •
•   •

Source: Robert D. Gatewood and Hubert S. Feild, *Human Resource Selection* (New York: CBS College Publishing, 1987).

used for the job of personnel research analyst. For each task, the T&E form asks if the applicant has any relevant training or experience for the task. If the answer is "yes," then the form would require the date and specific training program or the job that provided the experience. Reviewing the finished form allows a manager to determine what training/experience relates to specific job behaviors.

The *accomplishment record* technique was developed by a government regulatory agency to be applied to attorneys. Lawyers describe their professional achievements by illustrating specific dimensions, such as "using knowledge." Each description has a date, a general description of the outcome of the accomplishment, a summary of exactly what the applicant did to contribute, any awards or recognition, and the name of a reference to verify the accomplishment. One study also prepared scoring keys for the managers who reviewed the accomplishment record summaries, to improve consistency.[22]

Validity

Training and experience ratings seem to produce validity levels of about 0.13, with education producing validities of about 0.10. Biographical inventories produce validities of about 0.37 across many studies.[23] Accomplishment records have produced higher validity levels, when used to predict attorneys' job success, and have "face validity" because applicants believe they are appropriate and valid.[24]

Legality

As the *Griggs* v. *Duke Power* case showed, blanket application of broad educational or training requirements, such a high school diploma, can be legally vulnerable, because they produce adverse impact and are difficult to link to job behaviors. Experience and education requirements are less vulnerable when they clearly relate to job knowledge, involve high-level or safety-related positions, and do not perpetuate past discrimination.[25] Biographical inventories and accomplishment records have been shown to produce less adverse impact.

Interviews

John T. Phillips, my relentless interrogator, barrages me with questions. "Have you led any task forces or committees? Where you didn't have any position power, but where you were the leader?" I hesitate. "How did you go about getting the work done?" Silence.

Finally, I ask, "Does this have to be something from work?" Luckily not, so I find myself talking, and talking. Soon, Mr. Phillips is listening to true confessions: How I tried to defuse cold-war hostilities in my extended family, how I convened a meeting to reorganize our annual holiday bash, how I lobbied cousins and commandeered an uncle into menu-planning. From this, Mr. Phillips, who is director of training and development as S. C. Johnson & Son, Inc., hopes to know whether

I would fit into his company, if I were really looking for a job. —[Jolie Soloman, "The New Job Interview: Show Thyself," *The Wall Street Journal,* December 4, 1989, p. B1.]

The interview is virtually always part of employee selection.[26] Fifty-six percent of companies in one survey stated that interviews are the most important aspect of their selection process, and 90 percent reported that they had more confidence in the interview than any other selection method.[27] Yet, for decades psychologists and other researchers have published studies showing that the interview has low validity.[28] Why would presumably rational managers persist with an expensive and time-consuming process that doesn't predict job performance? In fact, emerging evidence suggests that the interview may be a much better predictor than widely believed, when conducted carefully and properly.[29]

The Interview Process

Exhibit 8.7 describes the employment interview as a "script," proceeding through five scenes, with clear expectations about the roles of the interviewer and the applicant. Every interview is somewhat different, but Exhibit 8.7 shows how both the interviewer and the applicant attempt to receive and send signals that present themselves or their company in a desirable way, and that provide clues to the match between the applicant and the organization (see Exhibit 8.2).

Exhibit 8.8 summarizes variables that research has investigated as affecting the employment interview. Although this model was proposed in 1982, it continues to form the basis for more recent interview research.[30] It divides the factors affecting the interview into applicant factors, situation factors, and interviewer factors. Moreover, it shows how important it is to consider the interaction of these factors when considering the causes of interviewer behavior and the likely results of employment interviews.

Applicant Demographic Characteristics

Applicants' qualifications and experience should, and usually do, affect selection decisions. But, is it possible that other applicant characteristics, such as sex, ethnic background, age, or disabilities, also affect interview decisions? In a recent sex discrimination case before the Supreme Court, *Price Waterhouse* v. *Hopkins,* Ann Hopkins joined Price Waterhouse in 1978, was the only woman nominated for partnership among 88 nominees in 1982, but was not among the 47 invited to become partners. Partners who recommended against her partnership used such phrases as "she is a lady using foul language" and advised her to "walk more femininely, talk more femininely, dress more femininely, wear make-up, have her hair styled, and wear jewelry." The Supreme Court, in a 6–3 decision, agreed that sexual stereotyping is barred by federal anti-discrimination laws, and it ordered a new trial in which Price Waterhouse must show that the firm would have reached the same employment decision even if there had been no bias.[31]

EXHIBIT 8.7 The "Script" of a Typical Selection Interview

Scene	Applicant Script	Interviewer Script
1. Precontact activities	Check appearance/dress. Enter locale. Announce arrival. Review notes while waiting.	Review résumé. Review interview guide. Make note of questions. Prepare setting.
2. Greeting and establish rapport	Shake hands. Sit when asked. Make good impression in small talk.	Shake hands. Seat applicant. Relax applicant with appropriate small talk.
3. Ask job-related questions	Provide educational history. Provide details of work history. Detail personal skills and abilities. Try to demonstrate proper motivation for the job.	Ask educational background. Seek relevant details about work history. Discuss special skills and abilities. Get to applicant's motivation to work.
4. Answer applicant questions	Ask about pay and benefits. Ask about opportunities for advancement. Ask about organization culture—work norms, and the like.	Answer applicant questions putting face on organization. Try to create positive impression about organization.
5. Disengagement	Wait for interviewer cue that interview is over. Discuss next step. Stand up and shake hands. Exit.	Show that interview is about to conclude. Suggest what the next step will be. Stand up and shake hands. Show applicant out.

Source: William L. Tullar, "The Interview as a Cognitive Performing Script," chap. 17, in Robert W. Eder and Gerald R. Ferris, *The Employment Interview* (Newbury Park, Calif.: Sage Publications, 1989), pp. 233–46.

Stereotypes occur when we assume traits about a person based on that person's membership in some group, such as sex, race, or age.[32] While the *Watson* case involved interviews, as well as other predictor information, it highlights the importance of considering whether stereotypes based on gender, race, or other applicant characteristics adversely affect interview decisions. This important question has occupied a great deal of research effort. Early results suggested that females often received lower ratings than males.[33] More recent research suggests that this occurs primarily when selectors are given little in-

EXHIBIT 8.8   Variables Affecting the Conduct and Outcomes of the Employment Interview

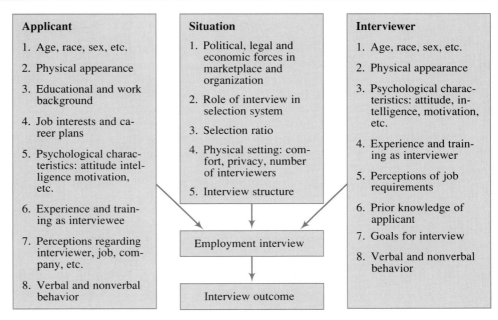

Source: Richard D. Arvey and James E. Campion, "The Employment Interview: A Summary and Review of Recent Research," *Personnel Psychology* 35, no. 3 (1982), pp. 281–322.

formation about employee qualifications, which correlate much more highly with hiring recommendations.[34] There is much recent evidence that applicant gender has little or no effect on interview ratings.[35]

Regarding applicant race, results are more mixed, with some studies finding that race does affect interview ratings but not to a very great degree.[36] Age also appears to affect interview decisions, but its effects are complex and depend on how accountable the interviewers are for their decisions, the gender of the interviewer, and the particular dimension being evaluated.[37] There is little evidence about the effects of applicant disability on interview decisions.[38]

Applicant Behaviors

Can applicants affect the interview decision by "managing interviewer impressions"?[39] Someone must think so, because every recruiting season witnesses a remarkable metamorphosis as students previously seen only in sneakers, white socks, jeans, and leather jackets suddenly appear in new blue suits, white shirts, stylish haircuts, shiny shoes, and carrying unscuffed mock-leather briefcases to their impending job interviews. Professors customarily attired in

---

EXHIBIT 8.9   Effective Interviewing: Guidelines for the Applicant

---

Dress appropriately.

Be punctual.

Know the interviewer's name and correct pronunciation.

Make sure your "body language" communicates your interest and attentiveness.

Do some research regarding the organization and the interviewer to ask pertinent questions.

Pause briefly and pensively before answering complex questions.

Try not to discuss salary in preliminary interviews.

Be responsive to each part of each question.

Ask how any personal or potentially illegal questions are related to job performance before responding.

Bring pencil and paper in case some information (for example, a telephone number) must be recorded.

Make some notes regarding high (and low) points of interview shortly after it ends in order to follow up in subsequent interviews.

Thank the interviewer for his or her time.

Be certain that any responses on application blanks or résumés are consonant with those provided in the interview.

Follow up with a letter thanking the interviewer.

Contributed by Milton D. Hakel, Department of Psychology, Ohio State University.

Source: Richard W. Beatty and Craig Eric Schneier, *Personnel Administration: An Experiential Skill-Building Approach*, 2d ed. (Reading, Mass.: Addison-Wesley Publishing, 1981). © 1981 by Addison-Wesley.

---

slacks, sweaters, and Birkenstock sandals can be found wearing suits and dress shoes in anticipation of meetings and lunches with visiting corporate recruiters.

Evidence suggests that nonverbal behavior (such as smiling, leaning toward the interviewer, eye contact), wearing scent, and "impression management" tactics (such as complimenting the interviewer, self-promotion, ingratiation) can affect ratings of applicant attractiveness and sometimes affect ratings of hiring suitability. However, the effects seem to depend on the situation, and the effects can backfire if impression management is overdone.[40] Exhibit 8.9 provides some general guidelines for you as you prepare and participate in employment interviews.

Interviewer Behaviors and Interviewer Training

Over the years, research suggests that, without training or some form of structure and guidance, interviewers may adopt potentially damaging strategies in interviews, such as:[41]

1. *Overemphasis on negative information.* Often, even finding a small amount of negative information can lead to rejection of a job candidate. Some have pro-

posed that this is because interviewers are seldom rewarded for selecting good candidates, but they are frequently penalized for hiring poor candidates. The logical reaction is to be very conservative, allowing not even a hint of possible negative information to affect the decision.[42]

2. *Confirmatory biases.* If you saw information on a person's application blank that suggested she or he had a history of theft, would you tend to ask that person more questions about theft than you would others with no such history? Research suggests that interviewers are biased toward asking questions that will confirm their initial impressions, which can be damaging if the initial impressions are false or if it leads the interview to generate little additional information.[43]

3. *Interviewer stereotypes.* As discussed above, interviewers may form incorrect impressions of applicants if they base judgments on stereotypes. This is especially legally vulnerable if such stereotypes lead to rejection of protected-group members.

4. *Failure to consider job information.* Lack of relevant job information can cause interviewers to rely more on less-relevant characteristics in their decisions.

5. *Different use of cues.* Interviewers may place more weight on some applicant characteristics than others or combine attributes differently.[44]

6. *Undue reliance on nonverbal cues.* As discussed earlier, applicant impression management may affect interview decisions, yet be unrelated to job success.

7. *Contrast effects.* Strong candidates who interview after weaker ones may appear even stronger by contrast, and vice versa for weak candidates following strong ones.

8. *Spending time discussing nonjob-related issues.* This may serve other purposes, such as "selling" applicants on the job, but it can also reduce the ability to choose good candidates.

9. *Making snap judgments about applicants early in the interview.* Some research suggests that interviewers make their decisions quickly, though recent research calls this into some doubt.[45]

Considering the well-known potential interviewer problems, you might think that research would have focused on how to train interviewers to improve. Unfortunately, very few studies of interviewer training exist.[46] One study trained interviewers for eight hours on general skills (such as note-taking and questioning methods), as well as avoiding rating errors (such as halo and leniency, see Chapter Four), but did not find an increase in agreement among interviewers. A second study found that training business students to avoid rating errors did reduce the errors.[47] Despite such mixed results, organizations continue to invest in interviewer training. Seventy-four percent of the 245 organizations responding to a recent survey indicated that they train their interviewers using their own personnel professionals, outside workshops, or the company training

---

EXHIBIT 8.10 Recommendations for Designing and Conducting Employment Interviews

---

Before the interview
Identify major interview objectives, such as:
1. Selecting.
2. Attracting.
3. Gathering information on what the applicant *can* do.
4. Gathering information on what the applicant *will* do.
5. Providing information.
6. Checking the applicant's "fit" with the organization.

Prepare interview content by:
1. Identifying major job responsibilities.
2. Writing hypothetical job situations to use as questions.
3. Planning and structuring the interview format consistent with its objectives.

Review each application form or résumé for information, such as:
1. Previous related work or nonwork experience.
2. Previous related training.
3. Previous related education.
4. Applicant work interests.
5. Applicant career intentions.

During the interview
Probe what the applicant can do through discussion and situational questions, such as:
1. Related work or nonwork experiences.
2. Related training.
3. Related education.

Probe work interests and career intentions to assess what the candidate will do.

After the interview
Use an applicant evaluation form to record evaluations of what the applicant:
1. Can do, based on existing skills and interests.
2. Will do, based on interests and intentions.
3. Applicant's personal "chemistry."

Record your level of interest in hiring each applicant on the *applicant evaluation form*.

---

department. Training times ranged from one-half hour to 60 hours, with an average of 9 hours.[48]

While there are few general guides to better interviewing, Exhibit 8.10 provides some general steps that interviewers can follow to ensure the interview is job related and that information is carefully assessed.[49]

Structuring the Interview

If interviews suffer because different interviewers adopt different questioning strategies and focus on potentially irrelevant information, a logical remedy would be to impose a consistent structure, with little interviewer opportunity to diverge from the prespecified format, and to base that interview structure on factors identified through job analysis as relevant to employment success. Many employers increasingly seem willing to accept this logic. Thirty-five percent of 245 companies responding to a recent survey said they use structured interviews, in which all applicants are asked identical questions. Twenty percent of firms that reported changing their interviews in the last three years did so to make them more structured.[50]

Interviews can be *unstructured,* in which the interviewer is completely free to cover any area; *semistructured,* where the interviewer prepares important questions in advance, but is allowed to probe those areas that seem to merit further investigation; or *structured,* where the interviewer's questions, and often their sequence, are prepared in advance, and the interviewer often fills out a form indicating applicant responses to the questions. Perhaps the ultimate in structured interviewing is to program a computer to ask the questions, record the responses, and analyze them mathematically.[51] For the moment, it is more typical to involve human beings in the process.

While structuring interviews may reduce spontaneity, there is strong evidence that structuring can produce more consistent and valid selection information. Three approaches to structuring the interview are: (1) *behavior description interview (BDI),* (2) *situational interview (SI),* and (3) *comprehensive structured interview (CSI).*[52]

Behavior description interviews (BDI)   This approach focuses on past behavior, based on the premise that "The best prophet of the future is the past."[53] Interview questions are based on a job analysis of situations or decisions likely to be faced on the job. Questions are constructed based on the "What did you do . . ." format. For example, to assess likely attendance, interviewers might ask, "Tell me about the most recent time you had to miss work and stay at home. What was the reason? What did you actually do?" In many ways, BDI is very similar to the life-history selection techniques discussed earlier, except that the interview format provides flexibility and the opportunity to probe further.

Situational Interviews (SI)   This approach derives from theories about goal setting, which suggest individual's intentions are related to their future behavior. Like BDI, the SI approach derives its interview questions from job analysis that identifies important situations and decisions likely to be faced by applicants, often in the form of "critical incidents" (see Chapter Four). The difference is that the questions focus on intentions, not past behaviors. For example, the same attendance-related question in an SI format might be, "Your spouse and two teenage children are sick in bed with a cold. There are no relatives or friends available to look in on them. Your shift starts in three hours. What would you do?"[54] By focusing on hypothetical but job-related situations and applicant intentions, the SI approach can potentially explore areas where job candidates may not have any actual previous experiences. SI approaches usually construct a scoring guide for interviewers, based on input from job experts, with the best example answers receiving the highest points. Exhibit 8.11 shows an example SI question and scoring guide for truck driver supervisors.

Comprehensive Structured Interviews (CSI)   The CSI can contain four types of questions:

1. Situational (such as the SI approach).
2. Job knowledge, such as "When putting a piece of machinery back together after repairing it, why would you clean all the parts first?"
3. Job simulation, such as "Many jobs require the operation of a fork-lift. Please read this (90-word) fork-lift procedure aloud."
4. Worker requirements, such as "Some jobs require climbing ladders to a height of a five-story building and going out on a catwalk to work. Give us your feeling about performing a task such as this."[55]

Like the SI, the CSI involves the construction of a scoring guide for interviewers.

Situational Effects on the Interview

As Exhibit 8.8 shows, interview structure is not the only situational factor that affects the conduct and outcomes of interviews. The interview takes place within the context of forces both within and outside the organization. Exhibit 8.2 illustrated the interactive nature of selection, and that interaction is especially apparent in the interview. Contextual factors, such as the complexity of the job and interview task, whether the purpose of the interview is to attract candidates to take job offers or to select among candidates,[56] the perceived cost of making a hiring mistake, and the interviewer's accountability for interview outcomes, all affect interview processes and results.[57]

Interview Validity

Though researchers have until recently lamented the low validity of the interview and cautioned employers against their tendency to use it so frequently, recent research advances and new evidence suggests that the interview can be a valid selection technique. Research suggests that interviews can attain validities in the range of 0.25 to 0.80, with structured interviews focusing on job-relevant experience, training, or interests producing higher validity coefficients than unstructured interviews or interviews based on personality characteristics or traits.[58] It appears that the interview, carefully constructed and implemented, has greater potential value than was previously believed.

Improving the Legal Defensibility of the Interview

Seventy-nine percent of people had been asked "intrusive" questions in their job interview, as discovered in a recent telephone survey of 1,000 people conducted by the National Consumers League, and most said they disapproved of

---

EXHIBIT 8.11   Structured Situational Interview Question and Scoring Guide

---

Interview question

You are in charge of truck drivers in Philadelphia. Your colleague is in charge of truck drivers 800 miles away in Atlanta. Both of you report to the same person. Your salary and bonus are affected 100 percent by your costs. Your buddy is in desperate need of one of your trucks. If you say no, your costs will remain low and your group will probably win the Golden Flyer award, because they will make a significant profit for the company. Your boss is preaching costs, costs, costs as well as cooperation with one's peers. Your boss has no control over accounting, who are the score keepers. Your boss is highly competitive, he or she rewards winners. You are just as competitive, you are a real winner!

Explain what you would do.

Record the applicant's answer in the space below

_____

_____

_____

_____

Scoring guide

(1 point)   I would go for the award. I would explain the circumstances to my buddy and get his or her understanding.

(3 points)   I would get my boss's advice.

(5 points)   I would loan the truck to my buddy. I'd get recognition from my boss and my buddy that I had sacrificed my rear-end for theirs. Then I'd explain the logic to my people.

Source: Adapted with permission from Gary P. Latham, "The Reliability, Validity, and Practicality of the Situational Interview," chap. 12 in Robert W. Eder and Gerald R. Ferris, *The Employment Interview* (Newbury Park, Calif.: Sage Publications, 1989).

an employer asking about living with a nonfamily member of the opposite sex and about elderly parents, religious preferences, and plans to have children.[59] Not only may such questions cause animosity among applicants, they create legal vulnerabilities should the organization's practices be found to exclude or differentially treat protected minorities or females. A review of court cases involving interviews suggests the following guidelines to minimize legal vulnerability:[60]

1. Develop job descriptions and use them to develop interview questions, procedures, and scoring systems.

2. Select interviewers to represent a mix of races and genders and train them to focus on job-related topics and to avoid potentially discriminatory questions.

EXHIBIT 8.12 Items Illustrating Mental Ability Tests

Tracing: draw a continuous line through each space without touching the lines.

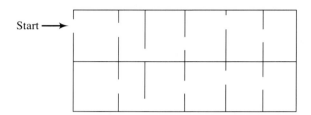

Tapping: put three dots in each triangle as quickly as you can.

Dotting: put one dot in each square as quickly as you can.

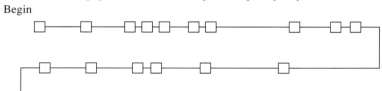

3. Ensure that interview questions and strategies are job relevant and are applied to all applicants.

4. Introduce review systems, such as interviewer panels, committees to review interview findings and recommendations, and systems for increasing accountability.

5. Keep records of interview procedures, evaluations, and decisions in case the organization is required to reconstruct them to demonstrate job relatedness.

6. Monitor disparate impact (see Chapter Six) and take specific steps to ensure fairness if disparate impact is detected.

Ability Tests

These tests assess general and specific capabilities or potential capabilities of individuals. Often called *aptitude* tests, they include paper-and-pencil measures of intellectual abilities, perceptual accuracy, spatial and mechanical abilities, and motor abilities. They indicate what a person might be able to do, given appropriate experience or training. Exhibit 8.12 shows items typical of a common aptitude test of mental ability. Testing is very big business. AT&T and IBM have developed and used their own tests for years. The Life Insurance Marketing and Research Association for 55 years has been providing members with a questionnaire that has more than 180 questions.[61] The United States Employment Service (USES) classifies applicants for job openings using the General Aptitude Test Battery (GATB).[62] Computerized ability tests are becoming increasingly sophisticated. A test developed for the Apple II® computer, for assigning helicopter pilots to different specialties, was based on a detailed task analysis and measured multilimb coordination, time sharing, short-term memory, selective attention, and kinesthetic memory.[63] Employers can purchase ability tests from a variety of consulting firms and testing services.[64]

Validity

One of the most important and widely accepted findings in recent psychological research is that "cognitive ability" tests appear to be valid predictors for a variety of different jobs. Moreover, as discussed later, research on validity generalization suggests that organizations can "borrow" validity evidence from past studies in different organizations to determine how well such tests will predict in their own organization. One theory is that such cognitive ability tests reflect a general intelligence, or "*g*-factor," that translates into superior performance across a wide variety of jobs.[65] Exhibit 8.13 shows validity coefficients based on many studies for several jobs and ability tests. The GATB has demonstrated a validity ranging from 0.2 to 0.4 in USES studies.[66]

Some claim that both cognitive ability and experience contribute to job knowledge, which, in turn, contributes to performance.[67] Others argue that the ability-performance relationship depends on the work-life stage. *Transition stages,* involving new or substantially changed job tasks, make the most use of cognitive abilities. *Maintenance stages,* involving executing well-learned procedures, draw more heavily on personality and motivational factors.[68] If this is true, maximum predictive power might come from combining ability and personality measures and from accounting for different work-life stages.

Legality

Tests risk litigation, because they often produce lower scores for some minorities.[69] The dilemma faced by the U.S. Employment Service in using the GATB to refer applicants for job interviews is a case in point.[70] Evidence suggested that black, Hispanic, and some Native American job applicants generally scored lower on the GATB and received correspondingly lower average performance ratings (the usual criterion in validity studies). Thus, such tests appear to validly predict performance for both black and white applicants, but they do so by predicting lower job performance for these protected groups. Re-

EXHIBIT 8.13   Validity Coefficients for Ability Tests in Various Jobs

Job	Ability	Estimated Average Validity Coefficient
First-line supervisor	General mental ability	0.64
	Mechanical ability	0.48
	Spatial ability	0.43
Mechanical repairman	Mechanical ability	0.78
Bench worker	Finger dexterity	0.39
General clerk	General mental ability	0.67
Computer programmer	Number series	0.43
	Figure analogy	0.46
	Arithmetic reasoning	0.57
Operator (petroleum industry)	Mechanical ability	0.33
	General mental ability	0.26
	Chemical comprehension	0.30
Maintenance (petroleum industry)	Mechanical ability	0.33
	General mental ability	0.30
	Chemical comprehension	0.25

Source: Robert D. Gatewood and Hubert S. Feild, *Human Resource Selection* (New York: CBS College Publishing, 1987).

ferring applicants for jobs based on test scores would tend to exclude larger numbers of black, Hispanic, and Native American applicants than white applicants. Yet, this is technically the most valid and job-related approach. A National Research Council Committee concluded that such an approach would exclude minority candidates who might have performed well more often than it excluded nonminority candidates who might have performed well.

The committee's compromise recommendations tried to satisfy both the nation's commitment to equal employment opportunity and the USES mission to help employers and job applicants achieve finding the best person-job match. The committee recommended that the USES avoid referring employees based on raw test scores, which would be lower for protected groups. Instead, the USES should adjust the scores to compare applicants only to others in their protected group. Thus, the best employees from within each minority and nonminority group would be referred to employers, but all protected groups would be represented in the referrals.

Employers may face a similar dilemma, if their tests also tend to exclude larger numbers of minority-group candidates. Should an employer so adjust the selection standards that a relatively equal number of minority and nonminority candidates is considered (thus avoiding adverse impact), or should applicants be treated precisely the same, competing only on the basis of their measured qualifications for the job? Though we have introduced this discussion here, as part of the ability test section, its implications are important for all of the tests

---

EXHIBIT 8.14   Example Job Knowledge Test Items for Different Occupations

---

Barber
1. A man with a prominent nose should have a:
   a. Pyramid mustache.
   b. Large mustache.
   c. Narrow mustache.
   d. Small mustache.

Bartender
2. Which one of the following drinks is always shaken?
   a. California Root Beer.
   b. Screwdriver.
   c. Gibson.
   d. Sombrero.

Building contractor
3. What should be painted first when painting a room?
   a. Walls.
   b. Window sills.
   c. Trim and moldings.
   d. Ceilings.

Massage therapist
4. The best type of heat to produce relaxation prior to a massage is:
   a. Electric.
   b. Dry.
   c. Prolonged.
   d. Moist.

Broadcaster
5. On a telephone call-in program, you should NOT:
   a. Clarify a topic for a listener.
   b. Place a time limit on the calls, as this inhibits those persons who wish to express their opinions.
   c. Express your own opinions on the topics.

Interior designer
6. What one element helps to give balance to a room?
   a. A window on every wall.
   b. A fireplace.
   c. Matching wallpaper and draperies.
   d. Furniture of varied heights.

Floral designer
7. Which design is NOT a sympathy design?
   a. Gates ajar.
   b. Spray.
   c. Cascade Bouquet.
   d. Cross.

Travel agent
8. To obtain the least expensive round-trip air ticket you should:
   a. Arrive at the airport two hours early.
   b. Buy two one-way tickets.
   c. Find three friends to travel with you.
   d. Book well in advance.

ANSWERS: 1b, 2d, 3d, 4d, 5c, 6d, 7c, 8d

Source: Allen D. Bragdon, *The Book of Tests* (New York: Harper & Row, 1989).

---

discussed in this section, because any of them may produce differences in average test scores between different racial or gender groups. There is no generally best way to resolve this dilemma, but employers should be aware of the problem so they can consider how to deal with it.

Job Knowledge Tests, Work Samples, and Job Tryouts

"Name an occupation, and there's probably a test that goes with it."[71] Exhibit 8.14 shows examples of job knowledge test items that might be used for several occupations. Job knowledge items are developed through job analysis to identify the key facts or rules that job incumbents must know to do their jobs. Work samples are miniature replicas or simulations of actual on-the-job behaviors, such as shorthand or word processing and blueprint reading. Perhaps the most realistic direct test of job knowledge is to select employees for trial periods on the job, as some auto plants do for their manufacturing employees.[72]

Validity

Work samples and job tryouts carefully constructed from job analysis have demonstrated validities in the mid 0.40s.[73] They perform best when they sample directly from the tasks that job incumbents actually do and when they reflect as much of the job situation as possible. Such selection devices are best suited to jobs with clearly observable and well-defined tasks.

Legality

Work samples and job tryouts have proven relatively free from discrimination.[74] They are also obviously job related if they contain actual job tasks. However, sometimes they will tend to exclude minority groups or females, especially in jobs not historically held by these groups. Therefore, they should be used only to assess skills and knowledge that applicants absolutely must have before starting the job. They should not reflect knowledge that is routinely learned on the job.

Physical/Physiological Requirements

About half of all organizations give preemployment medical examinations, and a similar percentage require drug tests.[75] However, more specific physical/physiological testing, such as physical abilities testing, polygraph tests, genetic screening, and AIDS tests, are much rarer.[76] Nonetheless, such measurements have stirred public and legislative attention and continue to generate controversy.

Physical Abilities/Medical Examinations

Most jobs don't exact such acute physical demands that applicant differences in physical abilities greatly affect job performance. However, for jobs that do exact such demands, a good deal of research has developed job-analysis methods to identify the necessary physical abilities, and tests to detect them. Tests of flexibility and balance have shown validity for some jobs, and tests of static strength (especially upper-body strength) show validity for others. Explosive strength and stamina are required in fewer jobs, but fire-fighter jobs do require prolonged cardiovascular activity, running, and jumping. One long-term research program reports validities for physical test batteries in the 0.50s and 0.60s.[77] However, a drawback to such tests is that they are likely to produce adverse impact for females and some racial groups, particularly tests of upper-body strength.[78]

Physicians can get guidance on factors relevant to job performance that can be observed in medical examinations. The *Manual for Identification of Joint Im-*

mobility provides a set of tests that a physician can use in his or her office to quickly determine if the individual possesses adequate range of motion at specific joints to perform general movement tasks.[79] The *Job Applicant Medical History Questionnaire* is completed by applicants and allows physicians to target a preemployment physical examination to the applicant's medical history, as well as the particular job requirements.[80]

A particularly controversial issue is whether employers may legally prohibit women of childbearing age from jobs that may pose risks to fetal health. Johnson Controls, a battery manufacturer, voluntarily adopted a fetal protection policy in 1982 at its Globe Battery manufacturing plant in Fullerton, California. The policy prohibited women from working in the production area unless they produced medical evidence of infertility, based on evidence that exposure to lead could endanger fetal health should the women become pregnant. Queen Elizabeth Foster applied for a job as a cast-on-strap loader at the plant, but declined to produce evidence of infertility and was denied employment at the plant. Johnson Controls argued that the policy was necessary to ensure worker health and safety. The United Auto Workers and others argue that such policies unfairly discriminate against women. The U.S. Supreme Court has agreed to hear this case, and its ruling may provide guidance for employers and job applicants.[81]

Drug Testing

"The formula for a high-paying top-of-the-line job today is 'six or seven interviews and a drug test,' " one Dartmouth College senior said in the days before graduation.[82] *Fortune* estimates that nearly half of all major U.S. companies, including IBM, Kodak, AT&T, Lockheed, 3M, and Westinghouse, require some or all job applicants to provide urine specimens. Large companies cite a responsibility to provide a safe, healthy, and productive environment for their workers. However, smaller companies employing lower-paid service workers may not be able to afford drug tests. One government agency in the northeastern United States tested 1,000 security guard applicants and 980 failed.[83] In the South and in some rural areas, employers cannot find enough drug-free workers to hire.[84] Evidence for the effectiveness of drug testing is sketchy and preliminary, as is evidence regarding potential legal vulnerability. Recommendations include: (1) test only applicants/employees whose jobs are considered "safety-specific" or "critical"; (2) use only valid measures of drug use; (3) obtain valid consent of the applicant or employee and then provide the examinee with the results of the tests; (4) strictly maintain confidentiality of test results; (5) use drug tests as a small part of a comprehensive drug abuse program.[85]

Smoking Bans

"The pay was good, the interview went well, and the job looked promising—until Art Hargreaves learned the hard way: no smokers hired." A half-pack-a-day cigarette smoker, Hargreaves was out of luck at Litho Industries, a printing company in Raleigh, North Carolina, which in January 1989 stopped hiring smokers—even those who agree not to smoke at work. Though estimated at only about 6 percent, the number of companies with such no-smoking policies appears to be growing, and urine tests are often used to detect evidence of smoking.[86] Such policies are frequently designed to cut insurance or medical costs, or to appease employees complaining about second-hand smoke effects. Clear evidence of the consequences of such policies does not exist, but there is a growing likelihood that such policies will be legally challenged as invasions of privacy or discrimination against the handicapped.

AIDS Screening

Acquired immune deficiency syndrome (AIDS) may be the most prominent medical crisis of the 1990s, with thousands of confirmed AIDS cases and over a million Americans carrying the AIDS virus.[87] A 1987 survey by the American Society for Personnel Administration (ASPA) reported that 33 percent of responding companies had employees with AIDS.[88] While the incidence of applicant or employee AIDS testing seems low among employers, it is possible that blood tests as part of medical examinations may be used to support such testing. One expert concludes that AIDS testing for employment purposes is not justified, because AIDS is a protected handicap, infection through routine work contacts is impossible, and presently available tests identify the antibody and not the disease.[89]

Genetic Screening

This type of testing involves examining an individual's genetic makeup, and it has been used to identify individuals with high susceptibility to workplace toxins and those genetically predisposed toward contracting various occupational diseases. Advances in genetic theory and understanding may expand the number of traits and characteristics that can be identified with such procedures. However, employers must proceed cautiously, because the techniques are intrusive, potentially discriminatory, and it is not clear whether such characteristics are job related.[90]

Polygraph (Lie Detector) Tests

These tests, used by thousands of employers prior to December 1988, were employed to help prevent employee theft or security breaches. However, effective December 27, 1988, the Employee Polygraph Protection Act of 1988 prohibits polygraph test use in selection except for state, local, and federal government employees and businesses with direct involvement in secret military, intelligence, or nuclear power.[91]

Personality, Honesty, and Graphology Tests

"Sometimes I tease animals. Also, I feel useless at times, and I occasionally feel that I'm about to go to pieces. Once in a while I like smashing things, is that weird?"[92] The world's most widely used personality test, the Minnesota Multiphasic Personality Inventory, uses 567 statements like these to determine individuals' degree of paranoia, depression, mania, or anxiety.[93] A wide variety of such tests is available through various psychological services, and they are used by about 17 percent of employers, especially for sales occupations.[94] Certainly, there is widespread belief that certain "types" of people make better salespeople, pilots, or actors than others.

With the prohibition of polygraph tests, there has been renewed interest in the use or written *honesty or integrity tests*. Such tests can either be specifically designed to ask applicants about their attitudes toward theft and dishonesty or about admissions of theft or illegal behavior. A second approach is to take items from more general personality inventories and score them in ways that distinguish those who are dishonest from others.[95]

Graphology, or handwriting analysis, has certainly prompted attention and, though rare, may be an increasingly used predictor. Before someone is hired at Thomas Interior Systems, Inc., the president of the Elmhurst, Illinois, office-furniture company has a handwriting analyst examine the candidate's writing to develop a personality profile. But, can an absence of "*i*" dots and a variance in pen pressure, for example, be indications of wandering attention and disregard for detail, as claimed by one handwriting analyst?[96] Psychological research has shown little support for the use of graphology, finding such analyses to have low reliability across analysts and little predictive power.[97] Exhibit 8.15 describes one "experiment" by a reporter on *The Wall Street Journal* and its results. Does your untrained analysis of the handwriting match the analysts? If a prospective employer uses the technique, it may be time to review those penmanship exercises from grade school.

Legality

Personality tests are subject to the same standards as all tests. If they result in differential treatment or adverse impact against protected groups, their job-relatedness comes into question. Target Stores, a discount department store chain, faces a class-action lawsuit in Alameda County, California, superior court challenging its psychological testing practices. Plaintiffs claim that Target's 700-question personality inventory containing such questions as "I believe in the second coming of Christ" and "I have had no difficulty starting or holding my urine" violates privacy protection guaranteed under the California constitution.[98] Honesty tests have been shown to produce little adverse impact for females or minorities.[99]

Who Am I? It Depends on Whom You Ask

As an unscientific look at the debate over the reliability of handwriting analysis, I submitted the same handwriting sample to three handwriting services: Graphological Services International in New York (whose motto is: "Handwriting Reveals What Resume Conceals"), Handwriting Resource Corp. in Phoenix, Ariz., and K.K.S. Graphoconsultants in Highland Park, Ill.

Listed here is a brief summary of some of the major findings of each analyst; one report included more than 100 traits. The profiles sometimes agreed and sometimes directly contradicted each other. But my editor, my wife and I all thought one profile, in full, was quite accurate.

> *My first-grade teacher, Sr. Miriam Francis, warned me to keep up with my penmanship — or I'd regret it someday. Turns out she was right.*
>
> *M. McCarth*

GRAPHOLOGICAL SERVICES	HANDWRITING RESOURCE	K.K.S. GRAPHOCONSULTANTS
A healthy nonconformist	Logical, objective and cautious	Logical, objective; clear and succinct
Original and independent thinker; very creative	Thinking is low in creativity and imagination	Not really into theory or abstraction but into facts
Good negotiator; adaptable to all kinds of people	Diplomatic; handles interpersonal politics tactfully	Sometimes blunt instead of charming; should not plan a career as a diplomat
Sensitive to criticism	Biggest weakness: indifference to criticism	Sensitive to personal but not professional criticism
Easygoing	Worried, anxious; stress-reduction efforts recommended	Anxious, intense, rather than laid-back or relaxed
Tends to have up and down moods corresponding to changing self-image	Emotions sometimes stable, sometimes inconsistent	Strong evidence of emotional stability; very much on an even keel

Validity

Can personality validly predict job behaviors? Many researchers have concluded that they cannot, or at least that their demonstrated validity is much lower than other available predictors, such as cognitive ability tests.[100] Yet, others point out that existing studies have not given personality tests a fair chance.[101] Studies continue to emerge that find significant relationships between personality and accidents, sales commissions, productivity, and occupational attainment.[102] Honesty tests have shown validities in the range of 0.50 with self-reported dishonest activity, though their relationship to objectively observed theft or discharge due to illegal activity is usually lower.[103] There is currently no clear evidence to generally reject or accept personality tests as selection predictors.

CONSTRUCTING THE EXTERNAL SELECTION PROCESS

No matter how valid the selection procedures, their effectiveness depends on how the organization uses their information. Properly constructing the process for gathering and combining predictor information often determines the success or failure of external staffing systems. Process designers make choices about whether to select for one job or several, who gathers and scores the information, and how to combine multiple selection procedures.

Single-Job Selection versus Classification

Most selection procedures are evaluated for their ability to predict performance or other behaviors on one particular job. More frequently, however, employee careers are expected to span several jobs, or to include learning many new skills and adapting to frequent work changes (see Chapter Three). Also, increasing labor shortages mean that employers will often face the task of assigning virtually all applicants to some job, with the decision focusing on for what job they are most qualified. Selection decisions involving choices about placing many job candidates into one of several employment opportunities are called *classification decisions*.

Consider the U.S. military, which tests thousands of applicants and assigns them to several hundred jobs based on their test scores. What priorities should be used in these assignments? Should a person who would make a superb cook but a pretty good tank gunner be assigned to the kitchen or the tank? How much weight should be given to the individual's stated job desires? How much should relative shortages in different assignments drive the assignment process? In principle, the system should place individuals by emphasizing the most important jobs, taking account of current and anticipated shortages, giving most weight to qualifications, but also making adjustments for their stated job aspirations. Putting such a system in practice, however, requires massive computer programs designed to consider a large number of complex alternatives.[104] Selection techniques for such a system must be evaluated not only for their ability to predict performance in each of the jobs but also for their ability to clearly sort individuals according to their relative qualifications for several different jobs.[105]

Gathering and Scoring Predictor Information

Unless a predictor is scored in a completely mechanical way, someone must observe and record the information about applicants and translate it into some sort of report or score. Usually, the personnel department handles this task, though interviews are often shared with other managers and the hiring supervisor.[106] The chairman of General Electric Company is reported to personally pore over thick volumes that contain detailed dossiers on prospects for top management jobs. He says that "selecting the right people is my most important job."[107]

Combining Multiple Selection Procedures

Would you hire a lifeguard based solely on information from an application blank? Probably not. You would most likely want to test the person's knowledge of relevant regulations, have him or her demonstrate strength and rescue skills in the water, and perhaps interview the person. Applicants are rarely selected using only one selection procedure. Using multiple procedures can provide more complete information, and it allows the selection process to be adjusted in response to particular situations. With multiple selection procedures, however, the organization must decide how to combine them to produce a single hire/reject decision for each applicant. In selecting lifeguards, for example, would everyone have to do well on the written test, the in-water demonstration, and the interview, or would you allow very good performance on one predictor to compensate for somewhat lower performance on others? Exhibit 8.16 describes three methods of using multiple selection methods: compensatory, multiple hurdles, and hybrid approaches.

Compensatory Processes
As Exhibit 8.16 shows, compensatory combination processes allow very high performance on one selection procedure to compensate for low performance on another. Applicants are tested on all selection procedures, and the scores on individual predictors are added before a judgment is made. This process is common in situations where there are few minimum requirements, and the objective is to get an overall picture of applicant qualifications. Usually, different predictors are given different weights, depending on their relevance and importance to different criteria. Computers can help with this weighting process.[108] Compensatory processes maximize the opportunity to combine all of the available data. They can be expensive, however, because each applicant must submit to all of the procedures before a decision is made.

EXHIBIT 8.16   Alternative Ways of Using Multiple Selection Procedures

Compensatory process

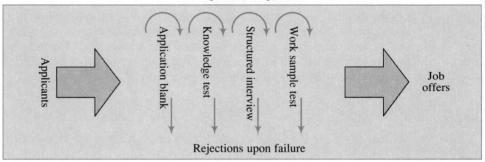

Multiple-hurdle process

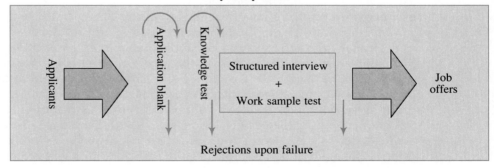

Multiple Hurdles

Multiple hurdles means that each predictor operates independently. Applicants must get past the first hurdles to proceed to the next, and failing any hurdle leads to rejection. In Exhibit 8.16, applicants must be minimally qualified on the application blank to proceed to the knowledge test and be minimally qualified on the knowledge test to proceed to the structured interview. Strength on one selection measure cannot compensate for weakness on another. Multiple hurdles make sense when the selection procedures reflect minimum required applicant characteristics. Accountants must have certain licenses, pilots must have experience in the aircraft they will fly, and lifeguards must know how to swim. Multiple hurdles processes can be used to cut selection costs, by using cheaper procedures first, to winnow down the applicant pool, and using more expensive procedures only on the smaller group of applicants who survived the first hurdles. Legally, such processes can be risky, however. The Supreme Court ruled in *Connecticut* v. *Teal* that every individual hurdle must avoid rejecting protected groups or be shown to be job related (see Chapter Six).

Hybrid Processes

As Exhibit 8.16 shows, a hybrid approach is simply the combination of hurdles and compensatory processes. Minimum qualifications that are essential for the job, such as licenses, skills, or certification, are used as hurdles. Applicants who survive the hurdles are tested with other procedures, whose results are so combined that some talents can compensate for others. In selecting lifeguards, for example, ability to swim and minimum endurance levels might be hurdles, but a combination of predictors measuring knowledge of regulations and motivation to do well might be used, with highly motivated individuals allowed to compensate for less knowledge, and vice versa.

VALIDATING THE SELECTION PROCESS TO DETERMINE WHAT WORKS

We have seen that there is a wide variety of available selection procedures, and that they can be combined in several different ways. How does a manager determine which procedures and selection processes give the best predictions? This question is important not only for evaluating existing selection processes but, perhaps even more important, before implementing a selection process.

Validation methods are the approaches used by organizations or researchers to determine whether one or more predictors are valid. Validation produces a prediction about the predictor—will the predictor accurately forecast the applicant's future behaviors. As Exhibit 8.2 and 8.16 showed, however, the selection process involves much more than scoring applicants on predictors. Validity depends as much on how predictor information is used as it does on what predictor information is gathered. For example, a fork-lift license may be a very valid predictor for loading dock performance but be virtually useless in predicting residence-hall advisors' performance (though a fork-lift might come in handy in some residence halls). Validation methods provide the most useful information when they focus on similar predictors, similar prediction criteria, and similar situations to those that the organization will actually encounter. Two general categories of validation methods are *criterion related,* which actually examines scores on both predictors and criteria, and *content based,* which examines similarities between the content of predictors and criteria.

Criterion-Related Validation Approaches

If you wanted to determine whether a friend's movie recommendations accurately fit your movie preferences, you would probably track several of the friend's recommendations, go to see movies both recommended and not recommended, and judge whether you liked the recommended movies better. Criterion-related validation approaches work in a similar way. These approaches actually measure scores on a *predictor,* which is usually a selection device, such as a test, interview, or biographical assessment. They also measure scores on a *criterion* or on a set of *criteria,* which is usually a job behavior, such as performance, absenteeism, and training success; or it may be a longer-run outcome, such as tenure or career progression. A predictor score and a criterion score is obtained for each person in the sample, and the statistical relationship between the two sets of scores is computed.

Choosing Predictors

Predictors in validation are usually chosen because they are similar or identical to the actual selection techniques the organization is considering. A good predictor will distinguish applicants from each other and do it *reliably* (consistently). Unless applicants are different, there can be no basis for choosing among them. However, making distinctions is not enough, for these distinctions must also be related to subsequent job behaviors or other criteria. For example, eye color provides a reliable and objective way to distinguish among the individuals in your class, but it is unlikely to relate to subsequent behaviors. It is also important to choose predictors that measure traits not routinely developed or learned on the job. For example, it does little good to select lifeguards based on their knowledge of CPR, if the county or state mandates that all lifeguards go through such training at the beginning of every season.

Choosing Criteria

Criteria must also be chosen carefully, and these choices are often much less obvious than the choice of predictors. Criteria can reflect a wide variety of individual characteristics, behaviors, or results, such as those discussed in Chapter Three. Good criteria should be: (1) affected by individuals, not determined largely by others or by technology; (2) relevant to the goals of key constituents in the organization, as discussed in Chapter Five; (3) measurable at reasonable cost, with adequate quality, and in practical ways; (4) affected by the individual differences reflected in the predictors; and (5) remain stable over time.[109]

The temptation is to choose criteria that are easily measured or that have been used in other validation studies. Sales performance might seem the perfect criterion for salesperson performance, because it is easily measured and clearly related to organizational goals. However, sales may be *contaminated,* because it reflects nonindividual causes, as when sales performance is largely determined by the territory assigned to the individual. Sales performance may also be *deficient,* because it fails to reflect important factors. For example, sales may fail to reflect effectiveness in training other salespeople or in completing paperwork. There is also evidence that typical and maximum performance are different phenomena, and that individuals high on one may not be high on the other.[110] Evidence also suggests that abilities and performance may not be stable over time.[111]

Different criteria may exhibit very different relationships to predictors. Evidence suggests that ability tests may predict promotional progress better than supervisory performance ratings.[112] Different personality traits predicted differently skills in selling, human relations, and organizing.[113] While a criterion, such as employee theft, may be important for retail or bank clerks, it may be quite unimportant for nuclear plant operators or managers. Thus, choosing criteria must be done carefully and must involve the key constituents who will be affected by selection decisions.

Predictive Validation versus Concurrent Validation

If you were validating your friend's movie recommendations against your own movie preferences, you could have your friend recommend for or against several movies, and then you could go see them to test whether the recommendations matched your preferences. Or, you could go to the movies with your friend and get his or her recommendations at the same time that you form your own preferences. This is the difference between predictive and concurrent validation.

Predictive validation methods use samples of job applicants, while *concurrent validation* methods use samples of current employees. Exhibit 8.17 compares the two. Both involve using job analysis to select or design selection techniques (predictors) and performance measures (criteria) in steps 1 and 2. The predictive validation method scores applicants on the predictor, hires them, and only then measures their criterion scores. Applicants may be hired randomly, or by using existing predictors, or by using the predictor being validated (the latter approach is not recommended).[114] The concurrent validation method scores current employees on the predictor and measures their criterion scores at the same time.

Predictive validation involves a delay between measuring the predictor and criterion scores, because applicants must be selected and allowed to perform on the job. It may also provide a smaller sample of individuals, because only a small number of applicants may be hired. Yet, by using actual applicants, predictive validation is likely to closely resemble the situation in which the predictor will be used.

Concurrent validation involves no delay, because predictor and criterion scores are obtained at about the same time. By using the entire group of current employees, it is also likely to generate a larger sample of individuals, providing more information than a small sample. However, current employees may or may not behave as applicants would. They may be less motivated to do well

EXHIBIT 8.17   Predictive versus Concurrent Validation

Predictive validation process

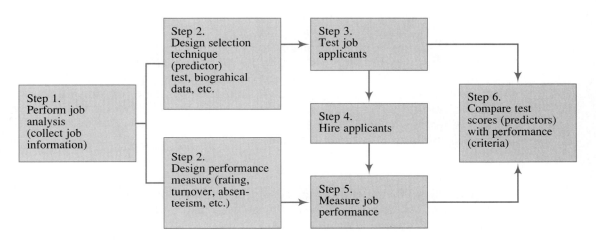

Concurrent validation process

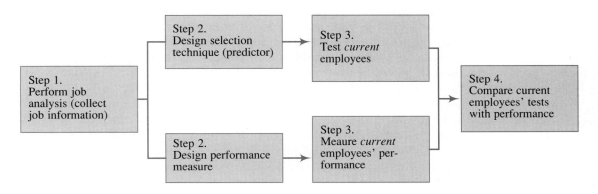

on the predictor, because they already have the job. They may have learned skills on the job that change their scores on the predictor. If the really good employees have been promoted and the really poor employees dismissed, the validity relationship may appear weaker than it would be with actual applicants.

Research suggests that validation results for mental ability tests are similar for both concurrent and predictive methods.[115] Considering the savings in time and the larger sample of individuals, a well-conducted concurrent validation study may well be preferable to a predictive study. The key is whether current employees are really different enough from applicants to bias the results severely.

Synthetic Validation

With small samples of applicants or current employees in one job, validity coefficients may not be very good estimates of how a predictor will perform in other applicant samples. *Synthetic validation* attempts to surmount the small-sample problem by relating predictor scores to the same job dimension, but across several different jobs with different employees.[116] For example, a typing ability test might be validated against the typing performance of not only secretaries but also of receptionists and clerks.

Validity Generalization

Individual predictive validation studies often encounter difficulties that may mask true predictor/criterion relationships. Small samples, error-prone measures, or an unusually small range of predictor or criterion scores in a particular sample can cause the results of any particular study to poorly represent what would actually happen if the predictor was applied to many future applicant samples. Individual studies differ in the degree of these difficulties, which can make validity coefficients appear to change with each study. This belief in "situational specificity" often led managers and researchers to assume that predictors found valid in one situation might be invalid if used in a slightly different situation. It prompted managers and researchers to place little credence in results of other validation studies and to undertake small-sample validation studies every time they introduced a new predictor or applied existing predictors to different situations.

Validity generalization combines the result of many validation studies, statistically removing the effects of "artifacts," such as small samples, unreliable measures, and restricted score ranges. Essentially, the correlation coefficient from each individual study becomes one data element in the larger validity generalization. This approach is also sometimes called *meta-analysis,* a term you will frequently see in the references at the ends of the chapters in this book. Validity generalization studies suggest that selection techniques are often equally valid in similar but not identical situations.[117] Human resource managers can use validity generalization to "borrow" validity coefficient results from other studies using similar predictors and similar criteria. This not only avoids the expense and time of conducting a situation-specific validation study, but it can produce more precise information if the studies are selected carefully. Validity generalization still arouses some controversy among researchers.[118] However, it is already being used by the U.S. Employment Service.[119]

Content-Based Validation

Another way to see if your friend's movie recommendations predict your preferences might never involve seeing any movies at all. You could discuss the aspects or content of movies that your friend likes and dislikes and make a judgment about whether the content of your friend's preferences corresponds to your own preferences. This is the idea behind content-based validation.

Content-based validation involves choosing and constructing selection techniques so they measure the knowledge, skills, and abilities (KSAs) used on the job.[120] Unlike criterion-related validation, content-based validation computes no predictor and criterion scores, nor a validity coefficient. Instead, it relies on judgments comparing the job content (based on job analysis, as discussed in Chapter Three) and the selection technique to determine the similarity between them.

For example, content validation for a word processing selection tool would involve listing the KSAs necessary for good word processing performance, such as: (1) ability to type at a keyboard, (2) ability to use standard business correspondence styles and formats, and (3) ability to turn on and operate an IBM-compatible computer. One predictor might be a short test on the procedures for starting and operating a computer, which would have high content validity with the third skill, but have low content validity for the other skills. A typing test on a typewriter would have high content validity for the first skill, but not for the other two. If the typing test involved taking a handwritten letter and producing a finished business letter in proper format, then it would have content validity for the first two skills, but not for the third.

Content validation works best when the job behaviors, KSAs, and predictor tasks are highly observable, because this minimizes the chance that judgments will be highly subjective and controversial. Many organizations use content validation to construct predictors that are later validated by using criterion-related methods.[121] An interesting variation on content validation involves having selection experts predict the validity coefficient that would be produced by a particular predictor and criterion.[122] One study found that the predictions of industrial psychologists compared favorably to the results of a typical single-organization criterion-related validation study.[123]

Extent of Test Validation

Validation does not appear to be a common practice. A Bureau of National Affairs (BNA) survey of 437 organizations found that only 16 percent had validated their procedures in accordance with the U.S. federal Uniform Guidelines on Employee Selection Procedures. Firms with more than 1,000 employees were more likely to validate than smaller firms. The most common validation criteria were formal performance evaluations, supervisory statements gathered specifically for validation, length of service, production rates, absence/tardiness, and success in training programs. Twenty-nine percent of those who validated used concurrent methods, while 18 percent used predictive methods. The other 53 percent used other methods, including some content validation, private consultants, or information from test publishers.[124] The last two sources may well base their estimates on validity generalization results. Apparently the time and energy required to conduct organization-specific validation studies is deemed too costly an investment, compared to other methods of determining whether selection procedures work, such as content validation or information from test publishers and consultants.

Government Regulation of Validation

Validity evidence can be a defense against findings of adverse impact (an unacceptably small proportion of women or minorities meeting hiring standards), as discussed in Chapter Six. Courts closely examine all aspects of the validation methods in considering such evidence, including:

The *predictor,* including the adequacy of job analysis, test content, and whether the organization considered predictor alternatives less harmful to the protected group.

The *criterion,* including adequacy of job analysis, measurement quality, rating processes, and rater training.

The *validation procedure,* including sample sizes, validation strategy, and job groups used.

The *data analysis,* such as the size and statistical significance of the validity coefficient, cost/benefit evidence, setting passing scores, fair predictions for minority groups, and evidence of validity generalization.[125]

The *Wards Cove* decision[126] (see Chapter Six) has stirred some controversy about the necessity of validation studies as a defense when adverse impact exists. The Supreme Court suggested that plaintiffs must not only show that adverse impact exists but must demonstrate that the practices contributed to the adverse impact. Nonetheless, the court did not reject the requirement that employers' selection practices be job related, and validation evidence is frequently presented to support a job-relatedness assertion.

INTERNATIONAL PERSPECTIVES ON EXTERNAL SELECTION

The increasing number of Japanese-style manufacturing plants in the United States has given American workers new insights into the differences between the two cultures. The 90,000 Kentucky residents who applied for 3,000 available jobs at the Toyota plant in Georgetown found that even the lowest-paid job on the shop floor required undergoing at least 14 hours of testing—in reading, math, manual dexterity, job fitness, and work place simulations—as well as a drug test and a physical. At the Smyrna, Tennessee, auto plant, applicants hoping to be hired must go through at least 40 hours of unpaid "preemployment" training. Mazda hired only about 1,300 of nearly 10,000 applicants who passed its five-step screening process. It says that it spends about $40 million—roughly $13,000 per employee—to staff its U.S. plants.[127] As we saw in Chapter Seven, Japanese companies in Japan can frequently rely on stringent school standards to handle the initial screening. In the United States, however, they adopt selection systems that expose applicants to a battery of work samples, tests, and interviews. The approach resembles the *assessment center,* used by U.S. companies primarily for their managerial employees, and discussed in Chapter Ten. Can such expensive and thorough selection systems really pay off for auto assembly line workers? These companies believe that it can, because they are looking for people who won't just do their job and go home. At Diamond-Star, a joint venture between Chrysler Corporation and Mitsubishi Motor Corporation, applicants are told they must learn several jobs, change shifts, work overtime, make and take constructive criticism, and submit a stream of suggestions for improving efficiency.[128] When you design a job this way, it pays to select carefully.

EVALUATING EXTERNAL SELECTION ACTIVITIES

We have already seen that external staffing decisions affect the productivity and qualifications of the work force, as well as the legal vulnerability of the employment relationship. However, many different measures could be used to assess these two general variables. Exhibit 8.18 describes several alternative measures that reflect the efficiency and equity outcomes of external selection.

Efficiency

How can you tell if the money spent on selection is really worth it? Is the money spent developing and implementing a work-sample test a good investment? As Exhibit 8.18 shows, ultimately, organizations hope to improve such business results in profits, productivity, defect reductions, and cost reduction. However, selection doesn't affect these things directly—it affects them through the match between applicants chosen and the demands of the jobs they fill. Using different selection techniques produces different kinds of information. According to the definition of information value from Chapter Five, selection information is a good investment if it: (1) corrects many decisions, and/or (2) corrects decisions that have very important effects, and/or (3) can be gathered at low cost.

Selection Cost
Every selection technique has costs. The particular level of costs will vary from situation to situation, but they generally include the costs to develop the selection procedure, the costs to actually conduct the procedure with applicants, the

EXHIBIT 8.18   Possible Measures to Evaluate External Selection Activities

Efficiency-Related	Equity-Related
Cost:	**Legality:**
Cost per new hire	Adverse impact
Quantity:	Number of legal challenges
Number hired	Adherence to legal requirements
Number who stay for 5 years	**Applicant perceptions:**
Average tenure of new hires	Satisfaction with the process
Quality:	Knowledge gained about the company
Validity of procedures	Satisfaction with the company
Average new-hire qualifications	
Proportion of new hires who succeed	
Performance levels of new hires	
Career progress of new hires	
Business results:	
Profits	
Productivity	
Defects	
Production costs	

costs to process the information and prepare it for the decision makers, and the costs of having decision makers evaluate the information and make a decision about who should receive employment offers. It is not possible to predict the precise costs of any selection procedure in every situation. Exhibit 8.4 describes the relative cost levels of different selection devices.

How Many Decisions Will Be Corrected?

Whether a selection device or system helps to correct only a few selection decisions or many depends on the number of such decisions that are made. The more selections, the more opportunity for selection information to work. However, it also depends on the probability that the selection decisions will be improved. You can improve 10 percent of 1,000 selection decisions or you can improve 50 percent of 200 decisions and get 100 improved selection decisions either way. Three variables affect the probability that new selection information will improve selection decisions—the base rate, the validity, and the selection ratio. Exhibit 8.19 shows how these three variables affect selection. Each diagram shows an ellipse or circle, which represents the pattern of individual scores on both a predictor (the horizontal axis) and a criterion (the vertical axis). The top series of graphs shows the situation where selection can greatly improve the existing situation, and the bottom shows the situation where selection cannot greatly improve the situation.

The *base rate* is simply the status quo—how successful your predictions would be *without* the new selection procedures. In Exhibit 8.19, it reflects the

EXHIBIT 8.19 Situational Factors Affecting Selection Efficiency

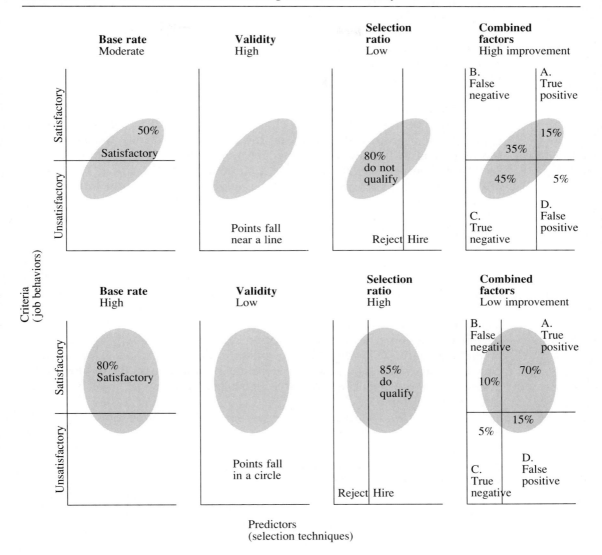

quality of the applicant population, compared to the dividing line between satisfactory and unsatisfactory performance. The high base rate in the lower part of the exhibit means that almost every applicant (80 percent) can already perform at a satisfactory level, so there's much less opportunity for a new selection procedure to improve decisions. The base rate of 50 percent, on the other hand, means that only 50 percent of applicants are currently satifactory if hired without the new procedure, so there's more room for a new procedure to improve on the base rate.

The *validity* of selection techniques has already been discussed. The top part of Exhibit 8.19 shows high validity, meaning the scores lie close to a straight line. Every predictor score associates with a relatively small range of criterion scores, making prediction more accurate. Higher validity means that a new selection procedure has a greater probability of correcting previously wrong hiring decisions. The opposite holds true with low validity, as shown in the bottom of Exhibit 8.19.

The *selection ratio* reflects how choosy you can be. It is the proportion of applicants who score high enough on the predictor to qualify for hiring. The top of Exhibit 8.19 shows a low selection ratio, where the reject/hire cutoff is set at a high level—only 20 percent of applicants qualify for hiring. The bottom of the exhibit shows a high seleciton ratio, meaning that the predictor cutoff for hiring is set low, so 85 percent of applicants qualify for hiring. Low selection ratios signify a more choosy selection process, because only the highest-scoring applicants are hired. So, low selection ratios provide the greater probability of correcting previously wrong hiring decisions.

The *combined effects* of these three factors determine how well selection corrects wrong decisions, as shown in the right-hand graphs of Exhibit 8.19. In both graphs, regions A and C represent accurate predictions, with A showing "true positives"—those applicants rated as qualified, who truly perform satisfactorily; and region C showing "true negatives"—those applicants rated as unqualified, who do perform unsatisfactorily. Regions B and D represent mistaken predictions, with D showing "false positives"—those applicants rated as qualified, but who would not perform satisfactorily; and region B showing "false negatives"—those applicants rated as unqualified who would have performed satisfactorily if hired.

The *success ratio* measures the proportion of those hired who actually do perform satisfactorily. Selection efficiency can be measured as the improvement between the base rate (without using the selection technique) and the final success ratio, if the selection technique is used. In the top part of Exhibit 8.19, we started with a base rate of 50 percent. By using the highly valid predictor, and being very choosy, we attain a final success ratio of 75 percent (15 percent in region A divided by the 20 percent in regions A and D). In the bottom of Exhibit 8.19, we started with a base rate of 80 percent. Using a less-valid predictor, and so setting our hiring cutoff that 85 percent of applicants qualify, we end up with a success ratio of 82 percent (70 percent in region A divided by the 85 percent in regions A and D). There are tables available for computing the expected success ratio, given a particular base rate, validity, and selection ratio.[129] Notice, however, that if you become very choosy with a less-valid predictor you increase the chance of false negatives, applicants who may be hired by your competitors.

How Important Are the Corrected Decisions?

Knowing the proportion of more-correct decisions you will make is useful, but it doesn't really tell you whether improved selection is a good investment. Would you spend an extra $10,000 per year to achieve the selection situation shown in the top of Exhibit 8.19 instead of the one shown in the bottom? You can't tell, without more information. Specifically, you need to know what difference the improved accuracy makes to organizational goals and outcomes. This is reflected in the *variability of applicant value*. For some jobs where decisions have huge implications or where mistakes can be disastrous, such as tanker captains, top managers, nuclear power plant operators, and airline pilots, the variability between high-value applicants and low-value applicants will be very great. For other jobs where decisions are highly constrained or where mistakes are easily corrected at low cost, such as very structured assembly line jobs, even the highest-performing employee may be only moderately more valuable than low-performing employees. When variability is high, selection systems that avoid false–positive errors are much more valuable than when variability is low. Recent research has begun to use this principle to measure the efficiency of improved selection in dollars. Though still somewhat controversial, estimates of selection system value in the million of dollars are not uncommon.[130] The dollar value, or *utility,* of new selection systems is higher when: (1) selection system costs are low; (2) large numbers of people will be hired with the system, and they stay with the organization a long time; (3) current base rates are near 50 percent; (4) the validity is high; (5) the selection ratio is low; and (6) the variability of applicant value in dollars is very high.

Equity

As we have seen, selection techniques have effects far beyond applicant productivity. They are seen as signals of the organization's treatment of its employees. Moreover, they are closely monitored by regulatory agencies, especially if they tend to exclude larger numbers of minorities and females than white males. Selection systems, in combination with external recruitment, are often key tools in increasing the rate at which protected group members are hired. Such affirmative action approaches may be seen as unfair when they give preference to lower-scoring minorities or females over higher-scoring white males.[131]

The use of clearly scorable and structured selection systems may have declined during the 1970s and 1980s, because of fears that minorities and females would score lower and be more frequently rejected. The question of whether it's "fair" to reject females and minorities who score lower on selection tests and perform somewhat well on the job remains hotly debated, with some arguing that the productivity reductions caused by failing to hire the best-qualified applicants are not worth the social benefits of preferential scoring.

Others argue that the productivity differences are small and may be due simply to biased supervisory performance ratings being used as selection criteria.[132] Human resource professionals will continue to be at the center of the effort to balance efficiency and equity through external selection.

SUMMARY

External selection activities provide the final filtering process before offering employment. The task is to measure applicant characteristics that will help the organization forecast which applicants will make successful future employees. A variety of external selection techniques exists, and many of them are the focus of heated debate about the balance between efficiency and equity at work. While validity is an important aspect of selection procedures, their true value is determined by the situation in which they are used. Clearly, human resource professionals, their employers, and society will continue to focus on this important human resource activity.

DISCUSSION AND REVIEW QUESTIONS

1. What choices must an HR professional make when designing an external selection strategy? How can these choices affect the organization from a legal standpoint as well as a long-run efficiency standpoint?

2. What is validity? Which purposes does validity evidence serve? What is a validity coefficient, and what are its characteristics?

3. Should application forms be relied on heavily in the selection process? Discuss the positive and negative impact they may have, and what an organization can do to make them more useful.

4. What effect can stereotyping, applicant behaviors, and interviewer behavior/ training have on employment interviews? What interview strategies are often found to have a damaging effect on the validity of interviews?

5. What does research suggest that can be done to improve interview usefulness? How can an organization protect itself from legal repercussions?

6. Discuss the uses and drawbacks of such selection devices as physical abilities/ medical examinations, drug testing, AIDS and genetic screening, personality and honesty testing. How can an organization balance efficiency and equity in using such techniques?

7. Discuss the role of predictors and criteria in validation. What characteristics should "good" criteria and predictors have? How might one avoid contamination and deficiency in predictors and criteria?

8. Distinguish predictive from concurrent validation. When might a well-conducted concurrent validation study be preferable to a predictive validation study?

9. Is high validity enough to justify investing in a new selection procedure? What other situational factors affect the value of improved selection information? What difference does it make if that value is measured in terms of prediction accuracy versus dollar-valued organizational outcomes?

10. Why do you think some minority groups score lower than nonminorities on common mental ability tests? If the tests still validly predict minority performance ratings (because low-scoring minorities also receive lower performance ratings), does this justify hiring all applicants based on their test scores even if this means excluding larger numbers of low-scoring minorities?

YOUR TURN
DRUG TESTING AT IBM

IBM Corporation has long been recognized as one of the most innovative and well-managed companies, especially with regard to its human resource management. Through 50 years of growth and innovation, it has maintained its core value of "Respect for the Individual." Today, it employs over 380,000 individuals virtually everywhere in the world. It's production processes for computers, semiconductor chips, and other products often involve highly trained employees handling products worth thousands of dollars and working with processes that are safe when handled properly but could have disastrous consequences if handled improperly.

William Colucci, IBM's vice president of personnel for the United States, described IBM's position in a 1986 interview:

> Simply stated, substance abuse is a national problem that must be addressed by society through coordinated actions by individuals, government, schools, medical professionals, and business. The evidence on substance abuse clearly indicates that the use of nonmedically prescribed drugs and alcohol abuse is harmful. For businesses, it is also costly. Safety and judgment can be impaired, interpersonal relationships damaged, and productivity lowered.
>
> At IBM, we want to balance our respect for an individual's right to privacy and the personal lifestyle of his or her own choosing against our objective to provide a safe, healthy, productive work environment.
>
> First, drugs and alcohol have no place in our business. The use, distribution, sale or possession of any drugs or other controlled substance for nonmedical reasons on company premises or in any IBM work environment is prohibited. We consider violations a serious breach of our policy, which normally result in dismissal. Second, employees under the influence of any nonmedically prescribed drugs are prohibited from company premises or any other IBM work environment. [International Business Machines Corporation, *Think,* no. 5 (1986), pp. 32–33.]

Put yourself in the position of the assistant to Colucci. He's asked for your ideas on an appropriate policy for IBM on drug testing for applicants. Should IBM test applicants for drug use? Should all applicants be tested, or only those for certain jobs? At what point in the recruiting/selection process should the test be given? Should it test for "hard" drugs only, or for all drugs? Should applicants be informed that they will have to undergo a drug test, and at what point in the employment process? What should be done if an applicant tests positive? Should applicants be allowed to take the test a second time? What if a very highly qualified applicant refuses to take the test? How can drug testing be justified as a "business necessity"? Your instructor has additional information about IBM's applicant drug-testing policy.

NOTES AND REFERENCES

1. Bureau of National Affairs, "Employee Selection Procedures," *ASPA–BNA Survey* no. 45 (Washington, D.C.: Bureau of National Affairs, May 5, 1983).

2. John W. Boudreau, "Utility Analysis," in *Human Resource Management Evolving Roles and Responsibilities,* ed. Lee D. Dyer (Washington, D.C.: Bureau of National Affairs, 1988).

3. Sara L. Rynes, "The Employment Interview as a Recruitment Device," in Robert W. Eder and Gerald R. Ferris, eds., *The Employment Interview* (Newbury Park, Calif.: Sage Publications, 1989), pp. 127–42.

4. For a particularly detailed example of an application blank, see *Recruiting and Selection Procedures,* Personnel Policies Forum Survey no. 146 (Washington, D.C.: Bureau of National Affairs, May 1988), pp. 68–71.

5. Allen Schuh, "Application Blank and Intelligence as Predictors of Turnover," *Personnel Psychology,* Spring 1967, pp. 59–63; Schuh, "The Predictability of Employee Tenure: A Review of the Literature," *Personnel Psychology,* Spring 1967, pp. 133–52; George W. England, *Development and Use of Weighted Application Blanks,* rev. ed., Bulletin 55 (Minneapolis: Industrial Relations Center, University of Minnesota, 1971); David Weiss, "Multivariate Procedures," in *Handbook of Industrial and Organizational Psychology,* ed. M. D. Dunnette (Chicago: Rand McNally, 1976), pp. 344–54.

6. Bureau of National Affairs, "Employee Selection Procedures."

7. John E. Hunter and Rhonda F. Hunter, "The Validity and Utility of Alternative Predictors of Job Performance."

8. England, *Development and Use of Weighted Application Blanks;* Raymond Lee and Jerome M. Booth, "A Utility Analysis of a Weighted Application Blank Designed to Predict Turnover for Clerical Employees," *Journal of Applied Psychology* 59 (1974), pp. 516–18.

9. Ernest C. Miller, "An EEO Examination of Employment Applications," *Personnel Administrator,* March 1981, pp. 63–70.

10. Bureau of National Affairs, *Recruiting and Selection Procedures.* Survey no. 146, May 1988.

11. "Reference Preference: Employers Button Lips," *The Wall Street Journal,* January 4, 1990, p. B1.

12. Ibid.

13. Hunter and Hunter, "The Validity and Utility of Alternative Predictors of Job Performance."

14. Kevin G. Love and Kirk O'Hara, "Predicting Job Performance of Youth Trainees under a Job Training Partnership Act Program (JTPA): Criterion Validation of a Behavior-Based Measure of Work Maturity," *Personnel Psychology* 40 (1987), pp. 323–41.

15. W. A. Owens, "Background Data," in *Handbook of Industrial and Organizational Psychology,* ed. Marvin D. Dunnette (Chicago: Rand McNally, 1976), pp. 609–44.

16. J. E. Rosenbaum and T. Kariya, "Market and Institutional Mechanisms for the High School to Work Transition in the U.S. and Japan," presented at the annual meeting of the American Sociological Association, Chicago, August 1987.

17. David Whitman, Joseph P. Shapiro, Ronald A. Taylor, Amy Saltzman, and Bruce B. Auster, "The Forgotten Half," *U.S. News and World Report,* June 26, 1989, pp. 45–53. Nancy J. Perry, "The New Improved Vocational School," *Fortune,* June 19, 1989, pp. 127–38.

18. Cindy Skrzycki, "Test of High School Graduates' Skills Planned," *Washington Post,* November 4, 1989, p. C1.

19. "NAB Chief Sees Business Problems in Growing Shortage of Qualified Workers," *BNA Labor Relations Week,* 4, no. 2 (January 1990).

20. John Bishop, "Why the Apathy in American High Schools?" *Educational Researcher* 18, no. 1 (January/February 1989), pp. 6–10; John Bishop and Suk Kang, "Vocational and Academic Education in High School: Complements or Substitutes?" *The Economics of Education Review* 8, no. 2 (1989), pp. 133–48.

21. Ellen H. Sides, Hubert S. Feild, William F. Giles, William H. Holley, and Achilles A. Armenakis, "Biographical Data: A Neglected Tool for Career Counselling," *Human Resource Planning,* 1984, pp. 151–56.

22. Leatta Hough, "Development of the Accomplishment Record Method of Selecting and Promoting Professionals," *Journal of Applied Psychology* 69, no. 1 (1984), pp. 135–46.

23. Hunter and Hunter, "Validity and Utility."

24. Leatta Hough, "Development of the Accomplishment Record Method."

25. Richard D. Arvey and Robert H. Faley, *Fairness in Selecting Employees,* 2nd ed. (Reading, Mass.: Addison-Wesley, 1988).

26. Bureau of National Affairs, "Employee Selection Procedures"; Bureau of National Affairs, "Recruiting and Selection Procedures."

27. Milton D. Hakel, "Employment Interview," in *Personnel Management: New Perspectives,* ed. K. Rowland and G. Ferris (Boston: Allyn & Bacon, 1982).

28. Richard D. Arvey and James E. Campion, "The Employment Interview: A Summary and Review of Recent Research," *Personnel Psychology* 35, no. 3 (1982), pp. 281–322; Eugene Mayfield, "The Selection Interview—A Re-Evaluation of Published Research," *Personnel Psychology* 17 (1964), pp. 239–60; Neil Schmitt, "Social and Situational Determinants of Interview Decisions: Implications for the Employment Interview," *Personnel Psychology* 29 (1976), pp. 79–101.

29. Michael M. Harris, "Reconsidering the Employment Interview: A Review of Recent Literature and Suggestions for Future Research," *Personnel Psychology* 42 (1989), pp. 691–726.

30. Susan M. Raza and Bruce N. Carpenter, "A Model of Hiring Decisions in Real Employment Interviews," *Journal of Applied Psychology* 72, no. 4 (1987), pp. 596–603.

31. Stephen Wermiel, "High Court Shifts Burden to Firms in Sex-Bias Cases," *The Wall Street Journal,* May 2, 1989, p. B1; John Bales, "Sex Stereotyping Data Valid, Brief Says," *APA Monitor* 19, no. 8 (August 1988), p. 23.

32. Richard D. Arvey and Robert H. Faley, *Fairness in Selecting Employees* (Reading, Mass.: Addison-Wesley, 1988).

33. Richard D. Arvey and James E. Campion, "The Employment Interview: A Summary and Review of Recent Research," *Personnel Psychology* 35 (1982), pp. 281–322.

34. J. S. Tosi and W. W. Einbender, "The Effects of the Type and Amount of Information in Sex Discrimination Research: A Meta-Analysis," *Academy of Management Journal*

28 (1985), pp. 712–23; Judy D. Olian, Donald P. Schwab, and Yitchak Haberfeld, "The Impact of Applicant Gender Compared to Qualifications on Hiring Recommendations: A Meta-Analysis of Experimental Studies," *Organizational Behavior and Human Decision Processes* 41 (1988), pp. 180–95.

35. Michael M. Harris, "Reconsidering the Employment Interview."

36. Michael A. Campion, Elliot D. Pursell, and B. K. Brown, "Structured Interviewing: Raising the Psychometric Properties of the Employment Interview," *Personnel Psychology* 41 (1988), pp. 25–42; T. McDonald and Milton D. Hakel, "Effects of Applicant Race, Sex, Suitability and Answers on Interviewer's Questioning Strategy and Ratings," *Personnel Psychology* 38 (1985), pp. 321–34.

37. Susan M. Raza and Bruce N. Carpenter, "A Model of Hiring Decisions in Real Employment Interviews"; Randall A. Gordon, Richard M. Rozelle, and James C. Baxter, "The Effect of Applicant Age, Job Level, and Accountability on the Evaluation of Job Applicants," *Organizational Behavior and Human Decision Processes* 41 (1988), pp. 20–33.

38. Michael M. Harris, "Reconsidering the Employment Interview."

39. Robert A. Baron, "Impression Management by Applicants During Employment Interviews: The 'Too Much of a Good Thing' Effect," chap. 15, in Robert W. Eder and Gerald R. Ferris, ed., *The Employment Interview*.

40. Michael M. Harris, "Reconsidering the Employment Interview"; Robert A. Baron, "Impression Management by Applicants."

41. N. Schmitt, "Social and Situational Determinants of Interview Decisions: Implications for the Employment Interview," *Personnel Psychology* 29, no. 1 (1976), pp. 79–101; Gatewood and Feild. *Human Resource Selection*.

42. P. M. Rowe, "Decision Processes in Personnel Selection," *Canadian Journal of Behavioural Science* 16, pp. 326–37.

43. Robert L. Dipboye, "Threats to the Incremental Validity of Interviewer Judgments," chap. 3, in Robert W. Eder and Gerald R. Ferris, eds., *The Employment Interview*.

44. Allen J. Schuh, "Interviewer Decision Styles," and Peter Herriot, "Attribution Theory and Interview Decisions," in Robert W. Eder and Gerald R. Ferris, eds., *The Employment Interview*.

45. M. R. Buckley and Robert W. Eder, "B. M. Springett and the Notion of the 'Snap Decision' in the Interview," *Journal of Management* 14 (1988), pp. 59–69.

46. Michael M. Harris, "Reconsidering the Interview."

47. Steven D. Maurer and Charles Fay, "Effect of Situational Interviews, Conventional Structured Interviews, and Training on Interview Rating Agreement: An Experimental Analysis," *Personnel Psychology* 17 (1988), pp. 329–44; Charles H. Fay and Gary P. Latham, "Effects of Training and Rating Scales on Rating Errors," *Personnel Psychology* 35 (1982), pp. 105–16.

48. Bureau of National Affairs, "Recruiting and Selection Procedures."

49. James G. Goodale, "Effective Employment Interviewing," chap. 22, in Robert W. Eder and Gerald R. Ferris, *The Employment Interview*.

50. Bureau of National Affairs, "Recruiting and Selection Procedures."

51. Brooks Mitchell, "Interviewing Face-to-Interface," *Personnel* 67, 1 (January 1990), pp. 23–25.

52. Michael M. Harris, "Reconsidering the Employment Interview."

53. Tom Janz, "The Patterned Behavior Description Interview: The Best Prophet of the Future is the Past," in Robert W. Eder and Gerald R. Ferris, eds., *The Employment*

Interview; Tom Janz, Lowell W. Hellervik, and D. C. Gilmore, *Behavior Description Interviewing* (Newton, Mass.: Allyn & Bacon, 1986).

54. Gary P. Latham, Lise M. Saari, E. D. Pursell, and Michael A. Campion, "The Situational Interview," *Journal of Applied Psychology,* 69 (1984), pp. 569–73.

55. Michael A. Campion, E. D. Pursell, and B. K. Brown, "Structured Interviewing: Raising the Psychometric Properties of the Employment Interview," *Personnel Psychology* 41 (1988), pp. 25–42.

56. Sara L. Rynes, "The Interview as a Recruitment Device," chap. 9, in Robert W. Eder and Gerald R. Ferris, eds., *The Employment Interview.*

57. Robert W. Eder, "Contextual Effects on Interview Decisions," chap. 8, in Robert W. Eder and Gerald R. Ferris, eds., *The Employment Interview.*

58. Michael M. Harris, "Reconsidering the Interview"; W. H. Weisner and Steven F. Cronshaw, "A Meta-Analytic Investigation of the Impact of Interview Format and Degree of Structure on the Validity of the Employment Interview," *Journal of Occupational Psychology* 61 (1988), pp. 275–90; George F. Dreher and Steven D. Maurer, "Assessing the Employment Interview," Steven F. Cronshaw and Willi H. Wiesner, "The Validity of the Employment Interview," in Robert W. Eder and Gerald R. Ferris, eds., *The Employment Interview.*

59. " 'Intrusive' Questions Are Plaguing U.S. Workers," *BNA Daily Labor Report,* no. 7, January 10, 1990, pp. 2–3.

60. James E. Campion and Richard D. Arvey, "Unfair Discrimination in the Employment Interview," chap. 4, in Robert W. Eder and Gerald R. Ferris, eds., *The Employment Interview.*

61. Claudia H. Deutsch, "A Mania for Testing Spells Money," *New York Times,* October 16, 1988, p. 4F.

62. Robert M. Madigan, K. Dow Scott, Diana L. Deadrick, and Jill A. Stoddard, "Employment Testing: The U.S. Job Service Is Spearheading a Revolution," *Personnel Administrator,* September 1986, pp. 62–69.

63. D. C. Meyers, M. C. Jennings, and Edwin A. Fleishman, *Analysis of Computer Interactive Tests for Assigning Helicopter Pilots to Different Missions,* ARRO Technical Report no. 3075/R838 (Bethesda, Md.: Advanced Research Resources Organization); Edwin A. Fleishman, "Some New Frontiers in Personnel Selection Research," *Personnel Psychology* 41 (1988), pp. 679–701.

64. One example is Consulting Psychologists Press, 577 College Avenue, Palo Alto, CA, 94306-1490, which will send a catalog of its ability and personality tests.

65. Linda S. Gottredson, ed., "The *g* Factor in Employment," *Journal of Vocational Behavior* 29 (1986), pp. 293–450.

66. John A. Hartigan and Alexandra K. Wigdor, eds., *Fairness in Employment Testing* (Washington, D.C.: National Academy Press, 1989).

67. Frank L. Schmidt, John E. Hunter, and A. N. Outerbridge, "Impact of Job Experience and Ability on Job Knowledge, Work Sample Performance, and Supervisory Ratings of Job Performance," *Journal of Applied Psychology* 71 (1986), pp. 432–39.

68. Kevin R. Murphy, "Is the Relationship between Cognitive Ability and Job Performance Stable over Time?" *Human Performance* 2, no. 3 (1989), pp. 183–200.

69. Richard D. Arvey and Robert H. Faley, *Fairness in Selecting Employees.*

70. John A. Hartigan and Alexandra K. Wigdor, *Fairness in Employment Testing.*

71. Gary Putka, "A Test For Every Task," *The Wall Street Journal,* February 9, 1990, p. B19.

72. "Job Tryouts without Pay Get More Testing in U.S. Auto Plants," *The Wall Street Journal,* January 10, 1985.

73. John E. Hunter and Rhonda Hunter, "The Validity and Utility of Alternative Predictors of Job Performance," *Psychological Bulletin* 96 (1984), pp. 72–98; Wayne F. Cascio and Neil Phillips, "Performance Testing: A Rose Among Thorns?" *Personnel Psychology* 30 (1979), pp. 187–97.

74. Wayne F. Cascio and Neil Phillips, "Performance Testing: A Rose among Thorns?"

75. Bureau of National Affairs, *Recruiting and Selection Procedures;* "Drug Testing Increases," *Human Resource Management News,* February 18, 1989, p. 3.

76. Bureau of National Affairs, "Recruiting and Selection Procedures."

77. Edwin A. Fleishman, "Some New Frontiers in Personnel Selection Research," *Personnel Psychology* 41 (1988), pp. 679–701.

78. Joyce Hogan and Ann M. Quigley, "Physical Standards for Employment and the Courts," *American Psychologist* 41, no. 11 (1986), pp. 1193–217.

79. D. L. Gebhardt and C. E. Crump, *Joint Mobility Evaluation Manual for Entry Level Natural Gas Industry Jobs* (Bethesda, Md.: Advanced Research Resources Organization, 1983).

80. C. E. Crump and D. L. Gebhardt, *Job Applicant Medical History Questionnaires* (Bethesda, Md.: Advanced Research Resources Organization, 1983).

81. "Fetal Protection Policies Challenged under New Legislation Proposed in House," *BNA Daily Labor Report,* no. 65, April 4, 1990; "Supreme Court Agrees to Review Legality of Fetal Protection Policies," *BNA Labor Relations Week* 4, no. 13 (March 28, 1990); *United Auto Workers* v. *Johnson Controls, Inc.,* US SupCt No. 89-1215.

82. "Graduates Face Drug Tests in Joining Job Market," *New York Times,* Sunday, June 21, 1987, p. 29.

83. Andrew Kupfer, "Is Drug Testing Good or Bad?" *Fortune,* December 19, 1988, pp. 133–40.

84. *Human Resource Management News,* January 13, 1990, p. 1.

85. Deborah F. Crown and Joseph G. Rosse, "A Critical Review of the Assumptions Underlying Drug Testing," *Journal of Business and Psychology* 3, no. 1 (Fall 1988), pp. 22–41.

86. Milo Geyelin, "The Job Is Yours—Unless You Smoke," *The Wall Street Journal,* April 21, 1989, p. B1.

87. "Spread of AIDS Is Abating, but Deaths Will Still Soar," *New York Times,* February 14, 1988, p. 36.

88. "Few Companies Have Policies to Cover Employees with AIDS," *Resource* 6, no. 12 (October 1987).

89. Judy D. Olian, "AIDS Testing for Employment Purposes? Facts and Controversies," *Journal of Business and Psychology* 3, no. 2 (Winter 1988), pp. 135–53.

90. Judy Olian, "Genetic Screening for Employment Purposes," *Personnel Psychology* 37 (1984), pp. 423–38.

91. James G. Frierson, "New Polygraph Test Limits," *Personnel Journal,* December 1988, pp. 84–91.

92. Cynthia Crossen, "Bulemics Take Note: Personality Testing Is Entering the 80s," *The Wall Street Journal,* September 13, 1989, p. A1.

93. *Minnesota Multiphasic Personality Inventory-2* (Minneapolis: University of Minnesota Press, 1989); Tina Adler, "Revision Brings Test into the 21st Century," *The APA Monitor* 10, no. 11 (November 1989), p. 2.

94. Bureau of National Affairs, "Recruiting and Selection Procedures."

95. Paul R. Sackett, Laura R. Burris, and Christine Callahan, "Integrity Testing for Personnel Selection: An Update," *Personnel Psychology* 42, no. 3 (Autumn 1989), pp. 491–529.

96. Michael McCarthy, "Handwriting Analysis as Personnel Tool," *The Wall Street Journal,* August 25, 1988, p. 19.

97. G. Ben-Shakhar, M. Bar-Hillel, Y. Bilu, E. Ben-Abba, and A. Flug, "Can Graphology Predict Occupational Success? Two Empirical Studies and Some Methodological Ruminations," *Journal of Applied Psychology* 71 (1986), pp. 645–53.

98. Richard B. Schmitt and Milo Geyelin, "Psychological Tests by Employers Are Challenged in California Court," *The Wall Street Journal,* September 12, 1989, p. B9; *Soroka* v. *Target Stores,* Calif SuperCt, Alameda County, Hayward Branch, no. H-143579-3.

99. Paul R. Sackett et al., "Integrity Testing for Personnel Selection."

100. John E. Hunter and Rhonda F. Hunter, "Validity and Utility of Alternative Predictors of Job Performance," *Psychological Bulletin* 96 (1984), pp. 73–98.

101. John R. Hollenbeck, Arthur P. Brief, Ellen M. Whitener, and Karen E. Pauli, "An Empirical Note on the Interaction of Personality and Aptitude in Personnel Selection," *Journal of Management* 14, no. 3 (1988), pp. 441–51; John R. Hollenbeck and Ellen M. Whitener, "Reclaiming Personality Traits for Personnel Selection: Self-Esteem as an Illustrative Case," *Journal of Management* 15 (1989), pp. 53–64.

102. John R. Hollenbeck et al., "An Empirical Note"; Curtiss P. Hansen, "Personality Characteristics of the Accident Involved Employee," *Journal of Business and Psychology* 2, no. 4 (Summer 1988), pp. 346–65; Fred M. Rafilson, "Development of a Standardized Measure to Predict Employee Productivity," *Journal of Business and Psychology* 3, no. 2 (Winter 1988), pp. 199–213; John W. Jones and Lisa J. Wuebker, "Accident Prevention through Personnel Selection," *Journal of Business and Psychology* 3, no. 2 (Winter 1988), pp. 187–98; James T. Austin and Kathy A. Hanisch, "Occupational Attainment as a Function of Abilities and Interests: A Longitudinal Analysis Using Project TALENT Data," *Journal of Applied Psychology* 75, no. 1 (1990), pp. 77–86.

103. Paul R. Sackett, Laura R. Burris, and Christine Callahan, "Integrity Testing for Personnel Selection: An Update," *Personnel Psychology* 42 (1989), pp. 491–529; Michael A. McDaniel and J. W. Jones, "A Meta-Analysis of the Validity of the Employee Attitude Inventory Theft Scales," *Journal of Business and Psychology* 1 (1986), pp. 31–50.

104. Joseph Zeidner, Cecil Johnson, Edward Schmitz, and Roy Nord, *The Economic Benefits of Predicting Job Performance,* IDA Paper P-2241 (Alexandria, Va.: Institute for Defense Analyses, September 1989).

105. Lee J. Cronbach and Goldine C. Gleser, *Psychological Tests and Personnel Decisions,* 2nd ed. (Urbana: University of Illinois Press, 1965).

106. Bureau of National Affairs, "Employee Selection Procedures."

107. John Welsh, presentation to Cornell Graduate School of Business, 1984.

108. Kenneth J. Calhoun, "Automated Objectivity for Subjective Hiring Decisions," *Computers in Personnel,* Winter 1989, pp. 5–10.

109. Robert D. Gatewood and Hubert S. Feild, *Human Resource Selection* (New York: CBS College Publishing, 1987), pp. 506–11; Gerald V. Barrett, Marilyn S. Caldwell, and Ralph A. Alexander, "The Concept of Dynamic Criteria: A Critical Reanalysis," *Personnel Psychology* 38 (1985), pp. 41–56.

110. Paul R. Sackett, Sheldon Zedeck, and Larry Fogli, "Relations between Measures of Typical and Maximum Job Performance," *Journal of Applied Psychology* 73, no. 3 (1988), pp. 482–86.

111. Rebecca A. Henry and Charles L. Hulin, "Stability of Skilled Performance across Time: Some Generalizations and Limitations on Utilities," *Journal of Applied Psychology* 72, no. 3 (1987), pp. 457–62.

112. Herbert H. Meyer, "Predicting Supervisory Ratings versus Promotional Progress in Test Validation Studies," *Journal of Applied Psychology* 72, no. 4 (1987), pp. 696–97.

113. Elaine D. Pulakos, Walter C. Borman, and Leatta M. Hough, "Test Validation for Scientific Understanding: Two Demonstrations of an Approach to Studying Predictor-Criterion Linkages," *Personnel Psychology* 41 (1988), pp. 703–15.

114. Robert D. Gatewood and Hubert S. Feild, *Human Resource Selection* (New York: CBS College Publishing, 1987).

115. Gerald V. Barrett, James S. Phillips, and Ralph A. Alexander, "Concurrent and Predictive Validity Designs: A Critical Reanalysis," *Journal of Applied Psychology* 66 (1981), pp. 1–6; Neal Schmitt, Richard Z. Gooding, Raymond A. Noe, and Michael Kirsch, "Meta-Analyses of Validity Studies Published between 1964–1982 and the Investigation of Study Characteristics," *Personnel Psychology* 37 (1984), pp. 407–22.

116. Robert M. Guion, "Synthetic Validity in a Small Company: A Demonstration," *Personnel Psychology* 18 (1965), pp. 49–63; John W. Hamilton and Terry L. Dickenson, "Comparison of Several Procedures for Generating J-Coefficients," *Journal of Applied Psychology* 72, no. 1 (1987), pp. 49–54.

117. See, for example, Frank L. Schmidt, I. Gast-Rosenberg, and John E. Hunter, "Validity Generalization Results for Computer Programmers," *Journal of Applied Psychology* 65 (1980), pp. 643–61; Frank L. Schmidt, John E. Hunter, and Kenneth Pearlman, "Task Differences as Moderators of Aptitude Test Validity in Selection: A Red Herring," *Journal of Applied Psychology* 66 (1981), pp. 166–85; Frank L. Schmidt, John E. Hunter, Kenneth Pearlman, and G. S. Shane, "Further Tests of Schmidt-Hunter Bayesian Validity Generalization Procedure," *Personnel Psychology* 32 (1979), pp. 257–81; N. S. Raju, and Michael J. Burke, "Two New Procedures for Studying Validity Generalization," *Journal of Applied Psychology* 68 (1983), pp. 382–95; Michael J. Burke, "Validity Generalization: A Review and Critique of the Correlation Model," *Personnel Psychology* 37 (1984), pp. 93–116; Frank L. Schmidt, and John E. Hunter, "A Within-Setting Empirical Test of the Situational Specificity Hypothesis in Personnel Selection," *Personnel Psychology* 37 (1984), pp. 317–26; Frank L. Schmidt, Benjamin P. Ocasio, Joseph M. Hillery, and John E. Hunter, "Further Within-Setting Empirical Tests of the Situational Specificity Hypothesis in Personnel Selection," *Personnel Psychology* 38 (1985), pp. 509–24.

118. Frank L. Schmidt, Kenneth Pearlman, John E. Hunter, and Hannah Rothstein Hirsh, "Forty Questions about Validity Generalization and Meta-Analysis," *Personnel Psychology* 38, no. 4 (1985), pp. 697–798; Paul R. Sackett, Mary L. Tenopyr, Neal Schmitt, and Jerard Kehoe, "Commentary on Forty Questions about Validity Generalization and Meta-Analysis," *Personnel Psychology* 38, no. 4 (1985), pp. 799–801; Ralph A. Alexander, Kenneth P. Carson, George M. Alliger, and Steven F. Cronshaw, "Empirical Distributions of Range Restricted SDx in Validity Studies," *Journal of Applied Psychology* 74, no. 2 (1989), pp. 253–58.

119. Robert M. Madigan, K. Dow Scott, Diana L. Deadrick, and Jil A. Stoddard, "Employment Testing: The U.S. Job Service Is Spearheading a Revolution," *Personnel Administrator,* September 1986, pp. 62–69.

120. American Psychological Association, Division of Industrial/Organizational Psychology, *Principles for the Validation and Use of Personnel Selection Procedures* (Washington, D.C.: American Psychological Association, 1979).

121. M. D. Dunnette, *Predicting Job Performance of Electrical Power Plant Operators* (Minneapolis: Personnel Decision Research Institute, 1983).

122. Pulakos, Borman, and Hough, "Test Validation for Scientific Understanding."

123. Frank L. Schmidt, John E. Hunter, Paul R. Croll, and Robert C. McKenzie, "Estimation of Employment Test Validities by Expert Judgment," *Journal of Applied Psychology* 68, no. 4 (1983), pp. 590–601.

124. Bureau of National Affairs, "Employee Selection Procedures."

125. Lawrence S. Kleiman and Robert H. Faley, "The Implications of Professional and Legal Guidelines for Court Decisions Involving Criterion-Related Validity: A Review and Analysis," *Personnel Psychology* 38 (1985), pp. 803–31.

126. *Wards Cove Packing Company* v. *Antonio,* 109 S. Ct. 3115 (1989).

127. Norma R. Fritz, "Culture Clash," *Personnel,* April 1988, pp. 6–7; William J. Hampton, "How Does Japan, Inc., Pick Its American Workers?" *Business Week,* October 3, 1988, pp. 84–85.

128. William J. Hampton, "How Does Japan, Inc., Pick Its American Workers."

129. H. C. Taylor and J. T. Russell, "The Relationship of Validity Coefficients to the Practical Effectiveness of Tests in Selection: Discussion and Tables," *Journal of Applied Psychology* 23 (1939), pp. 565–78.

130. Ibid.

131. Stephen Wermiel, "Workers Hurt by Affirmative Action May Sue," *The Wall Street Journal,* June 13, 1989, p. B1.

132. Linda S. Gottredson and James C. Sharf, "Fairness in Employment Testing," a special issue of the *Journal of Vocational Behavior* 33, no. 3 (December 1988), pp. 225–477; Hartigan and Wigdor, *Fairness in Employment Testing;* Brian D. Steffy and James Ledvinka, "The Long-Range Impact of Five Definitions of "Fair" Employee Selection on Black Employment and Employee Productivity," *Organizational Behavior and Human Decision Processes* 44 (1989), pp. 297–324.

CHAPTER NINE

Employee Separations, Work Force Reduction, and Retention

Employee Separations, Work Force
Reduction, and Retention

A Diagnostic Approach to Work Force
Reduction and Retention
Efficiency
Equity

Employee Separations in Staffing
Initiation by Employees or Employers
Measuring the Separation Rate
Validity in Separations/Retentions

Managing Resignations
Quits
Retirements

Managing Employee Dismissals

International Perspectives on
Employee Separations

Evaluating Employee Separations

Your Turn: Employment Security
at Digital Equipment Corporation

Do financial analysts ever really pay attention to human resource management decisions? Consider the case of IBM. By early 1990, the stock price continued to hover below $100 a share, a far cry from almost $150 per share before the stock market crash of 1987, and despite a general rise in stock prices. Market share had slipped from 88 percent in 1987 to an estimated 76 percent in 1991. Selling, general, and administrative expenses as a percentage of sales had risen from 40 percent in 1987 to over 42 percent. As a result, net income had fallen from almost $10 million in 1988 to about $9 million in 1989.

Of course, financial analysts pointed to IBM's product strategies (too much reliance on mainframes) and marketing strategies (emerging price competition with other computer companies). However, the financial analysts also began to profess a familiar theme: "Anything that takes employees out is a good thing" and "The best thing IBM could do would be to lose 30,000 to 50,000 people overnight."[1] Yet, three years earlier, IBM initiated an early retirement incentive that reduced the worldwide work force by 15,000 employees. In 1987, IBM also initiated a massive retraining and relocation program to shift personnel from administrative areas into sales and programming. In the summer of 1989, it initiated another retirement incentive, inducing 6,500 employees to leave.

In December 1989 the U.S. work force in IBM stood at 216,000. You can bet that John Akers, the CEO of IBM, had read and listened to the financial analysts' recommendations about reducing the work force. It's estimated that using retirement incentives to reduce the work force will mean a charge of $500 million against fourth-quarter earnings, or roughly $50,000 for each of the 10,000 employees you would hope to induce to leave.[2] Imagine that you are the vice president of personnel, or the executive charged with advising that vice president. Do you recommend yet another round of retirement incentives, despite the fact that it's possible all those who can be tempted by such incentives have already left? Or, do you begin to consider a major shift in your company's employment policies, and implement layoffs. You certainly wouldn't be the first company to resort to layoffs after a long history of avoiding them. Bank of America, Eastman Kodak, Hewlett-Packard, and R. J. Reynolds Tobacco have all resorted to layoffs in recent years.[3]

What would you do? Can you really achieve meaningful work force reductions through another early retirement incentive? Are there other ways to reduce the work force than resorting to layoffs? Is it really necessary to reduce the work force drastically, or would you just be losing valued employees who you'll need to replace two or three years down the road?

EMPLOYEE SEPARATIONS, WORK FORCE REDUCTION, AND RETENTION

Exhibit 9.1 shows that the staffing process does not end when employees are hired. If an organization loses its valuable employees, improved recruitment and external selection will do little good, because there will be too few long-term employees or their quality will be insufficient. In this chapter, we focus on what causes people to leave organizations, how this affects the quality and quantity of employees, and how that process can be managed.

◆

Employee separations occur when the employment relationship is ended and employees leave the organization. Employee separations affect *work force reduction* (a decrease of employees) and *employee retention* (the characteristics of employees who are retained).

A DIAGNOSTIC APPROACH TO WORK FORCE REDUCTION AND RETENTION

Similar to employee selection, employee separations affect the composition of the work force. Thus, managing employee separations, work force reduction, and retention fundamentally affect both the efficiency and equity goals of the organization.

Efficiency

When employees leave, it often means dollars walking out the door. Yet, organizations don't always want to keep every employee, and there are times when business conditions dictate a reduction in the size of the work force beyond what would occur with normal attrition. What is the "right" amount of employee separation? When is it cost-effective to encourage employees to leave?

Whether employee separations occur due to employee quits, retirements, layoffs, or discharges, administering the separations often incurs substantial costs.[4] Although employee separations are typically viewed as something to be avoided and reduced to lower such costs, in fact they can be beneficial.[5] Similar to employee selection, employee separations and resulting retentions can enhance work force value when the firm retains the best employees. Moreover, when separations are replaced, the interaction between the separation pattern and the quality of those acquired affects the productivity and efficiency of the work force. Therefore, organizations must base their management of employee separations, work force reductions, and employee retentions on efficiency-related objectives and information. Failure to recognize how employee separations affect organizational efficiency can lead to poor management and cause substantial negative effects on work force productivity.[6]

EXHIBIT 9.1   The Staffing Process as a Series of Filters

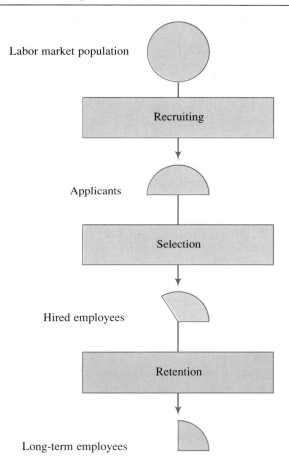

Labor market population

Recruiting

Applicants

Selection

Hired employees

Retention

Long-term employees

Equity

Employee separations have profound effects on individual self-esteem and security. Losing a job can be one of the most anguishing experiences. Is it fair to lay off employees who did nothing wrong and served loyally for many years? How much notice should employees get if they are to be laid off? What constitutes appropriate grounds for firing an employee? What if separation patterns cause an organization to lose the minorities and females that it has worked so hard to recruit and select? Not surprisingly, government regulations and courts pay close attention to the legality and fairness of separation policies. Fairness

---

EXHIBIT 9.2   Comparison between Employee Selection and Retention

---

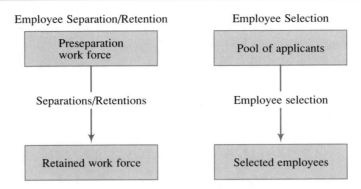

is examined not only for racial and gender groups but for age as well. Also, employees and job applicants will make judgments about an organization's attractiveness based on its approach to employee separations.[7]

THE ROLE OF EMPLOYEE SEPARATIONS IN THE STAFFING PROCESS

Most researchers and professionals treat employee separations as a negative outcome, to be reduced or avoided.[8] However, more recent research takes a broader view of employee separations, noting that they need not always be bad for organizations.[9] Employee separations are now seen as part of the staffing process, affecting work force composition just as employee selection does.[10] In fact, many of the principles of employee selection discussed in Chapter Eight apply as well to employee separations. Exhibit 9.2 illustrates the similarities.

As Chapter Eight showed, employee selection affects the composition of the work force by choosing some of the persons in the applicant pool to receive job offers and join the organization. The effect of selection on organizational goals depends on the relationship between the employees' skills, abilities, motivation, interests, and minority status and the staffing objectives. Validity in selection refers to the degree to which the inferences about applicants' performance are supported by evidence. Selection works to the degree that the characteristics of the chosen applicants conform to the desired employee characteristics.

At first glance, employee separations may seem to be the exact opposite of employee selection. In employee selection, employees join; in separation, they leave. Indeed this is the typical way of thinking about employee separations— in terms of how many employees are leaving. However, the effects of employee separations do not occur through those who leave. The leavers are no longer members of the organization and, therefore, have little effect on it (though they may become future customers). Rather, those who are retained as a result of the separations are the ones who affect future organizational goals. As Exhibit 9.2 shows, we can think of the pre-separation work force as an applicant pool. When separations occur, the organization retains some subset of the pre-separation work force, and this retained group determines the effects of the separations/retentions on future organizational goals. The characteristics of these retained employees determine the effects of separations/retention on the organization.

Separations Initiated by Employees versus Employers

Separations are choices made by employers or employees, or both, to terminate the employment relationship. One way to categorize them is according to whether they are initiated by the employer or the employee.

◆

Resignations are separation decisions initiated by the employee. They include *quits* (employee decisions to leave the organization when retirement is not a major factor) and *retirements* (employee decisions to leave the organization affected by retirement-related considerations).

Dismissals are separation decisions initiated by the employer. *Discharges* occur for individual-specific reasons, such as incompetence, violation of rules, dishonesty, laziness, absenteeism, insubordination, and failure to pass the probationary period.[11] *Layoffs* occur because of the need to reduce the size of the work force.

In fact, separation decisions are seldom solely at the discretion of either the employee or the employer. In most cases, both parties can affect the decision. For example, the employer may ultimately decide whether to dismiss or lay off employees, but such inducements as severance pay and outplacement assistance may encourage some employees to leave. The decision to quit or retire ultimately rests with the employee. Human resource activities, such as compensation, benefits, and career management, however, often manage to reduce or increase the attractiveness of resignation for employees.

Measuring the Separation Rate

Virtually every organization measures the quantity, or percentage, of separations, usually in an effort to minimize them or match the rate to that of competitors. The diagnostic approach to separations adopted in this book will focus on optimizing the level and pattern of separations to achieve the correct balance between positive and negative separation effects. The Bureau of National

Affairs (BNA) reports monthly "turnover" rates computed with the following formula:

$$\frac{\text{Number of total separations during month}}{\text{Average number of employees during month}} \times 100$$

The national separation rate per month is generally about 1 percent, implying a yearly separation rate of about 12 percent. Separation rates are higher in small companies, nonmanufacturing industries, and in the northeastern and western regions of the United States. In addition to measuring total separations, organizations could measure separately the quit, retirement, discharge, and layoff rates. Some organizations attempt to distinguish *unavoidable* separations—caused by factors beyond the organization's control, from *avoidable* separations—affected by organizational policies. Others attempt to distinguish *dysfunctional* separations—which involve losses of valued employees, from *functional* separations—which involve losses that are easily replaced or that remove the least-valued employees.

Like all information, the value of measuring the separation rate depends on its usefulness in improving managerial decisions, as Chapter Five showed. Thus, organizations must determine who will use the separation information, what decisions it is designed to affect, and what type of separation information best supports those decisions. Different organizations or organizational units will probably need different separation measures. *Benchmarks,* or comparisons to industry norms, will be useful for some organizations, but for others such comparisons will have little significance. It depends on the relationship between separations and work force value, or the "validity" of separations.

The Concept of Validity in Separations/Retentions

Chapter Eight noted that the validity in selection reflects the degree to which inferences about how applicants will behave after being hired are supported by evidence. When an organization uses information with high validity to select applicants, it is more likely that the predictions about the applicants' behavior will be correct. Validity is important in selection, because it enhances efficiency by helping to select applicants who better contribute to productivity. Validity also affects equity by providing a rationale for selection systems should they exclude a disproportionate number of minority applicants. Because employee separations/retentions also relate to employee behaviors, validity plays an important part in employee separations.

Validity Applied to Dismissals

When the organization initiates the separation decision, the information used to determine which employees leave or stay has a certain validity. The pattern of retentions affects the future productivity of the work force. Moreover, the

---

EXHIBIT 9.3   Separation/Retention Effects on a Work Force

Salesperson	Yearly Sales	Years of Seniority	Minority
Jeremy	$ 40,000	8	No
Rudolfo	40,000	8	No
Maggie	40,000	2	Yes
Manuel	40,000	6	Yes
Herbert	40,000	6	No
Karl	30,000	8	No
Donald	30,000	4	Yes
Lindsey	30,000	8	Yes
Ralph	30,000	6	No
Beuford	30,000	4	No
Arthur	20,000	8	No
Dorothy	20,000	2	Yes
James	20,000	6	No
Bertram	20,000	4	No
Jesse	20,000	4	Yes
Oliver	10,000	2	No
Anne	10,000	2	Yes
Enrique	10,000	2	Yes
Fred	10,000	6	No
Barney	10,000	4	No
Total	$500,000	100	
Average	$ 25,000	5	

retention pattern also affects work force characteristics related to equity, such as the minority composition of the work force.

Consider the situation shown in Exhibit 9.3, where an organization has 20 salespeople producing average yearly sales of $25,000 per person. The total yearly sales of this work force is $500,000 per year (i.e., 20 times $25,000). Individual sales levels vary between $40,000 and $10,000 per person. Seniority varies between two and eight years, and averages five years. The work force currently contains eight minorities (a representation rate of 40 percent). Suppose the organization decides to lay off 25 percent of the work force, or five people. It is considering laying them off based either on past performance or on seniority.

Performance-based layoffs will remove the five poorest-performing employees (Oliver, Anne, Enrique, Fred, and Barney). This will produce a retained work force containing 15 employees averaging $30,000 in yearly sales and producing a total yearly sales level of $450,000. Thus, performance provides a valid basis for layoffs. The minority representation rate remains unchanged under this scheme, because it leaves 6 minority-group members in the 15-person retained work force. However, such a layoff scheme removes two of the senior employees (Fred and Barney).

Seniority-based layoffs will remove the five least-senior employees (Maggie, Dorothy, Oliver, Anne, and Enrique). This will produce a retained work force containing 15 employees all with more than two years' tenure. However, because some low-tenure employees perform well, the average yearly sales level of those retained would be $27,333, producing a total yearly sales level of $410,000, which is lower than when layoffs are performance-based. Thus, seniority provides a less valid basis for layoffs. Because minority-group members fall primarily among the low-tenure employees, this scheme also removes four minority salespersons, producing a representation rate of 26.6 percent (4 divided by 15), which is lower than the 40 percent representation rate in the pre-layoff work force.

The same process occurs in decisions regarding discharges. But discharges are almost always based on poor performance, not seniority. The consequences of dismissals for both efficiency and equity are best understood by focusing on who is retained, rather than who is dismissed.

Validity Applied to Resignations

The analogies between selection and retention are readily apparent in the case of dismissals, because the organization initiates both actions. The validity concept applies as well, however, to resignations that are initiated by employees. Although the organization has less discretion regarding resignations, the quantity and pattern of resignations still affect the efficiency and equity of the retained work force. We refer to this relationship as the validity of resignations.

For example, suppose that the pattern of quits among the salespersons in Exhibit 9.3 was such that the best performers tended to leave. Specifically, suppose that the organization lost Maggie, Manuel, Ralph, and Beuford (a 20 percent quit rate). The retained work force of 16 employees would produce average yearly sales of $22,500, or total yearly sales of $360,000—a substantial drop from the $500,000 total in the work force prior to separations. Moreover, because two of the four separations involve minorities, the minority representation rate falls to 37.5 percent (i.e., 6 divided by 16).

Now, suppose an early retirement incentive causes the best-performing and most senior employees to leave. Specifically, suppose that Jeremy, Rudolfo, Karl, and Lindsey retire. This would have the same effect on productivity as the quit pattern. The retained employee group's average yearly sales would fall to $22,500—producing total yearly sales of only $360,000. Thus, performance-based resignations actually have *negative* validity. Because only one of these retirements involves a minority-group member, the representation rate would actually rise to 43.75 percent among the retained employees.

The view that employee separations constitute a staffing process has only recently been developed. Unlike employee selection, there is less information about the validity of retention patterns or the ability of human resource management decisions to affect them. Separations are managed through other staffing and HR activities, such as compensation and benefits. Therefore, our discussion focuses on the management decisions affecting each type of separation.

MANAGING RESIGNATIONS

When employees quit or retire, they initiate the separation decision. Understanding the reasons for their decision can suggest how to manage the process to achieve organizational goals.

Quits

The term *turnover* is often used synonymously with the term *quits*. However, turnover implies that the quit will subsequently be replaced (i.e., the organization "turns over" the position to a new person).[12] To avoid confusing issues of selecting replacements with issues of managing separations, we will use the term *quit* to refer to the employee's leaving the organization, regardless of whether the vacancy is subsequently filled.

The Decision to Quit

What makes someone want to leave their job and organization? This question has fascinated industrial psychologists and others for many years.[13] Exhibit 9.4 shows a very comprehensive model of the quit decision, based on years of research. Though it was proposed in 1980, it still represents much current knowledge in this area. Notice how the quit decision is affected by several factors, some of which are not easily controlled by the organization, including individual characteristics and labor market factors. Also notice the broad scope of organizational factors that can affect quit decisions. These three categories of factors affect individual perceptions of their job, and of the labor market for their skills. As Chapter Four showed, the comparison between job perceptions and individual values/needs leads to job attitudes/satisfaction. While satisfaction can affect decisions to quit, it is not the only factor. Individuals compare what they expect from their current job to what they expect alternative jobs might be like and to the probability of getting another job. These perceptions produce an attraction to the current job, as well as an attraction to try to find a new job. The interaction of satisfaction, attractiveness of the current job, and attractiveness of alternative jobs produces intentions to search for another job, which may lead to intentions to quit, which can lead to actual quits. Notice, however, that individuals who wish they could quit may engage in other "withdrawal" behaviors, such as absenteeism or reduced work effort.

Research has supported several of the links shown in Exhibit 9.4. Quits are higher in times of low unemployment.[14] Quits are negatively affected by pay,

EXHIBIT 9.4   A Model of the Employee Quit Decision

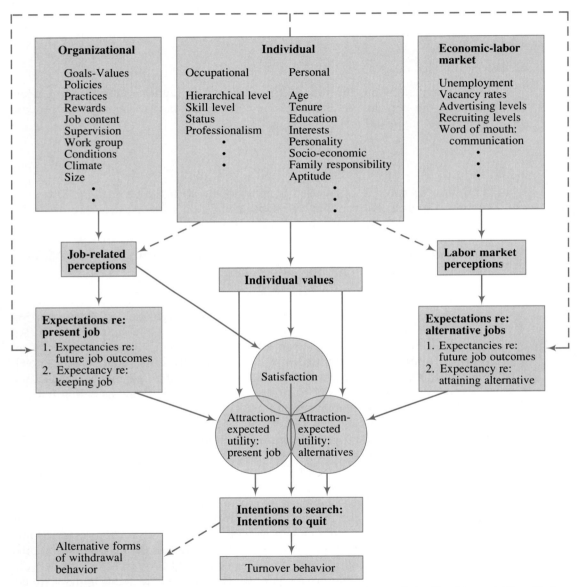

Source: William H. Mobley, *Employee Turnover: Causes, Consequences, and Control* (Reading, Mass.: Addison-Wesley Publishing, 1980), adapted with permission.

though one study of army reenlistment found that this was more true for highly skilled and high-demand occupations.[15] Quits are negatively related to role clarity, satisfaction, and organization commitment. Younger workers with fewer dependents quit more often, and biographical and demographic characteristics generally exhibit a strong ability to predict quit propensities.[16] Studies have also shown fewer quits in unionized situations. Perhaps unions give employees alternative ways to express their dissatisfaction, such as grievance procedures (see Chapter Sixteen, on Labor Relations).[17]

Implications for Reducing the Number of Quits

What does all this suggest for managing human resources? Organizations interested in reducing the number of quits might consider increasing pay, clarifying roles and job requirements, making work more satisfying, and improving relationships with co-workers and supervisors. Factors used to recruit and select employees, such as biographical information and realistic job previews (discussed in Chapters Seven and Eight) have also been shown to predict future quits.

A common tactic to find out why people are quitting is to interview them before they depart. One survey found that 84 percent of companies conducted exit interviews with separating employees to discover their reasons for quitting. Seventy-two percent of these companies later made changes in their HR activities to reduce quit rates. Common changes included:

Raising wage and salary levels (67 percent had made this change).

Improving orientation/induction procedures (60 percent).

Improving exit interview processes (57 percent).

Modifying employee benefits (54 percent).

Training supervisors (54 percent).

Changing selection methods (49 percent).

Training nonsupervisory employees (42 percent).

Improving upward communication (40 percent).[18]

How effective these actions might be is difficult to predict, because so many other factors can affect employee decisions to quit. However, a study summarizing 20 experiments that used either job enrichment or realistic job previews (RJPs) to reduce separation rates found that RJPs improved separation rates by an average of 9 percent, while job enrichment improved them by an average of 17 percent.[19]

The hospitality industry faces one of the highest quit rates and (as Chapter Six discussed) one of the tightest labor markets. Estimated quit rates for the hospitality industry are as high as 104 percent, which is still less than 210 percent in full-service restaurants and 270 percent in fast-foods. Still it has been estimated that it costs $2,500 to replace a hotel worker, so high quit rates can be costly. Holiday Inns has managed to reduce turnover to 65 percent per year through these methods: liberal use of bonuses; extensive training for all levels of employees—in other languages than English if necessary; creation and publicizing of career paths; and stepped-up training for managers in interviewing techniques, because half of all new employees quit in the first 30 days. At the Holiday Inn Crowne Plaza in White Plains, New York, manager Victor Vongs builds loyalty among new immigrant employees by enrolling them in English classes and finding them places to live.[20]

Nonetheless, many factors affecting quits are not easily managed by employers. To avoid the problems associated with sudden unexpected vacancies, employers often request or require notice from employees before they quit. Eighty percent of companies responding to one survey required two weeks' notice of resignation, though 59 percent of those companies imposed no penalties if such notice was not given.[21]

Implications for the Quality of the Retained Employees

Most organizations focus only on reducing the quantity (or rate) of employee quits to reduce the costs incurred to separate and replace employees. However, the quantity of quits is only part of the issue. The pattern of quits is what affects the value of the retained work force. As the example in Exhibit 9.3 showed, if quitters are the most valuable employees, even a low quit rate may be harmful. On the other hand, if quitters are among the least valuable employees, and they can easily be replaced with better employees, then even high quit rates may be no cause for alarm. Research evidence suggests that it is the lower performers who tend to quit, but the results are mixed and some studies have found higher performers among the leavers.[22]

When high performance is easily observable by competitors or when alternative opportunities are attractive and easy to obtain, the potential for losing high performers is substantial. For example, in California's Silicon Valley, computer programmers can easily leave one job and go to work for a competitor, often without changing the city in which they work. Thus, organizations would do well to measure not only the quantity of quits but whether the good or poor performers are among them.[23] Quit patterns also affect the minority composition of the work force. If minority-group members find the employment relationship less attractive than nonminority group members, they may also leave more frequently. It's much more difficult to attain EEO and affirmative action goals if minorities leave.

So, managers should not simply track the number of quits, hoping to see that number go down. They should also carefully examine the effects of quits on the performance and representation of the retained work force. Low quit rates may be masking serious problems for work force quality.

Retirements

Retirements are similar to quits, because they are initiated by the employee and result from a choice process similar to the one shown in Exhibit 9.4. Mandatory retirement ages of 65 or 70 used to be common, making retirement similar to a dismissal. However, in 1987, the Age Discrimination in Employment Act was amended to prohibit discrimination on the basis of age for anyone over age 40, removing the previous upper limit of age 70, and making retirement an option instead of a requirement for employees without work impairments, except in a few specific occupations, such as fire fighters, police officers and tenured university professors.

Retirements differ from quits, because they usually occur at the end of an individual's work career, though the trend is toward earlier retirement, often followed by a second career, especially for managers and top executives.[24] Retirements are also different from quits because retirees collect retirement benefits. From the employer, they usually receive pension benefits and continued insurance coverage (perhaps at increased premiums); from the government they receive Social Security and Medicare benefits, usually structured to reflect an "average" retirement age, such as 65.

While retirement decisions reflect many of the factors shown in Exhibit 9.4, they do differ on some dimensions. Individual factors, such as age, health, and family responsibilities, are different for retirees than for others, as are organizational factors, such as pension benefits and future promotion opportunities. Finally, instead of simply considering alternative employment relationships, retirees can consider the alternative of an employment-free lifestyle, with its unique attractions and concerns.[25]

Managing Employee Retirements

Virtually every human resource activity has the potential to affect retirement decisions. In industries with surplus workers, retirement income and benefits are often restructured to provide *early retirement incentives*. However, recent labor shortages and governmental scrutiny to age discrimination have led employers to attempt to *retain older employees* with human resource management (HRM) polices.

Early retirement incentives
An early retirement incentive opens the "window" of retirement eligibility for more employees by making retirement benefits available at a younger age or by adding retirement benefits, or both, so older employees can retire more comfortably without working longer. Typical early retirement packages include: (1) time added to age for pension computations (five years is typical), (2) cash separation or severance payment, (3) extra annual payments until Social Security payments begin, (4) continued health insurance coverage to age 65 or beyond.[26]

EXHIBIT 9.5   Flexible Retirement Policies That Can Lengthen the Contributions
of Older Employees

Retirement counseling programs.
Increased pensions for late retirees.
Supplements to pensions to bridge Social Security.
Use older workers as mentors or consultants.
Reassign older workers to less-demanding jobs.
Redesign jobs to reduce pressure.
Arrange for working at home.
Allow flexible work schedules.
Allow cutback to half-time schedules.
Use formal performance evaluations as input to retirement planning.
Use medical evaluations as input to retirement planning.
Provide for senior exempt employees to extend their careers.

Source: Benson Rosen and Thomas Jerdee, "Retirement Policies: Evidence of the Need for Change," *Human Resource Management* 28, no. 1 (Spring 1989), pp. 87–103.

IBM announced an early retirement incentive plan on September 18, 1986, with an election period ending on June 30, 1987. The IBM plan maintained the existing retirement benefit package and increased the pool of eligible employees by adding five years to each employee's actual age and service for retirement computations. For example, a 50-year-old employee with 10 years of service who was ineligible to receive a monthly income under the previous plan would become eligible to retire and receive a monthly pension calculated for a 55-year-old with 15 years of service. Retirement eligibility also includes postretirement participation in IBM's health and life insurance benefits.

For employees over 55 with more than 15 years of service who were already eligible for retirement, the incentive for early retirement is the increase in their monthly pension based on longer service and greater age. IBM also augmented its early retirement plan with training for managers to clearly and effectively communicate its implications to their subordinates, as well as company-funded financial counseling for eligible employees. After June 30, 1987, pension calculations no longer reflected the extra five years of age, though employees remain eligible for retirement and retain the extra five years of service for pension calculation purposes.

Early retirement windows were quite common in the mid to late 1980s in such firms as Xerox Corporation, IT&T, Hewlett-Packard, and Phillips Petroleum Company.[27] The windows have also appeared in the contracts of public school teachers.[28] NYNEX corporation recently announced an early retirement plan, affecting 10,000 of its 27,000 managers, which added five years of service and age credits and increased the salary periods on which retirement income is based, at an estimated cost of $45 million.[29] Some evidence suggests that such programs have the potential to induce substantial reductions in the work force and produce consequent cost savings. Both IBM and Xerox achieved their work force reduction goals.[30] A survey by Towers, Perrin, Forster & Crosby (TPFC) of 100 large employers offering retirement incentives in the mid-1980s found that retirement inducement costs averaged $50,000 per retiree, but first-year cost savings from reduced compensation and benefit obligations ranged between $61,000 and $60 million, with an average of $7.3 million.[31]

Early retirement incentives are not without their risks. The IT&T early retirement incentive failed to achieve the 50 percent reduction—from 850 to between 350 and 400—in headquarters staff needed, forcing the company to resort to layoffs.[32] Legal risks exist as well. The EEOC recently found age discrimination in Du Pont's early retirement program, because an age cap denied older workers the right to take full advantage of the incentive.[33] New York State recently faced an EEOC suit on behalf of judges affected by the mandatory retirement age of 76, seeking back pay for judges who had been forced to retire and reinstatement of retired judges. Justice Isaac Rubin, 76, whose appointment would expire under the current New York State policy, says, "The issue isn't age—age is just a number. The issue is one of a judge's experience, his competence, and his physical ability to serve on the bench."[34] Perhaps such sentiments partly explain the recent emphasis on retaining the older work force to enhance their contributions, rather than inducing them to leave.

Retaining Older Employees

For some organizations, age and performance are positively related. Daniel Knowles, Grumman's vice president of human resources planning, stated: "Between 1970 and 1977, Grumman laid off 13,000 people. The layoff was determined on the basis of performance, rather than seniority. When the layoffs were completed, the average age of the work force had increased from 37 to 45, suggesting a very positive correlation between age and performance."[35] Exhibit 9.5 lists several ideas for "flexible" retirement policies that allow and even encourage older employees to continue to contribute to organizations. Organizations facing increasing labor shortages may consider recruiting older workers (see Chapter Seven) but should not overlook the potential embodied in their own older employees.

Implications of Retirements for the Quality of Retained Employees

Though there has been a great deal of attention to the costs and cost savings resulting from early retirement incentives, we know little about the validity of early retirement incentives—that is, their effect on the value of the retained work force. Because pension benefits are calculated on the previous salary, it is possible that such incentives are most attractive to employees with the fastest-rising pay levels. Assuming these pay levels reflect employees' value, organizations may risk inducing their best senior employees to retire early, while retaining poor performers. The substantial salary and benefit cost savings produced by such incentives may be quickly offset by reductions in the value of the retained work force. On the other hand, if retirement incentives provide increased opportunities for the organization to promote talented younger employees, the productivity effects could be quite positive.[36]

MANAGING EMPLOYEE DISMISSALS

Unlike resignations, employee dismissals are initiated by the employer. They reflect the employer's choices, rather than the employee's. Because dismissals are the most extreme employment action that can be taken, a great deal of human resource activity attempts to avoid them. However, they are a fact of organizational life that must be managed effectively, not just ignored or avoided.

Discharges

"You're fired." Few of us ever hope to hear those words, because they signify the organization's most extreme action—capital punishment in terms of the employment relationship. *Discharges* occur when the employer terminates the employment relationship because the employee's behaviors are seriously harmful. A Bureau of National Affairs (BNA) survey showed that, among human resource managers reporting their most serious discipline problems, 60 percent cited attendance, 17 percent cited performance, 9 percent cited alcohol or drugs, and 14 percent cited a variety of other factors.[37]

The Decision Process for Discharges

Because discharges represent the most extreme disciplinary action, they are not undertaken lightly. In the vast majority of organizations, they represent the culmination of repeated unsuccessful efforts to resolve the behavior problem or conflict. We discuss conflict resolution systems in detail in Chapter Fourteen; here, we focus on their implications for discharging employees.

Virtually all organizations responding to the BNA survey adopted some form of progressive discipline involving oral and written warnings for initial conflicts. If the conflict is not corrected, more stringent disciplinary actions are taken, such as reprimands and suspension without pay, finally culminating in discharge. Discharges are rarely the only disciplinary step; however, a majority of the organizations in the BNA survey reported a one-step discharge decision for extreme infractions. These include computer fraud/security violations, falsifying work records, divulging trade secrets or proprietary information, willful damage to company property, falsifying an employment application, stealing company property, physical assault, possession of alcoholic beverages, possession of a weapon, and possession of illegal drugs. Fifty-four percent of companies with nonunion work forces included counseling in the process, and 71 percent included a formal appeals procedure. Those with unionized work forces were slightly more likely to include counseling (57 percent) and much more likely to have appeals procedures (98 percent). Discharges are more likely than any other disciplinary action to require approval by one or more managers at a higher level than the supervisor.[38] Thus, discharge is reserved for only the most serious conflicts.

A recent research review suggested that discharge rates are higher during economic prosperity, perhaps because increased hiring demands lead to selection errors. This review also found that unionized employees had similar discharge rates to nonunionized firms paying equal wage levels; that discharged employees have longer, more difficult job searches; and that discharge likelihood decreases with seniority and age.[39]

The Employment-at-Will Issue

Perhaps the most controversial issue regarding employee discharges involves the limits of an employer's right to dismiss employees at will.

The concept

When an employee is fired for cause, what constitutes sufficient or just cause? Indeed, is any "cause" required?

In early industrial England, both master and servant had obligations spelled out in law. A master could not discharge a servant unless that individual's conduct had been less than satisfactory. The servant could not quit without giving sufficient notice.

The U.S. industrial revolution modified this view, however. Rather than stressing the mutual duties of employment, the courts began to stress the right to freely choose an employer or employee. In 1910, The California Supreme Court described the employment-at-will rule:

> Precisely as may the employee cease labor at his whim or pleasure, and, whatever be his reason, good, bad, or indifferent, leave no one a legal right to complain; so, upon the other hand, may the employer discharge, and whatever be his reason, good, bad, or indifferent, no one has suffered a legal wrong.[40]

Changed attitude toward employment-at-will

The employer's right to terminate at will has been steadily eroding. The 1935 Wagner Act made it illegal for employees to be fired because of union activity. Collective bargaining agreements covering approximately 20 percent of the nonagricultural United States labor force forbid firing unionized employees, except for cause. Approximately 19 percent of the U.S. work force are federal, state, or local government employees, of whom the majority are protected from arbitrary dismissal by civil service rules. Title VII of the Civil Rights Act protects employees from being fired on the basis of race, color, sex, religion, or national origin. In addition, some legislation, such as OSHA and the Clean Air Act, includes protection against retaliatory discharge for employees who report employers' violations. However, unjust dismissal remains a potential problem for the 70 million employees in the United States who are neither civil servants, union members, nor members of protected classes.

In the 1980s, the courts began to limit the application of the at-will doctrine. Still, the treatment of wrongful or abusive discharge has been uneven. The court actions have examined the at-will doctrine in two ways: as a violation of public policy and as a violation of implied contracts between the employer and employee.

In special circumstances the firing of an employee *violates public policy*.[41] However, the "interest that the employee seeks to vindicate must be public, and not personal." For example, public policy protects:

1. An employee who refuses to commit an unlawful act; the court held that an employee was protected from discharge when she refused to submit false testimony at a trial and thereby commit perjury.

2. An employee who exercises the right to perform an important public policy obligation; an employee was protected from discharge when he blew the whistle on his employer's illegal conduct.

3. An employee who exercises a statutory right or privilege; an employee may sue his employer on the grounds that his filing of a workers' compensation claim resulted in retaliatory discharge in violation of the employee's statutory right.

However, a Florida court held that an employee could not sue when he was discharged for filing a workers' compensation claim, and an Alabama employer was permitted to fire an employee who refused to falsify medical records.[42] Without a national law, consensus in the state courts eludes us thus far.

Employee discharges can *violate employment contracts*. Personnel policies and manuals have been construed as implied, enforceable contracts. In *Toussaint* v. *Blue Cross/Blue Shield of Michigan,* the court held that an employee's discharge was improper, because the employer had discussed permanent employment during the interview and it was reinforced in the employee handbook.[43] So, simply referring to "permanent" employment may imply a contract, especially if the reference can be combined with statements on the application blank or oral statements during an employment interview.[44]

Some courts have also indicated that any action must be in the context of the total employment relationship. Thus, such factors as length of service or an employee's moving the family to work for an employer may imply a contract. For example, in *Clearly* v. *American Airlines,* the court ruled that termination without legal cause after 18 years of apparently satisfactory service amounted to "bad faith" because it would deprive the employee of pension and benefit rights.[45]

When discharges are subject to arbitration due to an employment contract, employers' decisions can be overturned by an outside arbitrator. Gould, Inc., fired a Minnesota man who harassed his former supervisor by dumping a load of dirt in his driveway, putting his house on the market with a real estate agent, and summoning paramedics to his home with a false report that the supervisor was having a heart attack. Seven months later an arbitrator reinstated the worker, concluding that the evidence that his actions caused the supervisor's work to deteriorate was insufficient.[46]

The EEOC is likely to take an expanded and quasi-judicial role in wrongful discharge cases in the future. More than 25,000 wrongful discharge cases were pending in state and federal courts in late 1989, according to the BNA.[47] A U.S. Federal Courts Study Committee noted that employment discrimination cases filed in federal courts increased from 336 in 1970 to 7,613 in 1989—an increase of 2,166 percent. The panel noted that the bulk of this increase is due primarily to an "enormous jump" in wrongful discharge cases, and it recommends that EEOC become a first-line adjudicator in such cases.[48]

Damages paid to wrongful discharge victims can be costly. One study examined 120 wrongful discharge cases in California between 1980 and 1986, involving employees whose average salary was $36,254. Plaintiffs won 67.5 percent of the cases and were awarded an average of $646,855, including an average back-pay award of $388,500 and punitive damages of $523,170.[49] Often, punitive damages involve claims of mental distress.[50] Another more recent report estimates average jury awards of $602,000.[51] However, the California Supreme Court decision in *Foley* v. *Interactive Data Corporation* may serve to limit such damages in the future by limiting the types of discharges for which punitive damages may be claimed.[52]

Implications for human resource management   As the state courts judicially redefine traditional employment-at-will, employers must become increasingly concerned about liability for wrongful discharge. Several lawyers specializing in the area have recommended the following guidelines to reduce potential liability.[53]

1. Wrongful discharge liability begins at the preemployment interview. Avoid any oral representation of permanent employment.

2. Revise employee handbooks to remove any implications that employment is other than at-will. Words such as "permanent" employee should be dropped. Include such statements as "this handbook is not a binding contract."

3. Job applications should list employer's rights and state that employment is at-will. For example, Sears Roebuck & Company has had a clause on its employment blanks for years which reads, ". . . my employment and compensation can be terminated, with or without cause, and with or without notice, at any time, at the option of either the Company or myself." All applicants sign this clause, which has consistently been upheld in termination and demotion lawsuits.

4. Document performance evaluations. Supervisors must be entirely truthful when they evaluate subordinates. They must document each instance of unacceptable behavior and the supervisor's response to it. Dissatisfaction must be communicated to the employees. They must be properly notified that their performance is jeopardizing their job.

5. The employer is in control of a discharge and, therefore, has the time and tools to handle it carefully and properly. In planning a discharge, an employer should list all potential issues raised by the decision, any prior disciplinary action, the investigation of the employee's conduct, and carefully document the charges. The discharge should be discussed with the employee to hear the employee's interpretation of events. Discrepancies should be investigated—the employee may be right.

6. Establish a conflict resolution procedure.

These guidelines are also important to avoid legal suits by employees who were discharged in legally appropriate ways. When the reasons for discharge are not well documented, employees can sue their former employers for libel based on the former employer's statements to the employee's prospective employers about past job performance.[54]

Attempts to achieve legal safety may often lead employers to constantly stress that employees understand the company's right to terminate at will. Repeatedly telling applicants and employees "we may fire you at any time" is a lot like having a divorce lawyer as the best man or as matron of honor at your wedding. Will employees really feel they should commit to a job or organization that emphasizes dismissals? Just instituting such practices can be risky. Consider Small Business Technologies (SBT), a Sauselito, California, software company that asked its 50 employees to sign an agreement saying they could be dismissed at any time for any reason. When Lee Pullins, an assistant manager with two years of tenure, refused to sign, he was fired. Now he's suing SBT for wrongful discharge.[55] Yet employers may face considerable liability if they do not take some precautions. Certainly, an effective and defensible performance evaluation and communication system is needed.

Implications for the Quality of the Retained Employees

Employees are seldom discharged without documented evidence, and often only after an exhaustive series of reviews and appeals. If past behavior predicts future behavior, such discharges are likely to rid the organization of employees who would have been poor performers or harmful influences in the future. The retained work force is likely to be better as a result of such discharges. Thus, it is in the employer's and the employees' interest to have a discharge procedure that reflects job-related behaviors and that makes decisions based on evidence. The performance assessment process (discussed in Chapter Four) becomes a critical activity for identifying and documenting this evidence.

Layoffs

When employees are discharged, it is usually because of something they did. When they are laid off, it is usually not because of something they did but, rather, because of "economic reasons," such as poor business decisions, poorly designed products, poor marketing, or unanticipated declines in markets that

---

EXHIBIT 9.6   Rings of Defense Strategies at Control Data Corporation

---

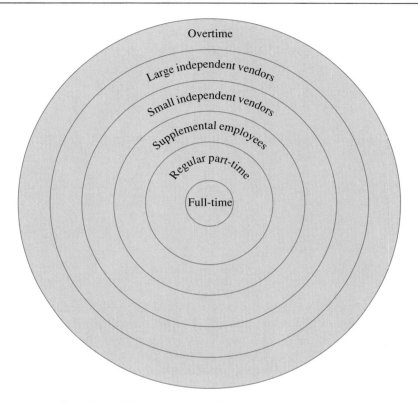

Overtime

Large independent vendors

Small independent vendors

Supplemental employees

Regular part-time

Full-time

Source: Control Data Corporation, Bloomington, Minnesota.

are out of the organization's or the employees' control. Thus, as difficult as discharges may be, layoffs are even more difficult, because the affected employees are often not at fault. Layoffs result from a very different decision process than discharges. Layoffs can be either permanent or temporary. Permanent layoffs obviously have more serious consequences; so, much of the following discussion applies to permanent layoffs. The general principles, however, apply to all layoffs.

The Decision Process for Layoffs

As with discharges, employers often go to great lengths to avoid layoffs.[56] For example, Control Data Corporation (CDC) attempts to avoid layoffs through its Rings of Defense Strategies, shown in Exhibits 9.6 and 9.7.[57]

The idea of these exhibits is that the company protects the inner rings by first using the strategies in the outer rings. The first defense is to cut overtime,

---

EXHIBIT 9.7   Inner Rings of Defense Strategies at Control Data Corporation

---

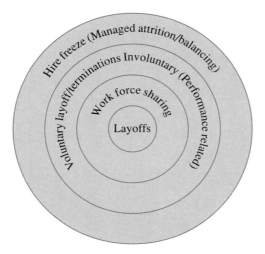

Source: Control Data Corporation, Bloomington, Minnesota.

then call back work that was subcontracted to outside vendors. Next, the company dismisses supplemental employees and part-time employees. Finally, if the surplus still remains, CDC must consider programs affecting its full-time work force—the Inner Rings of Defense, shown in Exhibit 9.7. Such programs as hiring freezes, voluntary layoffs, and dismissing poor performers are considered. Finally, CDC considers attempts to share work and reduce normal work hours. All of these options are considered before resorting to layoffs of full-time employees.

Many organizations include *redeployment,* or moving of employees between jobs within the organization, as an alternative to layoffs in surplus areas and hiring in areas of shortages.[58] Redeployment can be a potent addition to efforts to provide continuous employment for employees in organizations that believe employment security creates important corporate advantages.[59] We will discuss such internal movement in Chapter Ten. Employment stabilization and job security policies often seem to be adopted with little concern for their costs, but evidence suggests that avoiding layoffs can be cost-effective.[60] One study of U.S. government agencies found that the costs of layoffs, or "reductions in force (RIFs)," cost more than reduction through normal attrition, with excess costs amounting to over $1 million for some of the agencies.[61] Human resource managers would do well to consider other alternatives than "throw the crew overboard" when the organizational ship is sinking.[62]

It does not appear that work force reduction, or "downsizing," has become less frequent over recent years, though the number of employees affected by each downsizing effort has fallen. Less than half of organizations cite a business downturn (actual or planned) as the reason for downsizing, with "improved staff utilization" and "mergers and acquisitions" also motivating such efforts.[63] Increasing competition and industry maturity seem to bring inevitable shake-outs leading to layoffs, with recent headlines describing layoffs in high-technology and financial institutions, such as Hewlett-Packard, Bank of America, Chase Manhattan Bank, Ashton-Tate, and AT&T.[64] Meanwhile, layoffs in the auto industry continue.[65] Even tight labor markets can't prevent layoffs to rebalance the work force by eliminating workers with obsolete skills to hire those with more necessary skills. So, layoffs are likely to remain a fact of corporate life.

Human Resource Activities for Managing Layoffs

When organizations decide to reduce their work force, they must consider several activities, including: (1) giving notice of the layoff or plant closing; (2) order of layoff, and bumping; (3) income maintenance and extension of employee benefits; (4) job search assistance, or outplacement.

Notice of layoff or plant closing   The Worker Adjustment and Retraining Notification Act (WARN) requires employers with 100 or more workers to provide at least 60 days' notice of a plant closing or of mass layoffs to the affected workers or their representatives, to state dislocated worker units, and to the appropriate local government. This legislation became law on August 4, 1988, after passing both houses of Congress by more than a two-thirds majority. While this legislation was resisted by President Ronald Reagan and several business groups, evidence suggests that it has not drastically affected business operations or profits.[66] Advance notice appears to reduce unemployment among displaced workers and to moderate temporary increases in area unemployment rates.[67]

Order of layoff and bumping   Layoffs usually occur based on seniority, though job performance and transferability of skills are also frequently used. These factors may also be combined.[68] Such systems can create legal conflicts when minority-group members have less tenure than nonminority-group members. Even a neutral seniority-based system can seriously reduce the numbers of minority and female employees if they tend to have less tenure. Should an employer give preference to retaining females and minorities when layoffs occur? Supreme Court decisions suggest that preferential treatment for less-senior minorities may not be accepted as a way to maintain affirmative action progress.[69] When layoffs do threaten older workers, suits under the Age Discrimination in Employment Act are possible. Hoffman-LaRoche, Inc., was accused of terminating a disproportionate number of older workers in layoffs at its New Jersey plants. A group of employees, calling themselves Roche Age Discriminatees Asking Redress (RADAR) won the rights to use direct mail to gain the participation of other affected employees in a class-action lawsuit.[70] Even unions can restrict layoffs. Judge Barrington Parker ordered Eastern Airlines to keep 4,000 employees on its payroll at a cost of $7 million per month, though he allowed Eastern to eliminate the 12 percent of its flights for which the workers were employed. He charged that the flight cutbacks were calculated to hurt unionized Eastern while benefiting its sister subsidiary, Continental.[71]

Bumping refers to giving more senior employees whose jobs become obsolete the right to transfer into jobs of less-senior workers. It is frequently stipulated in collectively bargained labor contracts. Although it maintains jobs for long-service employees, it can cause problems if it leads to frequent job changes or to bumping unqualified individuals into some jobs.

Income maintenance (severance pay, supplemental unemployment benefits, and extended benefits) Organizations often establish policies to maintain the income of laid-off employees for some period after the layoff. The BNA survey found that 87 percent of the responding companies paid severance benefits to laid-off or terminated employees at some time. Eligibility and the amount of severance pay are usually determined by length of service, such as one week's pay for those with two to four years with the company, two weeks' pay for four to six years, three weeks' pay for six to eight years, and four weeks' pay for over eight years.[72] Supplemental Unemployment Benefits (SUB) are federal severance payments designed to supplement state unemployment insurance benefits.

Organizations may allow dismissed employees to remain eligible for employer-provided benefits, such as health and life insurance. Seventy-nine percent of the companies in the Conference Board survey continued health care benefits after plant closings, with 49 percent continuing them for less than five months.[73] The BNA survey found that 54 percent of companies continued health care coverage for dismissed employees and 32 percent continued life insurance coverage, though most of these organizations increased the workers' premiums.[74]

These strategies often have broader purposes than just assisting laid-off employees. *Tin parachutes,* so-called because they are lesser versions of golden parachutes offered to executives who are displaced by takeovers, can be potent weapons against takeovers. When employees are guaranteed severance pay, health and life insurance benefits, and outplacement assistance in the event they lose their jobs, it raises the takeover cost to any raider. However, many employers, such as Eastman Kodak, believe these plans also improve the morale and possibly the productivity of employees who feel the company cares about them enough to protect them.[75]

Job search assistance (outplacement) Most organizations offer employees assistance in locating and finding new employment.[76] This frequently includes individual or group counseling, recommendation letters, job market information, and secretarial and administrative support. Firms providing outplacement services grew rapidly in the 1980s, but it pays to consider carefully what you want them to do before hiring them.[77] Some suggest that many companies are satisfied because having the counselors around makes firing people easier.[78]

Emotional and physical effects can be severe for those who lose their jobs. However, providing advance notice and assistance can help, and many employees do manage to cope. Gerald C. Parkhouse used outplacement assistance to switch from being a manager with a global oil corporation to being a professor of international business.[79]

Implications for the Quality of the Retained Employees

Layoffs frequently remove much larger numbers of employees than any other form of employee separations, so they can have the greatest effect on the value of the retained work force, whether they are based on seniority, skills, performance, or job categories. Layoffs based on reverse seniority are common and can increase work force quality if senior employees are best suited to the organization's future work requirements. Often, however, it is the younger workers who possess the skills and flexibility needed in the future, so organizations may want to target layoffs to retain skills, rather than seniority. If bumping is allowed, the number of position changes will be far greater than the number of layoffs. This can be disruptive, but it does provide the opportunity to redeploy the work force in more productive ways, provided that the bumping requirements are flexible. Perhaps the greatest potential for layoffs to increase work force value is realized when other human resource activities, such as redeployment and training, are used with layoffs to enhance the value of those retained. Clearly, managers can overlook important consequences if they make layoff decisions simply based on the reduction in headcount or compensation costs.

The attitudes and equity perceptions of those retained will be affected by their perceptions of the layoff process.[80] Communicating the reasons for the downsizing is essential, and it should be done carefully. Ford maintains an in-house television network to broadcast a steady stream of up-to-the-minute company news, plus talks from chairman Donald Petersen. At BankAmerica, where the payroll has shrunk by 24,000 since 1984, the personnel department requires that executives audition before they are permitted to broadcast information about the company's plans.[81]

INTERNATIONAL PERSPECTIVES ON EMPLOYEE SEPARATIONS, WORK FORCE REDUCTION, AND RETENTION

We have seen in earlier chapters that Japanese corporations seem to spend more on recruiting and selecting good employees than typical American firms. There is also widespread evidence that Japanese firms work harder to guarantee "lifetime employment" for their core work force. This core work force may amount to only about 20 percent of the total Japanese work force and reside in the largest industrial companies, but it is widely believed that such a commitment contributes to employee loyalty and willingness to be flexible in times of change. Japanese firms use the "rings of defense" discussed earlier, often at the expense of their female employees, who tend to have low seniority or to occupy temporary positions. American observers often lament Japan's ability to manage employment security: "While laid-off Chrysler and General Motors Corporation workers protest their lot, employees at Honda, Toyota, Mitsubishi, Nissan, and Mazda factories in the United States are producing cars."[82]

Yet, all is not as simple as it may first appear. The flipside of job security often meant that Japanese workers were branded as traitors when they switched employers. This can cause inbreeding and reduce innovation. Recently, the culture of lifetime loyalty from employer and employee has begun to change. Japanese employees increasingly find that job-hopping can lead to increased pay, responsibility, and job satisfaction. Sony Corporation's general manager for hiring and training, Nobukazu Ohga, notes that this "stirring up effect" can be good for companies as they switch from perfecting mass production techniques to developing creative corporate strategies. One observer at the Mitsubishi Research Institute observed, "The one-company-for-life era has come to an end."[83] Also, Japanese companies operating in the United States seem to have trouble keeping their best American managers, because of perceived exclusion from decision making, absence of training, and lack of career opportunities.[84]

In Europe and Canada, it has long been traditional for the government to stipulate advance notice provisions for layoffs and terminations. Moreover, unions often stipulate strong employment security provisions. Exhibit 9.8 gives examples of advance notice provisions in different European countries. Most of these have been in existence for many years, while the United States passed advance notice legislation only in 1988. European laws and labor agreements also typically require consultations with employee representatives, with a view toward avoiding or mitigating the consequences of the dismissals.[85] Thus, managers accustomed to U.S. laws and rules are likely to find themselves even more severely constrained as companies increasingly expand their operations to Western and Eastern Europe.

EVALUATING EMPLOYEE SEPARATIONS, WORK FORCE REDUCTION, AND RETENTION

Employee separations continue to typically be evaluated solely by the quantity (or rate) of employees who quit, resign, are discharged, or laid off. In the case of layoffs, a typical additional evaluation approach is to estimate the savings in salary and benefits resulting from the smaller work force. We have taken a broader approach here, showing that separations are properly evaluated as part of the staffing process, and that many of their most important effects occur among those who are retained.

EXHIBIT 9.8 Requirements for Advance Notice for Collective Dismissals in European Legislation

Country	Definition of Collective Dismissals	Notice Requirements
Belgium	Within a 60-day period: *a.* 6 workers in 20–59 employee firms. *b.* 10% of work force in larger firms.	30 days
Denmark	Within a 30-day period: *a.* 10 workers in 21–99 employee firms. *b.* 10% of work force in 100–299 employee firms. *c.* 30 workers in ≥300 employee firms.	30 days
France	Within a 30-day period: *a.* 2 workers in firms of ≥ 11 employees.	45 days and up
Germany	Within a 4-week period: *a.* 6 workers in 21–49 employee firms. *b.* 10% of work force or greater than 25 workers in firms employing 50–499 workers. *c.* 50 workers in ≥500 employee firms.	30 days
Greece	2–10% of the work force in firms normally employing ≥50 employees (percentage changes each year).	30 days
Ireland	Within a 30-day period: *a.* 5 employees in 21–49 employee firms. *b.* 10 employees in 50–99 employee firms. *c.* 10% of work force in 100–299 employee firms. *d.* 30 employees in ≥300 employee firms.	30 days
Italy	On the same date: 2 workers in any firm employing ≥ 10 workers.	22 to 32 days
Luxembourg	Within a 30-day period: 10 workers. Within a 60-day period: 20 workers	60 to 75 days
Netherlands	Within a 3-month period: 20 workers.	30 days
Sweden	5 workers.	2 to 6 months
United Kingdom	1 worker.	30 to 90 days (if at least 10 workers are involved)

Source: Ronald G. Ehrenberg and George H. Jakubson, *Advance Notice Provisions in Plant Closing Legislation,* W. E. Upjohn Institute for Employment Research, 1988.

Efficiency

Costs

Separations and the programs to manage them can be costly. Separations involve such activities as exit interviews, outplacement assistance, counseling, and severance pay, as well as requiring administrative and clerical support. Exhibit 9.9 shows an estimate of typical outplacement costs. When the costs of hiring and training replacements are factored in (see Chapters Eight and Eleven), costs typically reach several thousand dollars per separation.[86] Such costs often tempt managers, consultants, and others to argue that separations—especially quits—should always be reduced. But programs to reduce separations also cost money, and focusing only on reducing separation rates misses potential benefits for productivity.

Productivity

Quits are not necessarily harmful to the organization. Quits can be functional when they improve the productivity of the work force by removing poor performers or allow replacement of highly paid employees with newer and lower-paid employees of similar ability.[87] As we have seen, the notion that separations can improve work force productivity applies not only to quits but to all separations. If employers so manage separations that the most valuable performers are retained, the productivity benefits can be substantial. By the same token, if the separation pattern is such that the most valuable performers leave, the potential productivity reductions are also substantial. The magnitude of these effects depends on the quality and quantity of the retained work force.[88] This perspective suggests that human resource managers would do well to look beyond simply the quantity and cost of separations, adopting an evaluation framework that encompasses productivity as well.

Equity

Employee separations are both a result and a cause of equity perceptions. Quits can result from low employee satisfaction; and the ways that organizations implement and communicate about dismissals, retirements, and layoffs serve as an index of their commitment to fairness and equity. Governments at the local, state, and federal levels carefully monitor the effects of separations on communities, older employees, minorities, and females. The "employment-at-will" doctrine continues to generate controversy in state courts, and federal legislation affecting separations continues to grow. The importance of the separation decision for employees and organizations means that decisions about separations must encompass both equity and efficiency.

SUMMARY

The employer or the employee, or both, can terminate the employment relationship. Employee separations have important impacts on the organization, because they affect the efficiency and equity of the retained work force. Beyond their effects on the work force, however, employee separations are widely debated and closely scrutinized by governments, communities, and potential em-

---

EXHIBIT 9.9   Estimated Costs of Outplacement Assistance

The following costs were estimated for terminating three clerical employees and seven professional employees in a 100-person organization, including counseling and seminars using the company's own human resources staff.

Cost to Company	Benefit to Employees
$ 30,000	Severance pay
56,000	Unemployment compensation
2,300	Insurance continuation
2,100	Office space
1,200	Clerical
1,000	Phone
11,683	In-house staff time and travel
Total $104,283	

Source: Adapted with permission from Donald H. Sweet, "Outplacement," chap. 5, in *Human Resource Planning Employment & Placement,* ed. Wayne F. Cascio (Washington, D.C.: Bureau of National Affairs, 1988), pp. 2-236–2-262.

ployees. The trend seems clear: Companies expect human resource managers to manage employee separations more carefully.

Such management requires a framework for objectives and evaluation that integrates employee separations/retentions into the staffing process. This chapter has proposed such a framework, demonstrating the similarities between external employee selection and employee separation/retention. Employee separation/retention constitutes a process through which a subset of the current employees are chosen to remain in the organization. Clearly, employee recruitment, selection, and separation/retention are an integrated set of staffing activities.[89] By understanding this fundamental similarity between employee selection and separations/retentions, human resource managers are better prepared to manage the external staffing process effectively.

DISCUSSION AND REVIEW QUESTIONS

1. Why can we characterize employee separations as "reverse selection"? How does the management of employee separations affect the staffing process?

2. How does the concept of validity apply to the four types of employee separations/retentions?

3. Give three examples of managerial actions that might reduce the number of employee quits, using the model in Exhibit 9.4 as your guide. Why might human resource activities fail to affect employee quit behavior?

4. Would a reduction in the number of quits necessarily be a good thing? Why or why not?

5. Under what circumstances does it benefit an organization to retain its older employees? Discuss some strategies for lengthening the contribution of older workers.

6. What is an early retirement incentive? What decisions are required for such an incentive, and how do they affect an organization?

7. Discuss why employee discharges are likely to be valid work force reduction strategies. What is the "employment-at-will" issue, and how does it affect how discharges are managed? Is it likely to affect the relationship between discharges and productivity? Explain.

8. What steps can an organization take to protect itself from liability for wrongful discharge? What effect could these steps have on an organization's ability to attract and keep employees?

9. Discuss the four human resource activities for managing layoffs in terms of their likely effect on the efficiency and equity goals of organizations. Do these goals always coincide? Give one example where they do, and one where they do not.

10. What's wrong with evaluating employee separations simply by tracking the separation rate, and by making sure it is at or below the average for your industry or geographic area?

YOUR TURN
EMPLOYMENT SECURITY AT DIGITAL EQUIPMENT
CORPORATION (DEC)[90]

Consider the situation faced in the late 1980s by Digital Equipment Corporation (DEC), a Boston-area computer manufacturer. Its founder, Kenneth Olsen, placed a high value on "employment security." The company's culture throughout the 1970s and early 1980s placed a substantial premium on maintaining employment security through swings in sales volume, making it a starting point for planning, rather than a policy whose merits were debated. DEC was also a rapidly growing firm, and its manufacturing strategy stressed the imperative of high-volume production to meet strong customer demand. New product introductions increased staff levels, with start-up surges handled by hiring temporary and contract workers, constituting about 20 percent to 50 percent of the direct labor. Labor surpluses were addressed by reducing temporary workers, by increased separations of poor performers, and by redeploying workers to new jobs (even if that took up to a year). This commitment to employment security partly explained employees' high organizational commitment and willingness to respond to changes in jobs.

In the late 1980s, things began to change: (1) *technology* was so changed that the same computer could operate with up to 75–80 percent fewer parts, requiring less labor; (2) *outsourcing*—buying, rather than making, parts—became necessary to compete on costs, and it reduced the demand for part-building labor; (3) *manufacturing policy* was changed, from one of reducing costs by producing high volume to reducing costs by using less resources, including labor; (4) *stock price crash* occurred on Tuesday, October 18, 1983, when low earnings caused the price to drop

12 percent in one day and another 17 percent over the next three weeks. A broad downturn in product demand seemed inevitable.

What would you advise in this situation? What options exist for DEC to reduce the work force without layoffs? In what order would you initiate those options? What could justify avoiding layoffs to reduce the work force further? If you decided to avoid layoffs, what further options exist to increase efficiency without reducing staff levels? What could justify initiating layoffs? If you decided to initiate layoffs, what characteristics would the layoff procedures have?

Your instructor has further information about what actually happened at DEC.

NOTES AND REFERENCES

1. Paul B. Carroll, "IBM Launches Retirement Plan to Cut Outlays," *The Wall Street Journal,* October 21, 1989, p. A4; John W. Verity, "What's Ailing IBM? More Than This Year's Earnings," *Business Week,* October 16, 1989, pp. 65–86.

2. Laurence Hooper, "IBM Announces Big Write-Off, Restructuring," *The Wall Street Journal,* December 6, 1989, p. A3.

3. John Hoerr and Wendy Zellner, "A Japanese Import That's Not Selling," *Business Week,* February 16, 1990, pp. 86–87.

4. Wayne F. Cascio, *Costing Human Resources,* 2nd ed. (Boston: Kent Publishing, 1987); T. F. Cawsey and W. C. Wedley, "Labor Turnover Costs: Measurement and Control," *Personnel Journal* 2 (1979), pp. 90–95; Dan R. Dalton, "Absenteeism and Turnover: Measures of Personnel Effectiveness," in *Applied Readings in Personnel and Human Resource Management,* ed. Randall S. Schuler, J. M. McFillen, and Dan R. Dalton (St. Paul, Minn.: West Publishing, 1981), pp. 25–42; E. A. Dyl and Timothy J. Keaveny, "Cost Minimization in Staffing," *Human Resource Planning* 6 (1983), pp. 103–13; F. J. Gaudet, *Labor Turnover: Calculation and Cost,* Research Study no. 39 (New York: American Management Associations, 1960); Eric G. Flamholtz, *Human Resource Accounting,* 2nd ed. (San Francisco: Jossey-Bass, 1985); H. L. Smith and L. E. Watkins, "Managing Manpower Turnover Costs," *Personnel Administrator* 23 (1978), pp. 46–50; Dan L. Ward, "The $34,000 Lay-Off," *Human Resource Planning* 8 (1982), pp. 35–41.

5. John W. Boudreau, "Utility Analysis: A New Perspective" in *Human Resource Management Evolving Roles and Responsibilities*, ed. Lee D. Dyer (Washington, D.C.: Bureau of National Affairs, 1988); John W. Boudreau and Chris J. Berger, "Decision-Theoretic Utility Analysis Applied to Employee Separations and Acquisitions," *Journal of Applied Psychology* [monograph] 70, (1985), pp. 581–612.

6. Boudreau, "Utility Analysis: A New Perspective on Human Resource Decision Making."

7. Catherine Schwoerer and Benson Rosen, "Effects of Employment-at-Will Policies and Compensation Policies on Corporate Image and Job Pursuit Intentions," *Journal of Applied Psychology* 64, no. 4 (1989), pp. 653–56.

8. Lyman W. Porter and Richard M. Steers, "Organizational, Work, and Personal Factors in Employee Turnover and Absenteeism," *Psychological Bulletin,* 80 (1973), pp. 151–76; Victory H. Vroom, *Work and Motivation* (New York: John Wiley & Sons, 1964).

9. Barry M. Staw, "The Consequences of Turnover," *Journal of Occupational Behaviour* 1 (1980), pp. 253–73;   Dan R. Dalton and William D. Todor, "Turnover: A Lucrative Hard Dollar Phenomenon," *Academy of Management Review* 7 (1982), pp. 212–18.

10. Boudreau, "Utility Analysis: A New Perspective on Human Resource Decision Making";   Boudreau and Berger, "Decision-Theoretic Utility Analysis Applied to Employee Separations and Acquisitions."

11. U.S. Bureau of Labor Statistics, *Handbook of Methods,* Bulletin 1919 (Washington, D.C.: U.S. Bureau of Labor Statistics, 1976).

12. John W. Boudreau and Chris J. Berger, "Toward a Model of Employee Movement Utility," in *Research in Personnel and Human Resources Management,* vol. 3, ed. Kendrith M. Rowland and Gerald R. Ferris (Greenwich, Conn.: JAI Press, 1985), pp. 31–54.

13. James G. March and Herbert A. Simon, *Organizations* (New York: John Wiley & Sons, 1958);   James L. Price, *The Study of Turnover* (Ames: Iowa State University Press, 1977);   William H. Mobley, "Intermediate Linkages in the Relationship between Job Satisfaction and Employee Turnover," *Journal of Applied Psychology* 62 (1977), pp. 237–40;   William H. Mobley, R. W. Griffeth, H. H. Hand, and M. M. Meglino, "Review and Conceptual Analysis of the Employee Turnover Process," *Psychological Bulletin* 86 (1979), pp. 493–522.

14. Barry Gerhart, "The Prediction of Voluntary Turnover Using Behavioral Intentions, Job Satisfaction, and Area Unemployment Rates" (Academy of Management, New Orleans, 1987).

15. Hyder Lakhani and Curtis Gilroy, *Army Reenlistment and Extension Decisions by Occupation,* Working Paper no. MPPRG 84-14 (Alexandria, Va.: U.S. Army Research Institute, 1984).

16. John L. Cotton and Jeffrey M. Tuttle, "Employee Turnover: A Meta-Analysis and Review with Implications for Research," *Academy of Management Review* 11, no. 1 (1986), pp. 55–70.

17. Daniel G. Spencer, "Employee Voice and Employee Retention," *Academy of Management Journal* 29, no. 3 (1986), pp. 488–502.

18. Bureau of National Affairs, "Job Absence and Turnover Control," *Personnel Policies Forum Survey no. 132* (Washington, D.C.: Bureau of National Affairs, 1981).

19. Wayne F. Cascio and Glen M. McEvoy, "Strategies for Reducing Employee Turnover: A Meta-Analysis," *Journal of Applied Psychology* 70 (1985), pp. 342–53.

20. "Grassroots Attack on Employee Turnover," *Human Resource Management News,* October 12, 1989, pp. 3–4.

21. Bureau of National Affairs, "Separation Procedures and Severance Benefits," *Personnel Policies Forum Survey no. 121* (Washington, D.C.: Bureau of National Affairs, 1978).

22. Boudreau and Berger, "Decision-Theoretic Utility Analysis Applied to Employee Separations and Acquisitions";   Ellen F. Jackofsky, "Turnover and Job Performance: An Integrated Process Model," *Academy of Management Journal* 9 (1984), pp. 74–83; John E. Mathieu and Joseph E. Baratta, "Turnover Type as a Moderator of the Performance-Turnover Relationship," *Human Performance* 2, no. 1 (1989), pp. 61–71.

23. Dan R. Dalton and William D. Todor, "Turnover Turned Over: An Expanded and Positive Perspective," *Academy of Management Review* 4 (1979), pp. 225–35;   Dan R. Dalton and William D. Todor, "Turnover: A Lucrative Hard Dollar Phenomenon";   Dan R. Dalton, David M. Krackhardt, and Lyman W. Porter, "Functional Turnover: An Empirical Assessment," *Journal of Applied Psychology* 66 (1981), pp. 716–21;   Boudreau and Berger, "Decision-Theoretic Utility Analysis Applied to Employee Separations and Acquisitions";   Boudreau, "Utility Analysis; A New Per-

spective on Human Resource Management Decisions"; John R. Hollenbeck and Charles R. Wiliams, "Turnover Functionality versus Turnover Frequency: A Note on Work Attitudes and Organizational Effectiveness," *Journal of Applied Psychology* 71, no. 4 (1986), pp. 606–11; D. C. Martin and K. M. Bartol, "Managing Turnover Strategically," *Personnel Administrator* 30 (November 1985), pp. 63–73.

24. Amanda Bennett, "Corporate Chiefs Calling It Quits Earlier," *The Wall Street Journal,* December 22, 1989, p. B1.

25. Herbert S. Parnes, "The Retirement Decision," chap. 5, in *The Older Worker,* eds. Michael E. Borus, Herbert S. Parnes, Steven H. Sandell, and Bert Seidman (Madison, Wis.: Industrial Relations Research Association, 1988).

26. Marc Frons, "Early Retirement: It Pays to Plan Early," *Business Week,* February 27, 1989, pp. 134–35.

27. "Incentive Program Accepted by More than 1,000 Xerox Employees," *Bureau of National Affairs Employee Relations Weekly,* February 23, 1987, p. 230; "ITT's Early Retirement Package Fails to Achieve Needed Staff Reductions," *Bureau of National Affairs White Collar Report* 60, no. 20 (November 19, 1986); "Hewlett-Packard Retirement Plan," *New York Times,* June 13, 1986, p. D3(L); "Phillips Petroleum Retirement Offer," *New York Times,* August 3, 1985, p. 32(L).

28. "Contracts Revise Early Retirement, Pensions, Health Care," *Bureau of National Affairs Pension Reporter* 12, no. 51 (December 23, 1985), pp. 1897–98.

29. Julie Amparano Lopez, "Nynex Managers Offered a Plan to Retire Early," *The Wall Street Journal,* December 22, 1989, p. A2.

30. International Business Machines Corporation, "Stockholders' Report, First Quarter 1987" (Armonk, N.Y.: International Business Machines Corporation, 1987); "Incentive Program Accepted by More Than 1,000 Xerox Employes, *Bureau of National Affairs Employee Relations Weekly,* February 23, 1987, p. 230.

31. "'Open-Window' Early Retirement Plans Seen Successful," *Bureau of National Affairs Daily Executive Report,* no. 48 (March 13, 1986).

32. "ITT's Early Retirement Package Fails to Achieve Needed Staff Reductions," *Bureau of National Affairs White Collar Report* 60, no. 20 (November 19, 1986).

33. "Age Bias Found in Du Pont Early Retirement Program," *Washington Post,* July 17, 1986, p. A4.

34. Wade Lambert and Arthur S. Hayes, "EEOC Suit Says New York State Shows Age Bias against Judges," *The Wall Street Journal,* October 31, 1989, p. B8.

35. Conference Board, Inc., "Older Workers: Dispelling Myths," *The Conference Board's Management Briefing: Human Resources* 4, no. 9 (September 1988), pp. 2–3.

36. Boudreau, "Utility Analysis," in Lee D. Dyer, ed.

37. Bureau of National Affairs, "Employee Discipline and Discharge," *Personnel Policies Forum Survey no. 139* (Washington, D.C.: Bureau of National Affairs, Inc., 1985).

38. Ibid.

39. Robert C. Rodgers and Jack Stieber, "Employee Discharge in the 20th Century: A Review of the Literature," *Monthly Labor Review,* September 1985, pp. 35–41.

40. *Union Labor Hospital Association* v. *Vance Redwood Lumber Co.,* 158 Cal. 551, 112, p. 886 (1910).

41. *Phillips* v. *Goodyear Tire and Rubber Company,* Ca5, No. 79-2011 (1981); *Tamory* v. *Atlantic Richfield Co.,* 27 Ca.3d 167 (1980); *Murphy* v. *City of Topeka-Shawunee County Dept. of Labor Services,* Kn Ct App. No. 57 (1981); *Palmateer* v. *International Harvester Company,* 85 Ill., 2d 124 (1981).

42. Clyde W. Summers, "The Need for a Statute," *ILR Report,* Fall 1982, pp. 8–12;   Paul Salvatore, "Legislative Action and Private Initiative: A Practical Solution," *ILR Report,* Fall 1982, pp. 13–15.

43. *Toussaint* v. *Blue Cross/Blue Shield of Michigan,* 408 Mich. 579 (1980).

44. Amy Dockser Marcus, "Courts Uphold Oral Pledges of Lifetime Employment," *The Wall Street Journal,* December 12, 1989, p. B1.

45. *Cleary* v. *American Airlines,* 111 Ca. App. 3d (1980).

46. Terry L. Leap, "When Can You Fire for Off-Duty Conduct," *Harvard Business Review,* January–February 1988, pp. 28–36.

47. Milo Geyelin, "Fired Managers Winning More Lawsuits," *The Wall Street Journal,* September 7, 1989, p. B1.

48. Bureau of National Affairs, "Time Is Right for Expanded EEOC Role in Handling Discharge Cases, Report Says," *BNA Labor Relations Week* 4, no. 2 (January 10, 1990), p. 2.

49. Milo Geyelin, "Fired Managers Winning More Lawsuits."

50. Eric H. Marcus, M.D., "The Cost of Mental Distress," *Personnel Journal,* August 1989, pp. 66–68.

51. *Human Resource Management News,* February 18, 1989 p. 1;   Bureau of National Affairs, *Without Just Cause: An Employer's Practical and Legal Guide on Wrongful Discharge* (Washington, D.C.: Bureau of National Affairs, 1989).

52. *Foley* v. *Interactive Data Corporation,* 47 Cal. 3d 654, 254 Cal. Rptr. 211 1988);   James L. Payne and Kevin M. Smith, "Establishing the Boundaries of Wrongful Discharge: California's *Foley* Decision," *Employee Relations Law Journal* 15, no. 1 (Summer 1989), pp. 35–47.

53. Lawrence Z. Lorber, J. Robert Kirk, Kenneth H. Kirschner, and Charlene R. Handorf, *Fear of Firing* (Alexandria, Va.: ASPA Foundation, 1984);   Robert H. Nichols, "Would Labor Oppose a Statute?", *ILR Report,* Fall 1982, pp. 21–23;   Ira M. Shepard and Nancy L. Moran, "'Wrongful' Discharge Litigation," *ILR Report,* Fall 1982, pp. 26–29;   "Court Says At-Will Clause in Sear's Application Form Allowed Managers to Discharge, Demote without Proving 'Cause'," *Human Resources Management Ideas and Trends,* November 24, 1982, pp. 209–10;   Anthony T. Oliver, Jr., "The Disappearing Right to Terminate Employees at Will," *Personnel Journal,* December 1982, pp. 910–17;   "At-Will Employment," *Human Resource Management Ideas and Trends,* May 19, 1983, pp. 73–80;   Robert Coulson, *The Termination Handbook* (New York: Free Press, 1981).   Also, William J. Holloway and Michael J. Leech, *Employment Termination: Rights and Remedies* (Washington, D.C.: BNA Books, 1985);   Jerome B. Kauff and Maureen E. McClain, *Unjust Dismissal, 1984* (New York: Practicing Law Institute, 1984);   Ralph H. Baxter, Jr., and Jeffrey D. Wohl, "Wrongful Termination Lawsuits: The Employers Finally Win a Few," *Employee Relations Law Journal* 10 (1985), pp. 258–75;   Koys, Briggs, and Grenig, "State Court Disparity on Employment-at-Will";   Koys, Briggs, and Grenig, "The Employment-at-Will Doctrine";   Sami M. Abbasi, Kenneth W. Hollman, and Joe H. Murrey, Jr., "Employment at Will: An Eroding Concept in Employment Relationships," *Labor Law Journal* 38, no. 1 (January 1987), pp. 261–79.

54. "Fired Employees Turn the Reason for Dismissal into a Legal Weapon," *The Wall Street Journal,* October 2, 1986, p. 33.

55. Aaron Bernstein, "More Dismissed Workers Are Telling It to the Judge," *Business Week,* October 17, 1988, pp. 68–69.

56. Lee Dyer, F. Foltman, and G. Milkovich, "Employment Stabilization," (Working Paper, Cornell University, 1984);   Mark Thompson, "The Permanent Employment

System: Japan and Mexico," Sixth World Congress of Industrial Relations, Kyōto, Japan, March 28–31, 1983; R. Fuller, C. Jordan, and R. Anderson, "Retrenchment: Layoff Procedures in a Nonprofit Organization," *Personnel,* November–December 1982, pp. 19–24; R. H. Ketchum, "Retrenchment: The Uses and Misuses of Life in Downsizing an Organization," *Personnel,* November–December 1982, pp. 25–30; Linda Wintner, *Employee Buyouts: An Alternative to Plant Closings* (New York: Conference Board, 1983); F. Foltman, "Managing a Plant Closing: An Overview" (Working Paper, ILR School, Ithaca, N.Y.: Cornell University, 1981); T. Bailey and T. Jackson, "Industrial Outplacement at Goodyear," *Personnel Administrator,* March 1980, pp. 42–48; D. L. Ward, "The $34,000 Layoff," *Human Resources Planning* 5, no. 1 (1982), pp. 35–43; Dick Schaaf, "Are You Training Yet for Outplacement and Retirement?" *Training,* May 1981, pp. 70–84; E. B. Silverman and S. D. Sass, "Outplacement," *Training and Development Journal,* February 1982, pp. 71–84; R. S. Barkhaus and Carol L. Mak, "A Practical View of Outplacement," *Personnel Administrator,* March 1982, pp. 77–85; C. H. Driessnank, "Outplacement—The New Personnel Practice," *Personnel Administrator,* October 1980, pp. 81–93; P. D. Johnston, "Personnel Planning for a Plant Shutdown," *Personnel Administrator,* August 1981, pp. 53–60.

57. Adapted from Dyer, Foltman, and Milkovich, "Employment Stabilization."

58. Leonard Greenhalgh, Anne T. Lawrence, and Robert I. Sutton, "Determinants of Work Force Reduction Strategies in Declining Organizations," *Academy of Management Review* 13, no. 2 (1988), pp. 241–54.

59. Ibid.; Leonard Greenhalgh, "Organizational Decline," in *The Sociology of Organizations* 2 (Greenwich, Conn.: JAI Press, 1983), pp. 231–76; James F. Bolt, "Job Security: Its Time Has Come," *Harvard Business Review,* November–December 1983; Leonard Greenhalgh, Robert B. McKersie, and Roderick W. Gilkey, "Rebalancing the Work Force at IBM: A Case Study of Redeployment and Revitalization," (Working Paper, Sloan School of Management, Massachusetts Institute of Technology, 1985); Rosalind Klein Berlind, "Cutting Costs without Cutting People," *Fortune,* May 25, 1987.

60. Dyer, Foltman, and Milkovich, "Employment Stabilization"; Work in America Institute, *The Continuous Learning/Employment Security Connection* (Scarsdale, N.Y.: Work in America Institute, 1987).

61. U.S. Government Accounting Office, "Reduction in Force Can Sometimes Be More Costly to Agencies than Attrition and Furlough," Report to the Director Office of Management and Budget (Washington, D.C.: U.S. General Accounting Office, July 24, 1985).

62. Rosalind Klein Berlind, "Cutting Costs without Cutting People," *Fortune,* May 25, 1987, p. 37.

63. Eric Rolfe Greenberg, "The Latest AMA Survey on Downsizing," *Personnel,* October 1989, pp. 38–44.

64. John Hoerr and Wendy Zellner, "A Japanese Import That's not Selling," *Business Week,* February 26, 1990, pp. 86–87; Marilyn Chase, "Ashton-Tate Is Cutting Its Work Force 15% to 20%, Predicting Wider Losses," *The Wall Street Journal,* August 16, 1989, p. B4; John J. Keller, "AT&T Plans to Trim Staff by 8,500 in 1990: Cuts for 1989 to Total 25,000," *The Wall Street Journal,* December 11, 1989, p. A3.

65. Joseph B. White, "GM Will Add 2,000 Workers to Lay Off List," *The Wall Street Journal,* December 27, 1989, p. A2; Joseph B. White, "GM to Reduce White-Collar Work Force," *The Wall Street Journal,* November 22, 1989, p. A3.

66. Matthew Cooper and Allan Holmes, "The Disaster That Never Happened," *U.S. News & World Report,* February 26, 1990, p. 47.

67. Ronald G. Ehrenberg and George H. Jakubson, "Advance Notification of Plant Closing: Does It Matter?," *Industrial Relations* 28, no. 1 (Winter 1989), pp. 60–71; Ronald G. Ehrenberg and George H. Jakubson, *Advance Notice Provisions in Plant Closing Legislation,* W. E. Upjohn Institute for Employment Research, 1988.

68. Joseph T. McCune, Richard W. Beatty, and Raymond V. Montagno, "Downsizing: Practices in Manufacturing Firms," *Human Resource Management* 27, no. 2 (Summer 1988), pp. 145–61.

69. *Firefighters Local Union No. 1784* v. *Stotts* 467 U.S. 561 (1984); *Wygant* v. *Jackson Board of Education* 40 FEP Cases 1321 (May 19, 1986); Bureau of National Affairs, *Affirmative Action Today* (Washington, D.C.: Bureau of National Affairs, 1986).

70. Bureau of National Affairs, "Court Approves Oversight of Notice to Age Bias Class" *Daily Labor Report,* no. 237 (December 12, 1989), p. 1.

71. Thomas Petzinger, Jr., and Michel McQueen, "Judge Blocks Eastern Air Cut of 4,000 Jobs," *The Wall Street Journal,* August 31, 1988, p. A3.

72. Bureau of National Affairs, "Severance Benefits and Outplacement Services," *Personnel Policies Forum Survey no. 143* (Washington, D.C.: Bureau of National Affairs, 1986).

73. Ronald E. Berenbeim, *Company Programs to Ease the Impact of Shutdowns* (New York: Conference Board, 1986).

74. Bureau of National Affairs, "Severance Benefits and Outplacement Services."

75. Carol Hymowitz, "Kodak Passes out 'Tin Parachutes' to All Its Employees," *The Wall Street Journal,* January 12, 1990, p. B1; "The 'Tin Parachute' as an HR Strategy," *Human Resource Management News,* December 2, 1989, p. 2.

76. Eric Rolfe Greenberg, "The Latest AMA Survey on Downsizing."

77. Donald H. Sweet, "Outplacement," in *Human Resource Planning Employment & Placement,* ed. Wayne F. Cascio (Washington, D.C.: Bureau of National Affairs, 1989).

78. Jeremy Main, "Look Who Needs Outplacement," *Fortune,* October 9, 1989, pp. 85–92.

79. Amanda Bennett, "One Middle Manager's Long Job Search," *The Wall Street Journal,* August 18, 1988, p. B1; Gerald C. Parkhouse, "Inside Outplacement—My Search for a Job," *Harvard Business Review,* January–February 1988, pp. 67–73.

80. Joel Brockner, Steven Grover, Thomas Reed, Rocki DeWitt, and Michael O'Malley, "Survivors' Reactions to Layoffs: We Get by with a Little Help for Our Friends," *Administrative Science Quarterly* 32 (1987), pp. 526–41.

81. Anne B. Fisher, "The Downside of Downsizing," *Fortune,* May 23, 1988, pp. 42–52.

82. John Hoerr and Wendy Zellner, "A Japanese Import That's not Selling."

83. "In Japan, Employees Are Switching Firms for Better Work, Pay," *The Wall Street Journal,* October 11, 1988, p. A1.

84. Wendy Zellner, "Help Wanted, Room to Advance—Out the Door," *Business Week,* October 30, 1989, p. 42.

85. Ehrenberg and Jakubson, *Advance Provisions in Plant Closing Legislation.*

86. Boudreau and Berger, "Decision-Theoretic Utility Analysis Applied to Employee Separations and Acquisitions"; Flamholtz, *Human Resource Accounting*; Dalton and Todor, "Turnover: A Lucrative Hard-Dollar Phenomenon"; Cascio, *Costing Human Resources;* Smith and Watkins, "Managing Manpower Turnover Costs"; Bureau of National Affairs, "Severance Benefits and Outplacement Assistance"; Ward, "The $34,000 Layoff"; U.S. Government Accounting Office, "Reduction in Force"; Michael W. Mercer, "Turnover: Reducing the Costs" *Personnel,* December 1988, pp. 36–40.

87. Dalton, Krackhardt, and Porter, "Functional Turnover: An Empirical Assessment."

88. Boudreau and Berger, "Decision-Theoretic Utility Analysis Applied to Employee Separations and Acquisitions"; Boudreau and Berger, "Toward a Model of Employee Movement Utility"; Boudreau, "Utility Analysis: A New Perspective on Human Resource Management Decisions."

89. Boudreau, "Utility Analysis: A New Perspective on Human Resource Management Decisions."

90. This "Your Turn" section is based on an extensive case study by Thomas A. Kochan, John Paul MacDuffie, and Paul Osterman, "Employment Security at DEC: Sustaining Values Amid Environmental Change," *Human Resource Management* 27, no. 2 (1988), pp. 121–43.

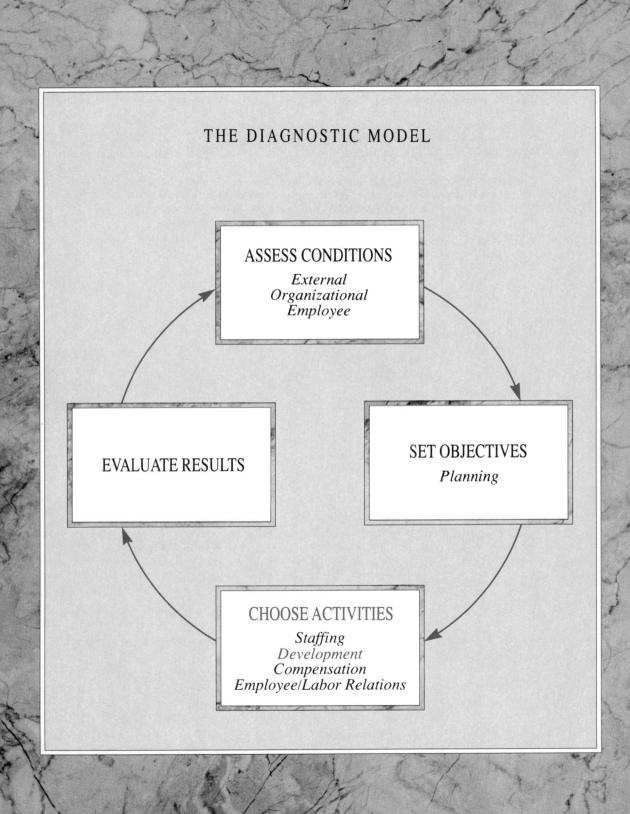

THE DIAGNOSTIC MODEL

ASSESS CONDITIONS
External
Organizational
Employee

SET OBJECTIVES
Planning

CHOOSE ACTIVITIES
Staffing
Development
Compensation
Employee/Labor Relations

EVALUATE RESULTS

PART FOUR

EMPLOYEE DEVELOPMENT

The United States faces a national crisis, because its workers are ill-prepared for future jobs by the educational system. With the drastic changes in the work force and critical skill shortages, described earlier in the section on External Staffing, organizations cannot expect to meet their labor force needs simply by managing external recruitment, selection, and separations. Most of the attention must be devoted to employees after they join the organization, providing them with experiences and training that will prepare them for the changing work roles of the future.

Employee development refers to the human resource activities designed to enhance the value of employees after they have joined the organization. It encompasses *internal staffing,* which involves moving people between jobs and work roles within the organization. It also includes *employee training and orientation,* which involves giving employees experiences designed to foster learning. These two activities go hand in hand, because they must work together if the work force is to be properly prepared. Internal staffing bears many similarities to external staffing, but, because internal staffing deals with existing employees, it also has characteristics similar to training activities. Employee training and orientation are based on principles of learning, but the methods that foster adult learning in the workplace are different from the classroom education experiences most familiar to college students.

A DIAGNOSTIC APPROACH TO EMPLOYEE DEVELOPMENT

The accompanying exhibit shows where development fits the diagnostic approach. Because internal staffing and employee training/orientation focus on developing existing employees, they must constantly strike a balance between organizational concerns for efficiency (optimal matches between skills and demands) and equity (perceptions that activities are fair, legal, and provide adequate opportunity). They are also keenly affected by factors outside the organization as well as organization and employee characteristics.

External Conditions

Markets Workplace skill demands are rapidly increasing, yet workers continue to leave schools ill-prepared in even the most basic skills. The increasing number of minority and female members of the work force present special challenges, because they often require different skill-building opportunities or opportunities to acquire business knowledge than the traditional white male. Global competition means greater flexibility and continuous learning among workers to produce better products and services every year. This can only be accomplished if training and internal staffing are targeted to organizational objectives.

Government Legal requirements affect employee development just as they affect external staffing. The same EEO legislation that regulates external recruitment, selection, and retention policies also affects internal staffing decisions. Moreover, affirmative action does not end when people are hired. Their advancement is also a critical requirement for meeting affirmative action goals. Organizationally supplied training and career experience is often the key to giving under-represented minorities and females the opportunity to advance. In addition, governments shape public education, from public schools to vocational training, to preschool programs, such as Head Start. Human resource managers have a stake in these programs, because their success often depends on how well they produce trainees that fit business needs. Finally, government regulations on occupational safety often mandate training and carefully designed job experiences to assure that employees are prepared to abide by safety rules.

Union Collective bargaining agreements and day-to-day contract administration are frequently more concerned with internal staffing and training opportunities than with external staffing. Most contracts award internal employment and training opportunities on the basis of seniority. Human resource managers increasingly bargain for more flexible staffing and training rules to allow the most qualified—not necessarily the most senior—employees to compete for opportunities. Unions are also key providers of training through their apprenticeship programs, especially for skilled crafts, such as construction.

Organizational Conditions

The organization's strategies and culture determine both the need and the nature of employee development. Organizations may restructure to eliminate management layers, push decision making closer to the production line or the customer, and cut costs by increasing labor productivity. These decisions must be supported by appropriate career paths, training experiences, and orientation activities if they are to succeed. It does little good to build a state-of-the-art manufacturing process if none of your employees knows how to read and calculate sufficiently to operate it. Organizational values also affect employee development. In organizations like IBM and Motorola, which choose to compete based on employment security and employee quality, massive amounts of resources are devoted to giving employees options to move between jobs and to get the training necessary to make them successful when they do move. Many organizations have adopted the concept of "continuous learning" to describe what they expect of employees in the future. For human resource managers, this often translates into "continuous training."

Employee Characteristics

Employee characteristics are especially critical to internal staffing. Unlike external staffing, where new pools of applicants can be developed with different attributes, internal staffing must focus on existing employees. It is their skills, interests, abilities, and knowledge that provide the raw materials for successful internal staffing decisions. Moreover, those rejected for internal staffing opportunities remain employed by the organization. Because internal staffing decisions determine career progress, pay, and status, the reactions of employees who are chosen as well as those who are not chosen will affect how well objectives are achieved. Both the need for and the success of training activities depends on individual characteristics. Employees must be motivated and able to learn for training to succeed. Moreover, the success of training is often evaluated by examining whether such individual characteristics as knowledge, attitudes, or behaviors have changed.

Objectives/Standards for Employee Development

Subsequent chapters will describe the goals and evaluation methods for employee development in detail. We will see that these activities often have affects that are not obvious at first. The goals of internal staffing may best be met by paying careful attention to the jobs that yield the promoted employees, not just the jobs that receive them. The goals of training programs may best be evaluated by calculating return on investment, even when you don't have any precise figures to use in the calculation. Like all human resource activities, the objectives/standards that are set for employee development must be inte-

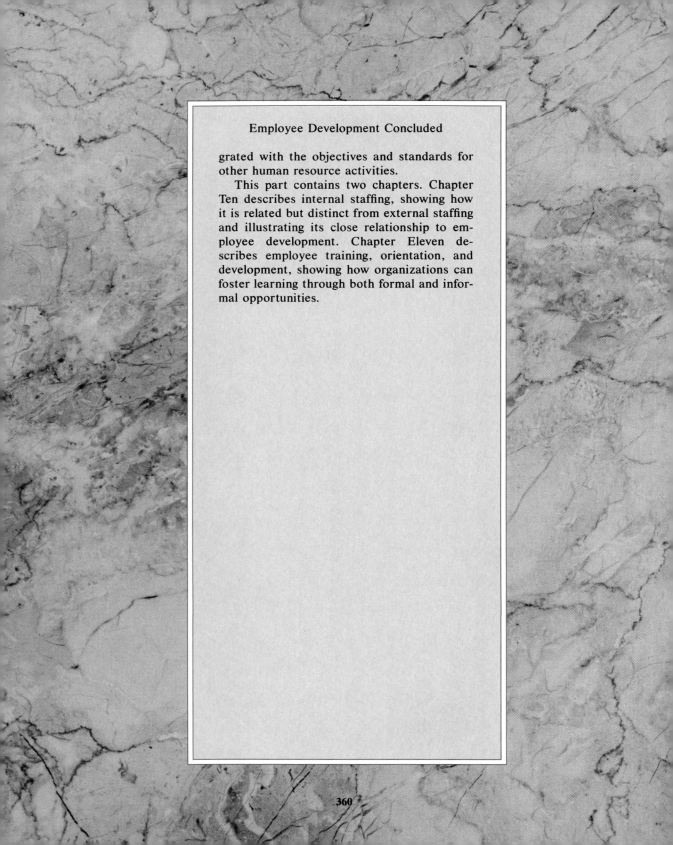

Employee Development Concluded

grated with the objectives and standards for other human resource activities.

This part contains two chapters. Chapter Ten describes internal staffing, showing how it is related but distinct from external staffing and illustrating its close relationship to employee development. Chapter Eleven describes employee training, orientation, and development, showing how organizations can foster learning through both formal and informal opportunities.

CHAPTER
TEN

Internal Staffing and Career Development

Internal Staffing and Careers
Objectives for Internal Staffing

Internal Employee Movement in Staffing

Career Management and Career Planning

Career Planning

Recruitment in Career Management
Job Posting
Skills Inventories
Replacement and Succession Planning
Nomination by Superiors and Mentors
Nomination by the Employees Themselves

Selection in Career Management
Past Performance, Experience, and Seniority
Selection Procedures Used for Internal Staffing
Assessment Centers

Separation/Retention in Career Management
Plateaued Careers
Dual-Ladder Career Progressions
The "Mommy Track": Opportunity or a Betrayal?

International Perspectives

Evaluating Internal Staffing and Careers

Your Turn: Breaking the Glass
Ceiling at Corning Glass Works

Imagine you attend a party being held in a six-cornered room. An aerial view of the room is shown in Exhibit 10.1. People with similar interests have all gathered in the same corner of the room, as signified by the letters R, I, A, S, E, and C. First, decide which corner of the room you would be drawn to, because that group contains the kind of people you would most enjoy being with for the longest time. Write down the letter signifying that corner of the room. Second, assume that, after 15 minutes, everyone in the corner you chose leaves, except you. Now, which corner would you move to, because that group contains the kind of people you would second-most enjoy being with for the longest period. Write down the letter signifying the corner to the right of the first letter. Finally, assume that, after 15 minutes, everyone in this second group of people you chose all leave, except you. Of the remaining corners, which one would you move to, because that group contains the kind of people you would third-most enjoy being with for the longest period. Write down the letter signifying your third corner to the right of the second letter. You now have a three-letter combination describing people who have the kinds of interests and with whom you like to associate.

Much research has been conducted in which people holding various jobs were asked the same kind of question, and the results suggest that people drawn to certain vocational interests tend to end up in certain kinds of jobs. The letters stand for: **R**ealistic, **I**nvestigative, **A**rtistic, **S**ocial, **E**nterprising, and **C**lerical. For example, **RIE** is commonly chosen by mechanical, petroleum, and mining engineers, as well as mechanics and machinists. **ISA** is often chosen by physicians, psychiatrists/psychologists, and medical technologists. **AES** is often chosen by advertising executives/managers, entertainers, fashion models, and public relations persons. **SIA** is often chosen by college professors, school counselors, nurses, and social workers. **ESC** is often chosen by city managers, personnel managers, labor arbitrators, and sales clerks. **CSA** is often chosen by secretaries, library assistants, and order clerks. There are several books and instruments available to help you pinpoint your interests and find what kinds of occupations they match.[1]

Did your choices seem to match the kind of career interests you think you'd like to pursue? Did the occupations listed above seem logical, or did they surprise you? Do you think that people can change their interests throughout their careers, or are they "anchored" to a certain kind of interest that keeps them in similar jobs/positions? Should organizations try to accommodate the vocational interests of employees as it makes staffing decisions, or should such decisions be dictated by finding the best person for the job, regardless of their particular interests?

EXHIBIT 10.1   Occupational Interests Arranged as a Six-Cornered Room

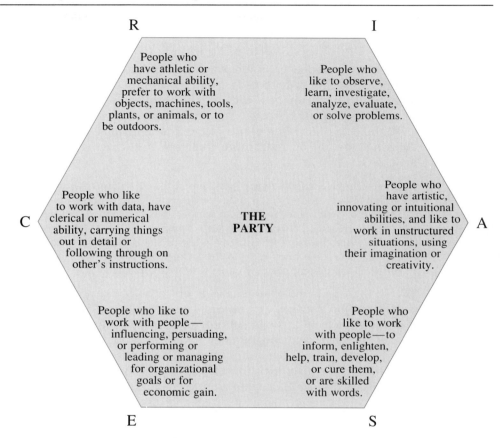

Source: Adapted and reproduced with permission of Psychological Assessment Resources, Inc., incorporated from the Self-Directed Search Professional Manual by John L. Holland, Ph.D. Copyright 1985 by PAR, Inc. Not to be reproduced further without permission from the publisher.

INTERNAL STAFFING AND CAREERS

Everyone faces questions about their career interests and aspirations throughout their working lives. While not everyone may address them as systematically as described above, one way or another people create and follow careers.

◆

A *career* is the evolving sequence of a person's work experiences over time.[2]

The particular sequence of jobs, organizations, and work roles a person pursues will be a function of both conscious choices based on interests, as well as constraints and opportunities, encountered throughout the person's work life. Careers include upward, lateral, and downward sequences of work experiences.

We tend to think of careers as related to individuals, but they are also vitally important to organizations and often are a key activity for human resource managers.

> Some employees left the predictable and found a team. Several employees went to Miami Beach. One person didn't switch and saw everything come up roses. Another did switch and, in his own words, "hasn't stopped smiling since."
>
> Who are these people and what's going on?
>
> They are, to use a term heard often in the company these days, IBM men and women who have been redeployed—who have set out with considerable optimism on what are essentially new careers in a new place.[3]

Twelve thousand employees changed jobs at IBM Corporation during 1986, and even more job changes are expected in the future. Many people changed careers, moving from areas of surplus, such as production, to areas of shortage—marketing, sales, and programming. Xerox Corporation's Reprographics Business Group retrains chemists, engineers, and other professionals to enter completely different high-demand fields, such as computer science and computer engineering. Pacific Bell maintains its policy of employment security with a companywide career planning system that updates employees on declining and rising job opportunities, and it trains those willing to relocate. And Hewlett-Packard Company moves production employees in surplus occupations to office jobs in high-demand areas, with a redeployment plan that includes career mentors to provide relevant on-the-job experience and conferences between supervisors from both the hiring and originating departments.[4] One recent study of population data forecasted that over a quarter of all workers in the U.S. labor force will work for the same employer for 20 years or more.[5] Most of them will hold many positions in the same organization.

Internal staffing decisions determine how employees move between jobs within the organization. Such decisions have always been a part of HR management, but they are becoming more important and frequent as organizations search for ways to maintain efficiency and equity in the face of rapidly changing economic conditions. Similar to external selection and reduction, such decisions can affect the organization for decades. Moreover, employee movements between jobs determine career progress, a major factor in employees' status, income level, and satisfaction with their jobs and lives. How can organizations identify internal employment candidates? Which factors affect individuals' willingness to accept certain employment opportunities, and how can they be induced to accept the changes necessary to keep the organization flexible and competitive? This chapter examines these and other issues related to the internal staffing process.

Setting Objectives for Internal Staffing and Careers

As we shall see, internal staffing and career choices affect what work roles are assigned to what employees. Thus, internal staffing shares many of the same effects on efficiency and equity as external recruitment selection, and separation/retention.

Efficiency

Internal staffing activities incur costs of attracting applicants for internal opportunities, assessing their characteristics and interests to determine their fitness for internal employment opportunities, moving employees from one assignment to another, and filling the vacancy created in the work role the employee leaves. Thus, all of the costs discussed in Chapters, Seven, Eight, and Nine apply to internal staffing as well, but they are incurred while focusing on existing employees. Such costs are not trivial. The executive vice president of Runzheimer and Company, a national consulting firm on employee relocation, estimated that about 500,000 employees were relocated by their companies in 1988, at an average cost of $37,000 for a homeowner and $10,000 for a renter.[6] This doesn't even include the activities related to attracting, selecting, and replacing those who moved.

Are such costs justified? As with external selection, this depends on how well internal staffing decisions place the right people in the right work roles at the right time. Recent research suggests that the difference between accurate and inaccurate placements can amount to millions of dollars over time in large organizations.[7] The effects are especially obvious when you consider that every internal promotion, lateral transfer, or downward transfer creates a vacancy that also must be filled. The sequence of staffing decisions initiated by internal staffing provides immense opportunities to add value or immense opportunities to do damage, if they are not considered carefully.

Equity

Because internal staffing affects current employees, decisions about internal staffing activities must be as much, or more, attuned to equity perceptions than external staffing activities. EEO/AA legislation and court decisions affect both internal and external staffing activities. So, managers must consider the effects of internal staffing on the minority composition of the organization.

Careers represent more than a series of employment opportunities for those who move; they are a signal to employees about the equity of organizational policies. Perceived career opportunities affect employees' attitudes and satisfaction. Because promotions often appear to be rewards, they are subject to the same equity scrutiny as pay and benefits. Moreover, employees' career decisions usually involve a concern for self-direction or control, family inputs, such as two-career planning, and a desire for assistance and information from organizations in planning and directing their own careers.[8]

Finally, because internal staffing decisions have fundamental effects on the employment security and pay levels of employees, they are a basic issue in most collective bargaining agreements. Unions desire to ensure that such decisions are made in objective and fair ways.

ROLE OF INTERNAL EMPLOYEE MOVEMENT IN THE STAFFING PROCESS

When most people think of internal staffing, they tend to focus on either the motivations and interests that cause individuals to be willing to move from one position to another or they focus on the organization's success in filling vacancies with internal job candidates who are already employed in other jobs. In this chapter we take a broader view, recognizing that internal staffing is part of the larger staffing process and must be integrated with external staffing (recruiting, selection, and separation/retention). In fact, evidence suggests that 99 percent of organizations use internal candidate sources, with many of them considering them more effective than external sources.[9] External selection is often used *only* after internal sources have been explored.

Exhibit 10.2 shows how the relationship between external staffing, development/career management, and exit differs depending on the nature of the organization. The vertical dimension reflects how open the staffing system is to external candidates, with more open systems at the top and more closed systems near the bottom. The horizontal dimension reflects how much individual competition there is for internal staffing opportunities. The **Academy** (similar to a college faculty) involves a fairly closed system, with entry typically only possible at entry-level jobs early in a person's career. This system emphasizes a high degree of training and career development, based on individual merit. The **Baseball Team** (similar to sports teams) involves a very open system, with entry possible at all career levels, as well as high individual competition for internal staffing opportunities. This produces a higher degree of turnover and career paths that often span more than one organization. The **Club** (similar to a fraternity, sorority, or country club) involves low openness, with entry typically possible only at entry-level jobs and low competition for opportunities among individuals. Career advancement is determined by standard steps at defined intervals. The **Fortress** (where those inside compete primarily with those attempting to join from outside) has low competition among individuals for internal staffing opportunities but high openness to external staffing at all levels. This system often characterizes industries with shortages in some areas but with surpluses in others, due to rapidly changing market demands. Notice how

---

EXHIBIT 10.2   Four Models of Career Systems

Highly open	**Fortress**	**Baseball Team**

	Entry:
	    Passive recruitment
	    Applicant self-selection
	Development:
	    Retain core talent
	Exit: Frequent layoffs
	        Seniority-based
	Examples:
	    Continental Airlines
	    Hotels
	    Retailing
		Entry:
		    High activity level
		    Emphasizes credentials
		    Select at all career levels
		Development:
		    Informal training
		    Little career management
		Exit:
		    High turnover
		    Careers cross employers
		Examples:
		    Entertainment
		    Advertising
		    Law/consulting firms

Openness to external selection	**Club**	**Academy**

	Entry:
	    Early career
	    Emphasizes tenure
	Development:
	    Builds general skills
	    Slow career paths
	    Required steps
	    Emphasizes commitment
	Exit:
	    Low turnover
	    Retirement is common
	Examples:
	    Utilities
	    Banks
		Entry:
		    Strictly early career
		    Emphasizes growth potential
		Development:
		    Highly emphasized activity
		    Extensive job training
		    Tracking and sponsoring high-potenital
		        employees
		    Elaborate career paths
		Exit:
		    Low turnover
		    Retirement is common
		    Dismissals are common
		Examples:
		    IBM
		    Kodak
		    General Motors

Low openness	Low competition	High competition

Promotion Competition among Individuals

Source: Adapted from Jeffrey A. Sonnenfeld and Maury A. Peiperl, "Staffing Policy as a Strategic Response: A Typology of Career Systems" *Academy of Management Review* 13, no. 4 (1988), pp. 588–600.

EXHIBIT 10.3   How Internal Movement Fits the Staffing Process

---

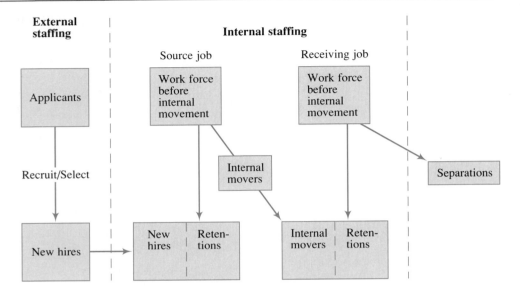

external selection, internal development, and exit are interrelated, depending on the conditions faced by the organization.

Another important and often-overlooked fact is that, when organizations move people between jobs, there are consequences not only for the jobs people move into but also for the jobs they move out of.[10] Exhibit 10.3 shows these relationships in a two-job system. The vertical dotted lines represent the organization boundary. The two boxes inside the lines represent two jobs within the organization, with the Source job providing employees to the Receiving job. The top set of boxes shows the situation prior to the employee movements, the bottom set of boxes shows the situation after the employee movements. The process begins on the right, with the Receiving job experiencing Separations of employees who leave the organization. The Receiving job's retained work force is smaller than before, so there are vacancies to be filled. These vacancies are filled with internal movers from the Source job, so, after the movements, the Receiving job's work force is a mix of Retentions and Internal movers. These internal movements have the same effect on Source job as separations, so the Source job work force is smaller than before. Source job vacancies are filled through external recruitment and selection, so, after the movements, the Source job's work force is a mix of Retentions and New hires. The relatively simple relationships shown here obviously become more complex with more than two jobs and when more than one job experiences external separations, or when many jobs can recruit and select from outside the organization. Research

---

EXHIBIT 10.4 Example Work Force Illustrating Internal Staffing Effects

---

Salesperson	Annual Sales	Years of Seniority	Minority	Predicted Managerial Performance (points)
Jeremy	$ 40,000	8	No	10
Rudolfo	40,000	8	No	6
Maggie	40,000	2	Yes	10
Manuel	40,000	6	Yes	8
Herbert	40,000	6	No	6
Karl	30,000	8	No	8
Donald	30,000	4	Yes	10
Lindsey	30,000	8	Yes	6
Ralph	30,000	6	No	10
Beuford	30,000	4	No	6
Arthur	20,000	8	No	10
Dorothy	20,000	2	Yes	4
James	20,000	6	No	8
Bertram	20,000	4	No	4
Jesse	20,000	4	Yes	4
Oliver	10,000	2	No	8
Anne	10,000	2	Yes	4
Enrique	10,000	2	Yes	6
Fred	10,000	6	No	8
Barney	10,000	4	No	4
Total	$500,000	100		
Average	$ 25,000	5		7

suggests that the combined effects of the retention and selection process can produce million-dollar effects, depending on how it is managed.[11] Because internal movement encompasses aspects of recruitment, selection, and separation/retention, its effects are more complex than simple selection or separation.

Internal Staffing Effects in Source and Destination Jobs

Let us expand the example from Chapter Nine to demonstrate how internal staffing affects the work force. Exhibit 10.4 depicts the same work force information contained in Exhibit 9.3. However, we have added a column of information—each employee's predicted performance as sales manager at this time. It is based on a scale of 2 to 10.

Suppose the organization has five sales manager vacancies and promotes solely on seniority, as is common in unionized situations. The firm would promote Jeremy, Rudolfo, Karl, Lindsey, and Arthur, producing an average predicted performance of 8 (out of a possible 10) points. It would achieve a 20 percent minority promotion rate (1 out of 5) and raise the minority representation rate among retained salespeople to 47 percent (7 out of 15). The 15 retained salespeople's annual sales performance would average $22,667, for a total of $340,000. Although this may seem equitable from a seniority perspective, high sales performers Maggie, Manuel, and Herbert may wonder whether it's worth working so hard or remaining with this organization if they have to wait up to six years to be promoted.

Now, suppose the organization promoted based on past performance, reasoning that high performers should be rewarded with higher status, more responsibility, and higher pay. Performance-based promotions would move Jeremy, Rudolfo, Maggie, Manuel, and Herbert up to sales manager, producing the same average predicted managerial performance level of 8. The minority promotion rate would be raised to 40 percent (i.e., 2 out of 5) and the original 40 percent representation rate among salespeople is maintained in the retained group (i.e., 6 out of 15 are minority-group members). However, the yearly sales level among the retained salespeople would drop to a total of $300,000 for an average of $20,000. This is far below the original average of $25,000. Moreover, as senior employees passed over for promotion, Lindsey and Arthur may wonder if they will ever get rewarded for their loyalty and long service.

Finally, suppose the organization promotes salespeople based on predicted performance as sales managers. This would promote Jeremy, Maggie, Donald, Ralph, and Arthur. They all have the highest predicted sales manager performance, so the average predicted performance rating of this promoted group is 10. This pattern achieves a 40 percent minority selection ratio (i.e., 2 out of 5 promoted employees are minority-group members), and it retains the 40 percent representation rate in the sales job (i.e., 6 out of 15 retained employees are minorities). However, such a promotion pattern still removes several high-performing salespeople, leaving a retained sales work force that produces yearly total sales of $340,000, an average of $22,667 per salesperson. Moreover, it promotes two low-tenure employees (Maggie and Donald) over others with up to eight years in the sales job. It also promotes lower performers Donald, Ralph, and Arthur over top-performing Rudolfo, Manuel, and Herbert. This may not seem very fair to the high-tenure and high-performing employees, especially if those promoted end up supervising them!

Clearly, internal staffing decisions produce broad consequences, and the effects on the sources of candidates are often different from the effects on destinations. These effects have implications for both efficiency and equity. This example used promotions, but the principles apply as well to lateral and downward transfers. In actual decisions, multiple destinations may compete for the best candidates and multiple sources may provide candidates. Actual decision implications also depend on the validity of the selection information—that is, how accurately the predicted managerial performance scores reflect eventual managerial performance and on the willingness of salespeople to accept promotion offers.

CAREER MANAGEMENT AND CAREER PLANNING

In external staffing, the organization may or may not be very concerned with the reactions and future employment behaviors of rejected applicants or separated employees. Though such people may affect the organization in the future (perhaps if they go to work for competitors), they are not part of the organization's work force. With internal staffing, however, all of the applicants—those chosen as well as those not chosen—remain with the organization, and the employees who separate from one position are employed somewhere else in the organization. The effects of internal staffing go well beyond those who are currently selected for internal movement opportunities.

Thus, internal staffing decisions must simultaneously consider both the employer's goals and the employees' goals. Careers develop through the interaction of individuals making choices that fit with their aspirations and through organizations providing opportunities that fit with organizational goals. This dual focus is reflected in the relationship between *career development, career planning,* and *career management.*

◆

Career development encompasses career management and career planning.

Career planning is the process through which individual employees identify and implement steps to attain career goals.

Career management is the process through which organizations select, assess, assign, and develop employees to provide a pool of qualified people to meet future needs.[12]

Exhibit 10.5 describes the different responsibilities of employees and employers in managing organizational careers. This exhibit focuses on career development once inside the organization; but career choices begin before employees join their first organization and continue as they move between organizations. The top portion illustrates how the employee, manager, and organization contribute to effective career planning, ensuring that careers match employee abilities and interests. The bottom portion illustrates how each contributes to effective career management—ensuring that internal staffing decisions assign individuals to roles that contribute to the organization's goals.

EXHIBIT 10.5 Integration between Career Planning and Career Management

---

Career Planning Activities

Employee's responsibilities:
- Self-assess abilities, interests, and values.
- Analyze career options.
- Decide on development objectives and needs.
- Communicate development preferences to manager.
- Map out mutually agreeable action plans with manager.
- Pursue agreed-on action plan.

Manager's responsibilities:
- Act as catalyst; sensitize employee to the development planning process.
- Assess realism of employee's expressed objectives and perceived development needs.
- Counsel employee and develop a mutually agreeable plan.
- Follow up and update employee's plans as appropriate.

Organization's responsibilities:
- Provide career-planning model, resources, counseling, and information needed for individualized career planning.
- Provide training in career development planning to managers and employees and career counseling to managers.
- Provide skills training programs and on-the-job development experience opportunities.

Career Management Activities

Employee's responsibilities:
- Provide accurate information to management as needed regarding skills, work experiences, interest, and career aspirations.

Manager's responsibilities:
- Validate information provided by employees.
- Provide information about vacant job positions for which the manager is responsible.
- Use all information provided by the process to: (1) identify all viable candidates for a vacant position and make a selection and (2) identify career development opportunities (job openings, training programs, rotation assignments) for employees and place them accordingly.

Organization's responsibilities:
- Provide information system and process to accommodate management's decision-making needs.
- Organize and update all information.
- Ensure effective usage of information by: (1) designing convenient methods for collecting, analyzing, interpreting, and using the information; and (2) monitoring and evaluating the effectiveness of the process.

Source: Frank J. Minor, "Computer Applications in Career Development Planning," in *Career Development in Organizations,* ed. Douglas T. Hall and Associates (San Francisco: Jossey-Bass, 1986), pp. 205–6.

CAREER PLANNING: EMPLOYEES FINDING AND PURSUING THEIR GOALS

Recall the opening case in which you chose which corner of the room you'd like to be in? That exercise illustrates the process of identifying the kinds of experiences you might find rewarding in a career. Researchers have identified two concepts to help understand the patterns of these career interests and how they may change over a person's lifetime—career orientation and career stages.

Career Orientation

Your career aspirations and interests form patterns, like those illustrated in Exhibit 10.1. People seem to be oriented toward certain kinds of competencies and experiences. These orientations reflect underlying motives and abilities formed before beginning work and during early work experiences. Research has suggested that these patterns can be organized into *career anchors*.

◆

A *career anchor* is a self-concept based on differing work motives and abilities. This self-concept guides, stabilizes, and integrates a person's work experiences.

People tend to pursue work roles that remain "anchored" around their self-concept, though like a ship at anchor they may move around the anchor as well. Changing to a new anchor would involve great effort and some fundamental rethinking of career motives. Five career anchors have been identified:[13]

1. *Technical/functional competence.* This anchor describes people whose primary orientation is the actual work they do and the wish to continue to use and develop their existing skills. They prefer to avoid positions that remove them from areas of established competence or that push them into general management, preferring growth through increasing skill, rather than increasing organizational level. A good example would be an engineer who wishes to pursue microchip design and has no wish to supervise others.

2. *Managerial competence.* This anchor describes people whose primary orientation is to develop managerial abilities of interpersonal competence, analytical competence, and emotional competence required at high levels of management. Aspirations to manage have been found to be strongly related to managerial career anchors and with specific activities, such as developing career contacts, developing organizationally specific skills, and accommodating boss's expectations.[14]

Perhaps because these studies were carried out on business school graduates, these two anchors occurred most. Even here, however, three other anchors emerged:

3. *Security.* An orientation toward working for a particular organization or in a specific geographic area.

4. *Creativity.* An orientation toward creating something that is entirely their own—whether it be a product, a company, a work of art, or a personal fortune.

5. *Autonomy/independence.* An orientation to avoid working under the constraints of organization life, with many of these people leaving to become consultants or start their own businesses.

Understanding the career orientations of individuals can make it easier to understand the kinds of internal staffing opportunities that will appeal to them. It can also help individuals better evaluate potential career paths.

Career Stages

We can also understand how individual career interests evolve by comparing career development to the biological and psychological model of birth, growth, development, and decline. The developmental phases are called *career stages.*

Career stages are phases of development that reflect the length of a person's work experience, as well as his or her stage of development as an adult. Research has suggested four career stages: (1) *exploration,* (2) *establishment,* (3) *maintenance,* and (4) *decline.*[15]

Exhibit 10.6 shows the four career stages. The top of the exhibit shows a curve depicting the relative level of involvement and influence associated with each career stage; the table below shows the activities, relationships, roles, and usual ages associated with each career stage.

Exploration
The young adult in the exploration stage is exploring activities, trying out different work roles, clarifying interests and skills, building skills through education and training, and reducing dependence on family and school. For college students, internships with companies can help crystalize career interests.[16] Such factors as the level and type of education, early career experiences, and even father's occupation may relate to ultimate career choices and success.[17] This searching usually results in seeking permanent employment, which leads to the establishment stage.

Establishment
Here, the individual successfully negotiates the permanent employment recruiting process, accepts a job, and becomes oriented to the chosen organization. Individuals learn their own capabilities, as well as those of the organization and co-workers, through exchanges of information about performance and feedback.

EXHIBIT 10.6 Career Stages

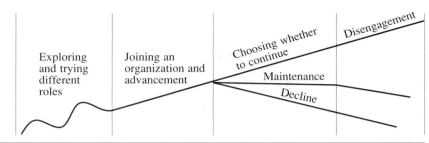

Issues / Stages	Exploration	Establishment	Maintenance	Decline
Central activity	Helping Learning Following	Being one's own person Independent contributor	Trainer and developer Resource allocator Shaping organization direction	Withdrawal
Relationships	Apprentice	Colleague	Mentor/Sponsor	Functionary advisory
Roles	Dependence	Independence	Assume responsibility for others Exercising power	Diminished power/role importance
Usual age	16–25	20–35	35–55	50–75

Maintenance

The individual becomes an important member of the organization, receiving assignments of a more vital nature. The organization draws on the individual's accumulated knowledge and experience, and the individual may serve as a mentor for newer employees. This is also the time when major changes in family, financial obligations, and recognized limits may precipitate a reevaluation of career choices. Many individuals at this stage choose to allow their current career to decline and cycle back to the exploration stage.

Decline

Researchers sometimes characterize the latter years of a career as a time of declining involvement and influence at work. Preparation for retirement may involve a psychological withdrawal from the organization long before any physical separation occurs. Reduced roles with less responsibilities may be assigned, as discussed later, and personal/work relationships may be adjusted according to their value to the individual and the amount of effort the individual is willing to expend on maintaining them.

Implications for Career Development

Understanding that individual career aspirations and interests will change and differ according to certain patterns, and, according to their career stage, can help individuals and managers understand what kinds of opportunities and assistance will be most effective in supporting individual career planning. For example, it suggests that matching career counseling information to the career anchor and the career stage of an individual can maximize the chance that it will effectively help the individuals plan their next move. These concepts can also help with career management, as the organization attempts to recruit, select, and retain promising candidates for internal movement opportunities. It may do little good for an organization to construct career opportunities that reflect a managerial career anchor and expect effort commensurate with the establishment career stage, if the pool of internal candidates generally has a technical/functional orientation and is still in the exploration stage of their careers. At McDonnell-Douglas Space Systems, the company gives managers and potential managers different kinds of "career rotation" through different jobs, depending on their career stage: rotation across units for those in the exploration stage, rotation across functions for those in the establishment stage, and rotation through upper-level corporate positions for those in the maintenance stage.[18]

McDonnell-Douglas hopes that, by reflecting individual career planning needs in its career system, it will improve the effectiveness of organizational career management activities that are designed to provide a pool of qualified people to meet future needs. This brings us to the other side of career development—the organization's attempts to manage careers through internal recruitment, selection, and retention.

RECRUITMENT IN CAREER MANAGEMENT

Just as in external staffing, candidates for internal movements must be identified and attracted to apply for employment opportunities. However, because internal staffing focuses on existing employees, the attraction/identification process is ongoing, with two-way communication throughout the individual's employment. Organizations can emphasize alerting employees to employment opportunities in hopes that they will pursue them, or the organization can keep records of employee characteristics and use these to identify promising candidates who are invited to apply. Combinations of these two approaches are also possible. Among the most prevalent methods of alerting employees to job openings is *job posting*. Among the most prevalent methods of recording employee characteristics and identifying promising candidates are *skill inventories* and *replacement/succession planning*. Finally, organizations must consider who nominates employees for internal staffing opportunities—employees themselves or their supervisors.

Job Posting

In the job-posting system, the organization notifies its present employees of openings, using bulletin boards and company publications. Employees who respond to these announcements are considered for the position.

Each week Bank of America, for example, publishes a job opportunities bulletin resembling the help-wanted section of a newspaper. The bulletin publishes various job openings with brief descriptions of the work involved and the qualifications required. Additionally, it lists salaries, grades, and the departments, subsidiaries, or branches offering the jobs. Copies are placed in staff lounges, hallways, and other points frequented by employees. On the back of the bulletin is an application form. Interested employees fill out forms and mail them to a coordinator to be considered.

Companies have widely adopted such systems. Most use them for office, clerical, administrative, and technical positions.[19] One reason for the popularity is the implicit openness of the system, enabling all employees, including EEO-protected groups, to nominate themselves for positions for which they consider themselves qualified. Posting is also a valuable tool incorporated in many affirmative action programs and consent decrees.

A useful set of guidelines for effective job-posting systems includes:

- Post all permanent promotion and transfer opportunities.
- Post the jobs for at least one week prior to recruiting outside the organization.
- Clarify eligibility rules. For example, specify minimum service in the present position; state decision rules used to choose between several equally qualified applicants, if such rules will be used.
- List job specifications. Make application forms available.
- Tell all applicants how the job was filled.[20]

How common is job posting? A recent survey found that, over all positions, 47 percent of respondents post listings for in-house applicants. Organizations were most likely to post lower-salaried positions (such as staff accountant and human resources specialists) than high-salary positions (such as general manager and senior financial officer).[21]

Skills Inventories

Skills inventories are lists of employees and their characteristics relevant to internal employment opportunities. Thus, skills inventories represent an ongoing method through which human resource managers learn about available internal employment candidates. As with any information system, the data in such skills inventories must be tailored to organizational needs. Some commonly included items are: name, employee number, present location, birthdate, employment date, current job code, prior experience, work experience with the organization, training completed, skill and knowledge ratings, education degree and major field, foreign languages spoken or written, health, professional qualifications, publications, patents, licenses, salary, and supervisory ratings of capabilities and promotability. Such inventories may also include employees' statements of career goals, geographical preferences, or anticipated retirement dates.

Skill inventories are a key tool in human resource planning, as discussed in Chapter Five. They can help managers anticipate shortages and surpluses of skills relevant to future anticipated skills needs. They become internal staffing tools when a shortage or vacancy is identified and when the organization begins to search for employees with appropriate skills to fill it.

Examples of Skills Inventories

IBM's system contains information on such data as career plans and educational goals for over 100,000 of its employees. This system allows IBM to project five-year engineering and other personnel needs for various rates of corporate growth. A monthly personnel transaction report for all divisions pinpoints possible imbalances within the total organizational system. The RCA Service Company uses its skills inventories to help management define which businesses it could be in.[22]

The U.S. Civil Service Commission has a skills inventory for all individuals above GS-14 (middle management)—about 25,000 executives. This database allows the U.S. government to examine age distributions by such factors as occupation, educational attainment, mobility, and reasons for entering and leaving, and to make these data available in a usable form for analysis. There are several uses of such a system:

> A carefully prepared skills inventory can be used as a basis for long-range personnel planning and development by providing precise definitions of the aptitudes and abilities available and needed by the organization. It can be used to assist in the evaluation of growth potential of the present executive work force and help to identify group strengths and weaknesses for future recruiting strategies. It may uncover interdivisional imbalances (e.g., understaffing), which could lead to future overall corporate personnel problems. Most importantly, it will serve as a motivating device by demonstrating through written feedback that the organization has a systematic approach to personal data utilization and that it is eager to develop each employee to full potential.[23]

Replacement and Succession Planning

Replacement planning involves having senior executives periodically review their top executives and those in the next-lower echelon to determine two or three backups for each senior slot. They sometimes call these *truck lists,* because they list replacements in case any executive is hit by a truck.[24] Succession planning not only focuses on those who might be candidates for current positions but also attempts to plan for possible changes in those positions, as well as the promotion and development needs of subordinates.[25]

EXHIBIT 10.7   Replacement Charts

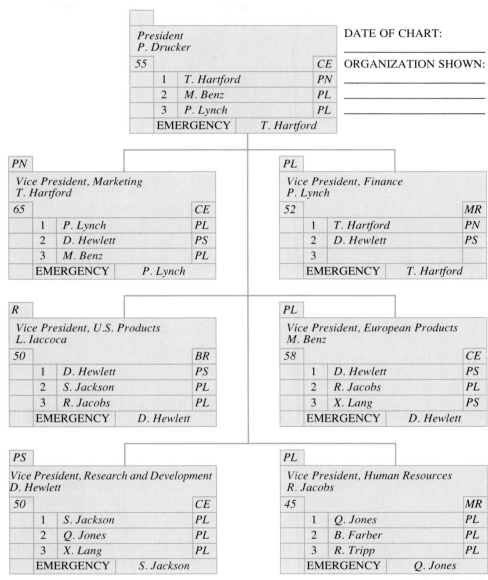

President P. Drucker			
55			CE
	1	T. Hartford	PN
	2	M. Benz	PL
	3	P. Lynch	PL
EMERGENCY		T. Hartford	

DATE OF CHART:
_____

ORGANIZATION SHOWN:
_____
_____
_____

PN

Vice President, Marketing T. Hartford			
65			CE
	1	P. Lynch	PL
	2	D. Hewlett	PS
	3	M. Benz	PL
EMERGENCY		P. Lynch	

PL

Vice President, Finance P. Lynch			
52			MR
	1	T. Hartford	PN
	2	D. Hewlett	PS
	3		
EMERGENCY		T. Hartford	

R

Vice President, U.S. Products L. Iaccoca			
50			BR
	1	D. Hewlett	PS
	2	S. Jackson	PL
	3	R. Jacobs	PL
EMERGENCY		D. Hewlett	

PL

Vice President, European Products M. Benz			
58			CE
	1	D. Hewlett	PS
	2	R. Jacobs	PL
	3	X. Lang	PS
EMERGENCY		D. Hewlett	

PS

Vice President, Research and Development D. Hewlett			
50			CE
	1	S. Jackson	PL
	2	Q. Jones	PL
	3	X. Lang	PL
EMERGENCY		S. Jackson	

PL

Vice President, Human Resources R. Jacobs			
45			MR
	1	Q. Jones	PL
	2	B. Farber	PL
	3	R. Tripp	PL
EMERGENCY		Q. Jones	

(continued)

Like skills inventories, replacement and succession plans also serve as tools for human resource planning, as discussed in Chapter Five.

Typically, replacement planning uses charts like the one shown in Exhibit 10.7. Replacement charts can be paper-and-pencil forms, or they can be imple-

EXHIBIT 10.7 *(concluded)* Codes for Replacement Charts

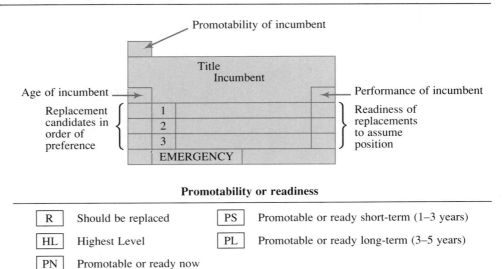

Promotability or readiness

R	Should be replaced	PS	Promotable or ready short-term (1–3 years)
HL	Highest Level	PL	Promotable or ready long-term (3–5 years)
PN	Promotable or ready now		

Performance

CE	Clearly exceeds requirements
MR	Meets requirements
BR	Below requirements

mented using computer programs. Based on organization charts, they provide a "snapshot" of the top key positions in the organization and show the availability of replacements from the current work force. Ratings of current performance, promotability, and readiness document judgments about employees' knowledge, skills, and abilities. This kind of formal record can improve decisions, compared to using only informal knowledge which may be less complete.

For example, in Exhibit 10.7, career planners might note that T. Hartford is a top candidate for both the vice president of finance job and the president's job, though she is 65 years old and may be considering retirement. They might also note that L. Iaccoca's promotability rating of "R" indicates that he may soon be replaced. If D. Hewlett replaces L. Iaccoca, all the candidates for promotion in Hewlett's job have promotability ratings of only "PL," meaning they need some development. It may be essential to develop at least one of these candidates very soon.

Replacement planning usually helps identify: the top 10–20 percent of managers, who are above standard and who can be promoted at a faster-than-average rate; the middle 60 to 80 percent, who should be developed through normal position growth; and the bottom 10 to 20 percent, who may not be qualified for present jobs and require some other personnel action.[26]

Several of the inherent shortcomings in replacement planning include:[27]

✦ There is little consideration of the actual requirements of the positions or of the prospective changes that occur in a job when a new person moves into it.

✦ Identification of backups or replacement candidates is largely subjective, based on personal knowledge of the nominating managers. There are rarely objective indicators of performance, individual capabilities, or past achievements.

✦ A high-potential candidate may be qualified for more than one management position, but he or she may be "boxed in" by the vertical line-oriented replacement planning or, alternatively, may be named as a backup for several positions, giving a false impression of management depth.

✦ The planning is fragmented and vertically oriented; rarely is there provision for lateral or diagonal moves across organizational units.

✦ There is rarely any input from the individuals themselves regarding their own self-assessments and career interests.

✦ Most significantly, the charts rarely result in the moves planned or in other developmental activities; the process is often a static, annual paperwork exercise.

Surveys of employment planning practices show that replacement and succession planning is widely practiced. Yet we know little about the payoffs from such practices. We do know of one case where a firm's succession plans from 10 years back did not include either the current CEO or the president. Several current vice presidents had received rather lukewarm evaluations. None of these employees were earmarked on previous plans as part of the future executive team.

The succession/replacement planning practices of 79 employers suggests that current practices tend to emphasize managers while often neglecting the nature of the work and the demand for employees.[28] Succession planning may also overemphasize identifying replacements at the expense of integrating learning experiences relevant to future positions.[29] This can occur through a lack of specific future position requirements, a tendency to select future managers who resemble current ones, underemphasizing learning versus development, insufficient follow-up to ensure learning activities take place, and too little candidate involvement.[30]

Nomination by Employees' Superiors and Mentors

Typically, one or more superiors of an employee plays a role in identifying and nominating the employee for internal job opportunities. The employee may not even know that the process is occurring, as when managers analyze skills inventories or succession plans. A second important supervisory role occurs because performance ratings are often a key factor in making internal staffing decisions, and it is usually the superior who makes these ratings.

Frequently, this nomination process becomes much more active, with managers serving as *mentors* for their subordinates, or protégés. A mentor serves as a kind of sponsor, using his or her influence and knowledge to support the protégé's development.

A *mentor* is a senior member of the profession or organization who provides support, coaching, feedback, acceptance, and friendship; who also creates opportunities for exposure, provides challenging and educational assignments, and serves as a role model and counselor.[31]

Mentor relationships usually evolve informally, but organizations can also encourage them.[32] Frito-Lay, Inc., added quarterly manager-subordinate development conferences to its performance assessment system.[33] Hawaiian Telephone Company has employees complete a workbook to help them identify their values, interests, and decision-making styles before meeting with their supervisors to discuss career possibilities.[34] Successful formal mentoring programs are characterized by top management support, careful selection of mentors and protégés, an extensive orientation program, clearly stated responsibilities for both the mentor and protégé, and established duration and frequency of contact between mentors and protégés.[35]

One danger of nomination by superiors, and of relying on mentoring relationships, is that they may be less effective for underrepresented groups, such as minorities and women. Factors contributing to ineffectiveness may include the lack of available mentors of the same sex or race, lack of access to information networks, perceived preferential treatment making mentors reluctant to associate with the person, stereotypes about women's or minorities' career preferences and performance, differences in socialization, and the danger of misperceptions about sexual intentions.[36]

Nomination by the Employees Themselves

Employees play a large role in identifying career opportunities and in nominating themselves for them. They can benefit from training in these processes.[37] Career development programs are available from consulting firms, and many organizations implement their own. At 3M Company, the department of career services includes a career information center, career services orientation, career growth workshop, individual counseling, supervisory development programs, and a career development library. All of these are available to employees during working hours.[38] At Dow Jones & Company, Inc., career planning assistance has evolved into the "Druthers Program." Employees write letters to their managers in the following format: "I'd druther do that than this." The letter outlines career objectives and preparation and serves as a starting point for career development activities. The letters are kept on file for current and future job openings.[39]

Increasingly, employees' decisions to nominate themselves for internal staffing opportunities reflect not only their own considerations but those of their spouse and family. These considerations are often called *dual-career considerations*. One study of families from 10 U.S. corporations suggests that employees' willingness to relocate was a key factor in their acceptance or rejection of internal staffing opportunities. The willingness to relocate, in turn, was affected by the number of children they had at home, the function in which they worked, their job involvement, and their general attitude toward moving. The wishes of a working spouse are also often critical to such decisions.[40] As the proportion of working women increases, it is likely that human resource managers will need to adopt specific policies designed to accommodate the dual-career aspirations of spouses and families, or risk having some promising candidates eliminate themselves from the internal promotion pool.

SELECTION IN CAREER MANAGEMENT

Just as in external selection, when there are more candidates than openings for an internal employment opportunity, information about the candidates must be used to determine who should receive the offer, and the value of this information depends on its validity. Moreover, internal selection decisions are subject to the same EEO legislation as external selection, so validity plays a part in justifying selection techniques that may exclude women or minorities. However, because internal selection focuses on existing employees, more information is available, and the information must be more carefully chosen because rejected candidates will continue to be employed.

Past Performance, Experience, and Seniority

What factors do you expect will influence your career advancement? Do you think that promotions should be solely a reward for good performance in the current job? Should promotions hinge on gaining certain "key" experiences that prepare you for future jobs? Or, should career advancement be a function of seniority, with those staying the longest getting preference when upper-level opportunities arise? Unions often stipulate that seniority, being the most objective and observable factor, plays a key role in internal staffing decisions.[41] Yet, evidence suggests that job seniority may not predict future performance and training times, as accurately as the similarity between past and future jobs and performance in past jobs.[42]

Although employees potentially always develop knowledge, skills, and personal characteristics as they progress through different work roles, organizations can capitalize on this process by creating specific sequences of experiences designed to prepare employees for future jobs. Exhibit 10.8 shows how a hypothetical sequence of jobs can allow individuals to build needed skills. In the middle of the exhibit is the career sequence, running from left to right. This career path begins with a foreman job that provides certain knowledge/skills, as shown in the top row. A foreman job's knowledge and skills might be related to the production process. The job also builds personal characteristics, as shown in the bottom of the exhibit. A foreman job might provide opportunities to use personal characteristics, such as commitment and loyalty. These attributes are carried with the individual when they move to Job 2, the production superintendent. Here, the individual might build skills in basic supervision, while using personal characteristics, such as responsibility for others. If the individual is successful, she or he can progress to assistant plant manager and, eventually, to plant manager.

At McDonnell-Douglas Space Systems, job rotation methods differ, depending on the type of manager being developed. Early in their careers, employees rotate among specialties within their discipline, to acquire skills in company procedures. For those in fiscal management, this might include accounting, overhead budgeting, and financial planning. Experienced employees below management rotate between operating units on a competitive basis, exploring options and mapping out five-year plans. Managers rotate for three-year stints outside their "home" division and functional discipline to provide the breadth of perspective needed for the highest level of management. As we will discuss later, organizations increasingly include "international" experience—working in foreign countries or with foreign markets—as an important element of career management. McDonnell Douglas personnel managers suggest that "yes" answers to the following questions help make a rotation system work:

1. Is the timing of rotation appropriate?
2. Will the program adapt to changing needs?
3. Are selection criteria well defined?
4. Are support systems, such as mentoring, adequate?
5. Are expectations made clear?
6. Are mentors and supervisors rewarded for career development activity?
7. Does development occur after rotation?[43]

The qualifications and background to be developed by past experience vary with the job and organization. Research suggests that among AT&T managers, those with college degrees advanced farthest.[44] Top executives from large U.S.

EXHIBIT 10.8 How Person-Work Interaction Builds Knowledge, Skills, and Personal Characteristics

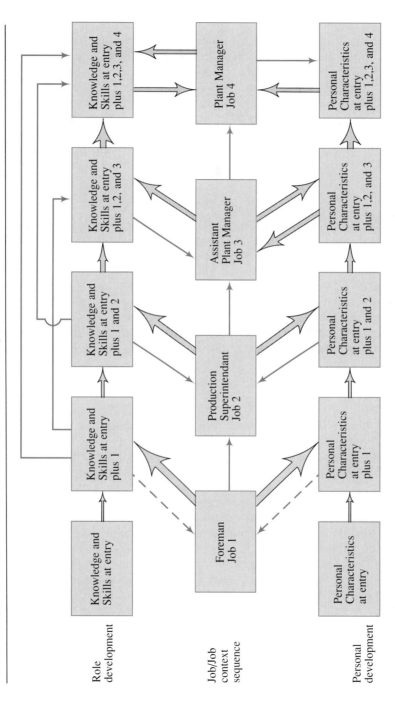

Adapted from Robert F. Morrison and Roger R. Hock, "Career Building: Learning from Cumulative Work Experience," in *Career Development in Organizations*, ed. Douglas T. Hall and Associates (San Francisco: Jossey-Bass, 1986), p. 241.

corporations indicated the following kinds of training or background as most important in their successors: sales and marketing (58 percent mentioned this), finance (40 percent), human resources (26 percent), legal (13 percent), data processing (12 percent), and general business (3 percent).[45] Of 93 human resource managers surveyed about their selection of first-line supervisors, over 50 percent mentioned the following factors: general competence, leadership ability, oral communication skills, human relations skills, initiative, decision-making ability, conscientiousness, written communication skills, and ability to control.[46]

Selection Procedures Used for Internal Staffing

Chapter Eight noted that reference/background checks and unstructured interviews are used most frequently for external selection. This pattern is even more pronounced with internal selection. One national survey of selection procedures used for promotion in the United States found that reference checks and unstructured interviews were used by about 60 percent of companies, structured interviews by about 25 percent of companies, and skills tests/work samples in 12 percent of companies for skilled employees, and in 37 percent of companies for office/clerical positions. Other procedures, such as weighted application blanks, ability tests, and personality tests, were used by less than 10 percent of companies.[47]

Assessment Centers

If you were selecting internal candidates, especially for supervisory/managerial jobs, it might seem logical to have them complete a work sample simulating the kinds of things that such jobs require. You might have them work on a typical set of letters, memos, notes, and statistical information from a manager's "in-basket." They could counsel a poor-performing subordinate, meet with an angry customer, analyze an organization's financial status, and compete for funds in a business meeting. With the recent emphasis on teams, you could also have them work with a team to accomplish a particular task. You might also interview the candidates. Finally, to improve accuracy and completeness, you might have all of these tasks observed by a team of assessors, who discuss and confer before giving their ratings.[48] This kind of selection procedure is called an *assessment center,* though it's not a location, but a set of selection tasks.

Less than 10 percent of companies reported using assessment centers for promotion in one national survey,[49] and 12 percent reported using such centers for *external* selection, especially for managers/supervisors.[50] Yet, because many of the largest U.S. organizations have used assessment centers, these have frequently been investigated and described by academics and professionals.[51] Assessment centers are usually more expensive than simpler selection procedures, but they have been shown to strongly associate with later promotions, with validity coefficients of about 0.40.[52] Even expensive assessment centers can pay off when applied to many hiring decisions, as Chapter Eight showed,[53] though it is not clear that assessment centers are actually better predictors than less-expensive alternatives.[54]

There is also some debate about why assessment centers really work, with the following explanations frequently suggested:

1. Assessment centers are good measures of the traits needed for success.

2. Those who make future promotion decisions know who did well on the assessment center; so such centers don't add any information, they just "crown the prince or princess."

3. Assessment centers just measure the factors the organization eventually uses to make promotions; so, they don't add any information beyond what would have been used anyway.

4. Being selected to participate in assessment centers, and doing well, gives managers a feeling of self-confidence that causes them to do well; so, the center's value is not for selection as much as for building attitudes and motivation.

5. Assessors simply react to the candidates' past performance, not the traits measured by the center.

6. Assessment centers measure candidates' intelligence.[55]

Assessment centers may also provide valuable training for the assessors themselves, by helping them better understand the traits and characteristics expected of successful managers. Assessors may go on to be better at appraising managerial performance or better at their own managerial tasks, or both.

Organizations also have a responsibility to those who participate in assessment centers and fail to achieve assessments justifying promotion to higher levels. Such individuals often can make valuable contributions, but the opportunity to make those contributions may be reduced if they are seen as "failures." The assessment center must be seen as one of many ways future potential is assessed, and there must be a commitment to providing opportunities for valued employees who may not be suitable for promotion.

SEPARATION/RETENTION IN CAREER MANAGEMENT

It's tempting to think about internal staffing solely in terms of its success in finding well-qualified candidates to move into new jobs. However, as Exhibit 10.3 showed, every time someone moves into a receiving job, they must move out of the source job. This causes changes in the employees who are retained in the source job, and these changes can have profound effects on the productivity and other characteristics of the organizations' work force.[56]

In one organization, "All salespeople hired off a campus are evaluated in terms of what kind of managers they will make," much to the "annoyance of those who wanted to create a professional sales force."[57] IBM's managers were concerned that redeployments to reduce IBM's work force in Burlington, Vermont, would leave the plant with only the poorest performers. Therefore, although other locations were encouraged to recruit and hire Burlington workers, the corporate policy included the "10–80–10" rule: managers could opt to retain workers in the top 10 percent, at least for six months; they could not transfer workers in the bottom 10 percent to other sites; and the middle 80 percent were fair game.[58]

Concern with the quality of the work force in source jobs, and the desire to retain employees in some jobs while still encouraging career movement, is at the heart of several important issues in career management, including plateaued careers, "dual-ladder" career progressions, "mommy-track" opportunities, and chief executive officer (CEO) succession.

Plateaued Careers

Role models and transfers are useful ways of developing young managers; a more compelling problem is maintaining the commitment and productivity of middle managers. These long-term employees, who have reached their highest career levels,[59] have "plateaued" and may stay that way for another 10 to 20 years. At IBM, for instance, 80 to 90 percent of the managers are long-term employees. At General Electric Company, the problem's dimensions are huge. Of 83,000 GE managers and professionals, more than 11,000 have been with the company more than 30 years, almost 26,000 have been there more than 20 years, and more than 48,000 for more than 10 years.

One study divided 30 engineering managers into two groups: those who were actively and enthusiastically involved in the organization and those who were passive.[60] The passive managers did not express extreme dissatisfaction, but they expressed no particular interest or enthusiasm for their jobs or the company. Both groups had 16 to 25 years of service with the employing organization. What accounted for the differences in motivation? The self-reports of what happened many years before suggest that the most important difference between the two groups was whether their early job assignments were connected to the mainstream of the company's activities. A sense of doing a task that is important to the company may carry through later career stages: early challenging positions boost confidence in ability to handle new hurdles.

The second factor affecting middle management motivation, according to this study, is openness and candor about a person's career prospects. Obviously, not everyone can be a general, no matter how good she or he is—there is a greater supply than demand. Supervisors can, though, provide clear and honest feedback about performance and prospects, however limited. When they do, employees are more likely to believe they have been fairly treated by the organization and maintain their commitment and productivity.

While further research is called for, it's clear that maintaining skills to avoid obsolescence, and maintaining motivation to produce, are two training issues that will only increase in importance as the U.S. work force ages.

Dual-Ladder Career Progressions

In many organizations, highly skilled engineers, programmers, scientists, or salespeople face a career dilemma. While they may be excellent performers in their skill area, and have a strong desire to grow within that area (a *technical/ functional* career anchor), the organization's career system has an "early ceiling" for such positions. Individuals can advance quickly within their technical skill, but they soon reach a point where further advancement requires taking on more supervisory or managerial tasks.[61] Not all engineers, for example, have the "aspiration to manage."[62]

The organization also faces a dilemma, because, by forcing its best technical people to leave their technical career in order to advance, it may find itself removing its top technical performers only to produce mediocre managers who really don't desire their managerial responsibility. The overall value of the work force may actually decline, due to a policy of promoting the "best" technical performer.

In an effort to retain technical experts in jobs that use their professional skills and still provide advancement and reward opportunities, such organization as IBM, Texas Instruments, Inc., Mobil Corporation, Union Carbide Corporation, and Westinghouse Electric Corporation have adopted "dual-ladder" or "two-track" career progressions.[63] Such a system establishes two parallel career progressions: one reflecting advancement through a managerial career and one reflecting advancement as a technical professional or staff member.[64] Movement up the managerial ladder means greater power and decision-making authority; movement up the technical ladder means greater autonomy in practicing the profession. Thus, they reflect the different career orientations of employees.

Exhibit 10.9 contains a diagram often used in recruitment information for technical/professional occupations. It demonstrates how technical/professional employees can choose to follow a management or a nonmanagement career ladder, and that movements between the two ladders are possible. The dual-ladder approach demonstrates how career management decisions account for both the employees' goals and the organization's goals. Though no formal studies exist, dual-ladder career paths are common in many large technically oriented organizations. With the declining number of college-age students producing fewer entry-level technicians, external staffing may not be able to fill future needs, and internal staffing through dual-ladder career paths may become more prevalent.

EXHIBIT 10.9   A Dual-Ladder Career System

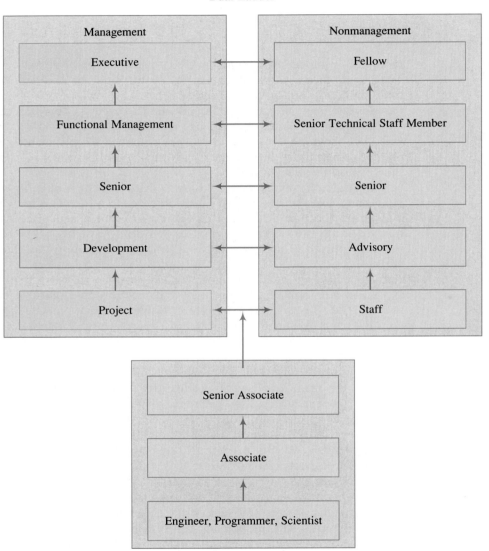

Is the "Mommy Track" an Opportunity or a Betrayal for Women Managers?

In 1989, an article by Felice Swartz, "Management Women and the New Facts of Life," appeared in the *Harvard Business Review*.[65] This article suggested that it may be more costly to employ women, especially as managers, because they separate more often, due to maternity and other dependent-care demands. It also suggested that corporations should provide more flexible arrangements, including options for different career positions, for women who want to combine career and family. For organizations, the dilemma is that, while women are often very high performers as managers, they may feel greater pressure to refuse career opportunities unless accommodations are made for their commitment to family. An "up or out" mentality, whereby all middle managers are expected to prove their full-time commitment to the company, may cause women to separate more often. Yet, providing special accommodations for family responsibilities, such as allowing a period of part-time work during child-rearing years, may seem discriminatory if applied only to women. Many men are also opting for a period of reduced career activity during childrearing years. Can employers afford the costs of allowing slower career advancement for some employees? Does stepping off the "fast track" necessarily mean employees can't ultimately catch up and advance to higher levels?[66]

The controversy over this issue will undoubtedly continue, but, in fact, many organizations, such as IBM, Mobil, and Du Pont, already have arrangements that allow greater flexibility in work hours and career progressions. Baxter International cut employee turnover to about 14 percent a year from about 24 percent after beefing up leadership training for women and promoting 4 of 21 women who took the course in one year. Mobil asked division managers to identify high-potential women and minorities, and it gave them training and on-the-job exposure, increasing the number of management and professional women from 17 percent in 1985 to 19 percent in 1989 with no increase in the overall number of managers. Yet, USX finds it "much tougher," to get women to accept transfer opportunities, and only 18% of Federal Express's transfers in 1988 were women.[67] It seems likely that men and women will not always fall neatly into mommy-trackers and fast-trackers, so dealing with these issues will require specific actions tailored to specific situations.

Chief Executive Officer (CEO) Succession

Many organizations have traditions or policies stipulating that top officers step down at a certain age, usually in their early 60s. If properly planned, this can be an advantage, because it opens up room for upward mobility, provides continuity, and brings in new ideas from below. If unplanned, or if CEOs are unwilling to relinquish their positions when they should, it becomes much more difficult to manage this separation process. It is often difficult to remove a CEO

EXHIBIT 10.10 Career Mobility of 71 Japanese Executives Staying over 13 Years

---

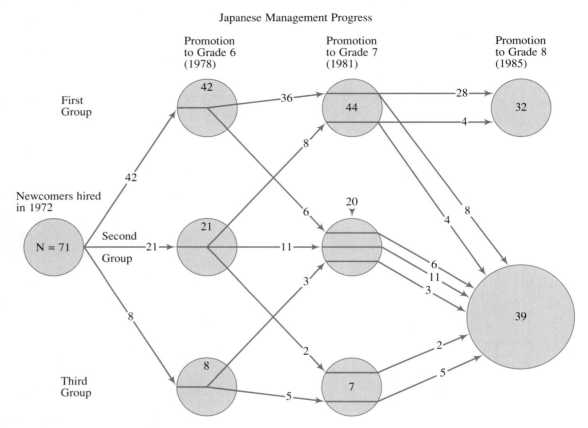

Japanese Management Progress

Source: Reprinted from "Japanese Management Progress: Mobility into Middle Management," by Mitsuru Wakabayashi, George Graen, Michael Graen, and Martin Graen, 1988, *Journal of Applied Psychology* 73, p. 221. Copyright 1988 by the American Psychological Association. Reprinted by permission.

if she or he doesn't want to go, because she or he is the top corporate officer and there are few in a position to encourage them to leave. Difficulties that must be overcome include: (1) the *denial of death,* or reluctance to accept the end of a successful career; (2) *loss of control* may hamper an executive's ability to allow successors to take over critical duties; (3) *fear of reprisal* from those not chosen as successors may make a CEO reluctant to decide who among his or her subordinates should succeed to the position; and (4) *romancing the past* by inflating memories of past accomplishments, thus making it difficult for the successor to institute needed changes and improvements.[68] Though mandatory retirement ages for CEOs are prohibited by the Age Discrimination in Employment Act, many organizations often promote an informal understanding among top executives that the CEO is expected to step down when he or she reaches a certain age, such as 65.

INTERNATIONAL PERSPECTIVES ON INTERNAL STAFFING AND CAREERS
Japanese Management Career Paths

Large Japanese corporations are widely known for their commitment to long-term employment and attention to career growth. "Those who succeed stay with the mother company and can look forward to the status, challenge, influence, and the material and social rewards bestowed on the most valued contributors to the corporation. The others can anticipate a comfortable position for a short time, and an early retirement."[69] How do Japanese companies accomplish this internal movement? Two competing views have been proposed. One holds that Japanese companies, like American Companies, emphasize characteristics of new hires and early career experiences. Those who succeed in the first three years have clear advantages in subsequent career competitions.[70] Others have argued that, in Japanese firms, young college graduates may be treated similarly for the first seven years, undergoing job rotation through tasks designed to build their skills. The more competitive and challenging career decisions are made after the initial seven-year period.

A study that followed 85 male college graduates in a leading Japanese corporation suggests that the three-year model is supported, with early career factors affecting both early and the late career success. Exhibit 10.10 shows the career progression of the 71 Japanese college graduates who stayed with the organization for 13 years. Notice how the managers were separated into three distinct groups, shown vertically, with the first, second, and third groups signifying the order in which managers received promotions. The three promotion grades and their timing are shown horizontally, with the second and third groups combined in the big circle under 1985. As the diagram shows, the groups are formed within the first six years, and there is very little movement between them. Twenty-eight of the 42 managers in the first group in 1978 made it to grade 8 by 1985, while only 4 of the 21 managers in the second group and none of the 8 managers in the third group progressed to this level.

Further research in this organization suggests that the degree of leader-member exchange (such as supervisor approachability, willingness to help newcomers, and clear leader expectations) has an important effect on career success at all stages. Moreover, it appears this corporation maintains a carefully planned career system, emphasizing developmental job experiences and established methods of assessing career development.[71]

International Management Assignments

Organizations increasingly foresee greater needs for an international perspective among their top managers. Dow Chemical is setting up a worldwide panel of senior executives to determine what the CEO of the 21st century will be like. Douglas Danforth, former chairman of Westinghouse Electric Company, advises future CEOs to "meet with the prime minister, the ministers of trade and commerce. Meet with the king of Spain and the chancellor of West Germany. Get yourself known."[72] With increasing business opportunities in Western and Eastern Europe, this trend seems likely to accelerate.

Yet, U.S. organizations do not seem to do a good job of choosing candidates for international assignments. It has been estimated that between 20 and 50 percent of those sent abroad return prematurely from their overseas assignment, at an average cost of between $55,000 and $150,000.[73] Though such factors as ability to deal with alienation, realistic expectations, nonverbal communication skills, and tolerance for ambiguity have been related to success and productivity overseas, U.S. firms seem to emphasize only the technical competence of candidates.[74] To improve the success of expatriate placements, organizations should focus on a broader set of selection factors, assist the candidate's spouse and family with the transition, make international assignments clearly fit a long-term strategic plan, improve training programs, and link expatriate assignments to the individual's specific career plan.[75]

EVALUATING INTERNAL STAFFING AND CAREERS

Because internal staffing combines recruitment, selection, and separation/retention activities, it has broad implications for achieving organizational efficiency and equity goals. Both external and internal staffing affect the composition of the work force. But, internal staffing draws from different candidate pools, may use different selection information, and moves employees simultaneously into some positions and out of others.

Efficiency

Unfortunately, just as external staffing activities are often evaluated using deficient measures, such as vacancies filled, movement percentages, or program costs alone, internal staffing activities are also often evaluated deficiently and unsystematically. In fact, very little research has addressed the impact of internal staffing on organizational performance.[76] One survey of 217 companies found that none analyzed whether the performance ratings used for promotions validly predicted future performance.[77] Another survey of supervisory selection found that only 20 out of 93 respondents validated their internal selection methods.[78] Still, internal staffing has important implications for the productivity and costs of the organization, as Exhibit 10.4 demonstrated.

Costs

Internal staffing can involve job posting, computerized skill inventories, employee career counseling/training, and succession planning. All of these activities incur costs of administration, materials, and employee and managerial time. Relocation expenses have been estimated at $37,000 per move for a home owner and $10,000 for a renter.[79] Assessment center costs may include thousands in start-up activities plus a substantial cost for each person assessed.[80] But, the costs of internal staffing are often small, compared to the effects on future employee productivity.

Productivity

While organizations seldom fully evaluate whether their internal staffing activities produce a high return on investment, it is quite possible to estimate the value of internal movements using the framework shown in Exhibits 10.3 and 10.4 A computer simulation based on these principles suggested that internal staffing could have million-dollar effects on work force value when it involves large numbers of employees staying with the organization for many years. An interesting finding was that it is just as important to monitor the effects of internal movements on the positions that serve as sources of candidates as it is to monitor whether it produces good candidates in the *destination* positions.[81] Clearly, organizations that evaluate internal staffing according to whether they can fill their vacancies, or even by the quality of those who move into new positions, may be missing vitally important opportunities to achieve efficiency.

Equity

Like external staffing activities, internal staffing is subject to specific rules and guidelines regarding equal employment opportunity and affirmative action. Government agencies and courts monitor internal staffing processes to ensure that protected groups are not adversely affected and that internal staffing procedures that do seem to exclude them are job-related. Unions are also deeply concerned with internal staffing policies, with labor contracts frequently stipulating very specific internal movement patterns and relationships among jobs, especially for blue-collar workers.

The importance of internal staffing takes on increased significance, because of the changing nature of the work force. With the proportion of white males in the work force expected to decrease during the 1990s, most organizations will experience a drastic change in the makeup of their work force. Many organizations have implemented procedures to increase awareness of cultural diversity among their top executives and to increase the diversity of backgrounds in those holding the top positions. The objective is to break what is perceived as a "*glass ceiling,*" where females and minorities are successfully hired but may remain stuck near entry levels.[82] This situation is especially troubling when it cannot be explained by differences in female qualifications or performance.

Mobil Oil Corporation questioned managerial and professional employees and interviewed 400 departed employees and 100 spouses of current employees, finding that a woman's age may affect the career support she requires. Among Mobil's women executives between 35 and 45, less than half were married and 90 percent had no children. However, high-potential women *under 35* often left to start a family. US West, Inc., a Denver-based communications company, began a development program for "women of color" in 1987 after finding that one of every 21 white males reached middle management or higher positions but only one of 138 white women and just one of 289 nonwhite women attained such heights.[83] Xerox established a career-support network for its minority and female employees similar to the traditional "old-boy" network for white males.[84] Evidence suggests that women are still less favored for international postings, and that stereotypes about blacks and females can influence internal movement decisions.[85] Increasing the opportunities for minorities and females will undoubtedly be one of the more important challenges to internal staffing systems.

SUMMARY

Internal staffing determines how existing employees move between employment opportunities inside the organization. Because every internal staffing decision involves both a selection and a separation, managing internal staffing requires a broad focus and attention to effects beyond the job being filled. Because both the selected and the rejected applicants remain with the organization, internal staffing must also pay careful attention to employee perceptions of the fairness and logic of its internal staffing policies. We have seen that internal staffing can provide a powerful tool for enhancing both efficiency and equity or be a powerful force against these goals if not managed properly.

We have also seen, however, that internal staffing does not operate in a vacuum. Its proper management requires that it be integrated with other HR activities, such as compensation, job design, and employee relations. One of the most important integrations is between the internal staffing designed to identify and move promising candidates and the training activities designed to prepare them for their current and future positions. We discuss training in the next chapter.

DISCUSSION AND REVIEW QUESTIONS

1. How does internal staffing integrate the processes of recruitment, selection, and separation/retention? How is it different from external staffing?
2. Is it always best to promote the highest performers? Which other factors should be considered? Why must internal staffing activities be especially attuned to employee equity perceptions?

3. Distinguish between career development, career management, and career planning. How can the notions of career orientation and career stages assist employees and employers in carrying out their responsibilities in these activities?

4. How are internal recruiting activities similar to external recruiting? How could you judge the effectiveness of a job posting, skills inventory, or succession planning system? Could you use the same evaluation methods as used for external recruiting? Why or why not?

5. How does internal staffing affect internal employee separations/retentions? Why is this effect often overlooked? Could this effect ever offset what appears to be a valuable selection process, or is the effect of internal movements on the retained work force probably not very important?

6. What is a career anchor? How important is this concept in developing an internal staffing strategy? Should career stage be used to determine which employees will be offered new opportunities? What factors are important in this decision from an organization's viewpoint?

7. Under what circumstances should past performance, experience, and seniority be used to determine career advancement? Is one more important than the others? Give examples.

8. Discuss the use of job rotation and its possible value to both employer and employee. What criteria determine whether it will be worth the effort and expense to implement system?

9. Discuss dual-ladder career progressions and the mommy track. Why have they been introduced and are they producing the desired affects? Give examples.

10. What is a glass ceiling? What are its effects and how can the ceiling be broken?

◆

YOUR TURN
BREAKING THE GLASS CEILING AT CORNING GLASS WORKS

Corning Glass Works is known as a good employer, with many progressive programs, including competitive benefits, child care, and flexible-time schedules. So, why can't the company retain its female and black managers? Chairman James R. Houghton challenged his executives to figure this out and correct it, saying, "We do a good job at hiring but a lousy job at retention and promotion. And it's not good enough just to bring them through the front door." While just 1 in 14 white male professionals left the concern each year between 1980 and 1987, about 1 in 6 black professionals departed, as did 1 in 7 female professionals. Asked in company exit interviews why they had resigned, most women and blacks cited "lack of career opportunities." Corning's manufacturing activities range from space-age ceramic components to housewares to collector-quality glass. Most of its operations are located in or around its headquarters in Corning, New York, a rural town with so few minorities living locally that Corning attracted a black hairdresser to town at the request of black managers who said they were driving an hour or more to Ithaca or Rochester for a haircut.[86]

Imagine you are a top personnel executive at Corning. How will you help Corning respond to the chairman's challenge? What are the potential biases or cultural histories that may be causing the shortage of female and minority top managers? What kind of internal staffing policies could improve their attractiveness for upper-level positions? How can ingrained biases and ignorance be attacked? How would you convince line managers of the need to act? Finally, how would you measure your success?

NOTES AND REFERENCES

1. John L. Holland, *The Occupations Finder* (Palo Alto, Calif.: Consulting Psychologists Press, 1978); John L. Holland, *Professional Manual for the Self-Directed Search* (Palo Alto, Calif.: Consulting Psychologists Press, 1979); John L. Holland, *Making Vocational Choices,* 2nd ed. (Englewood Cliffs, N.J.: Prentice-Hall, 1985).

2. Michael B. Arthur, Douglas T. Hall, and Barbara S. Lawrence, "Generating New Directions in Career Theory: The Case for a Transdisciplinary Approach," chap. 1, *Handbook of Career Theory,* ed. Arthur, Hall, and Lawrence (New York: Cambridge University Press, 1989).

3. Richard Bode, "Moving People to Jobs: A Big Job in Itself," *Think* 53, no. 2 (International Business Machines Corporation, 1987), p. 30.

4. Work in America Institute, Inc., *The Continuous Learning/Employment Security Connection* (Scarsdale, N.Y.: Work in America Institute, 1986), as reported in *Human Resource Management News,* February 28, 1987, p. 2.

5. R. E. Hall, "The Importance of Lifetime Jobs in the U.S. Economy," *American Economic Review,* September 1982, pp. 716–24.

6. "Keeping a Lid on Moving Costs," *Human Resource Management News,* September 9, 1989, p. 4.

7. John W. Boudreau, "Utility Analysis: A New Perspective on Human Resource Management Decisions," in *ASPA Handbook of Personnel and Industrial Relations,* vol. 1, ed. Lee D. Dyer (Washington, D.C.: Bureau of National Affairs, 1988).

8. Douglas T. Hall and Associates, *Career Development in Organizations* (San Francisco: Jossey-Bass, 1986); "Self-Assessment Said to Be First Step in Employee Career Development Process," Bureau of National Affairs, *Employee Relations Weekly* 5, no. 18 (May 4, 1987), p. 547; Richard K. Broszeit, " 'If I Had My Druthers . . .' A Career Development Program," *Personnel Journal,* October 1986, pp. 84–90.

9. Bureau of National Affairs, *Recruiting and Selection Procedures,* Personnel Policies Forum Survey no. 146 (Washington, D.C.: BNA, May 1988).

10. J. E. Rosenbaum, *Career Mobility in a Corporate Hierarchy* (New York: Academic Press, 1984); Shelby Stewman and Suresh L. Konda, "Careers and Organizational Labor Markets: Demographic Models of Organizational Behavior," *American Journal of Sociology* 40 (1983), pp. 298–321; Victor H. Vroom and K. R. MacCrimmon, "Toward a Stochastic Model of Managerial Careers," *Administrative Science Quarterly* 13 (1968), pp. 26–46; George T. Milkovich and John C. Anderson, "Career Planning and Development Systems," in *Personnel Management,* ed. Kendrith M. Rowland and Gerald R. Ferris (Boston: Allyn & Bacon, 1982).

11. John W. Boudreau, "Utility Analysis Applied to Internal and External Employee Movement: An Integrated Theoretical Framework" (Working Paper, NYSSILR-Cornell University, 1988); John W. Boudreau, "Utility Analysis: A New Perspective on Human Resource Management Decisions"; John W. Boudreau, "Utility Analysis for

Human Resource Management Decisions," in *Handbook of Industrial and Organizational Psychology,* 2nd ed., ed. M. D. Dunnette (Chicago: Rand McNally, in press).

12. Douglas T. Hall and Associates, *Career Development in Organizations* (San Francisco: Jossey-Bass, 1986).

13. Edgar H. Schein, *Career Anchors: Discovering Your Real Values* (San Diego, Calif.: University Associates, 1985);   Edgar H. Schein, "A Critical Look at Current Career Development Theory and Research," in Douglas T. Hall and Associates, *Career Development in Organizations* (San Francisco: Jossey-Bass, 1986).

14. Sara L. Rynes, Pamela S. Tolbert, and Pamela G. Strausser, "Aspirations to Manage: A Comparison of Engineering Students and Working Engineers," *Journal of Vocational Behavior* 32 (1988), pp. 239–53.

15. John O. Crites, "A Comprehensive Model of Career Adjustment in Early Adulthood," *Journal of Vocational Behavior* 9 (1976), pp. 105–18;   Solomon Cytrynbaum and John O. Crites, "The Utility of Adult Development Theory in Understanding Career Adjustment Process," chap. 4, in Michael B. Arthur, Douglas T. Hall, and Barbara S. Lawrence, *Handbook of Career Theory* (1989).

16. M. Susan Taylor, "Effects of College Internships on Individual Participants," *Journal of Applied Psychology* 73, no. 3 (1988), pp. 393–401.

17. Joel E. Ross and Carab Unwalla, "Making It to the Top: A 30-Year Perspective," *Personnel,* April 1988, pp. 70–78.

18. "Grooming Managers through Rotation," *Human Resource Management News,* December 6, 1989, p. 3.

19. J. R. Garcia, "Job Posting for Professional Staff," *Personnel Journal,* March 1984, pp. 189–92;   G. A. Wallropp, "Job Posting for Nonexempt Employees: A Sample Program," *Personnel Journal,* October 1981, pp. 796–98.

20. Dave Dahl and Patrick Pinto, "Job Posting: An Industry Survey," *Personnel Journal,* January 1977, pp. 40–42.

21. American Management Associations, *Hiring Costs and Strategies: The AMA Report* (New York: American Management Associations, 1986).

22. William F. Glueck, *Personnel: A Diagnostic Approach* (Plano, Tex.: Business Publications, 1982).

23. Robert Smith, "Information Systems for More Effective Use of Executive Resources," *Personnel Journal,* June 1969, pp. 452–65.

24. Stewart D. Friedman, "Succession Systems in Large Corporations: Characteristics and Correlates of Performance," *Human Resource Management* 25, no. 2 (Summer 1986), pp. 191–213.

25. Douglas T. Hall, "Dilemmas in Linking Succession Planning to Individual Executive Learning," *Human Resource Management* 25, no. 2 (Summer 1986), pp. 235–65;   Gupta, "Matching Managers to Strategies."

26. Merck and Company, Inc., Rahway, N.J.: *HR Planning Portfolio,* 1984.

27. James W. Walker, *Human Resources Planning* (New York: McGraw-Hill, 1980).

28. J. Carnazza, *Succession/Replacement Planning: Programs & Practices* (New York: Center for Career Development, Columbia Business School, 1982), p. 5.

29. Friedman, "Succession Systems in Large Corporations."

30. Hall, "Dilemmas in Linking Succession Planning to Individual Executive Learning."

31. Kathy E. Kram, "Mentoring in the Workplace," *Career Development in Organizations,* ed. Douglas T. Hall et al.;   L. Phillips-Jones, *Mentors and Proteges* (New York: Arbor House, 1982);   Judy D. Olian, Stephen J. Carroll, Christina M. Giannantonio, and

Dena B. Feren, "What Do Proteges Look for in a Mentor? Results of Three Experimental Studies," *Journal of Vocational Behavior* 33 (1988), pp. 15–37.

32. David Jacoby, "Rewards Make the Mentor," *Personnel,* December 1989, pp. 10–14.

33. "Developing Management Talent Often Difficult," *Bureau of National Affairs Employee Relations Weekly* 4, no. 38 (September 29, 1986), p. 1197.

34. "Hawaiian Telephone Co. Career Program Encourages Employee Growth," *Bureau of National Affairs Employee Relations Weekly* 4, no. 44 (November 10, 1986), p. 1406.

35. Raymond A. Noe, "Women and Mentoring: A Review and Research Agenda," *Academy of Management Review* 13, no. 1 (1988), pp. 65–78.

36. Raymond A. Noe, "Women and Mentoring."

37. John D. Drumboltz, Richard T. Kinnier, Stephanie S. Rude, Dale S. Scherba, and Daniel A. Hamel, "Teaching a Rational Approach to Career Decision Making: Who Benefits Most?" *Journal of Vocational Behavior* 29, no. 1 (August 1986), pp. 1–6.

38. "Self-Assessment Said to Be First Step in Employee Career Development Process," *Bureau of National Affairs Employee Relations Weekly* 5, no. 18 (May 4, 1987), p. 54.

39. Richard K. Borszeit, " 'If I Had My Druthers . . .' A Career Development Program," *Personal Journal,* October 1986, pp. 84–90.

40. Jeanne M. Brett and Anne H. Reilly, "On the Road Again: Predicting the Job Transfer Decision," *Journal of Applied Psychology* 73, no. 4 (1988), pp. 614–20.

41. Bureau of National Affairs, *Basic Patterns in Union Contracts* (Washington, D.C.: Bureau of National Affairs, Inc., 1986); Craig A. Olson and Chris J. Berger, "The Relationship between Seniority, Ability, and the Promotion of Union and Nonunion Workers," *Advances in Industrial Relations,* vol. 1, ed. David B. Lipsky and J. M. Douglas (Greenwich, Conn.: JAI Press, 1983), pp. 91–129.

42. Michael E. Gordon and E. J. Fitzgibbons, "Empirical Test of the Validity of Seniority as a Factor in Staffing Decisions," *Journal of Applied Psychology* 67 (1982), pp. 311–19; Michael E. Gordon and W. A. Johnson, "Seniority: A Review of Its Legal and Scientific Standing," *Personnel Psychology* 35 (1974), pp. 255–80; Michael E. Gordon, John L. Cofer, and P. Michael McCullough, "Relationships among Seniority, Past Performance, Interjob Similarity, and Trainability," *Journal of Applied Psychology* 71, no. 3 (1986), pp. 518–21.

43. "Grooming Managers through Rotation," *Human Resource Management News,* December 16, 1989, p. 3.

44. Ann Howard, "College Experiences and Managerial Performance," *Journal of Applied Psychology* 71, no. 3 (1986), pp. 530–52.

45. Louis Harris and Associates, *Strategic Vision: A New Role for Corporate Leaders* (New York: Louis Harris and Associates, 1987).

46. "A Look at Company Supervisory Selection Systems," *Personnel* 65, no. 6 (1986), pp. 13–19.

47. Bureau of National Affairs, Inc., "Employee Selection Procedures," ASPA–BNA Survey no. 45, May 5, 1983.

48. Paul R. Sackett and Michael M. Harris, "A Further Examination of the Constructs Underlying Assessment Center Ratings," *Journal of Business and Psychology* 3, no. 2 (Winter 1988), pp. 214–29.

49. Bureau of National Affairs, "Employee Selection Procedures."

50. Bureau of National Affairs, *Recruiting and Selection Procedures,* Personnel Policies Forum Survey no. 146, May 1988.

51. William C. Byham, "Starting an Assessment Center the Correct Way," *Personnel Administrator,* February 1980, pp. 27–32; P. R. Sackett, "A Critical Look at Some Common Beliefs about Assessment Centers," *Public Personnel Management* 11, no. 1 (1982), pp. 140–47; Frederick D. Frank and James R. Preston, "The Validity of the Assessment Center Approach and Related Issues," *Personnel Administrator,* June 1982, p. 94; Milan Marovee, "A Cost-Effective Career Planning Program Requires Strategy," *Personnel Administrator,* January 1982, p. 30; Anthony J. Plento, *A Review of Assessment Center Research* (U.S. Office of Personnel Management, Washington, D. C., May 1980), p. 8; Stephen L. Cohen, "The Bottom Line on Assessment Center Technology: Results of a Cost-Benefit Analysis Survey," *Personnel Administrator,* February 1980, p. 57; Donald H. Bush and Lyle F. Schoenfeldt, "Identifying Managerial Potential: An Alternative to Assessment Centers," *Personnel* (AMACOM), May–June 1980, p. 69; Stephen L. Cohen, G. L. Hart and P. H. Thompson, "Assessment Centers: For Selection or Development—IBM Workshop Experience," *Organization Dynamics,* Spring 1979, p. 63; D. W. Bray and D. L. Grant, "The Assessment Center in the Measurement of Potential for Business Management," *Psychological Monographs* 80, whole no. 625 (1966).

52. Paul R. Sackett and George F. Dreher, "Constructs and Assessment Center Dimensions: Some Troubling Empirical Findings," *Journal of Applied Psychology* 67, no. 4 (1982), pp. 401–10; V. R. Boehm, "Assessment Centers and Management Development," in *Personnel Management,* ed. K. Rowland and G. R. Ferris (Boston: Allyn & Bacon, 1982); Janet J. Turnage and Paul M. Muchinsky, "A Comparison of the Predictive Validity of Assessment Center Evaluations versus Traditional Measures in Forecasting Supervisory Job Performance: Interpretive Implications of Criterion Distortion for the Assessment Paradigm," *Journal of Applied Psychology* 69, no. 4 (1984), pp. 595–602; George F. Dreher and Paul R. Sackett, *Perspectives on Employee Staffing and Selection* (Homewood, Ill.: Richard D. Irwin, 1983); John R. Hinrichs, "An Eight-Year Follow-Up of a Management Assessment Center," *Journal of Applied Psychology* 63 (1978), pp. 596–601; Paul R. Sackett, "Assessment Centers and Content Validity: Some Neglected Issues," *Personnel Psychology* 40 (1987), pp. 13–25; Manuel London and Stephen Stumpf, "Effects of Candidate Characteristics on Management Promotion Decisions: An Experimental Study," *Personnel Psychology* 36 (1983), pp. 241–59.

53. Wayne F. Cascio and Val Silbey, "Utility of the Assessment Center as a Selection Device," *Journal of Applied Psychology* 64 (1979), pp. 107–18.

54. John F. Hunter and Rhonda F. Hunter, "Validity and Utility of Alternative Predictors of Job Performance," *Psychological Bulletin* 96 (1984), pp. 72–98.

55. Richard Klimoski and Mary Brickner, "Why Do Assessment Centers Work? The Puzzle of Assessment Center Validity," *Personnel Psychology* 40 (1987), pp. 243–60.

56. John W. Boudreau, "Utility Analysis Applied to Internal and External Employee Movement: An Integrated Theoretical Framework" (Working Paper, NYSSILR–Cornell University, 1988); John W. Boudreau, "Utility Analysis: A New Perspective on Human Resource Management Decisions."

57. Rosabeth Moss Kanter, *Men and Women of the Corporation* (New York: Basic Books, 1977), p. 130.

58. D. Quinn Mills, *The IBM Lesson* (New York: Random House, 1988).

59. Jay W. Lorsch and Haruyo Takagi, "Keeping Managers Off the Shelf," *Harvard Business Review,* July–August, 1986, pp. 60–65.

60. Ibid.

61. Milkovich and Anderson, "Career Planning and Development Systems."

62. Sara L. Rynes, Pamela S. Tolbert, and Pamela G. Strausser, "Aspirations to Manage."

63. Laurie Michael Roth, *A Critical Examination of the Dual Ladder Approach to Career Advancement* (New York: Center for Research in Career Development, Columbia University, 1982); Lisa A. Mainiero and Paul J. Upham, "Repairing a Dual-Ladder CD Program," *Training and Development Journal* 40, no. 5 (May 1986), pp. 100–105; Joseph A. Raelin, "Two-Track Plans for One-Track Careers," *Personnel Journal,* January 1987, pp. 96–101; "Dual Career Paths in Sales," *The Conference Board's Management in Briefing: Human Resources* (New York: Conference Board, 1987).

64. H. G. Kaufman, *Obsolescence and Professional Career Development* (New York: AMACOM, 1974), p. 125.

65. Felice Swartz, "Management Women and the New Facts of Life," *Harvard Business Review,* January–February 1989, pp. 65–76.

66. Elizabeth Ehrlich, "The Mommy Track," *Business Week,* March 20, 1989, pp. 126–34; Elizabeth Ehrlich, "Is the Mommy Track a Blessing—Or a Betrayal," *Business Week,* May 15, 1989, pp. 98–99; Carol Hynowitz, "Stepping Off the Fast-Track," *The Wall Street Journal,* June 13, 1989, p. B1; Douglas T. Hall, "Moving beyond the 'Mommy Track': An Organization Change Approach," *Personnel,* December 1989, pp. 23–29; Victor Fuchs, "Mommy Track Is Good for Both Business and Families," *The Wall Street Journal,* March 13, 1989, p. A14; "'Mommies' Follow Many Different Tracks," *Human Resource Management News,* January 13, 1990, p. 1.

67. "Labor Letter," *The Wall Street Journal,* May 23, 1989, p. A1; Cathy Trost, "How One Bank Is Handling a 'Two Track' Career Plan," *The Wall Street Journal,* March 14, 1989, p. B1.

68. Manfred F. R. Kets De Vries, "The Dark Side of CEO Succession," *Harvard Business Review,* January–February, 1988, pp. 56–60.

69. Mitsuru Wakabayashi, George Graen, Michael Graen, and Martin Graen, "Japanese Management Progress: Mobility into Middle Management," *Journal of Applied Psychology* 73, no. 2 (1988), pp. 217–27.

70. J. E. Rosenbaum, "Tournament Mobility: Career Patterns in a Corporation," *Administrative Science Quarterly* 24 (1979), pp. 220–41.

71. Wakabayashi, Graen, Graen, and Graen, "Japanese Management Progress."

72. Amanda Bennett, "The Chief Executives in the Year 2000 Will Be Experienced Abroad," *The Wall Street Journal,* February 27, 1989, p. A1.

73. Mark E. Mendenhall, Edward Dunbar, and Gary R. Oddou, "Expatriate Selection, Training and Career-Pathing: A Review and Critique," *Human Resource Management,* 26, no. 3 (Fall 1987), pp. 331–45.

74. Mendenhall, Dunbar, and Oddou, "Expatriate Selection"; Rosalie L. Tung, "Selection and Training Procedures of U.S. European and Japanese Multinationals," *California Management Review* 25, no. 1 (1982), pp. 57–71.

75. Mendenhall, Dunbar, and Oddou, "Expatriate Selection"; "HR Should Do More, Survey Suggests," *Human Resource Management News,* January 13, 1990, p. 3; J. Stewart Black and Gregory K. Stephens, "The Influence of the Spouse on American Expatriate Adjustment and Intent to Stay in Pacific Rim Overseas Assignments," *Journal of Management* 15, no. 4 (1989), pp. 429–544; Madelyn R. Callahan, "Preparing the New Global Manager," *Training & Development Journal,* March 1989, pp. 29–32.

76. John W. Boudreau, "Utility Analysis Applied to Internal and External Employee Movement: An Integrated Theoretical Perspective"; Milkovich and Anderson, "Career Planning and Development Systems"; Jeffrey Pfeffer and Yinon Cohen, "Determinants of Internal Labor Markets in Organizations," *Administrative Science Quarterly* 29 (1984), pp. 550–72.

77. Robert I. Lazer, "The Discrimination Danger in Performance Appraisal," in *Contemporary Problems in Personnel,* ed. W. Clay Hammer and Frank L. Schmidt (Chicago: St. Clair Press, 1977).

78. "A Look at Company Supervisory Selection Systems."

79. "Keeping a Lid on Moving Costs," *Human Resource Management News,* September 9, 1989, p. 4.

80. Cascio and Silbey, "Utility of the Assessment Center as a Selection Device"; Wayne F. Cascio and Robert A. Ramos, "Development and Application of a New Method for Assessment Job Performance in Behavioral/Economic Terms," *Journal of Applied Psychology* 71 (1986), pp. 20–28.

81. Boudreau, "Utility Analysis Applied to Internal and External Employee Movement"; John W. Boudreau, "Utility Analysis: A New Perspective on Human Resource Management Decisions"; John W. Boudreau, "MOVUTIL: A Spreadsheet Program for Analyzing the Utility of Internal and External Employee Movement," (Working Paper, Cornell University, NYSSILR, 1986).

82. Leon E. Wynter and Jolie Solomon, "A New Push to Break the 'Glass Ceiling,'" *The Wall Street Journal,* November 15, 1989, p. B1.

83. Cathy Trost, "Firms Heed Women Employees' Needs," *The Wall Street Journal,* November 22, 1989, p. B1.

84. Wynter and Solomon, "A New Push to Break the 'Glass Ceiling.'"

85. Jolie Solomon, "Women, Minorities and Foreign Postings," *The Wall Street Journal,* June 2, 1989, p. B1; Madeline E. Heilman, Caryn J. Block, Richard F. Martell, and Michael C. Simon, "Has Anything Changed? Current Characterizations of Men, Women and Managers," *Journal of Applied Psychology* 74, no. 6 (1989), 935–42; Jeffrey H. Greenhaus, Saroj Parasuraman, and Wayne M. Wormley, "Effects of Race on Organizational Experiences, Job Performance Evaluations, and Career Outcomes," *Academy of Management Journal* 33, no. 1 (1990), pp. 64–86.

86. Carol Hymowitz, "One Firm's Bid to Keep Blacks, Women," *The Wall Street Journal,* February 16, 1989, p. B1.

Training, Orientation, and Development

Training and the Employee
Development Process

A Diagnostic Approach to Training

Assessing Training Needs
Organization Analysis
Job, Task, and Knowledge-Skill-Ability Analysis
Person Analysis
Comparison and Use of Needs
Assessment Methods

Identifying Training Objectives

Selection and Design of Training Programs
Establishing Supportive Conditions
for Learning
Choosing the Content of Training
Choosing Training Delivery Methods

International Perspectives on Training,
Orientation, and Development

Evaluating Training Outcomes
Evaluation Criteria
Efficiency: Costs
Efficiency: Benefits
Break-Even Analysis
Equity

Your Turn: Basic Skills Training
at Swift Textiles

Motorola, Inc., faced a critical dilemma. In 1982, its sales had been even with Texas Instruments, Inc., the world's largest maker of semiconductors. But in only five years its semiconductor sales had slipped to fourth place, and its other electronics products were under siege from innovative foreign competitors. While other companies might have turned to massive layoffs or plant closings, Motorola's chairman Robert W. Galvin and his successor George M. C. Fisher decided to bet that their employees could provide the necessary competitive edge. In 1984, Galvin mandated that at least 1.5 percent of each manager's payroll be devoted to training. By 1988, Motorola was spending $44 million annually, or roughly 2.4 percent of its payroll, on education—nearly twice as much as the average U.S. company. The aim was to sharpen the corporation's focus on "total customer satisfaction," says Fisher.[1]

Put yourself in the place of the top personnel executives at Motorola. Such a strong commitment to corporate education from the top officer is rare and valuable. It means you can probably design a companywide training strategy, get the resources and management support you need to implement it, and have a real impact on the organization's goals. However, it also means that you're probably going to be held accountable for showing that your strategy pays off by improving "total customer satisfaction." How would you design and implement such a strategy? How would you assess the organization's training needs? Is it possible some of the problems are not training issues at all but require interventions like staffing or compensation? How will you establish the right motivation among employees and tailor the training to their learning abilities? What areas of training will you pursue, and how will you choose them? Should everyone get similar training in "customer needs" or should training for different groups, such as managers and production workers, be different? Should the training groups comprise a mix of different kinds of employees or should they have similar jobs and organizational status? What training delivery methods would you use? Should you opt for modern high-tech methods, such as computer-based videodiscs, or stick with more traditional lecture and group discussion formats? Finally, and perhaps most important, how will you later show the CEO that the $44 million spent on training really paid off more than investing that money in new tools, plants, or technologies?

TRAINING AND THE EMPLOYEE DEVELOPMENT PROCESS

Eight hundred Motorola employees have full-time training duties, while 200 training vendors (outside suppliers) and 360 in-house subject-matter experts assist. Satellite television courses through the National Technological University

EXHIBIT 11.1   Dollars Budgeted for Formal Training by U.S. Organizations

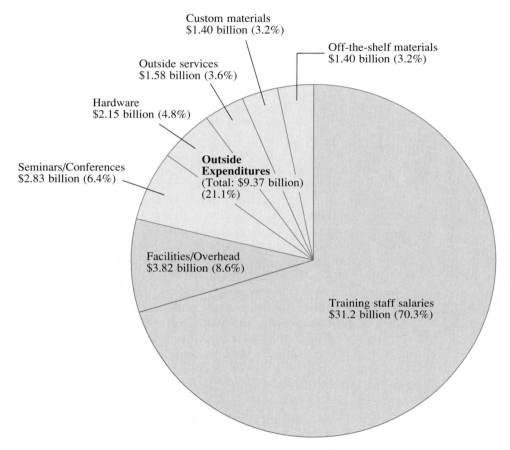

Custom materials
$1.40 billion (3.2%)

Off-the-shelf materials
$1.40 billion (3.2%)

Outside services
$1.58 billion (3.6%)

Hardware
$2.15 billion (4.8%)

Seminars/Conferences
$2.83 billion (6.4%)

Outside Expenditures
(Total: $9.37 billion)
(21.1%)

Facilities/Overhead
$3.82 billion (8.6%)

Training staff salaries
$31.2 billion (70.3%)

Total: $44.4 billion

allow Motorola as well as other employers to offer their students a master's degree in electrical engineering. Much of Motorola's training is tied to plant and office automation and to production process control techniques aimed at reducing product defects to practically zero. Motorola even trains workers for its key suppliers, many of whom lack the resources to supply training in such advanced specialties as computer-aided design and statistical defect control. Does all this training pay off? Motorola's head of training says, "We've documented the savings from the statistical process control methods and problem-solving methods we've trained our people in. We're running a rate of return of about 30 times the dollars invested—which is why we've gotten pretty good support from senior management."[2]

◆

Training is a systematic process of changing the behavior, knowledge, and motivation of present employees to improve the match between employee characteristics and employment requirements.

Companies now regard training as no less a part of their strategic investments than plants and equipment. It is seen as a vital component in building competitiveness.[3] An Ernst & Whinney survey of 300 midwestern manufacturers showed the top priority for the next five years will be employee training and motivation. "It's moved from virtually the bottom to clearly the top. . . . You don't dump technology on top of organizations whose employees aren't ready for it."[4] Training is clearly big business and getting bigger. Exhibit 11.1 shows that the total budgeted dollars for training in 1989 among U.S. organizations with more than 100 employees was $44.4 billion, a 12 percent increase over the 1988 figure. Notice that 70.3 percent of this expense went to pay training staff salaries, with the rest going toward materials, services, outside conferences, and overhead.

Training must be closely linked to other human resource activities. Employment planning can identify skill shortages, which can either be filled through staffing or by strengthening the skills of the current work force. Staffing can emphasize the trainability of those hired and promoted. Performance appraisal helps to identify gaps between desired and existing behaviors or outcomes, and these gaps often become the targets of training. Finally, motivating employees to acquire and use new skills often requires acknowledging this learning with pay and other rewards. Perhaps the closest link is between training and internal staffing. Career management often requires an integrated training strategy that prepares employees for future internal job opportunities, as does the program at New York Telephone.[5] Often, the first training experience employees have is their initial orientation to the organization. Moreover, employees generally report that most of their development occurs on the job, not in company-sponsored training programs.[6]

Yet, despite sizable budgets, good intentions, and real needs, many training programs fail to achieve lasting results. Too often, this is caused by vague training goals and poorly executed evaluation. If we don't know where we're going, it's impossible to tell if we ever get there. Many organizations spend millions on training and never know if it works, but techniques exist to link training to results.

EXHIBIT 11.2   Model of the Stages and Relationships in Training

---

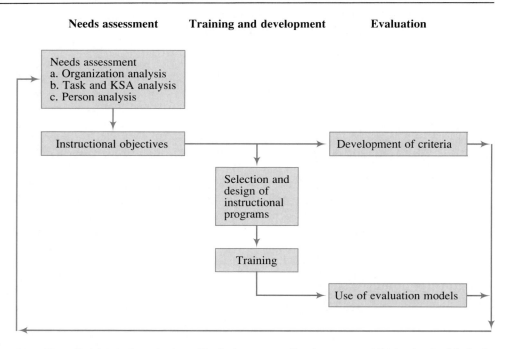

Note: From Training in Organizations: Needs Assessment, Development, and Evaluation (p. 16), by I. L. Goldstein, 1986. Pacific Grove, Calif.: Brooks-Cole Publishing Co. Copyright 1986 by Brooks-Cole. Reprinted by permission.

A DIAGNOSTIC APPROACH TO TRAINING

Exhibit 11.2 illustrates the three major stages in developing, implementing, and evaluating training activities. The needs assessment involves examining goals at the levels of the organization, the job/task/knowledge-skill-ability (KSA), and the person/individual. This process identifies gaps that become instructional objectives. In the training and development stage, the objectives are used to select and design the instructional program, and to deliver the training. Finally, the evaluation phase involves using criteria that reflect the objectives and evaluation models to determine whether the training achieved the original objectives. The results of this evaluation become the basis for a new needs assessment, and the process continues. A very similar model is used by IBM to organize its management system for its $900 million per year education system.[7]

Notice how closely this process matches the diagnostic model and the planning process discussed in Chapter Five. This is no accident. All of these processes should fit together to ensure that training and other human resource activities are integrated and aimed toward specific measurable goals. We'll now discuss each phase of the training model in turn.

ASSESSING TRAINING NEEDS

Have you ever been in a class where the instructor didn't set any specific goals, and no one seemed to know what they were trying to accomplish? If so, you know that it is quite possible to carry out training with no specific objectives, but you never know if it works. Needs assessment for training is a special case of the general process of setting objectives and evaluation standards as discussed in Chapter Five and illustrated in Exhibit 5.2. In fact, human resource planning objectives are the starting point for training needs analysis. Gaps between desired and actual organizational outcomes, unit achievements, employee performance levels, or other employee characteristics can become training objectives under two conditions: (1) they must be identified as important enough to merit organizational attention and (2) they must be addressable through training. Training is no panacea. Often, what at first appeared to be a training problem is better addressed through other activities. Sometimes, training is designed directly in response to a manager's request. More often, however, needs must be developed through the needs analysis process. Training needs can be identified at the organization, job/task/KSA or job-level, and the person/individual level.

Organization Analysis

Needs analysis at the organization level involves examining the organization's broad directions and needs to determine how training can fit in. The "learning organization" is heralded as a key to competitiveness, flexibility, and rising standards of living. While no consensus exists on the precise meaning of *learning organization,* many agree that such an organization will thrive on uncertainty, empower middle managers, constantly strive to become better, and foster corporate loyalty.[8] The learning organization provides examples of organizational-level needs that might be addressed through training. We can categorize organizational-level needs as organization maintenance, efficiency, and culture.

Organizational maintenance aims to ensure a steady supply of critical skills. It works closely with employment planning, discussed in Chapter Five, and succession planning, discussed in Chapter Nine. Skill imbalances may trigger a need for training to prepare individuals to move to new job assignments or to take on redesigned roles.

Organizational efficiency is related to the efficiency objective in the diagnostic model. Profits, labor costs, quality of output, and other measures might signal gaps that training can help to close. In fact, one important reason for increased training in many organizations is the realization that the existing work force must acquire the skills to make decisions, solve problems, work in teams, and exhibit other behaviors in support of "quality."[9] The Malcolm Baldrige award (see Chapter Five) emphasizes such activities in evaluating an organization's quality efforts.

Organizational culture reflects the value system or philosophy of the organization. Examining this factor can identify areas where training can help clarify or gain acceptance of organizational values among employees.[10] IBM's managerial training includes a hefty dose of the "IBM culture," including emphasis on respect for the individual and attention to quality. Team building and decision making also involve fundamental values that can be enhanced through training. However, such values must be reinforced on the job if they are to be maintained for long.[11]

An important factor in the effectiveness of training and needs analysis is how the training function is placed within the organization. When IBM discovered it was spending $900 million a year on education and training with no central planning, it restructured the entire education function, pushing it right to the top of the company and naming Ursula Fairbairn the director of education.[12] Other organizations create separate training profit centers or decentralize training decisions at the unit level.[13] The key is to so construct the training organization that it can accurately establish objectives and evaluate results in accordance with the organization's objectives.

Job, Task, and Knowledge-Skill-Ability Analysis

Chapter Three described the procedures for analyzing jobs and for developing job descriptions and specifications. These documents offer a valuable source of information on potential training needs, and several job analysis approaches can specifically provide information on the skills or knowledge needed to carry out job tasks.[14] Frequently, changes in the equipment being used or the production process will motivate a need for training. The state-of-the-art equipment planned for General Motors' Saturn Corporation plant in Spring Hill, Tennessee, led managers to carefully assess training needs. Gary High, Saturn's human resource training and development team leader said, "We'll concentrate on developing only what a team member needs. We aren't here to train for training's sake."[15] Warner-Lambert, Inc., introduced computer-integrated manufacturing processes that required mechanics and electricians with 15–20 years experience to change the way they work, calling the new B-type operators their "killer Bs."[16]

Person Analysis

Examining individual characteristics to determine whether they match those needed to accomplish organization and individual objectives can unearth training needs. The most obvious characteristic to examine would be employee performance, and the appraisal process would be a logical place to identify gaps between desired and actual employee behaviors. Yet, managers often are reluctant to conduct such developmental appraisals, because of the frequent negative employee reaction caused by identifying performance gaps. It is often better to conduct appraisals for reward and feedback purposes separately from appraisal for identifying training needs. Perhaps employees can identify their own training needs. Researchers at the Center for Creative Leadership have developed a self-assessment procedure called "Benchmarks" that focuses on how managers develop, rather than what they do, and examines such traits as resourcefulness, pragmatism, leadership, and team orientation. Managers can use the instrument to help identify their individual training needs.[17]

Comparison and Use of Needs Assessment Methods

Exhibit 11.3 compares several assessment techniques, in terms of the opportunity for involvement by the participants, the necessary involvement by management or supervisors, the time required, the cost, and whether the process produces data that can be quantified (expressed as numbers). Trainee involvement can be useful to promote motivation and a sense of responsibility for training success. Management involvement can help lay a foundation for supporting and encouraging trainees to use their new skills when they return to the job.[18] All things equal, methods that require less time, cost less, and produce information that can be documented as numbers would be preferable; but these factors are usually less important than trainee and management involvement. As Exhibit 11.4 shows, the most commonly cited reasons for training failures include a lack of managerial support and reward for the new behaviors, and a lack of employee motivation.

Though systematic needs analysis seems quite logical, indeed essential, for making rational training program decisions, in fact it does not occur frequently. One study found that 81 percent of companies surveyed had identified training needs only by reacting to problems as they occurred.[19] The most effective needs analysis will be closely linked to the planning activities discussed in Chapter Five.

IDENTIFYING TRAINING OBJECTIVES

As Chapter Five showed, objectives and evaluation standards (or "Criteria" in Exhibit 11.2) go hand in hand. Objectives must be measurable and specific enough to serve as measures of success. Moreover, objectives are not an end in themselves. Rather, they serve as information in the next stage of needs analysis, so better training decisions can be made in the future. Therefore, objectives and criteria for training must meet the same standards described in Chapter Five for all information: (1) they must reflect information that will correct future decisions; (2) they must correct important decisions; and (3) the

---

EXHIBIT 11.3   Needs Assessment Methods Compared

Technique	Potential Participant Involvement	Management Involvement	Time Required	Cost	Relevant Quantifiable Data
Advisory committees	Low	Moderate	Moderate	Low	Low
Assessment centers	High	Low	Low	High	High
Attitude (opinion) surveys	Moderate	Low	Moderate	Moderate	Low
Group discussions	High	Moderate	Moderate	Moderate	Moderate
Interviews with potential participants	High	Low	High	High	Moderate
Management requests	Low	High	Low	Low	Low
Observations of behavior (on-the-job performance)	Moderate	Low	High	High	Moderate
Performance appraisals	Moderate	High	Moderate	Low	High
Performance documents	Low	Moderate	Low	Low	Moderate
Critical incident method	High	Low	Moderate	Low	High
Questionnaire surveys and inventories (needs assessment)	High	High	Moderate	Moderate	High
Skills test	High	Low	High	High	High
Evaluations of past programs	Moderate	Low	Moderate	Low	High

Source: John Newstrom and John Lilyquist, "Selecting Needs Analysis Methods," *Training and Development Journal,* October 1979, p. 56. © 1979, *Training and Development Journal,* American Society for Training & Development. Reprinted with permission. All rights reserved.

cost of gathering the information must not exceed its benefit. Good objectives are measurable, specific, set a deadline, and reflect outcomes important to key constituents.

SELECTION AND DESIGN OF TRAINING PROGRAMS

The middle two boxes of Exhibit 11.2 describe the process of selecting and designing training, and then implementing it. This process involves establishing conditions conducive to learning, choosing the content of the training program, and choosing how training will be delivered and who will deliver it.

EXHIBIT 11.4   Why Training Fails

Reason for Failure of Training Programs	Percent Who Mentioned
No on-the-job rewards for behaviors and skills learned in training.	58%
Insufficient time to execute training programs.	55
Work environment does not support new behaviors learned in training.	53
Lack of motivation among employees.	47
Inaccurate training needs analyses.	40
Training needs changed after program had been implemented.	35
Management does not support training program.	30
Insufficient funding of training program.	21

Source: The Conference Board, *Trends in Corporate Education and Training* (New York: Conference Board, 1985).

Establishing Supportive Conditions for Learning

Effective training causes learning to occur.

◆

Learning is a relatively permanent change in knowledge, skills, beliefs, attitudes, or behaviors.

Notice that learning is defined broadly and includes much more than simply being able to declare facts or new knowledge. Before training ever takes place, certain preconditions must exist for learning to occur. Designing training programs requires establishing these preconditions.

Trainee Ability to Learn

Individuals enter training with different experiences, different familiarity with the material, and different innate mental and physical abilities. Training designers must ensure that their training demands match the abilities of trainees. Training that is either too difficult or too easy is likely to be less effective. General intelligence or other abilities can predict later performance, but the abilities that contribute to performance differ depending on what stage trainees are in the learning profess.[20] Testing trainees prior to beginning training can help ensure a good match.[21] Evidence suggests that work sample tests can predict trainability, though they predict short-term trainability better than long-term trainability.[22]

Trainee Motivation to Learn

Even the most able trainees will not learn well unless they are motivated to learn. While motivation theory is covered more fully in Part Four on Compensation, the basic concepts are important to training as well. Factors affecting trainee motivation include goal setting, reinforcement, and expectancies.

Goal setting Goal setting models postulate that individuals' conscious goals or intentions regulate their behavior. The trainer's job, then, is to get the trainees to adopt or internalize the training goals of the program.[23] Kenneth Wexley and Gary Latham identify three key points in motivating trainees:

- Learning objectives of the program should be conveyed at the outset and at various strategic points throughout the program.
- Goals should be difficult enough to adequately challenge the trainees and, thus, allow them to derive satisfaction from achievement, but not so difficult as to be unattainable.
- The final goal of program completion should be supplemented with subgoals (periodic quizzes, work samples), to maintain feelings of accomplishment and encourage anticipation of the next hurdle.[24]

Reinforcement Reinforcement theory says that the frequency of a behavior is influenced by its consequences. Behavior can be shaped by reinforcing progressively closer approximations to the goal behavior. Reinforcement needs to be administered as soon after the desired behavior occurs as possible. However, the same reinforcers are not effective for all people. The more familiar a trainer is with a group of trainees, the more likely it is that reinforcers can be tailored to the trainees.[25]

Expectancy theory Expectancy theory holds that individuals are motivated to choose a behavior alternative that is most likely to have desired consequences. There are two aspects to expectancy: First, the trainee must believe that improved skills or knowledge lead to valued outcomes; for example, to increased pay, promotions, or self-esteem. Second, the trainee must believe that participating in the training program can lead to improved skills and knowledge and, therefore, to the valued outcomes. This may seem obvious, but people who have been unemployed for a long time often do not have these expectancies. They may not expect that the effort expended to learn new behaviors in a training program can lead to meaningful employment. Trainers should not assume trainees have accurate perceptions of reward contingencies. Trainees must be told exactly what outcomes can be expected if the training program is to be successfully completed.[26]

Active Practice

For maximum learning, active practice of the skill to be acquired is necessary. Practice should continue beyond the point where the task can be performed successfully several times (overlearning). Distributed practice sessions (divided into spaced segments) are more effective than massed practice, a fact often ignored in training programs for the sake of expediency. And the size of the unit to be learned at each practice session affects the learning rate.

Should a training task be divided into subparts or taught as a whole operation? Whether to use "whole" or "part" learning depends on the difficulty of the task and on the degree of relationship between the subtasks. For example, you could probably learn an inventory clerk task by first learning to correctly identify the stock and then learning the computerized system for maintaining the inventory. On the other hand, you can't learn to turn a car unless it's moving, so you have to learn both turning-speed control and steering at the same time. Generally, when a task has highly related components and higher complexity, "whole" methods work better. When a task has low relationships and higher complexity, the "part" methods work better.[27]

Knowledge of Results

Imagine learning to bowl with a curtain preventing you from seeing whether your ball hits any pins. Without knowing the results of your tries, it would be very difficult to improve. Errors are eliminated faster when trainees have feedback about their mistakes and successes. Such feedback can come from the task itself or from role models or trainers. It's important that feedback occurs close to the actions that cause the outcomes, so learners can associate their actions with outcomes. The feedback should also be accurate, because there is evidence that, in the absence of feedback, learners will attempt to become consistent, even if this causes them to more consistently do the wrong thing.[28]

Retention

For training to be used, it must be retained long enough to be applied in actual work situations. The amount of retention depends on: (1) how well the task was originally learned, and repetition even after reaching proficiency will improve retention; (2) the meaningfulness of the material, which can be enhanced by constantly demonstrating how the training relates to the trainees' work, or by providing organizing frameworks, such as remembering that the order of musical notes on the spaces of the treble staff spell F–A–C–E; (3) the amount of interference either from previous knowledge that contradicts the training, or from subsequent events that distract or dilute from the training; (4) motives and perceptions that may cause us to avoid remembering unpleasant topics.[29]

Transfer between Training and the Job

When training for work behaviors, it is vital that the learning exhibited during the training be transferred and used in the actual work situation. Transfer is highest when the same tasks and the same responses are required by both training and the work situation, as when secretaries use the same computer and word processing software in training as they will use on the job. The transfer is least when the training task and the kinds of responses required are different from those at work. For example, leadership training that is accomplished by taking groups on outdoor rafting or rock-climbing adventures may not easily transfer back to an office situation. Transfer is affected by the training design, the trainee characteristics, and the work environment.[30] Active resistance or resentment at the work situation can also inhibit transfer. Top management commitment to training and its transfer to the job can help minimize these problems.

Instructional Environment and Instructors

The characteristics of the instructional environment and the instructors obviously affect the effectiveness of training.

Instructional environment Research suggests that the instructional environment can be designed around nine basic events:

1. Gaining attention.
2. Informing learners of objectives.
3. Stimulating recall of prerequisites.
4. Presenting the training stimulus material.
5. Providing learning guidance, such as verbal cues, hints, and context.
6. Eliciting performance, such as asking for a problem solution.
7. Providing feedback.
8. Assessing performance.
9. Enhancing retention and transfer, such as by providing a variety of different examples or problem types.[31]

Instructor preparation It's also important that the instructor be prepared. Instructors should ensure that they have:

1. Publicized the program.
2. Informed everyone about the time, place, and arrangements.
3. Arranged the facilities.
4. Checked the physical requirements, such as seating, food, and supplies.
5. Secured necessary equipment and ensured that it is working properly.
6. Established training objectives.

7. Studied the lesson plan to anticipate group responses and prepare experiences, examples, and stories.
8. Developed personal enthusiasm for the topic.[32]

While these may seem obvious, you can probably recall either giving or attending a class that was disrupted, because one or more of these things was overlooked.

Accelerated learning   *Accelerated learning* is an approach to the training environment that emphasizes such principles as: (1) being positive and accepting; (2) providing a natural and comfortable setting; (3) exalting the trainee; (4) reducing trainee anxiety or stresses; (5) being supportive of trainees and trainers; (6) using multiple learning approaches; (7) allowing for different learning styles, speeds, and needs, rather than forcing everyone to learn in the same way; (8) making learning fun; (9) emphasizing group-based learning; and (10) presenting material using pictures as well as words. Such training has received enthusiastic response in some organizations, and it has had descriptions of tremendous savings in learning time and costs in organizations, such as Bell Atlantic.[33] It has not yet received enough rigorous testing to know exactly how or why it might work. Still, it might be interesting to consider how many of these principles are followed in the classes you attend.

Choosing the Content of Training

Common Training Content Areas

Exhibit 11.5 shows the percentage of organizations with over 100 employees surveyed by *Training* magazine that provide formal training in various skills. Training in skills for executives, managers, and technical professionals is most common, while "those huddled near the bottom of the hierarchical ladder usually received less attention from the training department."[34] This does not mean that production employees don't get trained, but it means that they tend to be trained in ways that fall outside the organization's formal training budget. This trend may be changing, as work is redesigned to push decisions downward and layers of management are eliminated, as discussed in Chapter Three. Skills that used to reside with managers or technical professionals may become fundamental to effective production work.

Orientation

Often, the first training experience of new employees is their orientation to their new employer. You might wonder why we're discussing this here, rather than in Chapter Seven or Eight on recruiting and selection. Orientation does start before the person joins the organization, because such activities as recruiting, realistic job previews (RJPs), selection interviews, and other recruiting and selection activities send signals to potential employees.[35] The reason for

---

EXHIBIT 11.5   Types of Skills Taught by U.S. Organizations

Types of Training	Percent Providing
Management skills/development	84.2%
Supervisory skills	79.9
Technical skills/knowledge	79.8
Communication skills	75.7
Basic computer skills	69.3
New methods/procedures	68.8
Customer relations/services	66.4
Clerical/secretarial skills	65.4
Personal growth	61.9
Executive development	61.6
Employee/labor relations	52.1
Wellness	47.7
Sales skills	46.8
Customer education	42.2
Remedial basic education	31.7

Source: Beverly Geber, "Industry Report: Who, How, What," *Training,* October 1989, p. 50.

covering it here, however, is that orientation involves learning. It includes relinquishing certain attitudes, values, and behaviors as the new recruit learns the organization's goals, the means for attaining those goals, basic job responsibilities, effective job behaviors, and work rules. Much of this is learned on the job from co-workers and work teams.[36]

Orienting new employees has three objectives: One is simply learning job procedures. The second objective involves establishing relationships with co-workers, including subordinates and superiors, and fitting into the employer's way of doing things.[37] The purpose is to develop realistic job expectations and positive attitudes toward the employer. The third objective is to give employees a sense of belonging by showing how their job fits into the overall organization.

Transamerica Corporation recently implemented a new orientation program in its information system's group. It began by surveying a cross section of employees: managers, new hires, and people with different levels of experience. On the basis of information gathered from this group, it put together a 19-hour program. The program has proved so popular and the information presented so valuable that employees who are not new hires are signing up to attend. Among the factors Transamerica credits for the program's success:

1. Knowledgeable and enthusiastic presenters of information—the managers in charge of various areas are the presenters.

2. Top management's commitment—this motivates middle managers to participate and to send their new people to the sessions.

3. Follow up with participants to evaluate the program and revise its contents based on these evaluations.[38]

At Disney World in Orlando, Florida, the hourly fast-food and other service positions are called "roles"; and, to stress the employees' job of entertaining, the customers are called "guests." The recruitment and hiring process is called "casting." Orientation begins with a one-day program describing "Disney Traditions I," which presents the history of the organization with pride and enthusiasm. The second-day program is "Disney Traditions II," describing company procedures, policies, and rules. Finally, the new recruit spends several days or weeks in on-the-job training, working with an assigned buddy, who exposes the new employee to learning experiences that go along with his or her new "role."[39]

Rather than producing conformity to a single standard, orientation narrows the extremes in behaviors and attitudes. The goal is to avoid extreme behaviors or attitudes and thus avoid performing extremely poorly, rather than pressure to conform to one specific attitude or performance level. In fact, some have argued that many organization systems, including external staffing, orientation, and separation/retention, have the effect of producing similarities among organization members.[40]

Nonmanagement Skills Training

Many of the skills shown in Exhibit 11.5 are specific and observable, and they do not reflect supervision or management. Computer skills, understanding of procedures, customer relations, clerical, wellness, sales, and customer education are all examples of what is often known as *skills training*. Many of these skills are learned on the job and are outside of formally scheduled training programs.

Management Development

Skills for executives and managers are more commonly taught through formal training programs, though many of these skills are also learned through job experience as well. These skills are often less observable, and the manager being trained often shoulders a greater responsibility for developing them.[41] Eastman Kodak Company's management development program illustrates features found in many large organizations, such as IBM and General Electric, and is illustrated in Exhibit 11.6. The dimensions at the bottom of the pyramid were identified through intensive study of managerial jobs, and these were found to play a role in all levels of management. For example, problem analysis and planning skills would be provided for team leaders (at the bottom of the pyramid) at a basic level. As the person advances to become a supervisor, these programs are revisited but applied to the unit instead of simple team projects. As managers progress up the pyramid, the programs become more similar for everyone and apply to larger company units.

EXHIBIT 11.6   Eastman Kodak Company's Planned Approach to Management Education

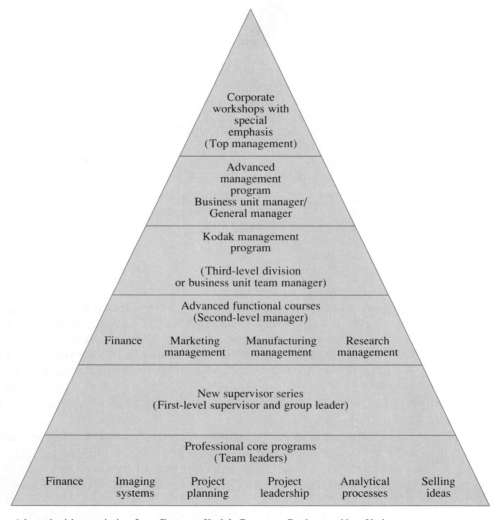

Corporate
workshops with
special
emphasis
(Top management)

Advanced
management
program
Business unit manager/
General manager

Kodak management
program

(Third-level division
or business unit team manager)

Advanced functional courses
(Second-level manager)

| Finance | Marketing management | Manufacturing management | Research management |

New supervisor series
(First-level supervisor and group leader)

Professional core programs
(Team leaders)

| Finance | Imaging systems | Project planning | Project leadership | Analytical processes | Selling ideas |

Adapted with permission from Eastman Kodak Company, Rochester, New York.

Basic Skills

Exhibit 11.5 shows that 31.7 percent of companies report they are providing remedial training in basic skills, such as reading and mathematics. Earlier chapters have noted the disturbing trends that suggest employers may soon frequently encounter shortages of applicants and employees having even the most basic level of skills needed to perform their jobs.

With public school often failing to prepare workers, U.S. companies often become the educators of last resort. Organizations, including major unions, the National Alliance of Business, and the Department of Labor, are increasingly calling on businesses to achieve an educational partnership with public and private schools.[42] The problem is especially acute for small service-oriented businesses.[43] A Virginia coalition of poultry processors lacking money and space for literacy training got a $300,000 state grant and invested $85,000 in a specially equipped van that brings educational resources to each worksite, accommodating 12 employees at a time.[44] However, even large companies renowned for their success in achieving quality and high-technology manufacturing face this challenge, spending hundreds of millions of dollars every year.[45] Motorola refuses to hire people who cannot do fifth-grade math and seventh-grade reading. In 1988, the company tested 3,000 applicants in Arlington Heights, Illinois, and half failed. As a result, Motorola will spend $35 million—four times its investment in a new state-of-the-art plant—to teach basic reading skills to employees by 1993.[46]

Choosing Training Delivery Methods

Once you've decided who will receive training, have established conditions for learning, and have decided what it is you plan to teach, you still must decide how to deliver the training.

On-the-Job Training

Most training takes place on the job, especially for nonmanagerial employees. In fact, on-the-job training is probably used more than off-the-job training, it is often informal, and it seldom shows up in formal estimates of training activity. If you ever held a job, you probably received some initial on-the-job training from your supervisor or co-workers.

A typical on-the-job training program places the trainee into the real work situation, where an experienced worker or the supervisor demonstrates the job and the tricks of the trade. On-the-job training avoids the major difficulties with off-the-job training: lack of relevance and reinforcement in the actual job situation.[47] For example, the literature offers many examples of managers who did well in formal classrooms but then made no changes in their behaviors at work. The importance of a job or task, how it fits in with other tasks and other jobs, and the consequences of improper performance are usually far easier to demonstrate to the trainee on the job.

On-the-job training is often accomplished by rotating employees through various jobs and by assigning employees to project teams that will use specific skills.

Although on-the-job training often requires few budgeted training resources, and can occur naturally on the job, there are risks. Novice workers can damage machinery, produce low-quality output, annoy customers, and waste materials.

EXHIBIT 11.7   Job Instruction Training (JIT) Procedure for On-the-Job Training

---

First, here's what you *must do* to *get ready* to teach a job:
1. Decide what the learner must be taught to do the job efficiently, safely, economically, and intelligently.
2. Have the right tools, equipment, supplies, and material ready.
3. Have the workplace properly arranged, just as the worker will be expected to keep it.

Then, you should *instruct* the learner by the following *four basic steps:*

Step I—*Preparation* (of the learner)
1. Put the learner at ease.
2. Find out what is already known about the job.
3. Get the learner interested and desirous of learning the job.

Step II—*Presentation* (of the operations and knowledge)
1. *Tell, show, illustrate,* and *question* to put over the new knowledge and operations.
2. Instruct slowly, clearly, completely, and patiently, one point at a time.
3. Check, question, and repeat.
4. Make sure the learner really knows.

Step III—*Performance tryout*
1. Test by having the learner perform the job.
2. Ask questions beginning with *why, how, when,* or *where.*
3. Observe performance, correct errors, and repeat instructions if necessary.
4. Continue until you *know* the learner knows.

Step IV—*Follow-up*
1. Check frequently to be sure instructions are being followed.
2. Taper off extra supervision and close follow-up until the learner is qualified to work with normal supervision.

Remember—if the learner hasn't learned, the teacher hasn't taught.

Stringent precautions must be taken to avoid endangering the safety of other workers. Moreover, on-the-job trainers must be chosen carefully. They should obviously be good performers, but they must also be capable trainers. The job instruction training procedure shown in Exhibit 11.7 is one framework for organizing training and ensuring follow-up.[48] You might find the technique helpful if you are ever called upon to train a friend or co-worker, even if it's not on the job.

Apprenticeships

Apprentice training combines on-the-job and off-the-job training. Apprenticeships require the cooperation of the employer, schools, government agencies (which frequently subsidize the apprenticeships and set standards for them), and unions.[49]

The apprentice commits to a period of training and learning that involves both formal classroom learning and practical on-the-job experience. These periods can vary from 2 years (barber, ironworker, baker, meat cutter) through 4

EXHIBIT 11.8   What Training Delivery Methods Are Used

Delivery Method	Frequency*
Videotapes	89.3%
Lectures	87.9
One-on-one instruction	70.3
Role playing	58.1
Slides	55.1
Films	47.2
Computer-based training	44.0
Games/simulations	43.9
Case studies	41.6
Self-assessment/self-testing	40.3
Noncomputerized self-study	32.4
Video conferencing	10.6
Tele conferencing (audio only)	8.9
Computer conferencing	4.1

* Percentages of firms with more than 100 employees using these methods.

Source: Beverly Geber, "Industry Report: Who, How, and What," *Training*, October 1989, p. 55.

or 5 years (electrician, engraver, tool and die maker, plumber) up to 10 years (steel-plate engraver). During this period, the pay is less than that for the master worker.

Popularity of Off-the-Job Training Delivery Methods

Exhibit 11.8 shows the percentage of firms with more than 100 employees who use several off-the-job training delivery methods. In formal off-the-job training, the traditional lecture remains a mainstay of training activity, but the variety of possibilities continues to increase.

Lecture

Lectures involve having an instructor present material to a group of learners. This is the most prevalent approach in schools and in most industrial training programs. Lectures are relatively inexpensive to develop and deliver, and they can be effective in imparting factual knowledge quickly and efficiently. Their shortcomings include the one-way nature of the communication; insensitivity to learner differences in learning style, ability, and interest; and the lack of feedback to the learner. Many of these difficulties can be overcome by a competent lecturer who effectively intersperses discussion into the learning session. One-on-one instruction, which pairs an instructor with one learner at a time, can also alleviate many of these disadvantages. Evidence on the effectiveness of the lecture compared to other techniques is sparse, but its familiarity and low cost argue against dismissing it simply because it is viewed as less exciting or glamorous than other techniques.

Audio-Visual Techniques

This group of techniques includes recordings, films, and slides that can be distributed to learners and used independently or be used in conjunction with other training methods. Increasing simplicity and decreasing costs of such things as video cameras and audio systems make it possible for organizations to produce their own training videos at relatively low cost. Professional-quality training videos are more expensive but can have greater appeal and impact. John Cleese, of "Monty Python" fame, has made quite a name for himself as an actor in videos that train managers to interview, provide feedback, and other tasks.[50] This category of techniques also includes video conferencing. In this, learners are located in remote classrooms equipped with televisions and microphones, and the instructor provides the training from a video studio, often linked to the learners via satellite. Learners can see the instructor and ask questions via audio links to the studio. Tele conferencing provides a similar arrangement, but uses only audio connections.

The advantage of audio-visual techniques is their ability to quickly distribute a consistent training experience to a large number of individuals, without being constrained by the time limits of instructors or the logistical requirements of getting instructors and learners to the same location. Professionally produced audio-visual techniques can also generate greater attention and involvement if constructed well. Once produced, films, slides, and recordings are less expensive to distribute.

Programmed Instruction (PI)

This approach refers to self-paced instruction that presents the learner with a series of tasks, allows evaluation of success at intervals throughout the training, and provides feedback about correct and incorrect responses as the learner advances through the training. PI approaches can be incorporated into books, machines, and, more recently, into computers, and PI is used to train everything from mathematics in elementary school to air traffic control rules. PI programs can proceed through a fixed sequence of experiences, or they can branch from one point to another, depending on how well the learner is grasping different parts of the material.

PI has advantages, including: encouraging careful attention to learning sequences and objectives; evidence suggesting that learners progress faster with PI than with lectures; materials that can be packaged and distributed, so learners can use the materials at their convenience and when they are ready; reinforcement can increase motivation; and self-pacing allows flexibility according to different abilities. It's major limitation is the expense of developing and preparing a PI course, as well as difficulty in teaching non-factual material (such as interpersonal interactions) and some learner isolation and resistance.[51]

Computer-Assisted Instruction

If you have ever spent several dollars on an arcade video game or spent several hours trying to get to the Upper Level of the Enchanted Swamp in a Nintendo® game, you know how engaging computer-assisted instruction (CAI) or computer-based training (CBT) can be. This type of instruction uses a computer to present material, assess learner responses, provide appropriate feedback, and make decisions about what should be presented next, often based on the pattern of the learner's responses. Obviously, such training is relevant to jobs where workers will work directly with computers. However, technological advances now make it possible to present material on virtually any topic. Computers can be linked to videodiscs, which store audio and video material that can be played like a television show or movie. Such *interactive videodisc* instruction allows learners to hear and see things they would hopefully never actually experience, such as what happens when a jet crashes, a nuclear plant melts down, or dangerous chemicals are mixed. Interactive video is a primary instruction method at Digital Equipment Corporation (DEC). Computers can also be combined with tele conferencing, with communication between instructors and students through their linked computers.[52] IBM has one of the most advanced-technology training facilities in Thornwood, New York, with miles of cables for audio, video, telephone, TV, data, security, lighting, and public address systems.[53]

Computer-based training shares many of the advantages of programmed instruction, while increasing the ability to tailor training to the learner, to use dramatic audio and video to illustrate learning points, and to provide an engaging training environment. Evidence from the U.S. Defense Department suggests that learning may occur faster with CAI than with instructor-led classes.[54] The drawbacks of CAI are also similar to those of programmed instruction, the main disadvantage being the expense of developing the training and equipping facilities with technology to use it. The addition of audio and video provides greater flexibility in teaching complex concepts, and the reduced expense of delivering the training may offset the initial development costs.[55]

Simulations

This training technique attempts to so copy the essential characteristics of real-world situations that learners' experiences transfer back to their work. Perhaps the most familiar version is a flight simulator, which duplicates the visual, audio, and sometimes movement cues that a pilot would experience in actual flight. However, the simulation principle also applies to less-dramatic training experiences, such as analyzing cases or playing a role in a hypothetical situation.

Physical simulations replicate physical machines or equipment, such as flight simulators or mockups of production processes. This category also includes team simulations, such as "war games" or airline cockpit team training that simulates actual situations requiring team solutions. Such "cockpit resource training" is believed to have helped the pilots of United Flight 811 successfully land their Boeing 747 after a cargo door and part of the fuselage ripped open in February 1988.[56]

Business games grew out of traditional war games, and they allow learners to make decisions about business variables, often competing against other individuals or teams. Computers are frequently used to track and compute the results. *Case study,* a method used throughout this textbook, presents the learner with a written report of a realistic situation, and the learners analyze the information and prepare solutions for discussion. *Role playing* involves having trainees act out simulated roles, sometimes interacting with other trainees who are also acting. This technique is often used to help trainees understand different points of view.

Behavior-modeling draws on learners' ability to imitate appropriate behavior, and it has been used extensively to improve managerial behaviors. This technique involves introducing the skills to be learned, viewing an example of successful behavior that has been related to the learning points, group discussion of the effectiveness of the behaviors, practice in the behaviors in front of others, and feedback about the effectiveness of the behaviors.[57]

Advantages of simulation-based training methods include the potential for a high degree of transfer to the work situation, high participant involvement, providing specific feedback, and helping learners deal with incomplete data and with realistic levels of complexity. However, there is little evidence to suggest whether this potential is actually achieved. Simulations can be expensive to develop, are very labor-intensive, and must be constructed very carefully to accomplish the realism necessary for high transfer to the job. For example, case-study methods are supposed to involve participants in confronting and questioning assumptions, to have only minimal dependence on faculty, to recognize that there is rarely one right answer, and to create drama to involve learners. Yet, one study of executive training found that faculty members frequently dominated the group interaction, failed to relate the case to situations on the job, and usually led the group to the "preferred solution."[58]

University, College, or Vocational School Education

Frequently, organizations use university, college, or vocational school programs to accomplish training. Executive development programs are a mainstay of many business schools, with several offering "professional" programs tailored to those working full time.[59] For those with little time to commute to the school and sit in a classroom, "online" university programs are emerging that provide training to students at remote sites through personal computers.[60] The National Technical University (NTU) provides a similar program for technical skills, through remote audio-video conferencing.

INTERNATIONAL PERSPECTIVES ON TRAINING, ORIENTATION, AND DEVELOPMENT

As organizations find themselves facing international markets and competition, they will increasingly need to move individuals successfully between countries and cultures. Unfortunately, as noted in Chapter Ten, such assignments are frequently unsuccessful. Can training help? Many people think so; but, for training to work, it must go beyond simple classes or programmed instruction in language skills. There is a growing appreciation of the complexity of international assignments and the training needed to make them successful. Elements leading to success include: (1) such job factors as technical skills, familiarity with host-country operations, and managerial skills; (2) relational skills, such as tolerance for ambiguity, flexibility, avoiding biased judgments, and cultural empathy; (3) motivational state, including belief in the assignment, interest in overseas experience and in the host-country culture, and willingness to acquire new behaviors and attitudes; (4) family situation, such as a spouse and children willing to move, and a stable marriage; and (5) language skills. While training cannot address all of these factors, such training techniques as simulations, role playing, meetings with previous international assignees, having families host international visitors, and even outward-bound adventure training with multicultural participants may help.[61] It has been argued that behavioral modeling training may be particularly effective.[62]

The potential of training has not been lost on international competitors, nor is there a reluctance to try new approaches. Toyota's sales training for its luxury Lexus product includes a marathon two-day seminar in Chicago, of lectures, quizzes, and role playing, emphasizing "personal attitudes, not product attributes." Testing on both days is accomplished like a game show, with a cheery host, multiple-choice questions appearing on a big-screen TV, and students feverishly entering their responses into touch-pads at their seats as the countdown clock ticks off seconds. Prescriptions include having receptionists greet customers, honest negotiations with buyers, and clean cars filled with gas after servicing (talk about radical innovations).[63]

U.S. organizations are strikingly different from their counterparts in Europe in the extent to which they use apprenticeship training. In the United States, apprenticeship programs are disproportionately composed of building trades programs. Although enrollments in registered apprenticeship programs are at historic highs, the proportion of the civilian labor force participating in apprenticeship training in the United States is extremely low—only 0.3 percent. If registered apprentices in the United States equalled the proportion of the labor force enrolled as apprentices in Austria, Germany, or Switzerland, there would currently be 7 million apprentices in the United States instead of 395,000. This is surprising, given the flexibility available to U.S. organizations in shaping apprenticeship programs. Apart from the requirement to conform to social policies, such as affirmative action and fair labor standards, employers and unions are relatively free to organize apprenticeships to suit their own needs.

EVALUATING TRAINING OUTCOMES

Evaluation is a vital part of the training process, as shown in Exhibit 11.2, just as it should be a vital part of every HR activity. While it is tempting to think of evaluation as the final stage of the training process, that is an incorrect view. Evaluation must be planned when objectives are set, and it must become a part of subsequent needs analysis to plan future programs. However, evaluation is like brushing your teeth after every meal—everyone advocates it but few actually do it. Managers often use training evaluation not as a planning tool but as a defensive mechanism to "sell" expensive training programs or to repel threatened program cuts. They often fear that evaluations may show some programs to be ineffective, thus threatening established procedures. They also often believe that the inability to perfectly measure all training outcomes makes it impossible to evaluate training at all.[64] Yet, an effective and ongoing planning and evaluation system for training is essential for ensuring adequate return on investment for the millions of dollars spent.[65]

Evaluation Criteria

The outcomes of training that can be used to judge success are as diverse as the goals of the organization. Evaluation on only one, or a small subset, of criteria can lead to biased and incomplete conclusions. We can generally place evaluation criteria into two categories: internal criteria and external criteria.

Internal criteria are associated with the content of the program. For example, a program offered by ComputerLand to train customers in the use of computer software could be judged on how fast and accurately the trainees can operate the programs. The criteria are found in the course content. A commonly used internal criterion is participant reaction—how the trainees feel about a specific training experience.[66] But it may not be the most relevant criterion, because it fails to address any skills, or behavioral or attitudinal changes. So, even though participant reaction is useful, it is not a sufficient evaluation.

External criteria are related to the ultimate purpose of training. Possible external criteria include performance evaluation ratings, changes in sales volume, or costs. They measure some aspect of performance and try to relate changes in performance to training.[67] For example, are sales up because use of computer software permits better tracking of potential customers?

Most researchers state the need for external measures of changes in job behavior and organizational effectiveness. Some even advocate multiple behavior indexes to capture the dynamic nature of the training process, with its multiple objectives for individuals and the organization.[68]

Four training evaluation levels have been advocated since the late 1950s, and they still remain the basis for training evaluation today:

1. Do the trainees feel good about the training? (Trainee reactions.)
2. Can the trainees recall and understand the concepts they were taught? (Learning.)
3. Do the trainees apply the concepts to their behaviors? (Behavior changes.)
4. Do these changed behaviors affect organizational outcomes? (Results.)[69]

The matrix shown in Exhibit 11.9 uses these four criteria to develop questions and general measurement approaches. Though this particular matrix was developed in the 1970s, it still provides a good general idea of how evaluation can be accomplished. When considering the fourth level—organizational results—evaluators frequently advocate cost/benefit analysis of training programs.

Efficiency: Costs

This chapter's introduction suggested that training has become big business. For individual human resource managers, even more compelling evidence of training costs comes from the budget allocated to training programs. Training costs can be divided into one-time costs of development and ongoing costs of implementation. One 1981 example calculated costs of $134,000 to develop an off-site training program (including training department overhead, staff salaries, consultants, equipment, and materials) plus $16,500 to deliver one two-day meeting for 20 people (including lost work time of participants, facility costs, and transportation).[70] A more recent study calculated the costs of a supervisory skills training program applied to 62 bank employees in five sessions. One-time costs involved developing materials and videotapes ($10,000) plus salaries, benefits, and travel for trainees for five days ($2,800). Total costs over the five sessions included trainers' salaries ($3,350), equipment and materials ($755), facilities ($580), and trainees' salary costs of $17,791. Thus, the total cost to train 62 bank employees was $35,276—that is, $569 per trainee.[71] Of course, the particular training costs differ with each training program. Exhibit 11.10 shows several training cost examples. Generally, training costs should include all resources that must be acquired or shifted from other uses to develop and conduct the program.

The substantial budget costs of training often lead managers to see only the cost per trainee and to consider cutting training programs to save costs. Although it may often be appropriate to cut ineffective training programs, it is

EXHIBIT 11.9 Training Evaluation Criteria and Measurement Approaches

What We Want to Know	What Might Be Measured	Measurement Dimensions	What to Look at (sources of data)	Alternative Data Gathering Method
I. Are the trainees happy? If not, why? a. Concepts not relevant. b. Workshop design. c. Trainees not properly positioned.	Trainee reaction during workshop.	Relevance. Threat. Ease of learning.	Comments between trainees. Comments to instructor. Questions about exercises. "Approach behavior" to exercises.	Observation. Interview. Questionnaire.
	Trainee reaction after workshop.	Perceived "worth." Relevance; or Learning energy.	"Approach behavior" to project. Questions about project concepts.	Observation. Interview. Questionnaire.
II. Do the materials teach the concepts? If not, why not? a. Workshop structure. b. Lessons: —Presentation —Examples —Exercises	Trainee performance during workshop.	Understanding. Application.	Learning time. Performance on exercises. Presentations.	Observation. Document review.
	Trainee performance at end of workshop.	Understanding. Application. Facility. Articulation.	Action plan for project. Use of tools on exercises. Presentations.	Observation. Document review. Interview. Questionnaire.

What We Want to Know	What Might Be Measured	Measurement Dimensions	What to Look at (sources of data)	Alternative Data Gathering Method
III. Are the concepts used? If not, why not? *a.* Concepts: —Not relevant. —Too complex. —Too sophisticated. *b.* Inadequate tools. *c.* Environment not supportive.	Performance improvement projects.	Analysis. Action plan. Results.	Discussions. Documentation. Results.	Observation. Interview. Document review. Questionnaire (critical incident).
	Problem-solving technique.	Questions asked. Action proposed. Action taken.	Discussions. Documentation. Results.	Observation. Interview. Document review. Questionnaire (critical incident).
	Ongoing management approach.	Dissemination effort. Language. People management process.	Discussions. Meetings. Documentation.	Observation. Interview. Document review. Questionnaire (critical incident).
IV. Does application of concepts positively affect the organization? If not, why not?	Problem solving.	Problem identification. Analysis. Action. Results.	Discussions. Documentation. Results.	Interview. Document review. Questionnaire (critical incident).
	Problem prediction and prevention.	Potential problem identification. Analysis. Action.	Discussions. Documentation. Results.	Interview. Document review. Questionnaire (critical incident).
	Performance measures. Specific to a particular workshop.	Output measures. Interim or diagnostic measures.	Performance data.	Document review.

Source: K. Brethower and G. Rummler, "Evaluating Training," *Training and Development Journal*, May 1979, pp. 14–22.

EXHIBIT 11.10   Training Cost Categories and Examples

Equipment	**Facilities**
Training devices:	Classrooms
Computer	Laboratories
Video	Offices
Trainers	Libraries/learning centers
Telecommunications	Carrels
Laboratory equipment	**Materials**
Personnel	Workbooks
Instructors	Texts
Managers/administrators	Slides, tapes
Clerks	Programs
Programmers	Tests
Analysts/designers	Paper
Evaluators	Film
Consultants	
Artists	

Source: Greg Kearsley, *Costs, Benefits, and Productivity in Training Systems* (Reading, Mass.: Addison-Wesley Publishing, 1982), p. 24.

impossible to judge effectiveness by costs alone. Very often, such shortsighted decision making may cost more in lost productivity than it saves in program expenses. Managers must pay attention to the benefits of training.

Efficiency: Benefits

Training produces many benefits for organizations. Exhibit 11.11 lists several examples of training program outcomes. Training outcomes roughly correspond to internal criteria discussed earlier, while operational outcomes correspond to external criteria, also discussed earlier. Though the internal criteria may provide useful information for monitoring how the training program is conducted or how participants react and learn from it, the external criteria are closer to organizational productivity outcomes.

However, the external criteria have two problems. First, they are hard to measure in the same tangible units as costs (i.e., dollars). Second, it is often difficult to be sure that the training program is responsible for changes in these outcomes. Regarding the first problem (measurement), there is no easy answer. However, several authors have recently proposed methods for attaching dollar values to such costly individual behaviors as turnover and absenteeism. Some have even attempted to value job performance in dollars (see Chapter Four). Though such estimates are bound to be crude and imperfect, exact precision is often not necessary.

EXHIBIT 11.11   Examples of Training Outcomes

Training Outcomes

Student throughput (number of graduates)	Achievement level (accuracy, speed)
Student completion time	Revision time
Testing time	Failure rate
Development time	Absence rate during training
Retention period	Accident rate during training
Attitude change	Amount of practice

Operational Outcomes

Production rate/quality	Quality/speed of service
Sales volume	Accident rates (on the job)
Equipment failure rates	Job proficiency
Job turnover rates	Customer or employee satisfaction

Adapted from: Greg Kearsley, *Costs, Benefits, and Productivity in Training Systems* (Reading, Mass.: Addison-Wesley Publishing, 1982), p. 60.

Regarding the second problem—establishing the program's effect—again, there is no easy answer. The key here is to design training evaluation to control possible extraneous factors and to isolate the effects of training.[72]

A recent statistical review of 17 studies suggested that training generally does have a positive effect on supervisors' ratings of behavior.[73] One study estimated monetary benefits from training 62 bank employees between $34,627 (assuming training effects last only one year) and $194,885 (assuming training effects last 20 years). And this is after subtracting the $35,276 cost of training 62 employees. Thus, it is possible (though rare) for training to be evaluated rigorously. However, even these studies could not obtain perfectly precise cost and benefit estimates. Fortunately, a method is available that makes such estimate precision less necessary.

Break-Even Analysis

Precise estimates of training costs and benefits are seldom, probably never, available. This is also true for virtually any human resource management activity. In fact, it is typically true for any management activity, including marketing, production, and finance (as anyone who had money in the U.S. stock market in October of 1987 can readily tell you). HR managers frequently lament this imprecision as making it impossible to do cost/benefit analysis, but such imprecision doesn't stop the finance, marketing, and production officers from using dollars to justify their programs. Perhaps human resource managers just aren't aware of systems for using imprecise information.

Exhibit 11.12 shows how *break-even analysis,* a system commonly used in management, can be applied to evaluate a training program even when the

---

EXHIBIT 11.12   Break-Even Analysis Applied to a Training Program

---

Computing Quantity/Leverage

Year	Trained Employees Added to the Work Force	Trained Employees Leaving the Work Force	Net Increase in Trained Employees in the Work Force	Total Trained Employees in the Work Force
1	200	0	200	200
2	25	5	20	220
3	25	5	20	240
4	25	5	20	260
5	25	5	20	280
Total person-years of productivity affected				1,200

Estimating Program Quality

Supervisors estimate the dollar value of the expected increase in employee service value from the training program, on a per person, per year basis, less the increased service costs that would have to be incurred to maintain that increased service value. The estimates of net value ranged from a low of $1,000 to a high of $10,000 per person-year.

Computing Program Costs

Year	Start-up Costs	Ongoing Program Costs	Total Costs
1	$500,000	$100,000	$ 600,000
2	0	100,000	100,000
3	0	100,000	100,000
4	0	100,000	100,000
5	0	100,000	100,000
Total program costs over 5 years			$1,000,000

Computing Total Program Returns

Total program returns = (Program quality × leverage) − Program costs

Program Quality	Leverage	Program Costs	Total Program Returns
$ 833/Person-year	1,200	$1,000,000	$ 0
1,000/Person-year	1,200	1,000,000	$ 200,000
10,000/Person-year	1,200	1,000,000	$11,000,000

Adapted from John W. Boudreau, "Utility Analysis: A New View of Strategic Human Resource Management," in *ASPA–BNA Handbook of Human Resource Management,* vol. 1, chap. 4, ed. Lee D. Dyer (Washington, D.C.: The Bureau of National Affairs, Inc., 1988).

training benefits are not precisely known. This system uses the "investment" analogy and the concept of Quality, Quantity, and Cost developed in Chapter Five.

Quality

The effects of a human resource decision on employee quality reflect two factors: First, they reflect any enhancements in employee service value to the organization, such as increased sales or better-quality production. Second, they reflect any additional service costs required to maintain and improve the enhanced employee value, such as increased inventories to support increased sales or higher productivity-based pay. The difference between enhanced employee service value and increased employee service cost is the net increase in employee value for the program. Thus, the effect of human resource activities on quality is the average increase in net employee value, per employee, per year. Though this concept is very difficult to measure, perfect precision usually is not necessary.

In Exhibit 11.12, assume that the most pessimistic managers said the training program could produce an increase in net value averaging at least $1,000 per person-year, while the most optimistic managers said it could increase net value as much as $10,000 per person-year.

Quantity

The number of employees and time periods affected by a human resource decision or activity is the quantity or "leverage" of human resource activities. Exhibit 11.12 depicts the leverage for a training program. The program is applied for five years and trains the existing 200-person work force in the first year. After that, five trained employees leave each year. The 25 new employees who join the work force each year are trained using the program—a gain of 20 employees. Therefore, the program puts 200 trained employees into the work force in the first year, 220 in the second year, 240 in the third year, and so on. By training 300 people, the organization reaps 1,200 person-years of productivity effects over the five years. When human resource decisions affect the productivity of employees for many years, they can quickly amass large leverage values.

Cost

The cost of a human resource activity refers to the value of the resources used in implementing that decision. These resources include the out-of-pocket expenses to develop and carry out the decision and the value of employees' time as participants, administrators, or in-house instructors. Relevant costs include those to develop and establish the activity, as well as those to keep it going.

In Exhibit 11.12, this training program requires building a state-of-the-art system of training studios capable of receiving closed-circuit audio-video transmissions of live training broadcasts and communicating with the instructors through a remote two-way audio system. Costs to build, maintain, and staff the studios, as well as to develop and carry out the training decision, would be $1 million for the five-year program, with half spent in the first year to build the studios.

Total Program Returns

The organization depicted in Exhibit 11.12 faces the decision of whether to spend $1 million to train 300 employees over five years, a cost of $3,333 per trainee. However, this cost level is misleading. Because of the leverage factor, the training program need only produce an average increase in net employee value of $833 per trainee, per year, to cover its costs (i.e., $1 million divided by 1,200). This is the break-even value of quality improvement.[74] If it produces the conservatively estimated $1,000 average increase in net employee value per person-year, the total return will be $200,000 ($1.2 million minus the $1 million cost), for a 20 percent return on the original $1 million investment. If it produces the optimistic $10,000 average increase in net employee value per person-year, the total return of $11 million ($12 million minus the $1 million cost) is a 1,100 percent return on investment.

Rather than dwell on the imperfections of the training effectiveness measures, we can focus on the minimum level of training benefits necessary to cover the training costs. This minimum return equals $833 (i.e., $1 million divided by 1,200). If the increase in work force value created by the training program (per person, per year) is greater than $833, the investment pays off, and vice versa. Several studies have suggested that break-even effect levels are often quite low.[75] When this is true, it may be possible that even imperfect training assessments based on only a portion of the possible training outcomes may be sufficient to justify the training investment. Such an approach is certainly superior to attempting to precisely measure training program effects down to the last dollar.[76]

Equity

Training has important effects on employee perceptions of fairness. Access to training that leads to advancement can be seen as a reward for good performance or loyalty. Being forced to undergo remedial training can be seen as a punishment. Training can arouse employee anger and even stimulate lawsuits. When employees were fired for refusing to participate in so-called new age training, which draws on Eastern mysticism or actively questions their religious values, the employees sued their companies for back pay and damages to compensate for "psychological trauma."[77]

Training is also a key tool as part of a complete EEO or affirmative action program, often providing protected groups with the skills they need to compete with others on equal footing. Though adverse impact analysis usually focuses on staffing decisions, training can be implicated as well when: (1) successfully completing training is a prerequisite for some jobs; (2) when persons are competitively selected for training; (3) when training performance is used as a selection predictor or to allocate compensation.[78]

Finally, training can affect equity objectives by enhancing community goodwill, when it increases the skills of the chronically unemployed or other disadvantaged groups.

SUMMARY

Exhibit 11.1 shows that U.S. organizations spend over $40 billion on formal training every year. When we include all the time, materials, and energy devoted to on-the-job training and educational partnerships, this figure is probably five or six times higher. We have seen how training plays a vital part in preparing and upgrading the work force, when it is carefully planned and integrated with other activities, such as external and internal staffing. Indeed, training and internal staffing are so closely tied that we have discussed them as two components of a single process—employee development. Many have argued that training holds the key to competitiveness and social equity by bringing previously excluded groups into the mainstream.

While the effort spent on training is astonishing, even more astonishing is that we know so little about how to effectively manage training investments. Financial, marketing, and production managers, who are responsible for the consequences of their decisions, devote considerable effort to ensure that comparable capital and financial outlays are well managed. Imagine the reaction if a manager proposed building a multimillion-dollar plant based only on the opinions of a few people, with little systematic analysis. Yet, of all the personnel activities, training seems most subject to passing fads and fashions.

Managers need to approach training decisions more systematically. They need to assess needs and objectives, design program alternatives to meet these needs and to achieve the objectives, and conduct cost/benefit evaluations. Until they deal with these issues, managers will remain unguided in their expenditure of the billions of dollars in training. As it now stands, the state of research in the management of training offers little comparative evidence by which to evaluate the impact or generalizability of various approaches to training the work force.

It is important to call out a basic premise underlying the discussion of training in this chapter. In training today, we tend to shape the individual to fit the job requirements. Perhaps training and development in the future must include managing the job design process, too. We need to study ways to design jobs differently—to build in future-needed skills in the present job, so employees can begin to prepare for future jobs. Human resource professionals need to create expectations in all employees that skills learning and change will be an ongoing process throughout their careers. Both employees and employers have responsibility to adapt to this change.

DISCUSSION AND REVIEW QUESTIONS

1. What is training, and why do organizations regard it as a strategic investment?
2. Discuss how training is linked to other HR activities used by organizations. How can these links be used to increase the value of training?
3. What is the diagnostic approach to training? How does it correspond to the planning process? Why is this relationship important? What can happen if it is ignored?
4. What are organization-level needs, and how can training address them? How can an organization maximize training benefits?
5. What factors affect whether trainees actually learn what is being taught? What does this imply for organizational efforts to improve learning?
6. Discuss the concept of "retention" in training, and the importance of transfer between training and the job.
7. What are the most common training content areas? How do different content areas affect the type of training chosen? Pick a content area and give an example of a very appropriate training delivery method, and an example of an inappropriate training delivery method.
8. Compare on-the-job training and apprenticeships. What are their similarities, differences, advantages, and disadvantages?
9. How important is training likely to be in the future? What changes are facing organizations that will increase the importance of training to human resource management?
10. How can the value of training be evaluated? Is it ever possible to evaluate training when so many of its effects are hard to predict or measure precisely?

YOUR TURN
BASIC SKILLS TRAINING AT SWIFT TEXTILES

Swift Textiles operates two plants in Columbus, Georgia, with a total of 1,125 employees. These plants have been in operation for over 100 years, make cotton into thread, and weave it into denim. In 1987, a $52 million upgrade and expansion was announced—to initiate computerized looms and packaging. Employees work 12-hour shifts, with an extra day off each week. While it might have been possible to get by on the job without reading and math skills, Swift determined that, without upgrades in math and reading skills beyond the sixth-grade level, its workers would not be able to handle the new production processes. Swift found that, for some employees, simply providing training enrollment cards was not enough, because they couldn't read them. They had to fill out the cards in advance and provide a place to check off the student's wish to participate in training.[79]

How would you structure a cost-effective basic skills training approach for Swift? Should it be conducted on-site during company time, or off-site? How will the nature of the work schedules affect this? What training content should be emphasized? How can it be made as relevant as possible to ensure transfer to the job? What are likely to be the most effective training delivery methods? How would you recruit participants without risking employee resentment? Would you require training or make it voluntary? Finally, how would you evaluate the program's costs and results?

NOTES AND REFERENCES

1. Lois Therrien, "Motorola Sends Its Work Force Back to School," *Business Week,* June 6, 1988, pp. 80–81.

2. Michael Brody, "Helping Workers to Work Smarter," *Fortune,* June 8, 1987, pp. 86–88.

3. Anthony P. Carnevale and Leila J. Gainer, *The Learning Enterprise* (Alexandria, Va.: American Society for Training and Development, and the U.S. Department of Labor, 1989).

4. "Manufacturing Spending Shifts toward Training and Motivation," *The Wall Street Journal,* October 10, 1988, p. 1.

5. Beverly McQuigg-Martinez and Edward E. Sutton, "New York Telephone Connects Training to Development," *Personnel Journal,* January 1990, pp. 64–71.

6. "How People Develop: An In-Depth Look," *HR Reporter,* July 1989, p. 1.

7. Patricia A. Galagan, "IBM Gets Its Arms around Education," *Training and Development Journal,* January 1989, pp. 35–41.

8. Walter Kiechel III, "The Organization That Learns," *Fortune,* March 12, 1990, pp. 133–36.

9. Ted Cocheu, "Training for Quality Improvement," *Training & Development Journal,* January 1989, pp. 56–62.

10. Chris Argyris, *Reasoning, Learning, and Action* (San Francisco: Jossey-Bass, 1982).

11. G. P. Latham and L. M. Saari, "Application of Social Learning Theory to Training Supervisors through Behavioral Modeling," *Journal of Applied Psychology* 61, no. 3 (1979), pp. 239–46.

12. Patricia A. Galagan, "IBM Gets Its Arms around Education."

13. Manuel London, *Managing the Training Enterprise,* chap. 3 (San Francisco: Jossey-Bass, 1989).

14. G. P. Latham and L. M. Saari, "Application of Social Learning Theory to Training Supervisors through Behavioral Modeling," *Journal of Applied Psychology* 61, no. 3 (1979), pp. 239–46.

15. "A New Work Force for a New Product," *Resource,* December 1988, p. 7.

16. "Automation: Training Is the Key," *HR Reporter,* August 1989, p. 2.

17. Cynthia D. McCauley, Michael M. Lombardo, and Claire J. Usher, "Diagnosing Management Development Needs: An Instrument Based on How Managers Develop," *Journal of Management* 15, no. 3 (1989), pp. 389–403.

18. James S. Russell, James R. Terborg, and Mary L. Powers, "Organizational Performance and Organizational Level Training and Support," *Personnel Psychology* 38 (1985), pp. 849–63;   James S. Russell, Kenneth N. Wexley, and John E. Hunter, "Questioning the Effectiveness of Behavior Modeling Training in an Industrial Setting," *Personnel Psychology* 37 (1984), pp. 465–81.

19. L. A. Digman, "Determining Management Development Needs," *Human Resource Management,* Winter 1980, pp. 12–17.

20. Edwin A. Fleishman and Michael D. Mumford, "Abilities as Causes of Individual Differences in Skill Acquisition," *Human Performance* 2, no. 3 (1989), pp. 201–23;   Beverly Geber, "The Limits of HRD," *Training,* May 1989, pp. 25–33.

21. Irwin L. Goldstein, *Training in Organizations: Needs Assessment, Development, and Evaluation,* 2nd ed. (Pacific Grove, Calif.: Brooks/Cole, 1986).

22. Ivan T. Robertson and Sylvia Downs, "Work-Sample Tests of Trainability: A Meta-Analysis," *Journal of Applied Psychology* 74, no. 3 (1989), pp. 402–10.

23. Dov Eden and Gad Ravid, "Pygmalion versus Self-Expectancy: Effects of Instructor- and Self-Expectancy on Trainee Performance," *Organizational Behavior and Human Performance* 30 (1982), pp. 351–64.

24. Wexley and Latham, *Development and Training.*

25. David A. Kolb, "Experiential Learning Theory and the Learning Style Inventory: A Reply to Freedman and Stumpf," *Academy of Management Review* 6, no. 2 (1981), pp. 289–96.

26. Wexley and Latham, *Development and Training.*

27. Irwin L. Goldstein, *Training in Organizations,* p. 81.

28. Ibid., p. 84.

29. Ibid., pp. 87–88.

30. Timothy T. Baldwin and J. Kevin Ford, "Transfer of Training: A Review and Directions for Future Research," *Personnel Psychology* 41 (1988), pp. 63–105.

31. R. M. Gagne and L. J. Briggs, *Principles of Instructional Design* (CBS College Publishing, 1979).

32. J. S. Randall, "You and Effective Training," *Training and Development Journal* 32 (1978), pp. 10–19.

33. Mary Jane Gill and David Meier, "Accelerated Learning Takes Off," *Training and Development Journal,* January 1989, pp. 63–65.

34. Beverly Geber, "Industry Report: Who, How, What," *Training,* October 1989, pp. 49–63.

35. Daniel C. Feldman, "A Contingency Theory of Socialization," *Administrative Science Quarterly* 21, 2nd quarter (1976), pp. 433–52;   Daniel C. Feldman, "The Role of Initiation Activities in Socialization," *Human Relations* 30, no. 4 (1977), pp. 977–90.

36. Jane S. Mouton and Robert R. Blake, *Synergogy: A New Strategy for Education, Training and Development* (San Francisco: Jossey-Bass, 1984).

37. Daniel C. Feldman, "A Socialization Process that Helps New Recruits Succeed," in *Current Issues in Personnel Management,* ed. K. Rowland, G. Ferris, and J. Sherman (Boston: Allyn & Bacon, 1983);   David F. Jones, "Developing a New Employee Orientation Program," *Personnel Journal,* March 1984, pp. 86–87.

38. Bureau of National Affairs, "Training and Development Programs," *Personnel Policies Forum Survey* no. 140 (Washington, D.C.: Bureau of National Affairs, 1985).

39. Manuel London, *Managing the Training Enterprise* (San Francisco: Jossey-Bass, 1989), pp. 33–34.

40. Robert D. Bretz, Jr., Ronald A. Ash, and George F. Dreher, "Do People Make the Place? An Examination of the Attraction-Selection-Attrition Hypothesis," *Personnel Psychology* 42, no. 3 (1989), pp. 561–82.

41. Douglas T. Hall and Associates, *Career Development in Organizations* (San Francisco: Jossey-Bass, 1986).

42. Kirkland Ropp, "A Reform Movement for Education," *Personnel Administrator*, August 1989, pp. 39–41; "Employers Are the Key to Basic Skills," *Human Resource Management News*, January 6, 1990, p. 4; Gary Putka, "Learning Curve: Lacking Good Results, Corporations Rethink Aid to Public Schools," *The Wall Street Journal*, June 27, 1989, p. A1.

43. Jeanne Saddler, "Small Companies Are Target of Efforts to Improve the Literacy of Employees," *The Wall Street Journal*, November 1, 1988, p. B2.

44. "Workplace Literacy Campaign on the Road," *Human Resource Management News*, November 1, 1989, p. 3.

45. Christine Gorman, "The Literacy Gap," *Time*, December 19, 1988, pp. 56–57.

46. Cindy Skrzycki, "Before You Can Work You Have to Read," *Washington Post National Weekly Edition*, October 2–8, 1989, p. 19.

47. Paul Ryan, "Job Training Employment Practices, and the Large Enterprise: The Case of Costly Transferable Skills," in *Internal Labor Markets*, ed. Paul Osterman (Cambridge, Mass.: MIT Press, 1984).

48. Fred Wickert, "The Famous JIT Card: A Basic Way to Improve It," *Training and Development Journal*, February 1974, pp. 6–9.

49. F. Foltman and V. Briggs, *Apprenticeship Research* (Ithaca, N.Y.: ILR Press, 1980); Jonathan S. Monat, Robert T. Patton, and Dean C. Elias, "Improving Management Training Using Apprenticeship Principles," *Training and Development Journal*, October 1975, pp. 20–24; Eugene Linden, "An Old Idea Makes a Comeback," *Time*, June 12, 1989, p. 71.

50. Video Arts, 4088 Commercial Ave., Northbrook, Ill.

51. Goldstein, *Training in Organizations*, pp. 190–99.

52. London, *Managing the Training Enterprise*, pp. 45–47.

53. Galagan, "IBM Gets Its Arms around Education."

54. N. Madlin, "Computer-Based Training Comes of Age," *Personnel* 64, no. 11 (1987), pp. 64–65.

55. Goldstein, *Training in Organizations*, pp. 206–09; London, *Managing the Training Enterprise*, pp. 43–54; John William Toigo, "Don't Dismiss CBT," *Computers in Personnel*, Winter 1989, pp. 41–45.

56. Judith Valente and Bridget O'Brian, "Airline Cockpits Are Not Place to Solo," *The Wall Street Journal*, August 2, 1989, p. B1; Joseph Oberle, "Teamwork in the Cockpit," *Training*, February 1990, pp. 34–38.

57. Goldstein, *Training in Organizations*, pp. 237–41; Gary P. Latham and Lise M. Saari, "The Application of Social Learning Theory to Training Supervisors through Behavioral Modeling, *Journal of Applied Psychology* 64 (1979), pp. 239–46; Marilyn E. Gist, Catherine Schwoerer, and Benson Rosen, "Effects of Alternative Training Methods on Self-Efficacy and Performance in Computer Software Training," *Journal of Applied Psychology* 74, no. 6 (1989), pp. 884–91; William M. Fox, "Getting the Most from Behavior Modeling Training," *National Productivity Review*, Summer 1988, pp. 238–45.

58. Chris Argyris, "Some Limitations of the Case Method: Experiences in a Management Development Program," *Academy of Management Review* 5, no. 2 (1980), pp. 201–98.

59. Lise M. Saari, Terry R. Johnson, Steven D. McLaughlin, and Denise M. Zimmerle, "A Survey of Management Training and Education Practices in U.S. Companies," *Personnel Psychology* 41 (1988), pp. 731–43; Philip J. Harkins and David Giber, "Linking Business and Education through Training," *Training and Development Journal* 43, no. 10 (October 1989), pp. 69–71; Beatrice E. Garcia, "'Executive' M.B.A. Getting High Marks," *The Wall Street Journal,* December 20, 1988, p. B1.

60. Len Strazewski, "Giving Workers Credit Where Credit's Due," *Human Resource Executive,* May 1989, pp. 48–49.

61. Simcha Ronen, "Training the International Assignee," in Irwin L. Goldstein and Associates, *Training and Development in Organizations* (San Francisco: Jossey-Bass, 1989).

62. J. Stewart Black and Mark Mendenhall, "Cross-Cultural Training Effectiveness: A Review and a Theoretical Framework for Future Research," *Academy of Management Review* 5, no. 1 (1990), pp. 113–36.

63. Wendy Zellner, "Two Days in Boot Camp—Learning to Love Lexus," *Business Week,* September 4, 1989, p. 87.

64. Cynthia A. Lombardo, "Do the Benefits of Training Justify the Costs?" *Training and Development Journal,* December 1989, pp. 60–64.

65. John W. Boudreau, "Utility Analysis," chap. 4, in *Human Resource Management: Evolving Roles and Responsibilities,* vol. 1 of the ASPA–BNA Handbook of Personnel and Industrial Relations, ed. Lee D. Dyer (Washington, D.C.: Bureau of National Affairs, 1988).

66. D. P. Hunt, "Effects of Human Self-Assessment Responding on Learning," *Journal of Applied Psychology* 67, no. 1 (1982), pp. 75–82; B. Mezoff, "How to Get Accurate Self-Reports of Training Outcomes," *Training and Development Journal,* September 1981, pp. 56–61.

67. Kenneth N. Wexley, "A Typology to Evaluate the Effectiveness of Training Programs to Improve Productivity and Quality of Work Life" (presented at 42nd annual meeting of Academy of Management, Dallas, Texas, August 1982).

68. David W. Mealia, "A Macro/Micro Decision Model for the Training and Development Specialist," *Relations Industrielles* 37, no. 3 (1982), pp. 657–68.

69. D. L. Kirkpatrick, "Techniques for Evaluating Training Programs," *Journal of the American Society of Training Directors* 13 (1959), pp. 21–26; George M. Alliger and Elizabeth A. Janak, "Kirkpatrick's Levels of Training Criteria: Thirty Years Later," *Personnel Psychology* 42 (1989), pp. 331–42.

70. W. J. McKeon, "How to Determine Off-Site Meeting Costs," *Training and Development Journal,* 1981, p. 117. Adapted in Wayne F. Cascio, *Costing Human Resources,* 2nd ed. (Boston: Kent Publishing, 1987), pp. 224–25.

71. John E. Mathieu and Russell L. Leonard, Jr., "Applying Utility Concepts to a Training Program in Supervisory Skills: A Time-Based Approach," *Academy of Management Journal* 30, no. 2 (1987), pp. 316–35.

72. T. D. Cook and Donald T. Campbell, *Quasi-Experimentation: Design and Analysis Issues for Field Settings* (Chicago: Rand McNally, 1979); Irvin L. Goldstein, *Training: Program Design and Evaluation,* 2nd ed. (Monterey, Calif.: Brooks/Cole Publishing, 1986); Jack J. Phillips, *Handbook of Training Evaluation and Measurement Methods* (Houston, Tex.: Gulf, 1983).

73. Michael J. Burke and Russell R. Day, "A Cumulative Study of the Effectiveness of Managerial Training," *Journal of Applied Psychology* 71 (1986), pp. 232–45.

74. John E. Boudreau, "Decision Theory Contributions to HRM Research and Practice," *Industrial Relations* 23 (1984), pp. 198–217.

75. Ibid.; John W. Boudreau, "Utility Analysis: A New View of Strategic Human Resource Management," in *ASPA–BNA Handbook of Human Resource Management,* vol. 1, ed. Lee D. Dyer (Washington, D.C.: Bureau of National Affairs, 1988); Beth C. Florin-Thuma and John W. Boudreau, "Effects of Performance Feedback Utility Analysis on Managerial Decision Processes," *Personnel Psychology* 40, 1987, pp. 693–713; Joe R. Rich and John W. Boudreau, "Effects of Variability and Risk on Selection Utility Analysis: An Empirical Comparison," *Personnel Psychology* 40 (1987) pp. 55–84; John W. Boudreau, "Utility Analysis in Human Resource Management Decisions," in *Handbook of Industrial and Organizational Psychology,* 2nd ed., ed. M. D. Dunnette (Palo Alto, Calif.: Consulting Psychologist Press); Mathieu and Leonard, "Applying Utility Concepts."

76. Boudreau, "Decision Theory Contributions to HRM Research and Practice."

77. Martha Brannigan, "Employers' 'New Age' Training Programs Lead to Lawsuits over Workers' Rights," *The Wall Street Journal,* January 9, 1988, p. B1.

78. C. J. Bartlett, "Equal Employment Opportunity Issues in Training," *Human Factors* 20 (1988), pp. 179–88.

79. Caricia Fisher, "Companies That Excel in Literacy Training," *WorkAmerica* 6, no. 9 (September 1989), pp. 7–9.

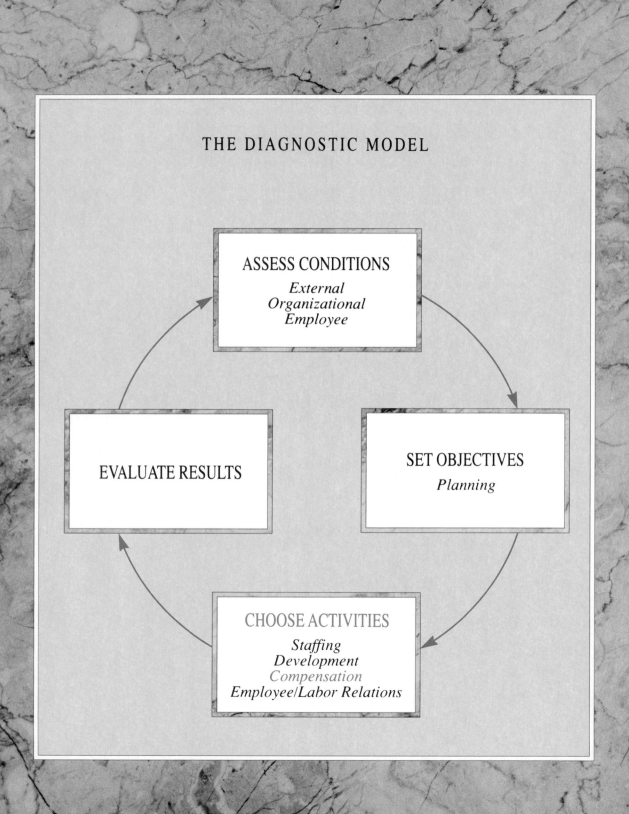

HUMAN RESOURCE ACTIVITIES

COMPENSATION

A paycheck is so wonderfully straightforward. The numbers are exact. The calculations behind the numbers are shown on the stub: deductions for health insurance, income taxes, Social Security, and pensions. Additions for regular hours, time-and-a-half for overtime, perhaps a bonus. These figures are the result of a great number of compensation decisions, which we discuss in the next three chapters. The preceding exhibit, the Diagnostic Model, shows how compensation fits into the diagnostic model. Pay is one of the most important means employers have to attract, retain, and motivate employees. Since pay is also a major cost of doing business, it requires careful management.

Traditional approaches for determining compensation are under challenge. These challenges come from managers who worry about competitive pressures, product quality, and labor costs; they question whether the pay system helps achieve objectives. When employees read about large executive bonuses and the difference in earnings between men and women, they challenge the equity of the entire pay system. Finally, stockholders question whether the compensation paid to employees in any way reflects the increased or decreased value of their investment. All these pressures are causing traditional, often bureaucratic, pay systems to be reexamined.

The three chapters in Part Five explore compensation: Chapters Twelve and Thirteen examine the decisions related to cash compensation; benefits decisions is the subject of Chapter Fourteen.

Before turning to these chapters, let's once again place the compensation activities into the diagnostic perspective. As shown in the exhibit, compensation objectives and the compensation activities managers choose may be influenced by external, organizational, and employee conditions. Managers need to assess each of these factors when making pay decisions.

EXTERNAL INFLUENCES ON PAY

Pay decisions may be affected by the economic conditions facing the firm, the firm's policies and practices, its relations with unions, and the types of people employed. Important external influences include the economy and government regulations.

Economy: Product and Labor Markets

Although some may feel that people should not be subject to forces of supply and demand, they are. During times of expanding demand for products and services, job opportunities expand and employers are more willing and able to increase pay to attract and retain employees with the needed skills and experience. Increased wages translate into increased costs of production. Organizations may try to pass increased costs on to consumers in the form of higher prices. This is easier to do during periods of strong demand for products or services. Even public sector employers, such as states or universities, pass on increased labor costs as tax increases or tuition hikes.

Increased competition also affects pay decisions. Managers faced with increased competition from foreign producers or surplus inventories must control costs to stay in business. So it is not too surprising that increased competition in product markets causes managers to think twice about the amount of pay and benefits to offer.

Labor market conditions affect pay, also. During periods of shortages of qualified employees, pay tends to increase to attract and retain needed workers. In recessions, or when surpluses of qualified employees are available, rates of pay increases are slowed; pay may even decrease.

Government Regulations

The government influences pay both directly through laws and regulations, and indirectly through its socioeconomic policies. For example, governments' monetary policies directly affect demand for goods and services, and subsequently the employer's demand for employees. These actions create economic forces that affect pay.

The government more directly affects compensation through wage controls and guidelines, which limit increases in compensation for certain workers at certain times, and laws that regulate wage rates, hours of work, prevent discrimination, and require certain benefits. These regulations are discussed in some detail in Chapter Twelve.

Unions

Although less than one in five workers are members of unions, it would be a mistake to conclude that their impact on pay is minor. Frequently, the threat of becoming unionized encourages managers to improve wages, benefits, and other conditions of employment.

In unionized organizations, the union is one of the main players in designing the pay system.

ORGANIZATION INFLUENCES ON PAY

The firm's objectives, strategies, its culture, the type of work which is performed, and the skills required to perform the work also affect pay.

Organization Strategies

All pay systems have a purpose. Answer the question—for what do we want to pay?—and you will begin to specify the objectives of the pay system. Some are clearly identified; others are implied. But the pay system objectives should support the organization's strategies.

The idea that compensation decisions are contingent upon the organization and the external environment is depicted in the next exhibit. It indicates that compensation decisions that "fit" or support the organization strategies and account for the environmental pressures are more likely to contribute to the desired employee behaviors and organization performance. The logic is that compensation contributes to an organization's success by signalling and rewarding behaviors that are consistent with the organization's objectives. The better the fit, the better the performance. Compensation decisions made in an ad hoc manner, without regard to organization, and external conditions are more likely to send mixed signals and are less likely to support desired behaviors and performance.

Culture and Values

Because pay is just one of the many systems that make up an organization, its design must be partially influenced by how it fits with the other structures and systems in the organization. A highly centralized and confidential pay system, controlled by a few people in a corporate unit, will not, according to this view, operate effectively in a highly decentralized and open organization. Unfortunately, little research has been done directly on the relationship between pay systems and the culture and values of organizations. Consequently, the influence of such factors as the degree of centralization, the decision-making style

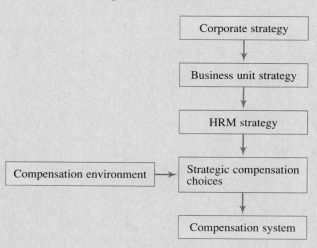

of management, or the maturity of the union/management relationship, is not well understood.

The importance of the congruency of pay programs with other management processes is perhaps most clear in the case of other human resource management programs, such as recruiting, hiring, and promoting. The pay tied to a job offer or a promotion must be consistent with other systems. Some employers do not maintain significant pay differences between manufacturing workers (such as assemblers or inspectors) and their first-line supervisors. This diminishes the incentive to acquire the training required to be a supervisor or to accept the promotion to supervisor. The situation is reversed for many engineering and research jobs, where the pay for managerial positions induces people to leave engineering and research positions. Pay coexists with other structures in the organization. An effective pay system can-

not be designed without taking the nature of the organization and its culture and values into consideration.

EMPLOYEE CHARACTERISTICS

The simple fact that employees differ is too easily and too often overlooked in designing pay systems. For example, older highly paid workers may wish to defer taxes by putting their pay into retirement funds, while younger employees may have high cash needs to buy a house, support a family, or finance an education. Dual-career couples who are overinsured medically may prefer to use more of their combined pay for child care, automobile insurance, financial counseling, or other benefits.

Employee needs raise four issues for compensation:

1. How to provide employees choices in their pay and benefits.

Compensation Concluded

2. How to keep employees informed about their compensation (increased communications).

3. How to offer employees the opportunity to participate in decision making (increased involvement).

4. How to provide employees a voice or dispute resolution procedures.

So a wide variety of external, organizational, and employee conditions affect compensation objectives and the design of compensation systems.

CHAPTER
TWELVE

External
and Internal
Comparisons

Multiple Perspectives

Forms of Pay

Compensation Legislation

Setting Compensation Objectives

Basic Policy Decisions

Translating Policy into Practice

External Competitiveness
Pay Level Effects
Market Surveys

Internal Consistency
Pay Structure Effects
Levels and Size of Pay Differences

Criteria for Pay Structures
Structures Built on Employee Attributes
Job-Based Structures

Job Evaluation Decisions
Purpose
Who to Involve?
Methods
Results of Job Evaluation

Your Turn: Evaluating Jobs

———————————————◆———————————————

Exxon employs a chief executive officer, chemical engineers, plant managers, nurses, market analysts, laboratory technicians, financial planners, hydraulic mechanics, accountants, guards, oil tanker captains, sailors, word processors, and so on. How is pay for these different jobs determined? Is the financial planner worth more than the accountant, or the mechanic more than the word processor? How much more? What procedures are used to set pay rates and who does it? How important are the characteristics of the employee—knowledge, skills, abilities, or experience? Should the potential consequences of job errors, like the 1989 Alaska oil spill, be considered in setting pay? How important are the characteristics of the work, the conditions under which it is done, or the value of what is produced? Do the procedures differ according to an employer's business strategies and its financial condition? What role do unions play? Would the employees be willing to postpone a pay increase in exchange for improved medical care?

The next three chapters address these questions. In this chapter we discuss the four basic decisions that need to be made when managing compensation. The major techniques used to determine employees' pay are described in this and the next chapter. Benefits, which account for almost 40 percent of labor costs, is discussed in the last chapter.

MULTIPLE PERSPECTIVES

Compensation means different things to different people. As employees, we may think of compensation as a return for our efforts or our investment in education and training or a reward for satisfaction or outstanding work.[1] For most of us, our pay is the major source of personal wealth; hence, it is an important determinant of our economic and social well-being.[2]

Managers have two views of compensation. First and foremost, pay is a major operating expense. Labor costs in many organizations account for more than 50 percent of total operational expenses. For this reason alone, pay requires sound administration. In addition to being an expense, pay can influence employees' work behaviors and attitudes. It may affect their decision to apply for a job, remain with an employer, work more productively, or seek training to qualify for a higher-paying job. If managed inequitably, pay may cause employees to diminish their efforts, to search for a different job and/or to form a union. This potential to influence employees' work attitudes and behaviors is another compelling reason for ensuring that pay systems are designed and administered fairly and equitably.

EXHIBIT 12.1 Forms of Compensation

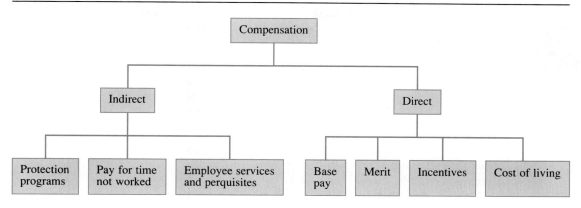

Source: George T. Milkovich and Jerry M. Newman, *Compensation,* 3rd ed. (Homewood, Ill.: BPI Irwin, 1990).

FORMS OF PAY

Compensation includes financial returns and tangible services and benefits employees receive as part of an employment relationship.

Exhibit 12.1 shows the variety of forms compensation can take. It may be received directly in cash (e.g., wages, bonus, incentives) or indirectly through services and benefits (e.g., pensions, health insurance, vacations).

This definition excludes promotions, recognition for outstanding work, feelings of accomplishment, choice office locations, and the like. Such factors may be thought of as part of an organization's total reward system. The administration of all these rewards should be coordinated with compensation, whenever possible.

COMPENSATION LEGISLATION

No matter its form, pay systems must comply with legislation. If an employer is operating in several different countries, there will be several different sets of legislation to comply with. In the United States, legislation affects wages and hours of work, and benefits. Antidiscrimination legislation, designed to ensure that all employees of similar ability, seniority, and qualifications receive the same pay for the same work, is discussed in Chapter Six. The effect of this legislation on pay systems in the past 25 years cannot be overestimated. Benefits legislation is discussed in Chapter Fourteen.

Wage Controls and Guidelines

Several times in the past quarter century or so, the federal government has established wage freezes and guidelines. Wage freezes are government orders that permit no wage increases; wage controls limit the size of wage increases. Wage guidelines are similar to wage controls, but they are voluntary, rather than legally required, restrictions.[3]

Economists differ on the usefulness of wage and price freezes. Critics argue that the controls are an administrative nightmare, that they seriously disrupt market forces and lead to frustration and strikes. However, during times of national emergencies, and for relatively brief periods, the controls can slow (but not indefinitely postpone) inflation. The important point for us is that managers must adjust their compensation decisions to fit any governmental wage guidelines or controls.

Wage and Hour Regulations

The Fair Labor Standards Act of 1938 (FLSA) is the basic labor act in the United States. Many countries have similar legislation. FLSA has been amended many times. It has a number of provisions, including the following:

Minimum Wages

All employers covered by the law must pay an employee at least a minimum wage per hour. In 1938, the minimum wage was 25 cents per hour. In April 1991, the minimum became $4.25, with a lower "training wage" for teenagers in their first 90 days of employment. The training wage provision expires in April 1993.

Economists sometimes argue that a minimum wage is harmful, because it can price workers with few skills out of the market. Others argue for a higher minimum, since people who work full time at the minimum wage earn only slightly above the federal poverty level.[4]

Fast-food firms and retailers who pay employees at or near the minimum wage are more affected by changes in the minimum wage than are auto and aerospace companies, who pay few if any employees at the minimum wage.

Overtime Pay

An employee covered by the law who works more than 40 hours per week must be paid one-and-one-half times the base wage.

Child Labor Prohibition

The law prohibits employing persons between 16 and 18 in hazardous jobs, such as meatpacking and logging. Persons under 16 cannot be employed in jobs in interstate commerce except for nonhazardous work for a parent or guardian. However, there are exceptions and limitations to the law.

In the 1980s, violations of the child labor act doubled. The supply of older teenagers was dwindling while the service sector of the economy grew. Restaurants, supermarkets, and retailers responded to the demand for longer shopping hours by hiring younger and younger employees—some as young as 14. While most of their jobs—stocking shelves, boxing groceries, ringing cash registers—are not particularly dangerous, others are: running meat slicers, compacting trash. The dramatic increase in violations has caused many states to take another look at child labor legislation.

Exemptions

For jobs covered by FLSA, strict record keeping of hours and pay is required so the Department of Labor, which enforces the act, can ensure compliance. However, FLSA does not cover all jobs. The list of exemptions is probably the most complex part of the act.[5] Most organizations make distinctions in their pay systems between "nonexempts" (jobs subject to FLSA overtime and hours provisions) and "exempts." In general, professional, executive, and administrative jobs are exempt. Most jobs in the transportation industry are also exempt, because of the practical difficulty of tracking exact hours of work.

The Department of Labor provides strict criteria for which jobs qualify for various exemptions. For example, to meet the executive exemption, employees must:

Primarily undertake management duties.

Supervise two or more employees.

Have control (or at least great influence) over hiring, firing, and promotion.

Exercise discretionary powers.

Devote at least 80 percent of their work hours to such activities.

Prevailing Wage Laws

Several laws, most notably the Davis-Bacon Act of 1931 and the Walsh-Healey Act of 1936, require that workers on covered projects receive at least a government-defined prevailing wage in an area. Covered projects include government-financed construction costing over $2,000 (Davis-Bacon) and production or supply contracts for government purchases over $10,000 (Walsh-Healey). The government theoretically surveys wages in the area and then sets the "prevailing rate" as the minimum to be paid on the government project. In practice, it takes the union rates in an area. So a government-set prevailing rate may correspond to the actual rate of only a minority of an area's laborers.

EXHIBIT 12.2   A Pay Model

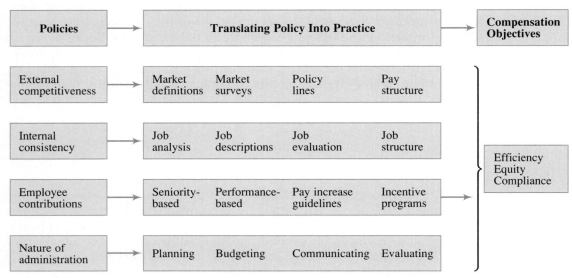

Source: George T. Milkovich and Jerry M. Newman, *Compensation,* 3rd ed. (Homewood, Ill.: BPI Irwin, 1990).

SETTING COMPENSATION OBJECTIVES

A Pay Model

The pay model shown in Exhibit 12.2 contains three basic parts: (1) the *policies* that form the foundations of the pay system, (2) the *techniques* that translate policy into practice, and (3) the *compensation objectives,* or desired results.[6] Each of these components and their interrelationships are discussed. The objectives and policy options are discussed first, then the techniques are described.

Compensation Objectives

Pay systems are designed to achieve certain objectives, shown at the right side of the pay model.[7] These objectives are broadly conceived. *Efficiency* is typically stated more specifically: (1) improving productivity and (2) controlling labor costs. Often these two can be found in an employer's statement of pay objectives, such as "to facilitate organization performance, to cost effectively attract and retain competent employees, and to reward employee contributions and performance."

Equity is a fundamental objective in pay systems. Such statements as "fair treatment for all employees" or "a fair day's pay for a fair day's work" reflect

EXHIBIT 12.3   Pay System Objectives

Hewlett-Packard

At Hewlett-Packard, our pay program is designed to be innovative, competitive, and equitable so that H-P will continue to attract and retain creative and enthusiastic people who will contribute to H-P's continuing success.

Your pay has been established to reflect the company's policy of "paying among the leaders."

Your pay will accurately reflect your sustained relative contribution to your unit, division, and H-P.

Your pay system will be open and understandable. You are encouraged to discuss the pay process with your supervisor.

---

the concern for equity. The equity objective recognizes both employee *contributions* (e.g., higher pay for better performance, experience, or training) and employee *needs* (e.g., providing a "living wage," or health care insurance).

Procedural equity, often overlooked by compensation managers, is concerned with the processes used to make pay decisions.[8] It suggests that the *way* a pay decision is made may be as important to employees as the *results* of the decision. As an objective for a pay system, procedural equity requires that employees be consulted in the design of pay plans and have an opportunity to voice any dissatisfaction with their own pay.

Compliance is part of the equity objective and involves conforming to various federal and state compensation laws and regulations. As these laws and regulations change, pay decisions often need to be adjusted to ensure continued compliance.

Multiple Objective Statements

There are probably as many statements of pay objectives as there are employers. In fact, some highly diversified firms, such as TRW and Dart-Kraft Industries, which compete in multiple lines of businesses, have different pay objectives for different business units. Hewlett-Packard's pay objectives are shown in Exhibit 12.3. It emphasizes innovative performance (productivity), competitiveness (costs), ability to attract and retain enthusiastic and creative people (productivity), and equity (relative contribution, employee communications, openness, and understanding).

BASIC POLICY DECISIONS

The policy decisions shown on the left side of the pay model in Exhibit 12.2 include (1) external competitiveness, (2) internal consistency, (3) employee contributions, and (4) administration. These policies form the four building blocks, the foundation on which pay systems are designed and administered.

---◆---

External competitiveness refers to how an employer positions its pay relative to what competitors are paying.[9]

How much do other employers pay accountants, and how much do we wish to pay accountants in comparison to what other employers would pay them? Some set pay levels higher than their competition, hoping to attract the best applicants. Of course, this assumes that someone is able to identify and hire the "best" from the pool of applicants. Another offers lower base pay but greater potential bonuses, better benefits, or more flexible working hours than those offered by other employers.

---◆---

Internal consistency, which is often called *internal equity,* refers to comparisons among jobs or skill levels *inside* a single organization.[10]

Internal pay relationships are based on the work content, skills required to do it, and the relative contribution of the work to the organization's overall objectives. How, for example, does the work of the word processor compare with the work of the computer operator, the programmer, and the systems analyst? Does one job require more skill or experience than another? Is the output from one job valued more than the output from another? Internal consistency is a factor in determining pay rates both for employees in similar jobs and for those in dissimilar jobs. In fact, determining what is an equitable difference in pay for people performing different jobs is one of the key issues in compensation management.

---◆---

Employee contributions refers to the relative emphasis placed on the performance and/or seniority of people doing the same job or possessing the same job skills.[11]

Should one programmer be paid differently from another if one has better performance and/or greater seniority? Or should a more productive team of employees be paid more than less-productive teams? Should managerial pay increases be based on corporate performance or on performance of the subunit they manage? On long-term or short-term results? Note that employee contributions focus on the people doing the jobs; internal consistency focuses on the *jobs* themselves, without regard to the people doing them.

◆

Administration includes planning the elements of pay that should be included in the pay system (e.g., base pay, short-term and long-term incentives), communicating with employees, and evaluating whether the system is achieving its objectives.

While it is possible to design a system that incorporates internal consistency, external competitiveness, and employee contributions, the system will not achieve its objectives unless it is administered properly.[12] The greatest system design in the world is useless without competent administration. Are we able to attract skilled workers? Can we keep them? Do our employees feel our system is fair? Do they understand what factors are considered in setting their pay? Do employees have channels for raising questions about their pay? Are there better ways? Such information is necessary to evaluate, adjust, or redesign the system, and to highlight potential areas for further investigation.

Balancing Policy Decisions

The relative emphasis among the four basic policies is also a key decision in any compensation strategy. Does it ever make sense to emphasize one policy concern over another? For example, many firms match outside offers from competing employers (an external competitiveness issue). These offers may be outside the range recommended by the pay system and, therefore, internally inconsistent. The relationship of an employer's pay level to a competitor's pay level directly affects the ability to attract a competent work force, to control labor costs, and, hence, to compete with products or services. Therefore, there are times when external competitiveness takes precedence. Ignoring internal consistency and employee contributions may increase dissatisfaction and vulnerability to lawsuits. If the person next to me is doing the same job but is paid more than I am, there had better be a good reason for this differential. Internal pay differences can affect employees' willingness to accept promotions, absenteeism, turnover, and unionization activity.

Compression

◆

Compression results when wages for jobs filled from outside the organization are increasing faster than wages for jobs within the organization.

An organization may develop a compression problem if external competitiveness is consistently emphasized. For example, if an increase in the minimum wage is mandated, an employer can either narrow the pay structure by raising wages only at the bottom, or pressure the structure by shifting all wages upward. Neither decision will satisfy everyone.

Thus, all four policy decisions—competitiveness, consistency, contributions, and administrative style—are critical. Achieving the desired balance and resolving conflicts among policies is part of making pay decisions.

TRANSLATING POLICY INTO PRACTICE

The middle portion of the model lists various pay techniques that translate policy into practice and link the policy decisions to the objectives. Uncounted variations in techniques exist; some of the most common ones are examined in this and the next two chapters.

EXTERNAL COMPETITIVENESS

External competitiveness refers to the pay relationships among organizations. It focuses attention on how our average pay or pay level compares to the average pay paid by our competitors.

◆

Pay level is the average of the array of rates paid by an organization.

There are three "pure" alternatives in setting a pay level—to set average pay so it (1) leads competition, (2) matches competition, or (3) falls below what others are paying. Evidence suggests that the most common policy is to match what is paid by competition.[13]

Pay Level Effects

What difference does the pay level make? The potential effects on compensation objectives are shown in Exhibit 12.4.

Match Competition

"Matching" organizations try to ensure that their wage rates are approximately equal to those of competitors. Equal wage rates place competing employers on an equal footing in their ability to attract and maintain a qualified work force.

Lead

Employers who offer higher pay rates than their competitors maximize their ability to attract and retain quality employees and minimize employee dissatisfaction with pay. The idea is that higher pay increases the number of applicants and permits the selection process to skim the cream of the applicants.

EXHIBIT 12.4   Probable Relationships between Pay Level Policies and Objectives

Policy	Compensation Objectives				
	Ability to Attract	Ability to Retain	Contain Labor Costs	Reduce Pay Dissatisfaction	Increase Productivity
Pay above market (lead)	+	+	?	+	?
Pay with market (match)	=	=	=	=	?
Pay below market (lag)	−	?	+	−	?

Source: George T. Milkovich and Jerry M. Newman, *Compensation,* 3rd ed. (Homewood, Ill.: BPI Irwin, 1990).

Higher-quality employees should exhibit greater productivity, thereby offsetting the greater wages. However, little research has been reported to support (or refute) these contentions. Some industries (e.g., petroleum and pharmaceuticals) do pay higher rates for similar skills (e.g., M.B.A. or accountants) than other industries, but this may be because they can pass these rates on to consumers and because labor costs are not a significant portion of total operating costs in these industries.

Lag

Letting pay rates fall below competitors' rates may hinder an employer's ability to attract or retain employees. However, the opportunity to work overtime, to secure promotions and avoid layoffs, or to secure a friendly work environment may offset lower pay rates for many potential employees.

No matter which pay level option is selected, it needs to be translated into practice. This is usually done by surveying relevant external labor markets and establishing a pay policy line. This policy line can be fitted to survey data through statistical procedures, such as regression analysis, or through scatterplots.

Market Surveys

Wage surveys tell us what other employers are paying for similar jobs and skills. They assess external pressures on wages.

The results of a market survey are shown in Exhibit 12.5. It reports the rates paid for "Word Processing Operator, Lead" by selected electronics firms in Dallas. A brief description of the job duties is given with the survey data. This aids survey users to match their jobs to the job in the survey. The survey also collects the minimum, mid (50th percentile or median), maximum, and average

---

EXHIBIT 12.5   Salary Survey Results

Word Processing Operator, Lead

Duties

Assumes responsibility for directing work flow through the word processing center and provides administrative support to principals to improve overall productivity. Uses word processor to type high priority and confidential work.

High school graduate or equivalent, plus three years of processing (diskette) experience required.

Company Code	Minimum Rate	Mid Rate	Maximum Rate	Average Rate	Employee Population
D	$9.34	$10.88	$12.40	$10.53	1
Y	8.23	9.69	11.14	10.53	1
E	8.53	10.07	11.60	10.17	3
Y	8.71	10.14	11.56	10.01	1
B	7.66	9.59	11.49	9.37	2
N	7.69	9.62	11.55	9.37	14
W	6.68	10.07	11.51	9.05	1
X	7.72	9.07	10.89	9.02	12
O	6.19	8.05	9.90	8.57	2
Q	7.22	9.63	11.46	8.49	3
M	6.38	7.99	9.59	8.29	2
G	6.14	7.59	9.05	8.24	1
R	6.94	8.55	10.14	8.24	3

Source: Dallas Area Electronics Survey. Survey sponsors: Recognition Equipment, Rockwell International, Collins Radio Group, and Texas Instruments, Inc.

rates paid from each participating firm. This provides a sense of the distribution of rates paid for the job within each firm.

Several features of the data are worth noting. First, there is no single "going rate" in Dallas for word processors. The rates paid by firms included in this survey vary from $6.14 per hour to $12.40 per hour. Differences in these rates may be attributable to differences in seniority or experience, but it also may reflect different pay level (lead, lag, match) decisions by the employers.

Pay surveys are conducted by employers, either individually or in associations, by consulting firms, and by government agencies.[14]

Data Collection

How are these surveys done? One method is the personal interview, which develops the most accurate responses but is also the most expensive. Mailed questionnaires are probably the most frequently used method, because it is cheapest. The jobs being surveyed by mail must be clearly defined, or the data may be suspect. Telephone inquiries can be used to follow up the mailed questionnaires or to gather additional data.

Key Jobs

In practice, employers do not seek market data for all jobs. Rather, only selected jobs, called *key* or *benchmark* jobs, are included in the survey. Key jobs
have the following characteristics:

+ The work content is relatively stable over time.
+ A large number of employees hold them.
+ They are common across a number of different employers.
+ They are free of discriminatory employment patterns.
+ They are not subject to recent shortages or surpluses in the marketplace.

Examples of key jobs may include data entry clerks, word processors, design
engineers, project engineers, compensation analysts, or even plant personnel
managers.

Judging Survey Results

Because survey data are adjusted according to the purpose of the survey and
the objectives of the organization, there is no standard approach to judging survey results. However, a number of critical questions can be raised: How well
does the sample of employers included reflect our competitors? are the jobs
accurately matched? what assurances are there that the data are accurate and
timely? do the data look reasonable?[15] One consultant, obviously referring to a
competing consultant's data, has suggested that, if they do look reasonable, it
is probably the result of two large offsetting errors.

The results gained from a survey are a distribution of rates paid by competitors for similar jobs. Exhibit 12.6 illustrates a set of hypothetical distributions
for five key jobs (A, D, G, M, and N). In the illustration, the pay level policy
line has been set to equal the average paid by the competition for each of the
key jobs: a matching-competition policy. We could establish a lead or lag policy
by simply shifting our pay level policy line up or down. Thus, market survey
data help translate the concept of external competitiveness into actual pay-set-
ting practice.

Once pay level has been determined, we turn to internal consistency.

INTERNAL CONSISTENCY

✦

Pay structures are the pay relationships among different jobs within
a single organization.

Pay structures are internally equitable if they pay more for doing jobs that require greater knowledge or skill to perform, are performed under less desirable
conditions, and/or whose output is more valued.

EXHIBIT 12.6 A Pay Level Policy Line That Matches Competitors

---

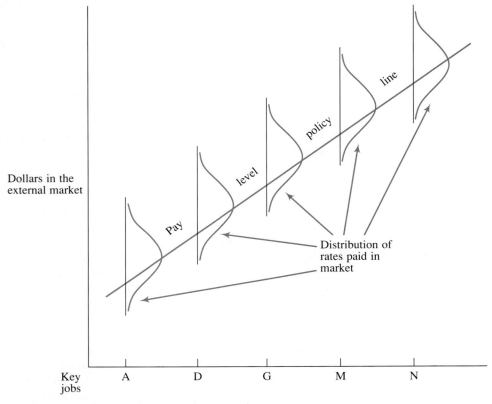

Source: George T. Milkovich and Jerry M. Newman, *Compensation,* 3rd ed. (Homewood, Ill.: BPI Irwin, 1990).

Pay Structure Effects

Pay structures focus attention on the link between employee perceptions and their work behaviors. Many compensation experts argue that equitable pay structures are related to everything from employee performance to strikes.[16] Exhibit 12.7 shows some of the potential effects of fair pay structures. Important among them are employee decisions to stay or leave the organization, and to invest in the additional training required from promotions or new assignments. Pay differences influence these decisions. Consequently, equitable pay structures can be a very important management tool.

EXHIBIT 12.7   Some Consequences of Equitable Pay Structures

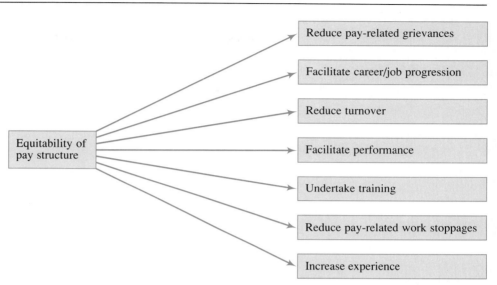

Source: George T. Milkovich and Jerry M. Newman, *Compensation*, 3rd ed. (Homewood, Ill.: BPI Irwin, 1990).

Levels and Size of Pay Differences

Pay structures differ widely across organizations. Relatively flat structures (e.g., fewer levels, small pay differentials) tend to obscure differences in work assignments. For example, rather than designating several levels of financial, marketing, and production analysts, a single broad title—management analyst—may be used. Changing assignments within a level does not require changing title or pay. Steeper structures require more detailed work rules and may require more frequent pay adjustments.

Considering their importance, it is surprising that so little is known about employee perceptions of what constitutes fair or equitable pay differences among jobs. A study of business school students and compensation administrators concluded "that a compensation differential of approximately 30 percent is considered appropriate for the higher two (adjacent) managerial levels."[17] A consultant reports that, of a sample of 350 employees, nearly half believed their own share of corporate profits was "about right," but two thirds thought chief executives got too big a share.[18] Data in Exhibit 12.8 support their beliefs. It shows that the top of the pay structure is rising. Executive compensation is discussed in more detail in the next chapter.

EXHIBIT 12.8   The Growing Disparity in Pay

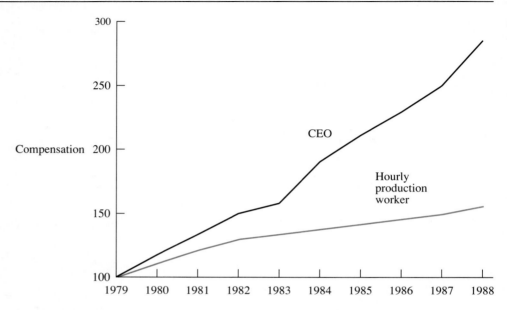

Index: 1979 = 100.
Source: Sibson & Co.

Within organizations, little is known about whether different employee groups (older versus younger, women versus men, office versus production workers, engineers versus accountants, and so on) hold different ideas about what constitutes fair pay differences among jobs. However, the number of lawsuits over pay discrimination seems to indicate that substantial disagreement exists.

CRITERIA FOR PAY STRUCTURES

An example of pay structures found within a single organization is shown in Exhibit 12.9. There are pay differences among jobs within each group, and there are differences among groups. In the example, the average pay for managerial work exceeds that for work in the technical-research job group.

Two criteria that are commonly used to establish pay structures are attributes of the individuals (i.e., how much skill or knowledge they possess), and attributes of the jobs.

EXHIBIT 12.9   Hypothetical Job Structure with Four Occupation/Skill Groups

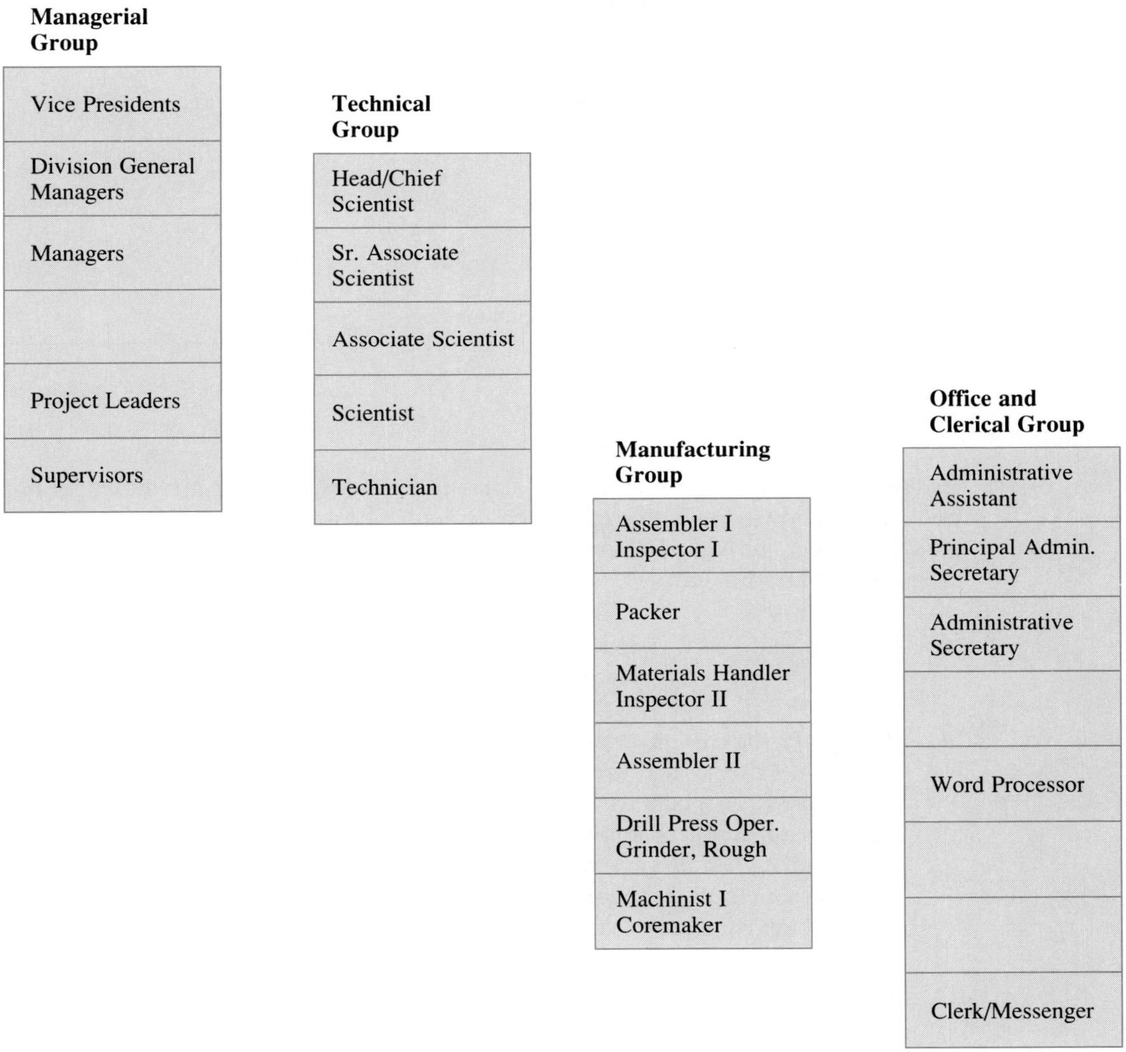

Managerial Group

| Vice Presidents |
| Division General Managers |
| Managers |
| |
| Project Leaders |
| Supervisors |

Technical Group

| Head/Chief Scientist |
| Sr. Associate Scientist |
| Associate Scientist |
| Scientist |
| Technician |

Manufacturing Group

| Assembler I Inspector I |
| Packer |
| Materials Handler Inspector II |
| Assembler II |
| Drill Press Oper. Grinder, Rough |
| Machinist I Coremaker |

Office and Clerical Group

| Administrative Assistant |
| Principal Admin. Secretary |
| Administrative Secretary |
| |
| Word Processor |
| |
| |
| Clerk/Messenger |

Source: George T. Milkovich and Jerry M. Newman, *Compensation,* 3rd ed. (Homewood, Ill.: BPI Irwin, 1990).

EXHIBIT 12.10   Borg-Warner Job Structure with Traditional and Knowledge-Based Pay System

---

Past	Current
Chain measurer	
Chain checker	
Stacker	
Ultrasonic tester	Cell operator C
Inspect/repair	
Chain cleaner/oiler	
Chain packer	
Assembler hand machine	
Auto assembler	Cell operator B
Riveter	
	Cell operator A

Structures Based on Employee Attributes

Basing pay differences on employee attributes, rather than job attributes, is not new. Skill, knowledge, and experience or seniority are commonly used characteristics. Some individual characteristics, such as minority status or gender, are illegal as a basis for pay.

Knowledge-Based Pay Systems

---◆---

Knowledge-based pay systems pay employees for the work-related skills they possess, rather than for the specific job they do. Knowledge-based pay plans can be of two types: *knowledge systems,* which link pay to depth of knowledge on *one* job (e.g., scientists or teachers); and *multiskill systems,* which link pay to the number of *different* jobs an employee is qualified to do. Employees increase their pay rates by learning new skills, even if they do not use these skills on the job they are presently assigned.

An example from Borg-Warner Corporation illustrates the system. Borg-Warner assembles drive chains for automobile transmissions. Exhibit 12.10 shows the firm's job hierarchy. Previously, 10 different jobs were involved in the assembly process, starting with riveters, and moving up through oilers, testers, and measurers. When Borg-Warner switched to a knowledge-based pay system, these 10 jobs were reorganized into three broad categories: Cell operators A, B, and C. Cell operator A is an entry level position. Once operator As are able to satisfactorily demonstrate that they have mastered the riveter, auto assem-

EXHIBIT 12.11   Knowledge-Based Compared to Job-Based Plans

	Job-Based	Knowledge-Based
Pay structure	Based on job performed.	Based on skills possessed by the employee.
Managers' focus	Job carries wage. Employee linked to job.	Employee carries wage. Employee linked to skill.
Employee focus	Job promotion to earn greater pay.	Skill acquisition to earn greater pay.
Procedures required	Assess job content. Value jobs.	Assess skills. Value skills.
Advantages	Pay based on value of work performed.	Flexibility. Reduced work force.
Limitations	Potential personnel bureaucracy. Inflexibilities.	Potential personnel bureaucracy. Cost controls.

Source: George T. Milkovich and Jerry M. Newman, *Compensation,* 3rd ed. (Homewood, Ill.: BPI Irwin, 1990).

bler, and assembler hand machine jobs, they become operator Bs, and they receive a pay raise. Operator Bs can be rotated among any of the jobs for which they have demonstrated mastery, and they will always receive the operator B wage rate. It is the same process to become an operator C. An operator C can do any job that the work schedule demands, including riveting, and still receive operator C pay. The advantage to Borg-Warner is that the assembly process may now be staffed by fewer people who are able to do a multitude of tasks. The greater flexibility in assigning employees means that production bottlenecks are less likely to develop, and so fewer employees are required to complete the assembly process. Previously, if Borg-Warner was short of riveters, delays would affect all others involved in the assembly process. With a multiskill system, work assignments are based on immediate production needs, and so work flows more smoothly.

Pay increases are earned by learning and by demonstrating mastery of various work-related skills. Once a skill is mastered, pay is immediately increased, and the employee may be rotated to jobs requiring that skill when necessary.

Exhibit 12.11 contrasts job-based versus knowledge-based systems. Under the job-based approach, the wage is assigned to the job, and employees move in and out of the job. Under a knowledge-based approach, the wage is assigned to an employee regardless of the job performed. Pay is based on the highest work-related skills employees possess (e.g., what they *can* do), rather than on the specific job performed (e.g., what they *are* doing). The manager has the flexibility to reassign individual employees to any tasks as long as the employees have the required skills and are paid at the rate of the highest skill possessed.

Advocates point to more flexible and better-trained work forces as one of the key advantages of knowledge-based plans.[19] For them, knowledge-based pay is part of a philosophy or culture that emphasizes teamwork and flexibility.

On the negative side of the ledger, pay for knowledge systems can be costly, both in terms of compensation and training costs. In fact, a program with General Foods costs about $50,000 per year in increased training costs for a group of 135 workers. Critics of pay for knowledge systems are also skeptical about claims for increased productivity and reduced labor costs.[20] How, they ask, can workers trained in several different jobs perform all of them better than a group of workers trained in only one job area? This flaunts a major tenant of industrial engineering (i.e., that specialization improves efficiency). Perhaps more experience with pay for knowledge systems and more reports on their effectiveness in the United States will resolve this question.

Beyond advocates' testimonials, more rigorous examination is required. All pay systems can become bureaucratic burdens and lose their flexibility. For example, the apprentice–journeyman–master system in craft occupations or the pay steps in contracts for elementary and secondary teachers are both knowledge-based systems, yet both have become procedure-ridden and inflexible. The recent knowledge-based plans are not inherently free of "creeping" bureaucracy. Some plans now have instituted "holding rates" for employees that have demonstrated mastery of a high paying skill for which there is no vacancy. Other plans have begun to develop elaborate peer review boards to assess skill mastery. Furthermore, the systems permit two employees doing equal work to earn different pay due to differences in their skill levels. Undoubtedly, some employees and their lawyers will want to test the legality of that practice if women or minorities receive the lower pay.

Job-Based Structures

Jobs are the most common unit of analysis used to determine the internally equitable pay structure. Choices among various job analysis and job evaluation techniques help shape these structures.

Job analysis, the systematic collection of information about jobs, was discussed in Chapter Three. The information collected is summarized into *job descriptions,* which serve as input into the job evaluation process.

◆

Job evaluation involves the systematic evaluation of the job descriptions. It compares the similarities and differences in the content and value of jobs.

Defining job evaluation beyond this can be controversial. Since the result of job evaluation is a job hierarchy, comparable worth advocates believe that job evaluation results ought to translate into wage rates, with pay differences among jobs directly corresponding to job evaluation differences.[21]

Others take the view that job evaluation merely provides a framework for combining job analysis with negotiations over pay.[22]

Both views may have some merit, depending on how job evaluation is designed and administered.

JOB EVALUATION DECISIONS

Some of the major decisions involved in job evaluation include (1) determine its purpose(s), (2) ensure involvement of relevant parties, (3) choose among alternative methods.

Purpose

Job evaluation emphasizes a systematic, rational assessment of jobs as a basis for deciding pay. But specifying and understanding what purpose(s) we want job evaluation to serve will influence its design and use. The plan that is designed should reflect its purpose. Varying perspectives on job evaluation have led to controversy over its role in setting pay differentials among jobs. So, the purpose of the evaluation should be clearly specified beforehand.

Who to Involve?

If job evaluation is really an aid to managers, and if gaining employees' understanding and acceptance of the pay structure is an important objective, then these groups need to be included in its design and administration. One common approach to gaining acceptance, understanding, and valuable ideas from managers and employees is by using compensation committees. Through these committees key managers, nonmanagerial employees, and/or union officials advise compensation professionals about job evaluation results and broader pay issues.

AT&T uses union/management task forces to design job evaluation. Their role is one of mutual problem solving. Other union leaders feel that philosophical differences prevent their active participation.[23]

Research strongly suggests that attending to the fairness of the procedures, rather than results alone, is likely to foster commitment, trust, and acceptance of results. Employee participation may help achieve this fairness. Researchers observe, ". . . if people do not participate in decisions, there is little to prevent them from assuming that things would have been better, if I'd been in charge."[24]

EXHIBIT 12.12 Job Evaluation Comparison Standards

Comparison	Nonquantified	Quantified
Job to job	Job ranking	Factor comparison
Job to a standard	Job classification	Point method

EXHIBIT 12.13 Typical Steps in Classification System

1. Determine jobs/units to be included in study.
2. Conduct job analysis/prepare job descriptions.
3. Select evaluators.
4. Define classes.
5. Identify and slot benchmarks.
6. Apply system to nonbenchmark jobs.

Source: George T. Milkovich and Jerry M. Newman, *Compensation,* 3rd ed. (Homewood, Ill.: BPI Irwin, 1990).

Methods

Four fundamental job evaluation methods are in use: ranking, classification, factor comparison, and point method. They can be distinguished by looking at (1) whether the evaluation is based upon the whole job or specific factors, (2) whether jobs are evaluated against some standard or against each other, and (3) whether the process is qualitative or quantitative. Exhibit 12.12 categorizes these comparisons.

A key feature is the extent to which the particular characteristics for comparison are called out. In ranking, jobs are compared against each other on some concept of relative value or job content. In classification, the job content and value are each divided into categories, and jobs are slotted into them. In factor comparison and point methods, content and value are broken down into factors, and jobs are evaluated by the degree of each factor the job possesses. While these are the four basic methods, uncounted variations exist. The following section offers some examples.

Ranking the jobs according to relative value is the simplest, fastest, easiest to understand, and the least expensive job evaluation method. However, ranking is seldom the recommended approach. The criteria on which jobs are ranked are usually so crudely defined that the results are subjective opinions, difficult to explain or justify. Furthermore, ranking requires familiarity with every single job under study. In larger, changing organizations this becomes a formidable task. Since its results are difficult to explain and defend, costly solutions are often required to overcome problems the ranking method creates.

Classification slots job descriptions into a series of classes or grades covering the range of jobs in the organization. Exhibit 12.13 lists the typical steps in this method. The method is similar to labeling all the shelves of your bookcase, and then sorting books according to those labels. Exhibit 12.14 contains some class descriptions used in manufacturing. This method is widely used in the public sector. It is also commonly used for managerial and engineering/scientific jobs in the private sector.

In practice, the most troublesome feature of the classification method is the need to describe each class properly. The description must be general enough to cause little difficulty in slotting jobs, yet capture sufficient detail to have meaning.

EXHIBIT 12.14   Illustration: Class Definitions and Benchmarks

---

Definition of Class IV Jobs

Ability to perform work of a skilled or specialized nature. Mechanically must have the ability to set up repair, overhaul, and maintain machinery and mechanical equipment without being subject to further check. Must have ability to read blueprints, material specifications, and the use of basic shop mathematics or comparable experience with the company layout to offset these requirements.

Work may be specialized or a nonmechanical nature requiring the ability to plan and perform work where only general operations methods are available and requires the making of decisions involving the use of considerable ingenuity, initiative, and judgment. Work under limited supervision.

Benchmark Jobs Class IV

Skilled machinist, packaging supervisor, skilled electrician, skilled mechanic, shipping supervisor.

Definition of Class V Jobs

Ability to perform work of the highest level in a trade or craft. This skill may be recognized with a license or other certification after formal apprenticeship training; or, after a considerable period of formal on-the-job training, by demonstrated competence to perform equivalent level of skill.

Other employees to be considered for classification into grade V must regularly supervise others in the technical and other aspects of the work, perform other supervisory functions and may, in addition, perform work of a nonsupervisory nature.

Benchmark Jobs Class V

Master electrician, factory supervisor, master (chief) mechanic, maintenance planner, power plant—chief engineer.

Factor comparison evaluates jobs on two criteria; (1) a set of compensable factors and (2) wages or points for a selected set of jobs. Typically, the compensation committee chooses compensable factors, based on what is judged to be important in the work.

---◆---

A compensable factor is a work-related job attribute that provides a basis for comparing relative worth. Common factors include skills, effort, responsibility, and working conditions.

The method is more complex than either ranking or classification, which limits its usefulness. Several versions exist; a typical example includes the following five steps.

1. Choose the key jobs to be evaluated. These may be the same key jobs used in the market survey. Characteristics of key jobs are discussed on page 463.
2. Rank the key jobs on compensable factors. For example, which key job requires the most skill? Which one second-most?
3. Divide the current pay among the compensable factors. If the job pays $13.75 per hour, how much of the $13.75 is allocated to each compensable factor?
4. Place the key jobs on a scale for each factor. Exhibit 12.15 shows a job comparison scale using mental requirements, skill, physical demand, supervision, and other responsibilities as compensable factors, which are listed across the top of the grid. Each factor is given a dollar value, running down the side of the grid. Jobs are slotted into the grid according to the allocation in step 3.
5. Slot in nonbenchmark jobs by comparing them to benchmark jobs on each compensable factor. In the exhibit, stocker, a nonbenchmark job, requires lower mental requirements than parts attendant but greater mental requirements than punch press operator. After the job is slotted on all compensable factors, a wage rate can be calculated by summing the dollar values assigned for all factors.

According to Nash and Carroll, only about 10 percent of employees that do a formal job evaluation use the factor comparison method.[25] The complexity of the above explanation demonstrates why. Some job evaluation methods seem so difficult to explain that their use to justify pay structure becomes very limited.

Point method, like factor comparison, is rather complex. But once designed, it is relatively simple to understand and administer. Exhibit 12.16 lists the steps in designing a point plan. Point methods have three common features: (1) compensable factors, (2) numerically scaled factor degrees, and (3) weights reflecting the relative importance of each factor.

Compensable factors were introduced in the factor comparison plan. The point plan refines the factors by scaling them (e.g., defining five different

EXHIBIT 12.15   Job Comparison Scale

$ Value	Mental Requirements	Experience/ Skills	Physical Demands	Supervision	Other Responsibilities
$0.00					
0.20					
0.40					
0.60			Truck operator	Parts attendant	Truck operator Machine operator Punch press operator Riveter
0.80	Punch press operator	Punch press operator		Truck operator	
1.00			STOCKER		STOCKER
0.20			Parts inspector	Punch press operator	Parts inspector
0.40	STOCKER			STOCKER	
0.60			Machine operator	Parts inspector	
0.80			Parts attendant		
2.00	Parts attendant				
0.20		Parts attendant			
0.40		Parts inspector	Punch press operator		
0.60	Riveter	STOCKER	Riveter		Parts attendant
0.80		Machine operator			
3.00		Riveter		Machine operator	
0.20		Truck operator			
0.40	Truck operator				
0.60	Machine operator				
0.80					
4.00					
0.20					
0.40	Parts inspector			Riveter	
0.60					
0.80					
5.00					

Source: George T. Milkovich and Jerry M. Newman, *Compensation,* 3rd ed. (Homewood, Ill.: BPI Irwin, 1990).

EXHIBIT 12.16   Steps in Design of Point Job Evaluation

---

1. Conduct job analysis.
2. Prepare job descriptions.
3. Choose compensable factors.
4. Establish factor scales.
5. Derive factor weights.
6. Apply to nonbenchmark jobs.

Source: George T. Milkovich and Jerry M. Newman, *Compensation,* 3rd ed. (Homewood, Ill.: BPI Irwin, 1990).

degrees of each factor, and giving examples of each degree). For example, the job evaluation plan in the appendix uses eight factors and 4 or 5 degrees for each factor. "Ability to read, write, add, and subtract basic mathematics" is part of the definition of the first degree of the Basic Knowledge factor. A job that required "Extensive specific skills training in a specialized field" would have four degrees of Basic Knowledge. A job's total point value is the sum of these numerical values.

Once the total points for all jobs are computed and a hierarchy established, the jobs are compared to each other to make certain that their relative place in the hierarchy makes sense.

The Hay Guide Chart-Profile Method, used by 5,000 employers worldwide, is perhaps the most widely used job evaluation plan. It uses the Hay factors—know how, problem solving, and accountability.[26] Because the Hay method is so widely used, these factors are almost universally accepted for describing managerial work.

Results of Job Evaluation

Some readers may feel by now that job evaluation is a bureaucracy run amok. There seem to be two overriding reactions. One is, Why bother with it? Why not simply set wages based on what competitors are paying in the market? Another reaction is a sense of building fences that limit employee and organization flexibility. Let's look at both these arguments.

Why Not Simply Pay Market Rates?

Market pricers match a large percentage of their jobs with market data. Opting for market pricing emphasizes external competitiveness and deemphasizes internal job relationships.

The problem with market pricing is that pay relationships among jobs are left to the vagaries of the external market and, therefore, competitors' decisions.

Job evaluation is based upon the need to develop an equitable pay structure. We said in our earlier discussion of external competitiveness that certain jobs—key jobs—can be compared across several firms in the market. However, all jobs are not key jobs—all jobs are not similar across firms. It becomes difficult if not impossible to set pay rates for dissimilar jobs based solely upon market data. The solution is to set the pay rates for key jobs based upon what other employers are paying; and set pay rates for all other jobs by slotting them around these key job rates. This slotting is accomplished via job evaluation.

An illustration In Exhibit 12.17 we have reproduced the pay level decision (competitiveness) made earlier. Recall that this decision was based on market data and the organization's policy decision to match competition. This permits us to set pay rates for the five key jobs, A, D, G, M, and N. What about all the other jobs? Enter job evaluation. Let's assume a point job evaluation method is in use. A job structure or hierarchy is established on the horizontal axis, based on the job evaluation points for key jobs A, D, G, M, and N. The hierarchy represents the similarities and differences among jobs based upon the compensable factors and the appropriate pay rates.

Based upon this hierarchy it is now possible to place each non-key job into the appropriate place on the pay level line. Note that the key jobs have the following job evaluation point totals: A (100 pts), D (150 pts), G (200 pts), M (250 pts), and N (300 pts). Next, the non-key jobs are evaluated and receive the following points: B (130 pts), C (140 pts), E (165 pts), F (170 pts), H (210 pts), J (230 pts), K (240 pts), and L (240 pts). Non-key jobs are placed into the structure established with the key jobs. Now all jobs A through N are in the pay hierarchy. Hence, job evaluation helps link internal and external market factors. Job evaluation helps determine pay rates for non-key jobs.

Obviously a point method of job evaluation is not required. Any of the job evaluation methods could be substituted to achieve a pay structure.

Building Fences

The other criticism of job evaluation is that it builds fences. During a project involving the design of a job evaluation system at 3M, several operating managers become concerned about the effects of job evaluation on creative, committed employees. 3M's corporate culture encourages innovation and risk taking. Managers felt that the job evaluation that was being proposed was inconsistent with that culture. "It places them in neat, bureaucratic boxes" and "It will inhibit them from going beyond their normal job, to adapt to changing and unanticipated events," were some typical comments. The plan was redesigned to address these criticisms.

EXHIBIT 12.17   Establishing a Pay Structure via Job Evaluation

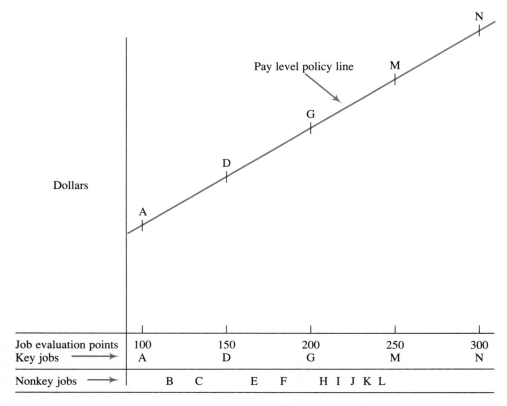

Source: George T. Milkovich and Jerry M. Newman, *Compensation,* 3rd ed. (Homewood, Ill.: BPI Irwin, 1990).

There is a danger that job evaluation can become a hindrance, rather than a tool, for a more effective management of human resources. Think back to the basic issue involved. We are trying to build a fair and equitable pay structure that will help achieve certain objectives. To achieve such a structure, some way must be devised to set pay equal to similar jobs and to ensure that differences in pay for dissimilar jobs are equitable. Setting equitable pay differences is the real issue. With them we can encourage employees to invest in training and to seek greater responsibility, thus maintaining an experienced work force. If differences in pay are not grounded in work and business-related factors then we run the risk of disgruntled employees, undesired turnover, grievances, strikes, and possible lawsuits.

Properly designed and administered, either knowledge-based or job evaluation-based systems can provide equitable pay structures. The challenge is to be sure that we do not inhibit creative and productive employees. In the next chapter, we will examine some approaches to reward such valued employees.

SUMMARY

A premise of this chapter is that no single pay program exists. Rather, the design and administration of pay programs are contingent on the organizational and environmental context in which they must operate.

Within this context, the pay model introduces several basic concepts. This chapter examined two of them. External competitiveness is established by setting a pay level. Market surveys are used to determine the pay policy line. The second concept is internal consistency in the pay structure. The structure, designed through a job analysis and job evaluation, focuses on pay differentials among similar and dissimilar jobs.

We have begun to develop the pay system. In the next chapter, we will develop it further to pay employees. Alternative methods of paying employees—merit pay, gainsharing, lump sums, and the like—are discussed. Administration and pay discrimination are also considered.

DISCUSSION AND REVIEW QUESTIONS

1. Distinguish among the four policy decisions contained in the pay model presented in this chapter. Give examples where organizations may adopt different policies, depending on the external and organization conditions they face.
2. What is a key job?
3. What is a pay structure? How do you construct one?
4. What are the four main job evaluation methods? What is the major advantage and disadvantage of each?
5. How does market pricing differ from job evaluation? How is it similar?
6. How can an organization adjust its pay system to its strategy?
7. What are the criticisms of evaluation? Do they have merit?
8. How should an organization decide who to include in a market survey?
9. How might an organization's culture and managerial style affect its compensation system?

---◆---

YOUR TURN
EVALUATING JOBS

Use the job evaluation plan included in the appendix to evaluate these six jobs. Include a chart that gives the points for each factor, as well as total points for each job. Rank the jobs according to points so results can be compared. Your instructor will share with you the company's actual decisions.

JOURNEYMAN TOOL AND DIE MAKER

General Purpose

Provide specific diversified tooling and assemblies to meet engineering and production requirements by performing various complex technical Tool Room functions with limited supervision.

General Duties

Journeyman Tool and Die Maker has a complete knowledge of all Tool Room operations and utilizes the skill and ability to perform complex layouts and complex machine tool setups for the purpose of adjusting, repairing, heat treating, and constructing various tools, dies, fixtures, gages, and the like. Must be able to work to extremely close tolerances, perform design and development without the aid of blueprints, assemble various tooling projects and electromechanical assemblies, and be able to setup and operate all Tool Room equipment with a general responsibility for work involved.

Job Specifications

Technical Know-How
Specific training and work experience equivalent to a Journeyman Trade Certificate, with the understanding of complex blueprints, assembly prints, and mathematics up to and including the fundamentals of trigonometry. Knowledge to setup, operate, adjust, and troubleshoot all Tool Room equipment and precision measuring devices is required. Understand the application of the principles of electrical circuitry, and the disassembly/assembly of machines and die equipment.

Training
Extensive specific skills training in the tool and die making field for a minimum of six (6) years, or Journeyman Certificate obtained through an apprenticeship program.

Decision Making/Accountability
The Journeyman Tool and Die Maker works in an environment that requires limited supervision, periodic guidance of others, and the latitude to deviate on Tool Room practices and procedures. Review of work results is usually after the fact.

Communication/Interpersonal Skills

Relationship usually involves discussion or recommendations, or both, on issues in regard to tooling practices. Impact is considerable and may be limited to an individual project or department or it could possibly affect the facility as a whole.

Safety

The Journeyman Tool and Die Maker performs work in a highly variable environment where safety principles and procedures need to be tailored to deal with unforeseen hazards to minimize high potential for serious injury, both to incumbent and others who will use equipment that is made/modified by incumbent.

Physical/Mental/Visual

The Journeyman Tool and Die Maker performs work with a high mental application and close visual attention required for extended time periods, with the possibility of exposure to hazardous conditions.

TOOL ROOM SERVICE OPERATOR

General Purpose

Provide perishable tooling to meet production requirements by performing specific machine tool functions under limited supervision.

General Duties

Operate specific machines in a Tool Room environment, performing repetitive, long-term basis operations required to maintain perishable tooling. Has a complete knowledge of various setup and operational functions of machines involved, skill and ability to work and inspect to very close tolerances. Must be capable of operating other basic machines in the Tool Room.

Job Specifications

Technical Know-How

Tool Room Service Operator will have specific training or work experience, or both, exceeding vocational trade school or high school. Knowledge to setup, operate, and adjust specific Tool Room Equipment with basic math and blueprint reading ability at a job-related intermediate level capable of working to close tolerances.

Training

Tool Room Service Operator requires minimum of two (2) years specific training to perform duties effectively.

Decision Making/Accountability

Supervision is usually limited and review of work results is after the fact. High potential for major impact on production if work quality is not of the highest standards.

Communication/Interpersonal Skills

Provide or receive technical information that may require an explanation or interpretation to proceed with a specific job involved.

Safety

Tool Room Service Operator works in accordance with a wide range of safety procedures to minimize potential for injury.

Physical/Mental/Visual

Extremely close mental and visual effort required for extended periods. Work environment is moderately disagreeable, with possibility of hazardous conditions.

TOOL ROOM MACHINIST

General Purpose

Provide tooling to meet engineering and production requirements by performing general or all-purpose machine tool setups and operations under limited supervision.

General Duties

Machinist has a general knowledge of various specific machine tool setups and operations. Inspection, print reading, setup, and machine operation is performed at an intermediate level with a general responsibility for work involved.

Job Specifications

Technical Know-How

Tool Room Machinist will have specific training or work experience exceeding vocational trade school or high school. Knowledge to setup, operate, and adjust a variety of Tool Room equipment, work to close tolerances, perform layouts, print reading, and math computations at an intermediate level.

Training

Tool Room Machinist requires a minimum of four (4) years specialized training in various machine operations and Tool Room functions to perform duties effectively.

Decision Making/Accountability

Subject to routine decision making based on established Tool Room practices and technical procedures. Progress of work is periodically checked by others.

Communication/Interpersonal Skills

Provide or receive technical information that may require an explanation or interpretation to proceed with specific job involved.

Safety

Perform work in accordance with a wide range of safety procedures to minimize potential for injury.

Physical/Mental/Visual

Close mental and visual effort required for extended periods. Work environment moderately disagreeable, with possibility of hazardous conditions.

MASTER JOURNEYMAN TOOL AND DIE MAKER

General Purpose

Provide specific diversified tooling and assemblies to meet engineering and production requirements by performing various complex technical Tool Room functions under limited supervision.

General Duties

The Master Journeyman Tool and Die Maker has an extensive knowledge of all Tool Room operations and utilizes skill and ability to perform complex layouts and complex machine tool setups for the purpose of adjusting, repairing, and constructing various tools, dies, fixtures, gages, and the like. Must be able to work to extremely close tolerances, perform design and development without blueprints, assemble various tooling projects, and have knowledge of setup and operation of all Tool Room equipment. Job duties place a strong emphasis on electromechanical assemblies, new die systems, and collaboration with designers and engineers on prototype projects. Extensive communication, evaluation, and decision making are required both in-house and outside the facility, which will at times include travel. Assistance in the education and training of other Tool Room employees and input on future tooling and projects is often required. Receiving, recording, inspecting, and advising changes in tooling, along with knowledge in the fields of electricity, hydraulics, heat treat, and fabrication is also required of this position.

Job Specifications

Technical Know-How

Minimum of eight (8) years extensive skills training or a Journeyman Trade Certificate with additional minimum of two (2) years extensive skills training. Knowledge in electrical, hydraulic, heat treat, tooling, and fabrication fields. Setup and operation of all Tool Room equipment and precision measuring devices. Knowledge of tooling, production, assembly, and manufacturing equipment in other departments is required. Knowledge of math up to and including trigonometry.

Training

The Master Journeyman Tool and Die Maker position requires eight (8) years as a minimum amount of training in the Tool Room and related skills to perform the duties effectively.

Decision Making/Accountability

The Master Journeyman Tool and Die Maker has the latitude to deviate on practices and technical procedures that encompass a wide range of department objectives or programs to meet an objective often with no review of work results by others.

Communication/Interpersonal Skills

The Master Journeyman Tool and Die Maker position usually includes extensive communication in a broad sense and will have considerable impact in areas both within and outside the facility. Extensive communications with other departments, vendors, engineering, sales, management, and so forth are usual.

Safety

The Master Journeyman Tool and Die Maker performs work in a highly variable environment both within and outside the department or facility that requires tailoring safety principles and procedures to deal with unforeseen hazards to minimize high potential for serious injury both to the incumbent and others who will use the equipment produced.

Physical/Mental/Visual

The Master Journeyman Tool and Die Maker position requires intensive mental application and visual attention for extended time periods, with the possibility of exposure to hazardous conditions.

MASTER DRAW DIE MAKER

General Purpose

Provide specific and prototype draw die tooling to meet production and engineering requirements by performing specialized draw die maker techniques under limited supervision.

General Duties

The Master Draw Die Maker develops and constructs drifts, laps, electrodes, draw dies, and so on pertaining to draw die tooling from sketches, prints, or verbal instructions. Operates profilers, die sizers, and EDM machines for the purpose of hand or machine lapping, sizing, polishing, and EDMing various new rough core dies and maintenance of existing draw dies and cut-off tooling. Inspects, records, and assists in ordering new draw die tooling. Investigates tooling problems in draw die area and makes recommendations for correction. Assists in the design and development of new draw die tooling in collaboration with engineering. Works to very close tolerances with a general responsibility for work involved. Assists in the education and training of other Draw Die Makers.

Job Specification

Technical Know-How

Specific skills' training exceeding vocational trade school or high school plus skills applicable to wire mill tooling requirements. Setup, operate, adjust, and troubleshoot all draw die making equipment plus Tool Room Equipment applicable to draw die making. Work to close tolerances, read drawings, develop layouts, grind and lap, follow instructions, and use math at a complex level. Must be totally capable of investigating, diagnosing, and correcting draw dies to satisfy close tolerances and form requirements.

Training
Extensive specific skills in draw die making requires up to five (5) years training in the draw die maker field plus one (1) year Tool Room Training to perform duties effectively.

Decision Making/Accountability
These positions have a degree of independence to deviate on certain practices and procedures in draw die making with often no review of work.

Communication/Interpersonal Skills
Master Draw Die Maker position involves discussion and recommendations in draw die making and could possibly affect the facility as a whole. Extensive communications with other production departments, Product Engineering, and Manufacturing Engineering are common.

Safety
Draw die making is performed in accordance with a wide range of safety procedures to minimize potential for injury.

Physical/Mental/Visual
Extreme physical effort, high mental application, or extreme close visual attention, or both, required for extended periods. Work environment highly disagreeable, with possible exposure to hazardous condition.

TOOL ROOM MACHINE OPERATOR

General Purpose

Provide basic machined parts by performing specific Tool Room functions under direct supervision.

General Duties

The Tool Room Machine Operator is an entry level position that performs a variety of basic machine tool setups and operations under direct supervision. Print reading, inspection, and machine operations are performed at introductory levels.

Job Specifications

Working from verbal/written direction, the Tool Room Machine Operator will have the skill, training, and abilities of the following degree:

Technical Know-How
The Tool Room Machine Operator will have knowledge equivalent to a high school diploma. Understand and follow basic drawings and instruction with a basic math background.

Training
Introductory level with no necessary training upon arrival. Training up and including two (2) years.

Decision Making/Accountability
This position is subject to routine decision making based on established practices and technical procedures. Progress of work is periodically checked by others.

Communication/Interpersonal Skills
Limited in nature to receiving and interpreting information on Tool Room tasks.

Safety
The Tool Room Machine Operator performs specific tasks with several specific safety procedures required.

Physical/Mental/Visual
Moderate physical/mental/visual application is required for short periods in this position.

APPENDIX
A Skill-Based Job Evaluation Plan for Manufacturing Jobs: Factor Definitions and Points

FACTOR 1: BASIC KNOWLEDGE

1st Degree (22 points)

Ability to read, write, add, and subtract basic mathematics, interpret and complete simple instructions.

2nd Degree (47 points)

Knowledge of higher mathematical calculations, such as basic decimal and fractional equations, ability to read and follow semicomplicated written instructions and to use basic measuring equipment.

3rd Degree (72 points)

Knowledge of a variety of manufacturing skills, specific training, work experience equivalent to trade school or high school, ability to read semicomplicated measuring equipment, graphics, technical or written reports.

4th Degree (111 points)

Extensive specific skills training in a specialized field; equivalent to one–two years of college or vocational (technical) training or master trade certificate.

FACTOR 2: ELECTRICAL/ELECTRONIC SKILLS

Application of the principles of electricity, electronics, electronic logic, and integrated transmission technologies, such as lasers. This includes understanding of circuits, their component parts, and how they work together.

1st Degree (7 points)

Operational knowledge of electrical/electronic equipment without understanding the electrical/electronic principles on which the equipment operates.

2nd Degree (15 points)

Operational knowledge of electrical/electronic equipment with understanding the electrical/electronic principles on which the equipment operates.

3rd Degree (23 points)

Application of principles of electronic circuitry and appropriate wiring procedures.

4th Degree (37 points)

Application of principles of miniaturized electronic circuits and digital and analog transmission concepts.

FACTOR 3: MECHANICAL SKILLS

The application of mechanical knowledge of how/why mechanical equipment works. It includes the operation, repair, or maintenance of machinery/mechanical systems.

1st Degree (5 points)

This includes the use of basic mechanical ability to operate/adjust single or multiple pieces of mechanical or electromechanical equipment. It includes, but is not limited to, such elements as clearing jams and setting feed speeds and/or pressure changes.

2nd Degree (12 points)

This includes all elements of 1st Degree basic mechanical ability, with the exceptions that the incumbent is required to have the skills to perform preventive maintenance, disassemble/assemble specific components, change tools, and the like.

3rd Degree (25 points)

Perform servicing and procedural repair activities on mechanical systems/machinery as the primary function.

4th Degree (31 points)

Apply advanced principles of mechanical skills to repair, rebuild, service to a close tolerance level of fit.

5th Degree (37 points)

Perform sophisticated diagnostic and repair activities on complex mechanical or electromechanical machinery/systems.

FACTOR 4: GRAPHICS

Reading, interpreting, and/or preparing graphic representations of information, such as maps, plans, drawings, blueprints, diagrams, schematics, and timing/flowcharts.

1st Degree (5 points)

Understand basic blueprints and/or prepare rough sketches.

2nd Degree (12 points)

Understand more complex blueprints and/or prepare simple graphic information.

3rd Degree (25 points)

Understand complex, technical graphic representations of information and/or prepare technical graphics.

4th Degree (31 points)

Prepare and/or interpret complex, technical graphic representations of a wide range of information.

5th Degree (37 points)

Develop, prepare, and/or interpret highly complex, sophisticated graphic representations.

FACTOR 5: MATHEMATICAL SKILLS

The selection and application of mathematical methods or procedures to solve problems or to achieve desired results.

1st Degree (8 points)

Simple arithmetic computations involving addition, subtraction, multiplication, or division.

2nd Degree (15 points)

Computations involving decimals, percentages, fractions, and/or basic statistics.

3rd Degree (23 points)

Computations involving algebra (e.g., solving for an unknown) or geometry (e.g., areas, volumes).

4th Degree (38 points)

Computations involving the use of trigonometry (properties of triangles and circles including sine, cosine, and tangent functions), logarithms and exponents, and advanced statistics.

FACTOR 6: COMMUNICATION/INTERPERSONAL SKILLS

This factor measures the scope and nature of relationships with others.

1st Degree (28 points)

Little or no contact with others. Relationships involve providing and/or receiving information or documents.

2nd Degree (56 points)

Some contact with others. Relationships often require explanation or interpretation of information.

3rd Degree (84 points)

Substantial contact with others. Relationships usually involve discussions with stakeholders or recommendations on issues regarding policies, programs, and so on. Impact is considerable and may be limited to individual departments/programs.

4th Degree (140 points)

Extensive contact with others. Relationships usually include decisions in a broad sense and will affect several areas within the manufacturing unit.

FACTOR 7: SAFETY SKILLS

This factor measures the requirements for adherence to prescribed safety and personal security practices in the performance of required tasks. These safety and personal security practices are generally required to minimize exposure to hazard or risk in the work environment.

1st Degree (10 points)

Perform work in accordance with a few simple safety procedures to minimize potential for injury.

2nd Degree (40 points)

Perform work in accordance with several specific safety procedures to minimize potential for injury.

3rd Degree (80 points)

Perform work in accordance with a wide range of safety procedures to minimize some potential for injury.

4th Degree (100 points)

Perform work in a highly variable environment where safety principles and procedures need to be tailored to deal with unforeseen hazards to minimize high potential for serious injury.

FACTOR 8: DECISION MAKING/SUPERVISION REQUIRED

This factor measures the degree of decision making required without being checked by others, and the degree to which immediate supervisor is required to outline the procedures to be followed and/or the results to be attained on the job.

1st Degree (36 points)

Limited decision making by the incumbent. Progress of work is checked by others most of the time, and/or 60–90 percent of activities are defined by other than the incumbent.

2nd Degree (89 points)

Routine decision making based on specific criteria. Progress of work is often checked by others, and/or 40–60 percent of activities are defined by other than the incumbent.

3rd Degree (112 points)

Significant decision making based on established guidelines and experience. Progress of work is checked by others some of the time, and/or 25–40 percent of activities are defined by other than the incumbent.

4th Degree (180 points)

Extensive decision making based on broad policies, procedures, and guidelines. Progress of work is seldom checked by others, and/or less than 25 percent of activities are defined by other than the incumbent.

NOTES AND REFERENCES

1. Edward E. Lawler III, *Pay and Organization Development* (Reading, Mass.: Addison-Wesley Publishing, 1981).
2. See any basic text in labor economics; for example, R. Ehrenberg and R. S. Smith, *Modern Labor Economics* (Glenview, Ill.: Scott, Foresman, 1988).
3. George P. Schultz and Kenneth W. Dam, "Reflections of Wage and Price Controls," *Industrial and Labor Relations Review,* January 1977, pp. 139–51.
4. Donald O. Parsons, *Poverty and the Minimum Wage* (Washington, D.C.: American Enterprise Institute, 1980); Lester Thurow, *Youth Unemployment* (New York: Rockefeller Foundation, 1977).
5. James Ledvinka, *Federal Regulation of Personnel and Human Resource Management* (Boston: Kent Publishing, 1982).
6. George T. Milkovich and Jerry Newman, *Compensation,* 3rd ed. (Homewood, Ill.: BPI Irwin, 1990).
7. George T. Milkovich, "A Strategic Perspective to Compensation Management," in *Research in Human Resources Management,* ed. K. Rowland and G. Ferris (Greenwich, Conn.: JAI Press, 1988); R. F. Broderick, "Pay Policy, Organization Strategy, and Structure: A Question of 'Fit,' " Paper for the Research Symposium of the Human Resource Planning Society, presented at Wharton School of Management, University of Pennsylvania, Philadelphia, 1985; D. Balkin and L. Gomez-Mejia, "Determinants of R&D Compensation Strategies in the High Tech Industry," *Personnel Psychology* 37, 1984, pp. 635–50; S. Carroll, "Business Strategies and Compensation Systems,"

in *New Perspectives in Compensation,* ed. D. B. Balkin and L. R. Gomez-Mejia (Englewood Cliffs, N.J.: Prentice-Hall, 1987), pp. 343–55.

8. Roger Folder and Mary Konovsky, "Effects of Procedural and Distributive Justice on Reactions to Pay Raise Decisions," *Academy of Management Journal,* March 1989, pp. 115–30; Jerald Greenberg, "Looking Fair vs. Being Fair: Managing Impressions of Organizational Justice," in B. M. Staw and L. L. Cummings, eds., *Research in Organizational Behavior,* vol. 12 (Greenwich, Conn.: JAI Press, 1990).

9. Bruce Ellig, *Executive Compensation—A Total Pay Perspective* (New York: McGraw-Hill, 1982); Jude T. Rich, "Strategic Incentives," in *1980 National Conference Proceedings* (Scottsdale, Ariz.: American Compensation Association, 1981).

10. Lester C. Thurow, *Generating Inequality: Mechanisms of Distribution in The U.S. Economy* (New York: Basic Books, 1975); Sara L. Rynes, D. P. Schwab, and G. H. Heneman III, "The Role of Pay and Market Pay Variability in Job Application Decisions," *Organizational Behavior and Human Performance* 31 (1983), pp. 353–64; Kenneth G. Wheeler, "Perceptions of Labor Market Variables by College Students in Business, Education, and Psychology," *Journal of Vocational Behavior* 22 (1983), pp. 1–11; Erica Groshen, "Sources of Wage Dispersion: How Much do Employers Matter?" Working Paper, Department of Economics, Harvard University, December 1985; Ronald G. Ehrenberg and George T. Milkovich, "Compensation and Firm Performance," National Bureau of Economic Research, Inc., Working Paper no. 2145, February 1987.

11. E. Robert Livernash, "The Internal Wage Structure," in *New Concepts in Wage Determination,* ed. G. W. Taylor and Frank C. Pierson (New York: McGraw-Hill, 1957); Ehrenberg and Milkovich, "Compensation and Firm Performance."

12. Edward E. Lawler III, "The New Pay," in *Current Issues in Human Resource Management,* ed. Sara L. Rynes and George T. Milkovich (Plano, Tex.: Business Publications, Inc., 1986); N. Gupta, G. D. Jenkins, Jr., and W. P. Curington, "Paying for Knowledge: Myths and Realities," *National Productivity Review,* Spring 1986, pp. 107–23.

13. Thomas A. Mahoney, *Compensation and Reward Perspectives* (Homewood, Ill.: Richard D. Irwin, 1979); Kenneth E. Foster, "An Anatomy of Company Pay Practices," *Personnel,* September 1985, pp. 67–71; John Barron, John Bishop, and William Dunkelberg, "Employer Search: The Interviewing and Hiring of New Employees," *The Review of Economics and Statistics,* 1986, pp. 43–52; Charles Brown and James Medoff, "The Employer Size Wage Effect," mimeographed, November 1985.

14. Thomas H. Stone and Sarosh Kuruvilla, "The Wage Comparison Process in a Local Labor Market" (University of Iowa: Working Paper, 1988).

15. Sara L. Rynes and G. T. Milkovich, "Wage Surveys: Dispelling Some Myths about the 'Market Wage,'" *Personnel Psychology,* Spring 1986, pp. 71–90.

16. Raymond A. Noe, Brian D. Steffy, and Alison E. Barber, "An Investigation of the Factors Influencing Employees' Willingness to Accept Mobility Opportunities," *Personnel Psychology,* Autumn 1988, pp. 559–80; Richard Ippolito, "Why Federal Workers Don't Quit," *Journal of Human Resources* 22, no. 2 (1987), pp. 281–99; Alan Krueger, "The Determinants of Queues for Federal Jobs," *Industrial and Labor Relations Review,* July 1988, pp. 567–81; Hyder Lakhani, "The Effect of Pay and Retention Bonuses on Quit Rates in the U.S. Army," *Industrial and Labor Relations Review,* April 1988, pp. 430–38; Timothy W. Lee and Richard Mowday, "Voluntarily Leaving an Organization: An Empirical Investigation of Steers and Mowday's Model of Turnover," *Academy of Management Journal,* December 1987, pp. 721–43.

17. Thomas A. Mahoney, "Organizational Hierarchy and Position Worth," *Academy of Management Journal,* December 1979, pp. 726–37.

18. Alan Farnham, "The Trust Gap," *Fortune,* December 4, 1989, pp. 56–75.

19. G. Douglas Jenkins, Jr., and Nina Gupta, "The Payoffs of Paying for Knowledge," *Labor-Management Cooperation Brief* (Washington, D.C.: Department of Labor, August 1985; Henry Tosi and Lisa Tosi, "Knowledge Based Pay: Some Propositions and Guides to Effective Use" (Working Paper, University of Florida, Gainesville, 1984); and Edward J. Lawler and Gerald E. Ledford, Jr., "Skill-Based Pay: A Concept That's Catching on," *Compensation and Benefits Review,* January–February 1986, pp. 54–61; Ian Ziskin, "Knowledge-Based Pay: A Strategic Analysis," *ILR Report,* Fall 1986, pp. 16–22; Also see the U.S. Department of Labor, *Exploratory Investigations of Pay-For-Knowledge Systems* (Washington, D.C.: Government Printing Office, 1986).

20. Bureau of National Affairs, "Changing Pay Practices: New Developments in Employee Compensation" (BNA: Washington, D.C., 1988).

21. Jerald Greenberg and Claire L. McCarty, "Comparable Worth: A Matter of Justice," in *Research in Personnel and Human Resource Management,* vol. 8, K. M. Rowland and G. R. Ferris, eds. (Greenwich, Conn.: JAI Press, 1990).

22. Myron Liberman, "The Conversion of Interests to Principles: The Case of Comparable Worth," *Journal of Collective Negotiations* 15, no. 2 (1986), pp. 145–52.

23. Mike Burns, *Understanding Job Evaluation* (London: Institute of Personnel Management, 1978); Harold D. Janes, "Union Views on Job Evaluation, 1971 vs. 1978" *Personnel Journal,* February 1979, pp. 80–85.

24. E. E. Lawler III and G. D. Jenkins, "Employee Participation in Pay Plan Development" (technical report to Department of Labor, Ann Arbor, Mich., 1976).

25. Allan N. Nash and Stephen J. Carroll, Jr., *The Management of Compensation* (Belmont, Calif.: Wadsworth, 1975).

26. For a copy of the Hay Guide Charts and a detailed description of their use, see Al Bellak, "Specific Job Evaluation Systems: The Hay Guide Chart-Profile Method," in *Handbook of Wage and Salary Administration,* ed. Milton L. Rock (New York: McGraw-Hill, 1984), pp. 15/1–15/16.

CHAPTER
THIRTEEN

Paying Individual Employees

Employee Contributions

Recognizing Employee Differences with Pay

Individual Pay Techniques
Flat Rates
Pay Ranges
Pay Increases Guidelines
Merit Awards
Lump-Sum Payments

Incentives
Individual Incentives
Group Incentives
Gainsharing
Profit Sharing

Evaluating the Results of Pay for
Performance Systems

Pay Administration
Cost Controls
Communication and Appeals
Participation
Special Groups

Executive Pay

International Differentials

Comparable Worth

Your Turn: Disney's CEO

The most important pay question for most of us is, How much of it do we get? The topics discussed in the previous chapter—external competitiveness, internal consistency, pay levels, and structures—seem abstract in comparison. This chapter examines various approaches to paying individual employees. It also considers a variety of issues associated with administering the entire pay system. These include budgeting, communication, pay discrimination, and paying special groups of employees.

How much should one employee be paid relative to another when both hold the same job in the same organization? For example, should all first-line supervisors working at Exxon Chemical's Baytown, Texas, facilities receive the same pay? Or should those with better performance and/or seniority receive more? Should the pay increase employees receive be based on their individual performance, the performance of a team to which they belong, or the plant or corporate performance?

An assessment of employee contributions, the third basic policy decision in the pay model presented in the last chapter (Exhibit 12.2), helps us to answer these questions. Policies on employee contributions refer to the pay relationships among workers doing the same work within a single organization. The policy is translated into practice through pay ranges, merit increase guidelines, individual bonuses and awards, and group incentives, such as gainsharing or profitsharing.

EMPLOYEE CONTRIBUTIONS

Several decisions go into determining the pay for individual employees. Two basic ones are:

1. Should different employees holding the same job or possessing the same skills be paid the same—or should managers be able to pay them differently?

2. What factors should be used to recognize differences in employees; that is, should differences in pay be contingent on performance, seniority or some combination of the two?

RECOGNIZING EMPLOYEE DIFFERENCES WITH PAY

Many employers do pay different rates to employees in the same job. The rates of the Dallas word processors in the last chapter are an example. These differences reflect external labor market pressures and organization policies.[1] Two external influences are:

1. Variations in the quality (skills, abilities, experience) among applicants in the external market (e.g., company A has stricter hiring requirements for word processors than does company B, even though the jobs are identical).
2. Recognition that employers place differing values on these variations in quality (e.g., word processing is more important at firms that specialize in word processing services than at Neiman-Marcus).

Differences in rates paid to employees on the same job also occur in response to the following organization factors:

1. Policies to recognize individual differences in experience, skill, and performance with pay. (Wordprocessor A does better and more timely work than does wordprocessor B, even though they have the same responsibilities.)
2. Employees' expectations that longer seniority and/or higher performance deserve greater pay.

So pay differences permit managers to recognize differences among employees.

INDIVIDUAL PAY TECHNIQUES

Employers use a wide array of techniques to determine the pay of individual employees. These include *flat rates,* which are used when the policy is to *not* use pay to recognize individual differences. Techniques designed to give managers discretion in making pay decisions about individuals include ranges, merit increase guidelines, and individual and group incentives.

Flat Rates

In cases where wages are established by collective bargaining, single flat rates, rather than different rates, are common.[2] An example might be if all senior machinists receive $14.50 per hour, regardless of performance or seniority. This flat rate is often set to correspond to some midpoint on a market survey for that job. Or it may simply reflect the results of the patterns established across various union/employer negotiations.

Existence of a flat rate does not mean that performance or experience variations do not exist. It means that the parties choose not to recognize these variations with pay. There may be several reasons for ignoring performance differences. Unions may argue that performance measures are biased. Or the work may be designed in a manner that requires cooperative team efforts, and different pay rates may hinder cooperation.

EXHIBIT 13.1   Establishing Ranges

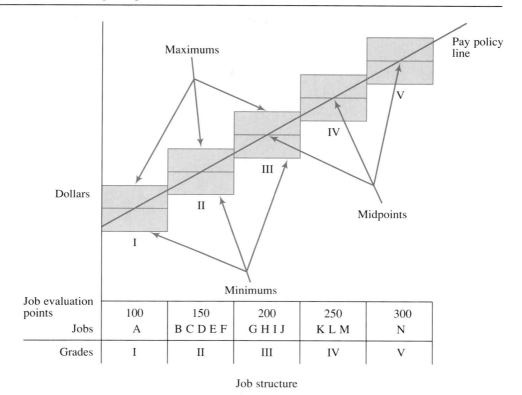

Source: George T. Milkovich and Jerry M. Newman, *Compensation,* 3rd ed. (Homewood, Ill.: BPI Irwin, 1990).

Some organizations may pay a flat rate for a job and then attach a bonus or incentive to recognize performance variations. Gainsharing systems follow this logic. Under these systems, differences in group or team performance, rather than individual differences, are recognized with pay.

Pay Ranges

Ranges set limits on the rates an employer will pay for a particular job. Exhibit 13.1 shows pay ranges constructed for the pay level and structure designed in the last chapter. Five pay ranges (I–V), one for each key job (A, D, G, M, and N), have been established. Designing ranges is relatively simple. There is no "best" approach, but two basic steps are typically involved.

EXHIBIT 13.2 Typical Pay Range

Grade II: Jobs B, C, D, E, and F

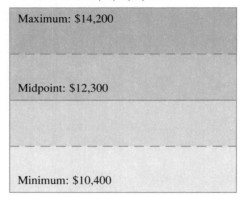

Maximum: $14,200

Midpoint: $12,300

Minimum: $10,400

1. Develop classes or grades In Exhibit 13.1, the horizontal axis is the job structure generated through job evaluation. A grade or class is a grouping of different jobs; thus, each grade may be made up of a number of jobs. There are five grades (I–V): grade I has one job (A) in it, grade II has jobs B, C, D, E, and F, and so on. The jobs in each grade are considered substantially similar for pay purposes. They may have approximately the same job evaluation points (e.g., within 30 to 50 points in a 700-point job evaluation plan).

Each grade has its own pay range and all the jobs within the grade also have that same range. Jobs within a grade (e.g., jobs K, L, and M in grade IV) should be dissimilar from jobs in other grades (e.g., jobs G, H, I, and J) and will have a different pay range.

What is the correct number of job grades? It simply depends on the circumstances. Designing the grade structure that "fits" each organization involves trial and error until one seems to fit the best without too many problems. The use of grades recognizes the imprecision in job evaluation.[3]

2. Set midpoints, maximums, and minimums Exhibit 13.2 shows a typical pay range, with a maximum, midpoint, and minimum. Ranges permit managers to pay on the basis of employee experience or performance. The pay range for any job should approximate the range of differences in performance and/or experience that managers wish to recognize. For example, a job of plant manager accommodates a wide variation in performance level and experience, so the pay range for this job may be quite large. But there is less latitude in the job of insurance claims processor, and consequently a narrower pay range. Ranges also act as control devices. A range maximum puts a ceiling on what the employer is willing to pay for the job; the range minimum sets the floor.

The midpoint rates for each range are usually set to correspond to the employer's pay policy line. The policy line represents the organization's pay level policy relative to what competition pays for similar jobs. The maximums and minimums (the range width or spread) are usually based on a combination of what other employers are doing and some judgment about what makes sense for a particular organization. Surveys usually provide data on both the actual maximum and minimum rates paid, as well as the established ranges (turn back to the previous chapter for examples). Some compensation professionals use the actual rates paid, particularly the 75th and 25th percentiles (if available) to establish the maximum and minimum; others use the average of the established ranges reported in the survey as a starting point to design the ranges. The range spread can vary from 10 percent to 50 percent on either side of the midpoint with ±20 to 30 percent of the midpoint most common.

Progression through Ranges

Once ranges are established, the next issue is to decide how employees will move through the range. Two criteria are commonly used, seniority and merit.

Seniority pay increases are based on experience or seniority on the job. Seniority-based pay increases recognize the value of an experienced, stable work force. However, as the work force grows older on the job, it also grows more expensive. So, without turnover or productivity increases, unit labor costs will increase under seniority-based systems.

Merit pay increases link pay to job performance. If pay is tied to productivity, then unit labor costs are less likely to increase than in seniority-based systems.

The choice of which criteria to use—merit, seniority, or some combination of the two—depends on the objectives of the pay system. If managers want to try to reinforce performance improvements with pay, then some part of pay must be linked to performance. If they also wish to ensure a stable, experienced work force, then seniority should be included, too.

Pay Increase Guidelines

Most employees have come to expect annual pay increases. A variety of pay increase guidelines exist. One, the *general increase,* typically is found in unionized firms. A contract is negotiated that specifies an across-the-board (equal for all employees) increase for each year the contract is in effect. Another, similar, increase method is based on *cost-of-living adjustments* (COLA). Under it, increases are triggered by changes in the consumer price index (CPI).

Another increase guideline, the automatic, or *seniority,* increase, was discussed above. For example, a pay range might be divided into 10 equal steps and employees moved to higher steps based on their longevity or seniority on the job.

EXHIBIT 13.3 Excerpt from Bank of America's Pay-for-Performance Plan

---

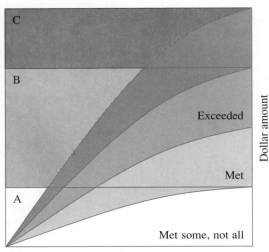

Your performance affects your pay in two ways.

First, it affects the size of the raise you receive. For example, if two employees started in the same job at the same time, at the same salary, over time the salary level of the one whose performance far exceeds will be greater than the salary level of the employee whose performance is rated as only having "met" an acceptable level of results. So, the better you do your job, the higher your salary can grow.

Second, the timing of your salary increase will be based on your performance and your position in your salary range. If two employees are in the same sector of their salary range, the better performer can expect to receive an increase sooner than the employee performing at a lower level. Thus, your performance determines how much of an increase you receive, as well as when you receive it.

By far the most common pay increase guideline for managerial and professional employees (about 90 percent are covered by it) is one based on merit.[4] An example of *merit increase* guidelines used by the Bank of America is shown in Exhibit 13.3. The pay ranges are divided into performance levels (Far Exceeded, Exceeded, Met, Met Some but not All Objectives) and the appropriate pay increase corresponding to each performance level is calculated. Lower performance ratings are tied to lower pay increases, and higher ratings get the largest increases. In many firms, the poorest performers may receive no pay increases under a pay-for-performance guideline. The case Merit Pay Decisions, pages 681–86, lets you design merit increase guidelines with the aid of a computer.

Merit Awards

AT&T, Digital Equipment, and other employers have turned to merit *awards* (contrasted with merit *increases* discussed above). Merit awards are pay increases that do *not* become part of the employee's base salary each year.[5] Several arguments have been advanced in favor of merit awards. They may offer management greater flexibility and reflect performance more accurately. They avoid one year's performance being part of a person's salary for an entire career.

But for all the pay-for-performance rhetoric associated with merit awards, they are primarily cost control devices. Recall our discussion on employment planning: we discussed options for reducing labor costs by making a portion of compensation costs variable. Merit awards do this in two ways. First, base pay is not increased each year. Second, since some benefits, such as pensions, are calculated on base pay, merit awards do not increase those benefits. Most firms that adopt awards are facing severe competitive pressures and are attempting to reduce labor costs.

Lump-Sum Payments

Lump-sum payments are a variation of merit awards. A quote from one company's manual illustrates this policy:

> The Lump-Sum Increase Program (LSIP) is a payment option offering you the flexibility to tailor part of your total compensation to your specific needs. Under this program you can elect to receive all or part of any salary increase—whether merit, promotional, or a special adjustment—in the form of one lump-sum payment (less a small discount for payment in advance). By making the full amount of your increase available as soon as it is effective, LSIP allows you to plan realistically for large expenditures without using retail credit plans having high interest rates.

To date, no research evidence has been reported on how effective the LSIP is. One writer estimates that 40 to 95 percent of eligible employees take advantage of the LSIP when given the opportunity.[6] Lawler states that "a lump-sum program represents one way in which employees are treated more as individuals by the organizations that employ them and, as such, it improves the quality of work life."[7] Yet, the effects of merit and awards of LSIP remain unknown; only research will tell whether this program will affect efficiency or equity.

INCENTIVES

The techniques of basing pay increases upon improvement in performance are old and well-established.[8] Hundreds of different formulas exist for calculating payments to employees based upon performance.[9] In all of them, the *level* at which performance is assessed is crucial. As Exhibit 13.4 shows, incentives can be based on an individual's performance or on the operating results of a work team, plant, or even the entire corporation.

Individual Incentives

Perhaps the oldest form of compensation is the individual incentive plan, in which the employee is paid for the quality or quantity of units produced, or both. Today the individual incentive plan takes several forms: examples include piecework and production bonuses, and commissions.

EXHIBIT 13.4 Incentive-Based Pay Plans

Performance Measure	Plan Type
Individual units of output	Individual Incentive Plan
Units of output for a small group	Small Group Incentive
Units of output or cost savings for a division or entire organization	Gainsharing Plan
Profitability of division or organization	Profit-sharing Plan
Value of stock	Employee Stock Ownership Plan

Piecework and Production Bonus

In piecework, an employee is guaranteed an hourly rate (probably the minimum wage) for performing an expected minimum output (the standard). For production over the standard, the employer pays so much per piece produced. The standard is set through work measurement studies and collective bargaining. The base rate and piece rates may be developed by surveys of compensation practices and financial analysis of revenues and expenses.

A variation of the straight piece rate is the differential piece rate. In this plan, the employer pays a smaller piece rate up to standard and then a higher piece rate above the standard. Yet another variation is based on standard hours required to perform a task successfully. For example, a car dealership may set a standard time required for replacing a fuel pump or the brakes in a specific type of car. The mechanic earns an incentive in addition to base pay for performing the task in less time. The dealer charge to you is based on the standard time, of course.

Commissions

Commissions are commonly used in sales jobs. Straight commission is the equivalent of straight piecework and is typically a percentage of the price of the item. A variation is to pay the salesperson a small salary and commission or bonus when the budgeted sales goal is exceeded. J. C. Penney, Neiman-Marcus, and other retailers make wide use of sales incentive schemes for their store sales force.[10]

Individual incentives are used more frequently in some industries (retail, mining, textiles) than in others (lumber, steel, autos) and more in some jobs (sales, production) than in others (managerial, clerical).

Results

The research results on the effectiveness of individual incentives are mixed; most studies indicate they do increase productivity. However, other performance aspects decline. For example, in sales, straight commission can lead to less attention being paid to servicing accounts. And that mechanic who re-

EXHIBIT 13.5   Factors Influencing Whether to Use Individual or Group Incentives

Characteristic	Individual Level of Incentives Appropriate	Group Level of Incentives (unit, department, organization) Appropriate
Performance measurement	Good measures of individual performance exist. Task accomplishment not dependent on performance of others.	Output is group collaborative effort. Individual contributions to output cannot be assessed.
Organizational adaptability	Individual performance standards are stable. Production methods and labor mix relatively constant.	Performance standards for individuals change to meet environmental pressures on relatively constant organizational objectives. Production methods and labor mix must adapt to meet changing pressures.
Organizational commitment	Commitment strongest to individual's profession or superior. Supervisor viewed as unbiased and performance standards readily apparent.	High commitment to organization built upon sound communication of organizational objectives and performance standards.
Union status	Nonunion. Unions promote equal treatment. Competition between individuals inhibits "fraternal" spirit.	Union or nonunion. Unions less opposed to plans which foster cohesiveness of bargaining unit and which distribute rewards evenly across group.

Source: George T. Milkovich and Jerry M. Newman, *Compensation,* 3rd ed. (Homewood, Ill.: BPI Irwin, 1990).

paired your car may be more interested in getting the job done in a short time than in the quality of the job. There is also evidence that individual differences play a role; some employees may want their pay based on their performance, others do not.

Incentive systems may be designed to affect other outputs than performance; for example, employers may use them to try to improve quality (reduce rejects) and lower absenteeism. Some incentive schemes have been designed to encourage early retirement of older workers. Others are designed to reduce turnover of highly skilled workers.[11]

Group Incentives

Incentives can also be paid to groups of employees.[12] Factors influencing whether to use individual or group incentives are shown in Exhibit 13.5. Group incentives are used when it is difficult to measure each individual employees' output, and/or when team work is important. The performance of a team of employees or the entire plant is used to determine pay increases. Employees who assemble pumps and electric motors at Dresser Rand, manufacture automobile components for TRW, and make toothpaste and soap for Colgate-Palmolive, receive group incentives.

Several types of group incentive schemes exist. Some focus on cost savings, others quantity of production, and still others emphasize quality of the units produced. The basic premise underlying these plans is to share the gains with employees. In the past few years, the use of these gainsharing plans has been increasing.

Gainsharing

According to its advocates, gainsharing is more than a group incentive scheme. It is part of a total management approach or philosophy.[13] Exhibit 13.6 lists the organizational characteristics favoring a gainsharing plan. Key characteristics include small-size operation, production and costs under employee control, trusting participative relationship between managers and employees, and a technically competent work force. Experience suggests that a plant manager totally committed to making the incentive plan work is also required.

An Illustration: The Scanlon Plan at Painted Post

Exhibit 13.7 highlights the key features of the gainsharing plan used in a manufacturing plant at Painted Post, New York. Employees earn a bonus by increasing productivity, improving quality, or saving shop supplies. This plan is a variation on the Scanlon Plan, undoubtedly the best-known group (plant or facility wide) gainsharing plan.[14] Plans of this type were developed by Joseph Scanlon, a union leader in the steel industry during the 1930s.

The Painted Post plan illustrates the three key features of a Scanlon plan. First, it includes a *philosophy* of management that is participatory and involves pay incentives and a suggestion system. Each unit in the plant has a production committee made up of foremen and employee representatives. Employee Involvement Teams (EIT) provide employees the opportunity to make suggestions for improvements.

The second key feature is that a *committee of employees and managers* administer the plan—including evaluating the improvement suggestions, applying the bonus formula, redesigning the formula, and so on. So the Bonus Committee at Painted Post screens the improvement suggestions made by employees and managers. If accepted, the gains (e.g., cost savings of improved production) are shared with the work group, not just the individual who suggested it.

Third, companies using the Scanlon Plan use widely varying *formulas for calculating the amount of bonuses employees receive* (usually a percentage of their pay). For example, some base the bonus on a ratio of total sales volume to total

---

EXHIBIT 13.6   Conditions Favoring Gainsharing Plans

Organizational Characteristic	Favorable Condition
Size	Small unit, usually less than 500 employees.
Age	Old enough so that learning curve has flattened and standards can be set based on performance history.
Financial measures	Simple, with a good history.
Market for output	Good, can absorb additional production.
Product costs	Controllable by employees.
Organizational climate	Open, high level of trust.
Style of management	Participative.
Union status	No union, or one that is favorable to a cooperative effort.
Overtime history	Limited to no use of overtime in the past.
Seasonal nature of business	Relatively stable across time.
Work floor interdependence	High to moderate interdependence.
Capital investment plans	Little investment planned.
Product stability	Few product changes.
Comptroller/Chief financial officer	Trusted, able to explain financial measures.
Communication policy	Open, willing to share financial results.
Plant manager	Trusted, committed to plan, able to articulate goals and ideals of plan.
Management	Technically competent, supportive of participative management style, good communications skills, able to deal with suggestions and new ideas.
Corporate position (if part of larger organization)	Favorable to plan.
Work force	Technically knowledgeable, interested in participation and higher pay, financially knowledgeable and/or interested.
Plant support services	Maintenance and engineering groups competent, willing, and able to respond to increased demands.

Source: Edward E. Lawler III, *Pay and Organization Development* (Reading, Mass.: Addison-Wesley Publishing, 1981), p. 144.

payroll expenses. This measure reflects labor cost changes (if corrected for inflation). Others focus on payroll costs for each type of product. The Painted Post plan utilizes three measurements to calculate the bonus payout:

Productivity (as measured by savings in labor costs).

Quality (as measured by reductions in spoilage and scrap).

Shop Supplies (as measured by reductions in costs for tools and aprons).

EXHIBIT 13.7   Key Features of the Painted Post, New York, Gainsharing Plan

---

✦ A productivity, quality, and cost reduction formula to recognize employees for their efforts.

Employees can earn a bonus by:

Increasing productivity.
Improve quality.
Saving on shop supplies.

This element of the plan gives employees a triple opportunity to be productive and, at the same time, conscious of quality, material, and shop supplies.

✦ An expansion of the employee involvement teams (EIT) to provide employees with an opportunity to solve problems that can increase productivity and quality, while reducing the costs of material and shop supplies.

✦ A Bonus Committee, composed of four employees and four management representatives, that is responsible for the overall administration of the program.

✦ Team work and employee participation are the key ingredients of the plan. Both require your support and commitment in order for the program to be successful.

Example

TOTAL ALL SAVINGS BONUS POOLS			$120,000
Labor	+	$50,000	
Quality	+	40,000	
Supplies	+	30,000	
		$120,000	
Less 1/3 as current quarter reserve provision*			40,000
Apply to prior quarter loss			0
Available for Distribution			80,000
Employee share of savings 65%			52,000
Participating payroll			1,000,000
Employee share—% of participating payroll			5.20%
(Participating payroll is total wages for all hours worked.)			

---

* The reserve is established to provide some safeguard for the plan against quarters with lower than normal efficiency where the stated labor costs, spoilage, scrap and reclamation, and shop supplies goals are not met. At the end of the gainsharing year, the money remaining in the reserve account will be distributed.

The plan permits gains in productivity to be enhanced by savings in scrap and shop supplies, as well as through suggestions for productivity improvements from the EITS. Thus, a bonus is determined by the following formula:

$$\text{Gainsharing bonus} = \frac{\text{Productivity}}{\text{(Labor costs)}} \pm \frac{\text{Quality}}{\text{(Scrap savings)}} \pm \frac{\text{Shop supplies}}{\text{(Cost savings)}}$$

In the example shown in Exhibit 13.7, the plant improvement in labor costs, product quality, and shop supplies yielded $120,000. One third of the bonus is set aside in a reserve, the remainder is divided between an employees' share (65 percent) and the firm's share (35 percent). The 65 percent employee share translates into about 5.2 percent per employee. So, if the average annual salary is $30,000, the bonus the average employee takes home is $1,560.

The main objective underlying gainsharing is to use pay to tie the goals of individuals to the goals of the organization and to emphasize that improved performance involves both individual and team effort. This is accomplished by sharing the gains from employee suggestions and technological improvements with the employees.

Profit Sharing

Essentially, profit sharing is the payment to employees of a portion of profits, after they have exceeded some preestablished level.[15] Many firms have recently adopted such plans. Union Carbide, for example, shares profits that reflect an 8 percent or better return on capital.

Profit-sharing plans vary in the timing of the payouts (e.g., quarterly, annually) and in the form the payout takes (e.g., cash or deferred payment until retirement or severance).

The assumption underlying profit sharing is that employees who have profit-sharing plans identify more closely with the company and its profit goal and, thus, reduce waste and increase productivity.

But there are problems with profit sharing. First, an organization cannot share what it does not have; and in bad years, there are no profits to share. The employees may have cut costs and worked hard, but perhaps a recession slowed sales and, thus, profits, or management chose an expensive but ineffective marketing program. Often, even in good years, it is difficult for the employee to see any connection between extra work and a share of profits received a year away, or worse, at retirement 40 years later.

Profit sharing is probably more successful in smaller firms where the employees can see the relationship between their productivity and company profits more easily. Plans restricted to executives have been more successful, as will be discussed later in the chapter.

Other forms of pay, such as stock ownership, are discussed in the next chapter, Benefits.

EVALUATING THE RESULTS OF PAY FOR PERFORMANCE SYSTEMS

From a decision-making perspective, pay-for-performance systems are evaluated in terms of their objectives—efficiency and equity.

Efficiency: Pay for Performance

Can the performance of employees and organizations be affected by properly designed and managed pay programs? One way to answer this question is to consider three subquestions: (1) Is pay important to employees? (2) Should pay increases be based on performance? (3) Does tying pay increase to performance affect employee and organization performance?

Is Money Important?

From the motivational theories discussed in Chapter Four, it is apparent there is no instinctive or basic need for money. Money becomes important insofar as it can satisfy recognized needs. Research suggests that money is capable of satisfying physiological, security, and esteem needs. If these needs are satisfied by other means, or if other needs are greater, then money is seen as having lower instrumental value and is not particularly useful in motivating performance.[16]

If different needs are, in fact, of varying importance across individuals, this information could be used to design a pay-for-performance system. Lawler argues for a two-step sequential process: (1) identify groups for which differential need strength is evident and (2) devise selection programs that will identify those individuals who have needs that can be satisfied through a pay system tied to performance.[17] Such a program, if successful, would permit organizations that subscribe to a pay-for-performance philosophy to implement a pay system designed to use pay for improved performance.

There is some evidence that organizations may be experiencing problems by assuming that employees place a high value on monetary rewards. One study suggests that managers overestimate the importance of pay to subordinates.[18] Given a belief that pay can motivate performance, supervisors become disillusioned when improved performance does not result from pay increases. This failure results in a general condemnation of pay as a motivator. In reality, however, it may be more advantageous not to view money as the supreme motivator, but rather as one of the numerous factors in the work environment that affects employee motivation.

Should Pay Increases Be Based on Performance?

Given that money can satisfy at least a subset of basic needs, the question now becomes *should* salary increases be based on level of performance? Substantial evidence exists that management and workers alike believe pay *should* be tied to performance.

One study asked 180 managers from 72 different companies to rate 9 possible factors in terms of the importance they should receive in determining the size of salary increases.[19] Workers believed the most important factor for salary increases should be job performance. Following close behind is the nature of the job and amount of effort expended.[20]

The role that performance should play in determining pay increases is also less clear-cut for blue-collar workers. As an illustration, consider the frequent opposition to compensation plans that are based on performance (i.e., incentive piece-rate systems). Much of the discontent with performance-based plans is a reaction to the specific type of plan and the way it is administered. One writer notes that "in many situations opposition to incentive pay comes about because the employees feel they cannot trust the company to administer incentive schemes properly."[21]

Are Pay Increases Related to Performance?

Do pay for performance plans work? Do they really affect employee behaviors and organization performance? Surveys report about 90 percent of large public and private sector employees claim to have at least a portion of their pay designed to link pay to performance. Even nonprofit employers are increasingly interested in such policies; 34 percent claimed to have pay-for-performance components in their pay systems.[22] But claiming or desiring to have a pay for performance plan does not necessarily mean they work.[23] So, let's turn to the evidence.

Gainsharing Results

Recently two well-controlled studies of gainsharing were completed. One, which included 28 different plants and used data over five years, reported improved productivity in about 60 percent of the plants. Unsuccessful programs tended to have (1) infrequent bonus payouts, (2) little employee participation, and (3) absence of union cooperation.[24]

In the second study, the effects of gainsharing were studied over 114 months at a foundry that made iron castings.[25] Exhibit 13.8 shows the trend in monthly productivity, with group incentive intervention occurring at the 45th month. Not only did productivity "step up" but also the rate of productivity improvement (slope of the trend) also improved. Similar effects on reduced labor costs and grievance rates were also reported.

Bonus Plans Research

According to a study of managerial bonus plans in 250 companies, improvements in the ratio of bonus to base pay for managerial employees resulted in improvements in the firm's return on assets (ROA) and returns on investments (ROI). For example, a 10 percent increase in bonus to base pay in one year yielded a 0.02 percent improvement in firms' ROA in subsequent years.[26] So, we are beginning to get hard evidence that incentive pay plans do seem to affect performance.

Why do these plans work? Unfortunately, little research is available to guide our decisions. What is available supports the belief that, to be effective, plans

EXHIBIT 13.8   Productivity Changes Associated with Gainsharing

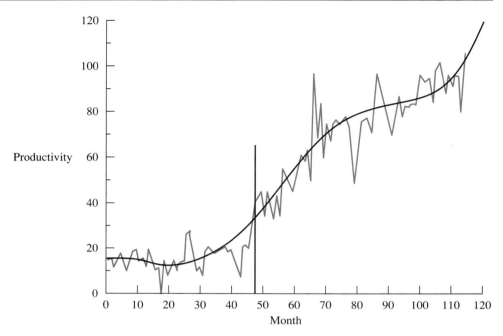

Source: John Wagner, Paul Rubin, and Thomas Callahan, "Incentive Payment and Non-Managerial Productivity: An Interrupted Time Series Analysis of Magnitude and Trend," *Organizational Behavior and Human Decision Processes* 42 (1988), pp. 47–74.

must clearly communicate the organization's objectives to employees, be part of a total human resource philosophy, and encourage employee involvement and commitment.

Negative Evidence

Most of the evidence arguing against a pay-for-performance system is based on problems encountered in implementing the system, particularly in the public sector.

The Civil Service Reform Act (1978) mandated that 50 percent of any pay increase for covered federal government employees be automatic (seniority-based) and the other 50 percent must be performance-based. But a study of managers in the Social Security Administration found merit pay had no effect on organizational performance. The authors note, however, that the plan was not trusted by employees. They challenged it in court, and its implementation was hamstrung by Congress and poor administration.[27] A summary of these problems is offered by Hamner.[28] He lists four problems that make it difficult to implement a performance-contingent pay system.

1. *Pay is not perceived as contingent upon performance.* Many employers adopt a policy of secrecy in their pay administration practices. The secrecy surrounding pay increases may lead employees to believe that there is no direct relationship between pay and performance.

2. *Performance evaluations are viewed as biased.* As noted in Chapter Four, if performance evaluations are based on subjective judgments by supervisors, and not on objective criteria (e.g., units produced) many employees feel that ratings have the potential to be biased.

3. *Rewards are not viewed as reward.* Assume, for the moment, that pay is supposed to be based on performance in company A. It would be expected that A's employees compare the pay increase they receive with that of other employees in company A. What happens if employees have an inflated view of their own performance relative to others in the company? They conclude that pay is not tied to performance; otherwise their pay would be higher.

This is exactly the problem uncovered in a study of several occupational groups in a number of companies. People were asked to rate themselves on job performance relative to other employees doing similar work. Across all occupational groups, in excess of 95 percent of the employees rated themselves above average. For each of the groups, at least 68 percent of the employees thought they were in the top 25 percent of all similarly situated employees in performance. This is statistically impossible. But the important point is that these employees expect a pay increase commensurate with their perceived performance.[29]

4. *Organizations fail to recognize other sources of motivation than money.* One of the difficulties faced in compensation is the belief that money is a general panacea, capable of compensating for all other human resource problems. If one thing has been learned from the problems with poor productivity, absenteeism, and sabotage in the automobile industry, it is that money may attract workers to unsatisfying jobs; it may also help to retain workers, at least in the short run. But the ability of money to motivate under conditions where numerous other factors work in opposition is limited at best.

Equity: Pay Satisfaction

Besides performance, pay is presumed to affect employee attitudes toward work. Particularly important is satisfaction and dissatisfaction, since certain employee behaviors may be related to these attitudes. Research supports the following findings:

1. Satisfaction with pay is a function of how much is received, how much others are perceived to receive, and perceptions of what should have been received.

2. Satisfaction with pay can influence overall job satisfaction as well as absenteeism, recruitment, and turnover.

3. Pay *dissatisfaction* is related to turnover. However, the two are not always highly related. The relationship seems to be strongly affected by the importance the employee attaches to pay.

4. The stronger causal tendency is *that performance causes pay satisfaction, rather than pay satisfaction causing performance*. Interestingly, pay satisfaction appears to be related to performance only when pay is based on employee performance.

5. The evidence quite clearly shows that pay dissatisfaction can lead employees to join unions, go on strike, and file grievances.[30]

Many researchers suggest that pay satisfaction is multidimensional. That is, there are a number of different aspects of pay that affect pay satisfaction. These multiple aspects make it a more difficult task to try to increase satisfaction; simply increasing pay may not necessarily increase satisfaction. Rather, the system adjustments need to be tied to the source of the dissatisfaction.[31]

In sum, there is evidence to support the premise that pay is linked to employee performance and satisfaction. However, certain potential problems often make it difficult to design a pay-for-performance system. The relationship between certain aspects of pay (level, structure, amount, and form) and satisfaction needs further research.

PAY ADMINISTRATION

The fundamental tenet of this book is that any human resource management system, including compensation, implies objective-directed behavior. Properly designed and administered pay programs help managers better achieve these objectives.

Rather than goal-directed tools, however, pay systems often degenerate into bureaucractic burdens. The techniques become ends in themselves. Operating managers may complain that pay techniques are more a hindrance than a help, and these managers are often correct. So, any discussion of compensation must consider the administration of the system, including (1) managing labor costs, (2) communication and appeals, (3) participation, and (4) special groups.

Cost Controls

One of the key reasons for being systematic about pay decisions is to control costs. A simple model of labor costs is shown below:

$$\text{Costs} = \text{Employment} \times (\text{Cash compensation} + \text{Benefits})$$

The model shows that there are three main factors that determine labor costs:

✦ Employment (both number of employees and number of hours worked).

✦ Cash compensation (wages and bonuses).

✦ Benefit costs (health and life insurance, pensions, and the like).

Chapter Five dealt with managing the numbers of employees through employment planning. Chapter Fourteen will deal with benefits costs. In this and the previous chapter, we dealt with cash compensation. However, the model points out that all three factors affect labor costs.

There are two basic types of cost controls in cash compensation: (1) those inherent in the design of the technique or policy and (2) the formal budgeting process.

Inherent Controls

Controls are embedded in the design of many pay techniques already discussed. A few examples illustrate the point.

Range maximums and minimums set the limits on the rates to be paid for each job. The maximum represents the top value the organization places on the output of the job. Presumably, some employees in this job may be qualified for other, higher-paying jobs. However, their extraneous qualifications do not affect the value of their present job. Balancing a ledger has a certain value for an employer whether its done by a high school graduate or a certified public accountant.

Think about the cost controls built into incentives and awards. These are examples of *variable* pay. Variable pay depends on performance and is *not* added to employees' base pay. The essence of variable pay is that it must be reearned each period, whereas conventional merit pay increases or across-the-board increases are added to base pay. From a labor cost perspective, conventional increases affect not only the average cash compensation but also the cost of those benefits contingent on base pay (e.g., pensions). Consequently, the greater the ratio of variable pay to base pay, the more variable (flexible) are labor costs.[32]

Communication and Appeals

The literature on pay administration usually exhorts employers to communicate pay information. One reason is that according to some research, employees seem to misperceive the pay system. For example, they tend to overestimate the pay of those with lower-level jobs and to underestimate the pay of those in higher-level jobs. In other words, they tend to think that the pay structure is more compressed than it actually is. What difference does that make? It is important because pay differentials were designed to encourage employees to seek promotions, to undertake added training, and to gain experience required for higher-level positions. Furthermore, there is even some evidence to suggest that the good will engendered by the act of being open about pay also affects employee satisfaction with pay.[33]

The danger in pay communications should be obvious. If the pay system is not based on work-related or business-related logic, the wisest course may be to avoid formal, detailed communication. Nevertheless, employees are constantly getting intended and unintended messages through the pay increase they receive and the gossip floating among co-workers.

Despite managers' best attempts to help employees understand how their pay is set, employees sometimes feel they have been unjustly treated. They may feel their performance was unjustly evaluated, their jobs improperly evaluated, or even that the external market comparisons excluded relevant firms. Many firms design procedures to handle these disputes. They provide employees a forum to voice their disagreements and to receive a hearing. These mechanisms are discussed in the Employee Relations chapter.

Participation

Lawler argues persuasively that employee participation can make a difference in the success of a pay system.[34] He cites two work groups doing the same kinds of jobs and operating under similar pay plans. One group had high productivity that continued to increase; the other had low and stable productivity. The first had a long history of participation in decision making; the second had the pay plan imposed by management.

A design process that includes employees can be successful in overcoming resistance to change. Employees are more likely to be committed to the system if they have some control over what happens.

All-Salaried Work Force

The all-salaried work force, an old concept, is often considered as part of a strategy to increase employee involvement and commitment. The all-salaried concept includes removing all time clocks, equalizing benefits and services for all employees, and converting hourly pay to biweekly rates. The objective is to improve employee's commitment to the organization by adopting a more egalitarian approach to pay practices.

TRW emphasizes that its all-salaried programs are part of a participative employee relations philosophy.[35] Such a philosophy goes beyond the pay system and involves the entire human resource management system. The fact that all employees are paid by the same method is not the critical variable—rather, what is important is the climate of respect, trust, and confidence.

Special Groups

Every organization has special groups of employees in unique circumstances. Often they are special because of the nature of the work performed. Examples include research scientists at Bell Labs, field sales jobs at Merck, or international assignments for any major employer. The unique external and organizational conditions facing these employees often require that the pay system for them also be unique. Probably the most obvious one is the pay system for executives. Executive pay will be discussed as an illustration of how pay systems are tailored for special groups of employees. The point is that firms typically have several pay systems, not just a single system.

EXECUTIVE PAY

For purposes of compensation, an executive is usually defined as any individual in a managerial position in the highest levels (e.g., top 5 percent) of the entire organization. A typical executive team appears in Exhibit 13.9.

Compensation Decisions

Designers of executive pay packages typically face some of the same issues discussed earlier. Only the answers may differ, because external and organization conditions differ. An important difference in executive pay is that it is often tied to the performance of the *entire organization*.

Executive Incentives

These incentive plans are based on notions from *agency theory,* which depicts executives as the "agents" of the owners (stockholders).[36] According to the theory, if executive pay increases are linked to the firm's performance via incentive plans, then the executives will make decisions consistent with the owner's interests.

Usually two types of incentives are used: short-term cash bonuses (based on one or two years, of performance), and long-term capital accumulation, such as stock options.

Stock options give the executive the right to purchase a fixed number of the company's shares at a fixed price (exercise price) by a fixed time in the future. The executive gains as long as the stock price increases in the future. For example: The chief executive officer of a company is given the *right* to purchase (not an obligation) 10,000 shares at $50 share within the next five years. If the market price of the common stock of the company increases to $65 and the executive exercises the option, a gain of $150,000 [($65 − $50) × 10,000] is realized.

Many types of stock options exist. Options are attractive to both executives and shareholders for the following reasons:

1. Executives must put up some of their own money as do the shareholders.
2. The value, the same as that of the shareholders' stock, is at risk with the price of the company stock.
3. Options are a form of profit sharing, which links the executive's financial success to that of the shareholders.[37]

EXHIBIT 13.9   Top Management Typical Organization Structure

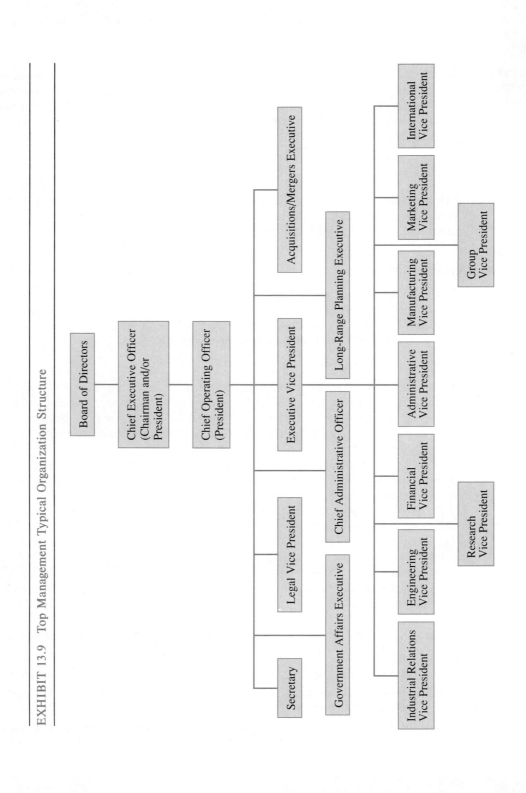

The Critics

Public skepticism about executive pay and its relationship to the performance of firms has a long history. Fifty years ago, President Roosevelt inveighed against corporate executives as part of the forces of "entrenched greed."[38] In the same year, *Fortune* reported the results of an opinion poll: "over half of those responding felt executives of large corporations were paid too much." Since then, executive pay continues to evoke skepticism. Recently a leading compensation consultant entitled his article, "The Wacky, Wacky World of Executive Pay."[39]

We sampled 50 years of media accounts and opinion polls on executive compensation and uncovered five recurring *beliefs:*

- ✦ U.S. corporate executives are overpaid.
- ✦ Corporate policies that determine executive pay ignore the interests of shareholders.
- ✦ Employment agreements such as golden parachutes shield executives from the sacrifices and risks faced by other employees and often run counter to the long-term interests of firms.
- ✦ Factors that might be expected to have an effect on firm performance— company size, the riskiness of the venture, the experience and training of individuals—do matter, but not as much as expected.
- ✦ Executives' pay continues to rise even when the firm's performance declines.

Exhibit 13.10 highlights one of the major criticisms underlying executive pay: Executives' pay level (base and bonuses) seem to suffer little or not at all, no matter what happens to company performance. Chief executive officer pay levels are not sensitive to declines in accounting measures of performance, such as return on equity.

Conflicting views seldom get much study, although some expectations do exist. Research suggests that the level of executive pay is correlated with the size of the firm as measured by sales and profits.[40] Summarizing their extensive research, Murphy and Larcker concluded that, "On average, compensation policies encourage managers to act on behalf of their shareholders and to put in the best managerial performance they can."[41]

Differentials

One highly publicized structural issue is the gap between returns received by executives and those received by other employees. For example, the chief executive officer at Disney received cash payments of over $7 million in 1987. This is 10 times more than a ride operator in the Disney theme park earns in an entire lifetime. Many people believe the gap between pay for executive and other employees is unfair.[42] This gap is most obvious when large cash bonuses

EXHIBIT 13.10   CEO Raises: They Just Keep Rollin' Along

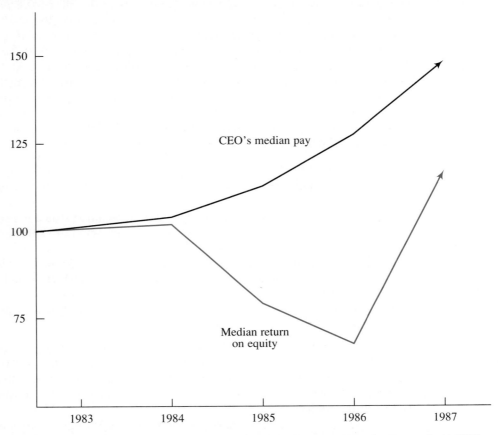

* Pay is salary and annual bonus. Companies: Burlington Northern, Champion International, CSX, Dow Chemical, First Chicago, W. R. Grace, GTE, Honeywell, ITT, Johnson & Johnson, Kroger, Tenneco, Texaco Petroleum, Unocal.

are paid to executives at the same time that concessions are demanded from other employees.

But such comparisons as the ones presented in Exhibit 13.10 or that between a Disney's CEO and a ride operator's are oversimplified. The effectiveness of executive pay is assumed to show up in later corporate results, in the returns to shareholders, and in more complex ways than a few financial indices. More rigorous research on these issues is underway.[43]

INTERNATIONAL DIFFERENTIALS

In international comparisons, pay structures may reflect labor market conditions. For example, if only a small percentage of the population possesses managerial/technical skills, those skills will command a substantial premium in the labor market. As the industrialization process continues, and the quality of the work force goes up, the economywide pay differentials ought to narrow. One consulting firm reports the greatest pay differences between executives and production workers in Argentina, Brazil, and Venezuela, and the lowest in Australia, Belgium, Canada, Germany, Japan, and Netherlands, Sweden, Switzerland, and the United Kingdom. The differentials in the United States were in the next-lowest category, along with France, Italy, Korea, and Spain.[44] However, all international comparisons require a great deal of caution in interpretation, because of the wide variety of perquisites that are standard in various countries (e.g., parents' allowance, company car or plane, country club memberships, household servants, cost of living adjustments, bonuses, and so on).

The point to remember about international and executive pay programs is that the basic issue faced in the design and administration of compensation plans must be readdressed in each application to each special group.

One final issue needs to be considered before bringing this discussion of pay administration to an end: pay discrimination, and, in particular, comparable worth.

COMPARABLE WORTH

Equal employment opportunity and pay discrimination were discussed in Chapter Six. Basically, the Equal Pay Act and the Civil Rights Act embody the principal of "equal pay for equal work." Equal work is defined by four factors: (1) equal skills, (2) equal effort, (3) equal responsibility, and (4) equal working conditions. These are strikingly similar to the compensable factors found in most job evaluation plans.

Differences in pay for equal work are permitted if they result from (1) differences in seniority, (2) differences in quality of performance, (3) differences in quantity and quality of production (incentives), or (4) some other factor than gender or race (e.g., premiums for night hours).

Earnings Gap

There is a continuing debate over the causes of the earnings gap between men and women and how to define and subsequently eliminate pay discrimination. The debate is not over whether all employees should be paid equally when they are doing the same jobs. This is required by the Equal Pay Act and the Civil Rights Act. What is at issue is pay differences for *dissimilar jobs*. Should jobs that are dissimilar in content but in "some sense of comparable value" be paid the same? For example, should nurses be paid equally with plumbers or office and clerical jobs equally with assemblers or carpenters? The question was so interesting to Mary Lemons, a nurse for the city of Denver, that she took her employer to court.[45] She felt that nurses (mostly women) should receive pay equal to tree trimmers (mostly men and unionized).

Several basic issues underlie the controversy:

1. Is the persistent gap in earnings between men and women (the average earnings of fully employed women is approximately 70 percent of the earnings of fully employed men) due to pay discrimination, or is it due to productivity-related factors (nature of the jobs, seniority, continuity of employment) and/or the collective bargaining process?
2. Should the currently accepted standard for pay determination (equal pay for equal or "substantially equal" work) be replaced with another standard—equal pay for work of comparable worth or value?
3. What is comparable worth and can it be assessed?
4. What are the consequences of adopting comparable worth as the standard for pay determination? Will the earnings gap between men and women be reduced? What will be the effects of adjusting the pay structure—on inflation, labor costs, or individual career decisions?

A Definition

Comparable worth, the principal mechanism suggested to reduce the earnings gap, has been defined as "jobs that require comparable (not identical) skill, responsibility, and effort."[46] It focuses on pay differences among occupations. Several state and local governments have developed approaches to establishing comparable worth. The appendix to this chapter describes the steps the American Federation of State, County, and Municipal Employees (AFSCME) recommends for establishing comparable worth. Basically the approach involves equal pay for all jobs with the same total job evaluation points. Thus, internal equality would dominate external market concerns. In the states of Washington and Minnesota, for example, such jobs as public health nurse and secretary received the same job evaluation points as carpenters and other craft jobs.[47] The rates paid to nurses and secretaries were raised to match those paid to crafts.

Consider Exhibit 13.11. The black circles are jobs held predominantly by women (i.e., female representation greater than or equal to 70 percent). The blue circles are jobs held predominantly by men (i.e., greater than or equal to 70 percent men). The policy line (solid) for the women's jobs is below and less than the policy line for male jobs (dotted line). A comparable worth policy would use the results of the single job evaluation plan (x axis) and price all jobs as if they were male-dominated jobs. Thus, all jobs with 100 job points would receive $700, all those with 200 points would receive $800, and so on.

EXHIBIT 13.11   Job Evaluation Points and Salary

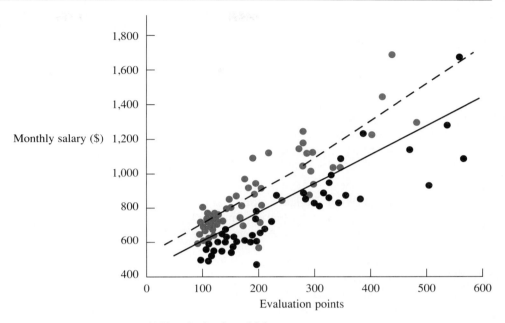

Critics, Politics, and Costs

Comparable worth is a political and emotional issue.[48] People who share a be-lief about how pay should be determined in society wish to convince a suffi-cient number of others that their approach is "fairer" or more "equitable." The courts have not interpreted present laws in a manner that encompasses com-parable worth. Consequently, comparable worth proponents continue to lobby for either new legislation or voluntary action on the part of employers that would include the comparable worth standard.

Since past pay legislation has outlawed lowering any wage to make pay equal, a comparable worth policy may require employers to pay all employees at the highest market line. This translates into the rate paid for jobs held predomi-nantly by men. Bellak raises a host of issues under such an arrangement:

✦ Would the unions give up their right to negotiate contracts independent of the pay arrangements in the other segments of the organization (i.e., would unions B, C, D, E, and so on have to agree to the same point/dollar relationship as union A, which signed the first agreement)?

◆ If the individual unions negotiated jointly for the same point/pay relationship, would there be any need for more than one union?

◆ How would an organization entice people into jobs where there were shortages because of distasteful work, if there were not premium pay for the same points, or more pay for fewer points?

◆ If one unit in a firm pays only base salary, will it have to increase its compensation level if another unit in the same firm introduces an incentive plan suitable for the business sector in which it competes?

◆ Must a state pay the same dollars for the same points to employees who work and live in a low-cost rural area as they do to employees in the high-cost large cities?

◆ Must a high-tech company raise the pay of its accountants (male-dominated) to equal the pay of its engineers (also male-dominated) for the same points?[49]

Underlying Bellak's points is a more basic one, which is whether legally mandating a job evaluation approach is defensible. Many employers do not use job evaluation at all. A mandated job evaluation approach simply does not fit all circumstances.[50]

Several other countries have adopted comparable worth as the standard for pay determination. Most notable is the Canadian Pay Equity legislation. For example, Ontario requires all employers, public and private, to adopt plans that are similar to the comparable worth approach already described. The experience in Canada may affect practice in the United States. Many major U.S. firms operate in Canada and must comply with its laws. It's only a matter of time before someone asks these firms, "If you can do it in Canada, why not here?"

SUMMARY

The last two chapters have examined the basic pay issues and illustrated alternative techniques designed to aid managers facing these issues.

This chapter examined pay for individual employees and some common techniques for varying pay: pay ranges, merit increase guidelines, merit awards, and lump-sum payments. Gainsharing deserves special attention. Even though it is not a new technique, it is enjoying renewed popularity as employers look for new ways to enhance competitiveness by increasing productivity and controlling costs. Gainsharing plans may be based on the work results of an individual, a work team, or the entire organization. They seek to share the gains that result from changed behaviors with employees.

Some employee groups, including executives, are likely to be paid under a separate pay plan. As with gainsharing, the objective of executive pay is to tie the pay system to the results of employee performance.

Comparable worth, the final topic in this chapter, refers to a pay system that gives job evaluation and internal job comparisons a greater role; market forces for jobs held predominantly by women are ignored. This proposal of "equal pay for jobs of comparable worth" differs from the legally required standard of "equal pay for equal work." The goal of comparable worth is to equalize salaries between men and women.

It is important to place compensation in perspective. It is only one, albeit an important one, of the human resource management activities. However, it does represent a major portion of the expense budget for most managers. Consequently, the systems used to determine and administer pay must be well designed. Unfortunately, much of contemporary compensation administration is bureaucratic and technique-oriented. The concepts and objectives are often replaced with forms and paperwork. But change is in the wind. Challenged by increased economic competition, managers are beginning to manage pay. Similarly, challenges from employees and comparable-worth advocates are also causing some of the current practices to be reexamined.

The next chapter examines a major form of compensation: benefits. Rising costs, concerns about their tax-free status, and questions about their value make benefits a timely topic.

DISCUSSION AND REVIEW QUESTIONS

1. In what circumstances may an employer wish to pay individuals on the same job different wages? In what circumstances may an employer wish to pay all individuals on the same job the same wages?
2. What are the most common employee differences used for individualizing pay?
3. What are some of the difficulties in a merit pay system?
4. When would you use group versus individual pay incentives?
5. What are "inherent controls?" Give an example.
6. Why is pay secrecy so prevalent?
7. What employee groups might need a separate pay system? Why?
8. What is comparable worth, and how does it differ from equal pay? What is legally required? What are some approaches to operationalizing comparable worth?
9. What are some difficulties in operationalizing it?
10. What are some alternative measures that the Painted Post plant could have used in gainsharing? What would be the advantages and disadvantages of each?

YOUR TURN
DISNEY'S CEO

You are the compensation director at Walt Disney. Your instructor will give you some additional information on how Mr. Eisner's salary is calculated. Look it over and prepare a memo for all employees explaining why it is in their best interests to have Mr. Eisner paid the way he is. Prepare an additional memo with the same objective for stockholders.

APPENDIX/AFSCME
Pay Equity Study

1. ***Gather information on the work force.*** What follows is a list of information that a union or an individual can request from an employer to discover whether his or her pay practices are discriminatory.

   ◆ The number of male and female employees in each classification and the wage rate for each classification.

   ◆ The number of males and females hired in each classification during the previous 12 months.

   ◆ The number of promotional examinations taken and the number of examinations passed during the past 12 months broken down by sex and the number of males and females that were actually promoted.

   ◆ Copies of any job evaluation studies done in the last five years.

   ◆ A copy of the employer's affirmative action plan and most recent EEO-4 reports.

   In the case of a government agency, the information should be available under either the state's Freedom of Information Act or the State Public Employment Relations Law.

   It may be necessary for you to make some accommodations, but if your employer is unreasonable you can pursue legal avenues to get the information.

2. ***Analyze the work force.***

   ◆ Of the total number of employees, compute the number and percentage that are male and the number and percentage that are female.

   ◆ Of the total number of position classifications, compute the number and percentage that are sex segregated (i.e., 70 percent and above of the incumbents in a position are of one sex). Of the classifications that are sex segregated, compute the number and percentage that are male and the number and percentage that are female.

+ Compute the average salary of the total work force, the average salary of all males, and the average salary of all females. Compute the average salary of all sex segregated classifications, the average salary of male-dominated classifications, and the average salary of female-dominated classifications.

+ To show salary range distribution, list the number and percentage of males and females for each job classification in descending salary range order.

3. *Select representative jobs (benchmark jobs).*

+ Include "male jobs" and "female jobs."
+ Include jobs with a large number of incumbents.
+ Include jobs that represent a range of wage levels.

4. *Get job descriptions for benchmark jobs.*

+ Make certain that descriptions are detailed, accurate, and current.

5. *Identify from each job description the qualifications required to be hired for the position.*

+ Education.
+ Experience.
+ Skills or knowledge.
+ Training.

6. *Group jobs by similarity of qualifications.*   Sample groupings:

+ No educational requirement, no experience required.
+ High school diploma (or equivalent), no experience.
+ High school diploma, specific skill training, no experience.
+ High school diploma, specific skill training, experience.
+ College degree, no experience.
+ College degree, experience.
+ College degree, graduate degree in specific discipline(s).

7. *Within each qualification grouping, separate the "male" jobs and "female" jobs and calculate an average salary for each sex.*

8. *Compare averages of pay for "male" and "female" jobs that require similar qualifications.*

9. *Summarize the findings.*   A pay equity problem exists if:

A pattern of sex segregated jobs and departments is found.

Average pay is lower for women than men.

"Women's" jobs are paid lower than "men's" jobs.

When salaries for "women's" jobs which require similar qualifications to "men's" jobs are compared, the women are paid less.

*10. **Prepare a concise report to highlight the results of the preliminary study.*** The report that results from the above analysis should be used to advance the overall strategy you or your union have chosen to work towards pay equity.

NOTES AND REFERENCES

1. George Milkovich and Jerry M. Newman, *Compensation,* 3rd ed. (Homewood, Ill.: BPI Irwin, 1990).

2. John A. Fossum, *Labor Relations,* 3rd ed. (Plano, Tex.: Business Publications, 1985; Arthur A. Sloane and Fred Whitney, *Labor Relations,* 6th ed. (Englewood Cliffs, N.J.: Prentice-Hall, 1988).

3. Hay Associates make this argument: that each job has its own evaluation point total and its own range. That is, each job evaluation point has a dollar value.

4. R. L. Heneman, *Pay and Performance: Exploring the Merit System* (New York: Pergamon Press, 1984); Charles Peck, *Pay and Performance: The Interaction of Compensation and Performance Appraisal* (New York: The Conference Board, 1984).

5. Carla O'Dell, *Major Findings from People, Performance, and Pay* (Houston, Tex.: American Productivity Center, 1986); Andrew Weiss, "Incentives and Worker Behavior: Some Evidence," NBER Working Paper no. 2194, March 1987.

6. C. A. Smith, "Lump-Sum Increases—A Creditable Change Strategy," *Personnel* 56 (1979), pp. 59–63.

7. Edward E. Lawler III, *Pay and Organization Development* (Reading, Mass.: Addison-Wesley Publishing, 1981).

8. James Lincoln, *Incentive Management* (Cleveland, Ohio: Lincoln Electric Co., 1969).

9. Max Bazerman and Brian Graham-Moore, "PG Formulas: Developing a Reward Structure to Achieve Organizational Goals," in *Productivity Gainsharing,* ed. Brian Graham-Moore and Timothy Ross (Englewood Cliffs, N.J.: Prentice-Hall, 1983); D. Rowland and B. Greene, "Incentive Pay: Productivity's Own Reward," *Personnel Journal,* March 1987, pp. 49–57.

10. C. F. Schultz, *Compensating the Sales Professional* (New York: Towers, Perrin, Forster and Crosby, 1985); N. Ford, O. Walker, and G. Churchill, "Differences in the Attractiveness of Alternative Rewards among Industrial Salespeople: Additional Evidence," *Sales Force Performance* (Wash. D.C.: Heath, 1985); John K. Moynahan, *Designing and Effective Sales Compensation Program* (New York: AMACOM, 1980).

11. Weiss, "Incentives and Work Behavior."

12. *Gainsharing: A Collection of Papers* (Norcross, Georgia: Institute of Industrial Engineers, 1983); Lawler, *Pay and Organization Development,* p. 144.

13. O'Dell, *Major Findings;* Martin Weitzman, *The Share Economy: Conquering Stagflation* (Cambridge, Mass.: Harvard University Press, 1984).

14. Robert B. McKersie, "The Promise of Gainsharing," *ILR Report,* Fall 1986, pp. 7–11; O'Dell, *Major Findings;* Lawler, *Pay and Organization Development.*

15. Nuti, "Profit-Sharing and Employment: Claims and Overclaims," *Industrial Relations,* Winter 1987, pp. 18–29.

16. A. Maslow, *Motivation and Personality* (New York: Harper & Row, 1954).

17. E. E. Lawler III, *Pay and Organization Effectiveness* (New York: McGraw-Hill, 1971).

18. F. A. Heller and L. W. Porter, "Perceptions of Managerial Needs and Skills in Two National Samples," *Occupational Psychology* 40, no. 1 (1966), pp. 1–13.

19. L. Dyer, D. P. Schwab, and R. D. Theriault, "Managerial Perceptions Regarding Salary Increase Criteria," *Personnel Psychology* 29, no. 2 (1976), pp. 233–42.

20. Peter D. Sherer, D. P. Schwab, and H. G. Heneman III, "Managerial Salary-Raise Decisions: A Policy-Capturing Approach," *Personnel Psychology,* Spring 1987, pp. 27–38.

21. E. E. Lawler III, "Managers' Attitudes toward How Their Pay Is and Should Be Determined," *Journal of Applied Psychology* 50 (1966), pp. 273–79; E. E. Lawler III and E. Levin, "Union Officer's Perceptions of Members Pay Preferences," *Industrial and Labor Relations Review* 21, no. 4 (1968), pp. 509–17.

22. Peck, *Pay and Performance.*

23. U.S. General Accounting Office, "Productivity Sharing Programs: Can They Contribute to Productivity Improvement?" AFMD 85-11, 1985.

24. Michael H. Schuster, "The Scanlon Plan: A Longitudinal Analysis," *Journal of Applied Behavioral Science* 20, no. 4 (1984), pp. 23–28.

25. John Wagner, Paul Rubin, and Thomas Callahan, "Incentive Payment and Non-Managerial Productivity: An Interrupted Time Series Analysis of Magnitude and Trend," *Organizational Behavior and Human Decision Processes* 42 (1988), pp. 47–74.

26. Barry Gerhart and George T. Milkovich, "Organizational Differences in Managerial Compensation and Financial Performance," Working Paper 89-11, Center for Advanced Human Resource Studies, Cornell University, Ithaca, New York, 1989; G. P. Baker, M. C. Jensen, and K. J. Murphy, "Compensation and Incentives Practice vs. Theory," *Journal of Finance* 43 (1988), pp. 593–616.

27. Jane L. Pearce and James L. Perry, "Federal Merit Pay: A Longitudinal Analysis," *Public Administration Review,* July–August 1983, pp. 315–25.

28. Clay W. Hamner, "How to Ruin Motivation with Pay," *Compensation Review,* Third Quarter 1975, pp. 88–98; Herbert H. Meyer, "Pay for Performance Dilemma," *Organizational Dynamics,* Winter 1975, pp. 71–78.

29. Lawler, *Pay and Organization Development.*

30. Herbert G. Heneman III, "Pay Satisfaction," in *Research in Personnel and Human Resources Management,* vol. 3, ed. K. M. Rowland and G. R. Ferris (Greenwich, Conn.: JAI Press, 1985).

31. Ronald Ash, Robert D. Bretz, Jr., and George F. Dreher, "The Measurement and Dimensionality of Compensation Satisfaction," Ithaca, N.Y.: Center for Advanced Human Resource Studies, working paper, 1990.

32. George T. Milkovich, "Gainsharing in Managing and Compensating Human Resources," paper presented at Conference on Participation and Gainsharing Systems, Johnson Foundation, Racine, Wisconsin, October 1986.

33. E. E. Lawler III, "Secrecy and the Need to Know," in *Managerial Motivation and Compensation,* ed. Henry Tosi, Robert House, and M. Dunnette (East Lansing: Michigan State University Press, 1972).

34. G. Douglas Jenkins, Jr., and E. E. Lawler III, "Impact of Employee Participation in Pay Plan Development," *Organization Behavior and Human Performance* 28, no. 2 (1981).

35. Ian Ziskin, "Knowledge-Based Pay: A Strategic Analysis," *ILR Report,* August 1984, pp. 16–22.

36. The February 1990 issue of *Industrial and Labor Relations Review* is a special issue on the topic "Do Compensation Policies Matter?"

37. Frederic W. Cook, "Lessons in Using Long-Term Incentives to Revitalize Earnings," January 26, 1990 newsletter, Frederic W. Cook & Co., Inc., New York; Bruce Ellig, *Executive Compensation—A Total Pay Perspective* (New York: McGraw-Hill, 1982).

38. George T. Milkovich and Bonnie Rabin, "Firm Performance: Does Executive Compensation Really Matter?" in Fred Foulkes, ed. *Executive Compensation,* Harvard Business School Press, 1991.

39. Graef Crystal, "The Wacky, Wacky World of CEO Pay," *Fortune,* June 6, 1988, pp. 68–78.

40. Baker, Jensen, and Murphy, Compensation and Incentives.

41. Kevin J. Murphy, "Top Executives Are Worth Every Nickel They Get," *Harvard Business Review,* March–April 1986, pp. 125–31; Kevin J. Murphy, "Corporate Performance and Managerial Remuneration: An Empirical Analysis," *Journal of Accounting and Economics,* April 1985, pp. 11–42; D. F. Larcker, "The Association between Performance Plan Adoption and Corporate Capital Investments," *Journal of Accounting and Economics* 5 (1983), pp. 3–30.

42. "The Trust Gap," *Fortune,* December 1989.

43. See the February 1990 issue of *Industrial Relations Review.*

44. TPF&C International Pay Comparisons, 1989.

45. *Lemons* v. *City and County of Denver* 1980, 620 F. 2d, 228.

46. D. J. Treiman and H. Hartmann, *Women, Work, and Wages: Equal Pay for Equal Value* (Washington, D.C.: National Academy Press, 1981), p. 9.

47. Helen Remick, ed., *Comparable Worth and Wage Discrimination* (Philadelphia: Temple University Press, 1984); George Milkovich, "The Nature of the Earnings Gap," Paper presented at Corporate Symposium on Pay Equity (New York: The Conference Board, 1987); GAO, "Pay Equity: Status of State Activities," U.S. General Accounting Office, 86–141, September 1986.

48. Henry J. Aaron and Cameron M. Lougy, *The Comparable Worth Controversy* (Washington, D.C.: Brookings Institution, 1986); W. Y. Oi, "Neglected Women and Other Implications of Comparable Worth," *Contemporary Policy Issues* 4, no. 2 (1986); J. O'Neill, "Issues Surrounding Comparable Worth," *Contemporary Policy Issues* 4, no. 2 (1986); J. Roback, *A Matter of Choice: A Critique of Comparable Worth by a Skeptical Feminist* (New York: Priority Press, 1986); Linda Subich, Gerald Barrett, Dennis Doverspike, and Ralph Alexander, "The Effects of Sex Role-Related Factors on Occupational Choice and Salary," and Randall K. Filer, "Occupational Segregation, Compensating Differentials and Comparable Worth," both in *Pay Equity: Empirical Inquiries* (Washington, D.C.: National Academy of Science, 1989).

49. Al Bellak, "Comparable Worth: A Practitioner's View," in *Comparable Worth: Issue for the 80's,* vol. 1 (Washington, D.C.: U.S. Civil Rights Commission, 1985).

50. David A. Pierson and Karen S. Koziara, *Study of Equal Wages for Jobs of Comparable Worth* (Philadelphia: Center for Labor and Human Resource Studies, 1981); Alice Cook, "Comparable Worth: Recent Developments in Selected States," *Proceedings of the 1983 Spring Meeting of the Industrial Relations Research Association,* Honolulu, March 1983, pp. 494–504. Some economists are beginning to model the costs and effects of comparable worth at an aggregated level, including Mark Killingsworth, "The Economics of Comparable Worth: Analytical, Empirical, and Policy Questions," in *Comparable Worth,* ed. H. I. Hartmann (Washington, D.C.: National Academy Press, 1985), pp. 86–115. See also Sandra E. Gleason and Collette Mosher, "Some Neglected Policy Implications of Comparable Worth," *Policy Studies Review,* May 1985, pp. 595–600.

CHAPTER FOURTEEN

Benefits

The Growth of Benefits
Unions

Setting Benefit Objectives and Strategies
Integrate with Human Resource Objectives
Entitlements versus Contributions
A Benefits Gap

Benefit Decisions

Competitiveness
Cost Comparisons
Actuarial Valuation

Compliance
Civil Rights Laws
Fiduciary Responsibility
Mandated Benefits

Coverage
Employer-Purchased Insurance
Paid Time Away from Work
Employee Services
Retirement Income

Communication

Choice

Evaluating the Results of Benefit Decisions
Effects on Costs
Effects on Employee Behaviors
Effects on Equity

Your Turn: National Health Insurance

June Betts, an Ohio speech pathologist, developed an Alzheimer's-related disease that left her unable to work at age 61. Ohio's pension plan included $350 a month disability pay plus medical benefits. But the law allowed disability retirements only through age 60. Since Ms. Betts was 61, she would have to take early retirement instead, and receive only $158 a month, with no medical benefits. Ms. Betts sued, charging that offering disability retirement only to employees age 60 or under was illegal age discrimination. The Supreme Court disagreed: age-based benefits differences are still acceptable, as long as they do not affect employment conditions outside of fringe benefits.[1]

Years ago, Continental Can negotiated an expensive pension plan that was payable to eligible employees in the event of a plant shutdown or extended involuntary layoff. Eligibility for the plan was based on age plus years of service. Once eligibile, an employee would receive full normal retirement benefits well before normal retirement age. Thus, there was a significant (and apparently irresistable) economic incentive to lay off employees *before* they became eligible and to protect the jobs of those who were already eligible so that the extra benefits would not have to be paid. Continental developed a sophisticated computer program to identify who was not yet eligible. These employees were not only targeted for dismissal, their names were continuously tracked so they would not be inadvertently recalled to work and allowed to become eligible. When these targeted workers found out about Continental's tracking, they filed suit.

Continental argued that the decline in demand for steel cans meant that the aggrieved workers would have been laid off anyway. Structuring layoffs with costs—including pension costs—in mind was good business sense. But a New Jersey federal district court judge said the firm went too far and its action was illegal. Potential benefit consequences had driven its business decisions, rather than the other way around.[2]

These two cases demonstrate some very important, and unresolved, benefits issues: the importance of employer-provided benefits to the social welfare of employees, and the importance of controlling benefits costs to employers.

Employee benefits are the indirect form of the total compensation; they include paid time away from work, insurance and health protection, employee services, and retirement income.

This chapter addresses the basic decisions managers make in the design and administration of benefits programs. We will consider the conditions affecting benefits decisions, discuss the objectives managers try to achieve with benefits, examine the alternative forms benefits taken, and then highlight what is known about their effects.

THE GROWTH OF BENEFITS

Although the first recorded profit sharing plan in the United States occurred at a Pennsylvania glass works in 1794, the big push for increasing benefits occurred during World War II.[3] War time needs created serious shortages of workers. Since increases in wages were controlled by the federal government, employers and unions came up with new ways to attract and retain employees. Managers offered inducements that were not subject to government controls. If the government would not permit managers to offer greater wages, then the managers offered to pay medical bills, to provide life insurance, and to subsidize cafeterias instead.

Tax policies encouraged the continued growth in benefits. Most benefits are nontaxable income to employees and are deductible expenses to employers.[4] Today, benefits constitute a major portion of labor costs. In 1929, they amounted to only 3 percent of total payroll; by 1969, they were 31 percent; and in 1989, they topped 39 percent.[5] The average employer pays almost $8,000 a year per employee for benefits. Exhibit 14.1 depicts this growth.

Unions

Unions have been a dominant force to improve benefits.[6] In the 1960s and 1970s, a major thrust of unions' bargaining strategy was for increased levels and new forms of benefits. Group auto insurance, dental care, eye glasses, and pre-paid legal fees became common issues at the bargaining table. Unions' success at the bargaining table has a spillover effect on nonunionized employees in the same facility. One study found evidence that benefits for nonunion employees improved 15 to 50 percent when blue-collar employees in that facility belonged to unions.[7]

At Chrysler, the company pays all health care insurance premiums for its workers and retirees, their dependents, and survivors. Those who are covered by the premiums pay nothing. The policy covers the entire cost of their hospitalization and medical tests, and almost all of the cost of outpatient dental, psychiatric, vision, and hearing care. For retired workers and their surviving spouses, the insurance pays nearly everything that Medicare does not. Workers who are laid off their jobs get full coverage for a year. The result is that, for every vehicle Chrysler produces, health insurance premiums cost $700. Chrysler's foreign competitors pay only $200 per car for health insurance.[8]

EXHIBIT 14.1   Total Employee Benefits as Percent of Payroll, 1951 to 1987

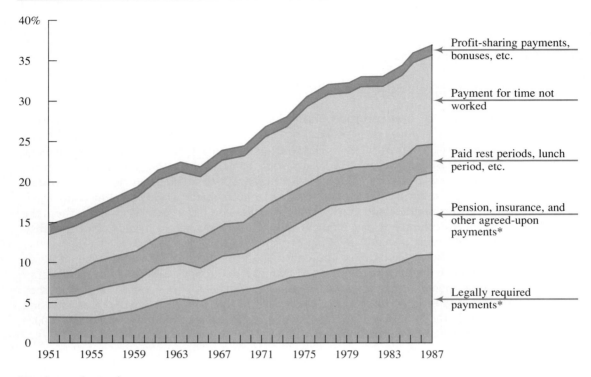

*Employers share only.
Source: *Monthly Labor Review,* May 1989.

Recently, unions have played a major role in employers' efforts to control health care costs.[9] Since most benefits are a form of tax-free income to their members, unions actively opposed Congressional efforts to tax benefits, particularly health insurance. And unions have actively worked with management in seeking approaches to contain rising health care costs, since many members view health care coverage as important as pay increases.

SETTING BENEFIT OBJECTIVES AND STRATEGIES

Organization strategies and objectives shape the benefit decisions managers make.[10] A large well-established employer in a growing or mature industry, for example, may offer a relatively generous benefit package. But a smaller newly formed emerging firm may find that the high fixed costs attached to many benefits, particularly pensions, entail too great a financial risk. Instead, such firms may emphasize incentive pay or profit sharing, where costs will vary with the firm's profitability, and deemphasize benefits with fixed costs. For example, Rolm, a midsized computer firm, did not provide pensions for its employees. Rather, all employees belonged to stock option programs and a profit sharing plan. Stock options and profit sharing supported Rolm's entrepreneurial strategy better than pensions, which focus on retirement, rather than firm performance. When IBM acquired Rolm, it phased the stock option plan into the IBM pension system. IBM was better able financially to undertake the fixed costs of a pension plan.

Typically benefits are designed to accomplish four objectives: (1) external competitiveness, (2) cost effectiveness, (3) insofar as feasible, tailored to individual employee needs and preferences (choices), and (4) comply with legal regulations. J. C. Penney's benefits objectives, shown in Exhibit 14.2, put costs in the context of sharing. The connections to productivity and specific employee behaviors are more tenuous. The reason is that benefits were intended to help protect employees' physical well being and provide for retirement. They were not intended to be tied to an individual's performance.

Integrate with Human Resource Objectives

As with all forms of compensation, the benefits offered need to be consistent with and support the organization's objectives and strategies. For example, benefits may emphasize the short term. Health insurance, generous vacation plans, or recreational facilities may help a growth-oriented employer attract new employees. Or the emphasis may be on long-term benefits that emphasize job security and encourage a stable, committed work force. In this case, more money would go to pension funds or tax-reduction strategies, in order to reward employees for years of service to the organization. The configuration of the benefits package should be designed to be consistent with the strategy of the overall compensation system and to help achieve the organization's objectives.

Entitlements versus Contributions

Benefit strategies are mirrored in the specific benefit decision managers make. Overemphasizing to illustrate the point, some organizations may foster a sense of caring and belonging as part of a family; it follows that all employees are entitled to benefits that help maintain their economic and physical well-being. Other employers pursue a strategy that is more performance driven; their compensation programs, including some benefits, would be linked to the performance of the firm and individual employees. In reality, many firms probably use a combination of these two extremes.

O'Toole draws out the implications of the two extreme strategies. He argues that as benefits increase, contribution, responsibility, and initiative are less and less linked to compensation and rewards.

EXHIBIT 14.2   Benefit Objectives

TO OUR PENNEY PARTNERS:

Teamwork, sharing, and mutual support—the same kind of cooperative effort that provides outstanding value and service for our customers—are all part of our benefits philosophy. Associates in the Penney family support one another's benefits during our active careers and in retirement. The Company shares in this team effort by contributing financial support where benefits help is most needed. Part of this help is by creating new plans responsive to associate needs, such as tax-deferred savings and the Penney Stock Ownership Plan (PenSOP). The result . . . a strong, vital program that gives substantial financial security—providing the greatest amount of protection at least cost to you.

> Workers have an expanding sense of what is due them as rights of employment. From pension, health care, long vacations to a high standard of living, the perception by workers of what constitutes their rights is inexorably being enlarged. Concomitant with the spiraling sense of rights has been a declining sense of responsibility.[11]

He offers the following example:

> The largest single item in the Los Angeles City operating budget: Pensions for police and fire fighters. It accounts for about 50 percent of all property tax revenues. The pension fund has an uncapped cost-of-living adjustment and is based on the salary of the worker on the last day before retirement—thus encouraging last-minute promotions to captain shortly before "retirement" at age 38.[12]

Consequently, O'Toole sees a basic trade-off when facing benefit decisions: entitlements versus contributions. The trade-off is between the proportion of total compensation received in the form of benefits (entitlements) for simply holding a job or belonging to the organization, versus the proportion allocated to increasing unit productivity, superior performance, innovation, and risk taking (contributions).

A Benefits Gap

A countering position to O'Toole's is that all members of society have certain rights, including the right to adequate health care and freedom from poverty. In 1987, 37 million Americans—18% of the labor force—had no health insurance.[13] Is it the government's responsibility to ensure coverage to every citizen, whether through welfare programs or through mandated employer-provided programs?[14] For those in society who are employed, employer-financed insurance and pensions provide a convenient method to ensure protection. For those not employed, employed in part-time jobs, or employed by small employers, a benefits gap between the haves and the have-nots exists. Some in society believe that employees should not be forced to choose between job and health, or between job and family; therefore, society's best interests are served if parental leave, day care, and other benefits are available to all employees who require them. It then follows that a minimal level of benefits should be a required part of any compensation system.

These are issues of public debate and dialogue. Benefit managers should be part of that dialogue.

BENEFIT DECISIONS

The typical decisions managers face in the design and management of benefit plans include:

+ Competitiveness: How should our benefits compare to our competitors?
+ Compliance: What are the legal requirements, and how can we meet them?
+ Coverage and forms: What types of benefits should we offer? Which employee should be eligible for each type?
+ Communications: How are employees best informed about their benefits? How is management informed of employees' needs?
+ Choice: What degree of choice or flexibility can be included? How can employee interests and concerns be accommodated?

COMPETITIVENESS

Competitive pressures impact benefit decisions in conflicting ways. On the one hand, labor costs must be controlled in order to price products and services competitively. At 39 percent of labor costs, approaches to reduce or manage benefits expenses have high priority.[15]

On the other hand, competition in labor markets to attract and retain productive employees creates pressure to match the benefits offered by other employers. If others include dental insurance and recreational facilities in their offer, employers who do not may be at a disadvantage.

Just as with cash compensation, an employer adopts a policy to position its total compensation, including benefits, in the marketplace. Traditionally, choices have been to lead, lag, or match competition. More often than not, benefits are designed to meet those offered by competitors. By offering employees choices among various benefits, some firms, such as TRW, Honeywell and others, emphasize a unique competitive posture regarding benefits. Their benefits programs can make them an "employer of choice."

Cost Comparisons

Assessing external competitors' benefits is accomplished through market surveys, which provide data on the different forms of benefits offered by competitors, their coverage, eligibility, and costs.

Comparisons can be made on total benefit costs, costs per employee, or percentage of payroll. These costs can then be compared to averages of competitors. The assumption underlying cost analysis is that, if an organization is spending the same amount on benefits as its competitors are, then its benefits package must be competitive.[16]

Actuarial Valuation

Rather than cost comparisons, Rosenbloom and Hallman propose using *actuarial valuations* to assess competitiveness.[17] Using the employer's actual employee population (or a targeted subpopulation), a standard set of actuarial assumptions is applied (e.g., likelihood of death or disability, need for medical care) and the value to the employees of a specific benefit package under these conditions is calculated. This value can then be compared to the value of various competitors' plans under the same conditions. The object here is to compare *values* of plans, rather than their *costs* to the employers. Exhibit 14.3 illustrates the approach. The average value of all benefits of all employers in the survey is set equal to 100. As the exhibit shows, the value of benefits provided by the employer for whom this chart was prepared is $174.80—substantially greater than competitor's.

A further external comparison is the configuration of the benefits offered, Exhibit 14.4. The top circle shows the percentage of the actuarial value of benefits alloted to various categories of benefits. This employer allots 26 percent of the total actuarial value of its benefits to vacations and holidays. The bottom circle shows the average for employers in the survey is 30 percent. While such data may not convince an employer to increase vacation pay by 4 percent, it does provide information on how others are allocating their benefits expenditures.

This actuarial valuation is an improvement over comparing employers' *costs* of benefits; however, there are some drawbacks. The approach is complex and, therefore, expensive to prepare and update. Additionally, all the caveats that apply to salary surveys apply here as well—relevance of comparisons, accuracy of data provided, and so on.[18] There is the further issue of appropriateness: What competitors offer may not be appropriate for a particular employer. For example, Exhibit 14.5 shows the age profile of Ford workers. Based on the aging of its work force, Ford expects its health care costs just for the company's hourly retirees and their spouses to jump to $300 million by 1990 from $160 million in 1984.[19] With the aging work force, an education reimbursement plan may not be suitable. Ford may be further ahead by offering Medicare supplements, no matter what its competitors do. In spite of these limitations, external comparisons do help assess the adequacy of benefits as well as the entire compensation package.

EXHIBIT 14.3 Illustration of Actuarial Benefit Value Comparisons—
Pension and Profit Sharing Plans

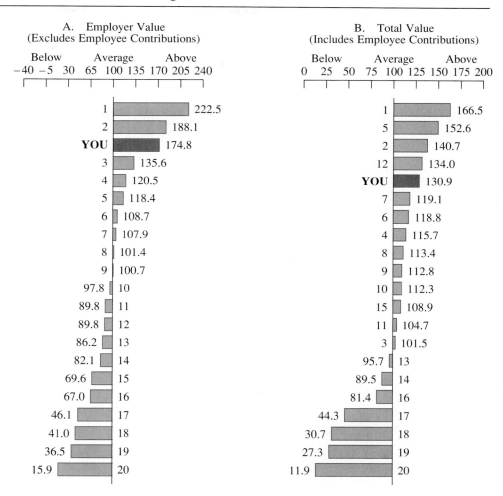

Source: Towers, Perrin, Forster & Crosby (TPF&C).

COMPLIANCE

Benefits may be one of the most heavily regulated areas of human resource management. Three categories of regulation exist: civil rights, fiduciary, and mandatory benefits.

EXHIBIT 14.4 Illustrations of Actuarial Benefit Value Comparisons—Total Value of Benefits

---

Component Plan Values As Percentages
of Overall Benefit Program

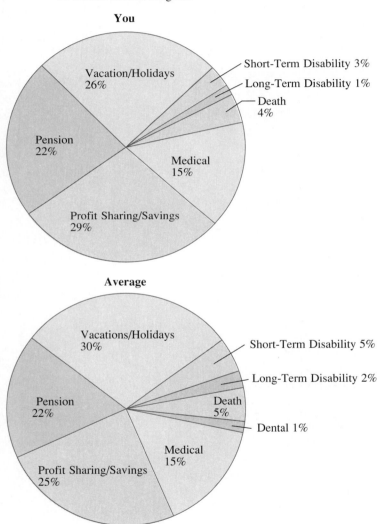

Source: Towers, Perrin, Forster & Crosby (TPF&C).

Civil Rights Laws

Three laws, Title VII of the Civil Rights Act, Age Discrimination in Employment Act (ADEA), and Pregnancy Discrimination Act are particularly important in benefits administration.

Title VII prohibits discrimination in terms and conditions of employment (including benefits) that is based on race, color, religion, sex, or national origin. Sex discrimination existed in two types of pension plans:

1. Plans that require women to contribute a higher premium than men in order to receive the same benefits as men, other things equal.[20]

2. Plans that require women to contribute the same amount but pay them smaller benefits than men, other things equal.[21]

The insurance industry justified such differences on the fact that women as a class live longer than men; therefore, the pension cost to the employer for the average retired woman was greater than the cost for the average retired man. But the Supreme Court ruled that Title VII of the Civil Rights Act applies to *individuals,* not classes. Since not *all individual women* live longer than *all individual men,* differential payments discriminate against those women required to pay more.

Women must also receive the same pensions. Lower benefits paid to women than to men who made the same contributions are illegal.

Thus, actuarial tables used to determine the cost of employer-provided insurance must be based on the combined illness, accident, and death rates for both men and women.

Age Discrimination in Employment Act (ADEA)

Passed in 1967 and amended in 1978 and 1986, the ADEA prohibits job-related discrimination against workers age 40 and above.

Mandatory retirement, formerly legal at age 70, is forbidden for all except fire fighters, police officers, and tenured professors.[22] These occupations are exempted because they apparently deal with public safety, although we have been unable to envision what threats to public safety a 70-year-old professor poses.

For people who work past age 65, however, special rules regarding pensions, life insurance, and health care may be applied:

1. *Pensions:* Age 65, a pension can be "frozen" at whatever level employees would have received had they retired at 65.

2. *Life insurance:* Coverage cannot be eliminated after age 65. However, reduction in the amount is permitted if an employer can demonstrate that continuing benefit coverage at the pre-65 age level results in higher costs.

3. *Health care:* Total health benefits cannot be reduced for those employees 65 and over. The employer may only reduce health insurance by the amount of Medicare coverage available.

The *Betts* case described in the chapter introduction shows the Supreme Court's narrow interpretation of this law. Ruling against *Betts,* they found that age distinctions in benefits are legal if they do not have a negative effect on employment conditions outside the benefits area. Legislation to overturn this interpretation is being considered.[23]

Pregnancy Discrimination Act

Should women be permitted health, disability, or sick leave benefits, or both, because of pregnancy? In 1976, the Supreme Court held that an insurance benefit that exempts pregnancy from disability coverage did not constitute sex discrimination under Title VII.[24]

This decision met with sufficient opposition from women's organizations, unions, civil rights groups, and sympathetic legislators to be overturned by law in 1978. The Pregnancy Discrimination Act "prohibits the denial of health, disability, or sick leave benefits to pregnant women temporarily disabled by childbirth itself or by a medical condition incurred before or after childbirth if such coverage is provided for nonpregnancy-related conditions." Such coverage only applies if a valid benefits plan is already in effect. It does not require an employer to offer a medical benefits program. But if a program is offered, pregnancy must be treated the same as any other medical condition.

In 1983, the Supreme Court applied the act to pregnancy benefits received by spouses of employees. The Newport News Shipbuilding Company had set a limit on maternity benefits for spouses of male employees. No limit was set on maternity benefits for female employees, nor was there a limit on any other medical condition for spouses. The court ruled that continuing this differential was discriminatory. Benefits that distinguish in coverage between employees and dependents, including spouses, are legal, but dependent coverage must be the same for all dependents, regardless of sex.[25]

Tax Laws

As we already stated, the tax-free status of benefits has been a major impetus for their growth. But tax law also affects benefits by insuring that they are nondiscriminatory.[26] In this sense, nondiscriminatory means that benefits must be received by a large portion of the firm's employees to qualify for favorable tax treatment. For example, very specific financial rules regulate capital accumulation plans (pensions, stock ownership, savings plans, and the like). The purpose of these regulations is to prevent the bulk of benefits being given only to executives.

Fiduciary Responsibility

In the early 1970s, thousands of retirees and workers who thought their pensions were guaranteed found out they weren't. When the former employers went bankrupt during a recession, the retirees were abandoned. As a result,

Congress passed legislation regulating private pensions and imposing strict financial measures on employers.

The 1974 Employee Retirement Income Security Act (ERISA), the 1984 Retirement Equity Act and the 1986 Tax Reform Act all regulate private pension plans. They do not require employers to provide pension plans, but, if one is offered, then it must conform to ERISA regulations.[27] ERISA has five main regulations.

Eligibility

All employee earnings from age 21 on must be included, and only 1,000 hours of work is required during a year to be eligible. Many part time employees are now covered by pensions.

Vesting and Portability

Full vesting means employees own the pension benefits if they leave the employer prior to retirement. Prior to ERISA, employees could lose all pension rights if they left (or were terminated) before retirement. Now they must be fully vested after five years of service with an employer.

Many pensions are also portable. That is, an employee changing jobs can transfer vested pension funds from one employer to another. ERISA does not mandate portability.

Funding and Fiduciary Liabilities

Because financial mismanagement of pension plans was the primary impetus for the passage of ERISA, an employer offering a pension must now conform to rigorous funding guidelines. These funding requirements combined with a runup of stock market values in the 1980s to create funding surpluses. As these surplus assets grew, many corporations terminated their plans, purchased annuities to cover the benefits already promised, and diverted the remaining funds to other purposes, including leveraged buyouts. Legislation has been introduced to tax funds so diverted. Opponents of legislation argue that overregulation will lead to the demise of private pensions altogether.[28]

Pension fund administrators have legal and financial obligations under ERISA. Pension funds are to be managed solely for the benefit of participating employees and their beneficiaries.

Termination Responsibilities

The Pension Benefit Guaranty Corporation (PBGC), a nonprofit agency, was formed under ERISA to protect employees whose employers failed to provide intended benefits. For example, in 1988, LTV, a steel conglomerate, declared bankruptcy and defaulted on its pension obligations to its current and retired employees. The PBGC assumed payments, but at a reduced level. These payments came from a reserve fund created by yearly premiums paid by all employers.

EXHIBIT 14.5   Tax Rates, Maximum Earnings Base, and Maximum Social Security Tax

Year	Taxation Rate on Covered Earnings		Total × Maximum Earnings Base		Maximum Social Security Tax (dollars)
	For Retirement Survivors and Disability Insurance (percent)	For Hospital Insurance (percent)	(percent)	(dollars)	
1978	5.05%	1.00%	6.05%	× $17,700	$1,070.85
1980	5.08	1.05	6.13	× 25,900	1,587.67
1983	5.40	1.30	6.70	× 35,700	2,391.90
1986	5.70	1.45	7.15	× 42,000	3,003.00
1990	6.2	1.45	7.65	× 50,400	3,856.00

* Automatic adjustments based on average earnings level.

Source: Social Security Administration (SSA) Bulletin no. 79-10044, 1979, and Annual Statistical Supplement, 1984–85.

Within months of terminating its original plan, LTV established a new plan that made up the difference between what PBGC was paying and what the employees had been scheduled to receive before the bankruptcy. In effect, LTV transferred a large chunk of its pension costs to other employers who were required to contribute to the reserve fund. In 1990, the Supreme Court ordered LTV to resume its original obligations, saying its actions were an abuse of PBGC resources.[29]

Mandated Benefits

Employers are legally required to offer certain programs to employees. These mandated benefits are Social Security, unemployment compensation, and workers' compensation.[30]

Social Security

The Social Security System, established in 1935, provides some income protection to employees who have retired, died, or are disabled. Payments are based on past earnings and years of work. Exhibit 14.5 shows the growth in social security tax rates. In 1990, employees paid 7.65 percent on incomes up to $50,400, for a maximum tax of $3,856. Employers pay an equal amount.

The benefits one receives depend on past earnings and length of work experience.[31]

Social Security provides income protection beyond pensions; these include survivor benefits for children under age 18, disability benefits, and Medicare health coverage for those beyond 65.

Unemployment Compensation

Unemployment compensation (UC) was set up in the United States as part of the Social Security Act of 1935. It is designed to provide a subsistence payment for employees between jobs. The employer pays in to the UC fund at a rate based on the average number of former employees who have drawn benefits from the fund.[32]

To be eligible for compensation, the employee must have worked a minimum number of weeks, be without a job, and be willing to accept a suitable position offered through the state Unemployment Compensation Commission. Some state laws permit payments to strikers.

To fund unemployment compensation, the employer pays a payroll tax to the state and federal governments on total wages paid. Currently the tax is 3.4 percent of the first $6,000 earned by each worker. However, if an organization has laid off very few employees, it may qualify for a lower tax rate. The state unemployment commissions receive the bulk of the funds.

Each state has its own set of interpretations and payments. Payments by employers and to employees vary because the benefits paid vary, experience ratings of employers may vary, and some states are much more efficient in administering the program than others.

Workers' Compensation Insurance

Workers' compensation is an employer-paid insurance program designed to compensate an employee for the expenses sustained from a work-related injury.[33] An injury is compensable if it is the result of an accident that arose out of, and while in, the course of employment. Diseases that result from occupations (e.g., black lung disease in miners) are also compensable.

Payments are made in the event of disability or death. Medical expenses are also covered. Disability payments are often based on formulas that take into account the employee's earnings, number of dependents, and other factors. Detailed accident and death records are also required of employers, in order to learn how to make the workplace safer.

Workers' compensation insurance laws exist in every state, and each is different.[34] Because each state offers its own program, the levels of protection, and consequently associated costs, differ considerably.[35]

COVERAGE

In addition to those legally required, four kinds of benefits are typically provided to employees: employer-purchased insurance, paid time away from work, employee services, and retirement income. Exhibit 14.6 ranks the popularity of various benefits. It shows that health insurance is one of the benefits employees value most.

EXHIBIT 14.6   Ranking of Different Employee Benefits

	Study		
	1	**2**	**3**
Medical	1	1	3
Pension	2	3	8
Paid vacation and holidays	3	2	X (not rated)
Sickness	4	5	
Dental	5	6	
Profit sharing	6	2	
Long-term disability	7	7	
Life insurance	8	4	

This exhibit was compiled from three different sources. Some of the reward components rated in some of the studies were not traditional employee benefits and have been deleted from the rankings here. The three studies were: *The Wall Street Journal,* "The Future Look of Employee Benefits," September 8, 1988, p. 23 (source: Hewitt Associates); Kermit Davis, William Giles, and Hubert Feild, *How Young Professionals Rank Employee Benefits: Two Studies;* International Foundation of Employee Benefit Plans: Brookfield, Wis., 1988; Kenneth Shapiro and Jesse Sherman, Employee Attitude Benefit Plan Designs," *Personnel Journal,* July 1987, pp. 49–58.

Employer-Purchased Insurance

The expenses associated with risks encountered throughout life—illness, accident, and early death, among others—can be diminished by pooling the risk through buying insurance. In addition to the tax advantage of employer-purchased insurance, employers can usually buy insurance cheaper because the rate is based on group risk, rather than individual risk. Insurance may be free to the employee (noncontributory) or the employee may pay a share of the premium (contributory).

Three major forms of insurance are common: health, disability-accident, and life.

Health insurance is costly, but as Exhibit 14.6 shows, it is extremely popular with employees.[36] Coverage may include prescription drugs, mental health services, and dental care. The Consolidated Omnibus Reconciliation Act (COBRA), passed in 1986, requires employers to continue coverage up to three years for employees who have been laid off. As Exhibit 14.7 shows, in spite of employer and government efforts to control increases, health care costs continue to go up far faster than other costs in the consumer price index.[37] Concerted efforts by employers and unions had slowed the rate of increase from an alarming 11.6 percent in 1982, but the discrepancy between the overall CPI and the medical care component continues to widen.

Group life insurance is one of the oldest and most widely available employee benefits. Yet, as Exhibit 14.6 shows, it is not particularly popular. The amount of insurance provided typically increases as salary increases.

EXHIBIT 14.7   Health Care Inflation

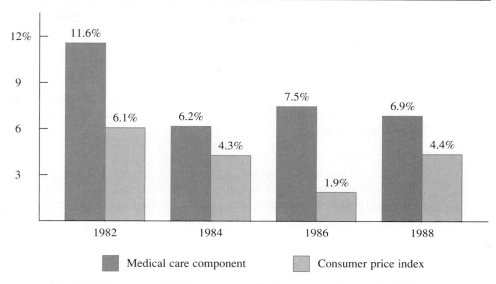

Source: *Monthly Labor Review*, U.S. Department of Labor, Bureau of Labor Statistics, May 1989.

Long-term sickness and accident/disability insurance protects employees who have accidents at work that leave them unable to work, temporarily or permanently. Workers' compensation pays a very small part of these costs, since it is designed primarily to take care of short-term disability problems. Employer-funded long-term disability insurance supplements benefits from workers' compensation, Social Security, and other agencies. About 75 percent of employers provide such coverage. Exhibit 14.6 shows that employees don't seem particularly attached to their disability insurance.

Paid Time Away from Work

As Exhibit 14.6 shows, paid vacations and holidays are a relatively popular benefit. However, they did not always exist. People used to work 12 hours a day, six days a week, 52 weeks a year.[38] Now most employers compensate employees for rest periods, coffee breaks, and time when they are not actually at work—holidays, vacations, or sick leave. Vacations with pay usually begins after a minimum period of employment. The cost of these benefits is influenced by the employees' base salary.

Employee Services

Services is something of a catchall category of voluntary benefits. It includes all other benefits provided by employers, such as cafeterias, saunas and gyms, free parking lots, commuter vans, infirmaries, discounts on company products, financial counseling, and child care assistance.

Educational Programs

Many organizations provide for off-the-job general educational support for their employees. Companies often use such plans as part of their employee development programs.

Social and Recreational Programs

Studies of the preferences of employees indicate that recreational services are *the least preferred* of all benefits and services offered.[39] However, the emphasis on controlling health care costs has increased employer interest in healthy lifestyles and various "wellness" programs.[40]

Child Care

The entry of record numbers of women into the labor force has dramatically increased the demand for quality child care centers. Working parents frequently list adequate child care as the most important problem they face.[41] Some 3,500 companies offer day care benefits.

There are several approaches to day care assistance. One is a flexible spending account, which lets employees put aside pretax wages for certain expenses, including help for elderly parents and child care. This arrangement saves the employee taxes on the money put into this account.[42] A second approach is corporation as caregiver. About 150 companies and 600 hospitals have set up operations at or near the office, but these arrangements may raise concerns about liability and possible favoritism in admissions.[43] Another alternative for many employers is to help subsidize community care providers both directly and indirectly through vouchers.

Parental Leave

This benefit is another response to women's entry into the labor force. While few employers presently offer it, bills have frequently been introduced in Congress mandating up to 18 weeks of unpaid parental leave. Many states are considering similar legislation.[44]

Retirement Income

Employees' retirement income comes from four sources—mandated Social Security benefits, private pensions, asset income, and earnings. Employers play a role in all of these categories.

Asset Income

Asset income is money generated by personal savings and investments. There are a wide variety of employer-assisted savings or capital accumulation plans.[45] Deferred compensation plans, such as 401(k) plans (named for the section of the Internal Revenue Code that authorizes them), permit employees to postpone income taxes on a portion of salary if that salary is contributed to a qualified plan.[46] Frequently, an employer will match an employee's contribution to a plan, typically on a 50 cents per $1 rate.

A number of compensation-deferred plans exist. Basically, all of them have the similar strategy of shifting income to postretirement years.[47]

Employee Stock Ownership Plans

Employee stock ownership plans are another approach to asset accumulation. Under these plans, employers make payments to a trust, which purchases the employer's stock, for the benefit of employees. Employers get a tax deduction for the contribution, and employees accumulate equity in the organization. Laws regarding tax treatment and requirements for such plans are periodically revised. Thus, ESOPs (employee stock ownership plans) preceded TRASOPs (Tax Reduction Act Stock Ownership Plan), which preceded PAYSOPs (so named because they are tied to the company's payroll, in order to provide greater benefits to labor-intensive industries). The 1986 Tax Reform Act allows corporations to use ESOPs to raise capital as well as transfer ownership to employees.

Employee ownership theoretically has the potential to "improve corporate performance, create a more equitable distribution of wealth, and build a society in which enriching one group will not automatically mean taking something away from another group."[48] However, the success of ESOPs in accomplishing such lofty objectives depends on the health of the organization before the transfer of ownership. A dying company is not made healthy by a change in ownership alone. Ownership may have nothing to do with problems that may exist.[49] But it does represent another retirement income option for employees and managers to consider.

In addition to stock ownership, incentive stock options (ISOs) are frequently used for executive in companies whose stock is likely to increase in value.[50] All of these variations on employee ownership are the result of legislation intended to accommodate a particular social goal or to curb a particular abuse. Thus, further revisions can be anticipated.

Private Pensions

Many employers provide pension funds to retired employees, with the amount usually based on years of service and income level while employed. There is an astounding variety in pensions, which cover about two thirds of all U.S. employees.[51] The most generous pensions are in the public sector: the federal government offers pensions that are double the rate of those in private industry. Some retirees are only 38 years old.

Most pension plans are "defined benefits." That is, the plan agrees to pay a certain amount a month to every retiree for life. Payments used to be financed from current income. But legislation in the 1970s required that money sufficient to pay the pension must be set aside during the working years of the employee. Because the total costs for a defined benefit plan would vary with life expectancy, many employers switched to "defined contribution" plans, which specified the amount of money paid in, rather than the amount paid out. Thus, the costs for defined contribution plans are easily calculated. This cost certainty is the reason why they have been more popular than defined benefit plans for new adoptions over the past 20 years.[52]

COMMUNICATION

Writer after writer bemoans the fact that employees do not appreciate or value their benefits, largely because they are unaware of them. But given the frequency of uncoordinated, haphazard administration, many employers seem equally unaware of them. Except for costs. Too many benefit departments are the purview of the Bob Cratchetts, who may be very good at managing forms, but lack either the talent or the authority to boost their effectiveness. Failure to understand benefits components and their value is a root cause of employee dissatisfaction with benefits.[53] So, perhaps some training in effective communication should be a prerequisite for benefits administrators. ERISA requires employers to communicate with employees by sending them an annual report on their pension plan and basic information on their pensions. J. C. Penney emphasizes how much employees would need to save to provide this coverage on their own in its annual report. Some employers even send employees copies of bills paid by the company for medical expenses on their behalf.

Communication is not a one-way process. A basic premise underlying benefits management is that employees need to be involved in choosing benefits; if some choice is available, then the chances are that (1) employees will understand their benefits and (2) they will be more satisfied with benefits. But employees can only choose an appropriate mix of benefits if they are given proper information and make a careful assessment of their own needs. Lack of interest or understanding by employees can lead to inappropriate and expensive choices that do not increase satisfaction.

CHOICE

The makeup of the work force—their age, sex, whether they have employed spouses, number of dependents, income level, time until retirement—affects what benefits are offered and how satisfied the employees are with them.[54] Employees close to retirement and with college age children will clearly have different benefit preferences than will newly hired employees with working spouses and preschool children. Yet, we really do not know which employees prefer tax-free benefits over taxable cash. It seems to depend in part on income level. A few studies found that employees at higher income levels preferred more benefits to cash, but the majority of employees prefer cash. For lower-paid employees, fewer tax advantages exist, or perhaps these employees may have more immediate needs that only cash can satisfy. But because benefits are so tied into a country's tax policy, these generalizations may not hold true outside the United States.

Employees do have preferences among different forms of benefits. But studies suggest that most preferences vary widely, and these change over time.[55] Failure to adjust benefits to demographic changes is one of the main causes of employee dissatisfaction with benefits.[56]

The degree of employee choice varies across organizations. Most firms allow employees to specify whether or not they wish health insurance to cover their dependents, or who their insurance beneficiary will be.

The greatest choice in contemporary systems is found in flexible benefit plans.

How Flexi Benefits Work

Although there are varying types of programs, the *core cafeteria plan* is the most common.[57] Under its provisions, employees have identical minimum levels of benefits (e.g., health and life insurance, pensions, and the like). They are then given a choice among additional life insurance, more vacation time, better health insurance coverage, dependent health insurance, long-term disability, dental coverage, child care services, and so on. Employees purchase these choices by using benefit "credits" designed into the plan. Different options require different levels of credits. NCR allows employees to increase their credits by "selling" back vacation days. Primerica's flexi-benefits plan is illustrated in Exhibit 14.8. Employees periodically recertify or revise their choices. In this way changes in employee needs are recognized.

Another approach to broadening the choices available is the use of *flexible spending accounts*. Employees specify the dollar amount they want deducted from each paycheck for their flexible account. They then use this fund to pay medical or dependent care bills, or both. The advantage to the employee is that these bills are paid with before-tax dollars. The disadvantage is the "use it or lose it" rule: any money left in the account at the end of the year goes to the employer.[58]

Advantages

The basic advantage of flexi benefits is that they are designed to meet employee preferences. If employees' benefit preferences are satisfied, they may be less likely to be absent, more reluctant to quit, have fewer accidents, and so on. But there is little research to support all these speculations.

EXHIBIT 14.8   Flexible Benefits at Primerica Corporation

The concept

The idea behind flexible benefits is very simple. It reflects our belief that each individual should have the ability to choose the benefits that are most meaningful to him or her. Under flexible benefits, you'll have a basic foundation — or core — of coverage and an allowance to use in putting together your own benefit program around that core.

The Development of Flexible Benefits

Think of our pre-flexible benefit program (the program we had before flexible benefits) as a circle divided into five parts — medical benefits, life insurance benefits, vacation, disability, and retirement and capital accumulation benefits. Over the past few decades, we worked hard to build a benefit program that stands among the best available in industry today. The trouble is, no one program — however rich — can ever meet everyone's needs equally well. People are too different for that.

Now picture an inner circle of benefits which we'll call the core. This core area represents fundamental protection that can't be changed under the flexible benefits system. It's a basic foundation of security for all employees — security no one can opt out of.

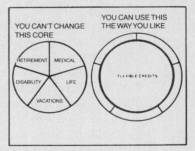

How Flexible Credits are Figured

The difference between the core and your pre-flexible benefits is transformed by insurance and actuarial calculations into flexible credits which are allocated to you in dollars. You can then use those dollars for benefit options. With them, you can build your own benefit program around the core. The amount of flexible credits you are allotted will vary from year to year. That's because they depend on your particular age, pay, family status, and years of service with the company. You'll be given your flexible credit allowance on the form you use to make your benefit option decisions. This same principle holds even if you joined us without having ever been covered by the pre-flexible program. Your flexible credit allowance will be figured the same way.

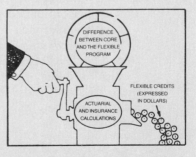

Disadvantages

Administering a flexible-benefit plan requires significant administrative effort. Administration includes extensive communications policies, employee counseling services regarding available choices, and sophisticated record-keeping and accounting systems. Computerized human resource information systems simplify these tasks.

An additional problem is "adverse selection." For example, employees may take extensive dental coverage in one year, then opt out of dental care the following year. For the next few years they may pay for routine dental care themselves and then opt back into the dental care program when major work is needed again. This results in erratic cost patterns for the company, as premiums increase according to the use or overuse of the provision.[59]

Flexible Benefits as a Cost Reduction Strategy

Employees also can face some disadvantages under flexi plans.[60] Many employers use the introduction of flexi plans as an opportunity to raise employee contributions and deductibles. However, flexible plans may also lower the costs of introducing new forms of benefits.[61] To illustrate, assume that a company has liberal life insurance and hospital/medical benefits, but no dental plan. By adopting a flexible approach, the company can offer a dental plan at no additional expense to the company. Employees pay the cost by reducing other benefit coverages. Thus, employees satisfy their needs while the employer does not increase the costs of providing an additional benefit.

Additionally, flexible benefits can be used to address unique concerns. For example, including day care services as part of a flexible-benefits package permits employees who need the service to select it. At the same time, the employer avoids the appearance of favoring one group of employees—those who require day-care services—over other employees. Flexible benefits permit a wider variety of benefits and a greater degree of employee choice than may otherwise be affordable.

There is evidence that flexible plans do reduce costs. A 1988 survey reports that sponsors of flexible plans spent $2,280 per employee for health care insurance, whereas sponsors of traditional plans spent $2,477—9 percent more.[62] However, it may be difficult to isolate the effects of flexible benefits from other cost reduction strategies instituted at the same time (e.g., improved communications, changed utilization patterns, and the like).

EVALUATING THE RESULTS OF BENEFIT DECISIONS

The previous section discussed the basic decisions managers face in the design and administration of benefits. These included competitiveness, compliance, coverage, communication, and choice. Certainly, managers do not make these decisions unilaterally. The government, employees, and their unions are very concerned with and often very involved in the process. The costs involved make these decisions salient to all parties. Given their relevance and costs, evaluating the results of benefits decisions deserves special attention.

From a decision-making perspective, benefits are evaluated in terms of their objectives. Three objectives deserve special attention. The first is the cost effectiveness of benefit decisions. A second is their impact on employee work behaviors and the third is the fairness or equity with which they are viewed by employees.

Unfortunately, much of the discussion that follows is drawn from "conventional wisdom" and beliefs. The lack of objective evidence to support the beliefs is disquieting, in light of the costs associated with benefit programs.

Effects on Costs

Controlling Costs

Because health care costs have experienced the greatest growth, increasing almost three times faster than overall price increases in the economy, they have received most of the attention. Tactics for controlling costs include changing employee consumption patterns, changing financing methods, and coordinating/managing benefits more efficiently.

Changing Consumption Patterns

Co-paid benefit plans require that employees pay a share of costs. For example, employees may be required to pay a share of medical insurance premiums, or they may be required to pay a part of total medical expenses. By requiring employees to pay a portion of costs, employers hope to heighten cost awareness and increase selectivity in using services. While this is currently one of the most popular cost containment strategies, it has the potential to backfire. Without effective communication, employees may see copayment and increased deductibles as cutbacks in benefit levels. Many employees are more willing to take a pay cut than reduce health care coverage. The number of strikes over health care benefits has been increasing dramatically. It was the primary issue in 1989's strikes against AT&T and the regional telephone companies. Employees felt that the level of profitability undercut the companies' arguments for sharing expenses. Management eventually dropped its demand, in exchange for a cap on coverage for retired employees.[63]

Case management—programs to plan and coordinate cost-effective medical care—is becoming a popular approach to managing consumption.[64] Emphasis is on exploring alternative sources of care and developing a plan to meet a patient's needs in the most cost-effective way. One study reports that one third of yearly health insurance claims stem from 2–5 percent of the insured population.[65] This is the population on which managers concentrate their efforts to manage consumption.

Requiring second opinions or preauthorization before covering certain medical expenses are other ways employers hope to motivate employees to be more selective in using medical services.

Changing Financing Methods

For employees whose health insurance premiums are based on communitywide claim experience, as little as 50 percent of the premium may go to pay providers of health care (doctors, hospitals).[66] Larger companies can often afford to set up a fund internally to cover health care claims. Expenses are then paid out of this fund, rather than by an insurance company. The advantage to the self-insured employer is increased control; and, if actual expenses come in under budget, the savings go to the employer, rather than to an insurance company. The down side of self-insurance is administrative problems and expenses, but much of this can be subcontracted to consulting firms.

Another way to change financing methods is to negotiate expenses. Kaiser Steel provides the classic example. Kaiser built its own hospitals for employees and hired its own doctors. While few employers go to this extreme, health maintenance organizations (HMOs), in which all medical services are provided for a flat monthly rate, have often been started at employer instigation.

More and more employers are negotiating rates with hospitals, doctors, laboratory services, and druggists.[67] Sometimes these special rates are in exchange for a certain volume of business. This approach, called *preferred provider,* is growing rapidly. Employees who use preferred providers pay little or nothing. Choosing nonparticipating doctors means high deductibles and copayments. Unfortunately, we don't know which, if any, of these cost-controlling methods are most effective. Further, the impact on the quality of medical care has so far been unexamined.[68]

Improving Coordination

Benefits are often not well managed. Many employers viewed them almost as a "fixed cost" and took them for granted, much the same as employees. But closer scrutiny and coordination can reduce costs. For example, two thirds of all employers do not coordinate pension levels with Social Security.[69] Yet, it is cost effective to do so. Within plans, employers rarely analyze coverage to see that it is internally consistent. For example, combining benefits from a sick-leave plan, a short-term and long-term disability income plan with workers' compensation and Social Security benefits may result in benefits at some times being greater than the pay they are meant to replace, while at other times they are far less.[70]

Effects on Employee Behaviors

Absenteeism

There is some evidence that vesting provision in pensions and health insurance curtails turnover and absenteeism.[71] General Motors and the UAW negotiated a link between absenteeism and reduced benefits.[72] Employees who were absent more than 20 percent of their scheduled work time during the first six months of the contract were offered counseling. If they exceeded the 20 percent rate during the second six months of the contract, their benefits were cut equal to the individual's absence rate. Cuts occurred in paid holidays, jury duty pay, and sickness and accident benefits. They reported an 11 percent drop in "controllable" absences the first year and 10 percent and 9 percent in subsequent years of the contract.

Early Retirement

Modified benefit programs are also used to reduce work force size, or to engineer an exit for a specific employee.[73] Health and disability insurance may be extended beyond the period of employment, or retirement provisions may be sweetened. For example, IBM added five years of age and service to employees' actual age and service for calculating retirement benefits, to induce employees to retire in 1986 and avoid layoffs. In 1989, IBM cut staffing levels again. Organizations must be sure their retirement incentives are consistent with age discrimination laws and that acceptance is voluntary.

Many companies require employees accepting early retirement programs to sign waivers indicating they will not file age discrimination charges. Nevertheless, some employees charge they are being coerced, since they face a possible layoff if they do not accept the retirement offer. Legal cases and legislation on the topic are pending.[74]

Performance

Benefits' effects on other behaviors, such as applicants' decision to join an employer, or work hard once employed, are less well researched. Some benefits may, at best, have an indirect effect on performance. The argument in support of an indirect effect is that unhealthy, worried, or troubled employees are not likely to perform at their best. Attention wanes, absenteeism increases, sustained effort at the job simply cannot be maintained. All of these work to lower productivity. Consequently, benefits designed to assist employees to maintain their health, financial security, and personal stability (drug counseling, child care, legal assistance) will help avoid these problems. Certain forms of retirement benefits, particularly ESOPs, are also thought to affect productivity. Partial ownership of the company is believed to have a positive effect on employees' motivation and, hence, their performance. Here again, these are based more on belief than on analysis.

Effects on Equity

An important objective of benefits decisions is to positively affect employee attitudes about the fairness and adequacy of benefits.[75] Research does show that the overall level of benefits is positively related to employees' satisfaction with their benefits. And there is also some support for the proposition that increased communication and choice increases employee's satisfaction with their benefits.[76]

However, more research is required to provide a better understanding of employees' reactions to various coverages and types of benefits. Opinion Research Corporation found a sharp drop in the satisfaction with benefits over the past decade.[77] They attribute this drop to a failure to restructure benefits in response to the changing demographics of the labor force.

SUMMARY

In spite of their hefty price tag—almost 40 percent of payroll costs—it has only been in the last few years that managing benefits has had a high priority for employers. Not only are benefits expensive, but they aren't always the benefits that employees want. Satisfaction with benefits has slipped dramatically in the last 10 years. Benefits have not kept step with changes in the demographics of the workplace.

The chapter has described the major benefits decisions: competitiveness, compliance, alternate coverage, communication, and choice. Competitiveness refers to structuring one's benefit package in relationship to one's competitors. Some of the issues here are similar to those discussed in the previous chapter on external competitiveness.

Some benefits are required by law: unemployment compensation, government pensions, and workers' compensation. In addition, most employers offer additional benefits, such as compensation for time off (holidays, vacations), employer-purchased insurance (health, life, and disability), private pensions, and other services, such as prepaid legal services, health club memberships, or child care centers.

Communication to employees about their benefit coverage deserves greater attention than most organizations give. Research shows that communication tends to increase employee satisfaction with benefits. This may occur because employees typically underestimate the value of their benefits.

One innovative approach to tuning benefits to individual preferences, as well as to control costs, is flexible benefits. Under these plans, employees are given a core group of benefits, plus credits for additional benefit coverage that they may allocate in any way they choose. The Internal Revenue Service has a number of requirements that must be met for such plans. Nevertheless, flexible benefit plans are becoming increasingly popular.

While the effects of benefits on costs are easily calculated, their effects on employee behaviors and on equity are less easily documented. Benefits may even be dysfunctional, since few of them are tied to performance. Rather, they are entitlements—given to employees as part of the conditions of employment. On the one hand, benefits provide a social good. But by steadily increasing them, fewer dollars remain to reward the risk-taking behavior or performance levels that may be required for an organization to maintain its competitive edge or profitability, or both.

DISCUSSION AND REVIEW QUESTIONS

1. Why do employers provide benefit plans?
2. How and why can benefits be tailored to individual needs?
3. Why are copayment strategies not always successful?
4. What effect does communication have on the various benefit objectives?
5. What effect will demographic changes have on benefits? How can an employer capitalize on such changes?
6. There is growing interest in legally requiring all employers to provide health insurance for their employees. From the perspective of the entire society, what are the advantages and disadvantages of mandating benefits? From the perspective of the organization, what are the advantages and disadvantages?
7. How can benefits be tailored to the strategic objectives of an organization?
8. What affects the form benefits take? How do you think benefits may vary among countries?
9. Which benefits discussed in this chapter correlate most strongly with seniority? Is this good or bad?
10. Why are defined contribution pension plans becoming increasingly common?

YOUR TURN
NATIONAL HEALTH INSURANCE

You are a member of the House of Representatives. The economy of your Michigan district is heavily dependent on the economy of the auto industry. The number one issue for a lot of your constituents, as well as fellow Representatives, is affordable health care.

Senator Kennedy's proposal on national health insurance is on your desk. The Heritage Foundation has sent over a copy of its proposal. One of your staffers has collected information on national health insurance plans in Canada and Japan. Compare the approaches and decide which of them you would vote for. (Your instructor will provide information on the various proposals.)

NOTES AND REFERENCES

1. *Public Employees Retirement System of Ohio* v. *Betts,* U.S. Sup. Ct. 88-389, June 23, 1989; 50 FEP Cases 104.
2. *McLendon* v. *The Continental Group, Inc.,* D.N.N., Civ. Act. No. 83-1340, May 10, 1989.
3. J. Cohen, "The Evolution and Growth of Social Security," in *Federal Policies and Worker Status since the Thirties,* ed. J. P. Goldberg, E. Ahern, W. Haber, and R. A. Oswald (Madison, Wis.: Industrial Relations Research Association, 1976).
4. Robert M. McCaffery, *Managing the Employee Benefits Program* (New York: American Management Association, 1983).
5. U.S. Chamber of Commerce, *Employee Benefits 1981* (Washington, D.C.: Chamber of Commerce, 1981).
6. Richard Freeman and James Medoff, *What Do Unions Do?* (New York: Basic Books, 1984).
7. Loren Solnick, "The Effect of Blue-Collar Unions on White-Collar Wages and Fringe Benefits, *Industrial and Labor Relations Review,* January 1985, pp. 236–43; and Richard B. Freeman, "The Effect of Unionism on Fringe Benefits," *Industrial and Labor Relations Review,* July 1981, pp. 506–07.
8. "Ouch! The Squeeze on Your Health Benefits," *Business Week,* November 20, 1989, pp. 110–22.
9. Ibid.
10. Dallas Salisbury, "What Challenges Do Benefit Managers Face?" *Employee Benefit News,* January 1990, pp. 25–30; Richard A. Rose, "Flexible Compensation: Supporting the Company Goals—Is Now the Right Time?" Presentation to 1988 Employee Benefits Conference sponsored by The Conference Board New York, March 1988.
11. James O'Toole, "The Irresponsible Society," in *Working in the 21st Century,* ed. C. Stewart Sheppard and Donald C. Carroll (New York: John Wiley & Sons, 1980), p. 156.
12. Ibid., p. 163.
13. "Questions and Answers about Employee Benefits," *EBRI Issue Brief,* April 1989, p. 1.
14. Linda Demkovich, "Covering Options through Mandated Benefits," *Business and Health,* January–February 1986, pp. 2–6.
15. Thomas Paine, "The Emphasis in Benefits Design Has Shifted from Enriching the Competitive Package to Cost Containment," speech given March 29, 1984, to Employee Benefits Conference sponsored by The Conference Board.
16. Bruce Ellig, *Executive Compensation—A Total Pay Perspective* (New York: McGraw-Hill, 1982).
17. Jerry Rosenbloom and G. Victor Hallman, *Employee Benefit Planning* (Englewood Cliffs, N.J.: Prentice-Hall, 1981).
18. George T. Milkovich and Jerry M. Newman, *Compensation,* Homewood, Ill.: Richard D. Irwin, 1990).
19. John Bussey, "An Older Work Force Burdens Big Producers in the Basic Industries," *The Wall Street Journal,* March 8, 1987, pp. 1, 21.
20. *Los Angeles Dept. of Water and Power* v. *Manhart,* 435 U.S. 702 (1978).
21. *Arizona Governing Committee* v. *Norris,* 32 Fair Empl. Prac. Cas. 233 (1983).
22. Jeanne M. Hogarth, "Accepting an Early Retirement Bonus: An Empirical Study," *Journal of Human Resources,* Winter 1988.

23. "U.S. Supreme Court: Age-Based Differences in Employee Benefits Plan Are Exempt from ADEA, "*Compflash,* August 1989, p. 6.

24. *Gilbert* v. *General Electric Corporation,* 429 US 125 (1976).

25. We must emphasize that these civil rights laws apply only in the United States. Every country will have its own set of laws regarding the treatment of employees and members of their family.

26. "Drive to Simplify Section 89 Accelerates as Congress Responds to Pressure," *EBRI Notes,* June 1989, pp. 1–4.

27. *Pension and Retirement Plans: Issues and Strategies* (Greenvale, New York: Panel Publishers, 1986).

28. "Fat Pension Fund Can Make Companies Tempting Targets," *Business Week,* November 10, 1986, pp. 106–08.

29. "High Court Will Review LTV's Pension Moves," *New York Times,* October 31, 1989, pp. D1, D3.

30. Salisbury, "What Challenges Do Benefit Managers Face?"; David E. Rosenbaum, "Prof. Moynihan Wakes the Class with Truth about Taxes," *New York Times,* January 21, 1990, p. E4.

31. Olivia S. Mitchell, "Fringe Benefits and the Cost of Changing Jobs," *Industrial and Labor Relations Review,* October 1983, pp. 70–78.

32. Elchanan Cohn and Margaret Capen, "A Note on the Adequacy of UI Benefits," *Industrial Relations* 26, no. 1 (1987), pp. 106–11.

33. Philip Polakoff and Paul O'Rourke, "Workers' Compensation: A New Look at an Old Problem," *Benefits Quarterly* 5, no. 1 (1989), pp. 27–41.

34. J. Paul Leigh, "Analysis of Workers' Compensation Using Data on Individuals," *Industrial Relations* 24, no. 2 (1985), pp. 247, 256.

35. (John Burton's newsletter).

36. Regina E. Herzlinger and Jeffrey Schwartz, "How Companies Tackle Health Care Costs: Part I," *Harvard Business Review,* July–August 1985, pp. 69–81; Herzlinger, "How Companies Tackle Health Care Costs, Part II, *Harvard Business Review,* September–October 1985, pp. 108–20; and Herzlinger and David Calkins, "How Companies Tackle Health Care Costs: Part III," *Harvard Business Review,* January–February 1986, pp. 70–80.

37. "Cost Containment," *Medical Benefits,* April 15, 1986, pp. 1–3.

38. Edwin Markham, Benjamin Lindsey, and George Creel, *Children in Bondage* (New York: Hearst's International Library, 1914).

39. Loren Falkenberg, "Employee Fitness Programs: Their Impact on the Employee and the Organization," *Academy of Management Review* 12, no. 3 (1987), pp. 511–22.

40. *Company Practices in Health Care Management* (Lincolnshire, Ill.: Hewitt Associates, 1985); Herzlinger and Calkins, "How Companies Tackle Health Care Costs: Part III"; Gary T. McIlroy, "Health Care Cost Containment in the 1980s," *Compensation Review,* Fourth Quarter 1983, pp. 15–31.

41. Oscar Ornati and Carol Buckham, "Day Care: Still Waiting Its Turn as a Standard Benefit," *Management Review,* May 1983, pp. 57–62; Jacquelyn McCroskey, "Work and Families: What Is the Employer's Responsibility?" *Personnel Journal,* January 1982; Sheilia B. Kamerman, "Child-Care Services: a National Picture," *Monthly Labor Review,* December 1983, pp. 35–39.

42. David E. Bloom and Todd P. Steen, "Why Child Care Is Good for Business," *American Demographics,* August 1988, pp. 22–27, 58–59.

43. Sandra L. Burud et al., *Child Care: The New Business Tool* (Pasadena, Calif.: National Employer Supported Child Care Project, 1983).

44. *California Federal Savings and Loan Association* v. *Guerra,* 107 S. Ct. 683 (1987).

45. Jon Sutcliffe and Jay Schuster, "Benefits Revisited, Benefits Predicted," *Personnel Journal,* September 1985, pp. 62–68; Gary S. Fields and Olivia S. Mitchell, "Earnings, Pensions, Social Security, and Retirement," Working Paper no. 44, Ithaca, N.Y., Cornell University, 1983; Jeanne Hogarth, "Accepting an Early Retirement Bonus: An Empirical Study," *Journal of Human Resources,* Winter 1988, pp. 21–33.

46. *Tax Aspects of 401(K) Plans: Information for Employers and Employees* (Chicago: Commerce Clearing House, 1983); Karen Ferguson, "How 401(K)'s Hurt Lower-Paid Workers," *New York Times,* April 27, 1986, p. 2F.

47. Carson Beadle, "Taxing Employee Benefits: The Impact on Employers and Employees," *Compensation Review* 17, no. 2 (1985), pp. 12–19.

48. Corey Rosen, "Growth versus Equity: The Employee Ownership Solution," *ILR Report,* Spring 1985; Polly Taplin, "ESOPs Meet the Needs of a Variety of Companies," *Employee Benefit Plan Review,* June 1983, pp. 10–14.

49. Ben Fischer, "A Skeptic Looks at Employee Buyouts," *ILR Report,* Spring 1985.

50. Bruce Ellig, "Stock Option Design Considerations," *Compensation Review,* First Quarter 1983, pp. 13–24.

51. Bureau of Labor Statistics, *Employee Benefits in Medium and Large Firms, 1988* (Washington, D.C.: Department of Labor, 1989).

52. Ibid.

53. George Dreher, Ronald Ash, and Robert Bretz, "Benefit Coverage and Employee Cost: Critical Factors in Explaining Compensation Satisfaction," *Personnel Psychology, 1988* 41, pp. 237–54.

54. Dana E. Friedman and Wendy B. Gray, *A Life Cycle Approach to Family Benefits and Policies* (New York: The Conference Board, 1989).

55. Richard E. Johnson, "Flexible Benefit Plans," *Employee Benefits Journal,* September 1986, pp. 2–7.

56. Towers, Perrin, Forster, & Crosby (TPFC) survey, "Corporate Benefit Communication . . . Today and Tomorrow," 1988; "How Do You Communicate? It May Not Be Nearly as Well as You Think," *Benefits,* December (1988), pp. 13–15; Kevin Greene, "Effective Employee Benefits Communication," in *New Perspectives on Compensation,* ed. David Balkin and Luis Gomez-Mejia (Englewood Cliffs, N.J.: Prentice-Hall, 1987).

57. "Viewpoint, Tax Reform: A Green Light for Flexible Programs," *On Flexible Compensation,* October 1986, monthly newsletter published by Hewitt Associates, Lincolnshire, Illinois.

58. Lance Tane, "Guidelines to Successful Flex Plans: Four Companies' Experiences," *Compensation and Benefits Review,* July/August 1985, pp. 38–45.

59. "Benefits Are Getting More Flexible—But *Caveat Emptor,*" *Business Week,* September 8, 1986, pp. 64–66.

60. Ibid., p. 64.

61. Robert Becker, "Utilization Review," speech given October 7, 1986, Lake Tahoe Health Care Cost Containment Seminar, sponsored by International Foundation of Employee Benefit Plans, Brookfield, Wisconsin. Also see numerous other references listed in this chapter.

62. "Despite Cost-Containment Efforts: Health Care Premiums Surge," *AMA CompFlash 88,* no. 3 (1988), p. 6.

63. The main point of contention in the 1989 strikes at the regional telephone companies (referred to as the *Baby Bells*) was over the companies' attempts to shift part of health care costs to employees.

64. C. Delaney and D. Aquilina, "Case Management: Meeting the Challenge of High Cost Illness," *Employee Benefits Journal* 12, no. 1 (1987), pp. 2–8.

65. Delaney and Aquilina, "Case Management."

66. C. Bradford, "Self-Funded Trusts: An Answer to Rising Benefit Costs," *Financial Executive,* July 1981, pp. 24–26; J. C. Milligan, "Firms Foresee Higher Costs, Move toward Self-Insurnace," *Business Insurance,* March 22, 1982, 3ff.

67. C. Jacobs, "Medical Case Management: A Program to Cut Costs and Enhance Care of the Seriously Ill," *Compensation and Benefits Management* 4, no. 2 (1988), pp. 123–28.

68. M. G. Henderson, B. A. Souder, and A. Bergman, "Measuring Efficiencies of Managed Care," *Business and Health* 4, no. 12 (1987), pp. 43–46.

69. T. N. Fannin and T. A. Fannin, "Coordination of Benefits: Uncovering Buried Treasure," *Personnel Journal,* May 1983, pp. 386–91; Marian Extejt, "Who Gets the Benefits after a Divorce?" *Personnel Journal,* October 1983, pp. 790–94.

70. William J. Wiatrowski, "Employee Income Protection against Short-Term Disabilities," *Monthly Labor Review,* February 1985, pp. 32–38; Rosenbloom and Hallman, *Employee Benefit Planning.*

71. Abby Brown, "The Retirement Game," *Personnel Administration,* November 1986, pp. 55–60.

72. George Ruben, "GM's Plan to Combat Absenteeism Successfully," *Monthly Labor Review,* September 1983, pp. 36–37.

73. Scott Macey, "Reductions in Force and Employee Benefits Considerations," Paper presented at Age Discrimination and Retirement Benefits Law Conference, November 21–22, 1985, Palm Springs, California.

74. Deborah L. Jacobs, "The Growing Legal Battle over Employee Waivers," *New York Times,* October 29, 1989, p. F12.

75. *EEOC* v. *J. C. Penney Co.,* DC, ED, Mich., Civil No. 79-74034; and *Colby* v. *J. C. Penney Co.,* DC, ND, Ill., No. 80-C-2032.

76. Dreher, "Benefit Coverage and Employee Cost."

77. Robert Levering, *A Great Place to Work* (New York: Random House, 1988).

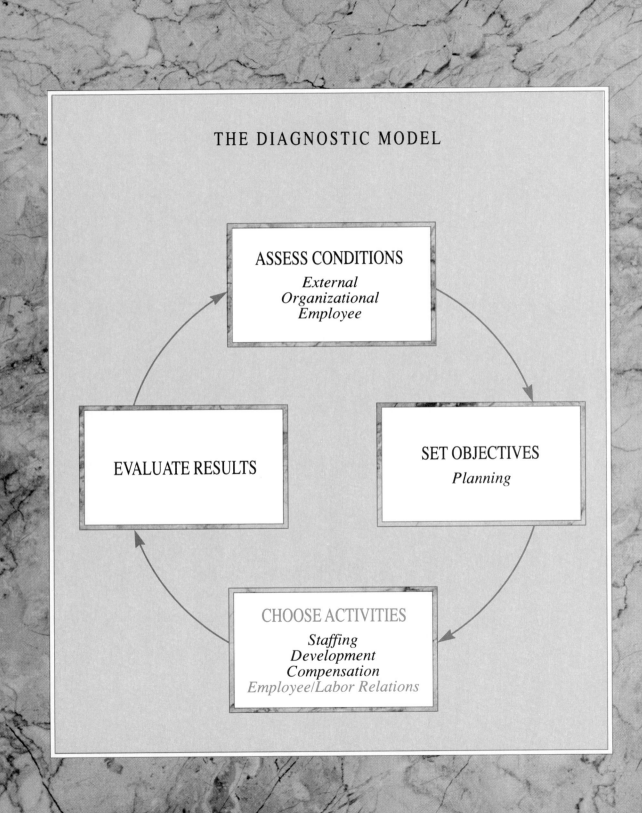

THE DIAGNOSTIC MODEL

ASSESS CONDITIONS
External
Organizational
Employee

SET OBJECTIVES
Planning

CHOOSE ACTIVITIES
Staffing
Development
Compensation
Employee/Labor Relations

EVALUATE RESULTS

PART SIX

HUMAN RESOURCE ACTIVITIES
Employee/Labor Relations

One-to-one relationships at work, the daily human relationships, are the focus of Part Six of the book: How to insure that managers treat employees fairly and with respect; How to help employees who come to work with personal or job-related problems (e.g., sick preschoolers, overburdening debts, or stress from marital problems or even drug abuse); How to convince managers that insuring safe and healthy working conditions are important to employees and society; and How to handle the disagreements that are inevitable in any organization.

Chapter Fifteen, Employee Relations, explores the ways managers and employees may relate to each other to insure fair treatment. All too often employers are not sufficiently concerned about the conditions and treatment employees face at work.

Rather than tolerate unfair conditions, employees may join together to form unions and collectively bargain improved employment conditions. In Chapters Sixteen, Collective Bargaining, and Seventeen, Labor Relations, we analyze the critical influences unions have on managing human resources.

Chapter Sixteen examines the collective bargaining process and its impact on employers and employees.

Chapter Seventeen analyzes the current status of labor relations in the United States and alternative ways for organized labor and employers to interact.

Unions' effects extend beyond their members; gains won during negotiations and the potential threat of union activity influence working conditions for all employees. Unions are part of the social and political fabric of this country.

A DIAGNOSTIC APPROACH TO EMPLOYEE/LABOR RELATIONS

The quality of employee/labor relations, as the diagnostic model shows (Exhibit VI–1), is affected by external conditions. Collective bargaining agreements are legal contracts subject to regulation by national laws. The whole unionizing and negotiating process is regulated, too, in order to provide some semblance of a balance of power among participants. Economic conditions affect these relations by limiting what options each side can afford to utilize.

External Conditions

Economic There is no doubt that a company that is making a profit and experiencing growth will find it easier to make a commitment to an open, supportive employee relations policy. Day care and elder care, drug rehabilitation, financial counseling—all become affordable. However, there is evidence that some employee relations activities may receive insufficient attention when there is extreme competitive pressures. For example, attention to health and safety may wane in an all-out effort to get products out the door.

A fundamental tenet underlying sound employee relations is that employees and management must have confidence in each other's intention to be fair and equitable. Fairness and trust are harder to maintain when the pie to be divided is shrinking and cutbacks are required. So, product market conditions play a significant role in setting the context for employee relations.

Perhaps more than any other human resource activity, labor relations is affected by economic conditions on a global scale. Foreign competition has had a devastating impact on union membership, employment, and wage scales in the auto and steel industries. Other industries, notably transportation and communications, have experienced the dislocations that have accompanied deregulation. For example, United Parcel Service, part of the deregulated trucking industry, has negotiated a two-tier wage structure under which newly hired package loaders and sorters receive only 60 percent of what currently employed workers receive for doing the same jobs.

Product market conditions have similar effects on the unions and employers. Hard times for an employer constitute hard times for the union. Membership declines when declining demand for a firm's products or services reduces employment levels. In contrast, labor market conditions can affect unions and employers differently. If the labor market is tight, the union's power may be enhanced. If unemployment is high, management may have an advantage: It can sustain a strike, and perhaps even benefit economically by replacing employees with new hires at lower pay rates. Hundreds of TWA cabin attendants, Cargill salt miners, and Geo. A. Hormel & Company meatpackers found themselves without jobs when their employers filled their jobs with lower-paid replacements following unsuccessful strikes.

Government The government creates the legal environment within which employee/labor relations takes place. The government's attitude toward labor relations has varied over time.

The courts continued to find collective activity illegal well into the 19th century.

However, a number of laws passed between 1926 and 1959 have given unions a more equal footing with employers. But many believe that the government has not given a high enough priority to protecting the interests of union members. Specific labor legislation will be covered in Chapter Sixteen.

Internal Conditions

Organization Culture and Values The employee/labor relations atmosphere reflects the values and culture of the organization. Many employee relations programs empha-

size safeguarding employees' rights. Others provide a forum for input into work and job decisions. Communication programs make employees aware of problems/objectives of the organization and make managers aware of problems/objectives of the employees.

Some organizations committed to strong employee relations programs evaluate managers on whether discipline procedures or conflict resolution systems are fairly administered, and women and minorities are given equal access to training, promotions, or other job rewards.

Unions play a substantial role in shaping employee relations. They can ensure the success of a quality of work life program by their support and participation, for example. But they also play an indirect role, in that many employee relations programs are motivated by a desire to maintain a union-free status for the organization. Many employers believe that they have more flexibility in the absence of a union. For example, promotions can be on the basis of merit or potential, rather than strictly on the seniority that most union contracts require. People can be switched among jobs, and jobs can more easily be changed to adopt new technologies or adjust to changing market conditions. Many employers believe that the services a union may provide—job security, grievance procedures, good wages—can and should be provided by an enlightened management without the intervention of a union.

So, assessing the conditions in which people are managed—the external, organization, and employee conditions—helps managers diagnose the situation, set objectives, and make proper HR decisions. We turn to examine employee relations decisions next.

CHAPTER FIFTEEN

Employee Relations

Set Employee Relations Objectives
and Strategies

Communication

Protection
Safety and Health Hazards
Co-Worker Relations

Employee Assistance
Approaches to Employee Assistance
Family/Job Conflict
Stress

Cooperation

Conflict and Discipline
Disciplinary Process
Conflict Resolution

Evaluating Results
Efficiency
Equity

Your Turn: Tradition or Team Approaches

Managers supervise a variety of employees as part of their jobs. Most employees perform effectively most of the time. But not always. What happens, for example, when the checkout cashier suspects he has been singled out unfairly for special scrutiny by his supervisor, and the stress from this possible scrutiny affects his job performance? What happens if the supervisor suspects the cashier is stealing? Suppose an employee is frequently late. Is it because of difficulties with child care arrangements, or drugs? These examples illustrate a time consuming and worrisome aspect of any manager's job—dealing fairly with troubled employees. Personal problems, both on and off the job, can affect employee work behavior. Because social as well as economic relationships are involved, an employer is frequently in the best position to motivate and provide assistance to employees at such times.

Many organizations go beyond changing negative behavior or assisting troubled employees. They wish to build on strengths: to provide a work environment where employees can flourish. They also wish to tap into employee expertise on how to do jobs better. Employee relations activities are those whose objective is to create an atmosphere of trust, respect, and cooperation.

Employee relations activities are those which seek greater organizational effectiveness by removing the barriers that inhibit full employee participation and compliance with organization policies.

These barriers may arise from organizational or personal factors. Whatever their source, employee relations activities seek to establish direct two-way communication to provide mutual assistance and involvement in overcoming them.

An employer's approach to employee relations permeates all other human resource activities. Job sharing, retraining programs, and career management could all be considered employee relations activities. So, while employee relations can be specific activities, it can also describe the intangible quality of management/employee relationships, part of the philosophy of the organization, that says an organization ought to treat employees with respect and ought to be responsive to the personal and family needs of employees. It is part of the organization conditions discussed in Chapter Three.

Survey after survey identifies family/work conflicts as a major problem for employees.[1] Dual career couples may be unable to make career-enhancing job moves. Whether managers can design alternatives for dual career couples reflects an organization's employee relations policy. So do work schedules; can they be adjusted to mesh with family demands? Participation in management is another way organizations can respond to employee needs. These topics are all discussed in this chapter.

SET EMPLOYEE RELATIONS OBJECTIVES AND STRATEGIES

Employee relations has been characterized by some as hardly more than a union avoidance strategy.[2] That is too simple. While union avoidance can certainly be an objective of employee relations activities, many organizations in which the likelihood of unionization is quite low still maintain strong employee relations. Union avoidance is not the only objective; indeed, it may be only an indirect effect. More typically, the objective is to provide an atmosphere in which all employees can perform their jobs to the best of their abilities and creatively contribute to the organization.

All HR decisions should be goal-directed. Consequently, employee relations activities should be designed and managed to help achieve specific objectives. Both efficiency and equity are affected by them. Employee relations activities affect efficiency, in that potential reasons for performance problems are confronted and help is offered to remove them. When the problem is an individual employee's behavior, employee assistance and conflict resolution systems seek constructive solutions. If the problem is the organization's behavior, employee/management committees or other two-way communication forums can identify possible changes that will remove the problem.

Equity is also affected. Much of employee relations is designed to send the message that the organization is a concerned institution that will help protect, assist, and deal fairly with all its members. How well this message comes through depends in large measure on how well employers deliver on these policies. Good intentions only go so far. Managers' decisions need to support these intentions.

The typical decisions that managers face in designing employee relations programs include:

- ✦ *Communication:* How best can we convey our philosophy to employees and solicit their opinions/suggestions on work issues?
- ✦ *Protection:* Are there aspects of the workplace that threaten the well-being of employees?
- ✦ *Assistance:* How shall we respond to special needs of specific employees?
- ✦ *Cooperation:* To what extent should decision making and control be shared?

EXHIBIT 15.1   Eroding Employee Confidence

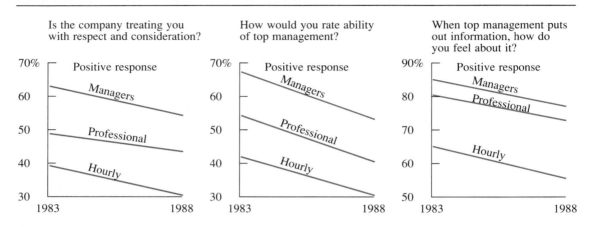

Source: Opinion Research Corporation.

♦ *Discipline and conflict:* How shall we deal with it?

While most of these topics have been touched on before, in this chapter we will focus more directly on their employee relations aspects.

COMMUNICATION

An employee handbook is a necessary part of communicating an employee relations program.[3] The handbook sets out the rules and policies within which employees and managers must operate. How the organization sets wages, allocates training and promotion opportunities, what services it provides, and what it expects from employees is discussed in the handbook. Later exhibits in this chapter provide examples from employee handbooks.

Organizations today are routinely advised to include a disclaimer that, although general policies, rules, and regulations are specified, the handbook does not form the basis of a binding employment contract. For example, attorneys representing discharged employees have successfully argued in courts that handbooks *can* imply a contract which forbids dismissal without just cause. However, interpretations vary among judicial districts.[4]

Obviously, merely writing a handbook is not enough. It must be continuously updated, publicized to employees, and supervisors must be thoroughly familiar with it, since they are the ones who translate policy into action. IBM gives all its new supervisors two weeks of intense training in implementing IBM's employee relations approach.

Handbooks provide communication in only one direction. Many organizations have formats for providing communication from employees to supervisors and managers. These can range from "speak-up" and open-door policies, work improvement suggestion systems, to "sensing" sessions, opinion surveys, or conflict resolution procedures. Unfortunately, there is evidence that there is a growing communications gap between employees and top management. Messages that managers think they are sending aren't being received by employees. Exhibit 15.1 shows a dramatic drop in employee confidence in top management.[5] The statistics are all the more unsettling because the decline accompanied an economic expansion. It is understandable that employees might be cynical about their treatment in a time of layoffs and economic downturns. But the middle 1980s enjoyed reasonable prosperity. Yet, employee trust in their employers eroded. Many employees felt they weren't being heard or that their concerns were not being factored into strategic decisions.

While organizations audit their financial resources regularly, only 45 percent of large employers make regular use of worker opinion surveys.[6] Many of those companies who do survey don't follow through with discussing results or explain what (if any) changes resulted from survey information. The result is that many top managers are sending crucial messages about strategy, innovation, and product quality to employees who aren't listening, because the managers don't listen to their employees.

Communication comes up again in this chapter when we discuss conflict. For now, let's move on to the topic of protection.

PROTECTION

Every manager and employee wants a healthy and safe work environment. The issue confronting contemporary organizations is, at what cost? What are the trade-offs between eliminating risks at the workplace and the costs involved?

In some organizations, work environments may be so bad that improvements are required by law. One required response to health and safety concerns is to compensate the victims of job-related accidents with workers' compensation and similar insurance programs. This is necessary, but reactive. An alternative strategy focuses on prevention.[7]

Prevention programs take many forms. They include redesigning jobs to diminish hazardous conditions, conducting safety training programs, even offering pay bonuses for good safety records. In an attempt to prevent accidents and improve overall safety records, Kerr-McGee considers applicants' accident records in selecting miners for work at its uranium and potash mines. However, the down side of this approach is the potential for blacklisting. Computerized data banks can provide information on whether job applicants have filed previous workers' compensation claims for such elusive ailments as back strain or stress. If such claimants have difficulty finding jobs, this may intimidate others from filing workers' compensation claims, however just their complaint.

Safety and Health Hazards

Safety hazards are those aspects of the work environment which have the potential for immediate and sometimes violent harm to an employee. Examples are loss of hearing or eyesight; cuts, sprains, bruises, broken bones; burns and electric shock.

Health hazards are those aspects of the work environment that slowly and cumulatively (and often irreversibly) lead to deterioration of an employee's health. Typical causes include physical and biological hazards, toxic and cancer-causing dusts and chemicals, and stressful working conditions.

Causes of Work Accidents and Illnesses

The causes of accidents and illness may lie in the job itself, the working conditions, or the employee.[8] Accidents and illnesses are not evenly distributed among jobs. Fire fighters, miners, construction and transportation workers, roofing and sheet metal workers, recreational vehicle manufacturers, lumber and wood workers, and blue-collar and first-line supervisors in manufacturing and agriculture face serious health and safety dangers on the job. A few white-collar jobs are relatively dangerous: dentists and hospital operating room personnel, beauticians, and X-ray technicians.

Working conditions that cause problems include poorly designed or inadequately repaired machines, lack of protective equipment, and the presence of dangerous chemicals or gasses.

Some employees seem to have more accidents than the average. The highest rate is for males under age 25, with a steady decline in following years. However, when older workers are injured, the costs per injury are higher. Females of all ages have substantially lower injury rates, due in large part to the differential occupational distribution of the sexes.[9]

In the mid 1980s, injury rates took a dramatic jump, as Exhibit 15.2 shows. Permanent work-related disabilities jumped 16 percent between 1986 and 1987 alone.[10] Safety experts attribute the cause to workplace changes made in response to competitive pressures and the expanding economy. Smaller work crews, excessive overtime, and faster assembly lines all contribute. So do inexperienced workers. The Los Angeles district attorney's office claims that half of the workplace deaths they investigate involve non-English speaking workers who were trained in English.

Occupational Safety and Health Act

The Occupational Safety and Health Act (OSHA) is intended to remedy health and safety problems on the job by establishing safety standards. The standards affect any aspect of the workplace. OSHA does not try to inspect all industries equally, but it creates priorities based upon known hazardous occupations. Similarly, all standards do not have equal emphasis. Those dealing with most hazardous conditions get highest priority.

EXHIBIT 15.2   Lost Workdays Due to Occupational Injuries (per 100 full-time workers)

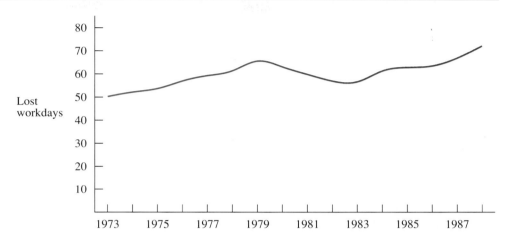

Unions have played a major role in lobbying the government for stricter enforcement of OSHA and its regulations. This is consistent with their long history of concern for employee safety.

Nevertheless, workplace safety continues to be a serious problem, for several reasons. Technology is constantly introducing new chemicals, whose potential hazards may not be fully appreciated for years. Additionally, OSHA focuses on design standards that dictate the physical characteristics of plant and equipment. But the chemical leak at Bhopal, India, which killed over 2,000 people, the radiation leak at Chernobyl in the Ukraine, whose damage is still occurring, and the Exxon oil spill at Valdez, Alaska, which killed wildlife and irreparably damaged the environment all show that human error is the usual culprit in large-scale disasters. People can circumvent almost any designed-in control system. OSHA at present ignores employee responsibility and places all responsibility on management. While it is clear that management bears complete responsibility for adequately training and enforcing the use of safe procedures, the employee's own responsibility for personal health and safety is not presently covered in OSHA's approach. For example, if employees wish to skip medical tests to determine if they are developing an occupational disease, OSHA has ruled they can.[11] If an employee refuses to wear safety equipment required by OSHA, the employer is held responsible. The employer can discipline or possibly fire the uncooperative employee. However, challenges by unions or in the courts for unlawful discharge make employers reluctant to impose penalties on employees.

To increase employee awareness of hazards, OSHA established a communication standard in 1986. Often referred to as "right to know," the standard is intended to protect the safety of workers by keeping them informed of the dangerous substances with which they are working, the hazards and symptoms of exposure, and the proper steps to take if they have been exposed. Manufacturers, importers, and distributors of petroleum, stone, textiles, food, paper, and chemicals are covered by the standard.

Applicant/Employee Screening

Because OSHA puts full responsibility for employee health and safety on management, many employers have begun screening people for factors that may affect health and safety on the job.[12] Screening for drug or alcohol use, or both, is the most common example. Medical screening is extremely controversial, for a number of reasons. First, many believe it to be an invasion of privacy.[13] Serious ethical issues arise if an employer has access to nonjob-related information about illnesses that carry a social stigma, such as sexually transmitted diseases or family histories of alcoholism or abuse.

This objection can be overcome if medical information is kept in the hands of the medical staff, and the employer is given only relevant data. But that brings up the second objection: Is the quality of data adequate for use in selection decisions? Predictive screening for susceptibility to certain conditions is not well developed scientifically.

Co-Worker Relations

What happens if the threat to health and safety, whether real or perceived, comes from co-workers: smokers, AIDS victims, alcohol or drug abusers, sexual harassers? Organizations must tread a narrow line here, so as not to trammel on the rights of one employee while protecting another. Court rulings generally provide guidance on how the employer may proceed.

AIDS

AIDS has surpassed cancer as the disease people fear most. The fear is partly rational, since the disease is nearly always fatal, and complete control has not yet been attained. But irrational fears exist, too, if people refuse to work with suspected AIDS victims. Legally, AIDS is considered a handicap; therefore, its victims are protected against job discrimination and cannot be fired or transferred, as long as they are able to perform their jobs.[14] But this stance does not allay co-workers who are fearful of contracting the disease. Even though medical experts agree that the disease is not transmissable under normal workplace conditions, managers must take a strong role in educating the work force to this fact. The San Francisco AIDS Foundation has developed written materials and a film entitled *AIDS in the Workplace: Epidemic of Fear* to assist employers in such efforts.[15]

Smoking in the Workplace

Company concern about employee health or comfort in conjunction with employee complaints about smoke have led to an increased interest in policies on smoking at work. To date, courts have generally rejected employees' claims to a right to a smoke-free work environment; however, a few states require organizations to have a smoking policy. One survey found that the most common employer response to complaints about smokers was to encourage employees to resolve the problem themselves. Only 1 percent refused to hire smokers, and less than 3 percent were willing to transfer either the smoker or the objecting employee.[16] However, a more recent survey found a higher percentage of employers who refused to hire smokers—6 percent.[17] Most of the companies who do not hire smokers are in the education/government/nonprofit industry.

While most companies rely on peer group pressure to police smoking among employees, some companies are structuring their health insurance to give smokers an incentive to quit. At PTC Aerospace in Garden Grove, California, smokers must acknowledge in writing that they smoke and pay $10 a month for health insurance that nonsmokers don't pay—or forfeit the insurance. Managers point to increased productivity and decreased health care claims to buttress their policy. But critics call this an invasion of privacy. Thus far, the courts have found that a policy reasonably intended to promote health outweighs a right to smoke.

Harassment

The Supreme Court has ruled that an employer is strictly liable for allowing a "hostile environment," even if an employer is unaware of any incidents of racial or sexual harassment.[18] Chapter Six discusses the legal foundation for this ruling. In 1987, K mart paid $3.2 million to settle a single case of sexual harassment.

Many people find harassment a vague concept. Exhibit 15.3 reveals the types of behavior that have led employees to file complaints. Because the employer alone has the power to promptly and irrevocably end harassment (through warning, transferring, demoting, or even firing the harasser), employer liability is justified. However, the employer can reduce its liability if its policy forbidding harassment is firmly stated and publicized, and a mechanism for employee complaints exists. A definition of sexual harassment, a policy statement, and a description of complaint resolution procedures should all be included in the employee handbook. Various approaches to resolve conflict are discussed later in this chapter.

Substance Abuse

Illegal drugs have become pervasive in American society. It's not surprising that they have also become an issue in the workplace. Yet, alcohol abuse is still far more common in terms of impaired performance and absenteeism than drug

---

EXHIBIT 15.3   Sexual Harassment on the Job: Types of Formal Complaints Received
by 160 Major Corporations*

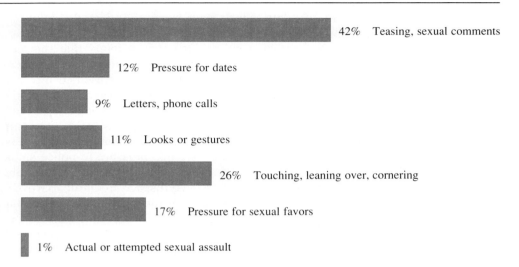

42%   Teasing, sexual comments

12%   Pressure for dates

9%   Letters, phone calls

11%   Looks or gestures

26%   Touching, leaning over, cornering

17%   Pressure for sexual favors

1%   Actual or attempted sexual assault

* Complaints from both men and women. Total is more than 100 percent because more than one
category could be selected per complaint.

Source: Opinion Research Corporation

abuse. The difference is that the mere possession of drugs is illegal, whether or
not work behavior is affected.

Some employers advocate mandatory drug testing of all employees. Over one
third of all companies use drug testing, according to one survey.[19] One fourth
of responding companies require drug tests of all new employees. Current employees are tested only when drug use is suspected. Applicants who test positive for illegal drugs are rarely told that this is the reason for not being hired.
However, current employees who test positive are given test results. Only 24
percent of them are fired; most are referred for treatment or counseling.

Testing may be justified for certain job classifications where the consequences of working while impaired are severe (e.g., bus drivers, pilots, or nuclear plant operators). But for many jobs, proper supervision may make drug
testing unnecessary. This does not imply the strict supervision and narrow employee discretion that was part of scientific management (see Chapter Three).
It does imply managerial awareness of employee well-being. For example, Hewlett-Packard has a policy of "Management by Wandering Around," shown in
Exhibit 15.4. The policy requires managers to be aware of how employees are
feeling about their jobs and of their personal well-being. The tone is positive.

EXHIBIT 15.4   Employee Relations Policy at Hewlett-Packard

MANAGEMENT BY WANDERING AROUND
AND
OPEN DOOR POLICY

Purpose

Through the years a fundamental strength of the company has been the effectiveness of communications both upwards and downwards within the organization. Two key ingredients for making this happen are:

I. Management by Wandering Around

   ✦ To have a well-managed operation it is essential that the managers/supervisors be aware of what is happening in their areas—not just at their immediate level, but also at several levels below that.
   ✦ Our people are our most important resource and the managers have direct responsibility for their training, their performance, and their general well-being. To do this managers must get around to find out how their people feel about their jobs and what they feel will make their work more productive and more meaningful.

II. Open Door Policy

   ✦ Managers and supervisors are expected to promote a working environment, within which employees feel free and comfortable to either seek individual counsel, express general concerns, or offer ideas.
   ✦ All employees have the right, if in their opinion they feel such steps are necessary, to discuss their concerns with higher-level managers. Any effort to prevent an employee from seeking higher-level managers through intimidation or any other means is absolutely contrary to company policy and will be dealt with accordingly.
   ✦ Therefore, the intent of the open door policy is to encourage employees to seek the "appropriate" management level. Appropriate is defined as that level that can best act with the information.
   ✦ Utilizing the open door policy will not in any way impact any evaluation of the employee or subject him or her to any other adverse consequences.
   ✦ Employees also have responsibilities—particularly in keeping their discussions with upper-level managers objective and focused on significant concerns.

The emphasis is certainly not on substance abuse, yet it puts managers on notice that they share responsibility for the well-being of all H-P employees.

Even though H-P does not test its employees for drugs, drug testing is big business at H-P: one of its products is a $100,000 mass spectrometer used by professional laboratories to test for various drugs. However, a new computer-based critical tracking test that quickly measures the ability to perform tasks requiring fine hand-eye coordination and quick reaction—similar to a video game—may make the spectrometer obsolete. The critical tracking test is far easier and quicker, and it focuses on ability to perform a job, rather than an employee's behavior off the job. Thus, it is not an invasion of privacy. However,

---

EXHIBIT 15.5   Excerpt from an Employee Assistance Policy

Policy

The EAP operates within the following framework:

1. A wide range of problems may affect employees' job performance adversely. These include alcohol and drug addiction, marital and family difficulties, and emotional distress. The EAP will assist employees to resolve these problems and others for which employees may seek help.
2. Employees' current jobs and future advancement will not be jeopardized by using EAP services.
3. As with all health and personnel documents, EAP records will be maintained in a confidential manner.
4. When necessary, sick leave may be granted for treatment and rehabilitation on the same basis as it is granted for other health problems.
5. Employees will be responsible for complying with the EAP service's recommendations and treatment plans.
6. The EAP service will also be available to employees' families.

Procedure

1. Employees who need professional advice are encouraged to use the EAP's counseling services, and those whose personal problems adversely affect their work are encouraged to seek help voluntarily from the EAP services.
2. Supervisors are responsible for confronting employees about their unsatisfactory performance and helping them to improve their work.
   a. Supervisors bring employees' unsatisfactory work to their attention and encourage them to solve the problem on their own or with the help of the EAP counseling services. Supervisors also point out to the employees that continued unsatisfactory performance will lead to formal discipline.
   b. If performance improves, no further action will be taken.
   c. If job performance continues to be unsatisfactory, regardless of whether or not employees have accepted help, regular disciplinary procedure will be followed, up to and including discharge.
   At each step of the procedure, supervisors will encourage employees to seek help from the EAP counseling service.

---

the test does not indicate why a person's performance is impaired, nor is it suited to complex jobs where decision-making ability is more important than hand-eye coordination.

EMPLOYEE ASSISTANCE

How does a manager respond when employees' personal problems impair their work behavior? It varies. One response is to search for ways to get rid of the troubled employee. Another is to assist employees either through internal programs or by putting employees in contact with outside professional assistance.

Various surveys report that referral to outside sources of assistance is the most common response of organizations, but some type of in-house counseling, especially for alcoholism, is also common.[20] Such counseling may range from a brief chat with a supervisor who warns the troubled employee that failure to seek outside help will result in dismissal, to private appointments with professional counselors at the work site.

Employer assistance with personal problems is not new. In 1917, the Ford Motor Company's Legal Aid Department assisted employees "free of charge for all matters involving legal questions, insurance, investments, settlements of disputes, purchase of real estate, and filling out and securing naturalization papers."[21] Its medical department had its own modern operating room and six-bed ward, and its English School taught reading, writing, and speaking simple English to thousands of employees. The bulk of these assistance programs ended in the 1920s, however, as the result of pressures accompanying the phenomenal growth of the company, the complexity and cost of the programs, and the loss of influence of top managers who supported them.

Today's assistance programs are structured in large part on the basis of research into alcoholism and effective ways to deal with employees who have this problem. Two components appear to be necessary for a successful program:

1. *A written policy*. While many of us do help our friends if we become aware of a personal problem, most of us are unsure how to proceed. Our intentions may be honorable, but lack of expertise on how to proceed limits our usefulness. So, too, in organizations. Co-workers and supervisors are typically the first ones aware of a problem, and they are in a position to provide the necessary emotional support and motivation to confront the problem. A written policy will guide them in how to proceed. Research has found supervisors' willingness to confront employees whose performance is impaired is highly related to a written policy outlining performance, discipline, and medical practices.[22] Exhibit 15.5 is an excerpt from an employee assistance policy, which clearly spells out the supervisors' role. A written policy also demonstrates full managerial support for the policy and the options organizations will pursue if performance does not improve.

2. *A program coordinator*. A coordinator ensures that procedures and policies are known and carried out throughout the workplace. A highly visible coordinator can advise supervisors, encourage them to confront the troubled employee, and can reassure employees as to the confidentiality of the service.

Approaches to Employee Assistance

There are two different approaches to intervention. Most assistance programs probably contain elements of both approaches.

Constructive Confrontation

This strategy evolved as a technique for identifying employed alcoholics and for counteracting the typical responses of guilt, denial, rationalization, and manipulation. It focuses solely on job performance and documents to the employee clear instances of impaired performance. Obviously, if job performance is not impaired, then there is no situation that warrants the organization's intervention. Confrontation is best combined with a progressive discipline strategy: Continued unacceptable performance will lead to progressively more severe discipline, culminating in dismissal.

That's the confrontation part of the strategy. The constructive part (1) expresses emotional support and group concern for the employee's welfare, (2) emphasizes that employment can be maintained if performance improves, and (3) suggests alternatives for the employee to regain satisfactory improvement. The support and the confrontation are offered in combination, and both focus heavily on job performance.

Counseling

Improved job performance does not necessarily mean that the underlying problems have been resolved. Additionally, job performance may not be affected until the problem has become severe. Rather than focusing on job performance, a counseling approach focuses on the cause of the problem—either in the individual or the social relationships surrounding the individual. Professionally trained psychotherapists are involved. In spite of its tantalizing promise of tackling problems before they become severe, counseling appears to be most useful when it becomes clear that problems are beyond employees' control. Before then, employees fear the stigma of being labeled "mentally ill" and so avoid contacting counselors.

Which approach, confrontation or counseling, has the better track record? Research indicates that programs that maintain a balance between the two approaches have better outcomes than single-approach programs.[23] Constructive confrontation motivates employees to change their behavior, and counseling provides one means of doing so.

Many organizations have established employee assistance or advisory programs. Programs range from 24-hour phone counseling and referral to classes on managing finances, stress, and health. Exhibit 15.6 shows the topics that come up most frequently at Control Data's Employee Advisory Resource (EAR). Personal problems account for about 60 percent of the calls; work-related problems account for 40 percent.

While these data help identify what aspects of the organization employees find troublesome, the program relies on employee-initiated contacts. Whether or not these contacts were associated with impaired job performance is not known.

Family/Job Conflict

Sometimes a problem lies not in the individual nor the workplace but in conflicting demands between family and job responsibilities. The increase in two-career couples makes it likely that a sizeable percent of students taking this course will experience family/job conflict. Such conflict is not limited to

EXHIBIT 15.6   Types of Problems Brought to Employee Advisory Service

Personal Problems

Category	Percentage of Calls
Financial (bankruptcy, financial difficulties relating to inflationary costs, poor financial management)	26%
Legal (most often family and tenant-landlord conflicts)	21
Chemical (10% alcohol; 3% drugs)	13
Mental health (mainly depression)	9
Familial (parent-child and parent-relative relationships)	8
Marital (difficulties with communication and problem resolution)	8
Personal (difficulties with identity, relationships, and sex)	5
Physical health	5
Miscellaneous (problems not characterized by one of the above groups)	6

Problems at Work

Category	Percentage of Calls
Compensation and benefits (sick pay, health insurance coverage, vacation, overtime, sick leave, retirement)	22%
Performance (disputes over the content of regular performance appraisals to specific disciplinary actions)	19
Transfers and promotions	7
Policies and procedures (requests for familiarization with specific written corporate policies)	14
Interpersonal relations (conflicts with supervisors or other employees)	10
Career counseling	8
Miscellaneous (including discrimination complaints, rehabilitation problems, complaints about working conditions, and other problems not characterized by another group)	20

Source: David J. Reed, "One Approach to Employee Assistance," *Personnel Journal,* August 1983, pp. 648–52.

women; one study identified such conflict in nearly one third of the men in a national sample.[24]

Conflict arises from simultaneous pressure to comply with competing demands. Pressure comes from several possible sources:

1. Time devoted to one role makes it difficult to fulfill requirements in the other.
2. Stress from participation in one role makes it difficult to fulfill requirements in the other.

3. Specific behaviors required in one setting are completely different from behaviors in the other.[25]

While there is little empirical evidence on this third point, an example might be conflicts between the self-reliant, aggressive kind of behavior expected at work and the nurturing behavior expected in the role of a parent.

Handling such conflict is essentially a personal matter, but an organization's employee relations philosophy and culture will influence its response to employees experiencing such conflict. A number of options exist: more flexible work scheduling, providing day care assistance, and increasing employee control over how their job requirements are met to make the work role requirements more flexible.

Work Schedule Adaptations

From the employee's perspective, an important aspect of a job is the number of hours of work required, the arrangement of the hours, and freedom (or lack of it) in determining work schedules. The work schedule affects the nonwork part of a person's life; the time with a family, in leisure and in self-development.

A sizable portion of job dissatisfaction may be related to lack of control over hours of work, forced overtime, and lack of freedom to adjust hours to personal needs.[26] Adaptations include flextime, permanent part-time positions, compressed work week, shift work, and home work.

Flexible Hours (Flextime)

Probably the most popular version of flextime provides for all employees to be present for a specified period (core time), but the rest of the required hours may be completed at their discretion within a specified period.

Within that specification, flextime can vary on a number of dimensions:

+ The total number of daily hours the employee must be at work.
+ The length of the work week.
+ Whether an employee can carry forward a surplus or deficit in hours from one day, week, or month to the next.
+ How much variation can be made without prior approval of supervisors.[27]

Exhibit 15.7 summarizes the results of research on the effects of flexible hours. Generally, the results are positive, particularly if employees have a role in designing the programs. However, flexible hours can pose administration problems:

All employees are not present when others want them.

There may be difficulty in keeping records of hours worked for pay purposes, and this can increase costs.

EXHIBIT 15.7   Summary of Flexible Working-Hour Effects

Criteria	Range of Reported Results	
Performance	No change	Positive change
Job attitudes	No change	Positive effect
Leisure-time satisfaction	No change	Positive effect
Stress symptoms		Decrease
Organizational attachment		Strengthen
Intention to quit		Weaken
Intention to be absent		Weaken
Attendance	No change	Improved
Turnover	No change	Reduction
Managerial effects	Very minor problems	Generally very favorable
Union reaction	Slow acceptance	

Source: Jon L. Pierce, John W. Newstrom, Randall B. Dunham, and Alison E. Barber, *Alternative Work Schedules* (Boston: Allyn & Bacon, 1989).

Middle management may perceive a loss of control.

Flextime may be hard to implement in interdependent jobs, and coordination may be difficult.

Part Time

Between 1950 and 1980, voluntary part-time employment grew over twice as fast as full-time employment. Fifteen to 20 percent of the work force were working part time in 1989, according to the Bureau of Labor Statistics, and women made up two thirds of this group. Principal advantages to employers include flexibility in scheduling workers to meet peak demand periods and reduction in costs of benefits and overtime.

While part-time work has been hailed as beneficial for working parents, it has also been severely criticized by some women's organizations. Part-time work is "marginal" employment, they say, because it pays low wages and forces workers to give up benefits. A better choice, the group suggests, would be for more employers to establish family-oriented workplace policies, such as parental leave, child care, and flexible scheduling, so "parents are not forced to choose marginal jobs to provide care for their families."[28]

Most part-time work is concentrated in the service industries, especially education, health care, personal services (e.g., beauty shops), business services such as advertising, and entertainment and recreation. The second most frequent location of part-time industry is in retail and wholesale trade, then agriculture, and finally manufacturing.

Job sharing, a special type of part-time work, occurs when a single job is divided between two workers. Because it requires schedule compatibility between the two people sharing the job, as well as roughly equivalent or complementary skills, most job sharing is initiated by the employees. More and more organizations seem willing to consider this alternative as they gain familiarity with its advantages.

Compressed Workweek

A compressed workweek is the scheduling of the normal hours of weekly work in less than five days. The typical compressed workweek follows a four-day schedule.

Research on the effects of compressed workweeks is uneven.[29] Some studies concluded it has positive effects on productivity, absenteeism, and other behaviors. Others conclude it does not. One pattern in the negative studies suggests that positive results occur shortly after the introduction of the compressed workweek; then they decline. Individual and job differences may explain many of the contradictions in the research findings. In general, older employees seem to find a compressed workweek undesirable, especially where the work is physically or mentally taxing.

Home Work

With the widespread use of computer terminals and telecommuting technology, many companies contract out routine forms processing. For example, Blue Cross/Blue Shield pays a flat rate per claim form processed to a number of clerks who do the processing on computer terminals in their own homes. Other work that can be done this way includes processing catalog sales or even writing computer software. People who have such work arrangements, mostly women, appreciate the convenience such arrangements provide. However, unions are unhappy. They argue that such arrangements weaken their organizations, erode wage standards, and open the way for exploitation of employees who lack the social support of other employees in a work group (see Chapter Three). For the immediate future, however, the practice is expected to spread, as technological change continues to exert its influence on organizations.

Ideally, all of these work schedule adaptations can work to the advantage of both the employer and the employee. However, many employers are reluctant to accede to employee requests for scheduling flexibility, especially if the employees are valued professionals. They take the position that family/job conflicts are the responsibility of the individual employee to manage, and the organization does not wish to get involved in private lives. Or they may feel that, if such options were made available to all employees, many more would take them. Productivity would plummet, as there would be no continuity to project management.

At the same time, these valued professionals are just the ones the company wants to hang onto. Therefore, demand for skilled employees may have already pushed companies to the point where flexibility can positively affect productivity. For example, when Corning discovered it was costing the company $2 million a year to replace female managers and professionals, who were twice as likely to leave as men, they offered the option of part-time or flexible hours, to reduce those replacement costs.

The costs of these work schedule adaptations vary. The lack of benefits and paid time off reduces labor costs for part-time employees; however, training costs may be higher. So the advantages to employers of work schedule adaptations will vary with the nature of the jobs and the employees.[30]

Day-Care Assistance

Eleven million children under the age of six have mothers in the labor force. One of the most frequently cited causes of work/family conflict is concern for adequate, affordable day care.

One survey of 35 companies found that each employee with children under age 13 misses an average of eight working days a year due to child care problems, and 39 percent of the parents had considered leaving their jobs because of child care problems.[31] Other studies have linked satisfactory day care with reduced absenteeism and turnover. So the presence or absence of satisfactory day care clearly affects work behavior.[32] The issue is, what role shall an organization play in this area? Corporations can provide options, ranging from care centers located at the work site, to coverage of expenses as part of flexible benefits, to referral services. Which approach an organization adopts will depend on its employee relations philosophy, as well as the needs of its employees. Day care probably is a more compelling issue in organizations that employ large numbers of young parents than in organizations with an aging work force. Thus far, only about 11 percent of employers provide direct assistance, although 60 percent say they provide indirect assistance (flexible work schedules, part-time work or information assistance).

IBM initially tried to address day care in its employee assistance program (EAP), but found that its more clinically oriented EAP staff was not equipped to provide day-care assistance. So the organization contracted with local referral providers around the country. Information on the referral service is mailed to the home of every IBM employee. The referral service then tells employees who inquire what day-care services are available, the costs, and so on. The referral agency must ensure that the day-care providers they list are licensed, insured, and meet certain standards. However, IBM emphasizes that it makes referrals, not recommendations. The parent must make the final decision.

Onsite day care has a rather poor track record. Levi Strauss provided onsite care, including an infirmary for sick children. The day-care center has since closed. Costs of downtown space, commuting patterns, and a limited number of eligible employees at a work site make this choice rarely affordable or appropriate. Other organizations report problems if there are more eligible children than spaces. Who gets the spots can cause tension among co-workers. Many people dislike taking their children out of their home or school area. Or perhaps some even dislike the idea of commuting with children.

Exhibit 15.8 presents an optimistic picture, in that many more companies say they *favor* various programs to reduce family/job conflict than presently provide them. For example, while 80 percent favor a child care information service, only 30 percent presently provide it. This implies that, if organizations knew how to locate and organize such information, they would be willing to provide it.

As discussed in the benefits chapter, child care assistance is becoming a competitive issue that may help to attract and hold employees. Legislation is under consideration to require employers to provide parental leave to care for newborn or sick children.

Stress

This topic is receiving a lot of attention, at least in the popular press. It is a difficult area to study, because what one person finds stressful another may find exhilarating. For example, there is no shortage of candidates (qualifications aside) to become astronauts, television talk show hosts, or presidents or prime ministers, occupations that surely involve stress.

One view of stress relates it to control: the lack of ability to make one's own decisions or use a range of skills. A recent medical study bypassed the popular picture of the executive under stress and found that workers in jobs that combine high psychological demand with low decision control (mail workers, telephone operators) are approximately five times more likely to develop coronary heart disease than those who have greater control over their jobs.[33] Exhibit 15.9 locates jobs along the two dimensions of psychological demand and decision control.

If an objective of employee relations is to assist employees under stress, this study is important not only for its job design implications but also because it points out the importance of control as a factor related to stress. Helping employees to identify and alter areas in which they feel a lack of control should be a major objective of employee assistance programs.

COOPERATION

The issue of control leads us directly into our next employee relations decision: to what extent will managers yield control in order to seek cooperative ways to solve workplace problems? And to what extent are employees interested in becoming involved in cooperative efforts? The highest degree of potential employee involvement in organizational decisions occurs when workers are also owners.[34] Employees buying plants to save their jobs is not unusual. But research has found that most of such owner/employees view their ownership only as a financial investment and rarely exercise their full decision-making rights.

EXHIBIT 15.8   Which Programs Do Companies Favor? (comparing corporate programs of today with attitudes about tomorrow)

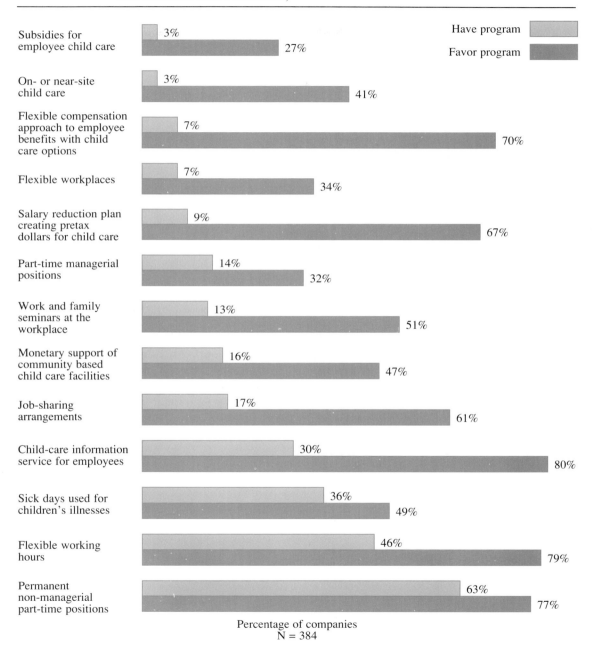

Have program

Favor program

Subsidies for employee child care	3% / 27%
On- or near-site child care	3% / 41%
Flexible compensation approach to employee benefits with child care options	7% / 70%
Flexible workplaces	7% / 34%
Salary reduction plan creating pretax dollars for child care	9% / 67%
Part-time managerial positions	14% / 32%
Work and family seminars at the workplace	13% / 51%
Monetary support of community based child care facilities	16% / 47%
Job-sharing arrangements	17% / 61%
Child-care information service for employees	30% / 80%
Sick days used for children's illnesses	36% / 49%
Flexible working hours	46% / 79%
Permanent non-managerial part-time positions	63% / 77%

Percentage of companies
N = 384

Source: Catalyst, 14 E 60th St., New York, NY 10022. Published in *Business Link* 1, no. 2 (Fall 1984), p. 5.

EXHIBIT 15.9   Stress at Work

Research suggests that workers whose jobs involve high psychological strain but little decision making are more subject to cardiovascular illness. Jobs at right of curve in model below are among the top 25 percent in combined risk factor of low control and high psychological demands.

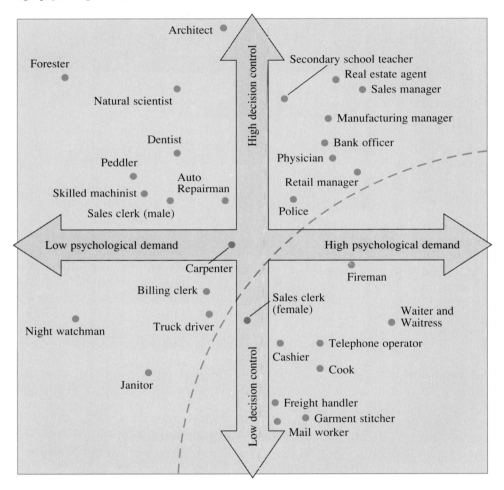

Source: Columbia University Department of Industrial Engineering and Operations Research.

EXHIBIT 15.10   Elimination of Barriers between Salaried and Hourly Personnel

---

Dress code	Casual dress. No neckties.
Parking	Executive garage closed. No reserved parking. Combined hourly and salaried lot.
Food service	No salaried/hourly distinction. No private dining. One cafeteria.
Rest rooms	No salaried/hourly distinction.
Overnight drive program	Open to all employees.
Committee	Open to both hourly and salary where appropriate.

U.S. tax law currently favors employee stock ownership plans (ESOPs) as a way to increase employee equity in a company. But even here, employee ownership does not typically alter the decision-making structure.

Encouraging employee participation is an idea everyone can be for. But translating the ideal into practice steps on people's toes. Control translates into power, and most people do not like giving it up. Managers and supervisors may feel the most efficient way to accomplish a task is to make a decision and act on it, rather than increasing the number of people involved in the process. Employees may also be wary if a managerial interest in working together does not square with past managerial behavior. So while cooperation is an appealing notion, it can be a hard sell.

Quality of Work Life (QWL)

Quality of work life initiatives, popular in the 1980s, stem from the recognition that the properly trained rank-and-file employee may be in the best position to identify unrecognized problems with product quality and how work is done. Shop-level worker committees are trained to use statistical and problem-solving analysis to improve quality and productivity in their particular work area. The focus is very much on the immediate work area; organization practices are of interest only in considering how they may interfere with product quality.

A program at General Motors is fairly typical. Its first efforts were to eliminate the subtle and not-so-subtle barriers between workers and managers (Exhibit 15.10). No neckties and one cafeteria may seem trivial, but they were signs of differential status that acted as barriers to cooperative efforts. Joint management/worker teams visited other facilities that were using QWL techniques, including some in Japan.

The QWL program at the Fiero Plant in Pontiac, Michigan, resulted in the complete reorganization of the managerial structure. An entire level of supervision was removed, which may explain why supervisor support for QWL is so sparse. Team members building the cars identified problems and solutions. The resources to implement the solutions were provided from higher levels. For example, if a supplier's door gaskets had a high rate of defects, that supplier met with team members to discuss how the problem could be resolved.

The program had two basic thrusts: training and quality control. Workers *and* suppliers entered training programs, especially those dealing with electronics or statistical quality control.

Reorganizing the inspection system was a critical component of quality control. Rather than inspection of the final product, a tally sheet stayed with the car from start to finish, and all workers inspected their own work. As each step was completed, the worker recorded on the tally sheet if the job was completed correctly, or if there were problems. Thus, workers were given more control over their work.

When the sporty Fiero automobile was introduced in 1984, it was a hit among car buyers, and its QWL program was a hit among business writers. But in 1988, production of the car ceased. A continuing series of safety recalls stemming from a basic design flaw made it "one of Detroit's greatest lemons ever, and perhaps a symbol of all that went wrong at GM in the mid-1980s."[35] Fiero illustrates why many United Auto Workers define QWL as a "Quick Way to Lose." All the participation, training, and quality control could not overcome the basic design flaw—an issue outside the workers' control. Too often, QWL has been introduced when a company is already in trouble for reasons that have nothing to do with employee participation.[36]

QWL programs in large part have been a response to the success of Japanese managerial systems, both in Japan and in other countries. But while Japanese "transplants" have been economically successful, others criticize their approach as leading to greater managerial control and elimination of employee rights. All the rhetoric about dignity and democracy translates into faster assembly lines, they say.[37]

Too frequently, key problems prevent QWL programs from having lasting positive effects.

1. The change effort is isolated—either confined to one area of the plant or treated as an experiment.
2. The change is piecemeal—no change is made in management hierarchies and decision-making modes to support the new approach.
3. Worker involvement is limited to only a few issues that are not connected to how work is actually done nor to critical business decisions.
4. First-line supervisors and middle managers are not involved in the change effort and so react negatively to employee participation.[38]

Supervisors must be intimately involved in the changes. They may require training in new ways to interact with employees. Support for the changes must exist at all levels in the organization, or it will be ineffective.

CONFLICT AND DISCIPLINE

Many of the policies and programs discussed in this chapter can go a long way to prevent discipline issues from arising. Prevention should be the objective of all organizations. However, when problems arise, having procedures in place to deal with infractions can help safeguard the rights of all concerned. There are four elements to assure adherence to generally acceptable work rules of such a system.

1. *Establish rules*. The first element in a discipline system is the establishment of work and behavior rules. The rules can concern behavior that is directly or indirectly related to work productivity.

2. *Communicate the rules to all employees*. The employee handbook is an appropriate forum. Unless employees are aware of the rules, it is unfair to expect them to follow the rules. Closely related is a willingness to accept the rules and their enforceability. Employee participation in the formation of rules may help ensure that rules are fair and appropriate. For example, rules regarding hair length are relevant to job safety in some settings but irrelevant in most others.

Though rules would ideally be kept to a minimum, they may need to be periodically revised to remain relevant.

3. *Assess behavior*. Performance evaluation typically assesses deficiencies in work behaviors at scheduled intervals; rule-breaking behavior is disclosed either as a result of observation or investigation (e.g., investigation of theft, falsifying records, and the like). Once again, the more constructive approach is to be aware of what's going on to forestall the need for discipline.

4. Finally, the disciplinary process includes assistance in *changing behavior* and administering punishment. Counseling and confrontation to motivate change may be part of the program.

Disciplinary Process

Discipline usually follows a progressive system, in that second or later infractions are dealt with more harshly than first offenses. The discipline policy in Exhibit 15.11 follows this approach. It progresses from a verbal reproach to a written warning, signed by the employee. A third offense within 12 months brings a final warning, with notification that additional problems will find the offender on the outside looking in.

A manager's first line of action is counseling; this is the most frequent method of disciplinary action. The supervisor determines if, in fact, a violation took place, explains to the employee why the violation significantly affects productivity, and suggests that it should not happen again. This approach works for most violations.

If a second or more serious violation takes place, the supervisor again counsels the employee, this time noting that the incident will be entered in the em-

---

EXHIBIT 15.11   Progressive Discipline Policy

---

1. With the exception of offenses requiring more stringent action, employees will normally be counseled once verbally before receiving a written warning.
2. In the event of another performance problem or a violation of any employer policy or rule, a written warning should ordinarily be issued.
   a. The warning should be signed and dated by the employee. If the employee refuses to sign the warning, another supervisor should be immediately brought in and asked to sign and witness that the employee has seen, but refused to sign, the warning.
   b. The warning should inform the employee of the possible consequences, including final written warning, suspension and/or discharge, should additional violations or performance problems occur.
   c. A written warning need not pertain to the same or similar offense for which the verbal counselling was given.
3. If a third offense occurs within 12 months of the previous written warning, a final warning should be issued.
   a. The warning should be signed and dated by the employee. If the employee refuses to sign the warning, another supervisor should be immediately brought in and asked to sign and witness that the employee has seen, but refused to sign, the warning.
   b. The warning should inform the employee that termination may result if further violations or performance problems occur.
   c. A final written warning need not pertain to the same or similar offense for which any prior verbal or written warning was issued.
   d. In addition to the final written warning, the supervisor may also suspend the employee without pay or take other disciplinary action deemed appropriate.
4. If the employee violates any policy of the employer or fails to improve his or her level of performance, termination may result.

Reproduced with permission from *Employee Handbook and Personnel Policies Manual* by Richard J. Simmons © 1983 Richard J. Simmons, Castle Publications, Ltd., P.O. Box 580, Van Nuys, California 91408.

---

ployee's personnel file. If the violation was sufficiently serious, the employee may also be given an oral or written warning of the consequences of a future recurrence.

If the incident concerns ineffective productivity, the employee may request transfer or be asked to transfer to another job. The employee may have been placed in the wrong job, there may be a personality conflict between the employee and the supervisor, or more training might help. In some rare cases, demotions or downward transfers are used.

If counseling and warnings do not result in changed behavior, and if a transfer is not appropriate, the next step is normally a disciplinary layoff. If damage resulted from the deviant behavior, the deductions may be made from employee's pay over a period to pay for the damage. Most disciplinary action will not require this severe a step. The layoff is usually of short duration, perhaps a few days up to a week.

The next most severe form of punishment is getting an employee to quit. Getting the unsatisfactory employee to quit has many advantages over termination, for both employee and employer. Both save face. The employee finds another job and then quits, telling the peer group how much better things are at the new location. The employer is satisfied because an ineffective employee has left, without recourse to firing.

While getting an employee to quit is not a forthright approach to discipline, many prefer it to the next step: discharge. To many inexperienced managers, discharge is the solution to any problem with a difficult employee. Often discharge is not possible, because of seniority rules, union rules, too few replacements in the labor market, fear of wrongful discharge lawsuits, or a number of other reasons. Discharge is also costly, both directly and indirectly. Direct costs include a loss of all human resource investments already made in the person: recruiting, selection, and training. Severance pay may be added. Indirect costs are the effect of the firing on other employees.[39] These may not occur if it is a blatant case of deviant behavior or severe inability, but frequently the facts are not clear, and employees may believe the action was arbitrary. If this is the case, productivity may drop, and valuable employees may leave, lest they become victims of arbitrary action, too, Thus, discharge is a final resort—when all else fails, or in very serious cases involving fraud or theft.

Documentation of actions and the behavior that precipitated them is required at every step of the way. This documentation may protect the employer from subsequent lawsuits accusing it of wrongful discharge, harassment, or violating employee rights.

Conflict Resolution

Conflict must be handled in a way that protects employees' rights. In addition to discipline issues, conflict on the job may arise for a host of reasons: sexual harassment, equal opportunity complaints, disputes over promotions, pay, admission to training programs. Some organizations have designed procedures that provide a mechanism for employees and managers to voice their disagreements.

Employees who belong to a union collectively bargain some of these disputes and take others through a formal grievance procedure.

Types of Systems

The type of system an organization uses may depend on the types of problems it deals with, and its compatibility with other organizational structures.

Procedures can vary on two dimensions:

1. *Degree of formality.*   High formality means explicit statements concerning appealable issues, steps to follow, and roles and responsibilities of parties.

2. *Degree of independence from management.*   Are workers forced to complain to their immediate superiors, or does the system use people further removed?

The most independent system would use an outside arbitrator, and it may even provide independent legal counsel to employees. At Wells Fargo Bank, the employee relations unit acts as an employee advocate within the organization. While many writers imply that the more formal and independent a process, the more accepted it will be, in fact no research has addressed this issue.

The hierarchical system is the most formal, the least independent, and also the most common.

Hierarchical Systems

Discipline is administered to most nonunion employees by the supervisor, who also evaluates the employee. When the employee is found to be ineffective, the supervisor decides what needs to be done. Hierarchical systems allow a supervisor, who might be arbitrary, wrong, or ineffective, to serve as cop, judge, and jury over the employee.

A person accused of a crime, such as speeding, in many of our courts can have counsel, the judge is not the arresting officer, and the penalty may be a $50 fine. In the employment situation, where the employee has none of these safeguards, the penalty for an infraction of work rules may be loss of job and salary. Even if the employee is convicted of speeding, appeal to a higher court is possible. What can employees do if they are unfairly treated by their supervisor?

Hewlett-Packard's "Open Door" policy in Exhibit 15.4 encourages employees to express their concerns to managers and supervisors and to go to higher level managers if they feel it is necessary. But an inherent limitation of hierarchical systems is that the whole value system of the hierarchy is based on mutual support among supervisors to build a good management team. So, while the system may offer *procedural* justice, in that employees are given the opportunity to be heard, *substantive* justice may be lacking if the system does not prevent arbitrary actions.[40]

A few organizations have taken steps to design systems to protect the employee from fear of supervisory action.

Peer Systems

In contrast to hierarchical systems, where employees complain to superiors, peer systems rely on independent or related peers to assess the situation and recommend action. They can be implemented in several ways.

General Electric Company's conflict system for 1,800 nonunion production workers at a Columbia, Maryland, electric-range plant uses a five-member panel, comprising the plant manager, a personnel officer, and three specially trained hourly employees. Thus, employees are in the majority.

An evaluation after five years' experience showed that, of 300 grievances filed, 100 went to the panel. The other 200 were resolved one-on-one with supervisors. This number was substantially higher than the complaints filed in the previous five years under an open door policy, where employees complained to management. Managers attribute the increase in complaints to greater employee confidence in fair treatment. They say the real value of the program is that it encourages better supervisor/employee interaction and makes supervisors more accountable.[41]

Ombudsmen

Another approach to resolving conflicts is the use of an "ombudsman," who will investigate complaints, hear all sides, and try to help the parties arrive at a solution they can all live with. The Intercom system at Chemical Bank of New York is an example. Bank employees from outside the personnel office receive special training and then serve a three-year term as an Intercom representative. Representatives are selected from all job levels and departments of the bank. Intercom representatives are trained to listen to employees and to talk to them about their job concerns. Management only becomes involved at the request of the employees.

To be effective, conflict resolution systems must appear more attractive than quitting or suing. This standard leads to four criteria for evaluating such systems.

1. *Fairness of settlement.*   Employees must perceive that an organization is both capable and willing to change a situation leading to the problem.
2. *Timeliness of settlement.*   Reducing the period of uncertainty and the loss of benefits stemming from continuance of the dispute is one of the main advantages of complaining versus suing.
3. *Ease of utilization.*   Time and effort required to file and follow through with an appeal must be minimal.
4. *Protection from recrimination.*   Future raises and promotions must not be perceived to be threatened by filing a grievance or complaint.[42]

EVALUATING RESULTS

The effectiveness of employee relations lies in its efficiency and its equity outcomes for employees and employers.

Efficiency

Efficiency measures of employee relations programs could include improved product quality (measured by reductions in reject rate), enhanced productivity (indicated by an increase in output per working hour), and reduced costs (measured in terms of cost per unit produced). Obviously, these measures could change as a result of other factors besides employee relations, which makes evaluation difficult.

One empirical study correlated QWL programs at 18 General Motors plants with economic performance (labor costs, product quality), which could be characterized as efficiency, and industrial relations performance (grievance rates, absenteeism, attitudinal climate of union/management relationship), which could be characterized as equity.[43] The authors were primarily interested in whether ongoing QWL programs could smooth collective bargaining relationships, as measured by the number of contract demands introduced in local, as opposed to national, bargaining. Despite having common technology, employer, and union, the 18 plants experienced extreme variations in grievance rates, discipline rates, and other industrial relations and economic measures.

While the industrial relations performance measures were strongly related to economic performance, the authors were hesitant to conclude that QWL programs caused any of these improvements, because of the incompleteness in data. The key test of QWL success, they say, is whether effective collaboration can be maintained at the workplace during periods of difficult negotiations at the bargaining table.

The utility approach to evaluation has been used to estimate the economic value of a job-based program. The economic value of a performance increase (or decrease) on a specific job is translated into an estimate of the program's value. The city of Phoenix used this approach to evaluate their alcoholism assistance program. Using public health estimates of the extent of alcoholism in the labor force (around 10 percent) and managers' estimates of the costs of impairment at various organization levels, the value of a program to reduce impairment was calculated.[44]

The program for city employees in Phoenix claims a higher degree of alcoholism rehabilitation than community treatment sources, because of the added clout of threatened job loss. They estimate cost savings due to their employee assistance program at over $2 million a year.

Control Data reports that a recent study of four workers' compensation cases projected a savings to the company of $705,000 through rehabilitation intervention by the EAR program. Only worktime loss was computed; the figures did not include medical expenses. So, their measure was an estimate of costs not incurred when workers were able to be placed in modified jobs, rather than kept on disability.

Equity

Studies of effects of employee relations activities are difficult, because employee relations reflects an overall philosophy. It is difficult to disentangle its effects from anything else. One study of discipline, for example, found that supervisory discipline behaviors were related to employee satisfaction with the supervisor, but the researchers were unable to link satisfaction with the supervisor to any overall job satisfaction or even grievances and absences.[45]

One way to examine effects is to consider employees' options absent strong employee relations. Valued employees who are disgruntled can easily leave an organization. Less-valued employees have fewer options to leave, but they can reduce their commitment and motivation, or even sabotage other employees' work efforts.

A second option for disgruntled employees is to unionize to pool their efforts to change the workplace. A third option for employees is to sue the employer. More and more employees are taking this option, and it is costly. Wells Fargo Bank's cost estimates for lawsuits filed by employees who felt they were unfairly fired range up to $6 million. Avoiding even one such suit would pay for a lot of employee relations activity.

Research to measure the results of cooperation programs viewed these programs as a variable affecting employee job satisfaction and motivation, or as an umbrella under which most organization development activities fit. The broadness of the definition makes it difficult to specify results. The fact is that most programs tend to be short-lived and have difficulty producing tangible, long-lasting results.

For more cooperative approaches to organization decision making to be successful, management must be willing to concede something of value to employees to obtain trust or credibility. The concession may be control over physical work conditions, or it may be job security. Additionally, there must be support for the new approach at multiple levels of the organization. The immediate supervisor may require training in how to make cooperative efforts a success.

With savings so difficult to document, you may ask yourself why employers bother to offer counselling assistance, conflict resolution systems, or day care. The fact is that good intentions and a show of concern may be all the justification that is required. Some employers may be committed to such programs, just as they are committed to the wider communities in which they are located. Nevertheless, effective human resource management helps ensure that employee relations programs are well designed and managed.

SUMMARY

There are a wide variety of activities in an organization aimed at enhancing the quality of the employment relationship. Some of the programs are formal, such as conflict resolution procedures. Other activities are more casual, such as organizing and funding an employee picnic. Encouraging a cooperative, rather than an adversarial, relationship is the goal. The underlying assumption is that such an atmosphere will better allow employees to perform their jobs and contribute a creative spark to the organization.

The effects of employee relations programs are difficult to assess. Most of their benefits take the form of cost avoidance—lawsuits not filed, turnover or absenteeism that did not occur, productivity that did not decline. Additionally, many of the programs contribute to a better atmosphere. They demonstrate that the employer is committed to cooperative relationships, respects the employees, views them as a source of profitable suggestions, and will make efforts to accommodate their preferences.

Because of the difficulty in justifying these programs on a cost basis, top management commitment to employee relations is essential. If this commitment falters (often through a change in management), it seems an easy choice to cut these programs to improve the bottom line. So, the human resource managers must be in touch with employees—to be sure that programs are working effectively—and with top management—to maintain their commitment.

DISCUSSION AND REVIEW QUESTIONS

1. A Minnesota jury recently awarded $60,000 to a former bank teller who said she had suffered emotional damage because she had been pressed by her employer to take a polygraph, or lie-detector, test. The teller, who had passed the test but said she had nightmares afterward, had been questioned about funds that were missing. With the advantage of hindsight, what would you advise your employer, the Suburban National Bank of Eden Prairie, Minnesota, to do when it suspects internal theft?

2. A Texas insurance company recently fired its auditor for failing to complete a timely audit. The auditor claims he could not complete the audit because his employer made claims that could not be verified and that the auditor believed were unrealistic. What would you do if you were the employer? The employee?

3. How might a successful assistance program for handling alcohol-impaired employees be structured?

4. Describe a progressive discipline system.

5. Is employee relations a good substitute for a union?

6. What other organization initiatives discussed in previous chapters could increase employee involvement?

7. How might a study of the cost effectiveness of a conflict resolution system be structured?

8. Why do you think many of the QWL programs begun in the 1980s no longer exist?

9. Whose responsibility do you think it is to manage family/work conflicts?

10. Do you think job stress should be a compensable factor on which pay systems are based?

YOUR TURN
TRADITION OR TEAM APPROACHES

Team concepts have slowly inched their way into some American work settings. The team approach can be successful in fostering a cooperative worker/management spirit that emphasizes common goals.

In general the team approach stresses the following: worker efficiency, detailed job design, worker interchangeability among jobs, and worker adjustment to output and system technology demands. The changes emphasize management control over design, scheduling, and work assignments. Workers are responsible for performance and team effectiveness. The team concept transforms the work setting into a web of *structured interactions* requiring member contributions and support. Each worker plays a major and predictable role in the team's performance. Proponents of this approach accent the value of group effort, satisfaction of team membership, and mutual gain. Recently, however, criticism has surfaced, which suggests that the stress and pressure team members experience may make the victory one-sided.

In the auto industry, supporters term the team concept *synchronous manufacturing*. They view such groups as a key to prosperity. Critics define it as *management by stress*. What do you think?

Select and define an organization. As the CEO, how would you defend the merits of the team approach? As an employee, how would you see your job changing? What criticisms would you raise?

This exercise was developed by Joseph Salamone, SUNY Buffalo.

NOTES AND REFERENCES

1. Daniel J. Koys, "Human Resource Management and a Culture of Respect: Effects on Employees' Organizational Commitment," *Employee Responsibilities and Rights Journal* 1, 1 (1988), pp. 57–68; Sheila B. Kamerman and Alfred J. Kahn, *The Responsive Workplace* (New York: Columbia University Press, 1987).

2. Thomas A. Kochan, Harry Katz, and Robert McKersie, *The Transformation of American Industrial Relations* (New York: Basic Books, 1986).

3. John P. Bucalo, "Successful Employee Relations," *Personnel Administrator,* April 1986, pp. 63–84.

4. Julius M. Steiner and Allan M. Dabrow, "The Questionable Value of the Inclusion of Language Confirming Employment-at-Will Status in Company Personnel Documents," *Labor Law Journal,* September 1986, pp. 639–45.

5. Survey in 1988 of 100,000 employees of Fortune 500 companies, conducted by Opinion Research Corporation, Chicago, Illinois.

6. Survey conducted by A. Foster Higgins & Co., benefits consultants, 1989.

7. John D. Worrall, ed., *Safety and the Work Force* (Ithaca, N.Y.: ILR Press, 1983); Robert S. Smith, "Protecting Workers' Health and Safety," in *Instead of Regulation,* ed. Robert W. Poole (Lexington, Mass.: Lexington Books, 1981); R. S.

Schuler, "Occupational Health in Organizations: Strategies for Personnel Effectiveness," *Personnel Administrator,* January 1982, pp. 47–56.

8. Ann P. Bartel and Lacy Glenn Thomas, "Direct and Indirect Effects of Regulation: A New Look at OSHA's Impact," *Journal of Law and Economics,* April 1985, pp. 1–25.

9. Alan E. Dillingham, "Demographic and Economic Change and the Costs of Workers' Compensation," in *Safety and the Work Force,* ed. John D. Worrall (Ithaca, N.Y.: ILR Press, 1983).

10. Clare Ansberry, "Workplace Injuries Proliferate as Concerns Push People to Produce," *The Wall Street Journal,* June 16, 1989, pp. 1, A8.

11. Kenneth Sovereign, *Personnel Law* (Englewood Cliffs, N.J.: Prentice-Hall, 1989).

12. Susan R. Mendelsohn and Kathryn R. Morrison, "The Right to Privacy in the Workplace, Part 2: Testing Applicants for Alcohol and Drug Abuse," *Personnel,* August 1988, pp. 57–60.

13. Patricia H. Werhane, *Persons, Rights, and Corporations* (Englewood Cliffs, N.J.: Prentice-Hall, 1985); Judy Olian, "The Changing Structure of Employment Relations," presentation at University of Maryland, College Park, October 1, 1985; Richard I. Lehr and David J. Middlebrooks, "Work-Place Privacy Issues and Employer Screening Policies," *Employee Relations Law Journal* 11, no. 3 (Spring 1987), pp. 407–21; Mark A. Rothstein, "Screening Workers for Drugs: A Legal and Ethical Framework," *Employee Relations Law Journal* 11, no. 3 (Spring 1987), pp. 422–37; Helen Axel, ed., *Corporate Strategies for Controlling Substance Abuse* (New York: The Conference Board, 1986).

14. *Privacy in the Workplace: When Employer–Employee Rights Collide* (New York: Alexander Hamilton Institute, 1987).

15. Information on the video "AIDS in the Workplace: Epidemic of Fear" can be obtained from the San Francisco AIDS Foundation, 333 Valencia St., San Francisco, CA 94103.

16. Elaine Gruenfeld, "Smoking in the Workplace," *ILR Report,* Spring 1986, pp. 9–17; ASPA–BNA Survey no. 50, *Smoking in the Workplace* (Washington, D.C.: Bureau of National Affairs, 1986).

17. Survey conducted by Administrative Management Society, Willow Grove, Pennsylvania.

18. *Meritor Savings Bank* v. *Vinson,* U.S. Supreme Court 40 FEP Cases 1826 (1986).

19. Eric Rolfe Greenberg, "Workplace Testing: Results of a New AMA Survey," *Personnel,* April 1988, pp. 36–44.

20. William J. Sonnenstuhl and Harrison M. Trice, *Strategies for Employee Assistance Programs: The Crucial Balance* (Ithaca, N.Y.: ILR Press, 1986); Bureau of National Affairs, *Alcohol and Drugs in the Workplace: Costs, Controls, and Controversies* (Washington, D. C.: Bureau of National Affairs, 1986).

21. *Essays on American Industrialism: Selected Papers of Samuel M. Levin* (Detroit: Wayne State University, 1973).

22. Jan Duffy, Stephen P. Pepe, and Beverly Gross, "Big Brother in the Workplace: Privacy Rights versus Employer Needs," *Industrial Relations Law Journal* 9, no. 1 (1987), pp. 30–56.

23. Janice Beyer and Harrison Trice, "A Field Study of the Use and Perceived Effects of Discipline in Controlling Work Performance," *Academy of Management Journal* 27 (1984), pp. 743–64.

24. R. L. Kahn, D. M. Wolfe, R. Quinn, J. D. Snoek, and R. A. Rosenthal, *Organizational Stress* (New York: John Wiley & Sons, 1964).

25. Jeffrey J. Greenhaus and Nicholas J. Beutell, "Sources of Conflict between Work and Family Roles," *Academy of Management Review* 10, no. 1 (1985), pp. 76–88.

26. Randall Dunham and Jon L. Pierce, "Attitudes toward Work Schedules: Construct Definition, Instrument Development, and Validation," *Academy of Management Journal,* March 1986, pp. 170–82; S. D. Nollen, *New Work Schedules in Practice: Managing Time in a Changing Society* (New York: Van Nostrand Reinhold, 1983); Graham Staines and Joseph Pleck, "Nonstandard Work Schedules and Family Life," *Journal of Applied Psychology* 69, no. 3 (1984), pp. 515–23; Thomas H. Patten, Jr., "Trends in Hours and Working-Time Arrangements in the United States of America, 1830–1985." Paper presented at International Industrial Relations Association, Hamburg, Germany, 1986; Paul Flaim, "Work Schedules of Americans: An Overview of New Findings," *Monthly Labor Review,* November 1986, pp. 3–6. Entire issue devoted to topic.

27. Jan Pierce, John Newstrom, Randall Dunham, and Alison Barber, *Alternative Work Schedules* (Boston: Allyn & Bacon, 1989).

28. "The Changing Workplace: New Directions in Staffing and Scheduling," BNA Response Center, 9435 Key West Ave., Rockville, MD 20850, 1986; Diane S. Rothberg, "Part-Time Professionals: The Flexible Work Force," *Personnel Administrator,* August 1986, pp. 27–39; Thomas J. Nardone, "Part-Time Workers: Who Are They?" *Monthly Labor Review,* February 1986, pp. 13–19.

29. Janina C. Latack and Lawrence W. Foster, "Implementation of Compressed Work Schedules: Participation and Job Redesign as Critical Factors for Employee Acceptance," *Personnel Psychology* 38 (1985), pp. 75–92.

30. Victor Fuchs, *Women's Quest for Economic Equality* (Cambridge, Mass.: Harvard University Press, 1988).

31. Martin O'Connell and David Bloom, *Juggling Jobs and Babies: America's Child Care Challenge* (Washington, D. C.: Population Reference Bureau, 1987).

32. Thomas I. Miller, "The Effects of Employer-Sponsored Child Care on Employee Absenteeism, Turnover, Productivity, Recruitment or Job Satisfaction: What Is Claimed and What Is Known," *Personnel Psychology* 37 (1984), pp. 277–89.

33. Columbia University Department of Industrial Engineering and Operation Research, reported in *New York Times,* February 21, 1987.

34. Ben Fischer, "A Skeptic Looks at Employee Buyouts," and Corey Rosen, "Growth versus Equity: The Employee Ownership Solution," *ILR Report,* Spring 1985, pp. 19–26.

35. Bradley Stertz, "Ill-Fated Fiero, Recalled Again, Returns to Haunt GM," *The Wall Street Journal,* January 22, 1990, p. B1.

36. Peter Cappelli and Robert McKersie, "Management Strategy and the Redesign of Workrules," *Journal of Management Studies,* September 1987.

37. Mike Parker and Jane Slaughter, *Choosing Sides: Unions and the Team Concept* (Detroit: Labor Notes/South End Press, 1988); Harry Katz, *Shifting Gears: Changing Labor Relations in the U.S. Auto Industry* (Cambridge, Mass.: MIT Press, 1985).

38. Ann W. Martin, "Work Restructuring in the 1980s: The View from PEWS," *ILR Report,* Fall 1988, pp. 6–11.

39. Dean Tjosvold, *Managing Work Relationships* (Lexington, Mass.: Lexington Books, 1986); *Employee Discipline and Discharge* (Washington, D.C.: Bureau of National Affairs PPF Survey no. 139, January 1985).

40. Lee Dyer and Donna Blancero Marron, "Procedural Fairness in Employee Relations: Theory and Research," Paper presented at the annual meeting of the Academy of

Management, August 1989, Washington, D.C.; Jerald Greenberg, "A Taxonomy of Organizational Justice Theories," *Academy of Management Review,* January 1987, pp. 9–22.

41. Martha I. Finney, "A Good Idea—Five Years Later," *Personnel Administrator,* 1988, pp. 45–46.

42. John D. Aram and Paul F. Salipante, Jr., "An Evaluation of Organizational Due Process in the Resolution of Employee/Employer Conflict," *Academy of Management Review* 6, no. 2 (1981), pp. 197–204.

43. Harry C. Katz, Thomas A. Kochan, and Kenneth R. Gobeille, "Industrial Relations Performance, Economic Performance, and QWL Programs: An Interplant Analysis," *Industrial and Labor Relations Review,* October 1983, pp. 3–17.

44. Janice Beyer and Harrison Trice, "The Best/Worst Technique for Measuring Work Performance in Organizational Research," *Organizational Behavior and Statistics,* May 1984, pp. 1–21.

45. Richard D. Arvey, Gregory A. Davis, and Sherry M. Nelson, "Use of Discipline in an Organization: A Field Study," *Journal of Applied Psychology* 69, no. 3 (1984), pp. 448–60.

CHAPTER
SIXTEEN

Collective
Bargaining

The Legal Framework for Collective
Bargaining

The Organizing Campaign
Authorization Cards
Hearings
Holding the Election
Success of Campaign Tactics

Negotiating a Contract
Preparation
Negotiation Issues
Refusal to Bargain
Bargaining Structures
Formalizing the Contract

Impasses in Collective Bargaining
Conciliation and Mediation
Strikes and Lockouts
Who Strikes—And Why?

Contract Administration
Steps in the Grievance Process
Arbitration

Your Turn: Arbitrating a Grievance

Ever since President Ronald Reagan fired striking air traffic controllers in the early 1980s, observers have predicted the imminent demise of organized labor. Unions have been portrayed as reeling from years of contract concessions, declining memberships, and the loss of manufacturing jobs to the Far East. Thirty years ago, more than a third of the nation's nonagricultural workers belonged to labor unions. Today, just over 16 percent of the work force is organized. Employers no longer quail before the thought of a strike; indeed, some even seem to be pushing for one, and begin hiring replacement workers before the picket lines are formed. Contract concessions accepted by the unions in the years of economic recession have in many cases not been made good in the days of recovery.

Yet, according to former international president of the United Auto Workers Douglas Fraser, if unions are down they are by no means out. Fraser acknowledged that unions are going to have to adopt some new strategies and to gain a lot of ground lost in the past.

"The traditional role of the union in our country is you let management make all of the decisions, and you challenge the decisions you don't like," Fraser notes. "That's not good enough if you are going to represent your workers. Suppose a company closes a plant? If you challenge that, it's too late. A union has to have a voice in councils where these decisions are made. We're very slow coming around to that."

If nothing else, corporations would gain new insight. "Take the Chrysler board. I was the only one who had ever worked in an auto plant and the only one that had contact with the Chrysler workers."[1]

So both unions and employers are adopting new approaches to their relationship and setting new objectives. At the same time, the external conditions that affect labor relations have shifted. Expectations of unions' role in society and in organizations are changing. In this chapter we will cover legislation that affects collective bargaining, and the collective bargaining process: organizing, negotiating, and administration. Chapter Seventeen analyzes managerial and union strategies, the union as an organization, and the status of unions in the United States and the world today.

Dealing with unions is frequently an emotionally charged activity. Few employers or employees get as emotionally involved over recruiting methods or selection techniques, for example, as they do over labor relations. The reason is that labor relations and collective bargaining go to the heart of employee relations problems—control. Control to hire, to pay, to judge performance, to fire— all translate into control to affect significant human needs. As we saw in the previous chapter, control over one's work life affects family relationships and even health. Many employees have turned to unions as a source of strength in numbers. By acting collectively, union members hope to gain greater power to influence employers' decisions and control their work life. In a nonunionized organization, management has flexibility in hiring and promoting people, establishing the nature of the work and work rules, and administering pay and benefits. Much of this changes when employees elect to join a union. Then, the union and the employer negotiate a contract, which spells out details of many personnel matters. Some unions have even become involved in the strategic decisions of the organization. Thus, labor relations and collective bargaining affect all other human resource management activities.

◆

Labor relations is a continuous relationship between a defined group of employees (represented by a union or association) and an employer. *Collective bargaining* is the process by which union representatives for employees in a bargaining unit negotiate employment conditions for the entire bargaining unit. The process includes the initial recognition of the rights and responsibilities of union and management, the negotiation of a written contract concerning wages, hours, and other conditions of employment, and the interpretation and administration of this contract over its period of coverage.

THE LEGAL FRAMEWORK FOR COLLECTIVE BARGAINING

In the United States, the history of unionism is inextricably intertwined with labor legislation.[2] The notion of collective action being a conspiracy was part of English common law. The legal principle that dominated labor relations laws into the 1800s was that of individual rights: Every individual was free to negotiate employment terms and to change employers at will. Unions were a criminal conspiracy that abridged the rights of individuals. Group attempts to regulate wages could have an adverse effect on not only the profits of the employer but also on free trade, the community in general, and workers who were not part of the union.

Criminal Conspiracy Theory

This theory was invoked in almost every case of unionism. The leading case was that of the Philadelphia Cordwainers. Prior to 1805, shoe merchants set the pay rate for cordwainers (shoemakers) on the basis of how the shoes were marketed: one price for making shoes to be wholesaled, another price for shoes to be sold at the merchants' shops, and a third price for custom-ordered shoes. In 1805, the cordwainers tried to establish a standard rate for each type of shoe, regardless of how the shoes were marketed. They asked all cordwainers to refuse to work except for this wage rate. But the courts declared that "the collective action of a few persons in pursuit of their selfish interests contravened the interests of citizens in general and was, hence, a criminal conspiracy."[3]

The courts continued to find collective activity illegal well into the 19th century. Employers and much of society refused to recognize unions as legitimate organizations. Even though the 1842 case *Commonwealth* v. *Hunt* allowed the association of workers, unions were legal only if their self-interest did not interfere with free market competition, and if the union did not use force against nonmembers. This interpretation still permitted judges to decide that almost any union action was an illegal interference with market competition.

Railway Labor Act This act, passed in 1926, is the first national labor law to be found constitutional that gives employees the right to choose whether or not to be represented by a union and to engage in union activity. Additionally, it encourages the use of arbitration and mediation as dispute resolution mechanisms. Although it applies only to the railway and airline industries, many of its provisions were later extended to other industries through additional legislation.

Norris-LaGuardia Act Severe economic disruption and massive unemployment in the 1930s aroused public sympathy to the plight of laborers and led to the passage of two important labor laws. The *Norris-LaGuardia Act,* passed in 1932, declared union membership to be a legal right of all employees. It limits the power of employers in two ways:

1. *"Yellow dog" contracts.* These are contracts that force employees to agree not to join a union or to participate in any union activity. Norris-LaGuardia forbids such contracts.
2. *Arbitrary injunctions.* The law also forbids federal judges from issuing injunctions against lawful union activities, unless there is a clear and present danger to life or property. (An injunction is a judicial order requiring or, more commonly, forbidding a specific behavior.) Unions must be given an opportunity to respond to charges before the injunction is issued; that is, to show cause why an injunction should not be issued.

The act applies to all private sector employees and unions. It does not require employees to bargain with unions, nor does it prohibit them from discriminating against employees for union activity. But it does establish employees' legal right to form a union, without reference to any public interest standard.

Wagner Act (commonly referred to as the *National Labor Relations Act*) Passed in 1935, this law finally put labor on a more equal footing with management. It guarantees employees' rights to organize and to bargain free from employers' interference. It requires employers to bargain with a union over wages, hours, and conditions of work, if a majority of employees desire such union representation. And it establishes the National Labor Relations Board (NLRB) to conduct representation elections and investigate charges of unfair labor practices. The NLRB's role in the collective bargaining process is further discussed in the next chapter.

For all practical purposes, modern labor relations in the United States began with passage of the Wagner Act.[4] After 1935, union membership boomed. But until the Supreme Court upheld the law in 1937, many employers simply refused to obey. They would not allow employees to join unions. They systematically spied on union activities, infiltrated union governments, and spent millions on spying, strikebreaking, and munitions. Youngstown Sheet and Tube Company is said to have amassed 8 machine guns, 369 rifles, 190 shotguns, 450 revolvers, 109 gas guns, 3,000 rounds of gas, and almost 10,000 rounds of shotgun shells and bullets in preparation for a strike. Republic Steel Company had purchased almost $80,000 worth of repellent gases and allegedly possessed the largest private arsenal in the United States, to be used against its employees.[5]

Taft-Hartley Act (the Labor-Management Relations Act) Some unions responded to this violence in kind, leading to passage of the Taft-Hartley Act in 1947. Technically an amendment to the Wagner Act, Taft-Hartley corrects union and, to a lesser extent, employer abuses.

There are five major elements to the act:

1. *Sweetheart contracts.* When faced with the threat of unionization, some employers had established their own union without consulting the majority of employees and signed labor contracts that were very favorable toward management. These "sweetheart contracts" were outlawed by Taft-Hartley; employers are now forbidden from assisting or establishing labor organizations.

2. *Exclusive representation.* Taft-Hartley also specifies exclusive representation. When a majority of employees desires a specific union, that union represents all employees in the bargaining unit, whether or not they are union members. Exclusive representation is a major difference between unions in the United States and many other countries.

3. *Federal Mediation and Conciliation Service (FMCS).* Additionally, Taft-Hartley established the Federal Mediation and Conciliation Service (FMCS), which offers assistance in contract settlement and maintains a list of arbitrators to help interpret contract language and resolve disputes.

4. *Closed shop and union shop.* Taft-Hartley specifies that the *closed shop,* which requires that employees be union members at the time of hiring, is now illegal. Requiring all employees in a bargaining unit to join a unit as a condition of *continued* employment is legal, if such a stipulation is agreed to by both employer and union. This is called a *union shop.* If the collectively bargained contract does not contain such a clause, then it is illegal for an employer to either require or forbid employees' union activity, or to use union status as a promotion decision factor.

5. *Emergency powers of presidents.* If a strike threatens the public welfare, the president of the United States has power to order an 80-day cooling off period. During this time, employees return to work, and a board of inquiry tries to settle issues.

Landrum-Griffin Act   Landrum-Griffin resulted from the charges in the 1940s and 1950s of labor racketeering. It was passed in 1959, and its main elements are:

1. *Union members' bills of rights.* Union members have the right to vote for union officers, the right to vote on dues increases, freedom of speech in union matters, and the right to sue their union. It also requires union officers to report certain financial transactions.

2. *Closed shop exception for construction trades.* Union membership is never supposed to be a basis for a hiring decision. However, in the construction industry, because of the relative strength of regional unions in comparison to individual employers, the bulk of hiring is done through union halls. The Landrum-Griffin Act permits union job referrals if the union agrees not to discriminate on the basis of union membership. Objective criteria, such as experience and training, must be used as a basis for referral. However, the only way to get the experience and training is through union apprenticeship programs.

"Right-to-Work" Laws

Many states have other laws that may further regulate the activities of unions or employers. One of the most common is right-to-work laws, which outlaw union shop clauses. Twenty-one states, mainly in the South and Southwest, now have such laws. Advocates of such laws claim that compulsory unionism in a union shop violates the basic American right of freedom of association. Opponents say nothing could be more basically American than the notion of majority rule.

THE ORGANIZING CAMPAIGN

When employees are not represented by a union, either the employees themselves or a union can initiate unionization. Union organizers who are not employees may assist employees to start a campaign if there is a good chance of success. A union will try to mobilize discontent and steer employees toward union formation as a solution.

Whether the employees or the union take the initiative, next comes a time of high drama: the organizing campaign itself.

Authorization Cards

Union organizers try to get the employees to sign cards, which authorize that union to represent them in collective bargaining. In the United States, 30 percent of the employees in the proposed bargaining unit must sign cards before the union can call for a representation election. In most Canadian provinces, if 60 percent of the workers sign authorization cards, the union is certified without a representation election. There is no "campaign" on either side. This may be one reason why union membership in Canada is increasing, while in the United States it is not.[6]

In general, the union tries to keep the initial stages of the campaign secret so it can get up momentum before management can mount a counteroffensive. During the organizing period, unions and management pursue campaigns to affect employee attitudes toward unionization. Typically, the union stresses how it can improve the workers' lot in terms of compensation, benefits, working conditions, and increased influence and control over decisions related to their jobs. Management mounts a countercampaign stressing how well off the employees are already and the cost of union membership in dollars and "loss of freedom." It is illegal for either side, in mass meetings, literature, or individual meetings, to threaten employees with discharge or violence. Both sides must be truthful, or the procedure can be set aside.

Hearings

After the authorization, the NLRB holds a hearing to decide if there is enough evidence to hold an election. The NLRB seeks to determine two things:

1. *Valid signatures.* Do the people who signed authorization cards actually work there, and do they constitute 30 percent of employees?
2. *Appropriate bargaining unit.* A bargaining unit delineates which group of employees will be involved in the representation election; for example, all employees in technician job categories at a particular plant location or all nonexempt employees at multiple locations.[7]

Typically, a union proposes a bargaining unit. The NLRB must determine if this unit is "appropriate," using two criteria: Will it ensure employees freedom of choice, and does it foster "industrial peace and stability"? It is not the NLRB's role to choose the "best" bargaining unit, only an "appropriate" unit. Employers frequently challenge the union's specification of a unit to influence which employees are eligible to vote in the election or just to delay the procedure.

Holding the Election

After determining that all requirements are met, the NLRB examiner schedules an election. The NLRB provides ballot boxes, counts the votes, and certifies the election. The union becomes the employees' representative if it wins the election.

To win an election, 50 percent plus 1 of the people who vote in the election must vote for the union. Occasionally, there may be more than one union on the ballot. If this is the case, they hold a runoff election between the two top

EXHIBIT 16.1   Benefits Stressed by Unions in Organizing Campaigns

Almost Always Stressed	Frequently Stressed	Infrequently Stressed
Grievance procedures	More influence in decision making	Higher-quality products
Job security	Better working conditions	Technical training
Improved benefits	Lobbying opportunities	More job satisfaction
Higher pay		Increased production

Source: Monty L. Lynn and Jozell Brister, "Trends in Union Organizing Issues and Tactics," *Industrial Relations*, Winter 1989, pp. 104–13.

choices; for example, either between the two unions, or between no union and the more popular union. When a union wins an election, the NLRB certifies that union's exclusive right to represent everyone in the bargaining unit. No other union may represent employees in the unit, and all employees in the unit are represented, whether or not they join the union.

Researchers have spent a great deal of effort trying to specify what factors affect the outcomes of union elections.[8] First, employees are more likely to unionize if an employer is perceived to have demanded different behavior than was expected, or failed to provide rewards expected. Second, an individual must believe that there is little likelihood of changing conditions except through collective bargaining. Third, some critical mass of like-minded activists is necessary to begin the unionizing attempt. Fourth, unionization by this activist coalition depends on their understanding of how collective bargaining works and their belief that the likely benefits of organizing outweigh the drawbacks.

Most union elections are very close. One study found that a shift of eight votes would have changed the outcome of the average election.[9] So, it is no wonder that participation rates are high—typically 90 percent—in union elections, compared to roughly 50 percent in major political elections. Employees accurately perceive that their vote *can* make a difference.

Success of Campaign Tactics

A variety of issues are emphasized in an election campaign. Exhibit 16.1 lists the issues that 97 union organizers said they stress during a campaign. Grievance procedures, job security, and better compensation (pay and benefits) were almost always stressed.[10]

But there is another side to the campaign. Employers have become increasingly aggressive in their communication campaigns and in their use of outside consultants to advise them.[11] Exhibit 16.2 presents the relative frequency of various employer activities as reported by union organizers. How successful

---

EXHIBIT 16.2   Frequency of Reported Employer Campaign Activities

---

Campaign Activity	Relative Frequency
Captive audience speeches	65%
Small group meetings	36
Supervisor training	38
Literature distribution	70
Employee surveillance	34
Excelsior-list irregularities	11
Administration of surveys	11
Employment discrimination	24
Wage increases during campaign	16
Threats of reprisal	10
Promises of gain/inducements	4
Directed election	22
Management consultant used	20

Source: John J. Lawler and Robin West, "Impact of Union-Avoidance Strategy in Representation Elections," *Industrial Relations*, Fall 1985, pp. 406–20.

are such tactics? It is hard to say. Economists who analyze aggregated data conclude that:

1. The amount of company communication influences election results, with unions winning most elections in which management opposition is light, but less than half of those in which opposition is severe.

2. The longer the delay between the initial petition and the actual election, the lower the union success.

3. Elections in which companies readily agree to the bargaining unit proposed by the union produce greater chances of wins than elections in which the NLRB stipulates the unit and, therefore, who can and cannot vote.[12]

4. From one quarter to half of the decline in union election success rates can be attributed to management opposition to organizing campaigns.

The problem with these conclusions is that they are based on nationwide data and do not consider what affects a particular election result. At the level of the individual union election, most employers' strategies have a relatively weak effect; however, their effects may be cumulative, and it may be that a weak effect is sufficient to change an election outcome.

Hiring an outside consultant appears to be the employer strategy that has the most strongly negative impact on union organizing success. However, there is also some evidence that an overly aggressive employer campaign can backfire and enhance the chances of union victory. Perhaps the most potent employer tactic is fair and effective human resource management, not only by the personnel department, but also by each manager in the organization.

Decertification

If a union has not served its members, or if employee membership has so changed that there is no longer support for the union, decertification is a possibility. The same group of employees who vote in a union can vote one out, using much the same procedure as in certification. An election, supervised by the NLRB, can be called for by either the employees in the unit involved or a labor organization acting on their behalf. Whoever requests the election must provide evidence that at least 30 percent of the employees want a decertification election. A petition signed by a majority of the bargaining unit employees is the most common evidence.

A decertification election cannot be held within 12 months of the certification election or while a labor contract is in effect.

NEGOTIATING A CONTRACT

Once a union is recognized as the bargaining representative for a group of employees, its officials are authorized to negotiate an employment contract. This contract differs in several important ways from a typical legal contract. It is unusual because:

1. So many people are bound by it. If you buy a car, you may feel a lot of people are involved: the salesperson, perhaps the salesperson's supervisor, the loan processor, and the license bureau. But a union contract involves all the people who are employed in the bargaining unit. This number may run into the hundreds.

2. The contract is not strictly voluntary, in that neither side can walk away from it. Workers are already employed, the union cannot say "I'll go get another employer," and the employer is legally required to bargain.

3. Most contracts specify all details of a one-time event. By contrast, the collective bargaining agreement governs a day-to-day relationship but may be incomplete and purposely vague. If there is no meeting of the minds, a statement of general principle may be given. For example, a statement supporting worker participation plans was contained in GM–UAW contracts for years before any programs actually began.

Preparation

Preparation for negotiation is an area in which little research has been done, mainly because the parties to the negotiation prefer secrecy. The more complex the bargaining, the further ahead preparations begin.

The beginning part of the preparation analyzes problems in contract administration and possible changes in contract language. If management or the union wishes to make changes in a contract, it must notify the other party and the Federal Mediation and Conciliation Service (FMCS) in writing of their desire to terminate or modify the contract at least 60 days before the contract expires. This notification also should include an offer to meet with the other side to discuss the issue.

Probably since the signing of the last contract, both sides have been compiling lists of issues to be brought up the next time. Management has asked its supervisors how they would like the contract modified to avoid problem areas. The industrial relations department has been studying patterns in grievances to identify problems. Management has examined the contract to identify undesirable sections, especially those that restrict its rights.

Based on these data, both sides gather statistical information and prepare bargaining positions. For example, management seeks information on economic conditions affecting the job (e.g., wage rates, productivity) from its staff, industry data, and published sources. Management also attempts to determine the cost of each likely union demand. Computer simulation can help here. Preliminary trade-offs are thought through.

Often there are differences within management groups over bargaining objectives. A common complaint is: "I'm having more trouble with my company than I am with the union." When these management differences are worked out before the negotiations start, the bargaining process is more effective. If an employer negotiates with more than one union, for example, different unions representing various bargaining units within the employer, careful preparation is essential, for what is negotiated with one union is brought up by the others. Typically, a careful balance of wage, benefit, and status differentials is maintained among unions.

The union also prepares for negotiations by preparing lists of problems with the contract. It, too, gathers statistical information, studies the issues likely to be raised, and coordinates with any other unions involved. Unions may also have internal differences, usually over what the bargaining objectives are; for example, younger workers may want job security, while older workers favor better pensions.[13]

Negotiation Issues

Any labor contract can have a large number of clauses; studies show that the number of items an employer must bargain over is increasing. They fall into five groups:

1. *Union security.* This is usually the first bargaining issue for a union. Most unions prefer *a union shop clause:* When workers take jobs in this bargaining unit, they must join the union after a certain time period. Union membership is a condition for continued employment. A union shop clause is legal. A *closed shop,* where union membership is a condition of hiring, is illegal.

If a union shop clause cannot be won, a union may settle for an *agency shop:* Even if workers do not join, they must still pay the equivalent of dues to the

---

EXHIBIT 16.3   Labor Contract: Agency Shop Clause

Section 1: Agency Shop
   A. Membership in the union is not compulsory. However, membership in the union is
      distinct from the assumption of equal financial obligations to all represented
      employees. Therefore, all represented employees, as a condition of employment, no
      later than ninety (90) calendar days after the beginning of their employment or the
      date of this Agreement, whichever is later, either become and remain members of
      the union in good standing or make payments to the union in an amount equal to
      the initiation fees and membership dues uniformly required by the union of its
      members.
Section 2: Checkoff
   A. The company agrees to deduct from the wages of those employees who so
      authorize by written assignment (on mutually agreed upon forms) regular monthly
      union membership dues and initiation fees or payments in lieu thereof.

EXHIBIT 16.4   Labor Contract: Administrative Details

ARTICLE II
Section 1: Strikes and Lockouts
   A. The union agrees that there shall be no strikes, picketing, boycotts, interruptions
      of work, or any other interferences directly or indirectly, with the operation of the
      plant so long as the grievance procedure under this Agreement is followed by the
      company.
   B. The company agrees that there shall be no lockouts, so long as the grievance
      procedure under this Agreement is followed by the union.
   C. Any violation of this Article, by any employee, shall constitute cause for immediate
      discipline and/or discharge.

ARTICLE III
Section 1: Grievance Procedure
   A. All differences, disputes and grievances that may arise between the union and the
      company out of this contract shall be taken up immediately under this grievance
      procedure.
      Any employee who has a complaint over the interpretation or application of this
      Agreement shall discuss the alleged complaint with his supervisor in an attempt to
      settle the alleged complaint. Any such complaint not so settled shall be processed
      according to the grievance procedure specified in this contract.

---

union. Exhibit 16.3 shows the agency shop clause from an agreement between
TRW, Inc., and the Globe Industries Employees' Independent Union.
   Another option is a *maintenance of membership clause:* Workers may or may
not join the union, but once they join, they must maintain (continue) their
membership for the duration of the contract. Membership can only be dropped

EXHIBIT 16.5   Labor Contract: A Two-Tier Wage Structure

Job	Pay Rate for Employees Hired on or after March 3	Pay Rate for Employees Hired before March 3
CNC chucker	$6.00	$12.00
CNC mill	6.00	12.00
Plating/painting technician	5.50	11.65
Punch press operator	5.00	12.44
Special machine operator	5.00	11.49

within 30 days of contract expiration. A maintenance of membership clause guarantees stability in numbers for a union.

2. *Contract administration.*   The contract specifies its duration, commonly two to three years, and procedures to ensure that it is applied/enforced as intended. Exhibit 16.4 shows part of the administrative details of the TRW contract. We return to contract administration later in this chapter.

3. *Compensation and working conditions.*   All contracts stipulate compensation and working conditions, such as direct compensation rates, benefits, and hours of work. Issues concern whether overtime should be voluntary, and the size of cost-of-living adjustments. Unions may bargain about not only payments for pensions but also the details of early retirement provisions, for example.

Two-tier provisions: One wage clause that has generated a great deal of controversy is the two-tier wage structure, in which the top rate of pay for new employees is substantially lower than that for previously hired employees. Exhibit 16.5 shows the size of these differentials in a TRW contract. The new employees may earn less than half as much as the previous employees on the same job.

Because employees with identical job titles, duties, responsibilities, and performance receive substantially different pay rates, two-tier structures seem particularly hard to reconcile with the objective of equity.[14] Fortunately, most such plans phase new employees into the higher rates after several years, so eventually the differential disappears. But pending renegotiation, about one third of such clauses specify permanent differentials. Current trends in contract negotiations indicate that both unions and management are having second thoughts about two-tier arrangements.[15] Equity issues among employees and membership pressures on union officials raise serious concerns about two-tier clauses.

4. *Employee security and seniority.*   Seniority is continuous service in a work unit, plant, or organization. Unions feel that seniority should be the determining factor in promotions, layoffs, and recalls. Management claims its right to make these decisions on the basis of job performance. Many contracts

stipulate that in cases of promotion and layoff, when efficiency and ability are substantially equal, the most senior employees shall be favored. Exhibit 16.6 shows part of the seniority clause from TRW's contract.

Seniority is an area of unresolved conflict between some union supporters and some EEO advocates. The Supreme Court has upheld the legality of seniority systems as long as the original intent of the system was not to discriminate.[16] Because minorities and women are more likely to have low seniority, layoffs on a seniority basis hurt them disproportionately.

5. *Management rights.*   This issue usually presents an especially difficult set of problems. Management lists certain areas or decisions as management rights or prerogatives, which are thus excluded from bargaining. Management tries to make these lists long, and unions try to chip away at them. In many cases, the wage concessions that unions made in the early 1980s were in exchange for reduction in the items of management's sole discretion.

Refusal to Bargain

What happens if an employer disagrees with the bargaining unit specified by the NLRB, or simply refuses to abide by the election results? The union can file a charge of unfair labor practice with the NLRB, which enforces labor law. If the NLRB finds a violation, it can issue a "cease and desist" order to the employer. Continuing refusal to obey results in the NLRB taking the employer to federal court to enforce the order.

In spite of the legal requirement to bargain in good faith, a lot of newly certified unions are unable to negotiate a contract. Of 2,656 union representation elections held in 1970, nearly a quarter of the units where unions were certified did not have a contract five years later.[17] Some units had decertified their union, some employers had gone out of business, and other unions had simply become inactive. Most of the unsuccessful unions in this study were small (fewer than 100 members). Another study restricted to larger-size bargaining units (over 100 employees) found that 63 percent obtained contracts within three years after the election, but only 56 percent were able to get a second contract.[18] Again, firms move or go out of business, unions get decertified or simply lapse into inactivity.

A study by Cooke examined the reasons why so many unions fail to negotiate a first contract.[19] He found that employer discrimination against union activists—mostly firings—and refusal by employers to bargain have substantial negative effects on the likelihood of obtaining a first contract. Even though employers are legally required to bargain, they can delay by throwing up legal challenges. A fledgling union rarely has the resources to fight or wait out these delaying tactics. However, when bargaining units are large and cohesive, and when national union representatives participate in the process, first contracts are more likely obtained. So, employers, in effect, don't bargain unless the union has the strength to force the issue.

EXHIBIT 16.6   Labor Contract: Seniority Clause

Section 1: Seniority Recognition
  A. Seniority is defined as length of service within the bargaining unit from the most recent date of hire. Length of service is defined as the length of employment with the company from the most recent date of hire.
  B. An employee shall be considered probationary during the first ninety (90) working days of employment. Such period may be extended for thirty (30) additional working days for illness only, by endorsement of the employee's work record and notification to the union of such extension. During the period of probationary employment, the company shall be the sole judge of the employee's qualification for continued employment without recourse to the grievance and arbitration procedure under this Agreement. Upon successful completion of the probationary period, the employee's seniority shall date back to the most recent date of hire.

Section 2: Promotion
  A. All job vacancies as indicated on the promotional chart will be posted on the bulletin boards, and any employee may apply for a job vacancy, as defined in paragraph B of this Section.
  B. There are three (3) types of job vacancies.
  "Type A"—Job will be awarded to the most qualified of the four (4) most senior applicants from the work group who are willing to accept the job.
  "Type B"—Job will be awarded to the most qualified of the two (2) most senior applicants from the work group who are willing to accept the job.
  "Type C"—Jobs in the Miscellaneous Work Group and entry level jobs will be awarded to the most senior bidding employee.

  Before a Type A or Type B job is posted for bid, employees with recall rights to such jobs must be recalled. This includes internal displacement as well as actual recall from layoff.

Bargaining Structures

A local union may be part of a national or even international union. There are also employer organizations. Thus, the parties negotiating a contract may not be single employers or single unions. For example, an *employer group,* such as the Bituminous Coal Owners Association, may negotiate with a single union, such as the United Mine Workers, or with several unions—United Mine Workers and Union Operating Engineers. *Multiemployer bargaining* is common in such industries as construction, trucking, and garment manufacturing, where large national unions face many small employers. *Coalition bargaining* involves several unions negotiating with a single employer. For example, the International Union of Electrical, Radio and Machine Workers (IUE), the United Auto Workers (UAW), and the United Electricians (UE) negotiate as a coalition with General Electric Company. These alternative structures result from one or the other parties to the negotiation trying to gain an advantage over the other.

Another way of gaining advantage is by *pattern bargaining*. Pattern bargaining is the use of a settlement in one setting as the "target" in another setting. Pattern bargaining was common into the 1970s, but it has declined in the 1980s, as local bargaining issues or problems have gained in importance over national agendas.[20]

Formalizing the Contract

An agreement comes about when both sides feel they have produced the best contract they can. Their perceptions are influenced by the negotiations, their relative power at the time, and other factors. Power factors, such as a weak union or a strong employer, are very important in the settlement of the contract.

After the two sides have tentatively agreed, the union leadership must receive the membership's support. The members must ratify the contract. Ratification is not automatic and union negotiators must keep an eye toward membership ratifications or the negotiation process will have to be repeated.[21]

The agreement or contract sets out the rules of the job for the contract period. It restricts some behavior and requires other behavior. Proper wording of the agreement can prevent future difficulties in interpretation. Both sides should thoroughly discuss the meaning of each clause to prevent misunderstanding, if possible.

Even if the contract is accepted at one level, it may require adjustments at other levels. For example, when Ford Motor Company signs a contract with the UAW at the national level, local plants must then settle disputes on work rules and other issues at each plant. Only when these are settled is the contract negotiation process over for a while.

IMPASSES IN COLLECTIVE BARGAINING

The description of contract negotiation above suggests a smooth flow, from presentation of demands to settlement. This flow is not always so smooth; impasses may develop that do not allow one or both sides to keep the process moving. Three things can happen when an impasse develops: conciliation or mediation, a strike or lockout, or arbitration.

Conciliation and Mediation

Conciliation or *mediation* is the process by which a professional, neutral third party is invited in by both parties to help remove an impasse to the contract negotiations.

All experts agree that it is better for the two parties to negotiate alone. When it appears this process has broken down, however, they can invite in a mediator, usually a government mediator, such as those provided by the Federal Mediation and Conciliation Service (FMCS). Some states also offer mediation services to both sides. FMCS offers such services as developing factual data if the two sides disagree, setting up joint study committees on difficult points, or trying to help the two sides find common grounds for further bilateral negotiations. Instead of waiting until an impasse, the FMCS also offers preventive mediation when the two parties anticipate serious problems prior to deadlines for strikes.

In general, fact-finding appears to work best when the negotiators are inexperienced and to be least effective when major differences exist between the expectations of each party to the dispute.

Mediators have no power to compel the two sides to reach an agreement. Instead, they seek to persuade employers and unions that it is in their best interests to reach an agreement without resorting to a strike.

Strikes and Lockouts

If an impasse in negotiations is quite serious, a strike or lockout can take place.

A *strike* is a refusal by employees to work. A *lockout* is a refusal by management to allow employees to work.

Strikes can be categorized by the objectives they seek. A *contract* strike occurs when management and the union cannot agree on terms of a new contract. More than 90 percent of strikes are contract strikes.

A *grievance* strike occurs when the union disagrees on how management is interpreting the contract or handling day-to-day problems, such as discipline. Strikes over grievances are prohibited in about 95 percent of contracts, but they occur fairly frequently in mining, transportation, and construction industries.

A *jurisdictional* strike takes place when two or more unions disagree on which jobs should be organized by each union. The Taft-Hartley Act gives the NLRB the power to settle these issues, and unions also have internal methods for settling them.

About 1 percent of strikes are *recognition* strikes. These occur as a strategy to force an employer to accept the union. *Political* strikes take place to influence government policy and are extremely rare in the United States.

Strikes differ, too, in the percentage of employees who refuse to work. A *total* strike takes place when all unionized employees walk out; if only a percentage of the workers does so, the result may be a partial strike, semistrike, or slowdown. In a *slowdown,* all employees come to work but they do little work; the union insists on all work rules being followed to the letter, with the result that output slows down. This is also called "working to the contract." This old tactic is being used with increasing frequency, as an alternative to a total strike, because many employers are simply replacing striking workers with new hires.[22] In a *partial strike,* many employees strike but others come to work. This type is especially prevalent in the public sector so essential services can be continued.

Public employees in the federal sector and in almost half of the states do not have the right to strike. Instead, impasses in negotiating contracts that cannot be resolved through mediation go to arbitration. However, arbitration is rarely used in negotiations in the private sector in the United States, although it is part of the contract administration process. Some countries do not make this sharp distinction between contract negotiation and contract administration. Their laws specify arbitration, rather than strikes, as the way to resolve any breakdowns in negotiations.

Anatomy of a strike   For a strike to take place, both sides must make decisions. Management must decide it can afford to "take a strike"; that is, it has built up its inventories, has sufficient financial resources, feels it will not lose too many customers during a strike, and believes it can win. The union must believe it will win more than it loses, that the employer will not go out of business, and that management will not replace the union employees with permanent replacements. The union members must be willing to live with hardships and worries about *no* paychecks and be willing to give the union a strike vote. When members give the union the authority to strike, its bargaining hand is strengthened, and it can time the strike to occur when it will hurt management the most.

During the strike, the union sets up the legally allowed number of pickets at the plants and tries to mobilize support among allies in other unions and the public.

What does management do if there is a strike? Lockouts are rarely used. In general, it tries to encourage the workers to return to work by advertising circulars, phone calls, and so on. The longer the strike, the harder it is on the strikers. If the union has only limited strike funds and workers' savings run out, a back-to-work movement can cause the strike to collapse. In recent years, management has tended to play a defensive "wait them out" game and to keep operating during a strike. Nonunionized employees, such as white-collar workers and managers, may try to keep things going, and, if management goes on the offensive, it can hire replacements or threaten to close the plant. A strike ends when both sides return to the bargaining table, or the weaker side gives in.

Who Strikes—And Why?

The threat of a strike is a powerful weapon. Managers need to assess the likelihood of a strike occurring. While only a small proportion of scheduled negotiations end in strikes, several factors correlate with the likelihood of a strike. Research shows that a strike is most likely if both sides are perceived to have equal strength, or that both sides will be hurt equally by a strike. If the sides are not equal, the weaker side is forced to submit to the demands of the other, so no strike will occur. If an industry is booming, an employer gives in to union demands, rather than losing production during a strike. If a local geographic area is booming (a tight local labor market), strikes increase because workers know they cannot be easily replaced, yet they may be able to pick up other jobs themselves. So, economically, it is a question of one side having more to lose than the other.

Organization conditions have a tremendous effect on the likelihood of a strike. Interestingly, the *variability* of the employer's profitability, rather than the *level* of profitability, affects strike activity.[23] If profit levels are volatile, both the incidence and duration of strikes increase. Perhaps this is because the uncertainty of the profit picture makes management less willing to make concessions and makes employees less confident in the competence of management.

The organization condition that appears to make the biggest difference in strike frequency is, not surprisingly, the quality of employee relations.[24] Employee relations is not only for nonunion employees. Dealing with union leadership is not the same as dealing with employees. Many employers learn this lesson the hard way. For example, the Timken Company negotiated a contract with United Steelworkers of America leadership in the fall of 1981. Union leaders confidently made many concessions, in return for which the company pledged to build its new $500 million steel plant in Canton, Ohio, rather than in the Sunbelt. But the union failed to present the pact effectively, and its membership rejected the contract.

Then Timken mounted a communications program aimed at rank-and-file members and their families. They held face-to-face meetings and also used newspapers and radio talk shows. The company encouraged employees and their spouses to ask questions, and it even set up an information hotline. The original proposal was resubmitted to the membership several weeks later, and this time it was ratified by a 10-to-1 vote.

One study compared differences between 28 companies that had experienced strikes and 28 unionized similar "nonstrike" companies.[25] In the strike companies, supervisors made no effort to resolve problems before they blossomed into formal grievances that took a long time to settle. Although both strike and nonstrike plants used overtime, the strike plants made overtime compulsory and made little effort to assist employees with the attendant family and job conflicts that inevitably resulted. In contrast, the nonstrike plants attempted to mitigate the unpleasant aspects of working long hours, and management and union leadership met periodically but informally. The study concluded that "most strikes have little to do with money or benefits. Workers vote for a strike only when they are frustrated because their needs, wants, and ideas go unheard, unheeded, or unanswered." Nonstrike plants established a quality of trust through demonstration of good intentions. Unfortunately, trust does not lend itself to statistical reports. Therefore, it is easy for managers to place more emphasis on labor costs or hours worked when analyzing human resources, because these factors are readily quantifiable. The nonquantifiable factors are too easily overlooked.

CONTRACT ADMINISTRATION

The labor contract governs the day-to-day employment relationships; it is a living document. The union steward and the supervisor are the principal interpreters and enforcers of the contract. Differences in interpretation are resolved through the grievance process. The grievance process is a mechanism for employees to voice their disagreement with the way the contract is administered; hence it is a key part of administering the contract. The ability to provide a channel for grievances is a key selling point for union organizers.

A *grievance* is a formal dispute between an employee and management on the conditions of employment.

Grievances arise because of (1) differing interpretations of the contract by employees, stewards, and management; (2) a violation of a contract provision; (3) violation of law; (4) a violation of work procedures or other precedents; or (5) perceived unfair treatment of an employee by management. The rate of grievances may increase when employees are dissatisfied or frustrated on their jobs or they resent the supervisory style, or because the union is using grievances as a tactic against management.[26] Grievances may also be due to unclear contractual language or employees with personal problems or who are otherwise "difficult."

The U.S. Department of Labor has found that the most frequent incidents that lead to the filing of a grievance are employee discipline, seniority decisions at promotion or layoff time, work assignment, management rights, and compensation and benefits.[27]

The grievance process has at least three purposes and consequences. First, by settling smaller problems early, it may prevent larger problems from occurring in the future. Second, properly analyzed, grievances serve as a source of data to focus the attention of the two parties on ambiguities in the contract for negotiation at a future date. Finally, the grievance process is an effective communication channel from employees to management.[28]

Steps in the Grievance Process

The employee grievance process involves a systematic set of steps for handling an employee complaint. Most union contracts provide the channels and mechanisms for processing these grievances, though the process varies with the contract.

1. *Initiation of the formal grievance.* An employee who feels mistreated or believes that some action or application of policy violates rights in the contract files a grievance with the supervisor. It can be done in writing or (at least initially) orally. The grievance can be formulated with the help and support of the union steward. If the steward feels no grievance has occurred, the process ends here. Most grievances are settled among the steward, the employee, and the supervisor.

The supervisor must attempt to accurately determine the reason for the grievance. The effective approach is to try to solve the problem, rather than assess blame or find excuses. The supervisor should consider what the contract says as modified by the employer's policies and past precedents in such cases. When the supervisor has a good working relationship with the steward, they can work together to settle the problem at that level.

2. *Department head or unit manager.* If the steward, supervisor, and employee together cannot solve the grievance, it goes to the next level in the hierarchy. At this point, the grievance must be presented in writing, and both sides must document their cases.

3. *Arbitration.* If the grievance cannot be settled at this intervening step (or steps), an independent arbitrator may be called in to settle the issue.

Arbitration

◆

Arbitration is the process by which two parties to a dispute agree in advance of the hearing to abide by the decision of an independent quasijudge called an *arbitrator*. In the United States, arbitration is typically used to settle grievance issues arising from contract *administration*. Bargaining impasse arbitration is only used in the public sector, where strikes are illegal.

No other topic in labor relations has more confusing jargon and labels. Arbitration refers to a process that ends in a *decision,* not a recommendation. Exhibit 16.7 clarifies the different forms of arbitration. Under voluntary arbitration, the parties agree to submit their differences to arbitration, whereas under compulsory arbitration the law requires the parties' impasses to be submitted to arbitration. Compulsory arbitration in the United States is common only in the

EXHIBIT 16.7   The Terminology of Alternative Forms of Arbitration

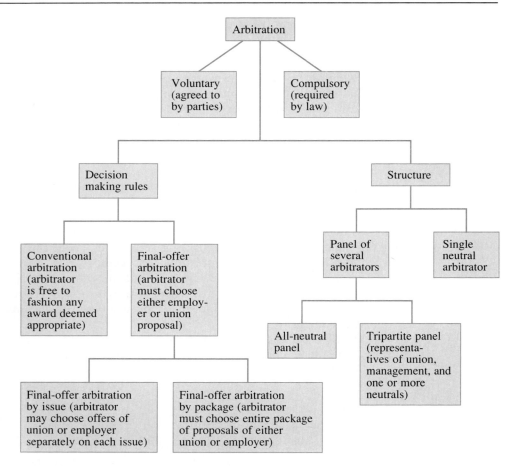

Source: Adapted from Thomas Kochan, *Collective Bargaining and Industrial Relations* (Homewood, Ill.: Richard D. Irwin, 1980), p. 290.

public sector, where employees may be legally forbidden to strike. Australia and some other countries specify compulsory arbitration for all labor disputes; no one has the right to strike. In these circumstances, arbitration resolves disputes arising from contract administration *and* contract negotiation.

Under conventional arbitration, the arbitrator is free to generate any resolution that seems appropriate. Final-offer arbitration requires the arbitrator to choose either the employer's or the union's last proposal. Arbitrators may deal with a single issue or the total contract, and it may be done by a single individual or by a panel of arbitrators.

After hearing all the evidence, the arbitrator writes the arbitration award, which is binding on both parties. The award normally reviews the facts in the case prior to stating the decision and usually is presented within 30 days of the hearing. The arbitrator writes the award in language understandable to all parties concerned, including the employee involved in a grievance. The award attempts to clarify the situation to prevent future problems from arising. The arbitrator usually looks over previous arbitration awards in similar cases but need not be bound by them.

More than 75 percent of grievances are settled at the first step and another 20 percent are settled at the second.[29] Only about 1 percent go to arbitration. Studies of the personal characteristics of those who have filed grievances, as contrasted with those who have not, revealed some differences. In general, those who filed grievances were younger, had more formal education, and got more wage increases. One study found gender differences in the handling of grievances: female employees are more likely to have disciplinary actions overturned than are male.[30] Of course, all these characteristics are probably secondary to the role of the union steward. The steward functions as a "gatekeeper" who can either encourage employees to file grievances (or even file in their behalf). Or the steward can seek to resolve problems informally, in consultation with management.

Handling grievances is time consuming and expensive for both unions and management. A study of 15 grievances that went to arbitration and 15 that were taken only to informal mediation found that management and the union spent only a third as much money on mediation as on arbitration, and both spent less time in preparation for mediation.[31] Neither side showed a high level of dissatisfaction with mediation, though the two sides reported differing levels of satisfaction: The employee who filed the grievance and the union representatives were more satisfied with mediation than were the management representatives. Mediation resolved 11 of the 15 grievances. Those that were unresolved proceeded to binding arbitration, as specified in the union contract. So the sooner and more informally grievances or just complaints or inquiries can be handled, the better.

SUMMARY

Many employees feel managers will be more responsive to their concerns if they join together to form a union. Unions can often negotiate better conditions of work and pay than can individual employees. Unions can also protect members from arbitrary actions of supervisors and managers.

Although few employers invite a union to organize workers, most labor/management relationships evolve to a position of mutual respect. However, managers have become more active and successful in resisting union organizing activities lately; in fact, their resistance is sometimes seen as a major factor in the decline in union membership.

If a union is certified, then union and management representatives begin the collective bargaining process. Collective bargaining involves both contract negotiation and administration. If the parties disagree during the negotiations, mediation may help them. If not, a strike or lockout may result. If the parties disagree about contract administration, the arbitration process provides a means to resolve the issue.

Although it does not always live up to its potential, collective bargaining can provide the forum for a tremendous flexibility in labor/management relations. Contracts are revised on a regular schedule, and employees and employers can structure the contract to suit their particular objectives.

The next chapter continues the discussion of labor relations. It examines the present status of unions in the United States and in the world, and their structure. It also discusses the variety of organization strategies for dealing with unions.

DISCUSSION AND REVIEW QUESTIONS

1. Which factors seem to influence the outcome of a union certification election?
2. Contrast different methods of dispute settlement.
3. What changes in collective bargaining legislation could be made to encourage union growth? Do you think such changes are a good idea?
4. What determines whether an issue is negotiable?
5. Why is the definition of a bargaining unit important?
6. Why did the doctrine of "criminal conspiracy" last so long?
7. Do you believe present labor law is equitable to both labor and management?
8. How might the two-tier wage system be incompatible with the Equal Pay Act? How would you resolve any difficulties?
9. How does a collectively bargained grievance procedure differ from those discussed in the previous chapter?
10. It has been proposed that only lawyers certified by the government be permitted to arbitrate labor cases. Do you agree with this proposal? Why or why not?

◆

YOUR TURN
ARBITRATING A GRIEVANCE

Collective bargaining involves examining, discussing, agreeing on, and maintaining the employment relationship. Balancing the rights of employees, management, and the public is no easy matter, given the differing objectives of the parties. This inevitable conflict is best and most frequently displayed in grievance arbitration.

In 1981, arbitrator Adolph Koven decided on the following issue: "Was the grievant discharged from employment for just cause?" The grievant was a member of Local 670 Rubber Workers, who had been employed for 13 years by Armstrong Rubber.

He was discharged for allegedly (1) being intoxicated at work, (2) damaging machinery, and (3) threatening a supervisor. Company witnesses testified that grievant was wobbly and incoherent, stumbled against a machine which caused extensive damage, and threatened to "cause trouble" for a foreman. Grievant testified that he had had nothing to drink for four hours prior to his shift and nothing during the shift, that the machine simply malfunctioned, and that he told the foreman, "The only thing you can do is stir up a bunch of trouble." Other union witnesses corroborated grievant's testimony.

Koven began by noting that it is the company's burden to prove both that an offense was committed and that it warrants discharge. If you were Koven, what kind of evidence would you look for? How would you evaluate the evidence? What would you decide?

This exercise was written by Joseph Salamone, SUNY Buffalo.

NOTES AND REFERENCES

1. Claudia Montague, "State of the Unions," *Ithaca Times,* May 10, 1990, pp. 1, 8.
2. Joseph G. Rayback, *A History of American Labor* (New York: Free Press, 1966).
3. John Fossum, *Labor Relations,* 3rd ed. (Plano, Tex.: Business Publications, 1985).
4. Arthur A. Sloane and Fred Witney, *Labor Relations* (Englewood Cliffs, N.J.: Prentice-Hall, 1988).
5. Irving Bernstein, *The Turbulent Years: A History of the American Worker, 1933–1941* (Boston: Houghton Mifflin, 1970).
6. Seymour Martin Lipset, "Comment," *Industrial and Labor Relations Review,* April 1988, pp. 447–49.
7. John E. Abodeely, Randi C. Hammer, and Andrew L. Sandler, *The NLRB and the Appropriate Bargaining Unit* (Philadelphia: Industrial Research Unit, University of Pennsylvania, 1981).
8. Jeanne M. Brett, "Why Employees Want Unions," *Organizational Dynamics,* Spring 1980, pp. 316–32; Cynthia Fukami and Erik W. Larson, "Commitment to Company and Union: Parallel Models," *Journal of Applied Psychology* 69, no. 3 (1984), pp. 367–71; Mary D. Zalesny, "Comparison of Economic and Noneconomic Factors in Predicting Faculty Note Preference in a Union Representation Election," *Journal of Applied Psychology* 70, no. 2 (1985), pp. 243–56; H. G. Heneman III and Marcus H. Sandver, "Predicting the Outcome of Union Certification Elections," *Industrial and Labor Relations* 36 (1983), pp. 537–59.
9. William T. Dickens and Jonathan S. Leonard, "Accounting for the Decline in Union Membership," 1984, National Bureau of Economic Research, 1050 Massachusetts Ave., Cambridge, Mass. 02138.
10. Monty L. Lynn and Jozell Brister, "Trends in Union Organizing Issues and Tactics," *Industrial Relations,* Winter 1989, pp. 104–13.
11. John J. Lawler and Robin West, "Impact of Union Avoidance Strategy in Representation Elections," *Industrial Relations,* Fall 1985, pp. 406–20.
12. Richard B. Freeman, "The Effect of the Union Wage Differential on Management Opposition and Union Organizing Success," *American Economics Association Papers and Proceedings,* May 1986, pp. 92–108; Barry T. Hirsch and John T. Addison, *Economic*

Analysis of Labor Unions—New Approaches and Evidence (Boston: Allen & Unwin, 1986).

13. Sanford M. Jacoby and Daniel J. B. Mitchell, "Development of Contractual Features of the Union-Management Relationship," *Proceedings of the Industrial Relations Research Association, Spring Meeting,* April 28–30, 1982, pp. 512–17; Carl Gersuny, "Origins of Seniority Provisions in Collective Bargaining," *Proceedings of the Industrial Relations Research Association, Spring Meeting,* April 28–30, 1982, pp. 518–23.

14. Lee Balliet, "Labor Solidarity and the Two-Tier Collective Bargaining Agreement," Paper presented at the IRRA Meetings, Dallas, Texas, December 30, 1984; M. Schuster, *Union–Management Cooperation: Structure, Process, and Implementation* (Kalamazoo, Mich.: W. E. Upjohn Institute for Employment Research, 1984).

15. Peter Cappelli and Peter D. Sherer, "Satisfaction, Market Wages and Labor Relations: An Airline Study," *Industrial Relations,* Winter 1988.

16. *Teamsters* v. *United States,* 431 U.S., 324 (1977); *Memphis Fire Department* v. *Stotts,* No. 82–206 (Decided June 12, 1984). For a discussion of seniority and affirmative action, see Louis P. Britt III, "Affirmative Action: Is There Life After *Stotts?*" *Personnel Administrator,* September 1984, pp. 96–100; and Lawrence Z. Lorber, "Employers Should Not Take Precipitous Action in Affirmative Action Cases," *Personnel Administrator,* September 1984, pp. 101–2.

17. Richard Prosten, "The Longest Season: Union Organizing in the Last Decade," *Proceedings of the Industrial Relations Research Association,* Winter 1979, pp. 240–49.

18. Charles McDonald, "Study of the Success in Obtaining Contracts after Winning an NLRB Election and after Obtaining a Bargaining Order," memorandum to the National Organizing Committee of the AFL–CIO, February 18, 1983. The study covered elections conducted in April 1979 through March 1981.

19. William N. Cooke, "The Failure to Negotiate First Contracts: Determinants and Policy Implications," *Industrial and Labor Relations Review,* January 1985, pp. 163–78.

20. Sloane and Witney, *Labor Relations.*

21. Peter F. Drucker, "Are Unions Becoming Irrelevant?" *The Wall Street Journal,* September 22, 1982, p. 34.

22. Alex Kotlowiz, "Finding Strikes Harder to Win, More Unions Turn to Slowdowns," *The Wall Street Journal,* May 22, 1987, pp. 1, 8.

23. Joseph S. Tracy, "An Investigation into the Determinants of U.S. Strike Activity," *The American Economics Review,* June 1986, pp. 423–36.

24. Tom Kochan, Robert McKersie, and Harry Katz, *The Transformation of American Industrial Relations* (New York: Basic Books, 1986); Dennis Maki, "The Effect of the Cost of Strikes on the Volume of Strike Activity," *Industrial and Labor Relations Review,* July 1986, pp. 552–63.

25. Woodruff Imberman, "Who Strikes—And Why?" *Harvard Business Review,* November–December 1983, pp. 18–24.

26. Thomas A. Kochan, Mordechai Mironi, Ronald G. Ehrenberg, Jean Baderschneider, and Todd Jick, *Dispute Resolution under Factfinding and Arbitration: An Empirical Analysis* (New York: American Arbitration Association, 1979); Stephen B. Goldberg and Jeanne M. Brett, "An Experiment in the Mediation of Grievances," *Monthly Labor Review,* March 1983, pp. 23–30.

27. *Federal Mediation and Conciliation Service, Thirty-Sixth Annual Report, Fiscal Year 1983* (Washington, D.C.: U.S. Government Printing Office, 1984).

28. David Meyer and William N. Cooke, "Economic and Political Factors in Formal Grievance Resolution," *Industrial Relations,* pp. 318–35; "Avoiding the Arbitrator:

Some New Alternatives to the Grievance Procedure," *Proceedings, 30th Annual Meeting Washington, D.C.: National Academy of Arbitrators,* 1977; Steven Briggs, "Beyond the Grievance Procedure: Factfinding in Employee Complaint Resolution," *Proceedings of the Industrial Relations Research Association, Spring Meeting,* April 1982, pp. 454–58; Mollie H. Bowers, Ronald L. Seeber, and Lamont E. Stallworth, "Grievance Mediation: A Route to Resolution for the Cost-Conscious 1980s," *Proceedings of the Industrial Relations Research Association, Spring Meeting,* April 1982, pp. 459–63.

29. Dan R. Dalton and William D. Todor, "Antecedents of Grievance Filing Behavior: Attitude/Behavioral Consistency and the Union Steward," *Academy of Management Journal* 25, no. 1 (1982), pp. 158–60.

30. Dan R. Dalton and William D. Todor, "Gender and Workplace Justice: A Field Assessment," *Personnel Psychology* 38 (1985), pp. 133–51; Dan R. Dalton and William D. Todor, "Composition of Dyads as a Factor in the Outcomes of Workplace Justice: Two Field Assessments," *Academy of Management Journal* 28, no. 3 (1985), pp. 704–12. Brian Bemmels, "Gender Effects in Discharge Arbitration," *Industrial and Labor Relations Review,* October 1988, pp. 63–76.

31. Sylvia Skratek, *Grievance Mediation of Contractual Disputes in Washington State Public Education* (Federal Way, Wash.: Washington Education Association, 1986).

CHAPTER SEVENTEEN

Labor Relations Objectives and Evaluation

Labor Relations Objectives
Union Suppression
Maintain Union-Free Status
Collaboration

Why Employees Join Unions

The Union Organization

Union Strategies
Involvement in Employer's Strategic Decisions
Cooperative Programs
Alternative Forms of Representation

Public Sector Unions

Labor Relations in Other Countries

Interaction of Business, Labor,
and Government

Evaluating the Effects of Labor Relations
Activities
Efficiency: Union Impact on Wages
Efficiency: Union Impact on Productivity
Equity: Union Impact on Employees' Voice

Your Turn: Play or Pay

"Even hardcore union activists had to admire the success of Nissan's tactics."[1] When a bitter 18-month-long union campaign ended in July 1989, the 2,400 hourly workers at the Smyrna, Tennessee, plant rejected the United Auto Workers (UAW) by better than two to one.

In the final weeks of the campaign, Nissan showed videotapes of strike violence and called the UAW a disruptive outsider that was ineffective in preventing layoffs in the plants it already represents. Focus groups of 10 to 15 employees, from which suspected union sympathizers were excluded, were told that the union was a threat to the existing atmosphere of team work and workplace flexibility.

The union alleges that Nissan's union avoidance strategy began even earlier, with psychological screening prior to hiring. "Nissan's psychologists identified people who would be very pliable, and very acceptable to company authority."[2]

In fact, the union avoidance strategy probably predates hiring. The location of the plant itself—in a southern state with a right-to-work law—is consistent with a union-avoidance strategy, as is Nissan's pay plan: higher than the prevailing manufacturing wage in the region, plus better benefits.

But the UAW will likely be back. It has already successfully organized three "transplants"—Japanese-owned facilities operating in the United States. Union watchers feel the UAW will try to encircle the Smyrna plant by organizing auto workers at major plants in surrounding states and then target the smaller employers whose products go into Nissan automobiles.[3]

Additionally, the pressure on Nissan will continue. During the 1989 Smyrna campaign, the UAW alleged that injury rates there were as high as 20 percent of the employees, due to assembly line speedups. Nissan refused to allow union representatives to examine the plant's injury logs, which, according to federal regulation, are supposed to be available to any worker. The Tennessee safety and health board fined Nissan $5,000 for this refusal, but Nissan has appealed.

The UAW vows to continue to watch this issue and support the 711 Nissan employees who voted for the union. A spokesman calls the loss a delay, rather than a defeat. "We didn't organize General Motors or Ford overnight. We learned a long time ago that one vote does not an election—or a union— make."[4]

Smyrna illustrates a number of issues relevant to understanding the current status of the union movement in the United States. Membership is declining, as jobs have slipped away from the traditional U.S. auto and steel manufacturers, who are heavily unionized. Additionally, many employers are taking steps to avoid and even get rid of unions. This chapter discusses actions an employer may take to reach its objectives for labor relations. We also discuss why employees join unions, how unions operate, and union strategies for labor relations. After that, we evaluate the results of labor relations activities.

EXHIBIT 17.1   Union Membership as a Percentage of the Nonagricultural Labor Force, 1930–1990

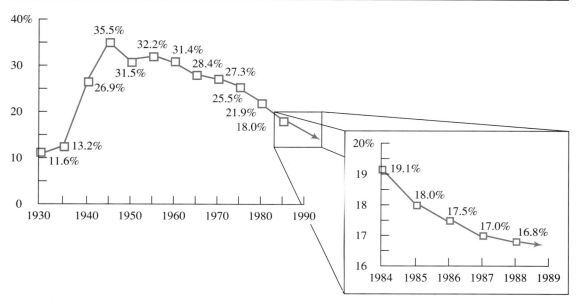

Source: *Employment & Earnings,* January 1990.

LABOR RELATIONS OBJECTIVES

Exhibit 17.1 shows the long decline in union membership. In 1957, one out of every three nonagricultural worker was a union member. Today, the figure is one in six. There are a number of reasons postulated for the decline: an economic restructuring that shifted jobs away from heavy manufacturing, greater employer resistance, and a work force whose expectations changed faster than unions could accommodate them. However, many people believe that a major cause of the decline is a change in organization objectives. More and more employers have made remaining (or becoming) nonunion part of their business strategy, and they have taken human resource actions consistent with this strategy.

Union Suppression

Some employers view a move by workers to organize as a personal challenge. Often they believe they have been a benevolent employer, betrayed by ungrateful employees. They may also believe that a union will constrain their flexibility

EXHIBIT 17.2   Employer Unfair Labor Practices against Unions, and Number of NLRB
Representation Elections, 1950–1980

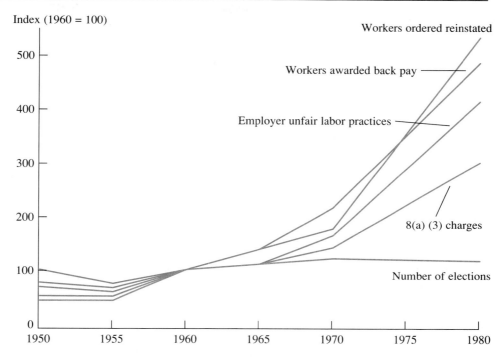

Source: National Labor Relations Board, *Annual Reports,* 1950–1980.

and thus their ability to operate effectively. For whatever reason, murmurs of
organizing are viewed as a call to battle.

Anti-union tactics include a variety of actions, not all of which are legal. The
most extreme behavior is to fire employees who are perceived to be union activists. While such a move is clearly and absolutely illegal, it unfortunately continues to occur. There is even some evidence that it is becoming more
common.[5] Exhibit 17.2 shows that, from 1968 to 1980, the number of all employer unfair labor practices charges rose fourfold, and the number of workers
awarded back pay or ordered reinstated to their jobs rose fivefold. The reason
for this increase may be that the penalties for such activity are slight. If the
NLRB rules that an employee was illegally fired for union activity, the employer must reinstate the worker and pay any difference between wages the
worker would have earned absent the firing, and wages actually earned.

But the appeals process takes time. It may be several years before the union
activist is back. This delay typically works to the employer's advantage and so

makes many of them willing to run the risk. The payoffs of remaining nonunion are viewed as greater than the financial penalties of illegal behavior.

During an organizing campaign, employers may launch a communication campaign. They try to convince employees that, not only is a union not necessary, it will actually be harmful because of union dues, possible strike, subservience to union officials, and the like. It is illegal for an employer to promise future benefits in return for voting against a union or to threaten election result consequences.

In addition to communicating with employees, employer tactics include delaying the organizing campaign. Some research shows that delaying the organizing campaign works in the employer's favor, though other studies found it made no difference.[6] The employer may delay by objecting to the proposed makeup of the bargaining unit. For example, when the United Auto Workers sought to organize technicians at Cornell University, the union defined the bargaining unit as those technicians in the Ithaca, New York, area. But Cornell insisted that agriculture school employees who conduct drug tests at race tracks across the state also be included. To include them would hinder the union campaign, because it would be impractical for union organizers to expend money and effort trying to secure their vote. Their inclusion could potentially dilute union strength. In this case, the NLRB ruled that technicians in the Ithaca area were an appropriate bargaining unit; and the UAW did win the right to represent them. However, challenging the bargaining unit definition can delay the organizing process, and it frequently allows the employer time to mount a more effective communication campaign.

Once employees decide to join a union, some employers still refuse to accept it. Although they are legally required to bargain with union representatives, they may try to get the union decertified through another election.

Or, employers may refuse to sign a labor agreement. Recall from the previous chapter that, even though they are required to "bargain in good faith," it can be a long way to a signed first contract.[7]

Maintain a Union-Free Status

Many employers who are not unionized make it an objective to maintain a union-free status.

In Chapter Fifteen, we acknowledged that employee relations programs may be motivated in part by such a desire.[8] Such programs have the objective of demonstrating concern and respect for employees and giving them substantial control over their work lives. The philosophy here is that "employees do not need a union, they are part of the organization which is as fair and equitable as possible." Nissan told employees the UAW was a threat to the existing workplace atmosphere.

A number of organization conditions appear to be related to whether or not a union is present. Three important ones are the location and size of the facility and the nature of the work.

Plant Location

In the United States, union membership is concentrated geographically. New York is the most highly organized state, with almost half of its nonfarm workers in unions or associations. Michigan, West Virginia, and Pennsylvania follow. In contrast, the southern states have relatively few union members and share a strong anti-union bias. For example, union membership in South Carolina is around 6 percent. Southern textile companies were infamous for their resistance to union organizers. A study of private sector clerical workers correlated organizing success with the strength of union presence in the state.[9] However, there was a negative correlation with the statewide level of strike activity.

Within a geographic region, small towns or the outskirts of large cities are also viewed as less favorable for unions.

Plant Size

For a number of reasons, including technical and economic, many companies have shifted from large, centralized organizations to smaller business units with more independence from the corporate headquarters. The smaller size gives organizations greater flexibility to respond quickly to market changes. Smaller plants are also less likely to be unionized. Perhaps their size and multiple locations make it less cost effective for an outside union to mount an organizating campaign.

Nature of the Work

Some occupations have historically contained a high percentage of union members. Printing is one example; truck driving is another. Some nonunion employers subcontract their own printing and trucking to avoid having printers or truck drivers on their payroll. By doing so, they hope to reduce the likelihood of a union campaign. If subcontracting is not possible, some employers go to great lengths to ensure that its employees in those occupations enjoy wages, benefits, and working conditions that are directly comparable to those earned by union members doing the same jobs for different organizations.

Union membership also varies among industries. Over one third of federal, state, and local government employees, and transportation, communications, and public utilities employees are union members—twice the national average.[10] In the services and financial industry groups, less than 8 percent of employees belong to unions. Of 14,000 U.S. banks, just 28 have collective bargaining agreements.[11]

Collaboration

Although labor relations disputes—strikes, violence, and allegations of illegal behavior—capture the attention of the public, the vast majority of contract negotiations and day-to-day administration is done in an atmosphere of mutual respect. If not harmonious, most relationships are at least cooperative, though

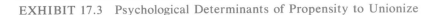

EXHIBIT 17.3   Psychological Determinants of Propensity to Unionize

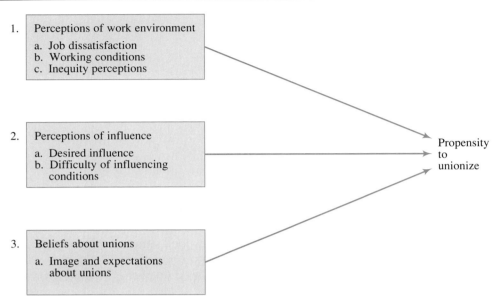

1. Perceptions of work environment
    a. Job dissatisfaction
    b. Working conditions
    c. Inequity perceptions

2. Perceptions of influence
    a. Desired influence
    b. Difficulty of influencing
       conditions

3. Beliefs about unions
    a. Image and expectations
       about unions

Propensity to unionize

Source: Thomas Kochan, *Collective Bargaining and Industrial Relations* (Homewood, Ill.: Richard D. Irwin, 1980), p. 144.

some employers do not become cooperative until they have exhausted all other possibilities. "Resigned to the inevitable" may be more descriptive.

A more positive approach is collaboration, in which "management attempts to improve labor/management relations through joint union/management committees, employee involvement, and, in a few cases, giving union leaders input into strategic business decisions."[12]

Which objective—union avoidance, maintain union-free status, or collaboration—or mix of objectives, is most common? It's a safe bet that almost all non-unionized firms in the United States prefer to remain so. They believe that a union will reduce their flexibility in making HR as well as capital decisions. Of those firms that are already unionized, one study found that whether they pursued an avoidance or a collaboration strategy (or a mix of the two) was heavily dependent on market pressures.[13] When the market worsens, as measured by "impact penetration" and industry employment levels, companies are more likely to choose union avoidance. The higher the proportion of plants unionized, the more likely the organization will choose collaboration. So external and organizational conditions clearly affect the choice of a labor relations strategy.

WHY EMPLOYEES JOIN UNIONS

Pragmatically, people join unions if they perceive the benefits to be greater than the costs. At the extreme, potential increases in wages must be greater than the amount of dues paid. Psychologically, however, there are more important reasons for joining. Probably the most important one has to do with gaining control over one's work life.

Thomas Kochan has developed a model, shown in Exhibit 17.3, which summarizes the research on the topic. An individual's decision to join or avoid a union, according to the model, is influenced by three critical determinants.

1. *Perceptions of the work environment.* Dissatisfaction with bread-and-butter aspects of the job, such as wages and benefits, dissatisfaction with supervision, or with the treatment of one group of employees versus another, all can translate into a greater interest in unionism.

2. *Desire to participate or influence* the job and the employment conditions surrounding the job. According to Kochan, a key here is that the lack of other effective alternatives for influence turns employees to unions.

3. *Employee beliefs about unions.* Employees who are dissatisfied have certain expectations about what a union can do for them. If they are predisposed or convinced through organizing efforts that a union will improve their situation, employees are more likely to join.

Why People Don't Join Unions

Some researchers have taken this theme a step further and analyzed why people *don't* join unions. Generally there are three reasons people do not join unions.

1. *They identify with management.* Those who work with or are close to management tend to identify with it and consider the union as an adversary. If they experience job dissatisfaction, however, they will lose this identification and consider joining a union.

2. *They do not agree with the goals of unions.* Other employees may disagree with the objectives of unions politically and organizationally. For example, they may prefer merit to seniority rules, may fear union social or political power, may resent dues paying, and may feel unions interfere in free enterprise and individual initiative.[14]

3. *They see themselves as professionals and unions as inappropriate for professionals.* For years, many employees such as engineers, nurses, teachers, and others saw themselves as independent professionals working for an organization. The concepts of union member and independent professional were viewed as opposites.[15]

The overall conclusion from the research is that there are no substantial differences between people who do and do not join unions. Rather, the work situation seems to make the biggest difference. That is why union organizers sometimes say that employers' personnel practices are the unions' greatest organizing weapon.

Union Jobs

Greg Hundley takes a different approach. Reasoning that most employees join unions because they accept jobs that are part of already organized bargaining units, he focuses on job characteristics and union membership.[16] If union jobs remain so, regardless of who does them, then what are the characteristics that increase the likelihood that a job will be unionized?

Hundley found that the likelihood of unionism depends on what advantage collective action can provide for a specific job over individual bargaining. Where job skills are generalized (e.g., managerial or administrative) or skilled craft, then individuals perceive that their careers will be enhanced through individual negotiation and the external market (i.e., it is relatively easy to switch employers). But where jobs are repetitive and less complex, or when they require training that is occupation-specific (e.g., telephone cable installer), then employees are more likely to perceive an advantage in collective action.

In addition to jobs, there are a number of employee attributes that have long been believed to be related to interest in unionism. For example, women have long been perceived to be more anti-union than men in their outlook.[17] Women have been characterized as not wanting to get involved in the politics of a union, or as less committed to a career and, therefore, more tolerant of unpleasant conditions. Women's increasing commitment to the labor force and unions and an increasing sensitivity to issues of particular concern to many women (pay differentials among jobs, day care, flexible work arrangements, parental leave) have probably changed this perception. Recent surveys are finding that women are more favorably disposed to unions, and union organizers are adjusting strategies to address concerns of women. Even the Teamsters now sponsor conferences on women in the workplace.

A high percentage of professional employees is also perceived as a hindrance to unionization. Professionals have historically been less interested in unions, but, like the attitudes of women, this, too, may be changing.

THE UNION ORGANIZATION

To become a union member in the United States, a person joins one of the 70,000 or so local unions. The local is a subunit of one of the 173 national unions, of which 110 belong to the American Federation of Labor–Congress of Industrial Organizations (AFL–CIO). This federation represents 80 percent of unionized employees. The AFL–CIO provides research, education, lobbying, and public relations services. A number of the larger unions are independent of the AFL–CIO, including the teamsters and the mine workers. Very large unions that are members of the AFL–CIO are steel workers, electrical workers, carpenters, machinists, and hotel and restaurant workers.

National union headquarters provides many services to subsidiary unions: training for regional and local union leaders, organizing help, strike funds, and data to be used in negotiating contracts. Specialists available for consultation include lawyers, public relations specialists, and research personnel. Under the national union are regional groups of local unions, which may provide office space and facilities for local unions.

The keystone of the trade union movement is the local unions, representing all the union members in a geographic area for a craft union (e.g., all carpenters in San Francisco) or in a plant for an industrial union (e.g., UAW members at GM's Saturn plant in Spring Hill, Tennessee). Therefore, our major focus is on the local level.

The Local Union

In general, the local union is a branch of the national union and has little legal autonomy. In many unions, the local must get permission from the national union before it can strike. The national can charter or disband a local, suspend it, or put it under national trusteeship. In Austin, Minnesota, a lengthy and bitter strike at Hormel, the city's largest employer, ended in 1986 with the national removing the local leadership. Local P-9 of the United Food and Commercial Workers' union had rejected a federal mediator's recommended settlement. Hormel hired replacements and resumed operations. When P-9 leadership refused an order from the national union to end the strike, the national union took over the local and ended the strike. The entire community was affected by the strike, and hard feelings continue to persist in the relatively small, rural community.

Union Leaders

Just as there is a great variety in the size and power of nationals, so there is great variety in locals. They vary in size from 8 or so members up to the 40,000 or so members in Local 32-B (New York City) of the Service Employees International Union. The local union elects officials, such as president, secretary-treasurer, business representative, and committee representatives. If the local is large enough, the business representative and secretary-treasurer are full-time employees. The business representative plays a crucial role in contract negotiations and grievances. The president and other officials hold full-time jobs in the trade or industry. Typically, they get some released time for union duties and are paid expenses.

Another local unit personality is the shop steward or job steward. This is equivalent to a first-line supervisor. The steward represents the union on the job site and is charged with handling grievances and disciplinary matters. Normally, the steward is elected by members in the unit for a one-year term. The effectiveness of the local is usually judged in terms of effective grievance handling.

Both employers and unions can be viewed as political entities. But politics are more fundamental to unions.

Union leaders, especially local union leaders, have much less power than their managerial equivalents. They are always subject to reelection, and the contracts they negotiate must be ratified by union members. Members can also keep union leaders in line by voting their union out or by engaging in wildcat strikes. But the union member is typically apathetic about union affairs except in times of crisis, such as the decision to strike. Usually only 10 to 15 percent of the members attend an ordinary union meeting. This gives more freedom and power to the union leader during "normal" times.

In theory, unions are democratic; their members are supposed to influence their policies and decisions. However, the typical union is run by a small percentage of members.

The union leader often has a strong personality and can mobilize the members against the employer. The effective union leader realizes, however, that the demands made by the union must not put the employer out of business. Good union leaders help employers by policing the contract and keeping maverick members in line. The union leader's job should be "to discern, reconcile, and then represent the diverse and often conflicting demands and interests of the membership."[18] This is a significant point—the membership is frequently divided on what it wants. Managers usually exaggerate the power of the local union leader and overlook the pressures that members and union subordinates can apply.

In sum, there is usually more conflict and less power on the union side of the bargaining table. Conflicts within the management side can usually be settled by a decision from higher up the hierarchy. This is less likely in unions.

UNION STRATEGIES

The union movement today is in trouble. In the 1980s, many unions became victims of their successes in the 1950s and 1960s. The appalling working conditions and arbitrary employer behaviors that had gained them public sympathy earlier in this century had vastly improved. Legally, they were no longer the underdog. They had negotiated generous agreements for their members. Good times for employers meant that generous labor settlements could be passed on to consumers in the form of higher prices. A highly structured, formalized relationship between unions and management evolved with detailed contracts enforced through grievance procedures. But the base of the unions' power detailed contract, the uniformity of its administration, the narrow job rules, and the emphasis on stability—were the very factors that constrained employers' ability to respond to the economic dislocation and competition of the 1980s. Formalized procedures that could only be changed through lengthy negotiation made it difficult to react fast enough to changes in external conditions. Exhibit 17.4 shows this rigidity in structures. Comparing work practices among nonunion and union plants within the same firm, the compensation structure is vastly more flexible in new, nonunion plants. For example, the number of job classifications and wage grades is substantially lower. (The chapters on compensation define these terms.) Having fewer numbers of job classifications increase flexibility to the extent that movement of employees to other jobs within the same classification is much easier than movement to a job in another classification. If, for example, "maintenance" workers are separately classified as "electrical maintenance," "plumbing maintenance," "diesel maintenance," and so on, scheduling work for each maintenance employee is more difficult. But if most of the maintenance employees are in the same job classification, then employees can be redeployed according to the demands of the work and their skills.

While the exhibit shows the new, nonunion plant experiencing the greatest degree of flexibility, part of this may be due to plant size and age (e.g., a lot of bureaucracy, like sediment, builds up over time). However, even an old nonunion plant run by this employer had more flexible practices than the union plant. So, unions do appear to constrain an employer's flexibility and speed of response.

However, unions are changing. We can identify three main thrusts to changes many unions are making in the way they interact with employers.

1. Involvement in employer's strategic decisions.
2. Cooperative programs.
3. Alternative forms of representation.

Involvement in Employer's Strategic Decisions

For several years, former UAW president Douglas Fraser was on Chrysler's board of directors. This is the most vivid example of unions' participation in shaping employers' directions. However, this probably was a unique case brought about by the extreme financial distress of Chrysler, and the interest and capabilities of Fraser. A lot of people in and out of the labor movement in the United States remain uncomfortable with such arrangements.[19] They feel they stray too far from the traditional roles of adversarial participants in a capitalistic economic system.

Another way for strategic involvement is through employee stock ownership.[20] Stock ownership programs, by themselves, may give employees equity in the company but may not increase their role in strategic decision making. At the minimum, however, ownership provides employees the ability to vote for the board of directors.

A third way of affecting employer strategy involves enlisting outside allies to exert pressure to change or rescind a decision.[21] There have been several instances of plant closing decisions that were successfully overturned

EXHIBIT 17.4 Comparison of Work Practices in Union and Nonunion Plants of the Same Firm

Work Practices	Type of Plant	
	New Nonunion (N = 3)	Union (N = 3)
Number of job classifications	6	96
Number of wage grades	7	14
Number of maintenance job classifications	1	11
Percent maintenance workers in a "General Maintenance" classification	75%	1%
Supervisors prohibited from doing subordinates' work	No	Yes
Subcontracting occurs only after meeting with union/employees	100%	0%

Source: Anil Verma, "Union and Nonunion Industrial Relations at the Plant Level." Ph.D. dissertation, Sloan School of Management, MIT, 1983.

when coalitions of union and community leaders located new buyers. In New York state, professionals from Cornell's School of Industrial and Labor Relations Extension Service intervened to assist employers and unions change production methods to make old plants more productive, thereby reducing the decline in manufacturing jobs in the state. Other times, unions conduct corporate campaigns to mount public pressure on banks that have financial ties to an employer. They hope to induce the bank, or perhaps members of the board of directors, to put pressure on recalcitrant employers.

Cooperative Programs

Resistance to unions dies hard. Most employers, unless they have no choice, prefer to remain nonunion. If they are only partially unionized, they may try to redirect their business to favor growth in the nonunionized segments, often at the expense of unionized segments.[22] This is what has happened in the airline industry since deregulation. Unionized airlines have been taken over by nonunionized airlines. Planes and routes of the unionized segment are then diverted to support growth of the nonunionized segment of the business.

However, there are examples of union/management cooperation.[23] For example, the Communications Workers of America and AT&T formed a private organization, the Alliance, to help retrain and relocate CWA members whose present jobs are no longer needed in the restructured AT&T. Relocation may be within AT&T, or it may be in other companies. The executive team, drawn equally from the CWA and AT&T, assists the union local and company managers to design training programs and redeployment activities that fit the needs of the location. The team recently was able to successfully place 150 out of 170 eligible long distance operators from AT&T's Springfield, Massachusetts, location.

Union/management cooperation has been the topic of a lot of recent research. The conclusions are similar to that presented on participation programs in the previous chapter: after an initial rush, the high is difficult to sustain. But the greater the union involvement in the *design* of the program, and the more *direct* the involvement (individual union members, rather than committees), the greater the productivity improvements. Avoiding joint participation for fear of negative union effects becomes a self-fulfilling prophecy.[24]

Alternative Forms of Representation

The third union tactic is the least developed thus far. It is driven by the fact that about 28 percent of all nonunionized workers either voted for a union in an unsuccessful organizing campaign or are former union members.[25] Hence, a large reservoir of sympathy exists outside the union membership. This amounts to presumed support that the unions are currently unable to draw on. Present U.S. law requires that a majority of those who vote determine the outcome for the entire bargaining unit. The United States is one of the few countries to have such a requirement. But if legislation was so changed that those employees who wanted a union could have one, even though they constitute a minority in a bargaining unit, the decline in union membership could turn around.

Another alternative is to offer an "associate membership." The purpose of this membership could be to increase awareness of the positive contributions of unions and mobilize support for its political initiatives.[26]

The outlook for unions in the private sector is uncertain. In the early 1980s, unions appeared ready to launch a major drive to organize clerical employees, especially in the insurance and banking industries. But these efforts have had only limited success.

Nevertheless, a Harris poll conducted for the AFL–CIO found that the American public continues to see a need for unions. At the same time, a majority of nonunion workers view unions as unable to make a significant difference. The one third of nonunion employees who do express an interest in union membership face limited prospects of achieving it on their jobs because (1) union organizing activity currently covers less than 1 percent of those eligible to organize, (2) it is unlikely that a majority of a given employee's coworkers will agree that unionization is needed, so they will vote against a union in an election, and (3) employer opposition can substantially reduce the probability of a successful union election.

One segment of the economy that presents a brighter picture for unionism is the public sector.

PUBLIC SECTOR UNIONS

Public sector unions in the United States are relatively recent, although many other countries have had a long experience with them. President John F. Kennedy granted federal employees modified rights to unionize and bargain over nonwage items in 1962. His executive order was soon replaced by the Civil Service Reform Act, which established the Federal Labor Relations Authority (FLRA) to oversee labor/management relations in the federal government. Federal employees still do not have the right to strike or bargain over wages. They do have access to binding arbitration, however.

In 1981, the Professional Air Traffic Controllers Organization (PATCO) called a strike after negotiations broke down. Within hours, President Ronald W. Reagan appeared on national television and gave the workers 48 hours to return to work or be dismissed. About 11,400 of the strikers were dismissed, and PATCO's right to represent them was terminated, because it is also illegal to advocate a work stoppage among federal employees. In 1987, the air traffic controllers formed a new union with new leadership.

Almost all states have passed legislation providing state and local government employees the right to organize and bargain collectively. States with public sector laws tend to be those with a high percentage of unionized private sector employees.[27] States with lower wages and weak organized labor have yet to pass similar laws.

Growth in Public Sector Unionism

Earlier, we said that less than 16 percent of the nonagricultural work force was unionized. But if we separate the private from the public sector, a remarkable picture emerges. While private sector unionism is under 14 percent and shrinking, public sector unionism is over 33 percent—and growing. One study documented a 3 percent higher employment per capita for city and county governments with unions than for those without unions, despite higher compensation in the unionized cities and counties.[28]

Two unique attributes of public employment account for the phenomenal growth.

First is the lack of managerial opposition to union organization. Because public sector employees also are voters, managers who oppose the union run the risk of loosing their own jobs.

Second, the interests of public sector employees and managers frequently overlap. They may be allies in lobbying for increased government spending. Managers may welcome union help in obtaining larger budgets, which translate into employment growth and consequent higher union membership.[29]

LABOR RELATIONS IN OTHER COUNTRIES

As we have seen, labor relations in the United States is intertwined with political and economic history.[30] This is so for other countries, too. Different models have seemed appropriate at different times. After World War II, the United States system of free collective bargaining was considered the model for governments in Western Europe and Japan to follow as they reconstructed their economies and political systems. There was even interest in exporting the U.S. model as part of a larger effort to limit the growth of communism.

In the 1960s, Sweden became the "universal model" of a system that was able to achieve labor peace and one of the highest standards of living in the world.

In the 1970s, some of the credit for West Germany's rise from complete economic, social, and political ruin in the 1940s to one of the world's strongest economies went to its mechanisms for worker participation and to the German government's consultation with labor and business in economic policy making.

By the 1980s, Japan had become the model for producing labor/management consensus and cooperation, steady growth in productivity, high-quality goods, individual worker motivation, and adaptability to the changing world economy. In contrast to its earlier glory, the United States approach to labor relations was under a barrage of criticism as too adversarial, too slow to adapt to the world economy, and unable to respond to employee needs.

This shifting focus provides a caution against assuming that one optimal system exists. Instead, the diagnostic approach may provide guidance: each country's system must fit the unique conditions of its society and adapt over time to changes in those conditions.

Labor relations systems in the United States have been relatively slow to adapt to changes in external factors. Unions (and many organizations, too) have frequently continued to follow policies and practices long after they had become obsolete. The increase in international and multinational organizations provides an opportunity for us to compare innovations in labor relations in other countries.

INTERACTION OF BUSINESS, LABOR, AND GOVERNMENT

According to Kochan and Barocci, differences among labor relations decisions reflect variations in relationships among business, labor, and government. Exhibit 17.5 contrasts variations in relationships among countries. While it vastly simplifies reality, it may provide a framework for understanding differences.

Business/Government Relations

Traditionally, the U.S. government has not assumed an active role in business decision making within firms. European systems, by contrast, have long experience with consultation among business, government, and labor on broad eco-

---

EXHIBIT 17.5   International Contrasts

	Business/Government	Business/Labor	Labor/Government	HR Practices
United States	Government remains neutral in affairs of business.	Job-conscious unions; union and management support capitalist values.	Social welfare benefits left to private sector.	Large assortment of bargaining structures and firm-specialized practices; layoffs, discharges, and plant closings left to private sector.
Japan	Strong links between government and business; government maintains planned economy.	Consultation, rather than negotiation, but not on organizational strategic issues; only on work-floor issues; interprise unions.	Greater government-provided social welfare benefits.	Employment continuity holds high priority; networks of emporaries and subcontractors buffer against unemployment.
Europe	Consultation among business, government, and labor on economic policy and planning.	Industrywide bargaining structures; work councils substitute for detailed local contracts.	Unions seek some fundamental changes in economic or political system; unions are class conscious.	Industrywide bargaining and government structures are the norm; decisions are made by work councils; layoffs, discharges, and plant closings are regulated.

---

nomic policy and planning.[31] In Japan, government policy is a major influence in the growth and decline of various industrial sectors. In fact, their strong government role has been credited with the worldwide success of Japanese electronics industries, among others.

Labor/Government Relations

Distinctions in labor/government relationships among countries can be made on two dimensions. The first is social welfare, the second is class consciousness.

Social welfare   Most countries have a greater proportion of government-provided or mandated social welfare benefits—health care, maternity leave, child care, pensions—than does the United States. Although runaway costs for medical care have revived interest in a national health insurance, the traditional U.S. approach has been to leave most benefits determination to the private sector. In contrast, Canada's public health insurance plan covers 90 percent of its population. Japan's national health insurance covers the 39 percent of the population that is not covered by employer-provided insurance. Japanese employers even provide dormitories and mortgage assistance to attract new employees in areas where housing is scarce and expensive. The downside to this housing assistance is that it is not available to those employees who do not work for large firms. Those who work for subcontractors or as temporary employees get no housing assistance.

Class consciousness   In Europe and South America, unions may seek fundamental change in their country's political and economic system. This is called *class consciousness,* and contrasts with the job *consciousness*—limited economic goals—pursued by U.S. unions. Even though U.S. unions may endorse candidates and encourage their members to actively participate in the political process, their objectives always remain the economic betterment of their members. They do not seek an alternative economic or political system.

Business/Labor Relations
U.S. unions have long been strong supporters of the capitalist values that underlie our economic system. In fact, support for free market economic systems appears to be growing worldwide. The capitalist system, while amenable to collective action, offers sizeable rewards as well as risks to individual action. This reliance on the individual contrasts with a more socialistic perspective of unions in many other countries. For example, Gallup polls in Canada show between 30 and 40 percent support for socialistic movements. Many more Canadians describe themselves as "working class" than do Americans. Even though the United States and Canada have similar or even identical employers facing similar external pressures, Canadian unionism is above 40 percent and growing, while the U.S. rate continues to drop.

In Japan, employment continuity is a high priority HR activity for most firms. This employment continuity is made possible by training in a wide range of skills throughout an employee's work life, and a large network of temporar-

Although Japan has no formal structure for worker participation in business decision making or in government policy making, most large Japanese firms engage union leaders in informal consultations. Union gains are made through these consultations, rather than negotiation. This approach is consistent with Japanese values of conformity to group norms. So, a tremendous variation exists in the nature of relationships among business, government, and employees.

HR Practices
Variations in HR activities among countries have been discussed throughout this book. In the United States, a diverse assortment of plant, area, firm, and industry bargaining structures and firm-specific practices exist. Layoffs, discharges, and plant closings are, for the most part, left to private sector negotiation.

In Japan, employment continuity is a high priority HR activity for most firms. This employment continuity is made possible by training in a wide range of skills throughout an employee's work life, and a large network of temporaries and subcontractors that buffer against unemployment in time of economic downturns. These activities occur outside of Japan's "enterprise unions"— unions within each company that are to a large extent created by the company.[32] These enterprise unions include staff production workers, as well as supervisors. The unions are regularly consulted on a wide range of issues and strikes are rare.

In Europe, industrywide bargaining and governance structures are the norm. Decisions by work councils substitute for the detailed contracts negotiated by locals in the United States. In West Germany, for example, there is little or no union activity at the company and plant levels. With the coming common market, European-wide agreements crossing all industries and sectors may be possible. At present, the Charter of Fundamental Social Rights for the Common Market stresses the role of national laws and collective bargaining. Layoffs, discharges, and plant closings are closely regulated by the individual governments of most European countries.[33]

All of the above statements necessarily oversimplify a wide diversity of practices. However, they do allow interested readers to question many patterns and traditions that might otherwise be taken for granted. Additionally, they may make us more objective when we discuss criteria for evaluating labor relations decisions.

EVALUATING THE EFFECTS OF LABOR RELATIONS ACTIVITIES

Labor relations and collective bargaining affect both efficiency and equity either positively or negatively. Economic theory depicts unions as a constraint on the organization.[34] In a competitive market, unions attempt to obtain monopolistic control over the supply of labor to raise wages above the market-determined rate. Moreover, as unions are likely to attempt to establish restrictive work rules to protect their members, productivity is likely to fall. Consequently, people frequently view unions as promoting inefficiency and inequality in society. Is that view accurate? Let us examine the research on the impact of unions.

Efficiency: Union Impact on Wages

Does the presence of a union in an organization raise the level of wages for workers above what it would be if the company was not unionized? The commonly held belief among workers is that unions do have a wage impact. Over 80 percent of the respondents to a quality of employment survey conducted by the Survey Research Center of the University of Michigan believed that unions improve the wages of workers.[35] Efforts to determine if this perception is accurate have been a focus on research for at least 40 years.

Part of the reason for the continuing interest in this area is that the question of union impact on wages has not been totally resolved. Efforts to determine union impact on wages run into several measurement problems. The ideal situation would compare numerous organizations that were identical except for the presence or absence of a union. Any wage differences among these organizations could then be attributed to the unionization. Unfortunately, few such situations exist. But even if they did, one could make the case that employers pay nonunionized employees wages close to those paid to union members to reduce the attractiveness of unions to employees. This union influence on nonunion wages and benefits is called a *spillover* effect.

Nevertheless, the best evidence we have suggests that unions do make a positive difference in wage levels, and the extent of the union effect varies over time.[36] During the 1932–33 period, union presence meant much higher wages for union versus nonunion workers. As the Great Depression receded in the late 1930s, the differential declined.

An increased union premium in the 1970s may have provided the economic incentive for increased management opposition in negotiations and organizing campaigns and for subsequent drop in membership. Thus, unions may be victims of their own success.

The wage impact of unionization in the public sector appears to be smaller.[37] A summary of 13 public sector union studies concludes that the average wage effect of public sector unions is approximately +5 percent. This wage differential is smaller than typically assumed, and certainly smaller than the estimate for the private sector. The largest gains for public sector employees are reported for fire fighters, with some studies reporting as much as an 18 percent wage differential attributable to the presence of a union. At the other extreme, however, teachers (primarily affiliates of the National Education Association and the American Federation of Teachers) have not fared as well, with reported wage impact of unionization generally in the range of 1 percent to 4 percent.

A more recent analysis for union effect on wages by Gregg Lewis looked at unadjusted estimates—those requiring the least adjustment for such factors as nonrandomness and overweighting or omission of specific groups of workers—in 117 different studies.[38] The best estimates were then used to estimate union-nonunion wage difference estimates for every year from 1967 to 1979. The results are shown in Exhibit 17.6. They show a mean wage gap of approximately 15 percent, and Lewis calls this estimate the "upper bounds," meaning he does not rule out the possibility that the gap averaged as high as 15 percent, but he suspects that it was lower.

What Determines Union Wage Levels?

Our discussion here touches solely on the level of wages in unionized firms in comparison to the level of wages in nonunionized firms. Among the most important factors affecting wage levels in unionized organizations are the ability of an employer to pay, productivity, and changes in the cost of living.

EXHIBIT 17.6   Union Wage Effects Estimated by Lewis

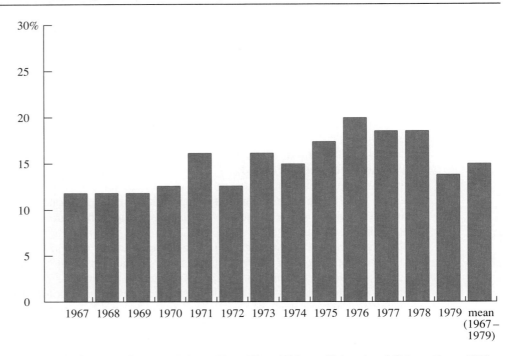

Source: H. Gregg Lewis, *Union Relative Wage Effects* (Chicago: University of Chicago Press, 1986), p. 9.

Changes in Employer's Ability to Pay

In profitable years, unions reason that part of the profits should accrue to the work force responsible for much of the organization's success. And in extremely unprofitable years, unions even offer wage concessions.[39] However, economists frequently describe wages as "sticky"; that is, they do not rise and fall readily, in response to changes in economic conditions.[40] Because of the time lag built into labor contracts, wages do not rise as fast as profits do, nor fall as fast. So changes in wages typically lag behind changes in an employer's ability to pay.

Changes in the Cost of Living

A second factor affecting wage levels in unionized organizations is the linkage of wages to the change in cost of living. Intent on maintaining and improving the buying power of membership, unions made a strong drive for wage escalator clauses during the 1970s. Cost of living adjustments (COLA) automatically in-

EXHIBIT 17.7   Unionism and Productivity

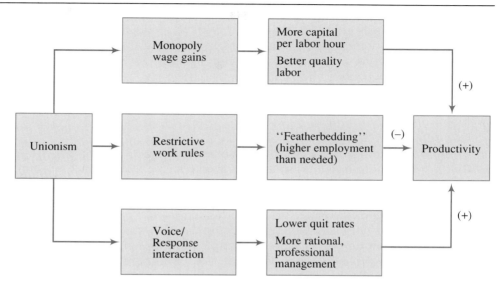

Source: Richard Freeman and James Medoff, *What Do Unions Do?* (New York: Basic Books, 1984).
©1984 by Basic Books, Inc., Publishers. Reprinted by permission of the publisher.

crease wages during the life of the contract as a function of changes in the consumer price index. By 1977, 61 percent of the workers covered by major bargaining agreements had COLAs in their contracts. Since then, the percentage has declined, partly because employment has been shrinking in some of the major unionized industries that have COLA clauses, and also because some unions have agreed to remove such clauses, in light of moderating increases in living costs.

Efficiency: Union Impact on Productivity

The model in Exhibit 17.7 indicates that unions can have a positive or negative effect on productivity, depending on the quality of the union/management relationship. The model suggests some specific ways that union and employer behavior can affect productivity. Based on their analysis of the research, Richard Freeman and James Medoff conclude that, "with management and unions working together to produce a bigger 'pie' as well as fighting over the size of their slice, productivity is likely to be higher under unionism. If industrial relations are poor, with management and labor ignoring common goals to battle one another, productivity is likely to be lower under unionism."[41]

Yearly increases in U.S. productivity have lagged far behind most other industrial countries over the past decade. Many industries have experienced losses in market share traceable to productivity problems. This has led to an increasing effort to tie wage increases to productivity increases.[42] Incentive systems, profit sharing plans, merit-based pay plans are all examples of efforts to make this productivity/wage link stronger. Even productivity bargaining and quality control circles show an increasing emphasis on the level of productivity in unionized and nonunionized organizations alike.[43]

Equity: Union Impact on Employees' Voice

In addition to its effect on members' wages, the other positive effect claimed for unionism is that it provides workers a collective voice on subjects affecting their work.[44] By providing workers with a voice in work-related decisions, unions are likely to have a number of positive effects for both employees and organizations. First, unions act as *information collectors* for organizations, obtaining a clearer picture of the preferences of all employees, rather than just new entrants to or leavers from organizations. As a result, employers are able to develop better personnel practices, which reflect the needs of the existing work force. Second, unions are likely to *increase worker satisfaction by reducing inequality* among workers and guaranteeing some degree of due process in organizational decision making. Researchers, for example, discovered that unions have a significant positive effect on employees' satisfaction with pay.[45] However, job dissatisfaction appears to be higher among union members than nonunion members.[46] Absenteeism rates may be higher among union members, too.[47] Since absenteeism can be interpreted as an expression of job dissatisfaction, it may be that any voice the union provides has only limited effect on job satisfaction.

Various writers have suggested that, by providing workers with a voice to change organizational conditions, the probability of turnover is likely reduced. Freeman and Medoff found consistent evidence that union membership increased tenure and decreased turnover. Some studies find turnover reductions as high as 50 percent attributable to the presence of a union.[48]

SUMMARY

Labor relations is a major activity in unionized organizations. It also is an activity of major interest in society as well. Cataclysmic events in the 1930s awoke the public to the wretched conditions faced by American workers. The public's identification with union goals led to a changed regulatory climate and phenomenal growth in union strength in the 1940s and 1950s. After that, unions began a long decline.

The industries that were most heavily unionized were typically the ones hit hardest by competitive pressures in the 1980s. Foreign competition, deregulation, and a changed climate of public opinion have severely weakened unions.

Many people continue to blame unions themselves, or at least the collective bargaining process as it presently exists in the United States, for unions' trouble. They cite high wage settlements that drove many jobs out of the country, and contracts that built up rules that eventually interfere with productivity. These costly side effects might be justified if the outcomes of the labor relations process were more palatable to the American public. Critics, however, say that unions that win the biggest settlements are not the ones whose members are "most deserving." Rather, they are the ones with the most effective bargaining power. They are less likely to be the $4-an-hour textile workers than $20-an-hour auto workers.

Perhaps it is this changed public opinion that has permitted employers to become more aggressive in their efforts to avoid becoming unionized. Private sector employers appear more willing to engage in behavior that is illegal, because they believe the benefits of being nonunion outweigh the penalties.

The public sector offers a brighter picture. Even though more public sector unions are forbidden to strike, public sector unionism is increasing to the point that it will be a major influence on the future focus and vitality of the U.S. labor movement.

Internationally, there is a wide variety of forms that unionism can take. In all cases, the nature of unionism is affected by the politics, culture, and history of a country. Many European and South American unions are political movements that seek major change in their societies. This contrasts with the focus on economic gains for members in U.S. unions.

Unions can be evaluated on how well they contribute to their members' economic well-being, and how well they help resolve conflict at the workplace.

Unions affect both efficiency and equity, because an effective union can provide employees a voice to change organization conditions and enhance equitable treatment of unionized employees. Having a more satisfied, stable, unionized work force can result in higher productivity for the employer. However, unions can have a negative effect on productivity if work rules hinder performance. Whether the effect on productivity is positive depends on the quality of the employer/employee relationship.

DISCUSSION AND REVIEW QUESTIONS

1. Why do people join unions?
2. Describe the various organization approaches to dealing with unions.
3. What factors have contributed to the past success of unions in the United States?
4. What factors have contributed to the recent decline in union membership in the United States?
5. How do unions differ in the public sector?
6. How do unions affect productivity?
7. How do unions affect wages?

8. What is "employee voice?" What are some indicators of employee voice in a nonunion organization?
9. What is "class consciousness?"
10. How and why do U.S. unions differ from those in other countries?

YOUR TURN
PLAY OR PAY

A strike by Musicians Local 369 in Las Vegas was dragging into its eighth month. The expired contract covered musicians at Bally's, Tropicana, Caesars Palace, Las Vegas Hilton, and Flamingo Hilton. The resorts employed musicians in two areas: the production rooms, where they play for the big dance numbers and extravaganzas, and the star rooms, where a smaller number of musicians provide music for the celebrity headliners. The old contract guaranteed 50 weeks of employment annually, and paid a weekly rate of $654, regardless of the number of nights worked per week.

The strike began when the musicians at the Tropicana walked off the Folies Bergere show to protest the stalemate in negotiations. The hotel responded by replacing the live musicians with taped music.

The extreme options to resolve this dispute are:

A. All-taped music:
   Advantage: Cheaper than live musicians.
   Disadvantage: Difficult to coordinate with a live performance.
   Lose the excitement and glamor of live musicians.
   Negative public relations.
   Obligation to former employees.

B. All-live musicians:
   Advantage: Flexibility.
   Disdavantage: Cost.
   May be of inconsistent quality.
   Less reliable.
   More difficult to manage.

What are some other staffing and pay options between these extremes? What are the advantages and disadvantages of those options? How can the disadvantages be overcome?

Your instructor can tell you what the actual settlement was.

NOTES AND REFERENCES

1. Sal Vittolino, "Nissan Drives 'Em Away," *Human Resource Executive,* October 1989, pp. 1, 24–27.
2. Ibid, p. 24.

3. Harry Katz, quoted in *Human Resource Executive,* October 1989, p. 26.

4. Vittolino, "Nissan Drives 'Em Away," p. 27.

5. Janice A. Klein and E. David Wanger, "The Legal Setting for the Emergence of the Union Avoidance Strategy," in *Challenges and Choices Facing American Labor,* ed. T. Kochan (Cambridge, MIT Press, 1985).

6. John Chalykoff and Peter Cappelli, "Union Avoidance: Management's New Industrial Relations Strategy," Paper presented at the 38th annual meeting of the Industrial Relations Research Association, December 1985, New York; Jack Fiorito and Christopher Lowman, "The Role of Employer Human Resource Policies in Union Organizing," Working Paper, University of Iowa, Iowa City, February 1986.

7. William N. Cooke, "The Failure to Negotiate First Contracts: Determinants and Policy Implications," *Industrial and Labor Relations Review,* January 1985, pp. 163–78.

8. Thomas A. Kochan, Harry C. Katz, and Robert B. McKersie, *The Transformation of American Industrial Relations* (New York: Basic Books, 1986).

9. Richard W. Hurd and Adrienne McElwain, "Organizing Clerical Workers: Determinants of Success," *Industrial and Labor Relations Review,* April 1988, pp. 360–73.

10. Richard Freeman, "Contraction and Expansion: The Divergence of Private Sector and Public Sector Unionism in the United States," Cambridge, Mass.: National Bureau of Economic Research Working Paper 2399, January 1988.

11. Rene Saran and John Sheldrake, ed., *Public Sector Bargaining in the 1980's* (Brookfield, Vt.: Gower, 1988).

12. William N. Cooke, "Improving Productivity and Quality through Collaboration," *Industrial Relations,* Spring 1989, pp. 299–319.

13. William N. Cooke and David G. Meyer, "Structural and Market Predictors of Corporate Labor Relations Strategies," *Industrial and Labor Relations Review,* January 1990, pp. 280–93.

14. Fred K. Foulkes, *Personnel Policies in Large Nonunion Companies* (Englewood Cliffs, N.J.: Prentice-Hall, 1980); John G. Kilgour, *Preventive Labor Relations* (New York: AMACOM, a division of American Management Associations, 1981).

15. Kay Deaux and Joseph C. Ullman, *Women of Steel: Female Blue-Collar Workers in the Basic Steel Industry* (New York: Praeger, 1983); Richard Freeman and Jonathan S. Leonard, "Union Maids: Unions and the Female Workforce," Cambridge: NBER, Working Paper, June 1985); Richard Moore and Elizabeth Marsis, "Will Unions Work for Women?" *The Progressive,* August 1983, pp. 28–30.

16. Greg Hundley, "Things Unions Do, Job Attributes, and Union Membership," *Industrial Relations,* Fall 1989, p. 335.

17. Freeman and Leonard, "Union Maids."

18. *The Changing Situation of Workers and their Unions,* Report of the AFL-CIO Evolution of Work Committee, February 1985.

19. Peter Cappelli and Robert B. McKersie, "Labor and the Crisis in Collective Bargaining," in *Challenges and Choices Facing American Labor* (Cambridge, Mass.: MIT Press, 1985).

20. Corey Rosen, "Growth versus Equity: The Employee Ownership Solution," *ILR Report,* Spring 1985, pp. 19–25.

21. Charles R. Perry, *Union Corporate Campaigns* (Philadelphia: Wharton School, 1987).

22. David J. Walsh, "Accounting for the Proliferation of Two-Tier Wage Settlements in the U.S. Airline Industry, 1983–1986," *Industrial and Labor Relations Review,* October 1988, pp. 50–62; Anil Verma, "Relative Flow of Capital to Union and Nonunion Plants within a Firm," *Industrial Relations,* Fall 1985, pp. 395–405.

23. Michael Schuster, "Models of Cooperation and Change in Union Settings," *Industrial Relations,* Fall 1985, pp. 382–94.

24. Anil Verma, "Joint Participation Programs: Self-Help or Suicide for Labor," *Industrial Relations,* Fall 1989, pp. 401–10.

25. John Joyce, "Codetermination, Collective Bargaining, and Worker Participation in the Construction Industry," in *Challenges and Choices Facing American Labor,* ed. T. A. Kochan (Cambridge: MIT Press, 1985); Paula B. Voos, "Managerial Perceptions of the Economic Impact of Labor Relations Programs," *Industrial and Labor Relations Review,* January 1987, pp. 195–208.

26. Paul Jarley and Jack Fiorito, "Associate Membership: Unionism or Consumerism?" *Industrial and Labor Relations Review,* January 1990, pp. 209–24.

27. William J. Moore and Robert J. Newman, "The Effects of Right-to-Work Laws," *Industrial and Labor Relations Review,* July 1985, pp. 571–85; Hurd and McElwain, "Organizing Clerical Workers."

28. Jeffrey S. Zax, "Employment and Local Public Sector Unions," *Industrial Relations,* Winter 1989, pp. 21–31.

29. Freeman, "Contraction and Expansion."

30. Much of this section is taken from Thomas A. Kochan and Thomas A. Barocci, *Human Resource Management and Industrial Relations* (Boston: Little, Brown, 1985), pp. 495–99.

31. John P. Windmuller et al., *Collective Bargaining in Industrialized Market Economics: A Reappraisal* (Geneva: International Labour Office, 1987).

32. Kazuo Koike, *Understanding Industrial Relations in Modern Japan* (New York: St. Martin's Press, 1988).

33. Leslie Lenkowsky, *Politics, Economics, and Welfare Reform* (Lanham, Md.: University Press of America, 1986).

34. Selig Perlman, "Labor and Capitalism in America," in *The Collective Bargaining Process,* ed., Jean A. Baderschneider, Richard N. Block, and John A. Fossum (Plano, Tex.: Business Publications, 1983).

35. John Fossum, *Labor Relations,* 3rd ed. (Plano, Tex.: Business Publications, 1985).

36. E. Kenneth Grant, Robert Swidinsky, and John Vanderkamp, "Canadian Union-Nonunion Wage Differentials," *Industrial and Labor Relations Review,* October 1987, pp. 93–107.

37. David Fairris, "Compensating Wage Differentials: Union and Nonunion," *Industrial Relations,* Fall 1989, pp. 356–72.

38. H. Gregg Lewis, *Union Relative Wage Effects* (Chicago: University of Chicago Press, 1986).

39. Ibid., p. 9.

40. Richard B. Freeman and James L. Medoff, *What Do Unions Do?* (New York: Basic Books, 1984).

41. Ibid., p. 165.

42. Walsh, "Accounting for the Profileration of Two-Tier Wage Settlements"; Zax, "Employment and Local Public Sector Unions"; Fairris, "Compensating Wage Differentials."

43. Cooke, "Improving Productivity."

44. Albert O. Hirschman, *Exit, Voice, and Loyalty* (Cambridge, Mass.: Harvard University Press, 1971); Richard B. Freeman and James L. Medoff, "The Two Faces of Unionism," *The Public Interest,* Fall 1979, pp. 69–93; R. B. Freeman, "The Exit–

Voice Trade-Off in the Labor Market: Unionism, Job Tenure, Quits, and Separations," *Quarterly Journal of Economics* 94 (1980), pp. 6433–74;   Francine Blau and Lawrence Kahn, "The Exit–Voice Model of Unionism: Some Further Evidence on Layoffs" (Paper, Champaign, University of Illinois, 1980).

45. Chris J. Berger, Craig A. Olson, and John W. Boudreau, "Effects of Unions on Job Satisfaction: The Role of Work-Related Values and Perceived Rewards," Working Paper, Krannert Graduate School of Management, Purdue University, 1983.

46. Michael E. Gordon, Laura L. Beauvais, and Robert T. Ladd, "The Job Satisfaction and Union Commitment of Unionized Engineers," *Industrial and Labor Relations Review,* April 1984, pp. 359–71;   Michael E. Gordon and Sandra J. Miller, "Grievances: A Review of Research and Practice," *Personnel Psychology,* Spring 1984, pp. 117–46.

47. Steven G. Allen, "Trade Unions, Absenteeism, and Exit–Voice," *Industrial and Labor Relations Review,* April 1984, pp. 331–45.

48. Francine D. Blau and Lawrence M. Kahn, "Unionism, Seniority, and Turnover," *Industrial Relations,* Fall 1983, pp. 362–73.

Cases

Human Resource Management
at Ithaca's Own

💻 *Starting Salary: Introduction to the PC*

Background Description of Ithaca's Own

Strategies and Staff

Setting Objectives

Employment Planning

💻 *Choosing Colleges for Recruiting: Using the PC*

Developing New Managers

💻 *Merit Pay Decisions: Using the PC*

Compression and External Experienced Hiring

The Jack Freelance Affair

Stand-Alone Cases

Strategic Human Resource Planning

Job Analysis

Ralph's Genuine French Cuisine

Gigantic Aircraft Company

Training Cost/Benefit Analysis at Massive Manufacturing Corporation

State Government

Lori Petersen

Collective Bargaining

Contract Costing

INTRODUCTION TO CASES

The cases provide you with the opportunity to develop your own analytical skills. Each exercise presents a realistic situation related to human resource management. The Ithaca's Own cases allow you to consider issues in a single organization. Setting the cases in the same organization allows you to explore how decisions regarding one HR issue may affect subsequent decisions on related issues.

Some of these cases require computer assistance. These are marked with a computer logo. You do not need previous computer experience to use them. They are designed to let you use the computer as a *tool* that performs your calculations. This allows you to concentrate on *why* you might take a certain action and on *what difference will it make*.

In solving these cases, try to follow the diagnostic approach used in this textbook. Consider factors in the external environment (product and labor market conditions, government regulations, union influences), organization conditions (business strategy, culture, nature of the work), nature of the individual employees, and the overall objectives of the organization.

HUMAN RESOURCE MANAGEMENT AT ITHACA'S OWN

---◆---

STARTING SALARY: INTRODUCTION TO THE PC

This case is different from the rest of the computerized exercises in that it does not contain data. You will enter the data to get the experience. The objective of the case is to become familiar with using the the HRM PC software by calculating a hypothetical 10-year salary progression. What you learn in this case will apply to the other computerized cases.

It is assumed that you:

◆ Know how to turn on the computer, monitor, and printer and set the printer to On Line.

◆ Know how to boot up the computer so you see the DOS prompt.

◆ Know how to enter a simple DOS command, like dir (directory).

◆ Are familiar enough with the keyboard to locate the letter, number, arrow, and Enter and Backspace keys.

◆ Know how to format a blank disk.

Tell your instructor if you do not know these things. Assistance will be provided to you.

Getting Ready

To use the computer cases, you will need:

◆ An IBM personal computer or a 100 percent compatible computer.

◆ DOS version 2.1 or higher.

◆ Your own copy of this book.

◆ The HRM disk containing the software.

◆ A printer.

◆ A monitor.

◆ A blank, formatted disk to save your work.

Some of the exercises display a graph. You will need a monitor connected to a graphics adapter to see the graphs. If this is not the case, you may still use the software; however, you will not be able to see the graphs.

These instructions apply to IBM or compatible personal computers with two disk drives, used as stand-alone work stations. If you are using another type of computer, a computer with a hard disk, or a computer that is connected into a network or laboratory, there may be different procedures for starting and running your computer. If so, your instructor will tell you what changes to make in the directions for this exercise.

Learning to use the HRM Software

The best way to learn how to use the HRM software is to complete the first case.

To start the program, turn on your computer, monitor, and printer. The computer boots up and you see the DOS prompt on the screen. The DOS prompt looks like A> or C>. If you have trouble getting to this point, your instructor can give you more detailed directions. (See instructor's manual.)

To start the HRM software:

✦ If you are using the software from a working disk:

1. Place the HRM disk into the A drive.
2. Make sure the DOS prompt says A>. If not, type a: {press the Enter key}.
3. Type hrm {press the Enter key}.
   If you get a message on the screen that says *Bad command or File not found, you did not put the Disk in the A drive. Try it again.*

✦ If you are using the software from the C drive of a hard disk:

1. Type cd \hrm {press the Enter key}. Be sure to leave one blank space between cd and \hrm.
2. Then type hrm {press the Enter Key}.

The screen then displays an introductory message, which includes copyright information. On the bottom of the screen is a *menu* box, with one choice highlighted. Just as in a restaurant, the menu provides a list of possible choices or options. However, the options included on the menu will change, depending on where you are in the software.

To choose an option, use the arrow keys on the right end of the keyboard to move around the menu. When the choice you want is highlighted, press Enter.

Press the arrow key a few times to become familiar with the way it works. Then, choose the exercise titled Starting Salary. Press any key to move to the next screen.

The next screen has two parts. At the top are labels for columns. On the bottom is a dialogue box giving you instructions to follow. Read and follow the instructions that appear on the screen.

The next screen has two boxes. The bottom box gives directions, the top box displays the data as you enter it. After you press any key, the cursor appears on the line where you are to enter information. Type in your name, then press Enter.

Type in the salary of $15000.25. *Note:* Do not type in commas or the dollar sign, but do type in the decimal point. That is, if you want to enter $15,000.25, enter it as 15000.25. Press Enter.

Type in 6.25 for a yearly percent increase of 6.25%. Press Enter, then press it again and the computer will automatically move to the next screen, where it displays its calculations.

As you can see, the computer program did the computations in seconds. One advantage of using computers is their speed in doing calculations, allowing you to quickly see the results.

To illustrate this, press ESC. The new menu on the screen lists some choices you can make. Use the arrow keys to move the cursor to Change Starting Salary or Increase. Press Enter, and the previous screen reappears. Type in new information for starting salary and annual raise, and then see how fast the computer calculated, organized, and displayed the new results. Try several more changes.

There are additional options available on the menu.

Save

Select this option to save what you have done so far on this exercise on your personal storage disk. NOTE: you MUST HAVE A BLANK, FORMATTED DISK to use this option.

To save your results, put your formatted disk into the A drive, and type in the command A:SALARY (Enter). *Remember the name you gave to your file.* You can retrieve this file if you wish to do additional work at another time.

If you get a message that says "write protect error writing drive a," you have tried to save a file onto a disk that is locked, or write-protected. Remove the disk. To unlock a 3.5 inch disk, slide the locking tab away from its edge. To unlock a 5.25 inch disk, remove the locking tab. Then reinsert the disk and type R (for retry).

Retrieve

Select this option to retrieve a file that you have previously saved. The computer will ask you for the name of the file you wish to retrieve. Insert your personal storage disk now.

Enter the letter of the disk drive (a, b, c) that contains your personal storage disk from which the file will be retrieved, followed by a colon, followed by your file name. Example: a:salary retrieves your work from the file SALARY on the disk in drive A.

Print

Every computer exercise in this book has a PRINT option. If you have a printer attached to your computer, choosing PRINT will produce a report of one or several pages summarizing the current information. Whether you have a printer or not, choose PRINT now.

After you choose the print command, you will have a number of options, depending on which exercise you are using. Your options may include:

0. Do not print. Choose this if you realize you are not quite ready.
1. Print data to printer. Choose this if you are hooked up to a printer.
2. Print data to text file. Choose this if you are using a computer that is not attached to a printer. To do this, give your printing file a name that is different from the name you used to save your results. A:PRINTFILE is a useful name. The A and the colon avoid inadvertently saving this file on the hard drive.

Then when you are at a computer hooked to a printer, simply insert your new disk and type in:

Print   A:printfile

Leave a space after the word print.

3. Print graphs to printer. This option is only available on the Merit Pay Decisions exercise.

Quit

You should now be familiar with the workings of the exercise software. If you wish to practice more, use the exercise options as you wish. When you are done, choose QUIT from the menu.

This option does *not* automatically save any data as you leave. If you want to save anything, use the SAVE option before exiting.

Before you choose QUIT, make sure the HRM disk is in the disk drive (unless you are a hard disk user or are on a network).

Summary

Through this guided tour of Starting Salary you have learned how to:

✦ Start the HRM software.
✦ Select an exercise from one of the three exercises available.
✦ Enter information into the computer.
✦ Use the exercise menu choices PRINT, SAVE, RETRIEVE, and QUIT, which are available in all of the exercises.

As you do the PC exercises, you will begin to discover the power and efficiency of computerized human resource management decision making. One word of caution is in order, however. The numbers and analyses you generate are not the answers to the case problems you encounter. Rather, they are tools to support and guide decisions. The best answer integrates what is learned from the computer analysis with your own experience and creativity. The computer supports you by making the computations and organizing the information, but you must supply the understanding necessary to turn the information into sound decisions.

◆

BACKGROUND DESCRIPTION OF ITHACA'S OWN

Ithaca's Own, Inc., founded in 1987, was begun as a small regional enterprise that specialized in health and natural food products. Since 1987, I–O has experienced reasonable growth. Last year its total revenues exceeded $10.2 million, and its net income was about $1.7 million. Today it can be said that I–O is unique in an industry dominated by giants, such as R. J. Reynolds, General Mills, Kellogg, and General Foods. I–O's advantage, according to its founder and chief executive officer (CEO), lies in its ability to innovate, based upon its research and development capabilities. For example, I–O's Research and Development Group developed an entire line of freeze-dried fruit snacks (Apple Bits and Bites is an example) to compete with candies and confections; other products developed by I–O are its Cayuga Coolers (a fruit-base drink), Frosty Fruits (fruit-based frozen bars), and a growing list of prepared products for microwave ovens (Quick Chick and Tastee Quick Popcorn are big sellers). I–O markets these products to wholesale distributors, as well as to institutions and restaurants.

During a recent interview with a national trade publication, the CEO described I–O as "an aggressive, technical-research-oriented enterprise whose competitive advantage lies in its relatively small size (approximately 410 employees) and its agility." Discussing the strategic thrust for the future, the CEO said, "Ithaca's Own will become a think tank for new consumer-oriented food products—I–O's principal product will be R&D—to generate new products, to develop new production and marketing approaches, and to sell those products and processes to other firms, or perhaps to spin them off as manufacturing affiliates."

Organization of Ithaca's Own

Ithaca's Own is organized functionally (Exhibit 1). The staff-support functions are performed in the Administrative Services Group reporting to the CEO through a vice president—Administrative Services. Operations has three groups: Research and Development, Production, and Marketing. The Human Resource Management (HRM) Department was added just six months ago.

While I–O has sold several of its new products to other firms, it decided to retain three products to manufacture and market on its own. These three are the freeze-dried Bits and Bites, microwave products (chicken and popcorn), and cooler drinks. Under the current business plan, these product lines are to be sold or established as affiliates of I–O. The R&D function remains the key to the firm's success. Currently, R&D has career progression arranged as a dual ladder, one for technical-research personnel and another for managers and project leaders. Marketing is organized in a somewhat similar manner, with market researchers on one career track and sales-account personnel on the other. Currently, the sales-account jobs mainly involve marketing products manufactured by I–O to wholesalers and institutional customers. The market researchers focus on new product development and on designing marketing strategies for them.

Work Flow

The general flow of work is as follows. Someone, typically in marketing research or R&D, initiates an application for a new idea. The application is reviewed by a new products team, consisting of management representatives from marketing, operations, and R&D. If the new idea is approved, further development in R&D and marketing usually is required. Once the product development is reasonably well along, operations assigns it to a unit to develop a production process or fit it into an existing process. Prototypes or pilot products are developed and tested in the labs and among consumer samples; then the new product is trial marketed. At any point in the development process, Ithaca's Own may sell the product (complete with market testing data and recommended production processes) to other firms, rather than go into full-scale production. However, as noted earlier, it does have full-scale production of some of its products.

Employment at Ithaca's Own

I–O is not currently, nor has it ever been, unionized. Two years ago, however, organizers from the Teamsters attempted to organize the hourly employees in the Operations Department. Although the attempt was unsuccessful, first-line supervisors believe another organizing campaign is likely.

I–O draws its work force primarily from the local area. Because it is one of the few industries in the Ithaca area, I–O has experienced few problems in meeting its employment needs. Recently, however, as I–O continues to grow, certain professional and managerial positions are becoming increasingly difficult to fill.

EXHIBIT 1 Organization Chart of Ithaca's Own

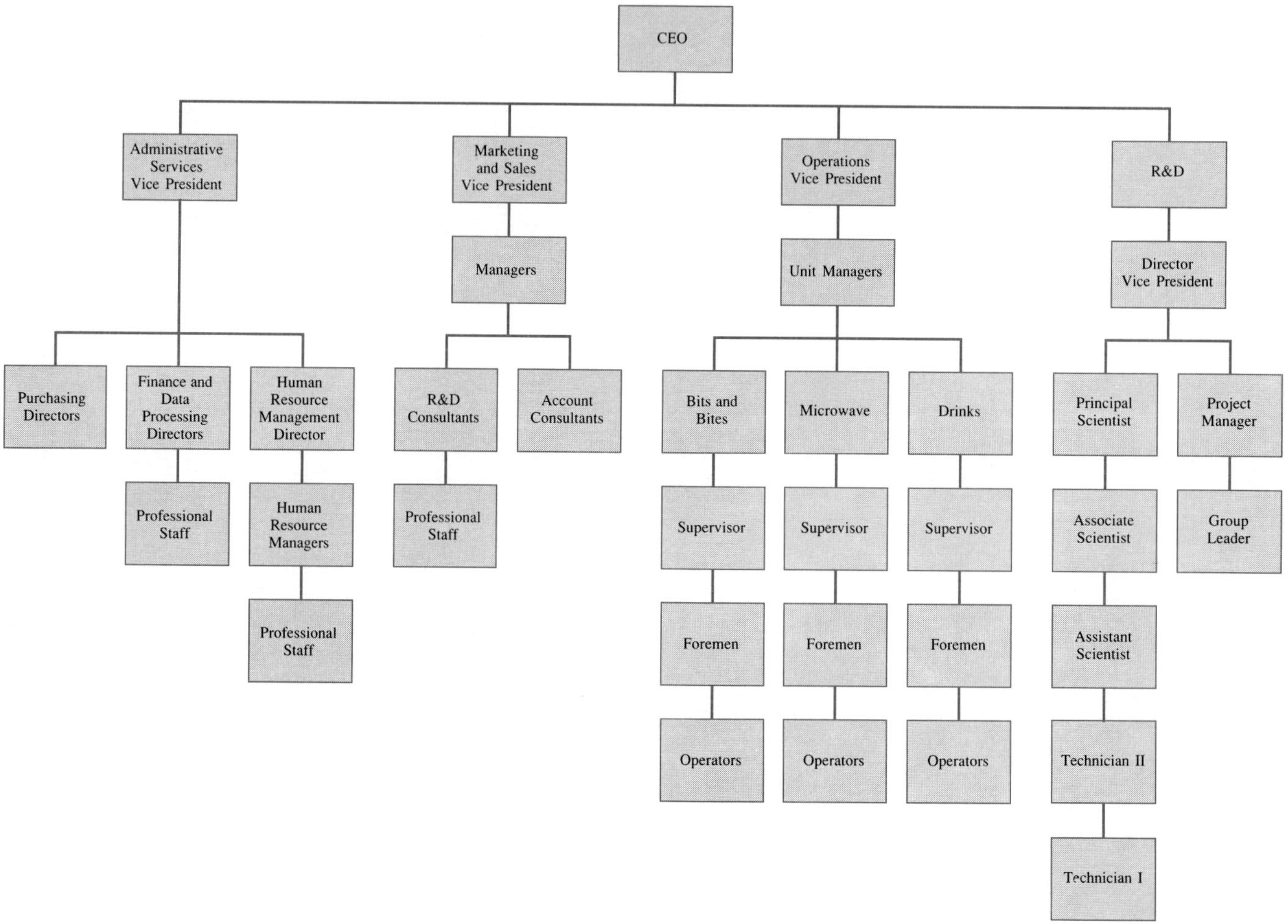

EXHIBIT 2   Administrative Services

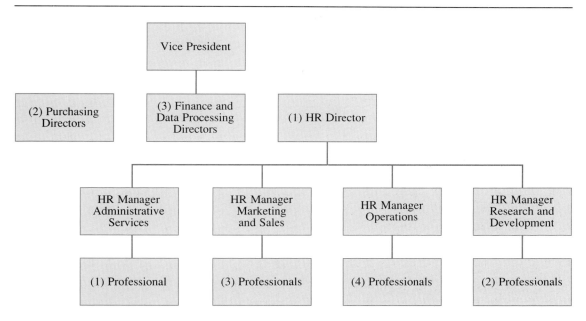

The organization has never been involved in a lawsuit regarding its human resource policies, although no formal analysis of these policies has ever been conducted. Documentation consists of employee portfolios, which include such information as the incumbent's name, position, number of absences, hiring date, sex, age, and date of termination, where applicable. Administrative Services maintain a separate file for each employee, and, to date, no effort has been made to compile and analyze this data for the work force as a whole. Accident rates are also documented. I–O has never been inspected for safety compliance, and internal safety audits are conducted on what can best be described as an ad hoc basis. While I–O considers itself an equal opportunity employer, no formal affirmative action plan exists.

The Human Resource Management Function

Growth and diversification at I–O necessitated establishing an HRM department. Four HRM generalists have been hired, one to address the needs of each functional area, and a director of human resources (also a generalist) has been hired to coordinate activities. The director reports to the vice president of Administrative Services (see Exhibits 1 and 2 for organizational charts).

Now that you have been introduced to the organization, you are ready to address more HRM decisions.

EXHIBIT 3   Human Resource Strategic Programming—Budget Allocation   (percents)

Strategic Programming	Functions			
	R&D	Operations	Marketing	Administrative Services
Total of Ithaca's Own (100%)	25%	60%	10%	5%
Training and development	15	40	30	20
Managerial	5	15	10	10
Technical	10	10	10	10
Skill-Craft	—	15	10	—
Staffing	45	10	30	20
Recruiting	35	10	20	10
Succession charting	5	—	5	5
Career planning	5	—	5	5
Performance evaluation	10	15	10	20
Compensation design	10	10	10	20
Equal employment opportunity	10	15	10	10
New programs	10	10	10	10
	100%	100%	100%	100%

◆

STRATEGIES AND STAFF

Exhibits 3 and 4 offer some information on I–O's employment plan for the next period, as well as data on their human resource budget allocations over the past few years. Exhibit 3 indicates the HR programming expenditures. I–O's total labor costs include salaries and benefits plus these programming expenditures on HR activities. In Exhibit 3, 25 percent of I–O's HR programming budget was allocated to the R&D group, compared to 5 percent to Administrative Services. Note also that the 25 percent allocation to R&D was distributed across nine activities, with staffing receiving the largest share: 45 percent.

Discussion Questions

You have been brought in as a consultant to advise Ithaca's Own top management regarding HRM issues. I–O top management has asked you to consider three major issues:

EXHIBIT 4   Human Resource Requirements and Turnover

	Planned Year			
	Current Year Employment	Forecasted Requirements	Estimates Turnover	Surplus/ (Shortage)
R&D:				
Principal scientist	10	7	0	3
Associate scientist	50	43	3	4
Assistant scientist	70	65	3	2
Manager	10	10	2	(2)
Group leader	20	23	4	(7)
Technician	30	32	4	(6)
Secretary and clerical	3	2	0	1
Total	193	182	16	(5)
Operations:				
Manager	3	3	2	(2)
Supervisor	9	8	1	0
Foreman	35	31	2	2
Operators	60	72	10	(22)
Secretaries and clerical	3	2	1	0
Total	110	116	16	(22)
Marketing and Sales:				
Managers	3	5	0	(2)
R&D consultants	10	6	2	2
Account consultants	8	11	1	(4)
Professional	30	38	2	(10)
Secretary and clerical	15	17	5	(7)
Total	66	77	10	(21)
Administrative Services:				
Human resource managers and director	5	5	0	0
Purchasing director	2	2	1	(1)
Finance and data processing director	3	4	2	(3)
Human resource professionals	10	10	1	(1)
Finance professionals	10	8	0	2
Secretary and clerical	11	9	4	(2)
Total	41	38	8	(5)

A. Considering what you know about organization and environmental conditions facing I–O,
  1. What, if any, strategies or patterns emerge from I–O's recent human resource decisions? Examine the budget allocations shown in Exhibit 3. How do these relate to the CEO's stated direction?
  2. What recommendations would you make to I–O with respect to the reallocation of its HR efforts? Discuss how these recommendations

may be more consistent with I–O's business directions and external conditions.

B. Consider organizational structure and staffing in the HRM department (refer to Exhibits 1 and 2).

    1. If a basic tenet of this book is correct—every manager is a manager of human resources—then what is the justification for employing human resource professionals?

    2. Is the current department structure consistent with I–O business strategy? For example, consider the Human Resource Department's relationship with Operations. Explore the advantages and disadvantages of alternative organization structures. Does having personnel report directly to general managers of each Operations unit have merit? Do you feel it is appropriate to assign generalists to each functional area? Would it be preferable to hire human resource managers with functional specialties (i.e., staffing, compensation, training)?

    3. What challenges/opportunities do you foresee facing the department in the upcoming year? Specifically, what external factors are affecting I–O? What internal factors? Select one external aspect and explain how changes in this area may affect the role and/or importance of the HRM function. Which HRM activity(s) would be involved? How would you adjust the allocation of the personnel budget to accommodate to that change?

C. Finally, what three or four pieces of additional data would you recommend collecting to better diagnose the situation at Ithaca's Own? Be specific about how you would use these data in your analysis.

SETTING OBJECTIVES

This project involves setting human resource objectives for Ithaca's Own.

    1. Develop a recommended list of five critical human resource objectives for I–O. To do so, refresh your understanding of the previous I–O case, Strategies and Staff, as well as I–O's actual budget allocations (Exhibit 3) and employment plan (Exhibit 4). Also, be sure to reread the additional background information on I–O on pages 664–68.

    2. Recall question A–2, page 669 in the previous Ithaca's Own case. That question asked you to make recommendations for how I–O could reallocate its HR efforts to be more consistent with its business directions and external conditions. Now, compare the recommendations you made at that time to the objectives you just set for I–O. Are the budget allocations consistent with the objectives you established? If they are not consistent, what adjustments would you make? Do your objectives fit I–O's business

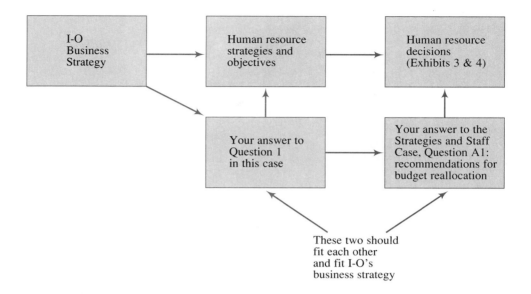

strategy? The chart above shows how your answers should fit with each other and with I–O's business strategy.

3. In the chart, the arrows go from business strategy to human resource strategy to human resource decisions. Are there any situations in I–O where the arrows go in the other direction? That is, do the HR decisions made in the past act as a constraint on possible I–O business strategies?

4. Which criteria would you use to evaluate the effectiveness of the HRM function?

EMPLOYMENT PLANNING

Ithaca's Own has begun to enlarge its share of the natural foods market. Projected sales this year have increased 17 percent over the previous year, and I–O products are appearing in stores nationwide. While top management is delighted, the organization's continued success has resulted in some headaches for the Human Resource Management Department.

Although a formal employment planning function does not yet exist at I–O, the director of HRM, Mr. Wable, forecast I–O's employment requirements, based on the anticipated productivity increases in each function. Wable then applied the historical rate of turnover to each position and calculated I–O's expected work force; these figures were then compared to employment require-

EXHIBIT 5   Recruitment Sources, Costs, and Yields

Recruitment Source	Cost (per hire)	Yield Rate (percentage)
Agencies	$8,000	30%
Advertising	1,000	10
College recruiting	5,000	10
Unsolicited walk-ins	200	2
Employee referrals	200	8

Note: Costs are averages over all hires obtained through each method over the last two years. Yield rates are the number of applicants identified through the method divided by the number receiving job offers. For example, if advertising produced 100 applicants and 10 received offers, the yield would be 10 percent. Both costs and yield rates vary across different positions. Not all methods have been used in all positions.

ments for the planned year. As Exhibit 4 indicates, I–O anticipates an overall shortage of 53 employees, but the employment mix within certain departments will change. For example, R&D is expected to have a net shortage of five employees, although certain positions in the department will require fewer employees in the plan year. In addition to the exhibit Wable developed, you have received a chart indicating the costs and yield ratios associated with various sources of recruits (Exhibit 5).

Regarding internal employee movement, you have noted the following general trends: (1) Secretaries and clerical workers are seldom promoted and are usually recruited externally. (2) In R&D, the promotion ladder runs up the jobs listed in Exhibit 4 (i.e., from technician to group leader and so on up to principal scientist). (3) In Operations, the promotion ladder runs up from operator to foreman to supervisor to manager. (4) In Marketing and Sales, professionals have been promoted either to account consultant or R&D consultant and then to manager. (5) In Administrative Services, directors have come from several of the other functional areas (R&D, Operations, and Marketing), but professionals are usually recruited externally.

Discussion Questions

1. Regarding internal staffing: For which positions are the traditional internal movement patterns likely to help alleviate these imbalances? For which are they likely to exacerbate the problems? What kind of internal movement pattern would alleviate some of the shortages and surpluses? How might you encourage these kinds of movement patterns?

2. Regarding external staffing: Which positions should be filled externally? Which of the four external recruitment methods are most appropriate for each position? Would you emphasize cost, yield, or both, in choosing recruitment methods? Justify your answer.

3. Which positions, if any, require national recruiting? Local labor market recruiting? Why? Would you recommend recruiting at additional sources to generate women and minority candidates? Give examples.

4. How would improved productivity affect the employment forecast? Which positions would be most affected? How will you handle expected surpluses in certain positions?

5. Which three additional pieces of information would be useful in preparing employment planning recommendations for I–O? Be specific about how you might use these data.

CHOOSING COLLEGES FOR RECRUITING: USING THE PC

Objective

In this exercise, you will use the PC to:

+ Analyze previous recruitment patterns and costs.
+ Forecast the likely effects of future recruiting strategies on the number of vacancies filled, new hire turnover and quit levels, performance, and costs.

The Issue

When employment plans identify important shortages of employee skills, decisions must be made on how to remedy them. While skill shortages can be addressed through many human resource activities, such as training and job redesign, they are often addressed through external staffing. An important first step in the external staffing process is recruiting. The quality of the recruiting strategy affects the entire staffing process. If the pool of candidates is unqualified, or if an insufficient number is attracted to accept offers, no amount of sophistication in the way new-hires are chosen can adequately fill the vacancies.

Though a variety of recruiting methods exists, college recruiting receives a great deal of attention and is frequently used to fill entry-level positions that will eventually provide candidates for important upper-level positions. College recruiting can also be quite costly. Therefore, it is important to carefully evaluate college recruiting strategies to achieve a balance among quantities and qualifications of candidates and cost levels. Though many organizations seem to plan and evaluate recruiting activities very informally, systematic attention to the recruiting process and the quality of candidates eventually selected can be quite valuable.

The Situation at Ithaca's Own

As a relatively young organization, Ithaca's Own has emphasized decisions and activities geared toward production, and its HR activities have been focused on the existing employee group. Certainly some external hiring has taken place, especially among marketing professionals where demand has been great and supply of internal candidates has been short. The quality of these entry-level marketing professionals is important, because many of them will become account consultants who manage very large and important marketing efforts. Moreover, they serve as an important source of customer information for improving Ithaca's Own products and generating ideas for new product developments.

In the past, Ithaca's Own has recruited from two nearby colleges, primarily in the business schools. Both colleges have fairly good programs in marketing and business. Because they are close to Ithaca and they tend to draw a student population from the immediate area, recruiting costs are low. It doesn't cost much to send a recruiter over; relocation costs for students are low; and students tend to be very receptive to job offers, since few organizations recruit at these two schools. However, neither school has a very large program (the maximum number of interviews per year is 24 at College 1 and 12 at College 2), so there is some concern that increased recruiting needs will not be met by limiting recruitment to just these two schools. Moreover, because these are small regional state colleges, management thought there should be some new blood from new schools injected into Ithaca's Own.

Two years ago, Ithaca's Own started recruiting from two additional colleges. College 3 is a very large business school at a state university in a major midwestern city. While it boasts a very large program (it is possible to conduct as many as 32 interviews per year there), competition among recruiters is somewhat greater and there is some belief that the quality of students who finally accept job offers may not be very high.

College 4 is a small but very exclusive and well-known business school at an Ivy League private university. Because it is some distance away and tends to attract students from around the nation, recruiting costs are higher. Moreover, although the quality of students interviewed is quite high (virtually everyone interviewed receives an invitation to visit), students from here are highly sought after and often do not accept visit invitations or do not accept job offers. Still, the quality of those hired from College 4 is generally believed to be quite high.

Your Assignment

As the assistant to the director of human resources at Ithaca's Own, you have been asked to analyze the present recruiting situation for marketing professionals and make recommendations for improvements.

No one at I–O has ever systematically gathered any information on costs, yields, or new hire quality across the four schools. Moreover, no one has ever attempted to systematically develop an interview strategy. Instead, recruiting

EXHIBIT 6   Recruiting Information for Marketing Professionals at Ithaca's Own for the Past Two Years

Recruitment Experience for Four Key Colleges (based on Previous two years' information)
College Number

	1	2	3	4
Interviews	38	22	58	12
Invitations	15	9	30	10
Site visits	13	8	22	5
Offers	7	5	12	4
Hires	6	4	8	2
Avg. performance	2.60	3.10	2.70	3.80
Quits in 2 yrs.	0	0	2	1
Fires in 2 yrs.	1	1	0	0
Cost of up to 16 interviews	$1,222	$764	$1,356	$1,664
Cost of 17–32 interviews	$2,525	$1,568	$2,769	$3,470
Cost per visit	$540	$512	$652	$750
Cost per hire	$622	$320	$688	$810
Max interviews yrs.	24	12	32	20

activities are driven by the current crisis. If costs are on managers' minds, recruiters are sent to the regional schools (Colleges 1 and 2). If quality complaints emerge, some additional effort is targeted to College 4. The director of HR believes there must be a better way to plan recruiting activities but wonders whether different recruiting strategies might make any real difference to the cost, quality, and yield obtained and has assigned you to find out.

Gathering the Data

As a first step, start compiling information on the past two years of recruiting activity at each college (shown in Exhibit 6). The data show that demand for new marketing professionals has been running steady at about 10 per year, and this is the number of new hires desired for the next year as well. The budget for recruiting in the upcoming year has a maximum of $28,000.

I–O's marketing account consultants have expressed a desire for higher-quality new hires who perform well and stay with the organization. However, they also don't like to waste their time conducting site interviews with clearly unqualified candidates or with candidates who don't accept subsequent job offers.

Doing the Analysis

The College Recruiting Process
The college recruitment process begins when a shortage is identified and a target number of needed college hires is set. Then, the organization determines

which colleges to visit, how many interviews to conduct, as well as other factors that affect the number and quality of the final pool of new college hires. The college recruiting process typically proceeds through five steps.

1. **Interviews** are conducted at college campuses, usually in the placement office of the university or college. Typically, the organization sends one or two representatives, who conduct half-hour interviews with students.

2. **Invitations for site visits** are offered to those candidates who are evaluated as most promising, based on the interview as well as on any other information compiled during the selection process. Those to be invited are chosen after the interviewer(s) has completed all the interviews and returned to the organization to analyze applicant information.

3. **Site visits** occur when invited candidates come to the organization site. This is usually the particular site where they will work or a headquarters site. In any case, the site visit involves having the candidate meet with prospective co-workers, supervisors, and HRM representatives to exchange information about qualifications and requirements.

4. **Offers** are extended to a subset of the candidates who visit the site. An employment offer stipulates the salary and other working arrangements and usually carries a deadline for reply.

5. **Hires** are the final step. Those candidates receiving offers and accepting them become employees of the organization. Once employed, their performance, tenure, and other outcomes can be evaluated to determine the quality of the recruiting effort.

Analyzing Past College Recruiting Efforts

The college recruiting process begins with an examination of information from past recruiting efforts. While conditions change and the organization may plan changes in its recruitment strategy, the past is often the best indicator of future outcomes. Exhibit 6 shows such historical college recruiting information at I–O. The data were compiled from the results of the last two recruiting seasons at the four colleges.

The first line of Exhibit 6 identifies the four colleges. The next four lines show the number of candidates at each stage of the process from each college. For example, the organization interviewed 38 students at College 1 over the last two years, yielding 15 invitations, which, in turn, yielded 13 site visits, 7 offers, and 6 hires. The next three lines show selected information about the outcomes of the recruiting/hiring process. For each college, the average two-year performance rating of the hires is shown (performance ranges from 1 = poor, 2 = below average, 3 = above average, and 4 = excellent). The number quitting and being fired in their first two years with the company is also shown.

The next four lines show the costs of the different recruitment stages. The cost of interviewing includes travel, lodging, and materials used, as well as the value of the recruiter's time. In Exhibit 6, the cost is shown for two levels of recruiting. One interviewer staying on campus for one day can complete 16 interviews. To complete 32 interviews, however, requires that the interviewer either stay an extra day or that an additional interviewer be sent to the campus. Therefore, the costs to conduct one interview are approximately the same as the costs to conduct 16 interviews.

The cost per visit is the expenses of the job candidate to visit the site, as well as the time and materials of those who interview and evaluate the candidate during the site visit. The cost per hire includes moving expenses and any initial orientation and other support. These two items are directly related to the number of students visiting and hired.

The last line shows the interviews per year for each college. This number is a function of the size of the graduating class at each college, as well as each college's recruiting regulations.

As a recruitment planner, you are interested in comparing different colleges about their "yields." For example, College 1 produced 6 hires for 38 interviews (a 15.8 percent hire-to-interview yield), while College 3 produced 2 hires for 12 interviews (a 16.7 percent hire-to-interview yield). However, yields tell only part of the story. The hires from Colleges 2 and 4 seem to attain a substantially higher performance level than those from Colleges 1 and 3. Still, the costs of recruiting at College 4 are somewhat higher than those at College 1.

Planning the College Recruiting Strategy

The objective of recruitment planning is to identify the colleges to use as recruiting targets and the intensity of the recruiting effort at each college. Information from past recruiting efforts is used to predict the results of this effort. You as the planner may wish to consider the possible changes in external conditions or organizational strategies that might improve the process. For example, perhaps providing more realistic information about the job and the organization during the interview would help candidates better determine whether they are qualified and interested. This might reduce the yield of hires somewhat, but it might also reduce the number of quits. Or, improving the site visits by making them less stressful or giving candidates more specific information about their initial job assignment might improve the number who accept offers.

The important outcomes of recruiting involve getting the right quantities of new hires (neither too many or too few), getting new hires of high quality (in terms of performance, as well as likelihood of staying with the organization), and doing so at the minimum cost. Of course, the particular strategic objectives of the organization will affect which of these factors is most important, but any recruiting plan should consider all of them to some degree.

You have been given this year's budget—$28,000—and goal—10 new hires. Propose a plan that meets these objectives. Decide what initiatives are most appropriate for I–O. Based on this, how many interviews will you conduct at each school, how many site visit invitations will you issue, and how many job offers will you make? Specify what you wish to accomplish by this plan, how it fits into I–O's circumstances, and what HRM actions will be required to carry out your recruiting plan.

Using the PC to Do the Analysis

The information in Exhibit 6, which represents the past two years' experience, has been entered into the exercise for you. To complete your assignment, plan an interview strategy, in light of the potential effects of changes in external conditions and organizational policies. By changing the number of interviews at each college, you can explore the effects of different recruitment strategies. For example, you might discover that the recruiting strategy spends more than the budget. You could examine the effects of emphasizing the less-expensive colleges. However, such a strategy might reduce average performance or increase quits or fires. Which goal should take precedence? Is there a way to reach all of the goals? You could continue to refine the strategy to answer these questions. There is seldom one correct answer. Many recruitment strategies can achieve similar goals.

Use the exercise software to perform needed computations and help organize the results. However, remember **you** must provide the decision-making and analytical skills to develop a feasible and desirable recruitment strategy.

If you need more information while you are using the software, refer to the Using the Software section following the Discussion Questions.

You may want to use the Discussion Questions, which follow, to guide your work.

Discussion Questions

1. What does the information in Exhibit 6 tell you about the four colleges? Your talks with I–O's managers suggested several beliefs, such as: regional schools (Colleges 1 and 2) are less expensive and easy to attract students from but may have lower-quality students; College 4 produces high-quality students, but they are very hard to attract and expensive to recruit. Are such beliefs supported or refuted by the information in Exhibit 6?

2. What will be the effect of your recruiting strategy? Will it meet the hiring goal of 10 new employees? Will it meet the budget goal of staying under $28,000? Will it meet the goal of obtaining high-quality recruits who stay with the company? Will it avoid managers wasting time on unproductive site visits?

3. Discuss the advantages and disadvantages of your strategy (e.g., if you opt for a low-cost strategy, do you have to sacrifice quality?).

4. What other HR actions are required to support your strategy, and what do you want these actions to accomplish? For example, realistic job previews might reduce acceptance rates but also reduce quit rates. Is this a good idea for I–O? Does the present computer program predict effects of such actions?

5. Why can evaluating and planning recruiting activities based only on meeting the hiring goals produce ineffective policies from the standpoint of

cost and quality? Why can evaluating and planning recruiting activities, based only on minimizing cost while meeting hiring goals, also produce ineffective policies from the standpoint of new-hire quality?

Using the Software

1. Start the HRM software by following the steps outlined in Starting Salary, page 661.
2. When the HRM introductory screen appears, use the arrow key to highlight Choosing Colleges for Recruiting: Using the PC. Then, press Enter.
3. The computer will display an introductory screen for the Choosing Colleges exercise. Press Enter again to see the data in Exhibit 6.
4. Press the ESC key to view your menu options. Use the arrow keys and the Enter key to choose your next step from the menu.
5. Remember that the menu options may change, depending on where you are in the exercise.
6. When you have completed a step in the exercise, use the ESC key to return to the menu for your next choice.

Menu Options

✦ *Look at historical data*
Select this option to view the results of past or anticipated recruitment outcomes for the four colleges (the data in Exhibit 6).

✦ *Plan a new strategy*
Select this option to enter the recruiting plan for the four colleges. Follow the on-screen directions to enter information.

✦ *Analyze forecasted results*
Select this option to view the results of the recruitment strategy.

✦ *Save your work*
Select this option to save what you have done so far on this exercise. Be sure to give the file a different name from the one you used in the Starting Salary exercise. If you type in A:college, you will be saving a file named college on the disk in the A drive.

✦ *Retrieve previous work*
Select this option to retrieve a file you previously saved. If you get a message "file not in correct format" the file you are trying to retrieve is not the correct one for this exercise.

✦ *Print your work*
Select this option to print the results of the calculations done by the computer.

✦ *Quit*
Select this option to leave the exercise. This option does NOT automatically save your work.

$\Large\diamondsuit$

DEVELOPING NEW MANAGERS

Human resource management at Ithaca's Own has increased requirements for competent managers to help meet the organization's objective. This coming year, I–O plans to promote 10 people to managerial jobs. None of them have had previous experience as managers. The HRM department is now faced with the challenge of helping to train the new managers.

Current Practices

As a relatively new company, I–O has not yet developed a formal training program, nor documented a policy regarding promotion to managerial status. In the past, when a managerial position was filled from within the organization, these promotions occurred on an ad hoc basis. Training is informal. It is usually on the job by an experienced manager familiar with the organization.

Top management at I–O feels that existing training practices are not appropriate to help prepare the work force for promotion to managerial jobs. In order to develop a more systematic approach to training, the CEO decided to allocate an additional $50,000 for managerial training.

Discussion Questions

Recommend a program designed to prepare employees to become managers at I–O. Your recommendations should consider four factors:

- a. Program objectives, their clarity and rationale.
- b. Content of the program.
- c. Appropriateness of the technique(s) selected.
- d. An evaluation strategy.

Based on these factors, design a development program for potential managers at I–O that includes the following concerns:

1. What are your recommended objectives for the program? Be as specific as possible.
2. What type of developmental experiences will these new managers need? Which training technique, or combination of techniques, would address these needs? What criteria would you use for selecting a method(s)?
3. Who should be responsible for conducting the training program? Why? Would you extend the training to existing managers at I–O? Why or why not?
4. How should I–O go about evaluating the program? What information would you need to evaluate it?

MERIT PAY DECISIONS: USING THE PC

Objective

In this exercise, you will use the PC to:

+ Analyze how merit pay is allocated at Ithaca's Own.

+ Construct a merit pay policy using a matrix called a *merit pay increase grid*.

+ Explore the implications of this grid for the total pay budget, as well as the specific pay raises for a group of I–O employees under varying external and organization conditions.

Issue

Pay increases are vitally important both to employees who receive them and to the managers who must determine them. For employees, increases can signal how their performance is valued by their managers. Greater-than-average increases are good signals, less-than-average increases are not so good. Increases in pay also help maintain employees' financial well-being. For example, increases greater than the increase in the cost of living mean an increase in real income, while less portends a decline.

From a manager's perspective, increases in pay can be used to reward desired employee behaviors and accomplishments (e.g., outstanding performance, innovative ideas, attendance, and so on). Increases must also help ensure that employees' pay remains competitive with that offered by other employers so valued employees do not leave. Finally, increases in pay affect labor costs, and, in highly competitive environments, any increase in costs may affect the organization's success. Determining pay increases is one of the most important human resource issues managers face.

The Situation at Ithaca's Own

The Human Resources Department develops a merit pay plan every six months. This plan guides operating managers and supervisors in allocating the portion of pay raises that are to be based on merit. The plan has two parts:

1. An overall merit increase budget target, based on projected costs, production, and revenue for the next six months. I–O's top managers set this target. This year the target is 7 percent.

2. Merit guidelines, which allocate increases on the basis of two dimensions: *(a)* existing pay relative to the *pay range* for the employee's job and *(b)* employee performance.

EXHIBIT 7   Pay Quartile Distributions of Current Employees

	Top 25%	Mid-High	Mid-Low	Bottom 25%
Percent of employees	10%	35%	35%	20%

The guidelines at I–O have always been based on the general principle that, among similar performers, low-paid employees should get higher percentage raises than high-paid employees, and good performers should get higher raises than low performers.

The actual merit pay raises in previous years have sometimes missed the budget target, and some managers have complained that the raise recommendations were inconsistent. The director of human resources wonders whether these problems are a natural part of the pay policy setting process, or whether a more thorough analysis would result in improved pay plans.

Your Assignment

As assistant to the director of human resources you have been asked to create a merit pay grid that matches the target pay increase budget of 7 percent.

Gathering the Data

As a first step, review the employee records to determine the distribution of employee performance ratings and pay quartile levels. The resulting distributions are shown in Exhibits 7 and 8. You will be entering these distributions into computer, using the merit pay increase program in the HRM software. Then you will use the software to design the pay increase guidelines that will distribute the targeted increase according to I–O's pay policies.

The Merit Increase Grid

As you recall from Exhibit 13.3 in Chapter 13, the increase grid functions as a control device to ensure that pay increases are distributed by managers throughout the organization according to established policy. The grid helps maintain a balance between control of costs and control of distributions of rewards in the organization.

Four variables make up a grid, as shown in Exhibit 9.

1. The distribution of employees at each level of performance. In I–O's performance scale, 1 = poor, 2 = below satisfactory, 3 = average, 4 = above average, and 5 = outstanding. The distribution is the percentage of all I–O employees who received a 1, the percentage who received a 2, and so forth.

EXHIBIT 8   Performance Rating Distributions of Current Employees

	High	4	3	2	Low
Percent of employees	30%	30%	25%	10%	5%

2. The distribution of employees in each pay range quartile. A pay range quartile is one 25-percent segment of the pay range, when you divide the range of pay for a job or job group into four equal segments. The distribution of employees in the quartiles is the proportion of all employees who fall into each quartile of the pay range for their job. In a typical distribution, most employees fall around the middle, but employees are distributed throughout the range. Chapter Thirteen provides more detail on pay ranges and merit increase grids.

3. The percentage pay increase associated with each combination of pay quartile and performance rating. These percentages can be adjusted by you. They are determined by considering both the need to reward high performance with higher pay, the need to keep employees within their pay range, and the financial constraints on I–O.

4. The size of the merit budget. This is the total percentage increase in the pay budget allowed for the merit increase. Multiply this percentage by the total pay budget for the previous period to get the total dollar amount available for merit pay. For example, if last year's pay budget was $500,000 and the current merit pay budget percentage is 7 percent, then there is a total merit pay pool of $35,000 to distribute.

Doing the Analysis

To better understand how grids work, look at the data in Exhibits 7 and 8. They show that 30 percent of I–O employees get high-performance ratings, and 10 percent of I–O employees are in the top quartile of their pay range. As you enter these distributions into the computer, the computer will multiply these two figures together and tell us that 3 percent of I–O employees satisfy both requirements: they get high performance ratings *and* are in the top pay range quartile (30% × 10% = 3%).

This group occupies the upper left cell in the merit grid.

Using the HRM software, you will specify a percent increase for this group of employees. Then you will move to another cell (e.g., employees who have received a "satisfactory" rating and are also in the top quartile of their pay range). What percent increase do you wish to give these employees? Be sure your decisions make sense and are consistent with I–O's pay policies.

As you enter a percent increase in each cell, the computer will tally your expenditures and display it as a percentage at the bottom of the screen. This is the portion of your pay budget that you have already allocated. For example,

---

EXHIBIT 9   A Merit Pay Grid

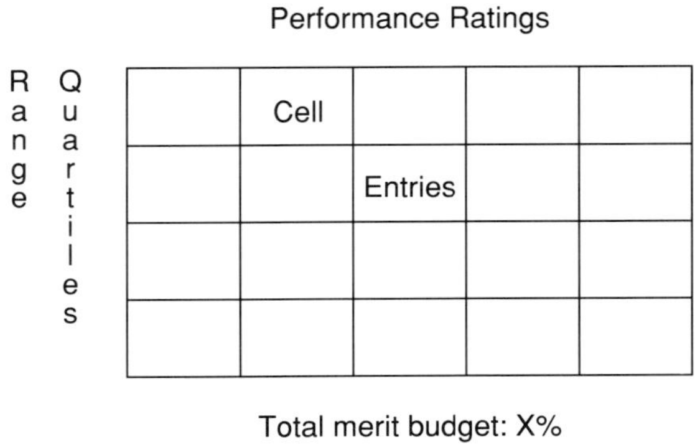

Performance Ratings

Range Quartiles

Cell

Entries

Total merit budget: X%

---

if the figure at the bottom is 8.10 and your budget target is 7 percent, you are already over your budget.

You can simulate (try out) a number of possibilities, while the percentage at the bottom of the screen serves as a cost control device, by telling you how much of your merit budget you have allocated.

Discussion Questions

1. Evaluate your pay grid with respect to the pay budget. Does it meet, exceed, or fall short of the budget? What would be the implications of each of these three outcomes? Use the program to adjust the pay grid percentages until you think they are optimum. Do you think there are other grids that could satisfy the budget criterion? If so, what other factors should be considered in establishing a pay increase grid?

2. Evaluate the implications of your grid for the pay increases of the Bits and Bites operators. What aspects of the resulting pay increase recommendations are likely to be favorably received by the employees and their managers? What aspects are likely to be unfavorably received? Why?

3. When you report to your boss, what three main points will you emphasize to argue in favor of your grid?

4. Consider the future uses of the computer for more strategic planning. For example, if an aging work force tends to shift toward the higher-pay quartiles and higher-performance ratings, what would the implications be if your pay grid were applied to such a work force? What conditions would cause employees to be low in their pay range?

5. Suppose I–O requires a forced distribution of performance ratings, for example, 5 percent fives, 20 percent fours, 50 percent threes, 20 percent twos, and 5 percent ones. Why might I–O adopt such a system? Simulate

this distribution with the software and discuss what effect it has on your budget.

6. Simulate a skewed distribution, for example, 35 percent fives, 50 percent fours, 10 percent threes, 5 percent twos. How might such a distribution develop? What difference will this make to your budget?

7. Discuss whether the grid should vary much from year to year. If not, how can changes in the pay plan reflect changes in employee characteristics, organizational goals, and budget requirements?

8. Discuss your boss's possible criticism that this entire process is too mechanical. After all, once the grid is designed and individual employee data is entered, the raises are determined by the computer program! Where does the manager enter the process? How could you use the program but ensure that pay increases are decided with the manager's input, as well as by the computer-applied formula?

Using the Software

1. Start the HRM software by following the steps outlined in Starting Salary, page 661.

2. When the HRM introductory screen appears, use the arrow key to highlight Merit Pay Decisions: Using the PC. Then, press Enter.

3. The computer will display an introductory screen for the Merit Pay exercise. Press Enter again. If you are using Merit Pay for the first time, type n (for no) when the computer asks if you have previously saved work for this exercise.

4. This will automatically take you to screen A, Employee Distributions. Follow the directions included on the screen to enter the pay quartile distributions in Exhibit 7 and the performance rating distributions in Exhibit 8.

5. After the distributions are entered, press ESC, then use the arrows and Enter keys to choose Go to Grid from the menu. This will take you to screen B. Screen B is the grid that results from the distributions you entered on screen A. Follow the directions on the screen to fill in the grid. At the bottom of the screen is a running total of the percentage of your merit budget as you distribute it among the cells. *Note:* You will not be able to get to screen B until you have completed the distributions on screen A.

6. Pressing the ESC key will return you to the menu for your next choice. Use the arrow keys and the Enter keys to choose your next step from the menu.

Menu Options

✦ *Save*
Saves your work on this exercise. Remember to use a file name that you have not used previously.

✦ *Retrieve*
Retrieves a file you have previously saved.

Return to Employee Distributions Screen/Change Employee Distributions
Allows you to change the pay and performance distributions on screen A.

Go to Grid/Return to Grid
Takes you to the grid (screen B) that results from the pay and performance distributions you entered on screen A.

Graphs
Displays data in pie charts.

Help
Suggests next steps.

Print
Lets you print your results, including graphs. To print the graphs, choose
#3 from the print selection, then tell the computer what kind of printer
you are using. If your printer is not listed, see your instructor.

Quit
This option does not automatically save your work.

COMPRESSION AND EXTERNAL EXPERIENCED HIRING

Ithaca's Own is committed to significantly increasing the staff levels in research
and development and sales. Finding the talent that I–O is seeking is a difficult
task; paying them appropriately without causing serious internal equity concerns is even more difficult. The point is illustrated in the following example:

	Salary after Fiscal Year 1991 Increase	Degree	Years Experience	Last Performance Rating
	Internal Comparisons			
Manager 1	$60,876	MS	12.0	Very good
Manager 2	60,974	BS	7.5	Very good
Manager 3	57,132	MS	11.0	Very good
Manager 4	59,251	BS	8.0	Fully qualified
Manager 5	61,302	BS	7.0	Outstanding
Manager 6	60,910	BS	7.0	Outstanding
	External Offer			
Outside Hire 1	64,500	BS	8.0	—

This scenario is repeated in nearly all external experienced offers that we
make. What alternatives does I–O have to fix the problem, and what are the
optimal solutions given its strategy and business conditions?

THE JACK FREELANCE AFFAIR

The director of human resource management is seeking your recommendation on what everybody in the office is calling the "Jack Freelance Affair." The director gave you the assignment late Friday afternoon and asked you to have a recommendation on his desk first thing Monday morning. All the data on the affair are in the materials which follow. Unfortunately, you will not be able to contact any of the parties involved over the weekend.

There are five pieces of information in the file the director gave you:

1. Case background.
2. Jack Freelance Case Review (prepared by a HR staff person).
3. March 15, memo to file from M. Hill (Freelance's manager).
4. April 20, memo to file from M. Hill.
5. May 6, memo to the HR director from M. Hill, manager of R&D.

Discussion Questions

You are to read the following case file and prepare a recommendation for the director. During your review, consider the following:

1. How fairly was Jack Freelance treated?
2. What steps for "due process" should be followed?
3. Which options in addition to termination are open to Ithaca's Own?
4. What are potential consequences if Jack is not terminated, as M. Hill recommends?
5. What are potential consequences if Jack is terminated?
6. What is your specific recommendation? (Choose one and support your decision.)
   a. Terminate now.
   b. Add supportive data to the file and then terminate.
   c. Demote.
   d. Reassign.
   e. Investigate more extensively (be very specific about how long you would investigate and what data you would collect).
   f. Suspension (how long?).
7. What procedures should I–O consider putting in place to help handle situations like this in the future?

Case Background

Jack Freelance is an associate scientist who has worked at I–O for four years. During this time, he worked for the same manager and received consistently "good" ratings each year. One year ago a new manager was assigned to supervise Jack. Due to changing I–O strategies and goals, the new manager decided to review and revise the department's objectives. The new manager noticed that all of his staff, with the exception of Jack, were relatively new in their jobs. In fact, all except Jack had less than one year's experience. Considering this experience, he felt Jack should perform at a higher level. He met with Jack at the beginning of the year and agreed to change the expected number of projects completed from 8 for the year to 12 in order to achieve a good rating. The rest of the staff, based on experience level, was kept at around 8 projects.

About halfway through the year, Jack and he met again to review how things were going. Jack was well behind the agreed-upon target. So the manager counseled him and made suggestions on how the performance might be improved. An agreement was made to check progress three months later.

At this progress review, the performance was still less than the expected level. When questioned about the matter, Jack responded by saying, "Why should I be expected to complete 12 projects when everyone else only has to finish 8?" The manager responded by saying, "As we agreed at the beginning of the year, your experience and contacts in this area should enable you to perform at a higher standard." The entire meeting was documented, and Jack was warned that he must bring his performance up to standard by year's end. He was given written notice of his performance problem and the potential consequences of it—that is, conditional performance rating and possible dismissal.

At the year-end performance review, Jack's performance level still did not meet the supervisor's expectation. He received a conditional rating. Prior to the meeting with Jack, his supervisor consulted with the human resources manager. It was decided to tell Jack that he had 60 days to correct his performance. If it did not improve, a recommendation for termination would be made. In the meeting, Jack was given final counseling, clearly stating the problems, and steps to resolve the issue. The meeting was documented, and, although the documentation was reviewed by Jack, he refused to sign it as he felt the manager had set too high a standard for evaluation.

It is now 50 days into the 60-day period, and the manager has asked the director of HR to agree with a recommendation for dismissal.

Jack Freelance Case Review

Jack Freelance is a white male, age 46, with a heart condition (angina pectoris—a condition marked by recurrent pains in the chest and left arm, caused by sudden decrease of blood supply to the heart). Medication required: nitroglycerin tablets.

Married, with three children, ages 18, 16, and 12.

Education

B.S. in chemistry from Rutgers University. Two years ago he began taking courses at Syracuse University for a master's degree in chemistry but stopped midway through his second semester.

Past Employment

Jack was first employed as a laboratory technician at Downstate Medical Center for three years while completing his B.S. degree. Upon completion of his degree he moved to Rochester and worked in New Product Technology at Ko-

---

Memo to File: Counseling Session with Jack Freelance

On March 15, Jack Freelance was counseled by me regarding his job responsibilities as an Associate Scientist at I–O. Specifically, he was told that his behavior of March 14, not informing me that he was leaving for the remainder of the day, was conduct not appropriate for his level and would not be tolerated.

Jack was informed that if he demonstrated this type of behavior again, it could possibly result in termination.

Jack was asked for his comments. He stated that the action being taken against him was extremely unfair and that he thought it was happening not because he left for the day without informing me, but because I suspected that he had informed OSHA of the violation.

I stressed to Jack that he was being counseled for leaving for the day without informing me of his whereabouts and the session ended.

_____

Jane Johnson, Human Resource Manager, R&D

_____

M. Hill, Manager, R&D

_____

Jack Freelance, Assoc. Sci., R&D

---

dak for 10 years. Jack supervised eight employees in the department while at Kodak. He later joined the R&D group in Corning Glass as an associate researcher, where he remained for the nine years prior to coming with Ithaca's Own. At the time he was hired as an assistant scientist at I–O, Jack received excellent recommendations from former employers.

Employment History with Ithaca's Own

Jack has been employed with the organization for four years and six months. He was originally hired as an assistant scientist at I–O and was promoted to associate scientist two and a half years ago. His performance history has been

---

Memo to File: Counseling Session with Jack Freelance
April 20

Jack Freelance was again counseled regarding his responsibilities as an Associate Scientist at I–O. Jack did not adhere to proper operational procedures. Specifically, he had neglected to follow through on a product-testing project assigned to him and instead delegated the project to another Associate Scientist. Four days after the situation was brought to his attention, Jack has not yet approached the other scientist regarding his intention to resume the project. This type of neglect is intolerable in light of the stringent deadlines for completion of each project. In addition, Jack admitted that he had not assumed nor assisted in another project since his disposal of the product-testing project.

I further advised Jack that as a result of his negligence of April 20, if another infraction of any kind occurred, I would have no other alternative but to recommend his termination. Jack was given an opportunity to comment and he indicated that he had none.

_____
Jane Johnson

_____
Mervin Hill

_____
Jack Freelance

---

good. Jack is currently the senior associate scientist in the R&D department. Although his actual job duties do not include supervision of other scientists, Jack assisted in training new recruits in the department and informally directs less-experienced scientists on projects.

Two months after his promotion to associate scientist and prior to the new manager taking over, Jack was reprimanded for leaving hazardous chemicals at his work station after closing. This was discussed with him and he was told that it was not to happen again.

Seven months after the incident, his manager changed, as did the focus of his job. More emphasis was placed on individual project work, as opposed to training and assisting other scientists. Everyone felt that he had the background and experience to continue in a largely self-directed, highly technical position.

May 6

TO: Director of Human Resources
FROM: M. Hill, Manager R&D

Jack Freelance was counseled today as he again did not adhere to proper operational procedures. Jack committed a serious infraction by signing the results of a product-safety testing project, implying that he was responsible for the results, while another scientist had in fact completed the project. Due to the emphasis on integrity in research at I–O, Jack knew this was an infraction which could have very serious consequences.

I had previously informed him that if another problem of any kind occurred, I would recommend termination. Jack was asked if he had any comments and he responded:

> "I have personal knowledge that it is not uncommon for experienced scientists to delegate the final stage of a project to a co-worker in order to begin a new project. Principal Scientists do this from time to time and are still employed at I–O."

I informed Jack that these Principal Scientists were not in my realm of responsibility, but he was, and although this is unfortunate, he did violate I–O procedures and demonstrated conduct and poor judgment not appropriate to his level. Therefore, my decision to terminate him stands.

Jack was told that if he wished, he could contact higher authority or the human resource manager of R&D.

It was also decided that there was no need to write a job description, since this was merely a change in priorities.

When the new manager assumed responsibility, Jack informed him of a safety problem in the facility. Specifically, the building was old and it had a deteriorating asbestos ceiling about which Jack claimed he received several complaints from fellow employees. Jack further stated that he had reported this problem to his previous supervisor on several occasions and nothing had been done.

The new manager told him to ignore the complaints as no problems had resulted thus far. It seemed like a minor detail at the time.

About two weeks later, an OSHA representative formally investigated an anonymous complaint and determined that the ceiling was in fact made of asbestos, was in a deteriorating condition and constituted a serious health hazard. OSHA ordered immediate correction of the problem, which required implementing $150,000 worth of repairs to the ceiling. The new management wasn't sure that Jack had informed OSHA of the problem, but very strongly suspected that he had.

When the facility reopened, Jack was directly accused by his manager of informing OSHA of the safety violation. Jack became so upset over the accusation that he had to take his angina medication, and he left the facility without informing his supervisor. Upon his return the next day, he was immediately counseled by his supervisor. At the close of the counseling session, his manager stated that it had come to his attention that Jack was on medication for a heart condition. It was further stated that this was of concern as the job is changing and the job is going to become more stressful.

One month later it was discovered that Jack had neglected to finish a project involving product safety testing, and he had, instead, turned it over to a fellow associate scientist for completion. The incident was brought to the attention of Jack's manager, who instructed Jack to resume the project himself and complete it within the three-week deadline. Both Jack and the manager agreed that the situation had been a misunderstanding caused by some ambiguity in the division of work assignments.

Four days later, however, the manager learned that Jack had not contacted the other scientist with regard to the safety testing project, nor had he begun the preliminary research for the next project. Jack again was counseled regarding the incident.

Three weeks later, Jack's manager received the product-safety testing project with Jack's signature on the final results, but he soon discovered that the other associate scientist, not Jack, had actually completed it. Jack was again counseled and the incident was documented. Jack's manager then called R&D's manager of human resources, informed him of the last incident, and requested termination.

STAND-ALONE CASES

STRATEGIC HUMAN RESOURCE PLANNING

Background

In Chapter Three, we discussed business strategies and presented Miles and Snow's three strategic types: Defenders, Prospectors, and Analyzers. Two points were emphasized: first, that organization units may differ in their financial and marketing directions (i.e., strategies); and second, that different business strategies may require different human resource strategies. We have also suggested that there is no single best approach to human resource management. Rather, the best depends in part on the organization's strategies and objectives. Hence, the manager must consider the strategic directions of the organization when designing HR actions.

Strategic Grids and Screens

The use of analytical techniques to guide strategic decisions has grown rapidly over the past decade. A typical technique is the planning matrix shown as Exhibit 10. The matrix relates an *organization's strength and weakness* to certain environmental characteristics, such as *industry attractiveness,* which yields opportunities and risks for the organization. For industry attractiveness, the vertical axis is determined by such factors as the size of the potential market or the growth rate in consumer demand. Organization strengths (the horizontal axis) are determined by technology, market share, financial conditions, or human resources. In the case of nonbusiness establishments (government units, universities, United Way), the dimensions on a strategic matrix may become "strength of the demand for services provided" and "the organization's strengths and weaknesses."

Several possible stages of cells emerge in the matrix. We have identified three strategic stages for illustrative purposes: Invest (grow), Evaluate (manage selectively), Disinvest (harvest). The characteristics of each stage are included in the exhibit. For example, a business unit in an invest stage is often a highly attractive business (high growth potential, profitability, or high service demand) and has a relatively high business strength (proven management, or good labor

---

EXHIBIT 10   Strategic Planning Matrix

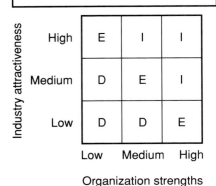

I = Invest (emerging, growth).
Strong revenue, market share potential.
Cash scarcity.
Individual decision makers.
Entrepreneurial managers.
Long-term orientation.
Invest for future.

E = Evaluate (manage selectively).
Revenue potential unclear.
Control expenses.
Formalizing management systems.
Intermediate to short-term orientation.

D = Disinvest (harvest).
Revenue potential weak.
Control expenses.
Formalized management systems.
Short-term orientation.

---

relations). According to this conventional strategic analysis, such a business unit should be considered a good risk and may receive increased deployment of resources to take advantage of the opportunity. Conversely, the disinvest stage combines a less attractive business (shrinking market or highly competitive) with low business strength (obsolete plant). Such a unit may be a drag on the enterprise and eliminated.

Such analysis, employed by General Electric and a host of other organizations, should help to direct the deployment of resources within the organization and to protect developing business directions. Even though there is little rigorous empirical research that supports such models, many industrial and consulting firms subscribe to some variation of the framework.

Discussion Questions

Speculate about the personnel actions that are most consistent with each business strategy. Exhibit 11 provides a framework for your comments.

1. Is planning formalized or not? Is the personnel function likely to be centralized in all strategies?

2. Which strategy is most likely to go outside for talent? Which is most likely to "grow their own"—promote from within and develop employees?

3. Which type would emphasize paying whatever is necessary to hire (competition is key)? Which would emphasize internal pay relationships? Which would focus on incentive plans?

EXHIBIT 11   Strategies

Human Resource Activities	Invest (I)	Evaluate (E)	Disinvest (D)
Planning			
Staffing			
Compensation			
Training			
Labor relations			

4. Would the types of training (e.g., technical, managerial, specific, general) emphasized differ by strategy?

5. Is the management's approach to unions at all related to the strategy it is following? How would the presence of a union affect the ability of the firm to pursue its strategy?

6. You may wish to return to this project after you have finished this book. Compare your answers after you read Chapter Three to those you give after reading the entire text.

JOB ANALYSIS

1. Use the job analysis questionnaire in the appendix to Chapter 3 to describe a specific job you presently hold or have held in the past. This can be a part-time job or volunteer work for which you were not paid. Be sure to put your name on the questionnaire.

2. After you have completed the questionnaire, pick a teammate (or the instructor will assign one) and exchange completed questionnaires with your teammate.

3. Write a job description for your teammate's job. Does the questionnaire give you sufficient information? Is there additional information that would be helpful?

4. Exchange descriptions. Critique the job descriptions written by your teammate for your job. Does it adequately capture all the important job aspects? Does it indicate which aspects are most important? Would it be useful for specifying the hiring and training requirements for your job? How about for performance evaluation or determining pay?

RALPH'S GENUINE FRENCH CUISINE

Ralph's Genuine French Cuisine is a food service company that provides regular catered meal service to organizations in western Texas and New Mexico. The bulk of its service consists of preparing and delivering lunches to office buildings without food service. For the offices, the service is convenient and alleviates the need for an in-house cafeteria. It is especially attractive to offices in outlying areas where a variety of food service is not available. However, many large office buildings in major cities (such as El Paso, Las Cruces, Lubbock, and Albuquerque) also use the service, because it offers their employees better-quality food than available nearby, as well as the convenience of dining on-site.

Lunches consist of such delicacies as scampi Provencale, veal a la Ralph, and Maxime's broccoli with Grand Marnier sauce. Ralph's also does some limited dinner catering for organizations that have a two-shift schedule or employees who work longer hours.

The service is purchased by one or more organizations in a particular office building, and Ralph's agrees to deliver a specified number of catered lunches for a flat fee per month. A key to Ralph's success (sales are up to $12.5 million per year) is an effective sales force to communicate the benefits of the service to the purchasing managers for the companies in the office.

Ralph recently hired Megan Caldwell as his new personnel director, and he called her in to discuss a problem:

"We've really got to get a handle on this turnover problem with our sales representatives, Megan. I've just received the records for the last three years, and we average 30 turnovers every year. With our work force of 100 sales representatives, that means each year we have to hire and train 30 replacements, not to mention the lost productivity while the positions remain vacant. How can we get the turnover rate down?"

Caldwell verified Ralph's statistics. Thirty of the 100 sales representatives per year left for various reasons. Sometimes, they got better offers (Juan's Genuine Cajun Catering is a fierce competitor), but more often they discovered they didn't like the job, relocated for personal reasons, retired, or were dismissed. The average cost of separation plus recruiting, selecting and training one replacement was $7,000.

Caldwell also gathered some sales information on the present work force and on new hires. Her data appear in Exhibits 12 and 13. Exhibit 12 shows the sales of the existing work force by quartile. The variability in sales is rather large (the bottom 25 percent average only $50,000 per year, while the top 25 percent average $200,000 per year). Exhibit 13 shows the pattern of sales over the first four years of a sales representative's tenure. While all sales representative's

EXHIBIT 12   Sales Information on Current Work Force

Quartile	Sales Level
Top 25%	$200,000 average sales per year
Next 25%	$150,000 average sales per year
Next 25%	$100,000 average sales per year
Bottom 25%	$ 50,000 average sales per year

EXHIBIT 13   Sales Information on New Hires

Quartile	Year 1	Year 2	Year 3	Year 4
Top 25%	$50,000	$100,000	$175,000	$200,000
Next 25%	$30,000	$60,000	$100,000	$150,000
Next 25%	$20,000	$40,000	$60,000	$100,000
Bottom 25%	$20,000	$30,000	$40,000	$50,000

sales rise, those who turn out to be the best generally start higher and rise somewhat faster. Sales representatives are currently paid a base of $15,000, plus 8 percent commissions.

Discussion Questions

1. What is the yearly turnover cost? What factors should Caldwell have included in computing her $7,000 per year turnover cost?

2. Based on the model of the Employee Quit Decision in the text, what are three methods Caldwell might use to reduce the turnover rate?

3. Is the 30 percent turnover rate really "too high?" How much could be saved in turnover costs if it were reduced to 20 percent? How much could be saved if it were reduced to 10 percent?

4. What are the sales implications if average performers separate and are replaced by average new hires? (*Hint:* To compute the average of any column in Exhibits 12 and 13, just add up the figures and divide by 4.) What are the sales implications for the worst possible turnover pattern (i.e., the pattern where the highest-performing sales representatives leave and are replaced from the bottom 25 percent of applicants)? What are the sales implications for the best possible turnover pattern (i.e., the pattern where the lowest-performing sales representatives leave and are replaced from the top 25 percent of applicants)?

5. Is it true that the 30 percent turnover rate is necessarily bad? How does your answer to this question suggest an integration between employee

separations and external selection? List and describe three additional pieces of information Caldwell could gather to properly evaluate the turnover implications.

◆

GIGANTIC AIRCRAFT COMPANY

Gigantic Aircraft Company is a large firm with a plant near Santa Barbara, California. The personnel manager has called in Jusef Piersol, a management consultant specializing in personnel, for advice on selection policies. Bill Fabris invited Piersol to come in the first thing in the morning. When Piersol arrived, Fabris said: "Jusef, I'm glad you're here. I've been having a lot of trouble in selection recently. My long suit has always been collective bargaining. I'm a lawyer by training, and I think I need help. Briefly, let me outline how we handle selection here now."

Blue-collar employees—Screening interview to separate out the misfits; then a test battery—mostly abilities tests—and then interview the best of the lot. For crucial jobs, either security-wise or if the job involves expensive equipment, get two letters of reference from prior employers.

White-collar employees—Clerical, and so forth—same as blue-collar procedures except references always are checked out.

Managerial employees—Multiple interviews, intelligence test, personality tests, and references.

Fabris added: "I've also been making a list of what's happened in selection is the last six months since I've been in this job."

1. Our best managerial candidate was lost because she refused to take the personality test we use, the Minnesota Multiphasic Personality Inventory. She said it was an invasion of privacy.

2. For employees who handle expensive supplies, we use a polygraph test, too. We've had a few refuse to take it. Our thefts are high. We wonder if it's any good! My boss feels the polygraph is essential.

3. One man we hired is doing a good job. We accidentally found out he has a prison record. His supervisor wants to know how we missed that and wants to let him go. We have no policy on this, but I feel he's proved himself in three months on the job.

4. We're having a lot of trouble on the reference letters. When we ask people to rate the applicants on the basis of all factors, including references, we find the supervisors read different things into these letters.

5. Our turnover has been high. My boss thinks it's because we aren't matching the best people to the right jobs. I need your help.

Discussion Question

You are Jusef Piersol. Make a list of additional information necessary to help Gigantic. How would you go about acquiring the information? Based on what you know now, what are the biggest problems, and what would you do about them?

◆

TRAINING COST/BENEFIT ANALYSIS AT MASSIVE MANUFACTURING CORPORATION

Spend $3,333 per trainee in a fancy new training system when we could spend $1,000 and use a good old classroom system? You've got to be kidding! We're facing tight budgets and worsening foreign competition, Petrie. The time has passed when you can get support for any bells and whistles fad that comes down the pike. This company has allowed training to run unchecked for too long, and this is a perfect example of the problem.

—Vice President of Marketing, Carol Rose

So went the last comment about a proposed new training system for Massive Manufacturing Corporation. Rob Petrie, the vice president of training, was surprised. In the past, he had enjoyed strong support from top management, but, with increasing competition, his training group was asked to account for their contribution to the organization's competitive position. More and more, managers were questioning whether training was necessary. Several managers had threatened to refuse to send their employees to many of the standard training programs, claiming that competitive pressures were too tight for that luxury. This was understandable, because the managers saw training as simply an additional cost added to their budget.

However, Petrie felt his programs really were contributing. This latest proposal was an example. He had proposed delivering training to manufacturing engineers through an innovative two-way audio and one-way video system that would greatly speed training. Of course, it required funds to build the network, but the payoff could be tremendous. Clearly, however, management was not buying it on faith. He needed some hard numbers. The problem was, he did not have time for a full-blown scientific study with precise statistics and cost figures.

You were recently hired as Petrie's assistant. Petrie was impressed with your training in management and personnel, and he hoped you would bring a much-needed analytical perspective to the training organization. He asked you to put together an analysis within 10 days. You had learned about break-even cost/benefit analysis in your personnel class and knew that it could provide quick and concise analysis in this situation. So, you gathered some information.

EXHIBIT 14 Cost and Leverage Information for the Audio-Video Training

Computing Quantity/Leverage

Year	Trained Employees Added to the Work Force	Trained Employees Leaving the Work Force	Net Increase in Trained Employees in the Work Force	Total Trained Employees in the Work Force
1	200	0	200	200
2	25	5	20	220
3	25	5	20	240
4	25	5	20	260
5	25	5	20	280

Total person-years of productivity affected = 1,200

Estimating Program Quality

Program effectiveness is unknown, but these engineers earn an average salary of $40,000 and make product design decisions that affect millions of dollars in production costs and profits.

Computing Program Costs

Year	Start-Up Costs	Ongoing Program Costs	Total Costs
1	$500,000	$100,000	$600,000
2	0	100,000	100,000
3	0	100,000	100,000
4	0	100,000	100,000
5	0	100,000	100,000

Total program costs over five years = $1,000,000

Computing Total Program Returns

Total program returns = (Program quality × leverage) − Program costs

Program Quality	Leverage	Program Costs	Total Program Returns
$833/person-year	1,200	$1,000,000	$0
1,000/person-year	1,200	1,000,000	200,000
10,000/person-year	1,200	1,000,000	11,000,000

Adapted from: John W. Boudreau, "Utility Analysis: A New View of Strategic Human Resource Management" in ASPA–BNA *Handbook of Human Resource Management*, vol. 1, ed. Lee D. Dyer (Washington, D.C.: Bureau of National Affairs, 1988).

Exhibit 14 shows the analysis for the proposed new audio-video training program. (This analysis is the same one shown in Chapters Seven and Eleven. Details are in those chapters.) Its large training capacity allows all 200 currently employed engineers to be trained in the first year, with 25 new engineers trained in each following year. Assuming a 5-engineer separation rate, this puts 20 new engineers into the work force after the first year, producing a leverage of 1,200 person-years (see Exhibit 14). However, this option is costly, involving a half million construction and set-up commitment before the first training program can even start, and requiring ongoing program costs of $100,000 per year. The marketing manager divided the total $1 million cost by the number of trainees over the five-year program (i.e., 300) to get the $3,333 per trainee figure. You computed an equation for total program returns as shown, and you tried out a couple of hypothetical productivity improvements ($833, $1,000, and $10,000) to see their implications. You found that to break even (i.e., produce benefits that just cover costs), the audio-video training program must improve engineering performance by $833 per person-year, but that at higher productivity levels the benefits increase quickly.

Exhibit 15 shows similar information pertaining to the current classroom training program. In the top part of Exhibit 15, you see the effects of severely limited classroom space—the program can be offered only to 45 engineers per year. Thus, it trains only 225 engineers over the five-year period. However, it costs only $1,000 per trainee, or $45,000 per year, for a total cost of $225,000. The marketing manager divided this $225,000 figure by the total number of trainees (i.e., 45 × 5, or 225 to get her $1,000 per trainee figure). Ms. Rose, the marketing manager, insists that classroom training is as effective or maybe a little more effective than audio-video training, and its lower cost per trainee makes it the clear value. (Also, if you don't get the extra $775,000 for your project, some of it will be available for a new ad campaign featuring Rose's daughter.)

You don't have any comparative training effectiveness information, but you do know that these engineers are paid an average of $40,000 per year. They make product design decisions that affect millions of dollars in manufacturing costs and profits.

Discussion Questions

1. Compute the leverage of the classroom training option (in Exhibit 15). Copy the information on the number of trainees from Exhibit 15 and follow the same logic developed in Chapter Seven to come up with a figure for the total person-years of productivity affected by filling in the blank information in Exhibit 15.

2. Compute a payoff function showing the relationship between total program returns, program leverage, and program quality. Use the symbol $P2$ to represent the unknown program quality per person-year from the classroom training, and follow the same logic as shown in Exhibit 14.

EXHIBIT 15 Cost and Leverage Information for the Present Classroom Training

Computing Quantity/Leverage

Year	Trained Employees Added to the Work Force	Trained Employees Leaving the Work Force	Net Increase in Trained Employees in the Work Force	Total Trained Employees in the Work Force
1	45	5		
2	45	5		
3	45	5		
4	45	5		
5	45	5		____

Total person-years of productivity affected =

Estimating Program Quality

Program effectiveness is unknown, but these engineers earn an average salary of $40,000 and make product design decisions that affect millions of dollars in production costs and profits.

Computing Program Costs

Year	Start-Up Costs	Ongoing Program Costs	Total Costs
1	$0	$45,000	$45,000
2	0	45,000	45,000
3	0	45,000	45,000
4	0	45,000	45,000
5	0	45,000	45,000

Total program costs over five years = $225,000

3. Draw a graph with total program returns on the vertical axis and dollar productivity improvement per person-year on the X axis (i.e., the variable left unknown in Exhibit 14). Graph the payoff function for audio-video training and the payoff function for classroom training. For example, when both programs have zero payoff per person-year, the audio-video payoff is −$1 million and the classroom payoff is −$225,000.

4. What is the break-even point for each of the two programs (i.e., the total program cost divided by total leverage)? Where does it appear on your graph? What do the two break-even values mean?

5. Which program is the better investment if both training methods produce equal benefits and the improved productivity per person-year equals $1,000 per person-year? (*Hint:* Use the value $1,000 in each of your pay-

off functions and compute total program payoff for each option.) Which is better if both produce a payoff per person-year of $3,000? What if the classroom training produces a payoff per person-year of $4,000 and the audio-video training produces a payoff per person-year of only $3,000?

6. What are the implications of your analysis? Is it true that the audio-video training must be more effective in improving productivity per person-year to justify its cost? Explain your answer.

7. Name three additional factors Petrie should consider in choosing whether to present your findings to argue for support for the new program. Name three additional pieces of information you would like to have, and say how you would use them.

STATE GOVERNMENT

Shirley Fleenor is responsible for personnel for a state in the western United States. An official in the state government has a problem.

State Senator Roger McAreavy, a Republican, had just made a fiery speech on the floor of the Senate. He was attacking inefficient and ineffective government. In his speech, which was widely covered throughout the state, he said:

> I suppose that a simple businessman like myself just can't comprehend really complex matters like state government. But I'll tell you that any business which had the record this administration does would be bankrupt by now. If Republicans were running the state, it would be run on a businesslike basis. Instead, we have the wholesale incompetence and waste of this Shaw administration which I'm sure when the people wake up will be thrown unceremoniously out the front door of the statehouse and the governor's mansion. Until that happy day, I guess the people will have to swallow hard and pay higher taxes for the incompetence in Capital City.

Even the TV picked it up. Rarely does the electronic media give much play to state government administration.

The facts the esteemed senator cited were excerpted from the recently published report by the Good Government League. Normally, these reports are filed in libraries without much comment. But this is an election year—three months from the primaries and six months from the election. Governor Shaw has announced that he will run for reelection. Senator McAreavy is running unopposed in the Republican primary.

The Good Government League's report covered many aspects of the state administration. The part that the senator cited was on page 10. It criticized the state administration for having the worst employee turnover in the area. The report showed that this state had a higher turnover than the other nine western states. It compared the state to *overall* turnover and in each category of employment as well. The report said:

> It is distressing to learn that our beloved state finishes absolute last in every category of employment turnover. Turnover is important because it is expensive and leads to gross ineffectiveness. It is expensive because every time an employee leaves, the state must incur recruiting costs, selection costs, and training costs. It is ineffective because everyone knows that there is a period during which all new employees have not reached their peak effectiveness. During that time, the employee makes mistakes. Something *must* be done to stop this waste of the taxpayer's money!

About an hour after the speech was on TV, the governor's office called, and the governor's administrative assistant requested that Fleenor be in the governor's office at 7:30 A.M. the next morning to brief the governor prior to his regular Wednesday press conference. Governor Shaw knows he will get a question about McAreavy's speech, and he wants to be ready.

That's why Fleenor is still at her desk at 10 P.M. Tuesday trying to prepare a briefing for the governor.

The trouble is that the figures are true. The state has had terrible turnover. Why? Well, the pay the state government offers has been poor for years. Often, what happens is that the government winds up with those employees who cannot get employment elsewhere. This may be so because they had a bad work record or because they are not adequately trained. Once they are trained, they leave for better jobs, or the less-desirable employees get fired.

One supervisor in the conservation department has characterized his plight this way: "They send us people who come into my office and say 'Oh! What is that machine there?' I reply that it is a typewriter. As soon as they are adequately trained for clerk typists, they go cross-town to the mining company or the lumber company at a 30 percent raise."

The state has always had this problem, but it has gotten worse in the last few years. For one thing, more industry has come into Capital City. Second, the older industry has expanded. Since the population hasn't increased that much, the salary structure of private industry has risen to attract the people. The legislature was made aware of this, but in the spirit of "economy in government" did not raise the salary scale enough.

What the state does have is a very generous benefit plan. Most of the items in the plan are nontaxable income. In fact, the state's plan is more generous than most of the industry in the area. Too often, state employees have left for a raise in industry but fewer benefits, so they are really behind after taxes. But that is a hard message to get across to large numbers of employees.

Fleenor has run a series of articles about the matter in the house organ, *The Stater*, but readership studies of the magazine are depressing. Most people don't read it. She has encouraged supervisors to discuss this, but follow-up studies find that most supervisors don't do it. Their excuse is that the benefits are complicated and hard to explain to employees, many of whom are not interested.

Fleenor wonders what to tell Governor Shaw in the morning.

Discussion Question

1. You are Shirley Fleenor. Prepare the brief for Governor Shaw. Prepare a program to improve the turnover situation. Assume for Plan 1 that the legislature refuses to increase wages; for Plan 2, that it raises them one half of the difference between the present salaries and salaries for comparable jobs in private industry. Include in your program a plan for taking better advantage of your benefits plan.

LORI PETERSEN[*]

Lori Petersen has worked for WipeEm, a medium-sized manufacturer of cleaning products, for six years. Lori's recent promotion to traffic manager came as quite a surprise to many of her co-workers, who wonder how well she will be accepted in this new job. Lori believes the promotion is recognition for her diligence and hard work as an administrative assistant to the previous traffic manager. Besides, she knows that top management is eager to get more women into warehouse and manufacturing jobs. Lori recognizes that all previous traffic managers have been men, but she is eager to develop managerial experience.

Lori's rapid adjustment and managerial approach quickly gained the support of other managers with whom she worked. However, on a daily basis, Lori saw her formerly cordial relationships with clerical co-workers being replaced by limited cooperation, inefficiency, and subtle forms of insubordination. She sensed that some resented her taking a managerial position and were trying to undermine her performance. Lori ignored the resentment and gradually disassociated herself from the clerical group.

Warehouse and manufacturing personnel considered Lori's promotion to be an opportunity to gain the work schedule changes that were being sought in the next contract. But they soon found Lori's diligence annoying. When Lori came down hard on the warehouse supervisor regarding unnecessary freight delays, the platform crew decided that it was time to put Lori in her place. They filed

---

*This case prepared by Professor Joseph Salamone, SUNY Buffalo.

a grievance, charging Lori did not wear the required safety gear—steel-toed boots, a hardhat, and protective goggles—when she came into the warehouse area. These rules had previously been only occasionally enforced; nevertheless, Lori was ordered to comply. Whereas at first the warehouse employees had been polite in Lori's presence, that, too, changed. They began to make comments that bordered on the obscene whenever she appeared.

To make matters worse, an illness in her family required Lori to deviate from her normal work schedule for several weeks. For many of her former supporters, this was the last straw. They became critical of her behavior, and said they were being forced to do her work. What had started as a great opportunity for Lori had evolved into a nightmare.

Discussion Questions

1. How could the grievance over safety gear have been avoided?
2. Has Lori been subjected to sexual harassment? Cite evidence to defend your answer. How strong is your evidence?
3. List the efforts you would make in designing and implementing an effective policy regarding sexual harassment.
4. List the events that require further investigation as matters of discipline.
5. Was Lori a good choice for the job of traffic manager? Why or why not?
6. How can Lori salvage her job?

◆

COLLECTIVE BARGAINING*

Arlo Gibbs was proud of the way he had handled management's opposition to the union he was helping organize at Tarjo. It hadn't been easy. Management had held numerous meetings with employees in production, maintenance, clerical, and the warehouse departments. So Gibbs was gratified when the NLRB notified him that 52 percent of the 386 employees had signed authorization cards.

He hoped Tarjo management would accept this show of employee preference, recognize the union, and avoid the necessity for an election. Instead, Tarjo began informing workers of the costs of becoming unionized. The company distributed results of job satisfaction surveys taken the previous year at Tarjo, and it said workers would lose their identity if they formed a union.

---

*This case prepared by Joseph Salamone, SUNY Buffalo.

Forced to respond, Gibbs and a dozen or so avid supporters countered management's propaganda with an informational campaign, which stressed group unity, worker voice, shared decision making, and increased fairness to workers. After long hours of publicizing and clarifying the issues, Gibbs was overjoyed with a 200-for, 186-against election outcome.

Aware that the battle had just begun, Gibbs mapped out the following set of objectives for the upcoming negotiations—initially, the union would want:

+ A short-term (one year) agreement so expiration would coincide with other similarly affiliated locals.
+ Union security requiring union dues of all employees.
+ Work assignments based on seniority and job classification.
+ Narrow seniority rights within the department.
+ A broadening of the benefits program, to be employer-financed.
+ An across-the-board wage increase.
+ A cost-of-living adjustment provision.
+ Limitations on management's right to subcontract.
+ A lengthy contract administration provision.
+ Seniority-based decision making.

Tarjo approached the situation in a different manner. All shifts were immediately scheduled for two or three hours of overtime; employee recruiting was stepped up; competitor firms were contacted and asked to supply their product and price lists; information detailing the benefits Tarjo already provided was mailed to the homes of all employees.

Puzzled by management's response, Gibbs called a meeting to develop a strategy for the upcoming negotiations.

Discussion Questions

One group of students should take the role of Gibbs and the other members of the union negotiating committee. They should discuss the following issues:

1. How strong is their support, as evidenced by the results in the organizing campaign? What difference will this make in their negotiating strategy?
2. How will the approach management is taking influence your bargaining power?

Other students should take the role of top management at Tarjo. They should discuss the following issues:

1. What difference does the size of the bargaining unit make to you?
2. What costs do you see associated with the presence of a union?
3. Which dimensions of the employment relationship may have created interest in union representation?

4. Which of the contract objectives Gibbs has specified do you think will be most expensive? Which would you be most willing to agree to, and why?

Each group should prepare a presentation to the class in which these topics are covered. Each group should respond to issues raised by the other group and by other students. They should also cover the proposed list of negotiation items.

◆

CONTRACT COSTING*

XXX Company is attempting to negotiate new contract terms with the IBPW—the union representing the employees. The old contract terms (with average hours worked) were as follows:

Job Category	No. of Workers	Hourly Wage	Average Hours Worked			Paid Vacation Days
			Regular	Overtime	Holiday	
Leadperson 1	25	$10.00	2,000	100	20	10
Leadperson 2	25	12.00	2,000	300	25	10
Production 1	200	6.00	2,000	200	50	10
Production 2	75	7.00	2,000	150	20	10
Production 3	50	8.00	2,000	400	10	10
Maintenance 1	50	9.00	2,000	100	50	10
Maintenance 2	75	11.00	2,000	200	50	10

Note: All employees work an eight-hour day.
Overtime rate = (Regular rate × 1.5).
Holiday rate = (Regular rate × 2.0).

The IBPW proposes that the new contract include:

1. A 5 percent across-the-board wage increase.
2. A new benefit package (costing on average $200 per worker).
3. An increase from 10 to 15 paid vacation days.

The management of XXX Company offers the following:

1. A 3 percent across-the-board wage increase.
2. A new benefit package (costing on average $150 per worker).
3. An increase from 10 to 13 paid vacation days.

---

*This case prepared by Joseph Salamone, SUNY Buffalo.

Discussion Questions

1. If the union's proposals are adopted, what will be the cost of the new contract?

2. If the management's proposals are adopted, what will be the cost of the new contract?

3. If the union proposals are accepted, what is the actual percent increase in wage package experienced by a Leadperson 1?

4. What is the difference in cost between the union's proposed 15 paid vacation days and management's proposed 13 vacation days?

5. Why might the production workers be unhappy with the method proposed by both the union and the management regarding wage increases?

NAME INDEX

A

Aaron, Henry, J., 528
Abbasi, Sami M., 352
Abodeely John E., 627
Abowd, John M., 170
Abraham, Lauren M., 122
Addison, John T., 627
Adler, Tina, 314
Ahern, E., 557
Akers, John, 319
Alexander, Ralph A., 315, 316, 528
Allen, Steven G., 657
Alliger, George M., 316, 442
Anderson, John C., 398, 401, 402
Anderson, R., 353
Ansberry, Clare, 257, 600
Aquilina, D., 560
Aram, John D., 602
Argyris, Chris, 439, 441
Armenakis, A. Achilles, 311
Arthur, Michael B., 398, 399
Arvey, Richard D., 122, 277n, 311, 313, 602
Ash, Ronald A., 88, 441, 527, 559
Atwater, D. M., 171
Auster, Bruce B., 254, 255, 311
Austin, James T., 315
Axel, Helen, 600

B

Baderschneider, Jean, 628
Bailey, T., 353
Baker, G. P., 527, 528
Baldwin, Timothy T., 440
Balkin, David B., 86, 256, 491, 492, 559
Balliet, Lee, 628
Balzer, William K., 120

Baratta, Joseph E., 350
Barber, Alison, E., 253, 256, 492, 583n, 601
Bar-Hillel, M., 315
Barkhaus, R. S., 353
Barocci, Thomas A., 656
Baron, James N., 19
Barrett, Gerald V., 121, 315, 316, 528
Barron, John, 253, 492
Bartel, Ann P., 600
Bartholomew, D. J., 171
Bartlett, C. J., 443
Bartol, K. M., 351
Bass, A. R., 119
Bass, Bernard M., 87
Baxter, James C., 312
Baxter, Ralph H., 352
Bazerman, Max, 526
Beadle, Carson, 559
Beatty, Richard W., 118, 119, 120, 278n, 354
Beauvais, Laura L., 657
Becker, Robert, 559
Bedeian, Arthur G., 119
Bellak, Al, 493, 521, 522, 528
Belous, Richard S., 256
Belt, J. A., 254
Ben-Abba, E., 315
Bennett, Amanda, 122, 253, 351, 354, 402
Bennis, Warren, 87
Ben-Shakhar, G., 315
Berenbeim, Ronald E., 354
Berger, Chris J., 349, 350, 354, 355, 400, 657
Bergman, A., 560
Berkman, Harold, W., 87
Berlind, Rosalind Klein, 353
Bernardin, H. John, 118, 119, 205
Bernstein, Aaron, 352
Bernstein, Irving, 627

Beutell, Nicholas J., 600
Beyer, Janice, 600, 602
Bies, R., 121
Biles, G. E., 170
Billings, Robert S., 236n, 256
Bilu, Y., 315
Bishop, John, 50, 255, 311, 492
Black, J. Stewart, 402, 442
Blake, Robert R., 440
Blau, Francine D., 204, 657
Block, Caryn J., 403
Block, Richard N., 255, 257
Bloom, David E., 559, 601
Bode, Richard, 398
Boehm, V. R., 401
Bolick, Clint, 254
Bolles, Richard N., 362n
Bolt, James F., 353
Booth, Jerome M., 310
Borman, Walter C., 316, 317
Borus, Michael E., 254, 351
Bouchard, Thomas J., 122
Boudreau, John W., 19, 167n, 170, 171, 172,
    255, 257, 349, 350, 351, 354, 355, 398,
    401, 402, 403, 442, 443, 657, 700n
Bowers, D. G., 170
Bowers, Mollie H., 629
Bradford, C., 560
Bragdon, Allen D., 287n
Brannigan, Martha, 443
Bray, D. W., 401
Breaugh, James A., 236n, 255, 256
Bres, E. S., III, 171
Brethower, K., 431n
Brett, Jeanne M., 400, 627, 628
Bretz, Robert D., Jr., 93n, 119, 120, 121, 441,
    527, 559
Brickner, Mary, 401
Brief, Arthur P., 315
Briggs, L. J., 440
Briggs, Steven, 629
Briggs, Vernon M., Jr., 49, 352, 441
Brister, Jozell, 610n, 627
Britt, Louis P., III, 628
Brockner, Joel, 354
Broderick, Renae L., 170, 172
Broderick, R. F., 491
Brody, Michael, 439
Broszeit, Richard K., 398, 400
Brown, Abby, 560
Brown, B. K., 312, 313
Brown, Charles, 492
Brown, D., 253

Bucalo, John P., 599
Buckham, Carol, 558
Buckley, M. Ronald, 120, 312
Buehler, Vernon M., 50
Buller, P. F., 120
Burke, Michael J., 316, 442
Burke, R. J., 120
Burns, Mike, 493
Burris, Laura R., 315
Burton, John, 170, 558
Burud, Sandra L., 559
Bush, Donald H., 401
Bush, George, 228
Bussey, John, 557
Butruille, Susan, 122
Byham, William C., 401

C

Cacozza, Albert F., Jr., 206
Caldwell, D. F., 255
Caldwell, Marilyn S., 315
Calhoun, Kenneth J., 315
Calkins, David, 558
Callahan, Christine, 315
Callahan, Madelyn R., 402
Callahan, Thomas, 510n, 527
Campbell, Donald T., 442
Campbell, D. P., 253
Campbell, John P., 118
Campbell, Richard J., 118
Campion, James E., 277n, 311, 312, 313
Campion, Michael A., 88
Capen, Margaret, 558
Cappelli, Peter, 601, 628, 655
Carnazza, J., 399
Carnevale, Anthony P., 439
Carpenter, Bruce N., 311, 312
Carroll, Donald C., 557
Carroll, Donald C., 557
Carroll, Paul B., 349
Carroll, Stephen J., 26n, 99n, 399, 491, 493
Carron, T. J., 87
Carson, Kenneth P., 316
Cascio, Wayne F., 172, 314, 347n, 349, 350,
    354, 401, 403, 442
Cavender, J. W., 121
Cawsey, T. F., 349
Cederblom, Douglas, 120
Ceriello, V., 172
Chalykoff, John, 118, 655
Chance, Paul, 88
Chase, Marilyn, 171, 353

Choate, Pat, 50
Churchill, G., 526
Cleveland, Jeanette N., 254
Cocheu, Ted, 439
Cofer, John L., 400
Cohen, J., 557
Cohen, Stephen L., 401
Cohen, Yinon, 402
Cohn, Elchanan, 558
Cole, Dianne, 254
Collins, M. M., 87
Conlon, E. J., 170
Connelly, Terry, 170
Constans, Joseph I., 119
Cook, Alice, 528
Cook, Frederick W., 528
Cook, T. D., 442
Cooke, Willaim N., 616n, 628, 655, 656
Cooper, Joseph N., 205
Cooper, Matthew, 353
Cooper, W. H., 120
Coovert, M. D., 119
Cornelius, Edwin T., III, 87, 118, 255
Cotton, John L., 350
Coulson, Robert, 352
Coyle, B., 257
Craft, James A., 170
Creel, George, 558
Crites, John O., 399
Croll, Paul R., 317
Cronbach, Lee J., 315
Cronshaw, Steven F., 313, 316
Crossen, Cynthia, 314
Crouch, Andrew, 87
Crown, Deborah F., 314
Crump, C. E., 314
Crystal, Graef, 528
Cummings, L. L., 492
Curington, W. P., 492
Cytrynbaum, Solomon, 399

D

Dabrow, Allan M., 599
Dahl, Dave, 399
Dahl, Henry L., Jr., 144n, 170
Dalton, Dan R., 349, 350, 354, 355, 629
Dam, Kenneth W., 491
Davis, Gregory A., 602
Davis, Kermit, 544n
Davis, Stanley M., 86
Day, Russell R., 442
Deadrick, Diana L., 313, 316

Deaux, Kay, 655
DeBejar, Gloria, 86
Decker, P. J., 255
DeCotiis, Thomas A., 119
Degregorio, MaryBeth, 120
Delaney, C., 560
Demkovich, Linda, 557
DeNisi, Angelo S., 120
Dertouzos, Michael L., 50
Deutsch, Claudia H., 313
Deutsch, S. J., 170
Devanna, Mary Anne, 87
DeWitt, Rocki, 354
Dickens, William T., 627
Dickson, Terry L., 316
Digman, L. A., 440
Dillingham, Alan E., 600
Dipboye, Robert L., 312
Dobbin, Frank R., 19
Douglas, J. M., 400
Doverspike, Dennis, 528
Dowling, Peter J., 50
Downs, C. W., 257
Downs, Sylvia, 440
Dreher, George, R., 401, 441, 527, 559, 560
Dreissnank, C. H., 353
Driscoll, Lisa, 118
Drucker, Peter F., 628
Drumboltz, John D., 400
Duffy, Jan, 600
Dumaine, Brian, 118
Dunbar, Edward, 402
Dunham, Randall B., 583n, 601
Dunkelberg, William, 492
Dunlap, John, 86
Dunnette, Marvin D., 88, 121, 205, 310, 317, 399, 443
Durick, Mark, 122
Duston, Robert, 118
Dyer, Lee D., 19, 26n, 28n, 29n, 49, 50, 57, 86, 88, 171, 172, 205, 253, 257, 310, 349, 351, 352, 353, 398, 443, 527, 601
Dyl, E. A., 349

E

Eason, L. W., 257
Eaton, N. Kent, 117
Eder, Robert W., 120, 276n, 283n, 310, 312, 313
Ehrenberg, Ronald G., 50, 254, 345n, 354, 491, 492, 628
Ehrenhalt, Samuel M., 50

Ehrlich, Elizabeth, 402
Einbender, W. W., 311
Elias, Dean C., 441
Ellig, Bruce, 492, 528, 557, 559
England, George W., 310
Ewing, David, 205

F

Fairbairn, Ursala, 410
Fairris, David, 656
Faley, Robert H., 311, 313, 317
Falkenberg, Loren, 558
Faludi, Susan, 206
Fannin, T. A., 560
Fannin, T. N., 560
Farh, J. L., 119
Farley, John A., 253
Farnham, Alan, 19, 466n, 493
Farr, James L., 121
Fay, Charles H., 119, 312
Fedor, Donald B., 120
Feild, Hubert S., 311, 316
Feinstein, Selwyn, 256
Feldman, Daniel C., 440
Feldstein, Martin, 253
Ferber, M. A., 204
Feren, Dena B., 400
Ferguson, Karen, 559
Fernandez, Linda, 253, 254
Ferris, G., 255, 256, 283n
Ferris, Gerald R., 88, 120, 171, 255, 256,
    283n, 276n, 312, 313, 350, 398, 401, 440,
    491, 493, 527
Festa, Ronald M., 254
Field, Anne R., 255
Field, Hubert S., 121, 312, 315, 544n
Fielder, Fred E., 86
Fields, Gary S., 559
Filer, Randall K., 528
Fine, S. A., 87
Fink, Laurence S., 256
Finney, Martha I., 18, 170, 602
Fiorito, Jack, 655
Fischer, Ben, 559, 601
Fisher, Anne B., 354
Fisher, Caricia, 443
Fisher, Cynthia D., 120
Fisher, George M. C., 405
Fitzgibbons, E. J., 400
Flamholtz, Eric G., 170, 349, 354
Fleishman, Edwin A., 87, 313, 314, 440

Florin-Thuma, Beth C., 19, 50, 120 121, 310,
    443
Flug, A., 315
Fogli, Larry, 118, 316
Folder, Roger, 492
Foltman, F., 352, 353, 441
Ford, J. Kevin, 440
Ford, N., 526
Fossum, John A., 526, 627, 656
Foster, Kenneth E., 492
Foster, Lawrence W., 601
Fox, William M., 441
Frank, Frederick D., 401
Franks, Marlene Strong, 204
Fraser, Douglas, 604, 641
Fraze, James, 18
Freeman, Kimberly A., 118
Freeman, Richard B., 204, 206, 557, 627,
    651n, 655, 656
Fried, Yitzhak, 88
Friedman, Dana E., 559
Friedman, Stewart D., 399
Frierson, James G., 118, 314
Fritz, Norma R., 317
Frtiz-Enz, Jac, 170
Frons, Marc, 351
Fuchs, Victor R., 49, 50, 402, 601
Fukami, Cynthia, 627
Fuller, R., 353

G

Gael, Sidney, 88
Gagne, R. M., 440
Gainer, Leila J., 439
Galagan, Patricia A., 439, 441
Galen, Michele, 118
Galvin, Robert W., 405
Gannon Martin J., 255
Garcia, Beatrice E., 442
Garcia, Joseph R., 86, 399
Garcia, M., 119
Gast-Rosenberg, I., 316
Gatewood, Robert D., 312, 315, 316
Gaudet, F. J., 349
Geber, Beverly, 418n, 423n, 440
Gebhardt, D. L., 314
Geisinger, Kurt F., 253
Gellerman, Saul W., 119
Gerhart, Barry, 86, 350, 527
Gerson, W. F., 254
Gersuny, Carl, 628

Geyelin, Milo, 314, 315, 352
Giannantonio, Christina M., 399
Giber, David, 442
Giles, William F., 311, 544n
Gilkey, Roderick W., 353
Gill, Mary Jane, 440
Gilley, D. W., 253
Gillispie, Jackson F., 171
Gilmore, D. C., 313
Gilroy, Curtis, 350
Gist, Marilyn E., 441
Gleason, Sandra E., 528
Gleser, Goldine C., 315
Glick, W., 88
Glisson, Charles, 122
Glover, M. Katherine, 139n
Glueck, William, 254, 399
Gobeille, Kenneth R., 602
Goel, Vindu P., 171
Goldberg, J. P., 557
Goldberg, Stephen B., 628
Goldstein, Irvine L., 408n, 440, 441, 442
Gomez-Mejia, Luis R., 87, 170, 172, 491,
    492, 559
Goodale, James G., 312
Gooding, Richard Z., 316
Gordon, Jack, 406n
Gordon, Michael E., 205, 400, 657
Gordon, Randall A., 312
Gorman, Christine, 441
Gottredson, Linda S., 313, 317
Graen, George, 392n, 402
Graen, Martin, 392n, 402
Graen, Michael, 402
Graham, Marcia, 205
Graham-Moore, Brian, 526
Grant, D. L., 401
Grant, E. Kenneth, 656
Gray, Wendy B., 559
Greenberg, Eric Rolfe, 353, 354, 600
Greenberg, Jerald, 121, 492, 493, 601
Greene, B., 526
Greene, Kevin, 559
Greenhalgh, Leonard, 353
Greenhaus, Jeffrey H., 403, 600
Grenier, Guillermo J., 50, 88
Grenig, Jay E., 352
Grestner, L. V., 254
Griffeth, R. W., 350
Grinold, R. C., 171
Groenman, S., 256
Groshen, Erica, 86, 492

Gross, Beverly, 600
Grossman, Morton E., 256
Grover, Steven, 354
Gruenfeld, Elaine, 600
Grune, Joy Anne, 206
Guest, Robert H., 88
Guion, Robert M., 316
Gupta, Nina, 492, 493
Gupta, Udayan, 252
Gutteridge, Thomas G., 253

H

Haber, W., 557
Haberfield, Yitchak, 312
Hackman, J. R., 88
Haight, Gretchen, 49
Hakel, Milton D., 118, 278n, 312
Hall, Douglas T., 372n, 385n, 398, 399,
    402, 441
Hall, H., 88
Hall, R. E., 398
Haller, Eleanor, 122
Hallman, G. Victor, 537, 557, 560
Hamel, Daniel A., 400
Hamilton, John W., 316
Hammer, Randi C., 627
Hammer, W. Clay, 403
Hamner, Clay W., 527
Hampton, William J., 317
Hand, H. H., 350
Handorf, Charlene R., 352
Hanisch, Kathy A., 315
Hannon, John M., 86, 170
Hansen, Curtiss P., 315
Hanson, J. C., 253
Harkins, Philip J., 442
Harris, Donald, 166n, 172
Harris, Louis, 400
Harris, Michael M., 119, 311, 312, 313, 400
Hart, G. L., 401
Hartigan, John A., 255, 313, 317
Hartke, Darrell D., 87
Hartmann, Heidi I., 51, 204, 528
Havemann, Judith, 257
Hayes, Arthur S., 351
Hedge, J. W., 119, 120
Heilman, Madeline E., 403
Helfgott, Roy B., 86
Heller, F. A., 527
Hellervik, Lowell W., 313
Henderson, M. G., 560

Heneman, H., Jr., 87, 170
Heneman, Herbert G., III, 492, 527, 627
Heneman, R. L., 526
Henry, Rebecca A., 316
Herriott, P., 257
Herz, Dane E., 254
Herzlinger, Regina E., 558
Hilgert, R. L., 257
Hill, Herbert, 205
Hill, R. E., 255
Hillery, Joseph M., 316
Hinrichs, John R., 171, 401
Hirsch, Barry T., 627
Hirschman, Albert O., 656
Hirsh, Hannah Rothstein, 316
Hitt, Michael, 170
Hock, Roger R., 385n
Hodgson, William G., 119
Hoerr, John, 349, 353, 354
Hofer, C. W., 86
Hogan, Joyce, 314
Hogarth, Jeanne M., 558, 559
Holder, Gerald W., 19, 57, 86
Holland, J. L., 253, 398
Hollenbeck, John R., 315, 351
Holley, William H., 121, 311
Hollman, Kenneth W., 352
Holloway, William J., 352
Holmes, Allan, 353
Holusha, John, 88
Holz, B. W., 171
Holzer, Harry J., 255, 257
Hooper, Laurence, 349
Hopkins, Kevin R., 254
Hough, Leatta M., 88, 311, 316, 317
Howard, Ann, 400
Huberty, C. J., 87
Hulin, Charles L., 120, 316
Hundley, Greg, 655
Hunt, D. P., 442
Hunter, John E., 310, 313, 314, 315, 316,
    401, 440
Hunter, Rhonda F., 310, 314, 315, 401
Hurd, Richard W., 655
Hymowitz, Carol, 354, 402, 403

I

Iaffaldano, M. T., 121
Ignatius, Adi, 120
Imberman, Woodruff, 628
Ippolito, Richard, 492
Ireland, R. D., 170

J

Jaccoma, Richard, 256
Jackofsky, Ellen, F., 350
Jackson, T., 353
Jacobs, C., 560
Jacobs, Deborah L., 560
Jacobs, Rick R., 121
Jacoby, David, 400
Jacoby, Sanford M., 87, 121, 628
Jago, Arthur G., 88
Jakubson, George H., 345n, 354
Janak, Elizabeth A., 442
Janes, Harold D., 493
Janz, Tom, 312
Jaques, Elliot, 88
Jaynes, G. D., 205
Jeannert, P. R., 87
Jenkins, G. Douglas, Jr., 492, 493
Jennings, M. C., 313
Jennings, P. Devereaux, 19
Jensen, M. C., 527, 528
Jerdee, Thomas H., 49, 332n
Jette, R. D., 118
Jick, Todd, 628
Johnson, Cecil, 315
Johnson, Eve, 206
Johnson, Richard E., 559
Johnson, Terry R., 442
Johnson, William A., 205, 400
Johnston, P. D., 353
Jones, David F., 440
Jones, John W., 315
Jordan, C., 353
Joyce, John, 656

K

Kahalas, Harvey, 171
Kahn, Alfred J., 19, 50, 599
Kahn, Lawrence, 657
Kahn, R. L., 600
Kalleberg, Arne L., 50
Kamerman, Sheila B., 19, 50, 558, 599
Kanabayashi, Massayoshi, 257
Kane, Jeffery S., 118, 119
Kang, Suk, 311
Kanter, Rosebeth Moss, 401
Kariya, Takehiko, 257, 311
Karren, Ronald J., 120
Katz, Harry C., 599, 601, 602, 628, 655
Katzell, R. A., 118
Kauff, Jerome B., 352
Kaufman, H. G., 402

Kavanagh, Michael J., 120
Kearns, David, 228
Kearsley, Greg, 433n, 452n
Keats, B. W., 170
Keaveny, Timothy J., 349
Keeley, Michael, 170
Keichel, Walter, III, 121, 439
Keller, John J., 353
Kendall, Daniel W., 18
Kendrick, John W., 88
Kernan, Mary C., 121
Ketchum, R. H., 353
Kets de Vries, Manfred F. R., 402
Keyhoe, Jerard, 316
Kikaoki, John F., 120
Kilgour, John G., 655, 656
Killingsworth, Mark, 528
Kingstrom, P. O., 119
Kinnier, Richard T., 400
Kirk, J. Robert, 352
Kirkpatrick, David L., 256, 442
Kirnan, Jean Powell, 253
Kirp, David L., 204
Kirsch, Michael, 316
Kirshner, Kenneth H., 352
Kleiman, Lawrence S., 317
Klein, Janice A., 655
Kleiner, Morris M., 255, 257
Klimoski, Richard, 401
Kochan, Thomas A., 118, 119, 355, 599, 602,
     628, 636n, 637, 655, 656
Koike, Kazuo, 656
Konda, Suresh L., 398
Konovsky, Mary, 492
Kopelman, R. E., 118
Kotlowiz, Alex, 628
Kotter, John P., 87
Koys, Daniel J., 86, 352, 599
Koziara, Karen S., 204, 528
Krackhardt, David M., 350, 355
Kram, Kathy E., 399
Krantz, James, 87
Kreuger, Alan, 492
Krzystofiak, F., 171, 172, 194n
Kupfer, Andrew, 118, 314
Kuruvilla, Sarosh, 492

L

Ladd, Robert T., 657
Laforge, R. L., 171
Lakhani, Hyder, 350, 492
Lambert, Wade, 351

Landy, Frank J., 121
Lannon, Lynn, 122
Larcker, D. F., 528
Larson, Erik W., 627
Latack, Janina C., 601
Latham, Gary P., 117, 118, 119, 283n, 312,
     313, 414, 439, 440, 441
Lavin, Mary Jo, 172
Lawler, Edward E., III, 118, 119, 491, 492,
     493, 505n, 508, 514, 526, 527
Lawler, John J., 253, 611n, 627
Lawrence, Barbara S., 398, 399
Lazer, Robert I., 403
Leap, Terry L., 352
Ledford, Gerald E., Jr., 493
Ledvinka, James, 171, 257, 317, 491
Lee, JoAnn, 87
Lee, Timothy W., 118, 492
Lee, Tony, 256
Leech, Michael J., 352
Lehr, Richard I., 600
Leigh, J. Paul, 558
Leininger, Wayne E., 171
Lemons, Mary L., 520
Lengick-Hall, Cynthia A., 86
Lengick-Hall, Mark L., 86
Lenskowsky, Leslie, 656
Leonard, Jonathan S., 205, 627, 655
Leonard, Russell L., 442
Lester, Richard K., 50
Levering, Robert, 18, 86, 88, 560
Levin, E., 527
Levine, Edward L., 88
Levy, Girard, 119
Lewis, H. Gregg, 650n, 656
Liberman, Myron, 493
Likert, R., 64, 87, 170
Lilyquist, John, 412n
Lincoln, James, 526
Linden, Eugene, 441
Lindsey, Benjamin, 558
Linger, J. K., 50
Lipset, Seymour Martin, 627
Lipsky, David B., 400
Lissitz, R. W., 87
Litterer, Joseph A., 120
Livernash, E. Robert, 204, 492
Loar, Michael, 119
Locke, Edwin A., 88, 118, 121, 122
Lodge, George, 19, 86
Lombardo, Cynthia A., 442
Lombardo, Michael M., 439
London, Manuel, 401, 440, 441

Lopez, Julie Amparano, 351
Lorber, Lawrence Z., 352, 628
Lorenzo, Frank, 56
Lorsch, Jay W., 401
Lougy, Cameron M., 528
Love, Kevin G., 310
Lowman, Christopher, 655
Luka-Siewiez, John, 45n
Lynn, Monty L., 610n, 627

M

McCaffery, Robert M., 557
MacCallum, R. C., 119
McCarthy, Albert H., 256
McCarthy, Michael J., 256, 292, 315
McCarty, Claire L., 493
McCauley, Cynthia D., 439
McClain, Maureen E., 352
McCormick, Ernest J., 67n, 87
MacCrimmon, K. R., 398
McCrosky, Jaquelyn, 558
McCullough, P. Michael, 400
McCune, Joseph T., 354
McDaniel, Michael A., 315
McDermott, Edward T., 51
McDonald, Charles, 628
McDonald, T., 312
McDuffie, John Paul, 355
McEvoy, Glen M., 120, 350
Macey, Scott, 560
McFillen, J. M., 349
McGee, G. W., 121
McGee, Lynne F., 253
McIlroy, Gary T., 558
McKenzie, Robert C., 317
McKeon, W. J., 442
McKersie, Robert B., 353, 526, 599, 601, 628, 655
McLaughlin, Steven D., 442
McNutt, Kathryn J., 88
McQuigg-Martinez, Beverly, 439
Madigan, Robert M., 313, 316
Madlin, N., 441
Mahler, Walter R., 170, 171
Mahoney, Thomas A., 26n, 49, 170, 171, 492
Main, Jeremy, 354
Mainiero, Lisa A., 402
Mak, Carol L., 353
Maki, Dennis, 628
Malm, F. T., 254
Mann, R. B., 255
March, James G., 350

Marcus, Amy Dockser, 352
Marcus, Eric H., 352
Markham, Edwin, 558
Markos, V. H., 87
Marovee, Milan, 401
Marron, Donna Blancero, 601
Marshall, K. T., 171
Marsis, Elizabeth, 655
Martell, Richard F., 403
Martin, Ann W., 601
Martin, C., 119
Martin, David C., 121, 351
Maslow, A., 526
Mason, N. A., 254
Mathieu, John E., 350, 442
Maurer, Steven D., 312
Mayfield, Eugene, 311
Mayo, E., 88
Mealia, David W., 442
Mecham, R. C., 87
Medoff, James L., 492, 557, 651n, 656
Megalino, M. M., 350
Meier, David, 440
Mendelsohn, Susan R., 600
Mendenhall, Mark E., 402, 442
Mendoza, Jorge L., 87
Mento, Anthony J., 120
Mercer, Michael W., 354
Metzenbaum, Howard M., 206
Meyer, Alan D., 51
Meyer, David G., 628, 655
Meyer, Herbert H., 316, 527
Meyers, D. C., 313
Mezoff, B., 442
Middlebrooks, David J., 600
Miles, Raymond E. Miles, 50, 86
Milkovich, George T., 26n, 36n, 49, 86, 88, 93n, 119, 120, 121, 170, 171, 172, 204, 205, 352, 353, 398, 401, 402, 453n, 456n, 464n, 465n, 467n, 469n, 472n, 475n, 476n, 478n, 491, 492, 497n, 504n, 526, 527, 528, 557, 561n
Miller, Ernest C., 310
Miller, H. E., 256, 257
Miller, Sandra J., 657
Miller, Thomas I., 601
Miller, William B., 172
Milligan, J. C., 560
Mills, D. Quinn, 401
Minor, Frank J., 372n
Mironi, Mordechai, 628
Mitchell, Brooks, 312
Mitchell, J. B., 628

Mitchell, K. J., 117
Mitchell, Michelle, 51
Mitchell, Olivia S., 558, 559
Mobley, William H., 328, 350
Mohrman, Allan M., Jr., 118, 119, 120
Monat, Jonathan S., 441
Montagno, Raymond V., 354
Montague, Claudia, 627
Montgomery, Linda, 254
Moore, Marat, 190n
Moore, Richard, 655
Moore, William J., 656
Moran, Nancy L., 352
Morgan, K. S., 171, 172
Morhman, Susan, 119
Morrison, Kathryn R., 600
Morrison, Robert F., 171, 385n
Mosher, Collette, 528
Moskow, M. H., 204
Motowidlo, Stephen J., 205
Mouton, Jane S., 440
Mowday, Richard, 121, 122, 492
Moynahan, John K., 526
Muchinsky, Paul M., 121, 401
Mumford, Michael D., 440
Munchus, George, III, 256
Murdick, R. G., 171
Murphy, Kevin R., 119, 120, 313
Murphy, K. J., 527, 528
Murrey, Joe H., Jr., 352
Myers, Louis B., 119

N

Nagle, David E., 118
Napier, N. K., 117
Nardone, Thomas J., 601
Nash, Allan N., 493
Nelson, Sherry M., 602
Nestleroth, Susan L., 254
Newman, Jerry M., 36n, 86, 194n, 453n,
     456n, 464n, 465n, 467n, 469n, 472n,
     475n, 476n, 478n, 491, 497n, 504n, 526,
     557, 561n
Newman, Robert J., 656
Newstrom, John W., 421n, 583n, 601
Nichols, Robert H., 352
Nieder, Linda L., 87
Niehaus, R. J., 171
Noe, Ann Wiggens, 254
Noe, Raymond A., 316, 400, 492
Nollen, S. D., 601
Nord, Roy, 315

Nowak, Margaret, 257
Nuti, Domenico Mario, 526

O

Oaxaca, Ronald L., 253
Oberle, Joseph, 441
O'Brian, Bridget, 441
Ocasio, Benjamin P., 316
O'Connell, Martin, 601
Oddou, Gary R., 402
O'Dell, Carla, 526
O'Hara, Kirk, 310
Oldham, G. R., 88
Olian, Judy D., 254, 312, 314, 399, 600
Oliver, Anthony T., Jr., 352
Olson, Craig A., 400, 657
O'Malley, Michael, 354
O'Neill, J., 528
O'Reilly, Charles, 64n, 86
Organ, Dennis W., 122
Ornati, Oscar, 558
O'Rourke, Paul, 355, 441
Oswald, R. A., 557
O'Toole, James, 533, 534, 557
Outerbridge, A. N., 313
Owens, W. A., 310

P

Page, Ronald C., 87
Paine, Thomas, 557
Parasuraman, Saroj, 403
Parker, Barrington, 342n
Parker, Mike, 601
Parkhouse, Gerald C., 343, 354
Parnes, Herbert S., 254, 351
Parsons, Donald O., 491
Patten, Thomas H., Jr., 601
Patton, Robert T., 441
Pauli, Karen E., 315
Payne, James L., 352
Payne, J. W., 254
Pearce, Jane L., 527
Pearlman, Kenneth, 316
Peck, Charles, 526, 527
Peiperi, Maury A., 367n
Pepe, Stephen P., 600
Perlman, Selig, 656
Perrin, 559
Perry, Charles R., 655
Perry, James L., 527
Perry, Nancy J., 50, 253, 255, 257, 311
Peters, Lawrence H., 87

Peters, Thomas J., 86
Petty, M. M., 121
Petzinger, Thomas, Jr., 354
Pfeffer, Jeffrey, 402
Phillips, Jack J., 442
Phillips, James S., 316
Phillips, Neil, 314
Phillips-Jones, L., 399
Pierce, Jon L., 583n, 601
Pierson, David A., 528
Pierson, Frank C., 492
Pinto, Patrick, 399
Pleck, Joseph, 601
Plento, Anthony J., 401
Pohlmann, John T., 87
Polakoff, Philip, 558
Pool, Robert, 120
Poole, Robert W., 599
Porter, Lyman W., 121, 349, 350, 355
Portman, Lisa, 205
Powers, Mary L., 440
Premack, S. L., 256
Preston, James R., 401
Price, James L., 350
Prosten, Richard, 628
Pulakos, Elaine D., 316, 317
Pursell, Elliot D., 312, 313
Putka, Gary, 313, 441

Q–R

Quigley, Ann M., 314
Rabin, Bonnie, 528
Raelin, Joseph A., 402
Rafilson, Fred M., 315
Ragins, Belle Rose, 87
Raju, N. S., 316
Ramos, Robert A., 403
Ramras, E. M., 87
Randall, J. S., 440
Rappaport, Stephen S., 254
Rayback, Joseph G., 627
Raza, Susan M., 311, 312
Reagan, Ronald W., 604, 644
Reed, David J., 581n
Reed, Thomas, 354
Reid, G. L., 254
Reilly, Anne H., 400
Remick, Helen, 49, 204, 206, 528
Resnick-West Susan M., 118, 119
Rhodes, Susan R., 112n, 121
Rice, Faye, 255
Rich, Joe R., 443

Rich, Jude T., 492
Roback, J., 528
Roberts, K., 88
Robertson, Ivan T., 440
Rock, Milton L., 493
Rodgers, Robert C., 351
Ronen, Simcha, 442
Rones, Philip L., 254
Roomkin, Myron, 255, 257
Roosevelt, Franklin D., 517
Ropp, Kirkland, 441
Rose, Richard, 557
Rosen, Benson, 49, 332n, 349, 441
Rosen, Corey, 559, 601, 655
Rosenbaum, David E., 558
Rosenbaum, James E., 257, 311, 398, 402
Rosenbloom, Jerry, 536, 557, 560
Rosenfeld, C., 253
Rosenthal, R. A., 600
Rosinger, Goerge, 119
Ross, Joel E., 399
Ross, Timothy, 526
Rosse, Joseph G., 314
Rosse, R. L., 88
Roth, Laurie Michael, 402
Rothberg, Diane S., 601
Rothfeder, Jeffery, 118
Rothstein, Mark A., 600
Rothwell, C., 257
Rowe, P. M., 312
Rowland, D., 526
Rowland, Kendrith M., 88, 120, 171, 255,
    256, 350, 398, 401, 440, 491, 493, 527
Rozelle, Richard M., 312
Ruben, George, 560
Rubin, Paul, 510n, 527
Rude, Stephanie S., 400
Rudelius, W., 171
Rumelt, R. P., 87
Rummler, G., 431n
Russell, James S., 440
Russell, J. T., 317
Ryan, Paul, 441
Rynes, Sara L., 253, 254, 255, 256, 257, 310,
    313, 399, 402, 492

S

Saari, Lise M., 119, 439, 441, 442
Sackett, Paul R., 118, 315, 316, 400, 401
Saddler, Jeanne, 441
Salamone, Joseph, 602, 629, 706n, 709n
Salipante, Paul F., Jr., 602

Salisbury, Dallas, 557, 558
Salsburg, Sidney W., 255, 257
Saltzman, Amy A., 254, 255, 311
Sandell, Steven H., 254, 351
Sandler, Andrew L., 627
Sandver, Marcus H., 627
Saran, Rene, 655
Sarri, Lise M., 313
Sass, S. D., 353
Scarpello, Vida, 257
Schaaf, Dick, 353
Schaeffer, Ruth G., 205
Schaubroeck, J., 119
Schein, Edgar H., 50, 88, 399
Schendel, D., 86
Scherba, Dale S., 400
Scherkenbach, William W., 122
Schinner, A. P., 171
Schmidt, Frank L., 313, 316, 403
Schmitt, Neil, 257, 311, 312
Schmitt, Richard B., 171, 315
Schmitz, Edward, 315
Schneier, Craig Eric, 99n, 119, 278n
Schoenfeldt, Lyle F., 401
Schrenk, Lorenz P., 28n, 29n, 49
Schuh, Allen, 310
Schuler, Randall S., 26n, 49, 170, 349, 599
Schultz, Charles, 526
Schultz, George P., 491
Schuster, F., 171
Schuster, Jay, 559
Schuster, Michael H., 527, 656
Schwab, Donald P., 255, 312, 492, 527
Schwartz, Howard, 86
Schwartz, Jeffrey, 558
Schwoerer, Catherine, 349, 441
Scott, K. Dow, 313, 316
Scwab, Donald P., 255
Seamans, Lyman, Jr., 172
Seeber, Ronald L., 629
Segal, Nancy L., 122
Seidman, Bert, 254, 351
Seybold, Geneva, 170
Shane, G. S., 316
Shapiro, Joseph P., 254, 255, 311
Shapiro, Kenneth, 544n
Sharf, James C., 317
Shaw, Karyll N., 254
Sheets, Kenneth R., 50
Sheldrake, John, 655
Shenkar, Oded, 50
Shepard, Ira Michael, 118, 352
Sheppard, C. Stewart, 557

Sherer, Peter D., 527, 628
Sheridan J. A., 171
Sherman, Jesse, 440, 544n
Shetty, Y. K., 50
Sides, Ellen H., 311
Silbey, Val, 401, 403
Silverman, E. B., 353
Silvestri, George, 45n
Simmons, Richard J., 592n
Simon, Herbert A., 350
Simon, Julian L., 49
Simon, Michael C., 403
Sistrunk, Francis, 88
Skratek, Sylvia, 629
Skrzycki, Cindy, 311, 441
Slaughter, Jane, 601
Sloane, Arthur A., 526, 627, 628
Smith, A. R., 171
Smith, C. A., 526
Smith, D. E., 120
Smith, H. L., 349, 354
Smith, Kevin M., 352
Smith, James P., 205
Smith, Patricia C., 119
Smith, Robert S., 50, 254, 399, 491, 599
Snider, Patricia, 193n, 205
Sniezek, Janet A., 257
Snoek, J. D., 600
Snow, C. C., 86
Solnick, Loren, 557
Solo, Sally, 257
Solomon, Charlene Marmer, 122
Solomon, Jolie, 122, 403
Solow, Robert M., 50
Sonnenfeld, Jeffery A., 367n
Sonnenstuhl, William J., 600
Sorensen, Aage B., 50
Souder, B. A., 560
Sourenian, Joan, 122
Sovereign, Kenneth, 600
Sowell, Thomas, 204
Sparks, Paul, 88
Spencer, Daniel G., 350
Spivey, W. A., 255
Staines, Graham, 601
Stallworth, Lamont E., 629
Staw, Barry M., 350, 492
Steele, Robert W., 120
Steen, Todd P., 559
Steers, Richard M., 112n, 121, 122, 349
Steffy, Brian D., 254, 317, 492
Steiber, Jack, 351
Steinbuch, P., 171

Steiner, Julius M., 599
Stephens, Gregory K., 402
Stertz, Bradley, 601
Stevens, D. W., 253
Stewman, Shelby, 398
Stock, John R., 119
Stoddard, Jill A., 313, 316
Stone, Thomas H., 492
Strausser, Pamela G., 399, 402
Strazewski, Len, 442
Stumpf, Stephen, 401
Subich, Linda, 528
Summers, Clyde W., 352
Susser, Peter A., 118
Sutcliffe, Jon, 559
Sutton, Edward E., 439
Swartz, Felice, 402
Swasy, Alecia, 257
Sweet, Donald H., 347n, 354
Swidinsky, Robert, 656

T

Takegi, Haruyo, 401
Tane, Lance, 559
Tannenbaum, Jeffery A., 252, 253, 254
Tanner, L. D., 204
Taplin, Polly, 559
Taylor, F. W., 88
Taylor, G. W., 492
Taylor, H. C., 317
Taylor, M. Susan, 257, 399
Taylor, Ronald A., 254, 255, 311
Tenopyr, Mary L., 316
Terborg, James R., 440
Terkel, Studs, 53, 86
Thayer, Paul W., 88
Theriault, R. D., 527
Therrien, Lois, 439
Thomas, Lacy Glenn, 600
Thompson, Mark, 352
Thompson, P. H., 401
Thurow, Lester, 491, 492
Tichy, Noel, 87
Tjosvold, Dean, 87, 601
Todor, William D., 350, 354, 629
Toigo, John William, 441
Tolbert, Pamela S., 399, 402
Tornow, Walter W., 87
Tosi, Henry, 493
Tosi, J. S., 311
Tosi, Lisa, 493
Towers, 559

Townley, Preston, 50
Tracy, Joseph S., 628
Treiman, Donald J., 51, 204, 528
Trice, Harrison M., 600, 602
Trost, Cathy, 402, 403
Tsui, Anne S., 170, 172
Tubbs, M. E., 118
Tullar, William L., 276n
Tung, Rosalie L., 402
Turnage, Janet J., 401
Tuttle, Jeffrey M., 350

U

Ullman, Joseph C., 253, 255, 655
Ulrich, David, 19
Unwalla, Carab, 399
Upham, Paul J., 402
Usher, Claire J., 439

V

Vagelos, Roy, 226
Valente, Judith, 441
Vance, R. J., 119
Vanderkamp, John, 656
Verity, John W., 349
Verma, Anil, 642n, 656
Vetter, 171
Vittolino, Sal, 654, 655
Voos, Paula B., 656
Vroom, Victor H., 88, 349, 398

W

Wagner, John, 510n, 527
Wakabayashi, Mitsuru, 392n, 402
Walker, A. J., 168n 172
Walker, James W., 399
Walker, O., 526
Walsh, David J., 655, 656
Walton, Richard, 19, 86
Wanger, E. David, 655
Wanous, John P., 256
Ward, Dan L., 349, 353, 354
Waterman, Robert H., Jr., 86
Watkins, L. E., 349, 354
Wedley, W. C., 349
Weisner, Willi H., 313
Weiss, Andrew, 526
Weiss, David, 310
Weitzman, Martin, 526
Welch, Finis R., 205, 253
Welsh, John, 315

Werbel, J. D., 119
Werhane, Patricia H., 19, 600
Wermiel, Stephen, 317
West, Robin, 611n, 627
Wexley, Kenneth N., 414, 440, 442
Wheeler, Kenneth G., 492
White, Connie, 190n
White, Harrison, 171
White, Joseph B., 353
Whitener, Ellen M., 315
Whitman, David, 254, 255, 311
Whitney, Fred, 526
Wiatrowski, William J., 560
Wickert, Fred, 441
Wigdor, Alexandra K., 255, 313, 317
Wilcox, D. S., 120
Wiley, W. W., 87
Williams, Charles R., 351
Williams, K. J., 120
Williams, R. M., Jr., 205
Williams, Robert E., 206
Windmuller, John P., 656
Wing, Hilda, 117
Wintner, Linda, 353
Witney, Fred, 627, 628
Wohl, Jeffrey D., 352
Wolfe, R. Quinn, 600

Woolley, Suzanne, 256
Wormley, Wayne M., 403
Worrall, John D., 599
Wroth, J. M., 171
Wuebker, Lisa J., 315
Wynter, Leon E., 403

Y

Yetton, Philip, 87
Yeung, Arthur, 19
Yoder, D., 87, 170
Young, John, 50
Yudof, Mark G., 204

Z

Zachary, G. Pascal, 171
Zalesny, Mary D., 627
Zax, Jeffery S., 656
Zedeck, Paul R., 118, 316
Zeidner, Joseph, 315
Zeira, Yoram, 50
Zellner, Wendy, 349, 353, 354, 442
Zimmerle, Denise M., 442
Ziskin, Ian, 493, 527
Zytowski, D. G., 253

SUBJECT INDEX

A

Abilities data, 70
Ability tests, 284–87
Absenteeism, 111–13, 554
  alcohol abuse and, 575
Accelerated learning, 417
Accounting, HR, 142–43
Active practice, trainee's, 415
Actuarial valuations, 536–37
Administering pay systems, 459
  communication/appeals and, 513–14
  cost controls and, 512–13
  participation, 514
  special groups and, 514–15
Adverse impact, 195
Adverse selection, 551
Advertising, 229–30
Affirmative action, 175
AFSCME (American Federation of State,
    County, and Municipal Employees), 520
  pay equity study, 524–26
Age discrimination, 187
Age Discrimination in Employment Act
    (ADEA), 187
  CEOs and, 392
  employee benefits and, 539–40
  recruiting and, 222–23
Agency shop, 613–14
Agency theory, 515
AIDS, 188, 574
AIDS screening, 290
Air traffic controller strike, 604, 644
Allegheny Ludlum, 65
All-salaried work force, 514
Alternation ranking, 102
AMA; see American Management Association

American Council of Life Insurance, 26
American Cyanamid Company, 103
American Management Association (AMA),
    229
Americans With Disabilities Act of 1990, 188
Anatomy of a strike, 620
Anti-union tactics, 633–34
Application forms/resumes, 268–69
Apprenticeship programs, 422–23
Appropriate bargaining unit, 609
Arbitrary injunctions, 606
Arbitration, 623–24
Assessment centers, 386–87
Asset income, 547
Associate memberships, 643
Attitudes/opinion assessment, 113–114
Audio-visual training, 424
Auditing HR activities, 141–42
Authoritarian leadership, 62
Autonomy/independence, 374
Availability analysis, 191–95
Availability measuring, 191–95
Avoidable separations, 324

B

Bank of America, 319, 500
Bargaining structures, 617–18
Base rate, 304–5
Basic skills training, 420–21
Behavioral costing, 156
Behavioral data, 70
Behaviorally anchored rating bars (BARS),
    101–2
Behavior description interview, 281
Behavioral discrimination scales (BDS), 102
Behavioral observation scales (BOS), 102

Behavior-modeling, 426
Benchmarks
  employee separations and, 324
  job classification and, 473
  managerial development and, 411
Benefit gap, 534–35
Benefits, employee
  actuarial valuations, 536–37
  benefits gap, 534–35
  choice in, 548–49
  civil rights laws and, 539–40
  communication and, 548
  competitiveness and, 535–37
  compliance and, 537–43
  cost comparisons, 535–36
  defined, 530
  employee behavior and, 554
  employee services, 546
  employer-purchased insurance, 544–45
  entitlements versus contributions, 533–34
  equity and, 555
  evaluating benefit decisions, 551–55
  fiduciary responsibility, 540–42
  flexi benefits, 549–51
  growth of, 531–32
  management decisions and, 535
  mandated benefits, 542–43
  paid time away from work, 545
  ranking of, 544
  retirement income, 546–48
  setting objectives/strategies, 532–33
  tax policies and, 531
  unemployment compensation, 543
  worker's compensation, 543
Betts case, 530, 540
BFOQ; *see* Bona fide occupational qualifications (BFQD)
Blacks, 3
  ability tests legality and, 285–86
  disparate impact and, 183
  earnings gap and, 176
  occupational attainment and, 176
  reverse discrimination and, 2
Bona fide occupational qualifications (BFOQ), 184
Borg-Warner Corporation, 468–69
Bounded rationality job approach, 221
Break-even analysis, 433–36
Budgets, HR, 142
Bumping, 341–42
Bureau of Labor Statistics, U.S., 583
Bureau of National Affairs (BNA), 111, 224
  employee turnover rates and, 323–24

Bureau of National Affairs—*Cont.*
  severance benefits survey, 342
  test validation and, 301
Business games, 426
Business/government relationship, 645–46
Business/labor relationship, 647
  productivity and, 651–52
Business planning, 136
  HR resource requirements and, 146–49

C

Career anchors, 373
Career development, 371
  implications for, 376
Career management, 371
  assessment centers, 386–87
  factors in selection, 383–86
  job posting and, 377
  nominations by superiors/mentors, 382
  replacement/succession planning and, 378–81
  self-nomination, 382–83
  separation/retention and, 387–93
  skills inventory, 377–78
Career planning, 371
  integration with management, 372
  orientation and, 373–74
  training strategy and, 407
Careers, 363–65
  career systems models, 367
  setting goals for, 365–66
  stages of, 374–75
Case study method, 426
Cease and desist order, 616
Cell entries, 151
Checklists, 99–101
Chernobyl accident, 573
Chief executive officer (CEO) progression, 391–93
Child labor laws, 454–55
Child care, 546
Chrysler Company, 531
  union contract and, 604
Civil Rights Act of 1964, 43, 174–75, 179, 519
Civil Rights Act of 1990, 184, 201
Civil rights laws, 539–40
Class consciousness, 647
Class definitions, 474
Classification decisions, 293
Closed shop, 613
Closed/union shop, 607
Coalition bargaining, 617
Cognitive test ability, 285

Collective bargaining, 335
 bargaining structures, 617–18
 case study, 706–9
 contract administration, 622–23
 impasses in, 618–22
 legal framework for, 605–8
 negotiating a contract, 612–16
 organizing campaign, 608–12
 refusal to bargain, 616–17
College recruiting, 226–27
 case study, 673–79
Commissions, 502
Commonwealth v. *Hunt,* 606
Communication, 570–71
 union organizing campaigns and, 634
Communications, 5
Communications Workers of America, 5
Communications Workers of America (CWA),
 642
Comparable worth
 critics/politics/costs and, 521–22
 definition of, 520
 earnings gap and, 519–20
Compensable factor, 474
Compensation, 4–6
 balancing policy decisions, 459–60
 comparative international hourly rates, 41
 defined, 453
 external competitiveness and, 446, 460–63
 foreign product markets, 39–41
 forms of, 453
 HMR activities and, 15
 internal consistency, 463–71
 legislation impacting, 453–56
 multiple perspectives of, 452
 parity approach and, 40
 policy decisions and, 457–59
 setting objectives, 456–59
 traditional approaches to, 445–46
Compensation/working conditions, 615
Compensatory job approach, 221
Compensatory process, 294
Competition
 benefit plans and, 535
 compensation and, 446
Competitive advantage, 138
Compliance, compensation, 457
Comprehensive structured interview (CSI),
 281–84
Compressed workweek, 584
Compression, wage, 459–60
 case study, 686
Compulsory arbitration, 623

Computer-assisted instruction, 425
Computer-assisted design, 60
Computerized testing, 265
Computers; *see also* Personal computers
 job applicant information and, 571
Conciliation/mediation, 618
Concurrent validation, 298
Conflict, 591
 conflict resolution, 593–95
 disciplinary process, 591–93
Connecticut v. *Teal,* 183, 296
Consolidated Omnibus Reconciliation Act
 (COBRA), 544
Construction trades closed shop, 608
Constructive confrontation, 579–80
Consumer price index (CPI), 499
 health insurance and, 544
Content, job, 66
 assessment of, 68–70
Content-based validation, 296–301
Contract administration, 615
Contract negotiation
 bargaining structures, 617–18
 contract cost case study, 708–9
 formalizing the contract, 618
 negotiation issues, 613–16
 preparation for, 612–13
 refusal to bargain, 616
Control Data Corporation, 339–40
 employee assistance and, 580
 employee/labor relations and, 596
Conventional arbitration, 624
Cooperative education (co-op), 227
Co-paid consumption plans, 552–53
Core cafeteria plan, 549
Corning Glass, 79–80, 114
Corporate-level strategy, 55
 culture and, 61–62
Correlation coefficient, 265
Cost-of-living adjustments (COLAs), 499
 linkage of wages and, 650–51
Costs of HR activities, 157
Counseling, 580
 conflict and, 591
Coverage, 543
 employer-purchased insurance, 544–45
Creativity, 374
Criminal conspiracy theory, 605–6
Criterion related methods, 296
 validation choices and, 297–98
Critical incidents, 101
Culture/philosophy, corporate, 61–62
 training and, 410

Cummins Engine Company, 80

D

Davis-Bacon Act of 1931, 455
Day-care assistance, 585–86
Decertification, 612
Decline stage, 375
Defense Department, U.S., 425
Defined benefits/contributions plans, 548
Demand analysis, 145–49
Democratic leadership, 62
Demographics, 2
  employee benefits and, 555
  employee characteristics assessment and,
    115
Department of Labor, U. S., 421
  wage legislation and, 455
Development, employee, 15
Diagnostic approach
  employee development and, 358–60
  external staffing, 210–13
  HRM and, 8–10
  human resource planning, 135–37
  job search and, 244–51
  planning and, 130–31
  training and, 408–9
Diagnostic model, 8–11, 20
  compensation and, 444–45
  planning and, 130–31
Diaz v. Pan American Airways, 185
Differentials, pay, 513
  executive compensation and, 517–18
  international comparisons and, 519
Digital Equipment Corporation (DEC), 40
  merit awards, 500
  training and, 425
Disabled workers, 223
Discharges
  decision process for, 334–35
  employment at will issue, 335–37
  quality of retained employees and, 338
Discrimination
  age and, 187
  behavioral discrimination scales, 102
  CEOs and, 392
  discrimination legislation, 179
  employee benefits and, 539–40
  job discrimination, 574
  pay discrimination, 180
  pregnancy and, 539–40
  recruiting and, 222–23
  retirement and, 187

Discrimination—*Cont.*
  reverse discrimination, 2, 200–201
  sex discrimination, 275
Dismissals, 323
  discharges, 334–38
  layoffs, 338–43
  validity applied to, 324–25
Disney World, 419
Disparate impact, 182–84
  proving, 210
Disparate treatment, 181–82
Dow Jones & Company, Inc., 383
Drug/alcohol screening, 574, 576
Drug testing, 289
Dual-career issue, 221
  compensation and, 448
Dual-career positions, 383
Dual-ladder career progression, 389–90
Dysfunctional separations, 324

E

Early retirement incentives, 326, 331
  EEOC and, 333
Eastern Airlines, 56
Eastman Kodak Company, 419
  management education and, 420
Economic conditions
  human resources and, 11
  labor market conditions and, 35–37
Education and external employee selection,
    272
Educational programs, 546
Educational Testing Service, 272
EEO-1 reports, 197
EEOC; *see* Equal Employment Opportunity
    Commission (EEOC)
Efficiency
  compensation objectives and, 456
  employee relations and, 595–96
  external selection and, 260–61, 303–7
  internal staffing/careers, 365–66, 394–95
  organizations and, 13–14, 409–10
  recruiting and, 238–39
  training programs and, 429, 432
  union impact on productivity and, 651–52
  union impact on wages and, 648–51
  work force reduction, 320–21, 345–46
Emergency powers of presidents, 608
Employee
  attendance and, 112
  attitudes/opinions of, 113–14
  demographic characteristics of, 115, 275–77

Employee—*Cont.*
  discrimination/harassment and, 200
  separation/turnover and, 113
Employee assistance, 578–79
  approaches to, 579–80
  family/job conflicts, 580–86
  stress, 586
Employee characteristics, 13
  assessment of, 90–91
  development and, 359
  performance criteria and, 96
Employee contributions, 458, 495
Employee development, 357
  diagnostic approach to, 358–60
  objectives/standards for, 359–60
  training, 405–8
Employee handbook, 570
Employee Involvement Teams (EIT), 504
Employee leasing, 231–32
Employee pay differentials, 495–96
Employee Polygraph Protection Act (EPPA),
    99, 290
Employee Polygraph Protection Act of 1988,
    211
Employee referrals, 224–26
Employee relations, 568–69
  communications and, 570–71
  conflict and, 591–95
  cooperation and, 586–90
  co-worker relations, 574–78
  diagnostic approach to, 564–65
  employee assistance, 578–79
  evaluation of results, 595–97
  protection and, 571
  safety/health hazards and, 572–74
  setting objectives/strategies, 569–70
Employee Retirement Income Security Act of
    1974 (ERISA), 541
Employee security/seniority, 615–16
Employee separation
  efficiency and, 320
  employee/employer initiated, 323
  equity and, 321–22
  evaluation of, 344–47
  international implications of, 343–44
  measuring rate of, 323–24
Employee services, 546
Employee stock ownership programs
    (ESOPs), 547
Employee training/development, 357–58
Employer campaign activities, 611
Employer group, 617
Employer-purchased insurance, 544–45

Employers
  affirmative action and, 175
  age discrimination and, 187
  internal grievance process and, 198
Employment-at-will issue, 335–38
Employment continuity, 647
Employment contracts, 336
Employment discrimination legislation, 179
Employment distribution, 177
Employment planning, 140, 145
  case study, 671–73
  demand analysis and, 145–49
  external supply analysis, 153
  internal supply analysis and, 149–52
  supply/demand reconciliation, 153–54
  training and, 407
English literacy requirements, 223–24
Enterprise unions, 648
Entitlements/Contributions, 533–34
Environmental scanning, 25–28
EPA; *see* Equal Pay Act (EPA)
Equal, definition of, 180
Equal Employment Opportunity Commission
    (EEOC), 43, 184
  early retirement incentives and, 333
  major activities of, 197
  organizational downsizing and, 211
  wrongful discharge cases and, 337
Equal employment opportunity (EEO), 12, 74
  availability analysis and, 191–95
  employee quits and, 330
  establishing goals for, 195
  evaluating performance of, 189–90
  external selection and, 261–62
  groups protected by, 179
  HR information and, 161
  internal grievance process and, 198–200
  internal staffing and, 365
  need for, 175–80
  performance assessment and, 110–11
  programming to achieve goals, 196
  protected groups, 377
  recruiting and, 239
  reverse discrimination and, 200–201
  settling disputes, 197
  training programs and, 436–37
  union seniority and, 616
  work force analysis and, 190–91
Equal Pay Act (EPA), 180, 519
Equal Pay Act of 1967, 46
Equal work, factors defining, 181
Equity, 14
  compensation objectives, 456–57

Equity—*Cont.*
 employee benefit programs and, 555
 employee/labor relations and, 596–97
 external selection activities and, 261–62,
  307–8
 internal staffing/careers and, 365–66,
  395–96
 labor relations and, 652
 recruiting and, 239–40
 training programs and, 436–37
 work force reduction and, 321–22, 346
ERISA; *see* Employee Retirement Income
  Security Act (ERISA)
Ernst & Whinney, 407
Establishment stage, 374
Europe 1992, 38–39
European Economic Community, 38–39
Exclusive representation, 607
Executive incentives, 515
Executive Order 11246, 186–87
 unions and, 199
Executive Order 12564, 99
Executive pay
 compensation decisions, 515
 critics of, 517–18
Exemptions, wage, 455
Exit interviews, 329
Expectancy theory, 414
Exploration stage, 374
External competitiveness of pay, 458
External conditions, 11–12
 assessing external pressures of, 25
 employee development and, 358–59
 employee/labor relations and, 564–65
 HR planning and, 136
 shaping of, 47
External criteria, training outcome, 428
External employee selection
 ability tests and, 284–85
 application forms/resumes and, 268–69
 case study for, 698–99
 choosing selection techniques, 265–66, 305
 constructing selection process, 293–96
 evaluating selection activities, 303–8
 international perspective on, 302–3
 life-history information, 270–74
 personality/honesty/graphology tests,
  291–93
 physical/psychological requirements, 288–90
 reference/background checks and, 269–70
 setting objectives for, 260–62
External staffing, 209
 diagnostic approach to, 210–13

External staffing—*Cont.*
 EEO and, 212–13
 employee characteristics and, 212
External supply analysis, 153
Exxon, 452
Exxon *Valdez,* 92, 573

F

Factor comparison job evaluation, 474
Fair Labor Standards Act (FLSA), 43
Fair Labor Standards Act of 1938, 454
Family/job conflict, 580–86
Federal Labor Relations Authority (FLRA),
  644
Federal Mediation and Conciliation Service
  (FMCS), 607, 619
Feedback, trainee, 415
 simulation methods and, 426
Fiduciary liabilities, funding of, 541
Fiduciary responsibility, 540–42
Final-offer arbitration, 624
Financial conditions, organizational, 54–55
Fixed costs, 553
Flexi-benefit plans, 549
 advantages/disadvantages of, 549–51
 cost reduction strategy and, 551
Flexible hours (flextime), 582–83
Flexible spending accounts, 549
Flexible work force, 46
Focus groups, 229
Foley v. *Interactive Data Corporation,* 337
Forced distribution, 102
Ford Motor Company, 579
Fortune, 211, 289
Four-fifths rule, 195
Functional-level strategy, 56
Functional separations, 324

G

Gainsharing systems, 497
 conditions favoring, 505
 key factors in, 506
 productivity changes associated with, 510
 results of, 509
General Aptitude Test Battery (GATB), 285
General Electrical Company, 388
 coalition bargaining and, 617
 conflict resolution and, 594
 management development, 419
General Motors Corporation, 45
 QWL and, 589–90, 596

General pay increases, 499
Genetic screening, 265, 290
G-factor, 285
Gigantic Aircraft Company case study, 698
Glass ceiling, 395, 397
Globalization of markets, 38–41
Government influences, 43, 45–46
    external staffing and, 210–11
Government regulations
    compensation and, 446–47, 453
    human resources and, 12
    organizational downsizing and, 211
    workforce reduction and, 321–22
Graphology (handwriting analysis), 291
Grievance process, 622–23
Grievance strike, 619
Griggs v. *Duke Power Company,* 182
Group life insurance, 544

H

Halo error, 106
Harassment, 575
    case study, 705–6
Harvard Business Review, 391
Hay Guide Chart-Profile Method, 476
Headcount ratios, 142
Headhunters, executive, 228
Health care
    changing financing methods, 553
    civil rights laws and, 539–40
    controlling costs, 552
    rising cost of, 532
Health insurance, 544
Health Maintenance Organizations (HMOs),
    553
Hewlett-Packard, 319
    career changes and, 634
    Management by Wandering Around, 576–77
    Open Door policy, 594
    pay programs and, 457
Hierarchical systems, 594
Hispanics, 3
    ability tests legality and, 285–87
    disparate impact and, 183
    earnings gap and, 176–79
    occupational attainment and, 176
Hoffman-LaRoche, Inc., 341
Holidays, 545
Home work, 584–85
Hostile environment, 189
Housing/transportation barriers, 223
HR; *see* Human resources (HR)

HRM; *see* Human resource management
    (HRM)
HRM PC software, 660–61
HR objectives, setting, 13–14
Human resource decisions
    business strategy and, 56
    cost of training, 435–36
    defined, 131
    employee benefits and, 555
    employee characteristics and, 91
    financial conditions and, 54–55
    leveraging training and, 435
    multiple stakeholders in, 5–6
    organizational planning framework and,
        135–36
    organization characteristics and, 54
    quality of training and, 435
Human resource department
    accounting and, 142–43
    auditing HR activities and, 141–42
    budgets for, 142
    headcount ratios and, 142
    planning and, 138–40
    reputational evaluations and, 143–45
    return on investment and, 143
Human resource information systems (HRIS),
    129, 159–61
    basic components of, 162–63
    customizing to user needs, 163–64
    data elements of, 166
    definition of, 160
    design process of, 164–68
    development profile, 167
    personal computers and, 169
    purposes of, 161
    security/privacy issues and, 169
Human resource management (HRM), 4–5
    action plans and, 140–41, 155
    activities of, 15–16
    assessing conditions, 11–13, 55
    benefits compliance and, 537
    diagnostic approach to, 8–10
    external selection and, 260
    financial analysts and, 319
    lobbying and, 47
    response to uncertainties and, 46–47
    specialization in, 17–18
    strategical purposes and, 57–60
    variation in issues, 6–8
    wrongful discharge cases and, 337
Human resource planning
    broader planning process and, 135–37
    case study, 693–95

Human resource planning—*Cont.*
  defined, 129, 132
  diagnostic approach and, 130–31
  functional level decisions and, 138–40
  integrating benefits objectives with, 533
  objectives/evaluation standards and, 132–33
  reasons for, 134–35
Human resources (HR)
  EEO implications, 189–90
  importance of, 2–3
  investment in, 155–57
  labor relation activities and, 647–48
  performance assessment and, 111
  valuing, 3–4

I

IBM, 212
  ability tests and, 285
  career enhancement, 364
  day-care assistance and, 585
  early retirement incentives and, 332, 554
  employee relations and, 570
  management development, 419
  redeployment and, 388
  Rolm acquisition and, 533
  skills inventory and, 378
  training system and, 408
  work force reduction, 319
Illegal drugs, 575–76
Immigration, 33
  recruiting and, 232–33
Immigration Reform and Control Act of 1986, 232–34
Incentives; *see* Pay-for-performance plans
Incentive stock options (ISOs), 547
Inducement strategy, 57
Inflationary pressures, 38
Information
  HR information system and, 161
  investment and, 133–34
Instructors, training, 416–17
Internal consistancy of pay, 458
Internal criteria, training outcome, 428
Internal staffing, 210–357
  careers and, 363–66
  effects in source/destination jobs, 369–70
  evaluation of, 394–96
  international perspective on, 393
  role of employee movement and, 366, 368–69
  setting objectives for, 366

Internal supply analysis, 149–52
International conditions, 38–41
  human resources and, 11–12
International economic comparisons, 42–43
International management, 39
International organizations, 40
Internship programs, 227
Interview, job
  diagnostic job search and, 251
  external employee selection and, 274–78
  interviewer behavior/training, 278–80
  scripted interview, 275–76
  types of, 280–82
  variables affecting, 277
Invasion of privacy
  drug testing and, 577–78
  smoking bans and, 575
Investment strategy, 57, 59–60
Involvement strategy, 60
Issue prioritization matrix, 29
Ithaca's Own case study
  background description of, 664–70
  college recruiting, 673–79
  compression/external experienced hiring, 686
  developing new managers, 680
  employment planning, 671–73
  Jack Freelance affair, 686–92
  merit pay decisions, 681–83
  setting objectives, 670–71
  starting salary case, 660–64
  strategies and staff, 668–70

J

Japan, 39
  career mobility in, 392
  employment continuity and, 647–48
  lifetime employment and, 343–44
  management career paths, 393
J. C. Penney, 533–34
  communication and, 548
Job analysis, 67–68
  case study, 695–96
  conventional method, 70–73
  information gathering procedures, 82–85
  performance assessment and, 95
  quantitative method, 73–74
  task data questionnaire, 69
  usefulness of, 75–76

Job applicant
  job/organization choice, 221–22
  occupation choice and, 219
  seeking job/organizational information,
    219–20
Job Applicant Medical History Questionnaire,
  289
Job bank, 31
Job-based pay structures, 470–71
Job comparison scale, 475
Job descriptions, 74–75
Job design
  defined, 76
  human relations and, 77–78
  job characteristics and, 78–79
  scientific management and, 76–77
  sociotechnical perspectives and, 79
Job discrimination, 574
Job evaluation
  building fences and, 477–78
  market rates and, 476–77
  methods for, 472–76
  persons involved in, 471–72
Job fairs, 227
Job instruction training, 422
Job knowledge, 287–88
Job opportunities, 245
  growing/declining occupations, 44–45
Job posting, 377
Job-related exception, 184
Job satisfaction, 114
Job search, diagnostic
  assessing conditions, 244–46
  case presentation, 249–51
  considering offers, 252
  interviews and follow-up, 251
  occupation/vocation decision, 243–44
  preparing case for, 246–49
  preparing resume, 246–48
Job-search behavior, 221
Job standards, 98–99
Job tryouts, 287–88
Jurisdictional strike, 619

K

Kaiser Steel, 553
Kerr-McGee, 571
Key jobs, 463, 477
K mart, 575
Knowledge-based pay systems, 468
  compared to job-based plans, 469

Knowledge/skills/abilities (KSAs) measures,
  301
KSA (job/task/knowledge-skill-ability), 408–9
Kuder Occupational Interest Survey, 219

L

Labor force, 2
  feminization of, 33–34
  growing roles in, 31
  quality of, 35
  social/demographic problems, 28–29
Labor/government relationship, 646
Labor legislation, 6
Labor/management relations, 636
Labor markets, 35–37
  current trends in, 210
Labor relations, 605
  collaboration, 635–36
  foreign markets and, 645
  union-free status, 634–35
  union suppression, 632–34
Laissez-faire leadership, 62
Landrum-Griffin Act of 1959, 608
Layoffs
  decision process for, 339–41
  income maintenance and, 342
  management of, 341–43
  quality of retained employees and, 343
Learning
  acceleration method, 417
  definition of, 413
  orientation and, 418
  trainee motivation and, 414
Learning organization, the, 409
Lecture training method, 423
Legality
  ability test and, 285–87
  application forms and, 269
  interviews and, 282–84
  life-history information and, 274
  personality/honesty/graphology tests and,
    291–92
  reference/background check and, 270
  work samples/job tryouts and, 288
Leniency error, 106
Levi Strauss, 585
Life-history information, 270–74
Life insurance
  civil rights laws and, 539
Lobbying, 47
Local union, 639

Long-term sickness/accident/disability insurance, 545
Lump-Sum Increase Program (LSIP), 501

M

McDonnell-Douglas Space Systems, 384
Maintenance stage, 375
Malcolm Baldrige National Quality Award, 138–39
Management by objectives (MBO), 98, 103
Management development, 419–20
  case study, 680
Management style, 62–64
Managerial competence, 373
Managerial organization structure, 516
Mandatory retirement, 539
Manual for Identification of Joint Immobility, 288–89
Marginal employment, 583
Market pricers, 476
Martin v. *Wilks*, 200
Massive Manufacturing Corporation case study, 699–703
Mediation, 625
Medicare, 331, 536
  supplementary insurance and, 531
Mentor, 382
Merit awards, 500–501
Merit pay, 499–500
  case study, 681–83
Meta-analysis, 300
Middle management motivation, 388
  orientation and, 418
Minimum wages, 454
Mixed standard scales, 101
Mommy track, 391
Motorola, Inc.
  basic skills training, 421
  training program and, 405–6
Multiemployer bargaining, 617
Multiple behavior indexes, 428–29
Multiple hurdles, 295–96
Multiple objective statement, 457
Multiple selection procedures, 294–96
Multiskill pay systems, 468

N

National Alliance of Business, 272, 421
National Association of Corporate and Professional Recruiters, 270
National Consumers League, 282

National Labor Relation Board (NLRB), 43, 611, 634
  anti-union tactics and, 633
  decertification, 612
  holding elections and, 609–10
  union hearings, 609
National Labor Relations Act of 1935, 606
National Labor Relations Board (NLRB), 607
National Science Foundation, 216
National Technological University, 405–6
  training and, 426
Native Americans, 285–86
NEC Information Systems (NECIS), 229
Needs assessment methods, 412
Needs improvement, 103
New Port News Shipbuilding Company, 540
Nonmanagement skills training, 419
Normative order, 61
Norris-LaGuardia Act, 606

O

Objectives/evaluation standards, 132–33
  case study, 670–71
  employee training and, 411–12
  formulation of, 133–34
Occupational attainment, 176
Occupational interests, 362–63
Occupational Safety and Health Act (OSHA), 572–74
Office of Federal Contract Compliance (OFCCP), 198
Off-the-job training, 423
Older workers, 30–31
  recruiting and, 222–23
  retention of, 331, 333
  technology and, 60
Ombudsmen, 595
One-to-one relationships, 563
On-the-job training, 421–22
Opinion Research Corporation, 555
Organizational commitment, 114
Organizational culture, 410
  pay systems and, 447–48
Organizational maintenance, 409
Organization conditions, 12
  employee development and, 359
  HR planning and, 136–38
Organization-level factors, 54
  human resource planning and, 135–36
Organizations
  characteristics and, 54

Organizations—*Cont.*
  downsizing of, 211
  efficiency and, 13–14, 409–10
  financial conditions and, 54–55
  organizational culture, 410
  quality objectives and, 138
  stakeholders and, 136–38
  training and, 409–10
Orientals, 183
Orientation
  career planning and, 373–74
  employee training and, 417–19
OSHA; *see* Occupational Safety and Health
    Act (OSHA)
Outplacement assistance, 342
Outplacement services, 323
Overtime pay, 454
Overutilization, 195
Owner/employee plans, 586

P

Pacific Rim countries, 39
Paid time away from work, 545
Paired-comparison, 102
Parental leave, 546
Parity, 195
Parity compensation approach, 40
Parity strike, 620
Participation rates, 29–30
Part time employment, 583–84
Pattern bargaining, 618
Pay-for-performance plans
  bonus plans research, 509–10
  factors influencing plans, 503
  gainsharing, 504–7, 509
  group plans, 503–4
  importance of money and, 508
  individual incentives, 501–3
  negative evidence and, 510–11
  pay increase-performance relationship,
    508–9
  pay satisfaction and, 511–12
  profit sharing, 507
Pay levels
  competition and, 464
  data collection, 462
  defined, 460
  effects of, 460–61
  market surveys and, 461–62
Pay model, 456
Pay structure, 463–64
  criteria for, 466–67

Pay structure—*Cont.*
  employee attributes and, 468–70
  job-based structures, 470–71
  size of differences and, 465–66
Pay system design, 459
Pay techniques, individual
  flat rates, 496–97
  lump-sum payments, 501
  merit awards, 500–501
  pay increase guidelines, 499–500
  pay ranges, 497–99
Pension Benefit Guaranty Corporation
    (PBGC), 541–42
Pensions
  actuarial valuations and, 537
  civil rights laws and, 539
  demographic changes and, 34
  eligibility and, 541
  private pensions, 547–48
  termination responsibility, 541–42
PepsiCo, 12–13, 46
  college recruiting and, 227
  demographic trends and, 30
  HR planning and, 27–28
Performance appraisal; *see* Performance
    assessment
Performance assessment, 91–92
  appraiser requirements, 104–7
  communicating results, 107–8
  criteria for, 94–96
  employee benefits and, 554
  employee training and, 407
  evaluating results, 108–11
  HR function and, 111
  methods for measuring, 96–104, 109
  reason for process of, 92–94
  timing of, 107
Performance based layoffs, 325–26
Performance Mentor, 105
Personal computers, 169
  college recruiting case for, 673–79
  HRM software introduction, 661–64
  merit pay decisions using, 681–83
  recruiting and, 241
  strategic HR planning case study, 693–95
Personal Journal, 159
Personnel Administration, 159
Personnel, 159
Personnel manager, 73
Person-work interaction network, 385
Physical simulations, 425–26
Piecework/production bonus, 502

Planning
  diagnostic decision making and, 130–31
  efficiency/equity integration and, 14
  research/analysis and, 27–28
Plant size/location, 635
Plateaued careers, 388–89
Point method job evaluation, 474–76
Political strike, 619
Polygraph (lie detector) tests, 290
Population
  age distribution and, 30–32
  immigration and, 33
Predictive validation, 298
Predictors, 263
  content-based validation and, 301
  gathering/scoring information of, 294
  government regulations and, 302
  selection techniques and, 305
  validation choices and, 297–98
Preferred provider insurance, 553
Preferential-quota system exception, 185–86
Pregnancy Discrimination Act (1978), 539–40
Prevention programs, 571
Price Waterhouse v. *Hopkins,* 275
Private employment agencies, 228–29
Private pensions, 547–48
Procedural justice, 594
Product/labor markets, 446
Product/service market conditions, 37
Professional Air Traffic Controllers Organization (PATCO), 644
Profit sharing, 507
  actuarial valuations and, 537
  benefits and, 533
Programmed instruction (PI), 424
Progressive system, 591
  discipline policy, 592
Public employment agencies, 228
Public sector laws, 644
Public sector unions, 644

Q

Qualifiable group, 193
Qualifications, job, 66
Quality
  HR activities and, 156–57
  labor force and, 35
  organizational-level objectives and, 138
Quality of work life (QWL), 589–90, 596
Quid pro quo harassment, 189
Quits
  decisions leading to, 327–29

Quits—*Cont.*
  implications for reduction of, 329–30
  low employment rate and, 327
  retained employee quality and, 330
Quota systems, 186
QWL; *see* Quality of Work Life (QWL)

R

Railway Labor Act of 1926, 606
Ralph's Genuine French Cuisine case study, 696–98
Ranking, performance, 102
Ranking jobs, 472–73
Rating scales, 100–101
Realistic job preview (RJP), 234–35
  employee orientation/training and, 417
Recognition strike, 619
Recruiting; *see also* External employee selection
  advertising and, 229–30
  applicant/employee screening and, 574
  applicant qualifications and, 222–24
  definition of, 217
  efficiency of, 238–39
  employee referrals, 224–26
  employment agencies, 228–29
  equity in, 239–40
  evaluation practices of, 240–41
  immigrants and, 232–41
  inducements, 233
  international perspectives on, 237–38
  professional societies/organizations, 228–29
  recruiting message, 233–35
  selection/training of recruiters, 235–37
  sources used by employers, 225
  temporary employees and, 231–32
  walk-ins and, 224
Redeployment, 340
Reference/background checks, 269–70
Reinforcement, training, 414
Replacement charts, 150, 379–80
Republic Steel Company, 607
Reputational evaluations, 144–45
Researching issues, 26–26, 65
Reservation wage, 221
Resignations, 323
  management of, 327–34
  validity applied to, 326–27
Retention of knowledge, trainee, 415
Retirement
  age discrimination and, 187
  civil rights laws and, 539

Retirement—*Cont.*
  early retirement incentives, 326, 331–33
  employee benefits and, 554
  income for, 546–48
  management of, 331
  quality of retained employees and, 333–34
  retention of older employees, 333
Retirement Equity Act (1984), 541
Retirement income, 546
Return on assets (ROA), 509
Return on investment, HR, 143
Rewards/returns, job, 66–67
Right to know, 573
Right-to-work laws, 608
Rings of Defense Strategies, 339–40
  Japanese firms and, 344
RJP; *see* Realistic job preview (RJP)
Role playing method, 426
Rosenfield v. *Southern Pacific,* 185

S

Safety/health hazards, 572–74
Safe work environment, 571
Scanlon plan, 503–4
Scatterplots, 263–64
Schultz v. *Wheaton Glass Company,* 180
Scientific management, 76–77
Security, 374
Security and Exchange Commission, 134
Selection ratio, 306
Self assessment, 244–45
Self-insurance, 553
Seniority based layoffs, 326, 341
Seniority clause, 617
Seniority pay, 499
Seniority system exception, 185
Separation/turnover, employee
  assessment of, 113
  RPJs and, 238
Severance pay, 323, 342
Sexual harassment, 188–89, 575
  case study, 705–6
  conflict resolution and, 593
Sexually transmitted diseases, 574
Sick leave, 545
Simulation training method, 425–26
Single-job selection versus classification, 293–94
Situational interview, 281–82
Situational specificity, 300
Skilled-based job evaluation
  basic knowledge, 486–87

Skill-based job evaluation—*Cont.*
  communication/interpersonal skills, 489–90
  decision making/supervision required, 490–91
  electrical/electronic skills, 487
  graphics, 488–89
  mathematical skills, 489
  mechanical skills, 487–88
  safety skills, 490
Skills inventory, 149
  career management and, 377–78
Slowdown action, 620
Smoking bans, 289–90
  work place and, 575
Social/demographic changes, 28–30
  HR effects of, 34
Social/recreational programs, 546
Social Security, 331
  coordinating benefits and, 553
  mandated benefit, 542
Social Security Act of 1935, 543
Social welfare, 646–47
Society for Human Resource Management (SHRM), 17
Southern Pacific Transportation Company, 99
Spillover effect, 649
Staffing, 15; *see also* External staffing; Internal staffing; Recruiting
  employee separations and, 323
  process of, 218
  series of filters and, 261, 321
Staffing, definition of, 209
Stakeholders, 133
  external-level decisions and, 136
  organizational-level decisions and, 136–38
State definitions, 150–51
State Government case study, 703–5
Stereotypes, 26
Stock options, 515, 533
Strategy, organization, 55–56
  culture and, 61–62
Stress, 586
  psychological strain and, 588
Strikes/lockouts, 619–20
  factors involved in, 621–22
Strong Vocational Interest Bank, 219
Substance abuse, 575–78
Substantive justice, 594
Summated scales, 101
Supervisors, 199
Supplemental Unemployment Benefits (SUB), 342
Supply analysis, 145

Supreme Court, U.S., 200
  disability retirement and, 530, 540
  disparate impact and, 183–84
  fetal health risks and, 289
  hostile environment and, 575
  labor legislation and, 607
  pregnancy leave and, 540
  quota systems and, 186
  seniority issue and, 616
  sex discrimination and, 275
Sweden's universal model, 645
Sweetheart contracts, 607
Synthetic validation, 300

T

Tachiscope evaluation, 229
Taft-Hartley Act of 1947, 607
Task data, 68
Tax Equity and Fiscal Responsibility Act
    (TEFRA) of 1982, 232
Tax laws, 531, 540
  stock ownership plans and, 589
Tax Reduction Act Stock Ownership Plans
    (TRASOPs), 547
Tax Reform Act of 1986, 547
Technical changes, 41, 43
Technical/functional competence, 373
Technology, 60–61
Tele conferencing, 424
Temporary employees, 231–32
Time interval, 151
Timken Company, 621
Tin parachutes, 342
Title VII, 174, 186
  application forms and, 268
  defining discrimination, 181–84
  EEOC and, 197
  employee benefits and, 539
  employment-at-will issue and, 335
  exceptions to, 184–86
  pay discrimination and, 180
  pregnancy under, 540
  sexual harassment and, 188–89
Total strike, 619
Tousaint v. Blue Cross/Blue Shield of
    Michigan, 336
Toyota, 427
Trainees
  ability to learn, 413
  goals/expectancy and, 414
Training, 9
  assessing needs, 409, 411

Training—Cont.
  break-even analysis for, 433–36
  cost/benefit case study, 699
  costs of, 429
  defined, 407
  diagnostic approach to, 408–9
  dollars budgeted for, 406
  employee development and, 404–8
  equity and, 436–37
  instructional environment and, 416–17
  international perspectives on, 427–28
  KSA and, 410
  objectives/standards and, 411–12
  organization analysis and, 409–10
  outcome evaluation criteria, 428–31
  person analysis and, 410–11
Training, 417
Training model, 408
Training programs
  choosing content of training, 417–21
  choosing delivery methods, 421–27
  establishing conditions for learning, 413–17
Training to job transfer, 416
Transamerica Corporation, 418
Transitional matrices, 150–52
Trend Analysis Program (TRP), 26
Truck lists, 378
TRW, Incorporated, 6–7
  labor contract, 615
  organization conditions and, 53
Turnover, employee
  case study, 696–98, 703–5
  definition of, 327
  rates of, 324
Two-tier provisions, 615

U

Unavoidable separations, 324
Underutilization, 195
Unemployment compensation (UC), 543
Uniform Guidelines on Employee Selection,
    184
Uniform Guidelines on Employee Selection
    Procedures, 301
Union Carbide, 507
Union-free status, 634–35
Union jobs, 638
Union members' bill of rights, 608
Union organization, 638
  local union, 639
  union leaders, 639–40

Union organizing campaign
  authorization cards, 608–9
  determinants for unionization, 637–38
  hearings, 609
  holding elections, 609–10
  success of campaign tactics, 610–12
Unions, 604
  affirmative action and, 175
  anatomy of, 638–40
  archaic policies and, 645
  comparable worth and, 521
  compensation and, 447
  definition of QWL, 590
  EEO and, 199
  employee/labor relations and, 565
  factors causing unionization, 637–38
  growth of employee benefits and, 531–32
  home work and, 584
  HRM activities and, 15–16
  human relations and, 12, 46
  impact on wages and, 648–51
  OSHA and, 573
  performance measures and, 497
  productivity and, 651–52
  public sector, 643–44
  staffing activities and, 211
  working conditions and, 564
Union security, 613
Union shop, 607
Union steward, 625
Union strategies, 640–41
  alternative forms of representation, 643
  cooperative programs, 642–43
  involvement in employer's strategic deci-
    sions, 641–42
Union suppression, 632–34
United Auto Workers (UAW), 590, 604
  Cornell University and, 634
  Nissan's Smyrna plant and, 631, 634
Unit-level strategy, 55
University/college training, 426
U.S.-Canadian Free Trade Agreement, 24
Utility analysis, HR, 157

V

Vacations, 545
Validation methods
  content-based method, 301
  criterion-related approaches, 297–301
  extent of usage, 301–2
  government regulation and, 302
  predictive versus concurrent, 298–300

Validation method—*Cont.*
  selection process and, 296
Validity; *see also* Validation methods
  ability tests and, 285
  application forms/resumes and, 269
  defined, 263
  employee interview and, 282
  interviews and, 282
  life-history information and, 274
  personality/honesty/graphology tests and,
    293
  selection techniques and, 306
  separations/retentions and, 324–27
  training experience ratings, 274
  work samples/job tryouts and, 288
Validity coefficient, 263–64, 300
  ability tests and, 286
  assessment centers and, 387
Validity generalization, 300
Validity information, 262
  external selection decisions and, 262–65
Valid signatures, 609
Variability of applicant value, 307
Variable pay, 513
Vesting/portability, 541
Vocational Rehabilitation Act of 1973, 188
Vocational school training, 426

W

Wages
  controls/guidelines, 454
  prevailing wage laws, 355–56
  rate/hourly regulations, 454–55
Wage surveys, 461
Wagner Act of 1935, 335, 606
Walk-in applicants, 220
  recruiting sources and, 224
Walsh-Healy Act of 1936, 455
Wards Cove case, 201
  validation studies and, 302
War games, 425
Weber v. *Kaiser Aluminum and Chemicals,*
    186
Weighted application blank (WAB), 268–269
Whistleblowers, 211, 335
Women
  earnings gap and, 176–79, 519
  feminization of labor force, 33–34
  mommy track and, 391
  occupational attainment and, 176
  pregnancy and, 540
  workforce reduction and, 321

Work, nature of, 65
Work accidents/illness causes, 572
Worker Adjustment and Retraining Notification Act (WARN), 341
Worker's compensation insurance, 543
  job applicant claims for, 571
Work force analysis, 190–91
Work force reduction; *see also* Employee separation
  efficiency of, 320–21, 345–46
  equity of, 321–22, 346
  government regulations and, 321–22

Work-level factors, 66
Work-related disabilities, 572
Work samples, 287–88
  training programs and, 413
Work schedule adaptions, 582
Work teams, 79–80

X–Y

Xerox Corporation, 364, 396
Yellow dog contracts, 606
Youngstown Sheet and Tube Company, 607